COLD WAR IN THE ISLAMIC WORLD

DILIP HIRO

Cold War in the Islamic World

Saudi Arabia, Iran and the Struggle for Supremacy

OXFORD

UNIVERSITY PRESS

OXFORD

UNIVERSITY PRESS

Oxford University Press is a department of the
University of Oxford. It furthers the University's objective
of excellence in research, scholarship, and education
by publishing worldwide.

Oxford   New York

Auckland   Cape Town   Dar es Salaam   Hong Kong   Karachi
Kuala Lumpur   Madrid   Melbourne   Mexico City   Nairobi
New Delhi   Shanghai   Taipei   Toronto

With offices in

Argentina   Austria   Brazil   Chile   Czech Republic   France   Greece
Guatemala   Hungary   Italy   Japan   Poland   Portugal   Singapore
South Korea   Switzerland   Thailand   Turkey   Ukraine   Vietnam

Oxford is a registered trade mark of Oxford University Press
in the UK and certain other countries.

Published in the United States of America by
Oxford University Press
198 Madison Avenue, New York, NY 10016

Library of Congress Cataloging-in-Publication Data is available
Dilip Hiro.
Cold War in the Islamic World: Saudi Arabia, Iran and the
Struggle for Supremacy.
ISBN: 9780190944650

Printed in the United Kingdom on acid-free paper
by Bell & Bain Ltd, Glasgow

CONTENTS

SPELLING AND TRANSLITERATION

A word about place names, and the spellings of Arabic, Persian and Urdu words. A foreign word written in italics at the first mention appears in roman later. There are many ways of spelling Hussain and the Islamic prophet's name. I have chosen Hussein and Muhammad, and stayed with these for the sake of consistency. There is no standard way of transliterating foreign words. In each case, I have chosen one of the most widely used spellings in the English-language print media—except when the spelling of an author is different from mine. There I have reproduced the published spelling in the quoted material. As someone familiar with Arabic and Persian, I know that the spelling Hizbollah is more precise than the alternative Hezbollah, and that the spelling of Iran's supreme leader as Khamanei is as accurate as Khamenei. While using Hizbollah and Khamanei for the first time, I mention the alternatives in brackets. In April 2015, when writing about two top Saudi princes—Crown Prince Muhammad bin Nayef and Muhammad bin Salman—Western journalists resorted to using their respective monograms, MBN and MBS. This practice is unsuitable for a book with an index. I have therefore opted for Bin Nayef and Bin Salman in the manner of Bin Laden used for Osama bin Laden.

The Epilogue, which takes the narrative to May 2018, is not indexed.

Dilip Hiro,
London, May 2018

PREFACE

The purpose of this book is to examine the ongoing rivalry between Saudi Arabia and Iran, the leading nations in the Gulf region, to trace its roots and analyse its evolution.

After being a rock of stability and conservatism in a volatile region, Saudi Arabia has generated more eye-catching headlines in the international media in the three-year rule of King Salman bin Abdul Aziz Al Saud than in the previous three decades.

I open my narrative with a Prologue which describes the totally unexpected elevation of the Deputy Crown Prince, Muhammad bin Salman, to the heir to the throne, in place of his cousin, Muhammad bin Nayef Al Saud, in June 2017. Moreover, Bin Nayef was divested of the Interior Ministry, which he had run for five years. Press TV of Iran described the Saudi monarch's surprise decision as "a soft coup."

The Introduction serves several functions. It compares and contrasts Saudi Arabia and Iran. Their claims to exceptionalism rest on different pillars. Since Iran's chronicles cover nearly 6,000 years, Iranians have a deeply ingrained sense of identity. In contrast, Saudi Arabia is a modern entity, with its existence in its present form dating back only to 1932. Its distant predecessor, the much smaller Emirate of Diriya in central Arabia, was established in 1744 when Muhammad bin Abdul Wahhab founded his Wahhabi school within the puritanical Hanbali jurisprudence of Sunni Islam. Hostility to Shia Islam was a core element of Wahhabism which is the official religion of the Kingdom of Saudi Arabia. I explain how Shias differ from Sunnis in doctrine, ritual, law, theology and religious organization.

PREFACE

In Chapter 2 I interweave the striking of oil in Iran in 1908 with its much later discovery in Saudi Arabia, and show how the Anglo-Persian Oil Company's lack of interest in exploring for petroleum in Saudi Arabia opened up opportunities for American oil companies from 1933 onwards. Since then petroleum from Saudi Arabia has been the chief reason why the United States maintains such close links with the Kingdom.

Given the primacy that the petroleum industry came to acquire in Iran, the ownership of its sole oil company became a point of contention between Britain, which owned the Anglo-Iranian Oil Company, and Iran, ruled by the democratically elected, nationalist Prime Minister Muhammad Mussadiq. During the crisis precipitated by Mussadiq's nationalization of Iran's sole oil company, he was overthrown by the American Central Intelligence Agency, aided by Britain's secret intelligence service, MI6. To fill the gap in oil supplies to the West, caused by Iran's oil nationalization, Saudi Arabia's oil corporation, Aramco, increased its production. Iran's loss proved to be Saudi Arabia's gain.

By contrast, the dramatic oil price hike in 1973–1974, resulting from the Arab oil boycott led by Saudi King Faisal during the 1973 Arab-Israeli War, benefited both countries. In Chapter 3 I deal with the consequences of this bonanza. Muhammad Reza Shah Pahlavi became over-ambitious. Among other things he gained influence in Afghanistan. In a similar vein, Faisal established a Saudi footprint in Pakistan. He was killed by the twenty-seven-year-old, American-educated, Faisal bin Musaid, whose father was Ibn Saud's twelfth son. The widely held belief in the Arab world was that his oil boycott of the US in 1973 had brought about his assassination, in which the CIA was allegedly involved.

Fueled by burgeoning petroleum revenues, the Shah accelerated the industrialization and militarization of Iran. That in turn prompted a large scale migration from rural areas to the cities and it was these conservative traditionalists who, being deeply religious and feeling alienated in an unfamiliar urban environment, found solace in the mosque. The secular opposition, suppressed by the dictatorial Shah for nearly a quarter century, in turn began to demand political reform. These two anti-Shah streams found a common leader in Ayatollah Ruhollah Khomeini, who demanded an end to the monarchy. He astutely tapped into Shia history and Iranian nationalism to engender and intensify anti-royalist militancy among a rapidly growing circle of Iranians. After the fall of the Shah, in February 1979, the succeeding Islamic Republic of Iran was founded along the lines of Khomeini's earlier book *Islamic Government: Rule of the Just Jurisprudent*. After outlining the essentials of the Islamic Republic, and the huge tasks facing it, Chapter 4 cites Saudi Arabia's Deputy Prime Minister Prince, Abdullah bin Abdul Aziz Al Saud. His declaration that every obstacle regarding manifold cooperation between the Kingdom and the Islamic Republic had been removed would turn out to be a gross misreading of the revolution in Iran.

Having overthrown the pro-Washington Shah, Khomeini set out to purge the Iranian state and society of American influence. In this campaign, he was aided by the surprise occupation of the US Embassy in Tehran in November 1979 by militant students. The capture of the secret CIA reports on the Middle East by the Iranian occupiers gave credibility to the regime's description of the Embassy as a "nest of spies," and created a rationale for taking fifty-two US diplomats hostage. The crisis lasted 444 days and ended with Ronald Reagan's inauguration as president in January 1981 after he defeated the incumbent, Jimmy Carter, a Democrat.

Quite independently, Saudi King Khalid faced an unprecedented challenge to the legitimacy of the House of Saud when on the eve of the Islamic New Year of 1400—20 November 1979—hundreds of armed militant Wahhabis, led by Juheiman bin Muhammad al Utaiba, seized the Grand Mosque in Mecca. They called for the overthrow of the royal family for having strayed away from Wahhabism. The Saudi government was able to retake the Grand Mosque after receiving assistance from the intelligence agencies of the United States and France, and the Pakistan armed forces. After restoring the status quo in Mecca, the regime examined the criticisms leveled at it by al Utaiba, most of which were subtly endorsed by Grand Mufti Abdul Aziz bin Abdullah bin Baz. As a result, the early 1980s witnessed the imposition of strict Wahhabi rules in the social-cultural life of the Kingdom's citizens.

Chapter 5 discusses these events and outlines the Islamization of state and society in Iran. In the region Khomeini focused on exhorting the Shia majority in Iraq to rise up against the regime of

President Saddam Hussein, the Sunni leader of the secular Arab Baath Socialist Party.

Encouraged by reports of low morale in the depleted Iranian military, and by the rulers of Saudi Arabia and Kuwait, Saddam Hussein invaded Iran in September 1980. His overly optimistic scenario visualized the ethnic minority in Iran's oil-rich Khuzistan province welcoming Iraqi soldiers as liberators, setting off a chain reaction that would culminate in the collapse of Khomeini's regime within a few months. In the event, the war lasted almost eight years, and is the subject of Chapter 6.

Iran fought the war using its limited resources. In stark contrast, Iraq received massive financial aid from Saudi Arabia and Kuwait which shipped their oil on Iraq's behalf as well as loans from Western nations and Japan. Nominally neutral America helped by passing on satellite and high resolution reconnaissance pictures of Iranian troops to Riyadh, knowing full well that the Saudi kingdom was transferring these to Iraq.

In the end, neither Iran nor Iraq lost much territory, and there was no change of regime in Tehran or Baghdad. The unintended consequence of the longest war of the twentieth century was that it enabled Khomeini to consolidate the Islamic Revolution.

In the background, competition between Riyadh and Tehran to influence Pakistan and Afghanistan sharpened (see Chapter 7). Riyadh backed the Islamization drive by Pakistan's military ruler General Zia ul Haq, a Sunni. Besides the official aid to Islamabad by Riyadh, there were contributions by Islamic charities, foundations, and mosque collections, and handouts by the Saudi princes.

When Zia ul Haq issued a decree for the compulsory collection of the religiously enjoined *zakat* charitable tax, as of July 1980, Shias mounted protest demonstrations. They argued that as believers they were required to pay one-fifth of their trading profits to a Grand Ayatollah of their choice. Zia ul Haq issued an exemption for Shias. That restored normalcy. But the military ruler and the armed forces' Inter-Services Intelligence (ISI) encouraged radical elements in the Society of Scholars of Islam political group to form a militantly Sunni organization, the *Sipah-e-Sahaba*. It secured the additional financial backing of Riyadh's General Intelligence Directorate. It ignited serious anti-Shia riots in Lahore in 1986, and resorted to killing prominent Shias. In return militant Shias formed the Soldiers of Muhammad to carry out tit-for-tat assassinations. The killing of the Iranian Counsel General in Lahore in December 1990 highlighted the fact that Saudi Arabia and Iran were engaged in a proxy war in Pakistan.

The rest of this chapter deals with Afghanistan. When the Kremlin intervened militarily in Afghanistan in December 1979, Khomeini condemned it vehemently. His government implemented its own anti-Soviet strategy in Afghanistan while staying clear of the US-Saudi campaign against the Moscow-backed regime in Kabul.

At the end of 1990, Saddam Hussein's invasion and occupation of Kuwait in August of that year dominated headlines internationally. US President George H. W. Bush, an oilman, saw that by annexing Kuwait, the Iraqi leader would control 20 per cent of the global oil reserves, putting him almost on a par with Saudi Arabia. That would deprive Riyadh of being the swing producer able to tweak a rise or fall in petroleum prices. Such an eventuality had to be aborted with the backing of the international community and Saudi Arabia was to be a key player in this project.

After convincing the Saudi King Fahd, on the basis of dodgy evidence, that Saddam was preparing to invade the Kingdom, Bush was invited by Fahd to send American troops to his country. It was thus that Saudi Arabia became the focal point of the century's last major war. By December 1990, the Pentagon, leading a coalition of twenty-eight nations, thirteen of them Arab or Muslim, assembled the largest and best armed military alliance since the Second World War to confront 545,000 Iraqi troops in Kuwait and southern Iraq. The fighting between 6 January and 18 February 1991 ended with Iraq's defeat and the liberation of Kuwait. This constitutes the bulk of Chapter 8.

In Saudi Arabia, the huge expenses incurred by the government to wage the war, the subsequent rearming, and the sharply reduced price of oil led Fahd's cabinet to raise foreign loans to balance the budget in 1994. In the region, Riyadh restored diplomatic ties with Tehran that had been broken off in 1987, a precursor to detente between the rivals, the subject of the next Chapter.

The rapprochement took effect in 1994 during the presidency of Ali Akbar Hashemi Rafsanjani whose personal envoys worked closely with Saudi Crown Prince Abdullah bin Abdul Aziz. It received a severe blow in January 2002 when US President George W. Bush bracketed Iran with Iraq (still ruled by Saddam Hussein) and North Korea as part of his "Axis of Evil" after Iran had covertly cooperated with the US in the overthrow of the Taliban government in Afghanistan in the aftermath of the 9/11 attacks on America. In between, at the behest of Saudi Arabia, Iran hosted the triennial Organisation of Islamic Cooperation summit in 1997, with moderate President Muhammad Khatami chairing the event. During the second term of US President Bill Clinton (1997–2001) a temporary thaw developed between Washington and Tehran. These events are covered in Chapter 9.

Khatami was quick to condemn the 9/11 attacks and called on the international community to act to eradicate such crimes. In comparison, the conventional wisdom accepted by senior Saudi princes was that it was all part of a broader Zionist conspiracy designed to dupe the American administration into launching a worldwide campaign against Islamic terrorism. Tehran clandestinely supplied intelligence on the Taliban during the Pentagon's anti-Taliban campaign in October–November 2001. Keeping its options open, Riyadh quickly adjusted to the downfall of the Taliban in Afghanistan. Meanwhile, Pakistan continued to be the battleground of choice where the Tehran-Riyadh proxy war was played out in inter-sectarian violence with militant groups conducting retaliatory assassinations of sectarian leaders.

Chapter 10 records these events, as well as Riyadh's shock at learning in August 2002 that Iran was concealing a massive uranium enrichment facility and other sites from the Vienna-based International Atomic Energy Agency. This killed off the detente between the two leading Gulf nations.

As the de facto ruler of Saudi Arabia, Abdullah was opposed to external aggression against any Arab country, including Iraq under Saddam Hussein. His stance made little difference to President George W. Bush's decision to invade Iraq, in March 2003. His overthrow of Saddam created a chain of events which, inadvertently, benefited Iran and damaged Riyadh's standing in the region.

In the succeeding Chapter 11, I examine how the Saudi Kingdom strengthened its ties with Pakistan, a declared nuclear power, in order to face the prospect of Iran succeeding in building an atomic bomb. Saudi influence extended to the domestic politics of Pakistan after Army Chief General Parwez Musharraf's coup against the democratically elected government in October 1999.

PREFACE

With the election of radical conservative Mahmoud Ahmadinejad as Iran's president in August 2005, the issue of Tehran's nuclear program turned into a crisis which was referred to the United Nations Security Council. This reassured Riyadh. On the other hand, it refused to face the reality that once the US, as the occupying power, had introduced free and fair elections in post-Saddam Iraq, the majority Shias, hitherto suppressed by Sunni rulers, would gain power through the ballot. This happened in late 2005. The alienated Sunni militants, operating as Al Qaida in Mesopotamia, bombed the sacred Shia shrine in Samarra in February 2006, triggering low-intensity warfare between Shias and Sunnis. Washington and Baghdad worked jointly to damp down sectarian violence, and succeeded by paying cash to win the loyalties of Sunni tribal leaders. In his secret cable to the State Department in September 2009, the US ambassador in Baghdad conceded that Iranian influence in Iraq remained pervasive. This meant the balance of power in the Saudi-Iranian Cold War had shifted decisively in Tehran's favor. Riyadh found this unacceptable but could do little to alter it.

In contrast, Saudi Arabia under King Abdullah played a significant part in rolling back non-violent, popular demonstrations for democracy and human rights that occurred in early 2011 in Tunisia, Egypt, Bahrain and Yemen. Chapter 12 deals with the "Arab Spring" revolution and subsequent counterrevolution, and the contrasting stances taken by Riyadh and Tehran. The election of Muhammad Morsi, a Muslim Brotherhood leader, as president in Egypt's first free and fair election in June 2012 went down badly in Riyadh. The Saudis welcomed the military coup against Morsi on 3 July 2013 and King Abdullah helped to put together a package of $12 billion in assistance to the military junta in Cairo.

Iran described the popular demonstrations in Egypt and Bahrain as an "Islamic Awakening". But it failed to attribute that description to the peaceful protests in Syria against the regime of President Bashar Assad, a follower of the Alawi sub-sect in Shia Islam.

Thereafter Syria became an active front in the Iranian-Saudi Cold War. In 2013 the Syrian civil war acquired an international dimension when the Assad regime used chemical weapons. The failure of US President Barack Obama to punish the Syrian government for crossing his so-called "red line" in August 2013 deeply disappointed King

Abdullah. He ignored the fact that the progressive tightening of economic sanctions against Iran by the US and the European Union were making Iran, ruled by moderate President Hassan Rouhani, amenable to a compromise on the nuclear issue. Obama was determined to scale down Iran's nuclear program through non-military means.

With the emergence of Islamic State in Syria and Iraq (ISIS) after its capture of the leading city of Mosul in northern Iraq in June 2014, Obama made it his top priority to eradicate ISIS, the overthrow of Assad becoming of secondary importance.

When rebel Houthis, affiliated to the Zaidi Shia code, captured the Yemeni capital of Sanaa in September 2014, and expelled the Sunni President Abd Rabbu al Hadi, alarm bells rang in Saudi Arabia. It simply could not allow a pro-Iran Shia force to take power in the Arabian Peninsula. The Deputy Crown Prince, Muhammad bin Salman, led a coalition of friendly Arab states to intervene in the long-running civil war in Yemen with a blitzkrieg of air strikes in March 2015, with the US supplying intelligence. He vowed to expel the Houthis from Sanaa in six months. This ignited protest by Shias in the Kingdom's Eastern Province. Their ire intensified when, ignoring international appeals for clemency, the Saudi government executed the highly respected Ayatollah, Shaikh Nimr al Nimr, in January 2016. An angry mob in Tehran attacked the Saudi embassy, smashed its furniture and computers, and set alight part of the building. This led to the severing of diplomatic ties between the two countries.

Chapter 13 tracks the three fronts of the rivals' Cold War: in Iraq, Syria and Yemen. Whereas Iran dispatched its trained Shia volunteers to fight ISIS in Iraq, all Riyadh did was to lend four jet fighters to the Pentagon in its fight with ISIS. When Bin Salman shored up opposition forces with cash and weapons in Syria, President Vladimir Putin of Russia, which had a long history of cordial relations with Syria, intervened militarily. He dispatched Russian air force units to Syria, and shored up the the government's much depleted weapons stocks. Iran also sent further contingents of Shia volunteers to fight for Assad. The recapture of Eastern Aleppo, an opposition stronghold for three years, in December 2016 was a turning point. With that, Iran established superiority over the Saudis in Syria.

Unlike the rest of the world except Israel, Saudi Arabia—which monitored closely Iran's negotiations with five permanent members of the UN

Security Council and Germany—received the news of an agreement on 14 July 2015, entitled the Joint Comprehensive Plan of Action (JCPOA), with disapproval. In sharp contrast, there were spontaneous celebrations in Tehran. Obama reassured Saudi Arabia and other Gulf monarchies that his administration was seeking only a transaction with Tehran on the nuclear issue and not a broader rapprochement.

Frustrated by its failure to defeat the Houthis in Yemen, the Saudi Air Force resorted to hitting civilian targets, including food production, distribution and storage facilities, thus soiling the image of Saudi Arabia in the West and the wider Muslim world.

In Chapter 14, I describe how the newly elected US President Donald Trump has stoked the Gulf rivals' Cold War. He conflated Tehran-backed Shia radicalism with Sunni jihadism, ignoring the theological conflict between Sunnis and Shias. In his speech to the Arab Islamic summit in Riyadh he lumped together Iran and Sunni jihadis as part of the same evil of terrorism. He referred to Iranians as their regime's longest-suffering victims a day after they re-elected Hassan Rouhani as president by a large margin.

Pumped up by Trump's rhetoric, Bin Salman led a diplomatic and commercial boycott of Qatar for maintaining normal relations with Tehran. His move proved counterproductive. It threw Qatar into the welcoming arms of Iran and strengthened its military cooperation with Turkey, a leading Sunni state.

The 7 June 2017 attack on the Iranian Parliament and Khomeini's mausoleum by ISIS gunmen and suicide bombers shattered Trump's thesis of Iran-backed Shia radicalism and Sunni jihadism being part of the same evil of terrorism. It is worth noting that ISIS lambasted Iran for protecting its 9,000 Jews, who are entitled to one seat in Parliament.

After declaring Lebanese Hizbollah a terrorist organization in March 2016, Bin Salman pressured Saad Hariri, the Sunni prime minister, to dismiss the two Hizbollah ministers included in his national unity cabinet. Instead, he advocated dialogue with Hizbollah. In early November 2017, he was summoned to Riyadh by Bin Salman. Hariri surprised the regional capitals by announcing his resignation via video from Riyadh in protest against Iran's undue influence in Lebanese politics, adding that he feared assassination. The brash, hasty Crown Prince failed to brief France or the Unites States of his move, a failing which would inter alia lead to his diplomatic defeat. He had failed to note that these Western powers were keen not to destabilize Lebanon partly because as a country with a population of mere 4.3 million, it had taken in more then one million Syrian refugees.

On 6 December 2017, Trump sprang a sensational surprise by recognizing Jerusalem as the capital of Israel, thus breaching the universal recognition of Tel Aviv as the state's capital.

By so doing Trump legitimized the annexation and colonization of East Jerusalem since the 1967 Arab-Israeli War, in clear violation of international law. His decision was criticized by the UN secretary general as well as the European Union. As the rotating president of the Organisation of Islamic Cooperation, Turkey called an emergency summit of the OIC in Istanbul on 13 December, which more than fifty heads of state or government attended. Among them were the Qatari Emir Tamim Al Thani and the Lebanese President Michel Aoun, a Christian. But neither the Custodian of the Two Holy Mosques, Saudi King Salman, nor his assertive Crown Prince, attended to speak up for safeguarding Islam's third holiest site, the Al Aqsa Mosque. Instead, they deputed the Minister of Islamic Affairs, Endowments, Call and Guidance to attend the summit. With that Saudi Arabia practically lost its claim to be *primus inter pares* among Muslim nations. The final communiqué declared East Jerusalem as the capital of the state of Palestine and invited all countries to recognize the state of Palestine and East Jerusalem as its occupied capital. It described Trump's move as legally null and void.

The last Chapter provides an overview and a set of conclusions.

PROLOGUE

The timing was perfect, and so too was the place. The issuing of the landmark royal decree by eighty-one-year-old King Salman bin Abdul Aziz Al Saud, the most dramatic in the history of Saudi Arabia, was accomplished with military precision.

On 21 June 2017, four days before the end of the holy month of Ramadan,[1] following a two-day cabinet session at Al Safa Palace in the sacred city of Mecca, King Salman removed his fifty-seven-year-old nephew Crown Prince Muhammad bin Nayef as heir-apparent, and elevated his thirty-one-year-old son Muhammad bin Salman from Deputy Crown Prince to Crown Prince. To allow his subjects full ample time to celebrate the stunning announcement, he extended the normal three-day Eid Al-Fitr (Festival of Breaking the Fast) holiday at the end of Ramadan to a week.[2]

Along with his decree to promote his son Muhammad, the Saudi monarch issued an order calling on senior royals to pledge their fealty to the new Crown Prince. Muhammad bin Nayef promptly did so at Al Safa Palace, and in return his young successor respectfully kissed his hand in full view of official cameras. Saudi news channels repeatedly broadcast the royal kissing ritual, and stressed that all but three of the Allegiance Council's thirty-four members, consisting of senior princes, had approved of the king's decision.[3]

In Washington, President Donald Trump was quick to call Bin Salman to congratulate him on his "recent elevation,"[4] albeit while failing to telephone his father first. But, well aware of diplomatic protocol, the rulers of the neighboring Gulf States offered their congratulations first to King Salman for choosing the new Crown Prince. This was done even by Emir Tamim bin Hamad Al Thani whose tiny emirate, Qatar, was ostracized by the Saudi-led Axis of four Arab countries which cut diplomatic and economic links with Qatar on 5 June. Al Thani sent a congratulatory cable to King Salman "on the occasion of the selection of His Royal Highness Prince Muhammad bin Salman Al Saud as Crown Prince" while expressing the prospect of "brotherly relations between the two brotherly countries".[5]

Across the Persian Gulf the state-run Press TV of Iran described the surprise decision by King Salman as "a soft coup." Iran's semi-official Fars news agency, affiliated to the elite Islamic Revolutionary Guard Corps, called the appointment "a political earthquake." It was left to Seyedhossein Naghavi-Hosseini, chairman of Iran's parliamentary committee on national security and foreign policy, to provide appropriate texture: "After the appointment of Bin Salman as the Crown Prince, we urge Saudi officials to act with prudence and according to international norms and they should know their limits," he said.[6] He was mindful that in his interview with the Dubai-based but Saudi-owned satellite television channel, Al Arabiya, on 1 May, Bin Salman had framed Riyadh's tensions with Tehran in sectarian terms, and claimed that it was Iran's goal "to control the Islamic world." He vowed to take "the battle" to Iran.[7]

The Saudi-Iranian battle for regional supremacy was ongoing. Riyadh and Tehran backed opposite sides in the wars in Syria and Yemen while supporting political rivals in Bahrain, Iraq and Lebanon.[8] Beyond the Arab Middle East, they supported different factions in Afghanistan and Pakistan.

As the favorite son of the Saudi monarch, Bin Salman had acquired the most prized rank in the Kingdom in two stages, which coincided with King Salman's successive steps to implement his soft coup.

Salman Upends the Dynastic Tradition

Within 100 days of his accession to the throne on 23 January 2015—during which posters showing Salman, Crown Prince Muqrin bin Abdul Aziz Al Saud, and the bespectacled and avuncular but clever, media-savvy and ambitious Bin Nayef had been displayed across the kingdom—King Salman stunned the country by elbowing out Muqrin. He claimed to have secured the approval of a majority of the Allegiance Council. This marked the first stage of Salman's palace coup.

Born to Baraka al Yemeniya, the Yemen-born eighteenth wife of King Abdul Aziz bin Abdul Rahman Al Saud (aka, Ibn Saud), the founder of the Saudi kingdom, Muqrin was socially regarded as being a notch below the offspring of Ibn Saud's Saudi wives. However, Muqrin was named the Deputy Crown Prince by King Abdullah (r. 2005–2015), with whom he had a long-lasting rapport, in March 2014. King Salman promoted Bin Nayef to Crown Prince. And, in his choice of the Deputy Crown Prince, he upended the long-established principle of seniority. Ignoring the eligibility of his four surviving sons, he promoted Muhammad to that position. As the first of the six sons born to King Salman's third and last wife, Fahda bint Falah bin Sultan al Hithalayn—nearly 20 years junior to her husband—he had been their favorite since infancy.

In dynastic terms, Salman accomplished three major aims. He restored royal authority to the Sudairi clan[9] whose hold on power was disrupted when Abdullah, a non-Sudairi, became the monarch in 2005. He paved the path for the transfer of absolute power to a younger generation more than six decades after the death of the dynasty's founder in 1953. And, in the absence of a male child of Bin Nayef, he assured the future of his favorite son, Muhammad, as the eventual King.

Salman implemented the second part of his palace coup by jettisoning Bin Nayef, depriving him even of the Interior Ministry which he had run with great efficiency for many years. Later he would be placed under virtual house arrest and his bank accounts frozen.

There seems also to be a third part to the grand plan: the abdication of the ailing Salman in favor of his son in the near future. This is most likely to happen during the holy month of Ramadan. By so doing Salman would be emulating the example of Qatari Emir Hamad bin Khalifa Al Thani who stepped down in June 2013 to allow thirty-three-year-old Crown Prince Tamim to ascend the throne.

1

INTRODUCTION

The contrasting histories of Iran and Saudi Arabia are aptly illustrated by their respective national museums.

Two complexes house the National Museum in northern Tehran: the Museum of Ancient Iran, inaugurated in 1937, and the Museum of the Islamic Era, set amid the lawns of the earlier museum, which opened in 1972. The seven-acre National Museum of Saudi Arabia containing eight galleries, located east of the main Murabba Square in Riyadh, and fronted by a sweeping wall of yellow limestone, is eye-catching. It is part of the vast Historical Center, which was unveiled by King Fahd bin Abdul Aziz on 23 January 1999 to mark the Islamic centenary of the establishment of the present (and the third) Saudi State, established on 15 January 1902,[1] by King Abdul Aziz bin Abdul Rahman Al Saud, also known as Ibn Saud.

The Museum of Ancient Iran, measuring 11,000 square meters, consists of three halls. These contain artifacts and fossils covering several millennia, starting with the lower, middle, and upper Paleolithic period and ending with the Sassanian empire. The Museum of the Islamic Era has had its interior altered several times. It was being remodeled when the 1979 Revolution swept the country. Its three floors exhibit the exquisite prehistoric pottery from the Caspian Sea littoral followed by some modern works. Overall, it contains various pieces of pottery, textiles, texts, artworks, astrolabes, and clay tile calligraphy from Iran's post-classical era. Given this long and distinguished history, it is no surprise that Iranians have a deeply embedded sense of national identity. They manifested this when tens of thousands of secular-minded Iranians volunteered to join the army of the newly established Islamic Republic of Iran to repulse the invasion of their country by Iraqi President Saddam Hussein in 1980.

By contrast, the northern wing of Riyadh's national museum hosts only three small pre-Islamic galleries before the birth of Prophet Muhammad in 570 CE. It is linked by a bridge to the much larger southern wing that displays the Islamic history of the Arabian Peninsula. After the gallery on Prophet Muhammad comes one on the rise and fall of the Islamic Caliphates, ending with the Ottomans, leading to the first Saudi State, in 1744. It lasted until 1818. It as well as the Second Saudi State (1824–1891) are the subjects of the next gallery. The collapse of the Second Saudi State comes at the end of Gallery Six. What follows is labeled "Unification." Here it refers to the unification of Najd and its Dependencies and the western region of Hijaz on 23 September 1932. However, the two words missing from the title of Gallery Seven are "through jihad".

Given this historical background, it is reasonable to expect the Saudi Kingdom to enjoy cordial relations with the "Islamic Republic" of Iran, established in April 1979. But an Islamic republic is radically different from a theocratic, absolute monarchy. As for relations between the Saudi kingdom and monarchical Iran, these have had a chequered history.

Claims to Exceptionalism

The common factor between Saudi Arabia and Iran is their claim to exceptionalism. Iranian identity as a nation has a recorded chronicle dating back six millennia. The origins of the modern Persian language lie in Old Persian, written in cuneiform characters and in use until the third century BCE, and Middle Persian, written in the Aramaic script in vogue between the third and ninth centuries BCE. After that modern Persian, using the Arabic script, became the literary and administrative language in Muslim ruled empires, from the Indian sub-continent to Ottoman Turkey.

INTRODUCTION

On 15 October 1971, Muhammad Reza Shah Pahlavi claimed to celebrate with extravagant lavishness 2,500 years of unbroken monarchy in Iran at Persepolis, once the capital of the ancient Achaemenid Empire, founded in c. 530 BCE. Barring a brief period of occupation by Britain and Russia during the Second World War, Iran has the distinction of being one of the four Muslim countries not colonized by a European power, the others being Afghanistan, Saudi Arabia and Turkey.

Iranian influence in architecture can be seen from Central Asia to South Asia. In recent times, Iranians overthrew the monarchy of Muhammad Reza Shah Pahlavi, a secular ruler, through a non-violent revolution in 1979. The leaders of the subsequent Islamic Republic claim to have married popularly elected representative government with Islamic tenets. They have held parliamentary and presidential elections at regular intervals. However the Paris-based Reporters Without Borders ranked Iran 165th out of 180 countries for freedom of the press, with Russia being 148th and India 136th.[2] But, with nine out of its ten citizens being Shia, a minority sect in Islam, Iran is one of the only four Shia-majority members of the 57-strong Organisation of Islamic Cooperation.[3]

The claims of Saudi Arabia's exceptionalism rest on different pillars. Unlike any other country on earth, its name is defined by the title of a family: Al Saud. The volume of its underground sea of petroleum is second only to that of Venezuela. Its state-owned Saudi Arabian American Oil Company (Aramco), is the largest oil corporation in the world, and its annual output of the commodity is the highest. Yet among the many oil giants, worldwide, it is the only one which does not publish its financial accounts. Globally, it is the number one exporter of oil, contributing one out of every four oil barrels traded on the international market, and therefore the single most important member of the Organization of Petroleum Exporting Countries (OPEC). And yet another exception is the vital importance of petroleum to its economy, which is large enough to secure it inclusion in G20—the group of twenty richest nations of the globe. Oil is the fuel for generating electricity. The subsidized power rates buttress energy-intensive cement factories, aluminum smelting plants, and energy-draining desalination plants. Commercial air-conditioners cool sprawling shopping malls while outside temperatures soar to 100°C and

3

children sled at Snow City in downtown Riyadh. Gasoline is cheaper than bottled water, and SUVs snarl in city traffic.

In 2015, Saudi Arabia set a record in peace time by spending 13.7 per cent of its gross domestic product (GDP) on defense. In absolute terms, its defense budget was the third highest after the United States and China.[4]

Politically, among the 51 authoritarian regimes in the world, Saudi Arabia is more repressive than 43 others, according to the Economist Intelligence Unit.[5] It has banned not only political parties and trade unions, but even photography clubs.[6] Reporters Without Borders ranked the Saudi Kingdom 168th out of 180 countries for freedom of the press.[7] Little wonder that in a region extending from Algeria to Bangladesh, it has proved to be an immovable rock of reaction, doggedly opposing democracy, secularism and gender equality.

It is the most theocratic state in the world. It punishes public celebration of non-Muslim religions, or even the wearing of a cross by a Christian or an Om sign by a Hindu. This restriction is based on the cardinal Saudi religious principle that all of the Kingdom's territory is a mosque, a derivative of Prophet Muhammad's last injunction about there being no two religions in Arabia. Saudi Arabia enforces strict segregation of sexes in public places. A royal decree lifting the ban on women driving issued in September 2017 is to be implemented nine months later. Every adult female must have a male relative as her "guardian" whose permission she is required to have in order to travel, study, or work. The guardian is legally entitled to make a number of critical decisions on a woman's behalf.[8] In mid-2017 an exemption was made when a woman wished to use a public health facility or educational institution. By stark contrast, in Islamic Iran hijab-wearing women are to be seen working in banks, airports, factories, hospitals, public and private offices, and supermarkets as well as in law enforcement agencies. They serve as government ministers. They drive cars and go skiing. And in the communal taxis plying along the main roads of Tehran, male and female passengers sit tightly together.

Although the Saudi kingdom is one among 58 countries where capital punishment is meted out, it stands out because of the decapitation of convicted criminals in public, thus re-enacting a practice dating back to the seventh-century Arabia of Prophet Muhammad.

INTRODUCTION

Saudi Arabia is home to the two most sacred sites of Islam in Mecca and Medina. While praying, Muslims the world over face Mecca. It is the only modern state established by holy jihad. Alone among the flags of the 195 members of the United Nations, its flag carries the creed of a religion—"There is no god but Allah, Muhammad is the messenger of Allah"—in Arabic. And it was at its initative that the first official pan-Islamic institution of inter-governmental cooperation of Muslim-majority countries, called Organisation of the Islamic Conference (later renamed Organisation of Islamic Cooperation) was formed in 1969.

Arabia Deserta, the Birth Place of Wahhabism

Until the nineteenth century, the Arabian Peninsula was widely viewed as comprising Arabia Felix and Arabia Deserta. Blessed with seasonal monsoon rains, the southwestern region of the peninsula was agricultural, supporting settled communities, amply earning the title of Arabia Felix. It was associated with the legendary Queen of Sheba, mentioned in the Old Testament—or Bilqis in the Arab tradition—arriving at the court of Solomon in Jerusalem at the head of an impressively long caravan. In stark contrast, Arabia Deserta, the peninsula's interior, was inhabited by nomadic tribes notorious for their periodic raids on Mesopotamia to the north and Arabia Felix to the south. It was only in 1888, with the publication of *Travels in Arabia Deserta*, by Charles Doughty (1843–1926), a British poet, writer and traveler, recording his trekking in the inhospitable region, that the outside world got some sense of the place. As a travel writer, however, Doughty was upstaged by Richard Francis Burton (1821–1890). His *Personal Narrative of a Pilgrimage to el Medinah and Meccah*, first published in 1855–56, was a bestseller.

Burton's description of the Hajj pilgrimage shows that he was granted an extraordinary favor. "I performed the seven circuits round the Kaaba, called the *Tawaf*," he wrote. "I then managed to have a way pushed for me through the immense crowd to kiss it. While kissing it, and rubbing hands and forehead upon it, I narrowly observed it, and came away persuaded that it is an aerolite [stony meteorite]. It is curious that almost all agree upon one point, namely, that the stone is volcanic... a 'block of volcanic basalt, whose circumference is sprinkled with little crystals, pointed and straw-like, with rhombs of tile-red felspar [dense igneous rock] upon a dark ground like velvet or char-coal, except one of its protuberances, which is reddish'. It is also described as 'a lava containing several small extraneous particles of a whitish and a yellowish substance'."

Today, as seen from the outside, the Kaaba is a 50 feet high boxlike structure of gray stone over a base of 40 feet by 35 feet. Covered with black and gold cloth weaved from silk and cotton and adorned with verses from the Quran, called the *kiswa* (Arabic: garment),[9] it is revered as the Throne of Allah (Arabic: Al means the; and lah, God). It contains the sacred Black Stone, regarded as the right hand of Allah. During the annual Hajj, an estimated three million Muslims, men and women, collectively circumambulate the Kaaba seven times, thus sym-bolically re-enacting an exercise of the angels in Paradise.

To this day, both Mecca and Medina, the burial place of Prophet Muhammad (570–632 CE), remain out of bounds for non-Muslims. This has to do with the Quranic verse (9.28), which reads: "O believ-ers, the idolaters are indeed unclean; and so let them not come near the Holy Mosque after this year of theirs". But the Saudi government has gone beyond the Quranic injunction. It has imposed a blanket ban on the entry of non-Muslims to Mecca, a city of 330 sq miles (850 sq km) with a population of 2.35 million—as well as Medina, occupying 127 sq miles (590 sq km) and home to 1.2 million people.

There are police check posts on approach roads to Mecca a few miles from the Holy City. Here lawmen check the documentation of the travelers. Those who fail to prove they are Muslim are turned away. On arrival at a Saudi airport, foreigners, Muslim or non-Muslim, are often informed that they must abide by the rules of the Sharia, Islamic Law. But the Saudi canon is of a specific Sunni variety, a sub-sect within the fundamentalist Hanbali school of Sunni Islam.[10] This sub-sect is commonly known as Wahhabism although its followers are officially called Muwahideen, Unitarian believers in the unity of Allah.

Wahhabi Doctrine

Wahhabism was founded by Muhammad bin Abdul Wahhab (1703–1792), a tall, high-cheekboned, fierce-looking native of the Uyayna oasis in southern Najd (lit., raised area), a bastion of the Hanbali code in Islam as explicated by Taqi al Din ibn Taimiya (1263–1328). Like Martin Luther (1483–1546), Wahhab advocated return to the earliest teachings of the faith, freed from later medieval accretions. Thus his teachings were akin to Salafiya, the doctrine which requires the faithful to follow the practices of the early converts to Islam, called *salaf al Salafin*, the pious ancestors.

The principal elements of Wahhab's version of Islam were respect and worship of unseen Allah only, refraining from worshiping man-made Allah's substitutes or human intermediaries, rejection of innovations in Islam, emulating the early converts to Islam with simplicity, and promoting virtue and forbidding vice. Deviating from the Hanbali practices, Wahhab made attendance at public prayer obligatory, and forbade minarets in the building of mosques.

In 1744, the Najd ruler Muhammad ibn Saud (ruled 1745–1765), a celebrated warrior with a hooked nose, large expressive eyes and a neatly trimmed beard, who had successfully defended the local date palm plantations in central Najd from marauding tribes, gave refuge to Abdul Wahhab from a nearby village after his expulsion for preaching his version of Islam. Ibn Saud accepted his guest's religious doctrine and married his daughter. Together they established the Emirate of Diriya, which is considered the first Saudi State.

The dynastic alliance and power-sharing arrangement between the two families has endured to this day. While the Al Saud lets the Al Shaikh descendants of Wahhab maintain authority in religious matters, the Al Shaikh supports the Al Saud's political power, thus imparting it Islamic legitimacy. In modern times Muhammad bin Ibrahim Al Shaikh (1893–1969) was the Grand Mufti of Saudi Arabia from 1953 until his death in 1969.[11]

The followers of Wahhab and Ibn Saud, known as Wahhabis, mounted a jihad which involved demolishing tombs, shrines, and even grave markers, and cleansing Islam of Shiaism since its excessive reverence for Prophet Muhammad's family was deemed to be verging on idolatry. Citing the Hadith (Sayings and Deeds of Muhammad), they banned music, dancing and even poetry, an integral part of Arab life. They prohibited the use of silk, gold, ornaments and jewellery. Regarding themselves to be the true believers, they lambasted all other brands of Islam.

It was the second ruler of the Emirate of Diriya, Abdul Aziz bin Muhammad bin Saud, who went far beyond demolishing shrines of local Shia saints. In April 1802, leading an armed force of 12,000, he sacked the Shia holy city of Karbala in present day Iraq, plundered the golden-domed tomb of Imam Hussein bin Ali (died in 680 CE), and butchered about 5,000 Shias, including women and children. "We took Karbala and we slaughtered," noted Uthman bin Bashir al Najdi, the chronicler of the Emirate of Diriya. "We took its people *sabaya* [as booty and slaves]. With the permission of Allah, we will not apologize for what we have done, and we will tell all *kuffar* [unbelievers], 'You will receive similar treatment'."[12]

Historic Sunni-Shia Divide

Hostility between Shias and Sunnis dates back to the events following the death of Prophet Muhammad in 632 CE. His first successor as caliph, Abu Bakr, chosen by an assembly of the Prophet's helpers, died two years later. Before his death he nominated Omar ibn Khattab, one of the fathers-in-law of the Prophet. He was later approved by community leaders. This disappointed Ali ibn Abi Talib, the Prophet's cousin married to his daughter Fatima. Omar was stabbed by an infuriated Iranian slave, Piruz Nahavandi, in 644 CE. On his death-bed he nominated an electoral college of six to name his successor as caliph. It included Ali and Uthman ibn Affan, married to two of the Prophet's daughters. The caliphate was offered to Ali provided he agreed to rule according to the Quran and the Prophet's Practice, Sunna, and accept all the recorded precedents set by the previous caliphs. Ali rejected the second condition. So the caliphate went to Uthman who accepted both conditions.

In June 656 CE, a group of rebel soldiers attacked Uthman's house and killed him. Ali condemned the assassination but made no effort to apprehend the killers. Calling Ali "the first among Muslims", the rebels and most of the adult male residents of Medina elected him the caliph. Those who recognized Ali as the only legitimate successor to Prophet Muhammad were called Shiat or Shia Ali, Partisans of Ali. And those who also recognized Abu Bakr, Omar and Uthman as caliphs came to be known as Sunnis, derivative of *Ahl al Sunna*, People of the Path of Prophet Muhammad. Since then the differences between Sunnis and Shias have widened and deepened.

INTRODUCTION

As caliph, Ali proved to be an inspiring leader of the Islamic community and a skilled general on the battlefield wielding his legendary forked tongue *zulfikar* sword. "There is no hero except Ali; There is no sword except his zulfikar," became the battle cry of Shiat Ali. However, Ali was killed in January 661 CE with a poisonous sword wielded by Abdul Rahman bin Muljam, a member of the Khariji sect, which denounced Ali's claim to the caliphate, declaring that that any pious Muslim was worthy of becoming caliph.

Ever since the original split, differences between Sunnis and Shias have widened. Shias differ from Sunnis in multiple ways. Differences have emerged even in the way a prayer is offered. Today Shias constitute 10 to 13 per cent of the global Muslim population of 1.6 billion. Most Shias are to be found in the Middle East, South Asia and Azerbaijan. In 2013, with 70 million Shias among its 77.5 million citizens, Iran had 40 per cent of the globe's Shia population.

Multiple Differences

Shias differ from Sunnis in doctrine, ritual, law and religious organization as well as the prayer ritual. The Shia credo consists of five basic principles and ten duties. Shias share three principles with Sunnis— monotheism, prophet-hood, which is a means of communication between Allah and humankind, and resurrection when the souls of dead human beings will be raised by God on their Day of Judgment and their deeds on earth judged. But Shias have two more: *imamat*, and *aadl* (justice), the just nature of Allah. Shias believe that only those in the lineage of Prophet Muhammad—and thus of his daughter, Fatima, and her husband, Ali—can govern Muslims on behalf of Allah, and that the Imams,[13] being divinely inspired, are infallible. By contrast, Sunnis believe that only Allah is infallible, with no exception made even for Prophet Muhammad. Finally, the ruler of Muslims must be just. The religious duties of Shias include daily prayers, fasting during Ramadan, *khums* (an Islamic tithe), *zakat* (alms tax), Hajj, encouraging virtue, discouraging evil, and loving Shia Imams and their followers.

Orthodox Sunnis consider the practice of some Shia clerics of cursing the first three of their four Rightly Guided Caliphs—Abu Bakr, Omar, Uthman and Ali—as un-Islamic. A Muslim must not curse the Companions of the Prophet.

Shia emotionalism finds outlets in mourning Imams Ali (assassinated), Hassan (poisoned) and Hussein (killed in an unequal battle), and in the heart-rending entreaties offered at their shrines. Shias believe that through asceticism and suffering one can remove the ill-effects of the humiliation and persecution inflicted on these Imams. During the Ashura (literally, Tenth, meaning Tenth of Muharram) ritual, the annual enactment of passion plays leading up to the martyrdom of Imam Hussein on 10 Muharram, 61 After Hijra[14]—17 May 681 CE—and self-flagellation by the faithful provide outlets for expiating the guilt and pain originally felt by the inhabitants of the southern Iraqi city of Kufa for abandoning Imam Hussein after having invited him to their settlement to take charge and fight the heavily armed, large forces of the interloper Yazid.[15] Sunni Islam offers no such outlets for its followers.

In fact, orthodox Sunnis argue that self-flagellation to commemorate the death of Imam Hussein runs counter to Prophet Muhammad calling on grieving women not to tear up their clothes and beat their breasts in grief.

Lastly, Shias and Sunnis organize religion and religious activities differently. Sunnis regard religious activities as the exclusive domain of the (Muslim) state. When the *ulema*—religious scholars—act as judges, preachers, or educators they do so under the aegis of the state. There is scant opportunity for the *ulema* to organize religion on their own. In contrast, in Shia Iran, leading *mujtahids* (authorities on Islamic Law), being recipients of the *khums* from their followers, maintain theological colleges and social welfare activities independent of the state. Also by adopting the custom of naming the most revered colleague as the *marja-e taqlid* (source of emulation), whose independent opinion on the compatibility of major state decisions with Islam had to be sought, the religious hierarchy underlined its independence. Unlike in the Sunni religious establishment, Shia clerics are ranked from *thiqatalislam* (trust of Islam) to *hojatalislam* (proof of Islam) to ayatollah (sign of Allah) to *ayatollah-ozma* (grand ayatollah). Among Sunnis, the religious hierarchy, starting at the top, runs as follows: *mujtahid*; Shaikh al Islam (wise man of Islam); Mufti al Azam (Grand Mufti, Deliverer of fatwas, religious decrees); Mufti; Qadi (religious judge); and Shaikh. It is the Muslim ruler in a Sunni-majority state who appoints the Shaikh al Islam or the Grand Mufti.[16]

INTRODUCTION

Divergent Prayer Rituals

Differences have emerged even in the way a prayer is offered—as described by Samra Hussain, a Sunni, who joined a Friday prayer congregation in the women's section in a Shia mosque.

"It was soon time for the Friday prayers (*salah* in Arabic), and the women got up" she wrote in her online post. "There were about 15 women present. I stood in line and noticed that everyone had a small round stone on the floor [or the prayer mat] in front of them. I wasn't sure what that was, but stood in line, my space void of the stone. I felt a little nervous, wondering if someone would ask me about my prayer stone, but surprisingly, nobody asked me about it. The salah was slightly different, but I followed others as it went on. For example, nobody folded their hands on their chest as is usual for Sunni Muslim women, but rather, everyone kept their arms comfortably against the sides of their body. Also, the prayer did not go directly into '*ruku*' (bending partly with hands on knees) as I am accustomed to do in a Sunni mosque. But rather a prayer was said during which everyone held out their hands (the symbol of asking God for something), followed by the ruku. The recitations were also slightly different during the ruku and the '*sujoo*' (full prostration with head bowed on floor). Once sitting, with legs folded, the imam went directly to reciting the '*shuhada*' (I bear witness that there is no god except Allah and that Muhammad is His messenger). The last difference I noticed was that upon the completion of the salah, after the imam said the salutations for the angels, nobody turned their head from side to side as Sunnis do. Everyone simply stopped the prayer, which was unusual for me, since I had never done that before. I thought about leaving, and then heard another call to prayer. Everyone got up. Confused, I got up. I simply joined the congregation for another round of salah. Were these extra prayers? A young woman explained that the second salah was '*asr*' (late afternoon prayer). So it turns out Shia Muslims pray asr right after the Friday [noon] prayers, by combining two prayers into one."[17] The "stone" mentioned by Hussain was in fact a small baked clay tablet of the soil from Karbala, the place where Imam Hussein was martyred on the 10 Muharram of 61st Islamic year, or 17 May 681.[18]

Although Shias combine two of the five daily prayers, Shia traders in Saudi Arabia are forced to close their stores during all five prayer times, in accordance with the Sunni practice. Shia mosques in mixed religious neighborhoods are required to recite the Sunni call to prayer, which is distinct from the Shia call, at prayer times.[19]

Shias in the Arabian Peninsula

In the Arabian Peninsula, once Ibn Saud had captured the eastern region of Al Hasa in 1913, he had to deal with the religious practices of Shias, given his Wahhabi affiliation. But he postponed the task while he focused on gaining more territory. Later, after capturing Hijaz along the Red Sea in 1924, he demolished the tombs worshipped by Shias. In the late 1920s, the armed followers of Ibn Saud, known as al Ikhwan, the Brotherhood, fired by their newly adopted Wahhabism, urged him to convert the Shias in Al Hasa forcibly to Wahhabi Islam. In response, he dispatched Wahhabi missionaries to the region to persuade the Shias to covert. The plan did not work. Consequently, Ibn Saud decided to allow the Shias to run their own mosques and exempted them from the Hanbali inheritance rules. This has continued. Many decades on, misconceptions about Shias among Saudi Sunnis are not uncommon. Many semi-literate Saudi Sunnis along with some literate ones believe that Shias hide their forked tails under their *thobes*, and that they indulge in unnatural sexual practices. Also, during the run-up to the Ashura, Shias of both sexes assemble in their *hussaiiyas* (meeting rooms) where they discard their clothes and engage in group sex. The subsequent babies are venerated by the community and grow up to become their *mullahs*.[20]

Living in the midst of a hostile, preponderant Sunni majority, Shias developed *taqiya*, or cautionary dissimulation, denying their sectarian identity—a defensive tactic sanctioned by their *mullahs*. Under Ibn Saud, they kept a low profile while their clerics practiced quietism. This would change in 1975, when young Shias gathered around Hassan al Saffar, a youthful, articulate cleric with downcast eyes and a round white turban, to form the Reform Movement clandestinely. Its aim was to counter discrimination against Shias and improve their socio-economic status. Its moderate demands included the right to publish Shia religious books and an end to the denunciations of Shias by Wahhabi preachers. In his sermons Saffar stayed strictly religious by stressing the determined resistance that Imam Hussein offered to injustice. But after the establishment of the Islamic Republic of Iran in 1979, the tone of Shia discourse in the Eastern Province would sharpen radically.

Ups and Downs of the House of Saud

The expanded land of the First Saudi state reached the Iraqi and Syrian borders, and included the western Hijaz region in the Arabian Peninsula, containing Mecca and Medina. This led the Ottoman sultan, a follower of the Hanafi school of Sunni Islam, to order the governor of Egypt, Muhammad Ali, to quell the Wahhabi movement. Defeated by the Ottoman troops, Abdullah bin Saud bin Abdul Aziz Al Saud, the great grandson of the founder of the First Saudi State, retreated from the Hijaz region to Diriya. After an interregnum of several years Ottoman general Ibrahim Pasha marched to Diriya and besieged it in 1818. Abdullah Al Saud surrendered. He was shipped to Constantinople. Tellingly, the Sharia court there found him guilty of heresy and brigandage, and sentenced him to death. He was taken to the gate of the Sultan's palace, and decapitated. His headless body was spiked on a tall pole and displayed, a sunken dagger pinning the sentence of excommunication to his bloodied chest, in a public square.[21]

Later, Abdullah Al Saud's son Turki managed to assemble a large enough army in the Wahhabi stronghold of Najd to retake Diriya and Riyadh from the Egyptian forces in 1824. He set up the Emirate of Najd, later titled the Second Saudi State. Its history was peppered with disputes among brothers about legitimate succession. A long, internecine warfare between two sons of Faisal bin Turki Al Saud, named Abdullah and Saud, which started in 1875, enabled their non-Wahhabi vassal in the north, Muhammad bin Rashid, to extend his power to most of the Najd region. He allied with the Ottoman Turks, and in the Battle of Mulayda in 1891 defeated the Al Saud ruler, Abdul Rahman bin Faisal, who took refuge in the neighboring independent Emirate of Kuwait. Thus ended the Second Saudi State.

After setting out from Kuwait with fifty armed men, the twenty-six-year-old Abdul Aziz bin Abdul Rahman Al Saud (aka, Ibn Saud) decided to retake Riyadh after capturing Diriya. On the night of 15 January 1902, he led forty men over the walls of Riyadh on improvised planks of assembled palm tree trunks. They surrounded the Masmak Fort, in the middle of the night, startling the sleeping forces of the Al Rashid governor, Ajlan. His ill-prepared resistance ended with his death in front of the fortress made of mud-bricks. Realizing the potential of the extraordinarily daring six-foot-four-inches tall son with a massive chest, Ibn Saud, who was injured in the raid, as a more effective leader than him, Abdul Rahman abdicated in his favor a week later.

At first Ibn Saud consolidated his power in Najd with the help of the sedentary population of oases. He then focused on winning over the leaders of the nomadic tribes by engaging the *mutawwa* (aka, Mutawween; meaning volunteers), religious volunteers later called police, to teach them the tenets of Islam as a step towards replacing their customary law with the Islamic Law, Sharia, and their traditional tribal bonds with religious ones. Thus Ibn Saud's regime came to rest on three pillars: Islamic education, enforcing the Sharia, and protecting public morality. This template has remained unchanged throughout the reigns of his six successors.

Then under King Salman the institution was reformed in April 2016 as outlined by the then Deputy Crown Prince Muhammad bin Salman. The government issued a set of guidelines which curtailed the powers of the mutawwa, then functioning as a semi-autonomous, 5,000-strong force. Till then they had patrolled parks, streets and shopping malls, sought to combat drug use, stopped unrelated men and women from mixing in public and ensured shops closed for daily prayers. Along with several government agencies they also monitored online activity. The new guidelines deprived the mutawwa of the right to see a person's ID or other documents and to entrap or arrest people—a procedure described as the sole right of the police and drug enforcement officials."[22]

During the early formative period, in order to protect his realm, Ibn Saud came up with the idea of forming a permanent fighting force. He encouraged nomadic tribes to settle in colonies, calling them *hijra* (Arabic: migration)—from a life of ignorance to one of enlightenment—and the settlers, al Ikhwan (Arabic: Brethren or brotherhood).

Each settlement of some 2,000 or so people included agricultural land, grazing pastures and reliable water supplies. In due course they became the religious, political, military, administrative and educational centers of Wahhabism. They enabled Ibn Saud to achieve something that no other power or leaders had so far done: impose a centralized rule over the forty major tribes inhabiting Najd. He kept many chiefs in the capital, Riyadh, under surveillance with the ostensible aim of educating them in Wahhabism.

The life in an Ikhwan colony, run jointly by an emir and a governor, was centered round mosques. The ulema played an important role as did the Mutawween who were trained in Riyadh. They punished those found smoking, singing or dancing, wearing gold or silk, or failing to perform the Islamic rituals. The emir, elected by the local all-male consultative assembly, reported to the Imam, the title given to Ibn Saud, and the governor, who dealt with the Sharia, and reported to the Shaikh al Islam, the head of the ulema, also based in Riyadh.[23]

The number of colonies would grow to 200. They would nurture the Ikhwan who were fired with fanatical zeal to spread the Wahhabi version of Islam to the farthest corners of the Arabian Peninsula and beyond. They were instrumental in Ibn Saud's capture of the region of Al Hasa in 1913. Three years later Ibn Saud secured the surrender of Saud bin Rashid, the most powerful among the Rashidis. After the downfall of the Ottoman Empire in 1918 at the end of the First World War, he conquered the Asir region on the Red Sea from Yemen in 1920. The next year he defeated his rival, Muhammad bin Rashid, and finally took control of the northern Hail region from the Rashid dynasty.

In 1924 he defeated Sharif Hussein bin Ali al Hashem in Hijaz, and deposed him. Though his Wahhabi soldiers did not sack Mecca and Medina, they demolished monuments and grave markers that were being used for prayers to Muslim saints by Shias.

Among other things, this incensed Shia Iran's monarch, Reza Shah Pahlavi (r. 1925–1941). He was wary of the Wahhabi Ibn Saud becoming the guardian of Islam's two holiest sites, and wondered if Ibn Saud would allow Shias to perform the Hajj in Mecca according to their own rituals. He expressed his fears publicly. As a result, protracted negotiations between the two monarchs followed. Besides the guardianship of Mecca and Medina, these covered the tricky issue of meddling in each other's domestic affairs, and the status of Bahrain where the majority Shias were governed by a Sunni dynasty since 1783. The end result was a friendly treaty between the two monarchies signed in Tehran in 1929.

Guardianship of the holy places would rest with the Saudi state; Hajj would be open to all Muslims, conducted in accordance with the rules of the Sharia. There would be no interference in countries' internal affairs. And since Bahrain was neither an Iranian nor a Saudi principality, it had sovereign status.[24]

Ibn Saud continued to couch his campaigns in Islamic terms, as a struggle to punish either religious dissenters or those who had strayed from true Islam as represented by the Wahhabi doctrine. From this flows the official claim that the Kingdom of Saudi Arabia is the only modern state to owe its existence to jihad.

Having declared himself King of Hijaz and Sultanate of Najd in January 1926, Ibn Saud sought international recognition. The following year Britain, the most powerful foreign power in the Gulf region, recognized him as the ruler of Hijaz and Najd. In return he accepted Britain as the protector of Oman and the Gulf principalities as well as the territorial integrity of Iraq and Transjordan, then under British Mandate.

Ignoring Ibn Saud's compact with Britain, some of the Ikhwan commanders continued to raid territories outside his domain. This led to a battle between the militant Ikhwan and Ibn Saud in March 1929 at Sabila, with 8,000 camel-borne Ikhwan—choosing to use only lancers and swords as in the days of Prophet Muhammad—facing 30,000 soldiers of Al Saud, equipped with motorized weapons supplied by the British. The rebels were defeated. Further battles followed, and it was not until January 1930 that the last of the defiant Ikhwan chiefs surrendered.[25] On 23 September 1932 Ibn Saud combined his domains, comprising about three-quarters of 1.12 million sq miles (3.1 million sq km) of the Arabian Peninsula—captured over the past three decades through a rich mix of daring, duplicity, co-option, coercion, punishment and persuasion—into the Kingdom of Saudi Arabia, and declared himself King of Saudi Arabia.

For more than seven decades the Saudi regime failed to celebrate the kingdom's founding date, 23 September, as the National Day holiday. The powerful Wahhabi ulema would not allow it. They argued that only Allah could grant holidays to Muslims. They made repeated references to the widely known Hadith (Sayings and Deeds of Prophet Muhammad) that the Prophet rebuked his followers when, on arriving in Medina, he noticed them celebrating two local, secular holidays dating back to the Age of Ignorance, the term used for the pre-Islamic era. "Allah has substituted what is better for you: the Eid al Adha [festival of sacrifice at the end of the Hajj] and the Eid al Fitr [festival of breaking of the fast at the end of Ramadan]," he declared. The Wahhabi ulema were opposed to even declaring Prophet Muhammad's birth day as a national holiday. None the less, King Abdullah bin Abdul Aziz Al Saud, resolved to forge a distinct Saudi identity, overruled them soon after ascending the throne on 1 August 2005. He decreed 23 September as a national holiday starting in 2006. This continues. In sharp contrast, nationalism is built into the DNA of Iran with a recorded history dating back to ancient times.

Broad Socio-economic Differences

The Kingdom of Saudi Arabia was the end result of the amalgamation of four distinct regions: Al Hasa in the east with a large Shia population; Asir in the west close to Yemen physically and culturally; Hijaz in the west exposed to a continual stream of pilgrims from the rest of the Muslim world; and Najd in the center, forming the core of Wahhabi Islam. In 1950 at least half of the Kingdom's sparse population of 3.2 million was nomadic or semi-nomadic where tribal identification was paramount. Based on common descent, a tribe (Arabic, *qabila*) is a political organization above the levels of extended family (Arabic, *faghaz*) and clan (Arabic, *masheer*), and maintains its cohesiveness through blood solidarity. In the Arab world, tribes are often classified as noble or common. The tribes of the same category combine to form a federation or confederation.

There were about 40 tribes or tribal federations in Saudi Arabia. The House of Saud belonged to the Ruwalla tribe of the Anaiza tribal federation spread over Najd, Iraq and Syria. The members of this federation are considered noble due to their claim to lineal descent from Yaarab, the eponymous father of all Arabs. Common (or non-noble) tribal federations such as the Awazim, dating back to the 15th century in the Najd area, were Arabized only by intermarrying with the noble bloodlines.[26] With the introduction of publicly funded education which started in 1941, and the simultaneous development of the economy caused by the growth of the oil industry, the new status categories began to undermine the importance of tribal affiliation to social status.

Whereas Tehran University was founded in 1934, the first privately funded Saudi institute of higher education in religion, called Al Taif

School of Theology in Taif, was established eleven years later. It was followed by Imam Muhammad ibn Saud Islamic University in Riyadh in 1953. It was in 1954 that the Ministry of Education was set up. And it was only in 1957 that the first university which was not religious, named after King Saud, was established in the capital. And whereas women were admitted to Tehran University in 1937, publicly funded education for girls at primary level started in the Saudi Kingdom only in 1960. A decade later the literacy rate for men at 15 per cent and for women at 2 per cent was the second lowest in the Middle East and North Africa, with Yemen being at the bottom.[27]

Stress on religion—"belief in the One God, Islam as the way of life, and Muhammad as Allah's Messenger"—starts at the elementary level. The average of nine periods a week on religion is the same as for Arabic, and there are twelve for geography, history, mathematics, science, art, and physical education combined. At the intermediate-school level, the corresponding figures are nine, twelve and nineteen. At the secondary level, the required periods of religious study are reduced while pupils are offered an option for a concentration in religious studies.[28]

The pro-religious bias continues all the way up to higher education, and has militated against producing enough Saudis well versed in science and technology to serve in the oil and related industries. To fill the gap, Aramco, which was established in 1933, discovered oil in 1938 and began developing oil fields after the Second World War, began importing foreign workers—primarily from Egypt, Yemen and the Palestinian territories. With the expansion of petroleum and allied industries, Aramco and its successor Saudi Aramco have continued the practice.

In stark contrast, the Iranian government nationalized the British-owned Anglo-Iranian Oil Company in 1951, and expelled its foreign employees. Although three years later, Western petroleum corporations were given the contract to manage Iran's oil industry, owned then by the National Iranian Oil Company, the number of non-Iranian workers in that sector was very limited. Since the 1979 Islamic revolution, the hydrocarbon industry has been run exclusively by Iranians.

In the Saudi public sector, the First Five Year Plan (1970–1975) involved spending $8 billion, while the subsequent Five Year Plan ballooned to $142 billion. Most of these funds were spent on building or expanding the infrastructure of roads, ports, communications, and power and water plants. Since the native population was too small, and, given their nomadic background, unused to working eight to ten hours a day, the government imported a vast pool of foreign workers not only from the Arab world but also the Indian sub-continent, Taiwan and South Korea.[29] The unprecedented influx of non-Saudi labor rapidly turned the Saudi workforce into a minority in a country with 9.74 million people in 1980. Five years later the number of foreigners was estimated at 4.563 million, with a total foreign workforce of 3.523 million.[30]

Saudi Arabia's trajectory of economic development is a contrast to Iran's. For starters, with a recorded history of six millenniums, Iran is akin to Egypt, rather than Saudi Arabia. That is also the case in the size of the Iranian and Egyptian populations. The last remaining trace of tribalism in Iran in the form of the small Bakhtiari tribe, based in oil-rich southwestern Iran, was eliminated by Reza Shah Pahlavi.

A steady drive to create a local manufacturing industry and spread literacy under Reza Shah Pahlavi and his son Muhammad Reza Shah Pahlavi led to the formation of clearly defined classes. It was Reza Shah Pahlavi who inaugurated the University of Tehran in 1934. By the time he abdicated in favor of his son seven years later, there were 3,300 higher education students.[31] The explosion in higher education can be judged by the fact that between 1963 and 1977 university numbers rocketed from 24,885 to 154,215 at 16 universities. The number of Iranian students studying abroad shot up from 18,000 to 80,000. The enrollment in vocational and teacher training colleges was even more dramatic during that period, rising from 14,240 to 227,500. Money to expand educational facilities came from rising oil revenue and US aid which ceased only in 1972.[32]

That explained why and how, at 650,000, the modern middle class in Iran had doubled in a generation among 7 million households. There were 304,000 civil servants, 208,000 teachers, and 61,000 white collar professionals and managers, forming 6.5 per cent of the labor force of 10 million.[33]

By the late 1970s the 60-odd families related to or associated with the Pahlavis were at the apex. Below them were 200 elderly aristocratic politicians and former military and police officers. Next in the hierarchy were non-aristocratic entrepreneurs. About a million families belonged to the traditional middle class, half of them from the bazaar.

Below them were those traders who functioned outside urban bazaars. Then in the social order were village workshop owners mainly producing carpets. Clerics and theological students completed the traditional middle class. In one generation the urban working class increased fivefold, with 900,000 in industry, 400,000 in the distribution trade and 1.2 million in construction, hawking and menial work. They aggregated 23 per cent of the working population.[34] Annual oil income at $20 billion in 1977 amounted to 79 per cent of the total government revenues. It was 34 per cent of the GNP in 1977.[35]

As a result of US and United Nations sanctions on Iran between 2006 and 2012 because of its controversial nuclear program, the Iranian government was compelled to diversify its economy. Therefore, in 2016, its oil and gas income at $41 billion was only 10 per cent of its GDP of $412 billion.[36] The Saudi kingdom provided a sharp contrast. It remained heavily dependent on expatriate labor which was never the case with Iran. In 1977 its oil income of $21.5 billion was 28.9 per cent of the GDP. In 2016, its petroleum sector accounted for roughly 87 per cent of its revenues and 42 per cent of its GDP, four times the figure for Iran.[37]

What both countries shared was the dominant role played by petroleum, struck in commercial quantities first in Iran and then in Saudi Arabia, in shaping their respective histories.

2

BLACK GOLD AND AMERICA SHAPE IRAN
AND SAUDI ARABIA

Crisscrossing the Zagros Mountains during my 3,000-mile journey
through Iran in the summer of 2004 proved to be an open air lesson in
geology, with the mountain range's surface changing from dusty, yellow particles to dun-colored rocks peppered with scrub, to soil car-
peted with pine trees, to sedentary rock—slate—laid out layer upon
layer like vast pieces of hard cheese. Near Shustar the mountainous
slate was often gray, sometimes reddish. "It is the red cheese time," I
said to Nemat Ali. He replied with a semi-audible grunt, focused as he
was on maneuvering expertly the narrow, winding road on our way to
Masjid-e Suleiman, the Mosque of Suleiman—the eponymous famous
holy man who once lived there—a town of 200,000 people, with a
military airport nearby.

In the town I was greeted by Mirza Javad Ahmadi, the public relations director of the National Iranian Oil Company (NIOC) at its spacious headquarters. A broad-shouldered man of medium height sporting a few days' dark stubble, he took me to the site of the pioneering
oil well, signposted in Persian and English: "MASJID-I SULAIMAN
WELL NUMBER 1. THE FIRST OIL WELL IN MIDDLE EAST." This
referred to the oil well and the original 75 feet drilling rig along with
its accompanying steam engine and boiler, all freshly painted in navy
blue, and resting on a raised platform, surrounded by a high fence wall.

Past a low, grilled steel gate, a large signboard by the steps to the drilling rig's platform provided the basic information in blue and red lettering in Persian and English:

WELL No.1 MASJID-I-SULAIMAN
COMMENCED JANUARY 23TH 1908
STRUCK OIL AND WELL COMPLETED MAY 26TH 1908
DEPTH 1179 FEET / 360 METERS

Credit for the pioneering find went to George Bernard Reynolds, a British geologist and petroleum engineer. A tall, robust figure, with a fleshy face, he was seldom seen in public without his pipe and solar hat, or his little dog. He managed to transport equipment weighing 40 tons from Chia Surkh near the Iranian-Iraqi border to the mountainous region of Maiden-e Naft (lit., Field of Oil), some 330 miles apart. He did so by shipping it first to Baghdad by road, deploying 900 mules, then to Basra by boat, next to Khorramshahr in Iran, on to the penultimate leg of the journey to Shardin. It took his men a whole year to fashion a road to Maiden-e Naft, which he had visited earlier to discover its rocks "saturated with petroleum". And one more year lapsed before Reynolds and his men reached the sites near Masjid-e Suleiman.

During the drilling phase, it was so hot that Reynolds slept outside his tent at the base camp some distance away from the noisy work sites where drilling continued round the clock. On the night of May 25, 1908 he went to sleep at his usual time but was woken around 4 am by a barrage of noise: a dramatic cacophony of men shouting, the rumble of machinery and the sound of oil gushing up 50 feet above the top of one of the derricks. Reynolds jumped up, dressed quickly, and rushed to the scene to savour every moment. The drill hole was less than 1,200 feet deep, barely three-quarters of the depth mandated by his directors in Glasgow. Unbeknown to him, he had tapped into a 100 sq mile field, the largest discovered so far in the world, containing nearly two billion barrels of oil.[1]

With the British Admiralty's decision in March 1913 to switch from coal to oil in order to make its battle ships more powerful and speedier than Germany's, the importance of petroleum rose sharply. To ensure adequate supplies to the Royal Navy, the British government decided to acquire a 51 per cent interest in Anglo-Persian Oil Company (APOC), which had originated as a subsidiary of the Glasgow-based

Burmah Oil Company in 1909. With that the fleet acquired an abundant supply of petroleum from a source virtually under British control. Thus began a link between oil and the armed forces which with time would become both more intimate and more fraught.

Britain realised that exploitation of Iran's oil resources by a British-controlled company would be facilitated only when there was a strong, centralised state in Iran. Ahmad Shah Qajar had proved to be a weak ruler, so the British encouraged Colonel Reza Khan, commander of the elite Cossack Brigade, to mount a coup against the civilian government, in February 1921. Reza forced the monarch to appoint his nominee as the Prime Minister, became the war minister in the first cabinet and later took over the premiership. By crushing tribal and other rebellions he raised his popular standing. In October 1925 the Majlis deposed Qajar and appointed him the regent. Two months later the freshly elected Constituent Assembly proclaimed Reza Khan Pahlavi as Shah-en-Shah (king of kings) of Iran.[2]

Having consolidated his supreme authority in Tehran, Reza Shah Pahlavi got tough with APOC, which had paid only $75,000 (£40,000) for the original sixty-year concession over a vast area, and a small share of the profits.[3] He signed a new agreement with it under the aegis of the League of Nations which stipulated a reduction of 80 per cent in the company's concession area in two stages. APOC was renamed Anglo-Iranian Oil Company (AIOC) in 1935. Reza Shah Pahlavi used the increased oil revenue to modernise the economy and reduce the traditional influence of mullahs by encouraging secularism.

Regional Ripples of Iran's Discovery of Oil

Britain's success in striking oil in Iran aroused the interest and envy of the Soviet Union and the United States. To the disappointment of their petroleum corporations, by then the oil concessions were available only in the five Northern provinces of Iran. The attempts by the Standard Oil Company of New Jersey (now Exxon) in 1920–1921 and by Sinclair Oil in 1923 to secure petroleum concessions in the north failed. The British were keen to keep the Americans out, as were the Soviets.

In Saudi Arabia Ibn Saud desperately wished to see oil struck in the eastern Hasa region of his Kingdom. Bidding started in February 1933 for oil concessions covering 300,000 square miles of land. He demanded £5,000 annual rental and an immediate loan of £100,000. The largely British-owned Iraq Petroleum Company (IPC), which had been active in the region for many years, found a rival in Standard Oil of California (Socal). However, IPC's geologists foresaw little, if any, prospect of striking oil in the Arabian Peninsula. Therefore, instead of making its bid in gold, as Ibn Saud had demanded, the IPC offered to pay in Indian rupees. It thus implicitly wrote itself out of the script.

Even though Socal found Ibn Saud's demand excessive, it sent a representative to deal with him because its subsidiary, Bahrain Petroleum Company, had discovered oil in nearby Bahrain in June 1932. It was the monarch's personal treasurer, Abdullah Suleiman, who struck the bargain. Having been born into a merchant family, he had learned accounting and book-keeping during a two-year stint in Bombay and had a sharp mind for numbers. He persuaded Ibn Saud to accept an advance of £5,000 in gold against future oil royalties, and a loan of £30,000, and witnessed the signing of the contract, valid for sixty years, on 29 May 1933—a landmark event.

After buying 35,000 gold sovereigns in London for $170,327, Socal transported them to a P&O steamer bound for Jeddah. The ship arrived there on 25 August.

The cash was delivered to the Netherlands Trading Society, the Kingdom's only bank, where Suleiman counted out the money by hand, sitting at the manager's table.[4]

Socal's directors rushed geologist Robert P. (Bert) Miller and Schuyler B. (Krug) Henry—then working in Bahrain, where they had grown beards and picked up everyday Arabic—to Saudi Arabia. They landed at the sleepy coastal village of Jubail, dressed as Bedouin Arabs, wearing long shirts, lightweight robes and cloth headdresses. It was 23 September, the first anniversary of the founding of the Saudi kingdom.

Ibn Saud provided their field party of seven with thirty escorts and four camel drivers. The oil corporation's transport included twenty-five riding camels and twelve baggage camels to carry their equipment, tents, furniture and provisions. Miller and Henry started looking for a group of limestone hills, as they had in Bahrain. Their first exploratory survey ended in June 1934.[5]

Socal's subsidiary, California Arabian Standard Oil Company (CASOC), focused on the Dammam Dome, sixty-five miles south of

Jubail. Of the seven exploratory wells that were drilled in the area in subsequent years, Number 7, atop the hill of Jabal Dhahran, proved wet. The discovery, made on 4 March 1938, was tested for several days with the well's daily yield settling down to 3,810 barrels. The directors of the two-year-old California Texas Oil Company (later Caltex)—the result of Texas Company (later named Texaco) buying half of CASOC—cabled from the head office in San Francisco that there was no further need for testing. Jubilation reverberated from Dammam Camp to Riyadh and San Francisco, according to Mary Norton writing in *Aramco World* to commemorate the fiftieth anniversary of the historic discovery.[6]

The commercial success of an American oil company led the US State Department to accredit the US Minister to Egypt to Saudi Arabia, thus formally establishing diplomatic relations with the seven-year-old kingdom. Ibn Saud remained neutral in the Second World War which led to a steep fall in the number of tax-paying Hajj pilgrims and wrecked his finances.

A desperate Ibn Saud appealed to Socal and Texaco presidents for financial assistance. They perceived the possibility of helping through the Lend-Lease law—officially titled "An Act to Promote the Defense of the United States"—enacted in March 1941. As a result of their lobbying the Franklin Roosevelt administration opened a one-man legation in Jeddah under James Moose as charge d'affaires in May 1942. At a State Department-sponsored meeting to discuss international oil policy in mid-February 1943, Socal and Texaco convinced the conveners of the need to exclude British oil interests from Saudi Arabia and ensure continued American monopoly in the Kingdom's petroleum industry. That meant aiding Ibn Saud. They also convinced Harold Ickes, the Interior Secretary, of the sagacity of this policy.

Over lunch on 16 February Ickes won over President Roosevelt—a handsome, wheelchair-bound patrician politician with a populist touch—who had been skeptical about aiding an absolutist monarch while the Allies were fighting for democracy worldwide. Two days later he signed an Executive Order saying, "I hereby find the defense of Saudi Arabia is vital to the defense of the United States", and authorized Lend Lease aid to its government. Soon after, the American mission in Jeddah was upgraded and Colonel William Eddy, fluent in Arabic, was appointed US minister.[7]

In September 1943, Prince Faisal (b. 1904) and Prince Khalid (b. 1913) were invited to Washington where US Vice President Henry Wallace organised a dinner for them at the White House. They stayed at the official guest house, Blair House, then visited the West Coast by a special train officially provided by the government.[8]

By then, on the battlefields, the tide had turned decisively in favor of the Allies, especially in North Africa.

Rivalry between British and American Oil Companies

During the Second World War, the earlier rivalry between British and American oil companies in the Middle East continued, albeit in a low key manner, even though the annual income of Caltex was a modest $2.8 million in 1944. In Washington Ickes recommended bilateral talks to reach an understanding with London on petroleum. But Lord Halifax, the British ambassador in Washington, found his discussions with the State Department so frustrating that he sought a meeting with Roosevelt. During their conversation on 18 February 1944, the President showed his interlocutor a rough sketch of the Middle East. "Persian oil is yours," he said. "We share the oil in Iraq and Kuwait. As for Saudi Arabian oil, it's ours."[9]

But this was not the end of the matter. While American oil companies had monopolised oil exploration in Saudi Arabia its king had a long history of political and military ties with London. That was why Roosevelt kept secret his planned meeting with Ibn Saud during his conference with Winston Churchill and Joseph Stalin at the Soviet sea resort of Yalta in early February 1945. His aircraft *Sacred Cow* carried him and his entourage to the Suez Canal Zone in Egypt, where an American cruiser, USS *Quincy*, was anchored in the Great Bitter Lake, halfway along the Canal between the Mediterranean and Red Seas. Soon after King Ibn Saud and his entourage arrived from Jeddah aboard the American destroyer USS *Murphy*.

The two leaders got along famously when they met on 14 February. They spent five hours together, interspersed by lunch, with US Minister Colonel Eddy, much trusted by Ibn Saud, acting as the translator. In 1954 Eddy would publish an account of the historic meeting, *F.D.R. Meets Ibn Saud*.[10]

Ibn Saud, walking with difficulty and carrying a cane, remarked that the two of them were of the same age and were afflicted with physical disabilities, his stemming from battle wounds to his legs which stopped him from climbing stairs, and Roosevelt's from polio which confined him to a wheelchair:

> Roosevelt: "You are luckier than I because you can still walk on your legs and I have to be wheeled wherever I go."
>
> Ibn Saud: "No, my friend, you are more fortunate. Your chair will take you wherever you want to go, and you know you will get there. My legs are less reliable and are getting weaker every day."
>
> Roosevelt: "If you think so highly of this chair, I will give you the twin of this chair as I have two on board."

Ibn Saud accepted the offer even though he saw that it was much too small for his large frame.[11]

They discussed oil, a Jewish homeland in Palestine, the post-war scene in the region, and the establishment of a US military base in Dhahran amid the oil fields of Al Hasa.

Ibn Saud was moved sufficiently by the Nazi atrocities against the Jews that on 1 March, soon after his return home, he declared war against Germany. He thus secured a seat for Saudi Arabia at the founding convention of the United Nations in San Francisco in April 1945. A month earlier, he was instrumental in getting the League of Arab Nations—a project conceived in London, better known as the Arab League—established in Cairo. (Besides Saudi Arabia, the other founding members were Egypt, Iraq, Lebanon, North Yemen and Syria.) Overall, though, the Ibn Saud-Roosevelt meeting laid the foundation for a Saudi-American compact whereby in return for Washington's protection of Saudi Arabia, its regime would guarantee continued domination of its oil industry by US corporations. This arrangement has held since then, overcoming several points of friction, the latest being the September 2001 terrorist attacks in New York and Metropolitan Washington.

After the Second World War there was a ten-fold jump in Saudi oil production between 1945 and 1949, with the annual revenue rising to $115 million, when the Kingdom's population was a little over 3 million.[12] This was the consequence of Aramco's co-opting of Standard Oil

Company of New Jersey (later Esso, then Exxon) and Standard Oil Company of New York (later Mobil) as partners, in 1948. Later that year, the enlarged Aramco hit a jackpot with the discovery of the Ghawar oil field. Measuring 3,300 sq miles, it had estimated reserves of more than 100 billion barrels, a world record. Seven decades later, its output of 5 million barrels per day (bpd) would account for more than half of total Saudi oil production.[13]

Ibn Saud's death on 9 November 1953 brought to an end the formative period of the Kingdom. As a domineering and militarily successful tribal chief, he had behaved as an autocrat. Following a surge in oil output after the war, the economic boom overstretched the rudimentary institutions of the state, supervised by him and his close aides. Yet it was not until October 1953 that he appointed a council of ministers, chaired by his eldest son, Saud—a handsome, dignified-looking man with a trimmed moustache, courteous and genial—as an advisory body.

Having married twenty-two times—while keeping the number of current wives to four in line with an Islamic injunction—Ibn Saud fathered 44 sons, with 35 of them surviving him. That crop proved so abundant that even 62 years after his death the throne was retained by one of them, Salman.

Oil Upturns Iran's Politics

After the outbreak of the Second World War in September 1939, Reza Shah Pahlavi kept Iran neutral. The Allies saw Nazi Germany's invasion of the Soviet Union in June 1941 as part of a pincer movement, its other arm being the German thrust into North Africa. In late August Soviet and British troops coordinated their invasion of Iran, with the Soviets entering the northern provinces of Azerbaijan and Khurasan. They forced the king to abdicate in favor of his son, Muhammad Reza, in September. He sailed first to Mauritius and then to South Africa. A small, slight man, Muhammad Reza, raised by an authoritarian father, had grown up as a timorous adult.

To encourage the Soviet Union to withdraw its forces from Azerbaijan at the end of the war in May 1945, Prime Minister Ahmad Qavam al Saltaneh concluded a deal with Moscow to form a joint Soviet-Iranian oil company with 51 per cent Soviet interest. It was signed by Muhammad Reza Shah Pahlavi. The Kremlin withdrew its troops from Azerbaijan the next month on the understanding that the final agreement would be ratified by the parliament, or Majlis, by October. With the backing of the United States, the Iranian forces quelled the existing autonomous governments in Kurdistan and Azerbaijan in December. Only then was the Shah was able to exercise authority over all of Iran.

Because of the deliberately staggered elections to the fifteenth Majlis, the agreement with the Soviet Union came up for ratification in October 1947. The deputies rejected it by 102 votes to two.

But rebuffing the Soviet Union was only part of the five-clause law passed by the Majlis. The last clause instructed the government to undertake necessary measures to secure "the national rights... in respect of the natural wealth of the country, including the southern oil."[14] It would prove to be the seed which would flower into a full blown oil nationalisation movement and bring the nationalist politician Muhammad Mussadiq to power.

Public opinion was inflamed further against AIOC when it announced a profit of £40m ($112m) in 1947 with Iran receiving a paltry £7m in royalties. In addition, AIOC sold Iranian oil at a substantial discount to the Royal Navy, while Britain was the majority owner of AIOC.[15]

The living conditions of Iranians working at the AIOC oil refinery in Abadan, as described by Manucher Farmanfarmaian, an Iranian oil expert, were shocking. "Wages were 50 cents a day," he reported. "There was no vacation pay, no sick leave, no disability compensation. The workers lived in a shantytown called *Kaghazabad*, or Paper City, without running water or electricity ...In every crevice hung the foul, sulfurous stench of burning oil—a pungent reminder that every day 20,000 barrels or one million tons a year, were being consumed indiscriminately for the functioning of the refinery, and AIOC never paid the government a cent for it. In Kaghazabad, there was nothing—not a tea shop, not a bath. Not a single tree. The unpaved alleyways were emporiums for rats."[16]

This was the case *after* strikes by oil workers in 1946 organised into trade unions by the Tudeh Party of Iran: Party of the Iranian Working Class. In the Majlis the Tudeh had eight members and 24 sympathisers.

The demand for oil nationalisation was made by the National Front, a coalition, formed in 1949. One of its co-founders, Mussadiq, was elected to the Majlis in February 1950. His stress on nationalising AIOC gained him popularity. By late April 1951 the Majlis and the Senate had passed the oil nationalisation bill and spelled out the details of the take-over of AIOC, including its oil concession covering a vast area of Iran, by the newly established National Iranian Oil Company (NIOC). When the Majlis chose Mussadiq as the Prime Minister on 28 April 1951 by 79 votes to 12, the Shah reluctantly appointed him to the high office. On 1 May the oil nationalisation bill became law, and Mussadiq formed the next government.

Britain's call for a boycott of Iran's oil was heeded by most Western nations. Consequently, Tehran's earnings from oil exports in 1951 fell by half from $45 million in the previous year, when they accounted for seven-tenths of its export revenues. Once Mussadiq had expelled the last British AIOC employee, in October 1952, Moscow contracted to buy petroleum from the NIOC. It also signed a commercial agreement with Iran.[17] But Mussadiq, a staunch anti-Communist, refrained from strengthening economic ties with Moscow, fearing that such a move would destroy any chance of economic and military aid from Washington—something he badly needed to maintain the living standards of 19 million Iranians. As a democrat and a constitutionalist, he remained hopeful to the last of separating the US from Britain, and of achieving the objective of destroying British economic domination of Iran with American help. This proved to be a pipedream.

To fill the gap in oil supplies to the West, Aramco increased its production. This pleased Ibn Saud particularly when the Iranian oil nationalisation crisis persisted for more than two years. Iran's loss proved to be Saudi Arabia's gain.

Faced with dwindling oil revenue, Mussadiq sought emergency powers from the Majlis, which agreed to grant them. The resulting hardening of Mussadiq's governance style alienated many Iranians. The deepening crisis culminated in a power struggle between him and the Shah. He won. The Shah and his wife Farah Diba fled to Rome on 16 August 1953. But his exile proved brief. Three days later, the generously-funded US Central Intelligence Agency (CIA), working with Britain's Secret Intelligence Service (MI6), and royalist Iranian military officers, mounted a coup against Mussadiq. The Shah staged a comeback. Across the Gulf, Saudi royals were pleased to see the Shah re-occupying the

Peacock Throne. Ibn Saud's successor, King Saud (r. 1953–64), would visit his Iranian counterpart in 1955.

The Shah Supreme in Iran

Far more importantly, the restoration of the Shah inaugurated a period in Iran's history when the US replaced Britain as the dominant Western power. Between August 1953 and December 1956, Washington provided Iran with military and economic aid worth $414 million.[18] With that came thousands of civilian and uniformed Americans—a development much resented by nationalist Iranians, both secular and religious. In the region the United States acquired pre-eminent influence in both Iran and Saudi Arabia.

As advised by Washington, the Shah kept the oil nationalisation law on the statute books, but downgraded the role of the NIOC. In 1954, it leased the rights to, and management of, Iranian oil for the next twenty-five years to a Western consortium, with the following share-out: AIOC 40 per cent; Royal Dutch Shell 14 per cent; five major US oil companies (Exxon, Gulf, Mobil, Socal and Texaco) 8 per cent each; and Compagnie Francaise des Petroles 6 per cent.

Iran's oil income jumped from $34 million in 1954–55 to $181 million two years later. With the state receiving such vast sums, corruption increased, as did the Shah's self-confidence. He showed his increasing ambition to arrogate all power, and resorted to dismissing prime ministers at will.

In 1955 the Shah formed a political police force under military officers to gather intelligence and repress the opposition, a prelude to the establishment of Savak—*Sazman-e Aminyat Va Ettilaat-e Keshavar*—Organisation of National Security and Intelligence. The law of March 1957 formalised the ad hoc arrangement, with Savak being attached to the Prime Minister's office, and its head given the status of a Deputy Premier. It maintained close contacts with the CIA, which had trained its operatives, and Israel's foreign intelligence agency, Mossad.

By 1957, the Shah had smashed the Tudeh Party as well as all the constituents of Mossadiq's National Front. But the overthrow in July 1958 of Iraqi King Faisal II by nationalist, republican officers, resulting in the end of the pro-Western monarchy in Iraq, rattled him. He invited President Dwight Eisenhower (r. 1953–61) to enter into a mutual defence pact. Eisenhower agreed to sign a more limited executive arrangement to assist the Shah in countering "overt armed aggression from any nation controlled by international communism" if he pledged to spend US non-military aid on economic development rather than imports of consumer goods, and liberalise the political system.[19] This set the scene for the emergence of state-controlled party politics in 1959, with the ruling party called Melliyun (Nationalist) and the opposition the Mardom (People's) Party.[20]

The Tehran-Washington military cooperation agreement in March 1959 created formal channels for close cooperation in military intelligence. By the end of that year the US was involved in every aspect of Iranian life, except religion. The US Embassy in Tehran became as important a center of power as the Shah's court. In the regional context, Tehran became aligned with Washington in the defence field, much like Riyadh almost a decade earlier.

Saudi-American Military Links

Just as exports of Saudi oil resumed in 1946, an American military advisory delegation arrived in Riyadh to reorganise Ibn Saud's regular army following his granting of a five-year-lease on the military airfield at Dhahran to the Pentagon. In 1950 the first US Air Force mission was posted at the Dhahran base. The next year, the Pentagon took another five-year lease on the Dhahran air base. But, sensitive to the rising Arab nationalist tide in the region and in his country, King Saud let the Dhahran agreement expire in 1956 and took to renewing it on a monthly basis. On the oil front, following the example of Venezuela, Saudi Arabia had achieved a 50:50 income sharing formula with Aramco, and that boosted its oil income from $39 million to $110 million in 1951.[21]

After President Eisenhower had pressured Britain and France to evacuate the Egyptian land they had occupied during the 1956 Suez War between Egypt and the Anglo-French-Israeli coalition, Saud signed a new military co-operation agreement with the US in February 1957. The Pentagon agreed to help double the Saudi army to 15,000 soldiers—and to add a navy and an air force to the Kingdom's armed forces—in return for being granted a five-year lease on the Dhahran air base.

The United States was now fully engaged in the geopolitics of oil. Following the inflow of American arms and other military aid into the Gulf, the US Navy had established a permanent naval presence in Bahrain in early 1949.[22] Its overriding objective was to safeguard petroleum supplies to the West from the region.

Overall, though, because of the ongoing Cold War between the Washington-led bloc and the Moscow-led bloc, the Pentagon came to pay far more attention to Iran, which shared a long common border with the Soviet Union, than to Saudi Arabia.

A six-year-long battle royal in Riyadh

On ascending the throne, King Saud named his forty-nine-year-old younger brother Faisal as the Crown Prince and heir apparent, as mandated by Ibn Saud twenty years earlier, on the assumption that family loyalty would be harnessed more securely around a partnership than a sole leader.

Faisal had the distinction of being the first member of what later became the House of Saud—the Al Sauds—to visit London as an official guest. After the defeat of the Ottoman Empire in November 1918, the British government invited Ibn Saud to London in appreciation of the assistance he had given Britain against the Turks from 1917 onwards, in lieu of an annual subsidy of £77,000.[23] But since Ibn Saud was preparing to capture the Asir region along the Red Sea, he sent his fifteen-year-old son Faisal instead. The teenage prince spent five months in the country and had an audience with King George V.[24] He was thus exposed during his adolescence to such aspects of Western life as drinking alcohol and pre-marital and extra-marital sex. His transgressions of Islamic injunctions would continue well into his middle age, and would be shielded assiduously from public view by a wall of bodyguards and a team of devoted aides.

Back home he was chosen by his father to mould himself as a valiant warrior. After proving his mettle on the battlefield, he was appointed viceroy of the Hijaz region in early 1926. During his second visit to London in the autumn he laid the foundation for the seven-year friendship treaty with Britain which was signed by Ibn Saud in May 1927. Five years later, Ibn Saud sent him on another important diplomatic mission—to Moscow. There he succeeded in convincing Soviet Premier Joseph Stalin to let Muslims in the Soviet Union make the Hajj pilgrimage to Mecca.[25] Later, as the Saudi monarch, Faisal would pursue rabidly anti-Soviet and anti-Communist policies worldwide.

In September 1943 Faisal, accompanied by his younger brother Khalid, became the first Saudi royal to visit the United States as an official guest. As foreign minister, he led the Saudi delegation at the two-month long founding conference of the United Nations (UN) in San Francisco in April 1945. In January 1946, he represented Saudi Arabia at the inaugural session of the UN General Assembly in Central London. When the time came for him to deliver his speech he was not to be found. A frantic police search traced him to a brothel in West London.[26]

As the Crown Prince in Riyadh, Faisal was disappointed to note that King Saud retained the premiership. But Saud proved incapable of handling the fiscal and administrative complexities arising from the sharp growth in oil revenues caused by increased demand for Saudi oil due to Iran's oil nationalisation crisis from 1951–1953.

Saud's personal profligacy was another negative factor. He built the Nasiriyah Palace Complex on the outskirts of Riyadh, enclosed by a seven-mile long high wall lit at night by thousands of colored electric lights for the benefit of the palace guards. Besides the vast, air-conditioned Royal Palace of pink concrete, with its reception hall large enough to accommodate 500 people, the complex contained many smaller air-conditioned structures for his four wives and numerous former wives. These were set amidst gardens, palm groves and fountains drawing water from artesian wells drilled by Americans. Traffic lights regulated the flow of hundreds of cruising air-conditioned Cadillac cars. The power needed to illuminate, cool and irrigate the numerous palaces and grounds exceeded that used by 150,000 residents of Riyadh.[27]

Saud continued the practice of his father, Ibn Saud, of dispensing cash as he wished without an accounting system. Following the resolution of Iran's oil crisis in 1954, and the subsequent drop in Riyadh's petroleum income, the financial state of the kingdom deteriorated. By 1955 his addiction to alcohol, particularly Cointreau, became the talk of the diplomatic circuit. By late 1957, his intemperate drinking compounded his stomach troubles and high blood pressure, with his sagging legs unable to carry his excessive weight due to poor blood circulation. His stable of concubines and many progeny had become a cause for adverse comment. Faced with the resulting economic crisis, and the absence of a budget, the state's administration came to a virtual halt by early 1958. Soon afterwards, Saud's reputation was tarnished by the discovery of his failed plot to bring about the assassination of Egyptian President Gamal Abdul Nasser—a charismatic doyen of Arab nationalists whose popularity transcended state borders—during his visit to Damascus on 24 February 1958. It severely damaged Saudi Arabia's standing in the region and beyond. At home, it gave other members of the royal family the opening they had been seeking. They called for a full transfer of domestic, foreign, and financial policies to Crown Prince Faisal. Days later, such an announcement was made on Mecca Radio.

The middle-aged Faisal's gnarled face with a large, hooked nose, and the mean-looking, downward twist of his lips over his straggly goatee beard, which gave him a dour, severe appearance, seemed to fit his public image of a pious and ascetic Muslim. Actually, his mid-life foxy face was a tell-tale sign of dissipation, resulting from his transgressions of Islamic injunctions against drinking and extramarital sex from his younger days while abroad on official business and well into his middle age. In 1957 he spent six months in America during which he underwent two operations, including one to remove a stomach ulcer. After that he had to stop drinking, and switched to consuming unappetising boiled food and endless cups of tea.

On assuming full executive authority, Faisal discovered that the public treasury was empty. He pruned the budget drastically and imposed austerity. As for Saud, he used his personal wealth to fund the projects popular with the tribes while promising to form a representative government. As a consequence, by December 1960, support for Faisal eroded so much that he resigned as the Prime Minister. But this did not put an end to internecine warfare.

In the midst of this struggle, the representatives of Saudi Arabia met with their counterparts from Iran, Iraq, Kuwait and Venezuela in Baghdad in September 1960 to form the Organization of the Petroleum Exporting Countries (OPEC) in order to make the most of their oil resources by coordinating their hydrocarbon policies. Though the CIA paid scant attention to the birth of OPEC, devoting a mere four lines to it in a report, in the coming decades OPEC came to play an important role in the world economy.

In Riyadh, King Saud formed a new cabinet and named himself prime minister. This lasted a year before failing health forced him to seek medical treatment abroad. Pressured by senior princes, he put Faisal in charge.

1962 was a make-or-break year for the House of Saud. Prince Talal, the twenty-fifth son of Ibn Saud, who had proposed the establishment of a national council in 1958—to no avail—defected to Cairo in early 1962 despite Nasser's statement that in order "to liberate Jerusalem, the Arab peoples must first liberate Riyadh."[28] In Riyadh, Talal's half brother Abdul Muhsin voiced support for Talal's call to transform the Saudi status quo into a constitutional democracy within a monarchical framework. When this proposal fell on deaf ears, Talal started broadcasting anti-royalist speeches on Cairo Radio.

The republican coup in North Yemen in September 1962 boosted the morale of liberal and democratic forces in Saudi Arabia. Nine Saudi pilots defected to North Yemen with their planes and Talal set up a Saudi government-in-exile.

In November 1962 the Council of Senior Princes decided (during the absence of Saud who was in the US for medical treatment) to invest Faisal with supreme executive authority. He immediately announced a ten-point program. Besides the promise of a written constitution and a Consultative Council, his list included strengthening Committees for Public Morality, and increased capital investment and economic growth. It was welcomed by different segments of society.

Having rallied all these forces, in March 1964 Faisal issued an ultimatum stating that he intended to retain full power and wanted to be named as regent, and that Saud's role should be purely ceremonial. This document was delivered to the monarch by Grand Mufti Muhammad bin Ibrahim Al Shaikh, the highest religious authority, related to Faisal's mother Tarfa bint Abdullah Al Shaikh. Saud refused.

Tensions rose and culminated in a confrontation between the guards respectively loyal to King Saud and Prime Minister Faisal which the Faisal partisans won. The ulema headed by the Grand Mufti sanctified the transfer of executive powers to Faisal with Saud continuing to hold the title of king. But Saud failed to reconcile with his new role of a figurehead.

The final denouement came on 29 October. Senior ulema met under the chairmanship of the Grand Mufti in Riyadh. Separately the thirty sons and fifteen grandsons of Ibn Saud assembled at the Sahara Palace Hotel. Both groups decided that Faisal should be the new monarch. Then a small delegation of clerics and princes traveled to see Faisal who was camped north of the capital to convey their unanimous decision. He asked if they had exhausted all means of persuading Saud to abdicate. After assuring him that they had done so, they declared him their king.

On their return to Riyadh they sought an audience with Saud. He refused. During the next three days, military commanders, tribal chiefs and provincial governors swore their fealty to Faisal. Unwilling to wait any longer, Muhammad bin Abdul Aziz, the most senior prince after Faisal, stormed Saud's palace, and warned him that if he failed to step down his property would be confiscated and he would be placed under house arrest. Saud did not budge.

But as the Royal Guards loyal to Saud surrounded Faisal's residence, Prime Minister Faisal ordered the much stronger Saudi National Guard to surround Saud's forces. The royal guard surrendered and the ulema issued a fatwa transferring executive powers to Faisal while still allowing Saud to remain king. It was only then that Saud signed his abdication decree.[29] He went into exile in Athens, Greece.

The National Guard, which had originated as the White Guard in 1932, had a liberal sprinkling of the former members of the Ikhwan, the armed Wahhabi zealots, who enabled Ibn Saud to expand his realm to seventy-eight per cent of the Arabian Peninsula in 1932, and name it the Kingdom of Saudi Arabia.

In the wake of the republican seizure of power in North Yemen, the White Guard was placed under the command of Prince Abdullah bin Abdul Aziz Al Saud and renamed the National Guard. Its rearming and retraining were assigned to British military experts who were later joined by the Americans. Its personnel were billeted outside the main urban centers and its officers were the most pampered after the royal family.

In the royal family, Faisal finally prevailed for several reasons. He was helped by Saud's long absences from the Kingdom because of ill health.

He had the backing not only of the vast majority of the royal family but also the leading Wahhabi ulema. To the last he maintained outward decorum by refraining from publicly calling on King Saud to abdicate, which greatly impressed the general public.

FAISAL'S ENDURING IMPRINT;
THE SHAH'S VAULTING AMBITION

To his string of firsts in the history of Saudi Arabia, King Faisal bin Abdul Aziz Al Saud added a final one. He became the only Saudi monarch to be assassinated. The date was 25 March 1975, which happened to be the birthday of Prophet Muhammad; and the place was his court in the historic Murabba Palace in Riyadh. His assassin was none other than his twenty-seven-year-old nephew, Faisal bin Musaid bin Abdul Aziz Al Saud.

Fast forward to May 2017. It was at the Murabba Palace that United States President Donald Trump concluded his busy day of diplomacy with King Salman bin Abdul Aziz Al Saud to join a festive banquet after participating, awkwardly, in an all-male sword dance.[1] If all the rooms of the Murabba Palace were made accessible to the public, historians would most likely make a beeline to the reception room where King Faisal was shot three times by his assassin's 0.38 caliber pistol.

As it was, four years after Faisal's violent end, the black steel gates of the Niavaran Palace of the last Pahlavi monarch, Muhammad Reza Shah, in the affluent suburban village of that name in the foothills of the Elborz Mountains in north Tehran were thrown open to all. The grounds of this complex consist of impressively well maintained pathways, memorable for the green-painted street lights that illuminated late nineteenth-century Paris, and exquisitely maintained lawns and flower beds. To reach the residence that the last Shah built for his family in 1957 I had to pass the one constructed by his father, Reza Shah Pahlavi, a tall, mustached man with stern looks, who had a dignified bearing despite his thin legs.

The two-story palace of his son, scarcely awe-inspiring, was permeated with melancholy, which lifted only when I came across the turquoise and yellow tiling in a part that was once used as an imperial living quarter. My gloom disappeared altogether when I entered rooms with walls decorated with mirror mosaics—thousands of small mirror fragments set at angles to one other to reflect light and distort images simultaneously—often found at religious shrines in Iran.

The basement was remarkable for the red, green, gold and white upholstered chairs which surrounded a large dining table, reflecting the haphazard way the Shah and his second wife Sorya Isfandiari had chosen the furniture, mixing the period pieces of France's Second Empire with the latest French fashion. A painting of Napoleon's retreat from Moscow confirmed the couple's Francophilia. Another place that drew my immediate attention was the last Shah's modest bedroom in a basement alcove. It was furnished with his daily diary written on large golden paper in Persian and English, and a small collection of books where the titles *Marathon* and *The Vantage Point* stood out. However, I had to cover my nose with a handkerchief to block the nauseating smell of phenol tablets scattered around the room to protect the books and fabrics from moths and other insects.

After the stink of the Shah's bedroom at the Niavaran Palace, a tour of the Saadabad Palace Complex in North Tehran, spread over a vast area of towering cedars, pines, cypresses, white birches and plane trees, well kept lawns, half-tended greenery, and gentle brooks was life-enhancing. This palace complex had become a popular spot for picnicking, especially in the sweltering months of summer. What immediately caught my eye after passing the gated entrance was a pair of huge bronze boots, a little higher than me, so more than six feet in height, near the entrance of a building with broad limestone steps. It was a remnant of the mammoth statute of Reza Shah Pahlavi that was toppled by revolutionaries in 1979.

A centerpiece of the complex was the palace built by his son to serve as an office and a residence during summer. Instead of attempting to incorporate the world renowned elements of Persian-Islamic architecture, which reached its apotheosis in the Taj Mahal in India, the last Shah settled for a bland concrete box. Its waiting hall was furnished in Louis XVI style with gold flocked wallpaper and crystal chandeliers crafted in Italy, and decorated with paintings by Henry Hadfield Cubley (d. 1934), a mediocre Scottish landscape artist. The bedroom of Farah Diba, a reedy, emaciated-looking woman who was the Shah's third and last wife, was furnished with a cream and blue bed and a large television set, and boasted an extraordinarily intricate silk carpet of over 273 sq meters (435 sq feet), the largest ever made, while her husband's gold satin bed was a replica of the one used by Napoleon.

What was truly remarkable about these palaces was the total absence of any Islamic imagery. There was no picture of the Kaaba, the centerpiece of the Grand Mosque in Mecca, nor of the shrine of Imam Ali in Najaf or Imam Hussein in Karbala. Nor was there even a calligraphic rendition of the word "Allah" or "Ali" in Arabic or Persian. Equally remarkable was the absence of a small mosque in these Palace complexes, or even a modest room in the royal residence set aside for prayers. It was hard to reconcile this absence with Article 39 of the 1907 constitution of Iran enjoining upon the monarch "to promote the Jaafari doctrine [of Twelver Shias]," and to seek "the spirit of the holy Saints of Islam to render service to the advancement of Iran."[2] Nobody in Saudi Arabia could have faulted King Faisal on a similar point because the Kingdom lacked a written constitution.

Faisal as King

On ascending the throne, Faisal retained the premiership after appointing his younger brother Khalid as Crown Prince and deputy prime minister. He reneged on the promise of political reform he had made in 1962—notably the promulgation of a written constitution specifying a predominantly elected Consultative Council. When reminded of his pledge, he retorted that "Our constitution is the Quran."[3]

Faisal rejected a proposal to merge the military and the National Guard mainly because having two separate armed services enabled him to maintain a balance between the competing clans inside his kingdom. Also the National Guard's role covered both domestic and foreign threats to the regime.

He strengthened the eight-year-old General Intelligence Presidency, the Kingdom's principal intelligence agency, in 1965, and appointed his brother-in-law, Kamal Adham, its head, who reported directly to him. Working closely with the CIA, and partly using the information supplied by it, Adham helped Faisal to crush dissent. Faisal quashed protests by Saudi employees of Aramco and outlawed labour unions in 1965. Over the years Adham became the godfather of Middle East intelligence, and came to act as the CIA's conduit for payments to potential and actual agents of the CIA.[4]

President Gamal Abdul Nasser despatched Egyptian troops to North Yemen from 1962 onwards to aid the Republican camp, which found itself on the defensive when the royalists gained backing from Saudi Arabia. This was the background to the escalating hostility between the Islamist Faisal and Nasser, an ardent advocate of pan-Arabism.

Nasser suppressed the Muslim Brotherhood, an advocate of pan-Islamism, after its activists made three unsuccessful attempts to assassinate him between 1964 and 1966. The mantle of pan Islamism was adopted by Faisal, who promoted it in the mid-1960s as a competing ideology to pan-Arabism. He started funding the branches of the Muslim Brotherhood, outlawed in Egypt, in various Arab states. Countering Nasser's drift towards Moscow, Faisal strengthened ties with Washington. He eschewed diplomatic or trade links with the Soviet Union or other members of the Soviet bloc, arguing that Communism and Islam were incompatible.

Opposed vehemently to the Soviet Union and socialism, he reinforced Saudi Arabia's ties with the United States by adding intelligence sharing to the previous mix of commerce and military cooperation. Opposed equally to Zionism, he advocated the cause of the Palestinians. Bizarrely, however, Faisal believed in the existence of an unholy alliance between Communism and Zionism, which he opposed. This obsessive conviction, bearing no relationship to evidence, led him to claim that the Zionists were behind the Palestinian terrorists.

Faisal's hostility towards Nasser sharpened when he invited the exiled Saud to come to Cairo in December 1966. Arriving there, Saud claimed that he had not abdicated, denounced Faisal as "an ally of colonialism," claimed that the CIA had assisted Faisal to depose him, and called on Saudis to overthrow "the usurper".[5]

Nasser's humiliating defeat in the Six Day War in June 1967 shattered his standing in the region. He cut diplomatic relations with the US for backing Israel in the war. Saud returned to Athens where he died in February 1969.[6] Much chastened, Nasser buried the hatchet with Faisal at the Arab Summit in Khartoum that August. He also withdrew Egyptian troops from North Yemen. By the end of 1968, Faisal had ended his military backing of the royalists, and later accepted a moderate Republican regime in the neighboring state.

During the Six Day War, Arab oil ministers, meeting in Baghdad, cut off petroleum supplies to America, Britain and West Germany to punish them for supporting Israel. Demonstrating against Washington's unqualified support for Israel, opposition forces in the Saudi Kingdom attacked American clubs and cultural centers as well as US military barracks in Dhahran, and called on the monarch to terminate oil supplies to the United States. This compelled Faisal to join the oil embargo,[7] which lasted only until the end of August. But it set the scene for the formation of the five-strong Organisation of Arab Petroleum Exporting Countries (OAPEC) in Kuwait in January 1968. (Later, its size would increase to ten members, including Egypt.)

King Faisal moved quickly to capitalise on the shock and anger that swept the Muslim world at the failed attempt by an Australian fundamentalist Christian, Michael Rohan, to set alight the Al Aqsa Mosque in Jerusalem, ranked just below Islam's holy sites in Mecca and Medina, on 21 August 1969. At his behest, King Hassan II of Morocco convened a conference in Rabat on 22 September to discuss the failed arson attack. It was attended by high officials of two dozen Muslim states, including Egypt—represented by Muhammad Anwar Sadat, one of the vice-presidents.

The convention called for Israel to relinquish the Arab territory it conquered in 1967. The subsequent Organisation of the Islamic Conference (OIC; later Organisation of Islamic Cooperation) established its secretariat in Jeddah. This enabled Faisal to claim that Saudi Arabia was *primus inter pares* among Muslim states (the OIC has been holding triennial summits in different Muslim capitals since then).

Few, if any, of the attendees at the Rabat convention were aware of the coup attempt in Saudi Arabia that June. It was led by the Saudi section of the Arab Nationalist Movement (ANM), advocating pan-

Arabism. The Saudi section had originated as a clandestine group in Dhahran in 1964 and had graduated into something bigger in early 1966. During the next three years the ANM built up a base among military officers, oil workers, civil servants and teachers. Its attempt at a coup in June 1969 was foiled only a few hours before its scheduled execution as a result of a tip-off by the CIA, which had managed to plant an infiltrator among the plotters. The resulting arrest of 200 conspirators, followed by scores of executions, destroyed the party. The Saudi government resorted to locating army bases far away from urban centers to prevent a military coup in the future.[8]

After the death of Nasser due to a heart attack, in September 1970, Sadat—who had been made the sole vice-president in December—became the acting president of Egypt. In mid-October he was elected president in a referendum in which he was the sole candidate.

Faisal Ascendant in post-Nasser Egypt, Riding the Oil Boom

With that, Faisal acquired leverage in Cairo. Of medium height, the dark, bespectacled Sadat, with short curly hair and a clipped mustache, was a pious Muslim whose slight bump on his forehead was often attributed to his regular prayers offered on a mat. He was appointed the secretary general of the Islamic Congress established in Cairo in 1965 by Nasser to rally Muslim opinion behind it. Sadat was then one of four vice-presidents. Nasser later made a sharp rightward turn in his domestic politics and made Sadat the sole vice-president. It was then that Adham started to channel CIA payments to Sadat, who was having financial problems. Later the Saudi government saw to it that he enjoyed a substantial regular income.[9]

At home, Faisal institutionalised religion by issuing a decree in August 1971 forming the twenty-strong Council of Senior Ulema (COSU), appointed by him, and the smaller Permanent Committee for Scholarly Research and Fatwas drawn from COSU. It was linked to the Higher Council of *Qadis* (Religious Judges), the Institute for Scientific Studies, the Supervision of Religious Affairs, and the Committee for the Promotion of Virtue and Prevention of Vice.

The last institution was based on the Quranic verse (3:100), which reads:

"Let there be one community [umma] of you, calling to good,
and bidding to honor, and forbidding dishonor;
those are the successful ones."

In the succeeding decades the monarch would consult COSU on vital issues. Its members, dependent ultimately on the king's goodwill for their four-year tenure, would prove pliant. With the arrival of the Internet in the Kingdom in 2001, several ulema started to post their public fatwas online. The problem became acute later in the decade. In August 2010, King Abdullah would limit the issuance of public fatwas to members of COSU.[10] By so doing he would severely curtail the power of non-establishment clerics irrespective of their popular standing.

In Egypt, President Sadat started peppering his speeches with verses from the Quran to underscore his religious piety and widen his base; he became known as "the believer president." He allowed many exiled Muslim Brotherhood members to return home from Saudi Arabia and introduced Islamic programs on the state-run television. He also amended the constitution such that the Sharia became the primary source of law. As for the Egyptians working in the Kingdom, they were encouraged to interpret the new wealth and power of Saudi Arabia as the divine vindication of Saudi-style piety. Riyadh financed many social projects and local Islamic groups in Egypt.

Faisal also encouraged Sadat to expel the 15,000 Soviet military personnel who had arrived in Egypt along with fighter aircraft, interceptors and surface-to-air missiles after the 1967 Arab-Israeli War. Sadat did so in July 1972. When early the next year Sadat began to implement a clandestine military strategy to retake the Sinai Peninsula lost to Israel in 1967, he made a secret trip to Riyadh on 27 August 1973 to inform Faisal of his plan. It was this close alliance of his with Sadat that led Faisal to use the oil weapon during the October 1973 Arab-Israeli War, launched during Ramadan, which was labeled a jihad by the Egyptian leader.

During the Arab-Israeli War,[11] OAPEC oil ministers met in Kuwait on 16 October. The next day, reacting to President Richard Nixon's decision to airlift weapons to Israel on a massive scale, they decided that "all Arab oil exporting countries shall forthwith cut production by no less than 5 per cent of the September production, and maintain the same rate of reduction each month until the Israeli forces are fully withdrawn from all Arab territories occupied during the 1967 [Arab–Israeli] War, and the legitimate rights of the Palestinian people are restored."They categorised the consumer countries as friendly, neutral or hostile to the Arab cause, with the friendly nations to be supplied at the September level, the neutrals at a reduced level and the hostile ones not at all. They also confirmed the steep price rise decided earlier by OPEC. King Faisal ordered a 25 per cent cut in Saudi output, running at 8 million bpd.[12]

In Tehran the Shah's refusal to join the OAPEC's boycott disappointed Faisal particularly when Iran emerged as the main supplier of oil to Israel. Moreover, encouraged by the self-reliant policies advocated by OPEC, the Shah had pressed the Western consortium to renegotiate the leasing agreement with his government. On the tenth anniversary of the White Revolution—a term he coined for a package of socio-economic reforms recommended by the US—in January 1973, he announced the nationalisation of the Western oil consortium. This duly occurred in July when the National Iranian Oil Company (NIOC) took over all the operations of the consortium as well as its ownership. After the October 1973 Arab-Israeli War, the Shah strongly backed the idea of OPEC raising petroleum prices.

By leading the Arab oil embargo in response to the United States' massive military assistance to Israel during the October War, Faisal displayed an independent streak which raised his stature among Arabs, who came to respect him as a leading Arab nationalist. By so doing he wielded petroleum as a weapon of war deployed during an armed conflict—an unprecedented accomplishment. The subsequent leap in oil prices gave Faisal access to huge funds which he deployed to extend Saudi influence beyond the Arab world.

With the cornucopia of petro-dollars at his disposal, Faisal promoted Islamic solidarity in the Middle East and beyond. This has continued—except that with the rising influence of Iran in the Arab world, Saudi rulers have resorted to emphasising sectarian affiliation. In short, Faisal's reign opened a new chapter in the chronicle of the Saudi Kingdom. All of his successors have pursued this goal, according it a leading role in their foreign policy.

Before his oil boycott strategy could realise its full potential, Faisal's resolve began to falter. Aware of his rabidly anti-Communist views,

Prime Minister Edward Heath of Britain, which had remained neutral in the war, dispatched a special envoy to Riyadh in late December 1973 to explain to the King that any prolonged oil boycott would weaken the West, and thereby strengthen Communism. Further help in that direction came when the ardently pro-Washington President Sadat worked in tandem with US Secretary of State Henry Kissinger, who had warned that the use of force by America to secure oil supplies from the Gulf region could not be ruled out. They succeeded in convincing Faisal to discontinue the boycott. Both Sadat and Kissinger then prevailed upon other OAPEC members to end the five-month embargo on 18 March 1974 "as a token of goodwill" to the West. They did so even though the Israelis were yet to withdraw from anywhere in the Arab occupied territories and the legitimate rights of the Palestinians had not been restored. Having deployed the oil weapon unexpectedly and therefore effectively, to the great consternation of Washington, Faisal failed to hold his nerve until he had achieved his loudly declared aim. He blinked first, thereby letting slip a once-in-a-generation opportunity.

In 1975, the Prophet Muhammad's birthday fell on 25 March, but it was a working day for Faisal at the Royal Palace, since his Kingdom only celebrated Eid al Adha and Eid al Fitr. In the morning he was scheduled to receive the Kuwaiti oil minister, Abdul Mutalib Kazimi. In the ante-chamber the twenty-seven-year-old Faisal bin Musaid appeared in the full regalia of a Saudi royal, and greeted Kazimi whom he had first met during his education at Colorado University, Boulder, in 1968. He was thus able to follow the foreign dignitary into the monarch's audience room.

As Kazimi was being introduced to Faisal by the Saudi oil minister, Zaki Yamani, Bin Musaid peered round his shoulder and fired three shots from his pistol. The first bullet hit the monarch in the throat and the other two grazed his head and shattered his ear. The assassin was instantly wrestled on to a nearby sofa. The efforts to revive King Faisal failed, and he died in hospital.[13]

The Saudi government declared three days of mourning, on which the Shah improved by announcing seven days of mourning in Iran.

A detailed investigation revealed that while studying for his undergraduate degree in political science in Colorado, Bin Musaid dressed in western clothes with his hair stylishly coiffured, and acquired a girlfriend,

Christine Surma. He later enrolled as a postgraduate student at the University of California in Los Angeles, and spent time with Surma, then an aspiring movie actress, before returning home in July 1974.

There was much speculation about the assassin's motivation. The popularly held belief in the Arab world was that King Faisal's oil boycott of the US in 1973 had brought about his assassination—in which the CIA was involved. This turned him into a martyr in the eyes of his admirers. But the key hint was implicit in Surma's prediction that Faisal bin Musaid would eventually be recognized as "the liberator of his country's people."[14] There was also an element of avenging the killing by Saudi police in Riyadh of his elder and more conservative brother, Khalid, during a demonstration against the newly launched television service.

In Riyadh, Faisal bin Musaid was beheaded by an executioner swinging a sword with a golden hilt in a central square in front of the palace of Prince Salman, the Governor of Riyadh. Salman was the only member of the royal family among the 10,000 spectators.[15]

Khalid's Reign Inaugurated

Watched by many surviving sons of Ibn Saud, led by Faisal's successor, King Khalid, and several foreign dignitaries—including President Sadat, Prime Minister Zulfikar Ali Bhutto of Pakistan, and President Muhammad Daoud Khan of Afghanistan—Faisal's corpse was buried in the fenced Al Oud cemetery about one kilometer from the center of Riyadh. It was the resting place of Ibn Saud and carried his appellation, meaning The Elder. As with Ibn Saud, the body of Faisal was laid along the north-south axis, with his face turned toward Mecca in an unmarked grave which happened to be next to the dynasty's founder.

On returning to his audience chamber, Khalid was overcome by grief and cried, and was comforted by Sadat. There was more to this gesture than simple human sympathy. As Egypt's president from September 1970 onwards, Sadat had forged a close friendship with Faisal: he had won the respect of the Saudi monarch by describing him as the Commander of the Faithful, *Amir al Mumineen*.[16] Among other things this relationship with Faisal gave Sadat leverage in his dealings with the US and West Europe. It was little wonder that on learning of

Faisal's assassination, Sadat was shocked and alarmed in equal measure. Instantly suspecting a conspiracy, he put the Egyptian army on alert and dispatched naval ships to the Red Sea. It was only after he had been assured by the royal palace in Riyadh that the murderous act was committed by a lone assassin and that the Saudi dynasty was not threatened that he relaxed.[17]

King Khalid bin Abdul Aziz Al Saud was a contrast from his predecessor in more ways than one. Endowed with pleasant looks, he was even-tempered and a conciliator. Suffering from ill-health, he underwent open heart surgery in 1972. On ascending the throne, he freed hundreds of political prisoners and appointed a cabinet in which fifteen of the twenty-five ministers were commoners, while ensuring that the crucial foreign, defence, interior and National Guard ministries stayed in the grip of members of the royal family. He underwent a second heart bypass procedure in October 1978, after which Crown Prince Fahd bin Abdul Aziz Al Saud (born 1921) became the de facto prime minister while Khalid spent more and more of his time rearing and training his hunting falcons.

Rising Importance of OPEC

In the mid-1970s OPEC's importance rose sharply, given that it produced more than half of the global output in 1976 and provided seven-eighths of world petroleum exports.[18] That year witnessed the first listing of North Sea oil, from the Forties field, on the exchange markets. Soon after, it acquired the name Brent, the largest oil field in the North Sea. Initially this price was used at the International Petroleum Exchange in London, but over the years Brent Crude became the main international benchmark, well ahead of the earlier West Texas Intermediate and the later Dubai Crude.[19]

Within OPEC, Saudi Arabia, possessing a substantial spare capacity at any given time, emerged as the "swing producer", able quickly to raise or reduce its production to balance the market and help maintain the price fixed by OPEC. This in turn enabled it to have the final say on prices. At home, enriched by the dramatic hike in oil prices, the Saudi government acquired 25 per cent of Aramco in 1974. It completed the total buy-out in 1980 after the overthrow of Muhammad Reza Shah Pahlavi of Iran in early 1979, caused partly by a strike in the country's oil industry which pushed the price from $14 to $28 a barrel within a few months. The renamed Saudi Aramco guaranteed supplies to the four US constituents of Aramco by giving them priority in buying its petroleum.

At that time OPEC was so powerful that it made its oil prices stick. By contrast, the position of the US had weakened as it became increasingly dependent on petroleum imports, a sixth of which came from the Saudi kingdom in 1978. Far from the self-sufficiency it should have acquired by 1979, as anticipated by President Richard Nixon, a mere shortfall of 2 per cent in its consumption—400,000 barrels per day—in mid-1979 led to panic buying and long gasoline lines.[20] But, overall, by 1979 the output in non-OPEC countries had started rising due to the high investment the Western petroleum giants had made in exploration after the oil price explosion. Yet non-OPEC output still lagged behind OPEC's total, albeit not for long.

Tehran Riyadh Washington Relations Get Complex

In the Persian Gulf region, in the early 1960s, whereas the internecine warfare at the top in Riyadh was in the final analysis an internal affair, the domestic agenda of the Shah in Iran came to be driven by Washington. With the arrival of John F. Kennedy in the White House in January 1961, US interference in Iran's domestic affairs grew. He urged the Shah to tackle corruption in the royal family and among his personal entourage, and initiate socio-economic reforms such as votes for women and agrarian reform. Indeed the availability of American weapons was made conditional on the Shah remaining on the reformist path. In 1962 total US military assistance to Iran during the past decade—or $20 per capita—was on a par with its economic aid.[21]

Washington's relations with Iran became a subject of public debate in mid-1964 when a bill to grant immunity to all US citizens working on military projects in the country was submitted to the Majlis. This bill had to be passed so that the US could loan Iran $200 million to purchase American arms.[22] Among those who bitterly opposed the legislation was Ayatollah Ruhollah Khomeini, who fourteen years later would lead the popular revolutionary movement which overthrew the Pahlavi dynasty.

Starting in the early 1960s, the geopolitical interests of Tehran and Riyadh began to diverge. Britain's withdrawal from Kuwait, in 1961, letting the emirate become an independent state, led the Shah to believe that it would withdraw from the Persian Gulf altogether within the next decade. He therefore started to improve relations with the Soviet Union so that he could shift his military forces from the north of the country to the south. He did so in March 1965. This set him on an arms race with the independent Arab Gulf states such as Iraq and Saudi Arabia. To pay for the additional costs of this build up, he pressured the Western oil consortium to raise output. Meanwhile, to fill the gap in the petroleum market following OAPEC's embargo after the Six Day War, Iran's Western oil consortium raised annual output from 770 million barrels in the previous year to 950 million barrels, and contributed $751 million to Iran's treasury.[23] And for the first time the consortium allowed the NIOC to market 100,000 bpd on its own.

In January 1968, Britain's Labour government decided to pull out of the Gulf by the end of 1971 as part of the general withdrawal from areas east of Suez given the adverse impact of the devaluation of the British pound.[24]

America and Britain assessed the comparative strengths of the economies and militaries of Saudi Arabia (population 5. 8 million) and Iran (population 28.5 million), and found Iran to be superior in every respect. Therefore Washington and London decided to transform the Shah into the policeman of the Persian Gulf. Iran's intelligence links with the US were so close that every Saturday morning the Shah had a two-hour briefing session with the CIA station chief in Tehran.[25]

Britain capped its respective withdrawals from Bahrain and Qatar in August and September 1971 with its supervision of the formation of the United Arab Emirates (UAE)—a federation of six principalities which had existed as British protectorates—on 2 December 1971.[26] A month earlier, the Shah, backed by Britain, pressed his claim to three islands at the mouth of the strategic Strait of Hormuz. Iran took over the two Tunb islands and partially occupied Abu Musa—much to the resentment of the UAE. Riyadh expressed its surprise and regret and called on the Shah to reconsider, but in vain.

When Sultan Qaboos of Oman requested Iranian aid to crush the leftist uprising in Dhofar province in 1972, the Shah attached naval units to the Omani island of Umm al Ghanem at the entrance of the Hormuz Strait. He also offered a joint defence of the Strait's navigable channels.[27]

In 1971, when the Shah regally entertained sixty-eight kings, queens, princes and princesses at the ancient site of Persepolis to celebrate the alleged 2,500[th] anniversary of the establishment of the Achaemenid Empire—a claim lacking historical evidence—he requested advanced weapons from the US. He got them thanks to the Nixon doctrine, under which the US President encouraged select American allies in the Third World to use Washington's military and economic aid to bolster their armed forces. America was to be more of an arms supplier and less of a gendarme outside the North Atlantic Treaty Organisation (NATO). As such, Iran continued to occupy the pre-eminent position it had acquired in Washington after the 1953 coup. Between then and 1969 it received as much US military assistance as all other countries combined. By late 1971 Iran asked Washington to cease its grants.[28]

In November 1972 the Shah declared that he was extending the "security perimeter" of Iran beyond the Persian Gulf to cover the north-western quadrant of the Indian Ocean, and combining this with a plan to expand the Iranian navy fivefold. This alarmed the Saudi government as did the Shah's dispatch of combat forces to Dhofar.[29]

While failing to join Gulf oil producers in their oil embargo of Western nations that supported Israel in the 1973 War, the Shah strongly supported the idea of raising petroleum prices. On 23 December 1973, at the meeting of Gulf oil producers in Tehran, his suggestion to double the oil price again was accepted, and later adopted by OPEC.[30] As a result, between mid-October 1973 and 1 January 1974 the price of oil was increased from $2.55 to $11.65 a barrel ($43 in today's terms) by OPEC, with the host government's average earnings rising fivefold, from $1.38 to $7 a barrel.[31] The resulting cash bonanza had an immense impact on the Saudi Kingdom as well as Iran.[32]

This was all the more so in Iran where, cajoled by the Shah, the NIOC increased its output to a record six million bpd in 1974 by overexploiting oil wells. Tehran's oil revenue jumped from $4.6 billion in 1973–1974 to $17.6 billion a year later. An overconfident Shah told a visitor to his Niavaran Palace, "I want the standard of living in Iran in 10 years' time to be exactly on a level with that in Europe today. In 20 years' time we shall be ahead of the United States."[33] In 1975 there was enough surplus foreign exchange in Tehran's treasury that the Shah granted a loan of $1 billion to Britain and the same amount to France, both then suffering stagflation because of the exponential rise in petroleum prices.[34] The overconfident Shah started talking of turning Iran into the fifth most powerful nation in the world after America, the Soviet Union, Japan and West Germany.

At the OPEC summit in Algiers in March 1975 the Shah and Saddam Hussein, then vice-president of Iraq, reached an accord on the land and fluvial boundaries of their countries. Iraq conceded Iran's demand, dating back to 1914, to demarcate the Shatt al Arab waterway according to the thalweg line (that is, along the median line of the main navigable channel). Both signatories agreed to end all infiltrations of a subversive nature. This agreement was formalised three months later as the Iran–Iraq Treaty of International Boundaries and Good Neighbourliness (1975).[35]

The Gulf monarchs said little about the rapprochement between pro-Washington Iran and pro-Moscow Iraq mainly because of their fear and dislike of the radical Baathist regime in Baghdad. However, the general feeling among them was that by agreeing to share the ownership of Shatt al Arab with Iran, Iraq had compromised historic Arab rights.

The Shah's Eastward Focus

On 17 July 1973 while Afghan King Zahir Shah was in Italy for medical treatment his cousin and the supreme commander of the military, Muhammad Daoud Khan, seized power in the name of returning Afghanistan to Islamic values. He abolished the monarchy and established a republic with himself as executive president.

In Tehran, bolstered by the riches that quadrupling of oil prices in 1973–1974 brought to the treasury, the Shah sought to influence policies and events in Kabul. Given the parlous economic state of Afghanistan, where foreign grants and loans accounted for more than 60 per cent of the 1977–1978 budget, Daoud Khan welcomed the Shah's offer of aid, which came with strings attached. Encouraged by Iran's intelligence agency, Savak, Daoud Khan's security agents resorted to murdering Marxist leaders who had backed his overthrow of the monarchy.

However, the assassination by state agents in 1978 of Mir Akbar Khyber, a respected trade union leader and a former editor of the leftist publication *Parcham*, altered the situation abruptly. The Marxist People's Democratic Party of Afghanistan (PDPA) mounted a massive anti-government demonstration in the capital. In response, Daoud Khan ordered the jailing of all PDPA functionaries. But Nur Muhammad Taraki, the top leader, escaped arrest. Advised by his radical colleague Hafizullah Amin, he activated the Marxist network in the military built up over two decades. The result was a coup by leftist military officers on 27 April 1978—an event officially called the Saur (April) Revolution. Daoud Khan was killed in the fighting at the presidential palace, and his official positions of president and prime minister went to Taraki. Amin became deputy Prime Minister.[36]

The coup was the culmination of the Marxists' efforts to recruit military officers over the past many years, and the policy of the Kabul government (initiated by Daoud Khan in the mid-1950s) of sending its officers for training to the Soviet Union. Since they received this training at the military academies in the Central Asian republics of the Soviet Union, they felt racially and culturally at home, and could not avoid comparing the economic, social and educational progress of the (Muslim) inhabitants of these republics with the backwardness of the Afghans. These experiences made them pro-Soviet and a suitable quarry for recruitment in the military network of the Afghan Marxists.

In the Gulf region the attention of Arab monarchs turned to the increasingly turbulent politics of Iran, precipitated by the Shah's headlong drive to industrialise Iran at a furious pace and inflate its arms arsenal. In response, King Faisal started to build close relations with his fellow monarchs in the Arabian Peninsula. By the spring of 1978 the Shah was grappling desperately with an increasingly popular anti-royalist movement at home, which ultimately succeeded in overthrowing the Pahlavi dynasty. The birth of a revolutionary, republican regime in post-Shah Iran threatened the region's status quo.

4

AN ISLAMIC REVOLUTION IN IRAN;

INITIAL MISREADING BY THE SAUDIS

"Welcome to the home town of Khomeini". So read the billboard greeting visitors to Khomein, 180 miles (290 km) southwest of Tehran, in white Persian and English letters against a green background on a concrete arch. The name refers to a cleric who, at the age of seventy-six, led the world's last great revolutionary movement in the twentieth century to victory by mobilising a disparate cast of anti-status quo forces around the most radical demand: the end of the Pahlavi dynasty.

At a road junction half a mile down the town's main thoroughfare, on a vast multi-colored billboard, was a portrait of Ayatollah Ruhollah Khomeini—a sharp featured face with a grey beard and stern eyes focused on the middle distance, capped by a neat black turban, indicating descent from Prophet Muhammad.[1] The caption in Persian and English read: "Imam Khomeini (PBUH)[2] was the reviver of religious government in the contemporary world."

Not far away stood a large mansion signposted Beit al Nour, the House of Light. A complex occupying 46,270 sq feet (4,326 sq meters), it consisted of four adjoining houses, each with a courtyard with a small pool and flower bed in the middle and a few trees on the perimeter, and a three-story watch tower.

As I walked through the well preserved rooms of the main house in 2004, I saw a tribute to Khomeini in Persian and English: "Imam

Khomeini first opened his eyes to the world and illuminated the Islamic world with his radiance and splendor in 1902 (1279 Iranian Year)." Equally eye-catching was the framed copy of the Identity Document issued to Khomeini by the Interior Ministry of the Islamic Republic of Iran: "'Number A/12/514514. Sayyid Ruhallah Mustafavi born in 1279 (Iranian year)... Issued by Ali Akbar Rahmani on 20.11.1358."

Ruhollah's childhood was unusual. He was only five months old when his father, Sayyid Mostafa Hindi, was murdered in February 1903. As a member of a deeply religious family, his instruction in the Quran started at the age of six. After finishing his Persian education at fifteen, he was tutored in Islam for four years by his elder brother Murtaza Pasandida. He then joined the seminary in Arak run by Ayatollah Abdul Karim Haeri-Yazdi. When, in 1922, his teacher moved to Qom, a Shia holy town 90 miles south of Tehran, to revive the seminaries there, Khomeini went with him. Three years later he graduated in the Sharia, ethics and spiritual philosophy.

The Rise of an Aging Revolutionary

He published his first book, *The Secrets Revealed*, anonymously in 1942. It upheld private enterprise and opposed secularism. "We say that the government must be run in accordance with God's law [i.e. Sharia], for the welfare of the country; and the people demand it," he wrote. "This is not feasible except with the supervision of the religious leaders. In fact, this principle has been approved and ratified in the [Iranian] constitution, and in no way conflicts with public order, the stability of the government, or the interests of the country."[3]

In 1945 he graduated to the rank of *hojatalislam* (lit., proof of Islam) in the Shia religious hierarchy. It allowed him to collect his own circle of disciples, who would accept his interpretations of the Sharia. This happened at a time when the most senior cleric of Iran, Ayatollah Muhammad Hussein Borujerdi, belonging to the quietist school, urged the clergy to shun politics. His stance went down well with Muhammad Reza Shah. Following a failed attempt on his life in 1949, he pressured Borujerdi to stop Khomeini's classes at a prestigious seminary in Qom. Khomeini then delivered his lectures first at Salmasi mosque and then at Mahmoudi mosque.

He decried the deal Muhammad Reza Shah made with the Western oil consortium in 1954, and deplored the government's over-dependence on foreign investments. After Borujerdi's death in 1961, his disciples urged Khomeini to publish his interpretations of the Islamic law. The result was his book entitled *Clarification of Points of the Sharia*. It offered "specific codification of the way to behave in every conceivable circumstance, from defecation to urination to sexual intercourse to eating to cleaning the teeth".[4] It led to his promotion to ayatollah.

The death of firebrand Ayatollah Abol Qasim Kashani in 1962 left the radical clergy leaderless. Given the status that sixty-year-old Khomeini had by now acquired, he emerged as Kashani's successor. In a series of sermons at the prestigious Faiziya Seminary in early 1963, he lambasted the Shah's White Revolution as phony. He went on to challenge the monarch and lost. He was exiled to Iraq in 1965, and took up residence in Najaf, one of the two Shia holy cities, the other being Karbala. There he kept up his campaign against the Shah—an enterprise that the leftist Baathists, who seized power in Iraq in 1968, found convenient since they too were opposed to the pro-Western Shah.

Khomeini made use of the Persepolis celebrations in 1971 to mark 2,500 years of the Persian Empire of the Sassanians, based in Persepolis, to attack the institution of monarchy openly and vehemently. "[Islamic] Tradition relates that the Prophet said that the title of King of Kings, which is [today] borne by the monarchs of Iran, is the most hated of all titles in the sight of God," he declared. "Islam is on the whole opposed to the whole notion of monarchy... Monarchy is one of the most shameful and disgraceful reactionary manifestations."[5]

Monarchy was also one of the subjects he tackled in his series of lectures published in 1971 as *Hukumat-e Islam: Vilayat-e Faqih* (Islamic Government: Rule of the Faqih). In it he argued that instead of prescribing dos and don'ts for believers, supervising welfare for widows and orphans, and waiting passively for the return of the Hidden (Twelfth) Imam, Shia clerics must strive to oust corrupt officials and repressive regimes and replace them with one led by just Islamic jurists.

Unhappy at the Iraqi Baathist regime's mistreatment of the Shia clergy, Khomeini sought permission in 1972 to leave for Lebanon, but was denied it. Three years later he decried the founding of the Rastakhiz (lit., Resurrection) as the sole ruling party in Iran. His call was taken up by many clerics and theological students.

Following the signing of the Iran–Iraq Treaty in 1975 the number of Shia Iranian pilgrims to Najaf and Karbala rose sharply, to 2,500 a week. This made it easier for Khomeini to guide his followers in their anti-Shah campaign through smuggled tape recordings. These audio tapes became all the more important as the revolutionary process, consisting of massive and repeated demonstrations and strikes, gathered momentum through several stages over two years, starting in February 1977. The discontent of the burgeoning middle class, created by rising literacy and living standards over the past quarter century, remained unexpressed because of the relentless repression of secular opposition. Only the mosque with its extensive networks remained intact. This, combined with the alienation experienced by a large underclass of recent rural migrants, fostered by an overheated economy, created a protest movement that began to stir in the autumn of 1977.

Mushrooming of Street Protest into Revolution

When Jimmy Carter, a strong advocate of human rights, became US president in January 1977, intellectuals in Iran were encouraged to urge the abolition of censorship. A reluctant Shah conceded their demand. This emboldened the dissenters, both secular and religious. A turning point in the protest movement came a year later when a scurrilous attack on Khomeini in the pro-government *Ettilaat* (Persian: Information) newspaper inflamed popular feelings and placed the initiative firmly with the Ayatollah as someone who had been viciously slandered. With all avenues of secular opposition blocked by the monarchical regime, more and more Iranians had turned to the mosque and clergy to express their growing discontent. Aware of this, Khomeini made astute use of Shia history and Iranian nationalism to engender and sharpen anti-royalist militancy among a rapidly growing circle of Iranians. He started to call those street protesters killed by police firings martyrs, an honor in Shia Islam associated with Imam Hussein, killed in a grossly unequal battle in Karbala in 681, and revered as the Great Martyr. He then called on his followers to commemorate the fortieth day of their death by staging ever larger demonstrations. These in turn resulted in creating more martyrs.

In June 1978 the Shah held out an olive branch by removing the much-hated Nematollah Nasseri, the head of Savak since 1965, and appointed him ambassador to Pakistan. He instructed his royal relatives to sever all their business connections. But by then, to his acute disappointment, the fifteen-year-long economic boom had ended, and annual growth was down to 2 per cent.[6]

On the eve of the holy month of Ramadan starting on 5 August, the Shah promised full and free elections to the Majlis due in June 1979. Nobody believed him. For the next twenty-nine days the faithful prayed daily at the mosques, and listened to the preacher's sermon—sometimes accompanied by Khomeini's taped speeches—before breaking the fast after sunset. "Preachers drew on the Shiite themes of struggle and martyrdom," noted the editors of *The Dawn of Islamic Revolution: Volume I*. "The Pahlavis did not have to be directly mentioned. It was not difficult to draw a parallel between the hated figures of Yazid and Muwaiya and the Shah, or between the Umayyad dynasty, with its bent for luxury and pomp, and the Pahlavi dynasty."[7]

The tide of anti-royalist militancy rose higher. To reverse the trend, the Shah changed course. At his behest the cabinet imposed overnight a six-month-long martial law decree in a dozen cities. Unaware of the curfew, a large crowd gathered in Jaleh Square in eastern Tehran on 8 September, a Friday. The protesters were gunned down by tank-mounted soldiers. By the time they cleared the square, some 1,600 people lay dead. More than 2,300 died of their injuries during the next few days.[8] The massacre of Black Friday convinced Iranians that the repressive Shah would go to any lengths to maintain his absolutist power. They were disgusted but not cowed even when the Shah reintroduced censorship. He arrested opposition leaders and extended martial law to yet more cities.

In mid-September the employees of the Central Bank of Iran released a statement showing that 177 affluent Iranians had recently transferred more than $2 billion abroad. The list included senior politicians, military officers, and high-ranking civil servants. By late September capital flight from Iran reached $50 million a day,[9] revealing that the super-elite had lost their confidence in the durability of the Pahlavi dynasty.

At the Shah's behest, Khomeini was expelled from Iraq. After an unsuccessful attempt to cross into Kuwait by road, he flew to France from Baghdad on 6 October after French President Valéry Giscard d'Estaing had received a tacit nod of approval from the Shah. Once installed in Neauphle-le-Chateau near Paris, he gave four to five interviews a day to the international media.

Inside Iran, by the third week of October, strikes had spread to almost all the banks, government ministries, post offices, railways, newspapers, internal air flights, radio and television stations, state-run hospitals, universities, high schools, and bazaars. Khomeini called on oil workers to stop working. On 31 October they began an indefinite strike. This meant a loss of $74 million a day to the state treasury, most of it in foreign currency.

On 4 November at Tehran University protesting students tried to demolish the Shah's statue at the main entrance. In the melee an army conscript handed over his rifle to the protesters. This incensed his sergeant, who fired his sub-machine gun, killing between thirty and sixty students.[10] The event was critical. It indicated that the loyalty of troops, consisting largely of conscripts, to the Shah was slipping. This unnerved the Shah, who responded by appointing a military government. Describing it as "contrary to the law of the land and Sharia," on 23 November, Khomeini called on the people to deny it taxes and assistance. "It is the duty of all oil company officials and workers to prevent the export of oil, this vital resource," he said. Alluding to the coming month of mourning, Muharram (starting on 2 December), he called on the faithful to organise their gatherings without deferring to the authorities.[11] During the first three nights of Muharram, thousands of men wearing white shrouds, showing their willingness to die, defied the curfew in various cities. More than 700 lost their lives to shooting by the military.

Prime Minister General Gholam Reza Azheri agreed to allow marches on 10 Muharram, the climactic day of Ashura, provided opposition figures led the marches along a prescribed route. At the end of a march by 2 million people in Tehran on 11 December, a 17-point charter was adopted by acclamation. It demanded an end to monarchy, acceptance of Khomeini as the leader, and the founding of an Islamic republic.[12] A call for a general strike on 18 December was a total success. Now the army started to show signs of serious cracks. In provincial capitals deserting soldiers defected to the opposition.

Having concluded that his military government had reached a dead-end, the Shah started a search for a civilian prime minister. On 29

December, Shahpour Bakhtiar, leader of the National Front, agreed to serve as the premier on the (unwritten) conditions that the Shah would immediately go abroad on holiday, and that he would act as a constitutional monarch in the future. None of this made any difference to Khomeini. But, realising that the paucity of heating oil in the midst of winter was causing hardship to millions of households, he instructed oil workers to produce enough to meet domestic needs. That meant an output of 700,000 bpd instead of the 5.3 million bpd before the revolutionary turmoil, which generated revenue of $19.5 billion, accounting for three-quarters of the government's annual income.[13]

The Shah did not go on holiday immediately. Instead, as was to be revealed later, he stayed on to finalise plans for a military coup to overthrow the Bakhtiar government and recall him from abroad. An impatient Bakhtiar announced on 11 January that the monarch would leave the following week, and announced the formation of a nine-member Regency Council. In response, two days later Khomeini announced the establishment of the Council of Islamic Revolution in accordance with "the rights conferred by the laws of Islam and on the basis of the vote of confidence given to me by the overwhelming majority of the Iranian people". It was charged with appointing a provisional government, convening a constituent assembly to produce a constitution for the Islamic Republic, holding elections and transferring power to the elected representative.[14] On 16 January the Shah and his entourage left for a holiday in the Egyptian resort of Aswan.[15]

On the evening of 31 January Khomeini, his aides, and journalists boarded a specially chartered plane in Paris. He arrived at the airport in Tehran the next morning. Three million people lined the streets to greet Khomeini. Finding the streets blocked, the officials of the Revolutionary Komitehs transported Khomeini by helicopter to a high school in east Tehran which became his headquarters for a month. He immediately appointed Mahdi Bazargan, leader of the Liberation Movement of Iran, as the Prime Minister of the provisional government.

To avoid a head-on collision with Khomeini, Bakhtiar agreed not to arrest the Ayatollah's provisional government and merely to call it "a shadowy administration". But, plagued by mounting desertions, the military was disintegrating. On 9 February a mutiny at Doshan Tapeh air base in east Tehran snowballed. When Bakhtiar ordered the elite Imperial

Guard to capture the air base, they found their path to it blocked by civilian guerrillas who attacked their tanks with hand grenades and machine guns. Having captured the armory at the air base the armed revolutionaries rushed weapons and ammunition to Tehran University campus where youthful citizens grabbed them. During the next 24 hours (10–11 February) armed revolutionaries and air force and army deserters went about destroying systematically what remained of the Shah's once formidable war machine. All told they distributed 300,000 weapons, including 75,000 machine guns. Thus armed, they fought the 30,000 strong Imperial Guards who, sitting in tanks and armored vehicles, were ill-equipped to engage in street fighting.

At 2 pm on 11 February, General Abbas Karim Gharabaghi, head of the Military Supreme Council, announced the armed forces' neutrality in the current political crisis, and ordered the troops to return to their garrisons.[16] Four hours later music on the National Radio of Iran was interrupted by an announcer to say that the station had been secured by the "the forces of the revolution."

When on 14 February the remnants of the Imperial Guards launched an attack on radio and TV stations, calls went out for popular support to repulse the assault. Thousands of armed revolutionaries appeared and defeated the royalists within an hour. Finally all of Tehran fell under the control of the revolutionaries. But in one of the provincial capitals, fighting between pro-Khomeini and pro-Shah forces did not end until 16 February, in favor of the revolutionaries.

Between the police firing in January 1978 and the overthrow of the Pahlavi dynasty in February 1979, the anti-royalists lost an estimated 10,000 to 40,000 lives. The army's strength fell from nearly 300,000 to less than 100,000 mainly because of desertions. Months of civil unrest and strikes against the background of economic boom, generated by the dramatic oil price rise combined with the doubling of output, followed by a recession, gravely crippled the economy. The indefinite strike by oil workers, still under the influence of the underground Tudeh party, delivered the coup de grace.

And yet the Shah gave up only in extremis. Had anti-royalists not been led by someone as astute and steadfast as Khomeini, then based abroad, they would have most likely failed to end the Pahlavi dynasty. It was hard to believe that the region's most powerful monarch, backed by a loyal military force of over 400,000, was dethroned by a movement of ordinary, unarmed citizens.[17] Between 1972 and 1978 the Shah had increased the military budget from $1.375 billion to $9.94 billion, consuming a quarter of the total. During that period he placed $20 billion worth of arms contracts with American corporations.[18]

Among other things this had created anxiety in Riyadh, even though the Desert Kingdom stood to gain financially and strategically. With the loss of Iran as an important and reliable supplier of oil, Washington became even more dependent for oil on Saudi Arabia, then the second largest petroleum producer in the world, behind the Soviet Union (at 11.4 million bpd), but well ahead of America (at 8.5 million bpd). With its imports running around 8 million bpd, the US was expected to pay a record sum of $61 billion for its oil imports in 1979, and Saudi Arabia to earn more than $66 billion from oil exports.[19]

The Pillars of the Islamic Republic

Politically, what set this historic upturn in the Middle East apart from previous radical changes after the Second World War was that the end of monarchy in Iran was achieved by millions of people taking to the streets. The earlier overthrow of the ruling dynasties in Egypt and Iraq was the result of military coups which received popular backing after the event. There were no grass roots protest demonstrations over many months in monarchical Egypt or Iraq, which generated rising tides of militant resistance to the status quo and resulted among other consquences in drastically reducing the local military into a passive spectator.

Among those who failed to grasp this crucial difference were the Saudi royals in Riyadh, where the ailing King Khalid sat on the throne, with his younger half-brother Fahd as the Crown Prince. They thought they would take in their stride the revolutionary overthrow of monarchy in Tehran just as they had done the overnight anti-royalist coups in Cairo and Baghdad. That was why in January 1979 Fahd, the de facto Prime Minister, expressed no alarm in public, stating merely that what was happening in Iran was a domestic problem that was best left to Iranians to resolve.[20] Senior Saudi royals failed to distinguish between coups carried out by plotting military officers, as had been the case in Egypt and Iraq, and a genuinely grass roots revolutionary movement gaining momentum month after month that succeeded in toppling a regime wholesale, while fatally weakening its armed forces, as happened in Iran between autumn of 1977 and February 1979.

So far as the Arab Gulf monarchies were concerned, Khomeini offered his interpretation of a verse in the Quran (*Lahul Mulk*), in the chapter titled "The Regime", that dynastic rule was un-Islamic. This argument alarmed the Gulf royal families, who had sought legitimacy within Islamic precepts. Khomeini's thesis, echoed by the state-run media in Iran, posed the most serious ideological challenge to them. This was particularly true of the Al Saud dynasty.

Earlier, it had dawned on King Faisal as well as the Wahhabi establishment that given the very small base of their creed it would prove hard to popularise it abroad. They became open to the Salafiya doctrine which had evolved at the oldest Islamic university, Al Azhar University in Cairo, under the leadership of Jamal al Din Afghani (1838–1897), who noted the militancy of the *salaf* (ancestors) in early Islam. His two Egyptian disciples, Muhammad Abdu and Muhammad Rashid Rida, showed how the sayings and deeds of Prophet Muhammad and his earliest followers could be applied to contemporary conditions. By so doing they laid the foundation of pan-Islamism which Faisal found politically expedient to adopt in order to counter the rival pan-Arabism being disseminated by Egypt's President Gamal Abdul Nasser. He thus succeeded in defusing the ideological threat posed by Nasser especially after the latter went on to embrace Arab socialism.

In the late 1970s, King Khalid and his advisors found it hard to dismiss or downplay such a towering Islamic figure as Khomeini. In the end they found solace in the Sunni-Shia divide, arguing that whatever Khomeini had to say applied to Shias and their rulers, and had nothing to do with Sunnis and their creed. Given the prevalent anti-Shia sentient among Sunnis in the Gulf region, this strategy proved effective.

The Khomeini regime faced the monumental task of defeating the inevitable attempts of the leading elements of the ancien regime to regain powe, and consolidating the revolution which, though led by the mosque operating through the local Islamic Komitehs (that is, Committees), contained substantial secular and leftist forces. In addition, it needed to disentangle Iran from the all-enveloping embrace of the United States, and expunge American influence from society as well as neutralise the remnants of the monarchical order. While maintaining what was left of the Shah's army, the new regime purged all the officers it considered non-Islamic or insufficiently Islamic. Besides the 11,000 officers who had undergone long-term training in America, there were many more thousands who had gone through short-term courses there.[21] It was also resolved to replace scores of secular laws with Sharia-based legislation.

The first priority was to order a referendum on the naming of the post-Shah political system. When Khomeini overruled the suggestions of "People's Democratic Republic," and "Democratic Islamic Republic," and opted for the question, "Should Iran be an Islamic Republic?", the leftist, secular and regional parties boycotted the referendum. The regime responded by lowering the voting age from 18 to 16. More than 98 per cent voted in favor. On 1 April 1979 the Islamic Republic came into being.

On 6 May Khomeini ordered the formation of the Islamic Revolutionary Guards, a special force, responsible to the Central Revolutionary Komiteh, to protect the revolution. Armed with submachine guns, they monitored the activities of leftists and liberals, and broke up demonstrations and strikes organised by them. They also kept a watch on army barracks and police stations.[22] A typical revolutionary guard came from a lower middle class or poor urban family and was totally dedicated to Khomeini and the revolution. Most observers saw revolutionary guards as a counter-force to army troops often led by officers whose loyalty to the Islamic Republic was suspect.

Within six months of the revolution, the Khomeini regime set up new institutions in the administrative, political, judicial, economic and security fields: the Revolutionary Komitehs, the Islamic Republican Party, revolutionary courts, the Mustazafin Foundation (which took over the assets of the Pahlavi Foundation and the affluent Iranians who had fled), and the Revolutionary Guards. In the cultural field, the Islamic regime stopped the purging of the Arabic words from Persian ordered by the Shah. Instead, it encouraged the learning of Arabic by providing lessons on one of the state-owned television channels. All Iranian clerics were fluent in Arabic, a compulsory subject in their curriculum, and studied the Quran in its original language.

In Riyadh, following Saudi Arabia's recognition of the Khomeini regime, its Deputy Prime Minister Prince Abdullah bin Abdul Aziz Al

Saud said in his interview with the Gulf News Agency that "The new established regime in Iran has removed every obstacle and dropped all reservations regarding all kinds of cooperation between Saudi Arabia and the Islamic Republic of Iran... The Holy Quran is the constitution of our two countries, and thus links between us are no longer determined by material interests or geopolitics."[23] This was a sweeping statement which would turn out to be a misreading of what had rocked Iran.

In Tehran, the immediate task of the provisional government was to arrange the election of an Assembly of Experts for the Constitution. It was held on 1 August. Of its seventy-three members, forty-five were clerics, and the rest laypersons.[24] It debated a draft constitution prepared in mid-June, and inserted the concept of *Vilayat-e-Faqih* (Persian: "Rule of the Religious Jurisprudent"). This doctrine was developed by Khomeini. In his book, *Hukumat-e Islami* (Persian, "Islamic Government"), published in 1971, he had argued that an Islamic regime requires an Islamic ruler who is thoroughly conversant with the Sharia and is just in its application: a Just Jurisprudent. In Shia religious hierarchy he would bear the title of *Marja-e Taqlid* (Arabic: "source of emulation"). As a ruler the Just Jurisprudent should be assisted by jurisprudents at various levels of legislative, executive and judicial bodies. The function of a popularly elected parliament, open to both lay believers and clerics, is to resolve the conflicts likely to arise in the implementation of Islamic doctrines. However, judicial functions are to be performed only by jurisprudents conversant with the Sharia. The overall supervision and guidance of parliament and judiciary rests with the Just Jurisprudent, who must also ensure that the executive does not exceed its powers.[25] The final version of the constitution, completed on 15 November, was endorsed by 98 per cent of voters in a referendum held on 2 and 3 December.

"The official religion of Iran is Islam, and the Twelver Jaafari school of thought," stated the Constitution while according "full respect" to the Hanafi, Shafii, Maliki, and Hanbali schools of thought in Sunni Islam, as well as the Zaidi code in Shia Islam. It recognized Christians, Jews and Zoroastrians as religious minorities and allocated them four seats in the Majlis.

Since "Allah has placed man in charge of his social destiny," read Principle 56, "No one can deprive man this Allah-given right, nor subordinate it to the interests of a given individual or group." This was a clear denunciation of monarchy and civilian or military dictatorship or a cabal of generals. The Just Jurisprudent is called the Leader of the Revolution.[26] The constitution declared Khomeini as the Just Jurisprudent and Supreme Leader for life, specifying that after him the Leader or Leadership Council, in office for eight years, was to be named by the popularly elected Assembly of Experts. The constitution specified that the legislative, executive and judicial powers of the government were independent of each other. Just below the Just Jurisprudent was the directly elected President, a cleric or a layperson, who was the chief executive. "In accordance with the command of the Quran contained in the verses 'Their affairs are by consultation among them,' and 'Consult them on [their] affairs,' councils and consultative bodies belong to the decision-making and administrative organs of the state," read Principle Seven. A Council of Guardians, part nominated by the Just Jurisprudent and partly elected by the Majlis, ensured that bills passed by the Majlis did not contravene Islamic tenets or the constitution. It also vetted candidates for public office.

The articles dealing with the basic rights of the individual provided for equal human, political, economic, social and cultural rights for men and women. The formation of political and professional parties and associations, as well as religious societies was allowed provided they did not violate the principles of independence, national unity or Islamic criteria.[27] In practice these noble principles were only partially implemented.

It seemed that senior princes in Riyadh had not yet bothered to get the Iranian constitution translated into Arabic and/or English and peruse it. This was the only conclusion to be drawn from what Crown Prince Fahd bin Abdul Aziz Al Saud said in his interview with *Al Hawadith* magazine on 10 January 1980: "It is not in our interest to have misunderstanding ... especially since the new regime in Iran is working under the banner of the Islamic faith, which is our motto in Saudi Arabia."[28] Even a cursory reading of Iran's constitution would have shown that there was a wide chasm between the Saudis and Iranians in how Islam was to be applied to administer a state and its citizens' affairs.

The Islamic Republic's foreign policy, as stated in Article 152, was based on "the rejection of all forms of domination, preservation of complete independence and territorial integrity of the country, the defense of rights of all Muslims.... [and] non-alignment with respect to the hegemonist superpowers." In fact, Khomeini had already set the republic on the non-aligned path. On 10 August his government terminated the 1959 military cooperation agreement with the United States, withdrew from the anti-Soviet Central Treaty Organisation (CENTO), formed in 1959, with Britain as its founding member, and cancelled three-quarters of its $12 billion worth of orders for US arms.[29] It severed Iran's ties with Israel, and recognized the Palestine Liberation Organization.

To Washington's distress, this ruptured the base of its strategy in the Middle East. Since the establishment of Israel in 1948, its anti-Soviet policy had come to rest on three pillars: Israel, Saudi Arabia and Iran. Despite their periodic differences with the Shah, Saudi royals were reassured by the fact that their Kingdom and the Shah shared the same US security umbrella. Now the fraying ties between the Khomeini regime and America made the ruling Saudi dynasty anxious.

Tehran's relations with Washington started souring during the revolutionary turmoil. The strength of the US Embassy in Tehran, at 1,000 during the heyday of the Shah, shrank to 60 in the spring of 1979. On 17 May the US Senate voiced its "abhorrence" at "the summary executions without due legal process." Tehran Radio retorted that the same Senate had said nothing against the massacre of hundreds of Iranian revolutionaries in the streets earlier in the uprising. On 25 May country-wide demonstrations were held against the Senate resolution, the theme being that "America is the number one enemy of the Islamic revolution." The situation deteriorated dramatically after 22 October, when the Carter administration allowed the deposed Shah, suffering from advanced cancer, to enter America for medical treatment, thus violating the promise it had given to Iran. The Khomeini regime called for his extradition to try him for treason for violating the 1907 Constitution, and ordering the killing of thousands of peaceful protesters. The Carter administration refused.[30]

On 1 November, three million people marched in Iran to demand the former Shah's extradition from the US. The next day Khomeini urged students to intensify their campaign against America to secure the Shah's return to Iran, and declared 4 November as the Students'

Day. At the planned student rally at the Tehran University campus, some 450 activists of the Islamic Associations at local universities never arrived. Instead, they seized the US Embassy within three hours.

IRAN'S SECOND REVOLUTION;

A MILLENNIAL CHALLENGE TO THE HOUSE OF SAUD

The size of the sprawling diplomatic complex of the United States matched its importance. So too did its location in central Tehran—at the junction of Takht-e Jamshid (Persian: "Throne of Jamshid") Avenue and Roosevelt Avenue. Housed inside a high brick-walled compound— a quarter of a mile in each direction—the old US Embassy included not only the main administrative building, a chancery, the ambassador's mansion and several houses for the senior diplomats, but also a warehouse, an electric power plant, tennis courts, a football field, a swimming pool, a parking lot, and a spacious garden.

"Nest of Spies"

Nowadays, the 30 acre complex houses Imam Hussein University and the Organisation of the Islamic Revolutionary Guard Vocational School, with the former chancery transformed into computing classrooms. Since admission to the site is denied to foreign journalists and writers, the only way a visitor can get some idea of the enormity of the place is to take a seat by the French windows of the third floor restaurant of Mashhad Hotel across Taleqani (former Takht-e Jamshid) Avenue.

That is what I did during my visit to Tehran some weeks before the 20th anniversary of the US Embassy takeover in November 1979. I broached the subject of Iranian-American relations with the head waiter, Shahriyar Isfahani, and a member of kitchen staff, Amir Zarkesh, a plump man with graying stubble and unkempt hair. "There were demonstrations for several weeks," he said, reminiscing without any emotion. "Some demonstrators slept in the street even though it was quite cold. The local shops were closed for several days due to these demonstrations."

Although I was there too, covering the event for the *Sunday Times*, I lacked the vantage point of Zarkesh. I could only watch and listen at street level—as did several American and European television camera crews camped out in front of the main entrance which was then at the middle of the wall facing Taleqani Avenue, and not at the corner—at the intersection of Taleqani Avenue and Martyr Moffateh (formerly Roosevelt) Avenue—as it is now.

All through the early weeks of the Embassy occupation there was enough in the air to make a foreign visitor feel that the nation was going through a "second revolution"—focused on purging the American influence that had permeated all facets of life in Iran, except the mosque. It was signaled by the fall of the laymen-dominated Provisional Government of Mahdi Bazargan on 6 November, with the 13-member Islamic Revolutionary Council, led by Ayatollah Muhammad Beheshti, containing six clerics, becoming the sole repository of power.

The occupied American Embassy became a rallying point and a place of pilgrimage. Its perimeter of black-painted steel bars and the buildings behind it, facing Taleqani Avenue, were bedecked with a huge portrait of Khomeini and many banners in English, Persian and Arabic, the most prominent being 'Allahu Akbar [God is Great]' and "NO NEGOTIATION, JUST DELIVERING SHAH". The whole area was lively round the clock, with the arc lights of the several Western camera crews banishing the night-time darkness.

During the day, it was almost like London's Speakers' Corner—without the speakers holding forth on top of soap boxes, interrupted by occasional, good-natured heckling from the audience, but with people hanging around in knots, talking politics, debating, distributing leaflets with information about the activities of respective parties or factions, or selling political literature. Every so often they would stop to watch columns of demonstrators march past the Embassy carrying placards and shouting slogans. One day it was factory workers march-ing; the next bazaar merchants and sales assistants; then it was the turn of students of secondary schools, boys or girls, followed by hospital staff, civil servants, journalists, employees of the National Iranian Oil Company, and so on.

My week-long straw poll conducted in different parts of Tehran in late November for the *Sunday Times* showed that a large majority of adult residents of Tehran had visited the US Embassy at least once, either individually, or as part of a marching, shouting column. The most frequent slogans that I heard were: "Give us the Evil Shah [then in an American hospital]", "Allahu Akbar, Khomeini *Rahbar* / God is Great; Khomeini is Leader", and "*Marg bar America* / Death to America".

Nearly two decades later at Mashhad Hotel, Zarkesh went further down his memory lane. "I remember the days when Americans visited Tehran and stayed at our hotel—during the Shah's time,' he said. 'Then you'd see half-naked American women at the swimming pool here. They used to be very noisy, those Americans. Some guests couldn't sleep due to the noise they made." The moment Zarkesh still savoured was when from his kitchen he saw the students "jump over the wall, and go inside quickly".

Inside the Embassy, the staff tried to destroy as many secret papers as they could using shredders and incinerators. But the forty or fifty hardcore assailants, who entered the main Embassy building with stun-ning speed and precision, captured most of the documents intact. They also preserved the shreds of paper which would later be painstakingly reconstituted and published as a series of fifty-four volumes in Persian and English under the title of *The Documents of the Nest of Spies*.[1]

During the following months, these documents proved to be a trea-sure trove to Islamic leaders while their description of the Embassy as the "Nest of Spies" caught on. They used the seized papers to discredit and eliminate most of its opponents, and even some of its lukewarm supporters.

After taking hostage sixty-seven US diplomats, later reduced to fifty-two after the release of fifteen female and black Americans, ordered by Khomeini, the militants—calling themselves Khat-e Imam (Khomeini), Partisans of the Imam—declared that they would exchange their hos-tages for the Shah. Such a deal was out of the question, said the Carter administration. But desperate to see the American hostages released, it pressured the Shah to leave. No country was prepared to take him. However, yielding to US pressure, Panama's ruler General Omar Torrijos agreed. The Shah flew out of New York on 15 December.

In the midst of this unprecedented crisis, the Carter administration received a further shock from its remaining favored state in the region. Every year the resources of the Saudi Kingdom are stretched to the full during the Hajj season. No matter what it thought of the revolution in Iran, it had to deal with the Hajj pilgrims from that country. Iran's new republican leader Ayatollah Ruhollah Khomeini attempted to use the annual ritual, due on 30 October 1979, to further Islamic revolution in the Muslim world. Thus instructed, the Iranian pilgrims conducted propaganda through leaflets. The Saudi authorities were ill-prepared to cope with this unprecedented tactic. Nearly three weeks later they were caught unawares, again, when an existential threat to the House of Saud suddenly materialised.

The Seizure of Mecca's Grand Mosque

The most serious domestic ideological challenge to the Saudi monarchy came on the eve of the Islamic New Year of 1400—20 November 1979, a Tuesday. Despite his faltering health, King Khalid was expected to offer dawn prayers in the Grand Mosque in Mecca. That was why hundreds of tightly organised insurgents had gathered among the mass of worshippers in the Grand Mosque for the first Hajj of the new Islamic century. They were led by Juheiman bin Muhammad al Utaiba and Muhammad bin Abdullah al Qahtani. The forty-three-year-old Juheiman, a hirsute man, with a lean, ascetic face framed by a mass of long, wavy black hair and an unkempt beard, belonged to the noble Utaiba tribe which, with three million members, was the Kingdom's largest. The surname of his twenty-seven-year-old brother-in-law, al Qahtani, a former student of the Islamic University of Riyadh, was a derivative of Qahtan, a legendary ancestor of Arabs.

Born in Sajir, an Ikhwan settlement in the northern Qassim province, Juheiman was a grandson of an Ikhwan militant who died in 1929 in a battle against Bin Saud. At the age of eighteen in 1954 he joined the National Guard, which inter alia encouraged religious learning among its recruits. He left the National Guard in 1973, signed up with the Salafi Group in Medina, and became a pupil of Shaikh Abdul Aziz bin Baz, who advocated a return to the letter of the Quran. The Group was funded by charitable foundations.

In early 1977, the Minister of Religious Affairs instructed a few pro-government ulema to wean away the members of the Salafi Group. They had partial success. Most members stayed and accepted Juheiman as their leader. His belief in the Wahhabi doctrine was so acute that he refused to use banknotes because they carried pictures of Kings, and limited himself to coins. Towards the end of that year, tipped of his imminent detention, Juheiman and his followers escaped to Qasim province. There he published a pamphlet "The State, Allegiance and Obedience: The Conduct of the Rulers". In it he attacked the Saudi rulers for their deviation from the Sharia, greed and corruption, misuse of laws for their own benefit, and socialising with atheists and unbelievers.[2]

In the summer of 1978 the government arrested him and his ninety-eight followers. After interviewing them Shaikh bin Baz, the leading member of the Council of Senior Ulema, concluded that what they had been propagating was not unreasonable. Their detention ended when they promised not to undertake subversive activities. Later, though under surveillance, they managed to slip away from Riyadh.

Juheiman developed the concept of *Mahdi* (messiah) and published his treatise in the pamphlet "The Call of the Ikhwan" in August 1979. In his brother-in-law, Muhammad bin Abdullah al Qahtani, bearing the same name as the founder of Islam, he found the Mahdi. To this doctrine he tagged the notion held by Sunnis that a *Mujaddid* (Arabic: one who brings renewal) appears at the beginning of an Islamic century to revive the faith and forbid innovation.

The Islamic New Year 1400 was to begin on 1 Muharram/20 November 1979. Juheiman and others expected King Khalid to attend the dawn prayer in the Grand Mosque, which would offer an opportunity to take him hostage, according to Juheiman's plan. At the start of the previous month—during which the faithful make the Hajj pilgrimage from the 8th to the 12th—Juheiman instructed his followers to converge on the Grand Mosque in Mecca on New Year's Eve.[3] In the preceding weeks they began to store arms, ammunition, and food and water in the many cellars and retreats of the Grand Mosque, using coffins to smuggle in weapons, including Kalashnikov assault rifles. It is customary for pious Muslims to bring a coffin of a dead relative on a stretcher covered with a sheet to the Grand Mosque for the Last Prayer before burial. The "corpse" in this case was a collection of small arms.

· After the dawn prayer, the armed militants quickly overpowered the official guards. In the absence of King Khalid at the Grand Mosque, Juheiman called on the imam to read out his denunciations of the royal family's corruption and religious deviations—and accept al Qahtani as the Mahdi to purify the Grand Mosque and the faith. When the imam refused, the rebels shut all thirty-nine doors of the Mosque and opened fire. While they allowed the foreign pilgrims among the nearly 100,000 devotees to leave, they instructed the Saudis to stay. By late afternoon they had posted themselves on the minarets and covered arches of the upper gallery.

King Khalid called the Council of Senior Ulema (COSU) to seek its advice on storming the Grand Mosque. In its emergency fatwa it referred to the Quranic verse: "Do not fight them near the Holy Mosque until they fight you inside it, and if they fight you [inside], you must kill them for that is the punishment for the unbelievers."[4] The fact that the armed rebels were not unbelievers was conveniently overlooked.

The government deployed the National Guard backed by tanks and helicopters. But the insurgents, occupying vantage points on all nine minarets, successfully targeted anyone approaching the holy site. Initially, army marksmen were reluctant to damage the minarets by shooting at the rebels. A series of assaults, involving police, the National Guard and the army—using different radio frequencies—ended in disaster. Astonishingly, the government did not possess the architectural plans of the Mosque. Saudi Binladin Group, a construction company, had one, and the other was with the Jeddah-based Hajj Research Centre whose director handed it to the commander of the assault troops.

On 24 November, Khalid ordered the National Guard to retake the Mosque. But when blowing up the minarets and storming by para-troopers failed to dislodge the insurgents, the army resorted to artil-lery while the National Guard battled their way slowly to the center of the compound where the Kaaba is located. Among those they killed was al Qahtani. The insurgents retreated to the labyrinthine basement where about a thousand rooms were connected by corridors and alleyways, the areas where they had stored their arms and ammunition, and food and water. The army's repeated offensives proved inadequate. After a week, the Saudis approached their ultimate savior: the United States, which readily offered the services of the CIA.[5]

According to Yaroslav Trofimov, author of the meticulously researched *The Siege of Mecca: The Forgotten Uprising in Islam's Holiest Shrine and the Birth of al Qaeda*, a team of CIA operatives was instantly converted to Islam. They entered Mecca and assessed the battle ground. They recommended using chemical agents. The Saudis pumped tear gas into the underground infrastructure through various entrances, but in vain. The insurgents prevented the spread of the gas into the narrow subterranean corridors by using thick mattresses, cardboard and cloth. By soaking their headdresses with water, they protected their breathing. In contrast, the bearded Saudi troops, wearing gas masks, failed to protect themselves as gas drifted upwards into the compound. With the tear gas spreading to the surrounding areas, the local residents had to be evacuated. In desperation, the Saudi government turned to France and its Foreign Legion. To let their forces enter Mecca, bin Baz allowed their temporary conversion to Islam. The French Captain, Paul Barril, opted for CS gas, an irritant that blocks breathing and leads to fainting, and is fatal if ingested in its concentrated form. He calculated that one tonne, or 1,000 kg, was needed, but he had only 300 kg on hand. To make the maximum use of the limited stocks, numerous holes were drilled in the compound and CS gas was pumped through them while soldiers entered the underground infrastructure from two ends of the Mosque.[6]

Following Saudi Crown Prince Fahd's urgent appeal to General Zia ul Haq, the military ruler of Pakistan since July 1977, a large contingent of the country's Special Services Group, led by Brigadier Tariq Mehmood, was flown to Mecca.[7] They too assisted the Saudi forces. Together, they succeeded in overpowering the rebels and capturing Juheiman on 4 December. Later these troops, lacking any roots in Saudi tribal society, would be deployed to guard strategic sites and senior princes' palaces.

Juheiman was tried in a Sharia court and found guilty, and brought before Shaikh bin Baz for his final ruling. When the accusations against the defendants were stated in full, bin Baz ruled that the accused were right in pointing out that a true Wahhabi state should not associate with unbelievers, that heresies and deviation from pure Islam should be removed, that images of all sorts were forbidden, and that consumerism and money had become the norm in society. Where the insurgents went wrong was to challenge the House of Saud and announce the arrival of the Mahdi. Therefore he declared that the decision to behead them was "the judgment of Allah".[8] The Wahhabi religious establishment nodded its agreement with bin Baz who was awarded the King Faisal International Prize for services to Islam the following year.

Khomeini Fishes in Troubled Waters

At the beginning of the crisis, against the background of patchy official news from Riyadh about the seizure of the Grand Mosque, the Carter administration, reeling from the fiasco of seeing its diplomats taken hostage in Tehran, hastily concluded that the insurgents were Shias who had acted in response to Khomeini's calls for a general uprising by fundamentalist Muslims in the Middle East. Citing a US intelligence official, the New York Times ran a front page story on 21 November headlined, "Mecca Mosque Seized by Gunmen Believed to Be Militants From Iran."[9] Unsurprisingly, this outraged Tehran. Iran's state-run radio aired a statement by Khomeini accusing America and Israel of orchestrating the despicable event in Mecca. Carter ordered a battle group from Subic Bay in the Philippines including the aircraft carrier Kitty Hawk to the Persian Gulf to enhance Saudi Arabia's sense of security.[10]

In the absence of a categorical denial from Saudi Arabia, Khomeini's assertion gained widespread currency in the Muslim world. Mobs in Pakistan, Bangladesh, Turkey, Libya, and Kuwait targeted American diplomatic mission and information and culture centers. During a five-hour siege of the US Embassy in Islamabad, the frenzied demonstrators burned down the building and killed two American marines guarding the premises.[11] Khomeini expressed his "great joy" at the news from Pakistan, and added that America and Israel were trying to seize the two holiest Islamic mosques in Mecca and Medina. "Muslims, rise up and defend Islam," he declared. "One of the biggest mistakes that Carter and his kind make is that they don't comprehend the depth of the contemporary Islamic movement," he added. "Our movement is Islamic, before being Iranian."[12]

Encouraged by the air of defiance engendered by the ongoing crisis in Mecca, the half a million Shia minority in the Kingdom, concentrated in the oil-rich province of Al Hasa, broke the long-established ban on the Ashura ritual. Between 25 and 30 November, Ashura processions were staged in Qatif and several other Shia-majority towns, defying the 65-year-long ban on all Shia festivals in the Kingdom.

The defiance was led by the Organisation of the Islamic Revolution in the Arabian Peninsula (OIRAP). It had originated as the clandestine Reform Movement and was led by Hassan al Saffar, a young, articulate Shia cleric. Its moderate demands included the right to publish Shia religious books and an end to the denunciations of Shias by Wahhabi preachers. In his sermons Saffar stayed strictly religious by stressing the determined resistance that Imam Hussein offered to injustice. But after the success of the Islamic revolution in Iran its tone hardened. This was encapsulated by a passage in one of its pamphlets: "When the people look at the squandering of the wealth while every area where they [Shias] live is deprived, miserable and suffering, is it not natural for them to behave in a revolutionary way, and for them to practice violence, and to persist in fighting for their rights and for the protection of their wealth from the betrayal of the criminal Al Saud."[13] The fact that almost all of the fourteen major oil fields of the Kingdom were in the Eastern Province, where one-third of the inhabitants were Shia, was a bitter pill for Saffar's followers to swallow. The newly named OIRAP won the active backing of Iran's official media and foreign ministry. In August 1979 Shia leaders in Qatif announced that that they would publicly celebrate Ashura in defiance of the official ban on all Shia festivals.

On 30 November in Qatif thousands of Shias, wearing black, beating their chests rhythmically or hitting themselves with chains, snaked their way to the Al Fatah (Shia) Mosque near the main bazaar and the fish market. Their emotion was heightened by the tearful nature of the Ashura sermons. The dramatic events in Iran added to the significance of this first Ashura in the new Islamic year. Listening to the heart-rending sermon of the mullah, the crowd gathered outside the mosque, beating their chests and sobbing, shouting: "No Sunni, No Shia! All Muslims together"—followed by the newly coined slogan, "Islamic Republic." Someone who had brought along posters of Khomeini dis-

tributed them, and these were hoisted high. This was enough to provoke the Wahhabi troops of the National Guard lined up across the
wooden barriers with their hands on the electric prods. They jumped
over the barriers and wielded their prods wildly, breaking the bones
and heads of those whose loyalty lay with "the Persians".[14]

Widespread rioting broke out with protesters attacking National
Guard troops with stones, wooden sticks and iron bars, and setting
alight the office of the state-owned Saudi airline, and the soldiers
resorting to firing live ammunition. This lasted three days. On 3
December there were large Shia protest marches which led to many
arrests. According to OIRAP, sixty of its members were killed, 800
were injured, and 1,200 arrested.[15] The official casualty figure was
twenty-four dead. Soon after, Saffar and other leaders of OIRAP fled
to Iran and Britain where the organization started publishing a monthly
magazine in Arabic from London.

In the wider, regional context, the vociferous Ayatollah's interpretation that dynastic rule was un-Islamic, repeatedly aired by Iran's Arabic
language radio, was viewed in Riyadh as an existential threat to the
House of Saud. Khomeini was scathing about the Gulf monarchs' policy
of depleting their oil resources to satisfy the ever-growing demands of
America, which he routinely described as the Great Satan, with Britain
being the Little Satan. He denounced them for depriving their subjects
of any role in the decision-making process. The creation of a representative system in the Islamic Republic, with a popularly elected president
and parliament, made his argument for republicanism attractive to many
in the Arabian Peninsula, irrespective of their sectarian affiliation.

Carter's Failed Military Mission Inside Iran

Whereas the seizure of the Grand Mosque ended in Mecca, the crisis
generated by the taking of American diplomats in Tehran lingered even
after the Shah had left the United States. The Khomeini regime had no
leverage to apply on Panama to extradite the Shah, hence it hung on to
its most powerful bargaining chip vis-à-vis Washington.

In March 1980 its government uncovered a secret network of pro-
American royalist officers. This in turn led to further discoveries during the next four months—a process accelerated by the Carter admin-

istration's unsuccessful attempt to rescue the hostages by mounting a military asssault inside Iran on the nights of 24–25 April. The plan was to sneak in six to eight helicopters to a disused air strip near Tabas, 380 miles southeast of Tehran, and fly in 90 specially trained American commandos in six C130 transport planes from Quna air base in Egypt, carrying among other things fuel for helicopters. The commandos would then fly to Damavand, 30 miles east of Tehran, where many of the 400 Iranian agents of the US had already gathered. There the commandos and the Iranians would board trucks, and head for the US Embassy in Tehran, which would by then have been infiltrated by other Iranian agents. The commandos would use nerve gas to incapacitate the Iranian guards at the embassy. Once they had secured it they would call the helicopters at Damavand. These choppers would then take the American hostages and commandos to Manzariyeh airport, 70 miles south of Tehran. There they would all transfer to the waiting C130 planes and fly out of Iran as other US aircraft, equipped with sophisticated devices, jammed Iran's radar systems.

But things went disastrously wrong. One of the six helicopters that had landed safely at Tabas air strip broke down, and could not be repaired. Then one of the arriving transport planes collided with a stationary helicopter, causing an explosion and the deaths of eight military personnel. Moreover, the secrecy of the mission was compromised by the totally unexpected passage of a bus with 50 passengers aboard, and its detention by the American officers on site. After this debacle the leader of the mission was ordered by President Carter to abort the mission. In their hurry to evacuate the air strip, the Americans left behind much incriminating material, including $1 million in Iranian currency. The sum was meant for American agents in Iran who were getting restive at not having been paid since the seizure of the Embassy in November 1979.[16]

A detailed report on the episode published two years later in the *Washington Post* stated that the raid was facilitated by a big gap in the Iranian radar and defences due to the CIA having recruited "a high ranking Iranian defense official". This official put "on maneuvers", or sent to Kurdistan, mobile ground-to-air missiles, anti-aircraft batteries, and some radar facilities around the areas of the planned American mission. He was most probably Major General Amir Bahman Bagheri, commander of the Iranian air force. It was not until early June 1980 that he was arrested.

Contrary to the official American leaks, the backup force waiting in Egypt was as large as "up to 2,500 men". Moreover, Carter was ready to authorize air cover or air strikes on military targets around Tehran to ensure the mission's success. In the case of crowds gathering outside the US embassy, the plan was for C130 aircraft to fire their machine guns and cannons at them. The whole exercise was so complicated that it required the active cooperation of Egypt, Oman, Bahrain, Turkey and Israel. Even then, according to outside experts, at best only half of the 52 hostages could or would have been rescued.[17]

The episode confirmed Khomeini's fears regarding America's intentions about the Islamic Republic. With this, Tehran and Washington turned into enemies. In the region this was unwelcome news for all the monarchies, particularly the Saudi Kingdom.

Aftermath of the Tremors in Mecca

Shaken by the Shias' celebration of Ashura in its eastern province, the Saudis sponsored a meeting of the information ministers of the Gulf monarchies in Riyadh in late December 1979. They agreed guidelines on the Iranian revolution for their state-run and state-guided media. These stressed "playing down the news from Tehran," and "demoting the Iranian revolution from the status of an all-Muslim one to a purely Shia one and then to downgrade it to a purely Iranian Shia one".[18]

At home, to refurbish the tarnished image of his government, King Khalid reshuffled seventeen top civilian and military positions. He appointed a committee to produce a draft constitution. Crown Prince and de facto Prime Minister Fahd promised a Consultative Council and a Basic Law "within a period which, I believe, will not exceed two months."[19] It would be another thirteen years before this pledge would be fulfilled, and that too in the aftermath of the 1991 Gulf War.

Having crushed the most serious ideological threat, backed by armed rebels, to the Al Saud dynasty since 1932, the regime considered it politic to examine the criticisms leveled at it by Juheiman and his ardent followers, most of which were subtly endorsed by bin Baz. It took note of the fact that a widely held view among its citizens was that Allah had intervened on the first day of Islamic Year 1400 to end the un-Islamic proliferation of photographs of human beings in the Kingdom.[20]

In the wake of the Grand Mosque seizure, many Saudi men trimmed their beards to distinguish themselves from the hirsute Juheiman. But in later years conservative men reverted to long beehive beards associated with the Salafiya doctrine, as a sign of piety as well as an instrument of intimidation. They became de rigueur for the members of the Mutawween, or religious police.[21] At the state level, knowingly or otherwise, the Saudi Kingdom entered into a race with the Islamic Republic of Iran as to who was more Islamic than the other.

The application of strict Wahhabi injunctions on society, then confined to the central Najd region, was extended to the rest of the realm. The change was most dramatic in Jeddah, a port city along the Red Sea, which had the distinction of being the diplomatic capital of Saudi Arabia since its inception until 1985. Before the landmark siege, Jeddah had five cinemas and two theaters. It was the site of arts exhibitions— as well as the celebrations of Valentine's Day, Halloween, and Christmas when lights were put in small trees which could not be seen over the compound walls from a street. "There were bazaars and plays and fashion shows—international events with the women from different countries wearing their national costumes," recalled Samar Fatany, who returned to Jeddah in January 1980 after her university studies in Cairo, to join the English-language service of Radio Jeddah.[22]

Even Aramco's Dhahran Residential Camp, within a gated compound measuring 22.5 square miles and home to 11,000 people, which had been exempted from the Kingdom's social rules since its inception in 1939, was no longer immune from this latest surge in Islamisation. It replicated a sprawling California suburb, complete with imported palm trees and lush lawns in front of low bungalows comfortably separated from one another along wide asphalted streets. It had its own schools, a small mosque without the iconic minaret, a cinema, swimming pools, golf courses, gymnasiums, libraries and supermarkets where men and women mixed freely. Women were free to drive or cycle. English was the common language and the street signs were in both Arabic and English. "When I think back on growing up in Dhahran [Residential Camp], it seems like a dream," said Ayesha Malik, a New York-based photographer in her *Time* magazine interview in February

2015. "Dhahran [Residential Camp] is in Saudi Arabia, but it's not really Saudi Arabia."

In the wake of the Grand Mosque seizure, the authorities cancelled the previous exemptions, and banned the consumption of alcohol and pork as well as the open celebration of Christian festivals.[23] In the rest of the Kingdom, the process continued for several years. In a series of social and educational steps taken by King Khalid and his successor King Fahd, the regime closed the gap that had developed over decades between its administration and the original Wahhabi doctrine. The rule about daily prayers was also tightened. Instead of letting a shopkeeper pray outside his store, he was required to shut his business and pray at the nearest mosque. As employees of the Committee for the Promotion of Virtue and the Prevention of Vice, the mutawwa, appearing in imposing General Motors vans, enforced the rule strictly.

Female members of the mutawwa ensured that women covered themselves in *abayas* (cloaks), which was not compulsory before the Grand Mosque seizure; a shawl around the shoulders was considered enough. Also women wearing the full-face veil, the *niqab*, started to appear in public. Segregation of sexes in public places which was the norm in the Wahhabi stronghold of Najd was extended to the rest of the Kingdom. Screens were erected between male and female sections of restaurants and cafes, which were required to have separate entrances for different sexes. The Committee for the Promotion of Virtue and the Prevention of Vice started inspecting construction plans to ensure these complied with "moral principles" of the Kingdom. In Riyadh, the opera house constructed before 1979 failed to stage an opera.[24] Husbands and wives had to carry their IDs with them in order to prove their married status. Since Arab and Iranian women keep their surnames after marriage, that requirement proved tricky. The government banned photographs of unveiled women in newspapers and on television. It injected more Islam and religious programs into the state-run broadcasting media, and it took women announcers off the screen. It closed all cinemas and theatres, and banned music and singing from television.

The ban on cinemas and theaters remained in force until late 2017. Cinemas were scheduled to open in April 2018. However, young movie addicts as well as older film makers had been circumventing Saudi censors by streaming movies online and watching films on satellite television. Also it was easy and quite inexpensive to travel to adjoining Bahrain and the United Arab Emirates to visit movie theaters.[25] Where a break with the past came was in having a solo woman performer sing before an all-female audience. This happened on 6 December 2017 in the case of the Lebanese singer Hiba Tawaji at the King Fahd Cultural Center in Riyadh.[26]

During King Fahd's rule, a decree in 1982 required the clerics delivering sermons in mosques to obtain an authorization certificate from the Ministry of Hajj and Waqf [Religious Trusts]. Pressured by the Wahhabi ulema, starting in the early 1980s, drastic changes were made to the curricula in schools and colleges. Study of geology, history of civilization, and European history was excised while the learning of maths, science and English was drastically curtailed in order to make space for the history of Islam and the House of Saud, and a larger dose of Islamic studies. Thus high-school students spent as much as a quarter of their time on obligatory religious studies. A similar approach was applied to university education. In the 1980s universities reverted to old curricula with a large dose of Islamic studies, as was the case in the 1950s when higher studies were first introduced in the Kingdom. As a result, in 1986, one out of six of the 100,000 university students were pursuing religious studies.[27] At the same time the government stopped sending students to Western countries. That explained why, unlike his much older two half-brothers, Prince Muhammad bin Salman, born in 1985, was not sent to a Western university, and ended up studying law at King Saud University, Riyadh.[28] As a result of these changes, most Saudi university graduates majored in Islamic studies, literary studies, sociology or Islamic history well into the first decade of the twenty-first century, according to Abdullah Dahlan, director of a professions training institute in Jeddah. This dovetailed with the finding that as of 2009, only about 20 per cent of the kingdom's graduates had majored in technical and scientific subjects.[29]

In the religious field the re-Islamisation drive helped the incipient Sahwa (*Al Sahwa al Islamiyya*, Islamic Awakening) movement to grow. Its origins lay in the arrival of Muslim Brotherhood activists from Egypt following the crack down on their organization by President Nasser in 1954. The professionals among them helped to build and sustain the educational and financial infrastructure in the Kingdom. They pledged their allegiance to the Saudi monarch and went on to meld the doctrinal conservatism of Wahhabism with the Brotherhood's participation in Egyptian politics. The resulting hybrid came to be known as the Sahwa movement.

The movement grew rapidly in the 1980s and threw up two out-standing leaders: Salman al Awda (also spelt Oudah; born 1955) and Safar bin Abdul Rahman al Hawali (born 1950). A bright-eyed cleric and scholar with an oval face, sporting a neatly trimmed mustache and a goatee beard, Awda was a native of the northern city of Buraidah. And the tight-lipped, bespectacled Hawali with a long, unkempt beard was the dean of Islamic Studies at the Umm Al-Qura University in Mecca.

Islamisation Under the Khomeini Regime

By focusing Iranians' attention on American misdeeds in Iran, the Embassy siege united the nation and strengthened radicals at the expense of moderates in the Islamic camp. It proved to young Iranians that Khomeini and his followers were as anti-imperialist as the competing left wing Mujahedin-e Khalq Organization and Fedai Khalq, thus draining away support for secular leftists. It enabled the regime to engage the masses politically and rally popular support for the Islamic constitution, which was approved in a referendum on 1 and 2 December.

At the popular level the leading role in Islamisation was played by the Islamic Republican Party (IRP) and Islamic Associations which had sprung up in workplaces, educational institutions, and the security forces. The IRP was formed in March 1979 by leading clerics, includ-ing Ali Husseini Khamanei and Ali Akbar Hashemi Rafsanjani. Its main aim was to guard the revolution and infuse Islamic principles into political, economic, cultural and military spheres of society. As well as encouraging individuals to join it, the founders of the IRP urged the local Islamic Associations to affiliate to it.

In the elections to the 73-strong Assembly of Experts for Constitution, 47 members either belonged to the IRP or were sympa-thetic to it. They were instrumental in getting Khomeini's concept of the Just Jurisprudent included in the constitution. In the poll for the first Islamic Majlis held between March and May 1980, the IRP won a majority of the 216 declared seats. Earlier, in the presidential poll in late January 1980, Abol Hassan Bani-Sadr—the forty-three year old son of an ayatollah, who had been one of the close aides during Khomeini's exile in a suburb of Paris, the base of Bani-Sadr for a quarter century—was the winner with 76 per cent of the vote. He owed the thumping majority to the backing Khomeini gave him. After his election, Khomeini appointed him commander-in-chief.

Iran's military was under his command when Iraq attacked in September 1980. Later he moved away from Khomeini and tried, unsuccessfully, to cultivate his own base. That led him to start aligning himself with the leftist Mujahedin-e Khalq (Persian: People's Mujahedin; MeK) which had fallen foul of Khomeini for failing to surrender its arms to the regime after the establishment of the Islamic Republic. The tension between Bani-Sadr and Majlis deputies would culminate on 20 June 1981 with the impeachment of Bani-Sadr who was then dismissed by Khomeini. In the subsequent presidential election in October, Ali Husseini Khamanei was the winner, gaining more than 16 million votes out of 16.847 million. The Majlis approved Mir Hussein Mousavi as the Prime Minister.

The Mousavi government intensified the purging of the governmental and revolutionary institutions of all those with "insufficient Islamic convictions." It dismissed those officers of the Islamic Revolutionary Guard Corps (IRGC), founded in June 1980, whose sons or daughters had been MeK members. The recently passed law on Islamic dress for women in public was implemented strictly. The purge of Islamic judges, which had so far affected thirty judges for accepting bribes to commute capital punishment to life imprisonment, was extended. Special judges were appointed to combat such impious acts as adultery, homosexuality, gambling, sympathising with atheists and hypocrites, and treason. [30]

Sunni-ruled Iraq's "Defensive" Offensive against Tehran

After their seizure of power in Iraq in July 1968, secular leaders of the Arab Baath Socialist Party from Sunni backgrounds censored religious publications and closed several Islamic institutions. They started harassing the clerics of Shia Islam, the majority faith in Iraq. When mullahs urged their followers to protest, further repression followed. It was in this context that *Hizb al Daawa al Islamiya* (Party of Islamic Call), commonly known as al Daawa, was formed clandestinely in Karbala. When the Baathist government tried to interfere with some Shia rituals and weaken the authority of the religious hierarchy, al Daawa gained ground. In December 1974 Shia religious processions turned into anti-government demonstrations. In response, the authorities executed five al Daawa leaders. At the same time they tried to placate the Shia masses by increasing the flow of public development funds to the Shia-dominated south.

In his congratulatory message to Khomeini, Ayatollah Muhammad Baqir Sadr, an outstanding Shia jurist and thinker, and the author of authoritative works on the Islamic state and economics, said, "Other tyrants have yet to see their day of reckoning." By "other tyrants," he meant Baathist rulers, especially Saddam Hussein, who was then Vice President. Tehran Radio's Arabic service referred to Sadr as "the Khomeini of Iraq" and called on the faithful to replace "the gangsters and tyrants of Baghdad" with "divine justice".[31] That such a move violated Iran's 1975 treaty with Iraq, which specified noninterference in each other's domestic affairs, did not seem to enter Tehran's revolutionary thinking.

On 10 June 1979 Saddam Hussein submitted a list of men to be executed to President Ahmad Hassan Bakr for his signature. It included not only the Shia leaders of the demonstrations but also a number of senior military officers alleged to have been secretly in touch with them. Bakr objected to the inclusion of military officers. On the eve of the eleventh anniversary of the Baathist take-over, on 14 July 1968, Saddam Hussein forced him to resign on health grounds and became President.

In March 1980 came the execution of 97 civilians and military men, half of them members of al Daawa, membership of which was now punishable by death. Al Daawa and its activists had resorted to attacking police stations, Baath offices and Popular Army recruiting centers. State repression of Shia militants had already compelled Ayatollah Sadr to issue a fatwa that the Baathist regime was un-Islamic and that dealings with it were religiously forbidden.

To avenge the execution of their cadres, al Daawa activists tried on 1 April, the first anniversary of the founding of the Islamic Republic of Iran, to assassinate Tariq Aziz (born Mikhail Yahunna), the Christian deputy premier of Iraq. The attempt failed, but it made Saddam Hussein more ruthless in his drive against the Shia underground. He decreed the execution of Sadr and his sister Bint al Huda. These sentences were carried out in the utmost secrecy on 8 April. It took about a week for the news to leak and reach Tehran. Khomeini was shocked as well as incensed. "The war that the Iraqi Baath wants to ignite is a war against Islam," he declared. He called on the people and army of Iraq to overthrow the Baathist regime because it was "attacking Iran, attacking Islam and the Quran," and added that "Iran today is the land of God's messenger; and its revolution, government and laws are Islamic."[32]

By now Baghdad had become an important center of activity by major political and military figures of the Pahlavi era. Shahpour Bakhtiar and General Gholam Ali Oveissi, joint chiefs of staff under the deposed monarch, were given a radio station in Iraq. Besides conducting anti-Khomeini propaganda, these stations broadcast specific advice to the partisans of Bakhtiar and Oveissi among the armed forces and Iranian tribals. The Bakhtiar-Oveissi camp wanted to set up an anti-Khomeini base inside Iran with a view to initiating a civil war.

After the failure of Washington's armed rescue operation to retrieve its diplomats on 24–25 April 1980, the pro-Shah camp tried to mount a military coup on 24–25 May. It was thwarted by Khomeini loyalists. On 9–10 July an attempt by pro-Shah military officers, orchestrated and funded by Bakhtiar, to topple the Tehran regime also failed. On 27 July the Shah, the inspiration of monarchist generals and politicians, died of cancer in Cairo.[33] That made no difference to Iran's position on American hostages. By continuing to make Washington appear helpless in securing the release of its diplomats, the Khomeini regime damaged Washington's standing in the region. This was detrimental to the interests of Saudi Arabia, which was tied closely with the US commercially, militarily and in terms of intelligence-sharing.

As for Saddam Hussein, until the Shah's demise, he had counted on the success of the repeated attempts by the US and/or anti-Khomeini Iranian forces to overthrow the clerical oligarchy in Tehran, or at least to destabilize it. Now there was no alternative to the Iraqi president performing the task himself.

Saddam was buoyed up by accounts of rapid military, political and economic decline in Iran. Persistent reports of conflict between Iran's President Abol Hassan Bani-Sadr and religious leaders and low morale among military officers who had seen thousands of their erstwhile colleagues purged went hand in hand with accounts of shortages of consumer goods, growing unemployment, and rising disaffection among the professional classes as well as such ethnic minorities as ethnic Kurds and Arabs, based in the areas adjoining Iraq. Without doubt, Iran was isolated diplomatically. Its refusal to release US diplomats had led to an economic embargo on it by Western nations. Its relations with Moscow had soured because of the Kremlin's military intervention in Afghanistan. Its virulent attacks on Gulf monarchs as unjust, corrupt rulers had left it friendless in the region.

Saddam Hussein decided to act before the US presidential election in early November, fearing that the new president might settle the hostage crisis and establish normal relations with Iran. After finalising his military plans he secured the active backing of the rulers of Kuwait and Saudi Arabia by signing secret agreements with them. The Saudi Kingdom and Kuwait agreed to raise their oil production by 1 million bpd and 800,000 bpd respectively, and contribute the revenues to Iraq's war effort.[34] Then he moved fast. On 2 September clashes erupted along the border. On 17 September, during his address to the recently-elected National Assembly, Saddam tore up the Algiers Accord and claimed full sovereignty over the Shatt al Arab. On 22 September Iraq invaded Iran at eight points on their 730 mile (1,200 km) common border with a third of its 240,000 troops, and bombed Iran's military installations and economic targets.[35] Iran then had only 100,000 men in its military, commanded by officers with a low morale, and depleted arms arsenals.

Bakhtiar and Oveissi provided Saddam Hussein with a guise to present himself as a liberator not only of the ethnic Arabs in the oil-rich Iranian province of Khuzistan but all Iranians suffering under the chaotic rule of the fanatical mullahs. Together they envisaged Iraqi forces being greeted as liberators of the ethnic Arabs of Khuzistan, capturing the oil-rich province in a week, linking up with Iranian Kurdish insurgents, and declaring the Free Republic of Iran under Bakhtiar. This would set off widespread uprisings against the Khomeini regime by discontented civilians as well as army officers, they predicted. Khomeini and his mullahs would be out in six to eight weeks. In reality, the Iran-Iraq War lasted ninety-five months, and became the longest conventional war of the twentieth century. It went through several phases before ending on 20 August 1988, with a United Nations-mediated truce.

For one thing, although the Iranian economy was still struggling to recover from a long period of instability, its income from oil exports was higher than before the revolution. This was so as a result of the loss of Iran's supplies to the world market, which spiked the price of a barrel of from $13 to $20. With the resumption of exports at 3.2 million bpd in the spring of 1979, Iran earned more than it did with much larger exports before 1979.[36] Saudi Arabia had fared well too. To fill the gap created by the Iranian revolution, Riyadh increased its output from 9.5 million bpd in 1979 to 10 million bpd the following year. With the oil price per barrel rising from $13 to $28 in March 1980, Riyadh's oil income shot up to a record $106 billion in 1980.[37] Little wonder that Saudi royals were in a bullish mood when Saddam Hussein attacked Iran in September.

6

THE IRAN-IRAQ WAR STEELS KHOMEINI'S REGIME

Though the Battle for Hill 270 near the Iranian border town of Mehran in September 1986 was merely a snapshot in the photographic album of the Iran-Iraq War, it reflected fairly accurately the wider picture of the ongoing conflict.

Soon after Iraq invaded Iran in September 1980, it captured Mehran—a settlement of 25,000 people—and destroyed or damaged 2,500 houses, 550 shops and fourteen mosques. The Iraqi occupation of the town and its surrounding hills, extending many miles into Iraq, ended in July 1982. Then, following the Iranian success in seizing Iraq's Fao Peninsula in February 1986, the Iraqis recaptured Mehran and its environs in May that year. Iraq proposed exchanging Mehran for Fao. Tehran rejected the offer. Its forces regained Mehran on 30 July, but to consolidate their gains, they had to retake the surrounding hills. On the night of 26–27 September, using surprise guerrilla tactics against the heavily fortified Hill 270, they did so.

An Eye-Witness Account

Arriving on the scene soon afterwards on a sunny morning, several foreign reporters and I witnessed the detritus of the recently expelled Iraqis—empty cans of French-made milk powder and Austrian-processed beef with potatoes, and Iraqi newspapers. What instantly grabbed our attention, though, were the boxes of mortars marked: 'CN 1860101 GHQ Jordan Armed Forces, Dir of Plng N Org, Amman, Jordan,' and Egyptian bombs with yellow casings. Another intriguing article was a gray plastic casing with the inscription: 'N5 Antipersonnel Mine, Mod. Valemarra 69. Contract N 1654/ A.S. /84 Lot N 004/85', with no indication of the country of origin. A few of these deadly weapons were still in place, as were several conventional mines. There were many more spent grenades and conventional mines scattered all around. The extensive barbed wire rolls, reinforced with steel spikes, testified to the hurdles that the Iranian forces had to overcome to seize their target. From the trench atop the hill, we could see the Iraqi bunkers barely 500 yards (meters) away. The fresh autumnal air crackled with periodic machine-gun fire as each side directed bursts at the other.

The visit to Hill 270 was arranged by the Iranian military headquarters at Salehabad, a 45-minute helicopter flight away. A spokesman there claimed that when their troops attacked the Iraqis at Hill 270 in the dead of the night, the Iraqis were asleep. "This was also the case in Fao," he added. He was referring to the peninsula in the deep south of Iraq which the Iranians had captured seven months earlier.

Later, when some eighty soldiers and civilians gathered for evening prayers, they were led by Hajji Mujtaba Namdar, a small, bearded, square-shouldered cleric, wearing a brown cloak and a white turban. After the prayers, Namdar delivered a sermon. "If we make peace with Saddam he will grow strong and attack us again. After six years of war, what we are we to say to the relatives of those who have been martyred or disabled? The Iranian people are shouting 'War, war until victory.' Even if it takes twenty years to secure victory, we will go on. Dying for Islam is as sweet to us as honey." The next day we saw the thirty-two-year-old cleric at Zaloo Aab command post near Hill 270. He had changed his tunic and cloak for a soldier's khaki fatigues. He was part of the political-ideological department in the military, which educated officers and other ranks in Islamic history and ideology.

The importance of clerics at the battlefront was underscored by Ali Akbar Hashemi Rafsanjani, the spokesman for the Supreme Defence Council and Speaker of the Majlis. "Your presence on the war front can be more effective than sending a million video cassettes there," he told a contingent of clerics departing recently for the battlefield. "Showing a cleric carrying an RPG-7 (rocket-propelled grenade) or riding a motorcycle along the front can boost the morale of millions of people, and encourage them to enlist for the war."[1] That explained why, at the Salehabad army headquarters, the mosque, housed in a large shelter, was the hub of activity. A full length picture of Ayatollah Ruhollah Khomeini, with his hand raised in blessing, dominated a wall. A green arrow near the podium at the far end of the hall pointed toward Mecca to which the faithful must bow during prayers. Verses from the Quran, printed on broadcloths, covered the walls. To this had been added black flags, signifying the current month of Muharram, when Imam Hussein, especially revered by Shias, was killed at Karbala some thirteen centuries before.

The Baseej volunteer units marching off to the war fronts from the Iranian hinterland were called "caravans to Karbala", and the war communiqués frequently described the Iranian forces as "Marchers to Karbala"—a place in southern Iraq then ruled by "infidel" Saddam Hussein.

Historically, competition and rivalry between Iran and Iraq dated back to the days of the Ottoman Turkish Empire (1517–1918) and the Persian Empire under the Safavids (1501–1732). Iraq, then called Mesopotamia, was the easternmost province of the Ottomans and Iran was the nucleus of the Safavid realm.

Iraq Invades Iran Amidst Ongoing US Hostages Crisis

On 22 September 1980, Iraq advanced into the oil rich Khuzistan province of Iran. Six days later the United Nations Security Council, treating the invader and the victim as equals, urged a truce. Iraq announced its readiness to cease fire if Iran accepted its claimed rights over the Shatt al Arab. Iran refused.

Khomeini argued that, by attacking the "Government of God" in Iran, Saddam had assaulted Islam, and therefore it was a religious duty of every Muslim to fight his regime and die, if need be, and become a martyr. In Shia Islam, martyrdom is a highly revered concept, with Imam Hussein called the Great Martyr. The appropriate verse in the Quran (3:163) reads, "Count not those who are slain God's way and dead,/ but rather living with their Lord, by Him provided,/ rejoicing in the bounty that God has given them,/ and joyful in those who remain behind and have not joined them."[2]

On the hostages front American officials and their Iranian counterparts reached a secret deal at the UN in New York. US President Jimmy Carter said on 18 October that the US would like to see "any invading forces withdrawn". On 26 October the Iranian Majlis decided to consider the recommendations of its committee on the hostages. Two days later Carter promised that if the hostages were released his administration would airlift the arms and spares that Iran had already paid for. Because of the time difference between Washington and Tehran, and the Islamic weekend in Iran, the Majlis debated the issue only on 2 November. By a majority the 185 deputies accepted its committee's recommendation to release the hostages subject to Washington accepting Khomeini's demands. The next day Carter called the decision "a positive basis" on which to end the crisis. The student captors handed over the hostages to the government.[3] But this was much too close to the presidential election day of 4 November to help Carter. He lost to his Republican rival Ronald Reagan. And it was just after Reagan was sworn in as US president on 21 January 1981 that the Iranian government ended the 444 days of American hostages' captivity by handing them over to US officials in Algiers. There was much relief in many capitals, but not in Riyadh, where the Saudi royals suspected that Reagan had made a secret deal with the Khomeini regime.

Most Iranians regarded Carter's defeat as a case of poetic justice. America had imposed Muhammad Reza Shah Pahlavi on them in August 1953, and made them suffer his repressive, autocratic rule for a quarter century. Now they had determined the outcome of an American presidential election. They had got even with Carter, who had been fulsome in his praise of the Shah and had backed him during the revolutionary crisis, and had finally let him enter the US. Furthermore, contrary to the promises of non-interference in the internal affairs of the Islamic regime, his administration had actively tried to destabilize it and instal a government congenial to American interests.

In the Gulf region, compared to the previous year, Iran's contingent for the Hajj pilgrimage in Mecca in mid-October 1980, numbering only 10,000, was subdued because of the outbreak of war with Iraq.

While the Organisation of Islamic Cooperation failed to condemn Iraq for its aggression, as demanded by Khomeini, and side with Iran, at home Khomeini succeeded in sublimating war with Islam. This was aptly captured by the slogan "War can be as holy as prayer when it is fought for the sake of Islam" displayed frequently in offices and on street walls.

Khomeini's appeals and the rallying of Iranians of all classes to defend their country, and the government's decision to turn the Baseej volunteer force into an auxiliary of the Islamic Revolutionary Guard Corps (IRGC), could not mask the weakness of the Iranian military, which had been shattered by the events leading to the Shah's over-throw. By mid-November it had ceded the oil city of Khorramshahr to the Iraqis who had besieged nearby Abadan, the site of a large oil refinery. Iraq now occupied 10,000 sq miles (25,900 sq km) of Iran in the southern and central sectors. Soon, however, weather, geography and Saddam's poor generalship came to Iran's rescue. The result was a military stand-off.

By now Washington was routinely passing on satellite and high resolution reconnaissance pictures of Iranian troops to Riyadh, knowing well that the Saudi kingdom was transferring these to Iraq. The same applied to the information collected by four American-manned Airborne Warning and Control Systems (AWACS), leased by the US to Saudi Arabia in September 1980, for round-the-clock surveillance of the Persian Gulf, a fact later confirmed by Saddam Hussein.[4]

As a result of considerable damage to the oil industries of Iran and Iraq, exports by OPEC fell. This pushed up the oil price, taking it to a peak of $47 a barrel in 1981 (or $125 in today's terms), when Saudi Aramco's oil income reached a record $119 billion,[5] later stabilising around $34 in the early 1980s.

The outbreak of the Iran-Iraq war hastened Saudi Arabia's earlier proposal for an internal security pact with fellow-monarchies on the Arabian Peninsula after the seizure of the Grand Mosque in Mecca. Meeting in Abu Dhabi, rulers of Bahrain, Kuwait, Oman, Qatar, Saudi Arabia and the United Arab Emirates (UAE) decided to form the Gulf Cooperation Council (GCC) on 25 May 1981. Its objectives were to coordinate internal security, arms procurement, and the national economies of member states, and settle border disputes under the leadership of the Supreme Council, consisting of the heads of member states.

By then, the Iranian military, much boosted by a surge of patriotism among Iranians, had blocked further Iraqi advances. In September, Iranian forces lifted the siege of Abadan. Various efforts by the UN and the OIC, strongly backed by Saudi Arabia, to end the conflict foundered. Iran refused to negotiate so long as Iraq occupied its land.

As a result of Saudi Arabia's pro-Iraq bias, tensions between it and Iran rose sharply. On 23 September 1981 Saudi security forces arrested two Iranians praying before Prophet Muhammad's Medina shrine to intercede on their behalf with God, which is strictly banned. The next day hundreds of Iranian pilgrims protested, and resorted to shouting slogans against America and Israel. In the subsequent fighting 22 Iranians and six Saudi soldiers were injured.[6] As a result, some 75,000 Iranian pilgrims, arriving for the Hajj, due on 7 October, were searched thoroughly and their books and pamphlets confiscated. In December, addressing GCC interior ministers in Manama, Bahrain, the Saudi Interior Minister Prince Nayef bin Abdul Aziz Al Saud said, "The Iranians, who after their revolution said they did not want to be the policeman of the Gulf, have become terrorists of the Gulf."[7]

During his visit to Riyadh on 8 February 1982, US Defence Secretary Caspar Weinberger persuaded the Saudi government to form a joint Saudi-American Military Committee—something it had been unwilling to do in the past. The change in its stance came because of its fear of the Iranian threat. This was the backdrop against which the Pentagon issued a secret directive in March which widened the scope of US military involvement in the Gulf.[8] This policy shift was authorized by Crown Prince Fahd, the Kingdom's de facto ruler, given the fast deteriorating health of King Khalid, who succumbed to a major heart attack in June 1982.

Fahd Enthroned

Fahd ascended the throne at a time when the Saudi Kingdom earned a record $113.2 billion in oil income in 1981.[9] This allowed the spendthrift Fahd to indulge his fancies uncontrolled in a brazen show of conspicuous consumption by freely dipping into state funds. He had a well-documented record of having been a womaniser and a familiar figure at casinos along the French Riviera. It was not until 1974, following spectacular gambling losses, which resulted in a severe reprimand from King Faisal, that he started to mend his ways. But his obesity persisted. To tackle it, in March 1979 he repaired to a health farm near Marbella, Spain, to undergo weight loss treatment centered on injections containing cells scraped from a lamb's fetus. It made little difference. By the time he became king, he was a grossly overweight, diabetic man—his ailment exacerbated by his daily habit of drinking sixty cups of sweet tea.

Lacking the widespread support that the ascetic-looking Faisal enjoyed, or the rapport that the avuncular Khalid had with his subjects, the unprepossessing Fahd centralised authority, blocked fresh advice reaching him, and came to rely on compulsion as a means of securing loyalty. His extended absences abroad and his decision to spend long stretches of time away from Riyadh to avoid the prying eyes of the ulema, and on his luxurious yacht, the size of a luxury liner, off the coast of Jeddah where he could live his dissolute lifestyle unobserved, made his subjects view him as "a high level captive of the West," deride him as a "hypocrite, a rogue masquerading as a pious Muslim," and prone to believe him to be "a heavy drinker and fond of foreign women."[10] He built a series of fabulous palaces at home and abroad: in Marbella; in Geneva; the $3 billion Al Salem Palace in Jeddah with white beach sand imported from Greece; in Taif, and between Riyadh and Diriya, draining the assets of the Saudi Arabian Monetary Agency. Fahd's personal failings and governance style were grist to the propaganda mills of the Islamic Republic of Iran particularly when there was no dip in Riyadh's financial backing of the Saddam Hussein government in Baghdad.

Iran Turns the Tide in the Iraq War

On the war front, on 24 May 1982 Iran retook Khorramshahr, then broke the Abadan siege, and drove the Iraqis back to the international frontier. Baghdad was plunged into crisis. On 9 June, Iraq announced its readiness for a truce, but in return Iran demanded the removal of Saddam Hussein from power. It knew this was out of the question. On

20 June the Iraqi President declared that Iraq's voluntary withdrawal from Iran would be completed within ten days. On 30 June the Iranians found that Iraqi forces had evacuated some indefensible positions to regroup elsewhere. In any case, Khomeini reckoned—rightly—that if he accepted a ceasefire the clerical and non-clerical politicians in Iran would resume their quarrelling and escalate it to the point of seriously weakening the still fledgling Islamic Republic he had founded.

The Iranian government then decided to march into Iraqi territory. This seemed to be in line with the strategic thinking of its leadership which had concluded that an effective way to defend the revolution was to go on the offensive to extend its influence abroad. Explaining this policy later, President Ali Khamanei said: "If the revolution is kept within the Iranian borders, it would become vulnerable."[11] Among the movements Iran backed at that time were the Organization of the Islamic Revolution in the Arabian Peninsula (OIRAP) and the Islamic League of Bahraini Students in Bahrain. Inadvertently, Iranian leaders were following the example of the secular Bolshevik leaders after their revolution in Russia in October 1917. Vladimir Lenin's regime formed the Communist International in March 1919 to fight "by all available means, including armed force", for the overthrow of the international bourgeoisie and for the creation of an international Soviet republic.

Now, in mid-1982, Iran's penetration into Iraq led the Kremlin to change its 1972 policy. As a signatory of its Friendship and Cooperation Treaty with Iraq, the Soviet Union reversed its position on arms supplies, which it had halted after Iraq's invasion of Iran. Its fresh shipments would include Scud-B surface-to-surface missiles with a 185 mile (300 km) range. In the region too Saudi Arabia, along with Kuwait, started backing Iraq openly—financially and logistically—while continuing to share their US-supplied intelligence on Iran with Baghdad. Riyadh and Kuwait started to supply the oil shipments that Iraq had signed with Western nations and Japan which it was unable to fulfil by itself.

Iran tried to conquer the southern Iraqi city of Basra in July 1982. With nine divisions locked in the largest infantry combat since the Second World War, fierce battles raged for a fortnight. Finally Iran managed to hold only 32 sq miles (83 sq km) of Iraqi land. Yet it stuck to its earlier conditions for withdrawal from Iraq: removal of Saddam

Hussein from the presidency, the appointment of an international tribunal to determine and punish the aggressor, and an acceptance of its claim of $150 billion as compensation for war damages.

Encouraged by Iran's successful performance on the battlefield in the spring of 1982, Khomeini instructed the head of the Hajj Pilgrimage Committee, Muhammad Musavi Khoiniha, to acquaint the fellow pilgrims of what was happening in crusading Iran and the oppressed Afghanistan, and inform them of their Islamic duty to confront aggressors and international plunderers. Saudi authorities countered by stressing that peace and amity had to be maintained during the holy pilgrimage, and that shouting political slogans violated this long-held tradition. Khomeini's acolytes ignored the Saudi instruction. After planting himself firmly inside the Grand, Khoiniha called for mass prayers to crush the conspiracies of "the deviated people"—a thinly disguised reference to the House of Saud. He repeated the exercise inside the Prophet's Mosque in Medina. Saudi security forces clashed with the Iranian pilgrims for violating the ban on holding public meetings inside the Two Holy Mosques. They arrested 100 Iranian pilgrims, including Khoiniha.[12] Subsequently, Khomeini instructed the Hajj pilgrims to remain peaceful and refrain from distributing printed political material and criticising Muslim governments. In response, Saudi authorities moderated their stance, and agreed to permit demonstrations *outside* the Two Holy Mosques at previously agreed places.

In March 1983 OPEC lost its monopoly to determine oil prices. In that month the New York Mercantile Exchange (Nymex) introduced crude oil futures. That meant oil price being fixed daily on the open market determined by the give and take of exchange traders, operating on the auction floor of the Mercantile Building with buyers and sellers monitoring their computer screens worldwide. This development, introduced against the background of falling oil demand in the West, weakened OPEC's price-setting clout further. Prices started sliding. Saudi Arabia, then ruled by King Fahd, curtailed its output sharply to stabilise the price at $29 a barrel in 1984.

Meanwhile, buoyed by its record annual oil income of $23 billion in 1983, Iran persisted with periodic offensives. On the third anniversary of the war in September 1983, the Iranian army was 320,000 strong, the air force 70,000, and the navy 23,000—the total reaching the pre-revolution figure; and the size of the Islamic Revolutionary Guard Corps (IRGC) had risen to 150,000.[13]

Iraq had boosted its military by importing a large number of foreign workers in order to release Iraqi men to join the armed forces. But the total strength of GCC militaries was only 150,000. In addition, Riyadh's National Guard was 41,000-strong.[14] Iraq started using chemical weapons from October 1983 onwards. Nevertheless, in February 1984, following its offensive in the Haur al Hawizeh marshes, Iran seized Iraq's oil-rich Majnoon Islands. By the fourth anniversary of the war, in September 1984, the Iraqi Army numbered 500,000 and the auxiliary Popular Army had 560,000 armed personnel.[15]

The demands of ongoing hostilities made many of Iran's industries self-sufficient. For its spare parts for US-made weapons, Iran turned to Vietnam with its vast stores of leftover US weapons and spare parts. Later it approached private firms in Amsterdam, Athens, Madrid, Seoul, and Singapore for these items. The Reagan administration covertly encouraged these sales to let the war drag on and make the conservative Arab monarchies, fearful of Iran's Islamic republicanism, more dependent on Washington for security. This changed after Washington included Iran in its list of countries that support international terrorism in January 1984. By contrast, Baghdad made diplomatic gains when the Reagan administration, having removed Iraq from the list of nations that support international terrorism in November 1983, restored diplomatic ties with it two months later after a seventeen year break.

Tanker Warfare and the War of the Cities

Iraq escalated its attacks on Iranian oil tankers, using French-made Exocet air-to-ship (surface-skimmer) missiles, and intensified its air raids on the Kharg oil terminal, which handled 85 per cent of Iran's petroleum exports, thus initiating a tanker war. Iran retaliated by hitting ships serving the ports of Kuwait and Saudi Arabia. For the Iranian year ending in March 1984, its oil income fell to $14.7 billion, well below the budgeted $21.1 billion. As a consequence of Iraq's sustained attacks on Iranian tankers and the Kharg oil terminal, Iran's oil exports fell to 1.6 million bpd, just enough to pay for the war.

In March 1985 Iraq hit a steel factory in Ahvaz, a civilian target, and announced that it was now treating Iranian air space as a war zone. Its modified Scud-B missiles hit Tehran. The rationale for the war of the cities, as given by Major-General Thabit Sultan, was that "We want to bring the Iranian people into the front lines of the war. We hope this will encourage the Iranian people to rebel against their government and bring the war to an end." Iran retaliated by hitting Baghdad with its missiles. Between March and June 1985 Iraqi warplanes struck Tehran forty-three times; in response, twelve Iranian missiles landed in Baghdad. Once the respective populations got over the initial shock they realised that the damage caused by these attacks was limited and bearable. So this installment of the war of the cities ended in July.[16]

Overall, however, the broader war of attrition continued. Washington started to intervene actively on the Iraqi side. The Iranian assault in February 1986 in the south, which resulted in the capture of 310 sq miles in the Fao Peninsula, broke the stalemate. A determined effort by Iraq, which mounted 18,648 air missions between February 9 and March 25 1986—compared with 20,011 missions throughout 1985—to regain Fao met with failure.[17] The Iranians claimed that throughout the Fao offensive, which included several unsuccessful Iraqi counteroffensives, they destroyed 141 Iraqi tanks and 86 Iraqi planes and helicopters. They put the number of Iraqi casualties at 35,000.[18] In March 1986, following a report by UN experts on Iraq's use of poison gases, the Security Council combined its condemnation of Iraq for deploying chemical weapons with its disapproval of the prolongation of the conflict by Iran.

Saudis Weaken Iran's Economy

The next month, flooding of the oil market by Kuwait and Saudi Arabia caused the price of petroleum to plunge below $10 a barrel, down from $27 the previous December. They did so primarily to meet the challenge of the price-cutting strategy of non-OPEC producers such as Britain and Norway to maintain their share of the world market. OPEC then decided to flood the oil market in order to counter the non-OPEC producers' strategy as well as ruin the Iranian economy. Their actions depressed the price from $28 to below $10 a barrel by July 1986.

Tehran's oil revenue shrank by half, to a mere $7.2 billion a year. Iraq suffered financially too, but it was cushioned by the $12 billion a year it received in aid from its Gulf allies, the West and the Soviet Union.[19]

During the visit of Iranian Foreign Minister Ali Akbar Velayati to Moscow in mid-February, 1987, the Kremlin tried to mediate between the two combatants. Saddam Hussein agreed to suspend the war of the cities if Moscow agreed to replace Iraq's lost warplanes with advanced Soviet combat aircraft. The Kremlin agreed. By the time the war of the cities was suspended on 18 February, 1987 it had affected thirty-five Iranian urban centers and killed 3,000 people. By contrast, the missile attacks and besieging of Basra had cost only 300 Iraqi lives.[20]

Saddam Hussein's repeated war of the cities led Khomeini to lift the veto he had imposed on the development and manufacture of weapons of mass destruction (WMD) which he had described as un-Islamic because of their failure to distinguish between combatants and non-combatants. The Iranian government approached Pakistan to purchase nuclear fuel-cycle technology from it. Pakistan, then ruled by General Zia ul Haq, refused. Tehran did not give up. Iran signed a cooperation agreement with Pakistan on civilian nuclear energy and a senior Pakistani nuclear scientist secretly passed on a sensitive report on centrifuges used to refine uranium. Later, Abdul Qadeer Khan, the "father of Pakistan's nuclear bomb," would confess to proliferating nuclear weapons to Iran by passing on several centrifuges to it.[21]

The Bloody Iranian-Saudi Clash in Mecca

The negative impact on Tehran of its war with Iraq impinged directly on Saudi-Iranian relations. The oil price plunge caused by the Saudi-Kuwaiti strategy in the spring of 1986 crippled Iran's war effort. Yet Khomeini rejected the UN Security Council Resolution 598, adopted unanimously on 20 July 1987, which called for a ceasefire and withdrawal of warring forces from occupied foreign territories. The ten-article text included a clause for an impartial commission to determine war responsibility, one of the major demands of Iran. Iraq said it would accept the resolution on condition that Iran did likewise. Tehran refused to do so.

On 24 July, a Kuwait oil supertanker, escorted by US warships, hit a mine believed to have been laid by an Iranian speedboat. Emotions ran high among the 155,000 Iranian Hajj pilgrims. Khomeini had urged them to perform the "disavowal of the pagans" ritual over the Iran-Iraq War, and hold a "unity rally" to seek "deliverance from infidels". This was encapsulated in the slogan, "Death to America! Death to the Soviet Union! Death to Israel!" The logic behind it was that America was the prime source of "corruption on Earth," the Soviet Union had intervened militarily in the Muslim nation of Afghanistan, and Israel had usurped Muslim Palestine. Mahdi Karrubi, the personal representative of Khomeini, leading the Iranian pilgrims, worked out the route for the pilgrims' march in Mecca, its terminal point being about a mile from the Grand Mosque.

On 31 July, after Friday midday prayers, when the Iranian pilgrims, led by women and invalids in wheel chairs, and holding aloft Khomeini's portrait, arrived at the agreed terminal point, they faced a phalanx of steel-helmeted Saudi riot police behind concrete barriers. During the subsequent stalemate the pilgrims were pelted with stones and rocks by a mob which had gathered at a neighboring carpark. Tempers rose as policemen wielded truncheons and electric prods to break up the vast crowd. After a brief lull, National Guard troops arrived. According to US intelligence reports (which became public knowledge later), they fired tear gas canisters, and then live ammunition from pistols and automatic weapons at the pilgrims. This, and the subsequent stampede caused by the firing, led to 402 deaths. These included 275 Iranian pilgrims, eighty-five Saudi civilians and security men, and forty-two non-Iranian pilgrims. Saudi authorities denied the firings and asserted that all the deaths were caused by the stampede that ensued. Saudi authorities failed to order an official inquiry into the bloody episode.[22]

There was outrage in Iran. Mobs in Tehran stormed the Saudi and Kuwaiti embassies, smashed furniture and set fires which led to the death of one Saudi diplomat. "This plot is a US-designed conspiracy," said Iran's President, Ali Khamanei. "No doubt the US shoulders responsibility for it. Of course the Saudi Government is also responsible because it was carried out through the Saudis and their police."[23] Khomeini was livid. In his message to Karrubi, he lambasted "the fanatic Saudis" driven by their own misguided beliefs to kill innocent Shia pilgrims. Referring to the Saudi rulers as "vile and ungodly

Wahhabis," who were "like daggers which have always pierced the heart of the Muslims from the back," he declared that Mecca was in the hands of "a band of heretics."[24]

The Saudi authorities denied that they had deployed tear gas or that the police had opened fire. Their narrative was that the deaths had occurred when dispersing demonstrators surged in retreat and trampled on each other. The Interior Minister Nayef bin Abdul Aziz Al Saud claimed that the real aim of the Iranian pilgrims was to create "sedition" inside the Great Mosque, thus making it impossible for non-Iranian pilgrims to circumambulate the Kaaba, which is the core of Hajj ritual.[25] He offered no evidence to support his statement.

Each side disseminated its version of the episode worldwide. Given that with a few exceptions all the member-states of the Organisation of the Islamic Conference (OIC) were Sunni, the Saudi version gained credibility. This became apparent at the OIC meeting in Amman in March 1988. Saudi Arabia secured the organization's consent to its plan to fix a quota of 1,000 pilgrims for one million Muslims living outside the Kingdom. The next month it cut its diplomatic ties with Iran, which duly reciprocated.

The War Ends Inconclusively; the Islamic Regime Remains Entrenched in Iran

After a Kuwaiti oil supertanker, escorted by US warships, was damaged by a sea mine planted by Iran there followed a naval build-up in the Gulf by America, Britain and France. At its peak, sixty warships were involved. In October 1987 the US Navy, in its Operation Nimble Archer, sank three Iranian patrol boats near Farsi Island, claiming that Iran had fired on an American helicopter; and US warships destroyed two Iranian offshore oil platforms in the Lower Gulf in retaliation for an Iranian missile attack on a US-flagged supertanker docked in Kuwaiti waters. Tehran's capacity to mount major offensives was much reduced due to its shortage of foreign exchange, needed for essential military purchases, and professionally trained soldiery, and the damage done to its bridges, factories and power plants by ceaseless Iraqi bombing—which was much improved, thanks to the expertise of US Air Force personnel seconded to Iraq.

In February 1988 Iraq renewed the war of the cities, this time targeting Tehran with long range missiles. This demoralised the residents of Tehran, prompting an exodus of people to outlying areas. Iran retaliated by targeting Baghdad with its missiles. By the time the revived war of the cities ended on 20 April, at least a third of Tehran's residents had decamped. Their fear was enhanced by what happened in Halabja in Iraqi Kurdistan.

On 13 March 1988, Iran and its Iraqi Kurdish allies captured the predominantly Kurdish city of Halabja, a town of 75,000, situated 15 miles from the Iranian border. Three days later the Iraqi air force attacked it with poison gas, killing between 3,200 and 6,800 people, and injuring another 10,000.[26] The pictures of men, women and children frozen in instant death, relayed by the Iranian media, shocked the world. In killing its own unarmed citizens with chemical weapons, the Saddam Hussein regime did something unprecedentedly abhorrent. This was a propaganda boost to Iran's leaders. But, by over-exploiting the episode, they demoralised their own people, especially in Tehran, where residents feared that Iraqi missiles carrying warheads filled with poison gas would hit the city.

In mid-April, Iraq recaptured the Fao Peninsula, once again using chemical weapons. After the frigate USS *Samuel B. Roberts* was damaged by an Iranian mine, the US Navy responded with Operation Mantis. It blew up two Iranian oil rigs, destroyed one Iranian frigate and immobilised another, and sank an Iranian missile boat and smaller gunboats. From 23 to 25 May, Iraq, using poison gases, staged offensives in the northern and central sectors, and then in the south, regaining Shalamche. Between 19 and 25 June Iraq recaptured Mehran in the central zone and then the Majnoon Islands in the south—using chemical weapons in both cases.

Iraq tried to seize Iranian territory but failed. On 3 July, USS *Vincennes*, an American cruiser, shot down an Iran Air airbus carrying 290 passengers over the Lower Gulf.[27] While the Pentagon explained that the cruiser's commanding officer had mistaken the aircraft for a warplane, Iranian leaders considered the event to signify that the US had intervened directly in the war.

Following extensive consultations in Tehran among the senior leadership, on 20 July 1998 Iran unconditionally accepted UN Security

Council Resolution 598. Two days later Khomeini stated that acceptance of a truce was "in the interest of the revolution and the system at this juncture".

From 22–29 July, Iraq mounted last-ditch offensives in the northern, central and southern sectors to capture Iranian land. It failed in the north but succeeded elsewhere. However within a week Iran had regained its lost territory. On 20 August, a truce came into effect under UN supervision. By then, Iraq had used 110,000 chemical munitions against Iran.[28]

By its official count, Iran suffered 194,931 fatalities during the war, of which 183,931 were combatants and 11,000 civilians. The unofficial estimate for Iraq was 160,000 to 240,000 dead. According to the Stockholm International Peace Research Institute, Iran spent $74–91 billion on weapons, plus another $11.26 billion on imports. The corresponding figures for Iraq were $94–112 billion, plus military imports of $41.94 billion. However, in July 1990 Iraq's Deputy Premier Tariq Aziz put the military imports bill at $102 billion.[29]

In the end, neither country lost much territory, nor was there a change of regime in Tehran or Baghdad. The unintended consequence of the longest war of the twentieth century was that it enabled Khomeini to consolidate the Islamic revolution. The demographic composition of Iran was such that each year 422,000 males, amounting to about 1 per cent of the total population, reached the conscription age of eighteen. The figure for Iraq was 161,000. In addition there was the Baseej volunteer force, operating from over 9,000 mosques, open to those below eighteen and above forty-five, along with women. By the spring of 1983 the Baseej had trained 2.4 million Iranians in the use of arms, and sent 450,000 to the front.[30]

The Baseej mobilised the deep religiosity of many Iranian Shias, above all their strong cult of martyrology. They considered it their religious duty to fight evil and oppression, which in this case was equated with Saddam Hussein. But they also viewed the struggle as part of another, much more ambitious project: to liberate Jerusalem from its Zionist occupiers and oppressors. The march on Najaf and Karbala in southern Iraq or Baghdad in central Iraq would inaugurate the advance on Jerusalem itself, the third holiest city of Islam, which in Arabic is called Al Quds (The Holy) or Bait al Muqqadas (The Holy

Place). Since Syria was an ally of Iran and a staunch anti-Zionist state, all that stood between the Islamic Republic and Jerusalem was the infidel regime of Saddam Hussein. To die in removing this hurdle was to ensure passage to heaven in the afterlife. On Iranian radio and television the audiences were constantly reminded of Prophet Muhammad's saying to the believers: "Wish death and welcome afterlife". One measure of the martyr complex of Iranian Shias was the disproportion between the figures for captives on each side. In early 1984 Iraq held only 7,300 Iranian prisoners of war, whereas Iran had over 50,000 Iraqi captives. The war had caused colossal losses in human lives and limbs, property and production. It distorted the economy, and channeled large sums into the military and weapons. It led to the postponement of rapid economic development. It increasingly isolated Iran in the world arena.[31]

On the other hand, it accelerated the drive for self-sufficiency. And with the counter-revolutionaries and the Mujahedin-e Khalq siding with Baghdad, the Iranian regime was able convincingly to label them as unpatriotic, and curtail their influence inside the country. The war unified the nation, and bolstered popular support for the government. Finally, it created an environment conducive to governmental control of the economy which in general worked in favor of the dispossessed.

With a million men in its military, Iraq emerged as the most powerful country in the region, outstripping Turkey and Egypt. While Saddam Hussein's aim of ending the Khomeini regime failed spectacularly, he did block the onward march of the Islamic republican revolution from Tehran. By so doing, he served the vital interests of not only Gulf monarchies but also the United States. In retrospect, however, this armed conflict sowed the seed for the largest assemblage of armed forces since the Second World War to expel the invading Iraqis from Kuwait.

During the war, both Saudi Arabia and Iran engaged in a race to extend their influence in the Muslim world at large. With its sparse population, the Saudi Kingdom had far more funds, generated by its unrivalled petroleum exports, to lavish on establishing its footprint abroad than Iran with four times more citizens than Saudi Arabia, while waging a war without having raised any foreign loans.

7

THE SAUDI-IRANIAN RACE TO INFLUENCE THE MUSLIM WORLD

It was Saudi King Faisal who had leapfrogged eastward into Pakistan. And it is in that South Asian country that his legacy is most visible in the form of an iconic mosque in the Pakistani capital of Islamabad. A traveller approaching Islamabad at night by car is likely to be struck by a unique architectural design, glowing like a jewel, safeguarded by four tall, slender, shining towers, at the foot of the hill. The absence of a dome would lead the visitor to rule out the building being a mosque. But he would be wrong. It really is a mosque where the highly imaginative architect has innovatively amalgamated contemporary lines with the traditional appearance of a Bedouin tent, to enclose a large triangular prayer hall, and planted four pencil-shaped minarets, each 80 meters (250 feet) high, the tallest in South Asia, to symbolise as many directions.

Shah Faisal Mosque, Islamabad

The idea for a national mosque in the purpose-built Pakistani capital of Islamabad (Urdu: "Place of Islam") was proposed during the visit of King Faisal in April 1966. He backed the idea with a pledge to fund the project. Progress was glacial. A decade passed before the final design by Turkish architect Vedat Dalokay was selected by a committee from the 43 submissions, and construction inaugurated with an Islamic prayer. Lasting ten years, it cost $120 million.

The initial criticism of the unconventional design and lack of a traditional domed structure died down when the skeptics looked at the striking scale and form of the finished white mosque, covering 54,000 square feet and resting on a raised platform, set against the dark, craggy Margalla Hills. The marbled interior of the tent-shaped hall is embellished with eye-catching mosaics and calligraphy and a chandelier of impressive proportions. The western wall facing Mecca is adorned with the Islamic creed in early Kufic script. Inside, the ceiling soars to 40 meters (125 feet) and the air hums with muffled recitations. With its capacity to accommodate 100,000 believers at prayer in its main prayer hall and courtyard, the locally named Shah Faisal Mosque became the largest place of its kind in Pakistan. But its claim to be the largest mosque on the planet lasted only seven years. However it remains the top attraction on the itinerary of tourists, domestic or foreign.

Faisal's prestige among Pakistanis soared after he had sided with their country in its war with India in September 1965 by proiding cash to fund arms purchases by Islamabad.[1] During his visit to Pakistan's first capital, Karachi, in April 1966, President Ayub Khan was fulsome in his admiration for the Saudi monarch as the admiring crowd shouted, "Long Live Islamic Unity," in Urdu.[2] The main highway in the city was renamed Sharah-e Faisal (Urdu: Faisal's Highway). More importantly, Faisal expanded military cooperation with Pakistan. As a result Pakistan's air force helped the Saudis to operate and maintain their newly acquired jet fighters. During the conflict between the Saudi Kingdom and the recently liberated South Yemen, ruled by Marxists, in November 1969, Pakistani trainers acted as combat pilots to help the Saudis retake the disputed town of Al Wadiah from the South Yemenis.[3]

Two months earlier, at the convention of two dozen Muslim leaders in Rabat called at the behest of Faisal, Pakistan, composed then of its eastern and western wings, was the most populous Muslim state, ahead of Indonesia. It therefore merited special attention by the Saudi monarch as he tried to promote pan-Islamism beyond the Arab world.

In December 1971, when war broke out between Pakistan and India in Pakistan's eastern wing, the Faisal government called the Indian action "treacherous and contrary to all international covenants and human values," adding that it found no justification for the Indian aggression except "India's desire to dismember Pakistan and tarnish its

Islamic creed".[4] When the Pakistani government feared an attack on its Western wing by India after its victory in East Pakistan, Faisal lent Pakistan seventy-five warplanes.[5]

But Muhammad Reza Shah Pahlavi of Iran lent US-made warplanes to Pakistan before Faisal did, at the behest of President Richard Nixon who was determined to prevent the dismemberment of Pakistan. In response to an appeal by General Yahya Khan on 4 December 1971, Nixon told Henry Kissinger, "If it is leaking, we can have it denied. Have it done, one step away." As it was, third party transfers of US arms were illegal "unless the US itself would transfer the defense article under consideration to that country." The CIA chief in Tehran met the Shah on 5 December and secured his agreement. Nixon confirmed it. On 10 December Kissinger told the Chinese ambassador to the UN, Huang Ha, that the US would supply arms to Pakistan through third parties including Iran.[6] The war ended on 16 December.

In the spring of 1972, Faisal played host to Pakistan's President Zulfikar Ali Bhutto, who was seeking funds for research and development of a nuclear weapon. It is unclear how much Faisal contributed. (Bhutto's approach to the Shah of Iran for the same purpose was rebuffed.) However, noting the Saudi monarch's wish, Bhutto, leader of the nominally secular Pakistan People's Party, ensured that the post-1971 constitution of Pakistan, drafted under his guidance, prescribed the official name of the country as the Islamic Republic of Pakistan—a departure from the Republic of Pakistan as in the 1962 constitution. In return, overlooking Bhutto's rhetoric about Islamic socialism, his luxurious lifestyle, and his public acknowledgement of consuming alcohol, Faisal approved his hosting of the Second Summit of the Organisation of the Islamic Conference in Lahore in February 1974. Having enlarged the armed forces of the much-reduced, post-1971 Pakistan, Bhutto signed a technical assistance agreement with the Faisal government which allowed the Saudi Kingdom to secure the services of Pakistan pilots, plane mechanics and tank technicians as well as military instructors.[7]

Khalid Follows Faisal's Footprints Abroad

Crown Prince Khalid bin Abdul Aziz Al Saud ascended the throne at a time when the ambitious Second Five Year Plan (1975–1980) worth

$142 billion had just been launched. The impact of a dramatic economic upturn fuelled by a sharp jump in oil prices was being felt in all spheres of Saudi life. The unparalleled influx of foreign workers was rapidly turning the indigenous workforce into a minority, diluting the ultra-conservative Wahhabi socio-cultural fabric of Saudi society.

The reaction to this phenomenon varied among the senior princes. While they and the monarch were all for economic development and modern technology, they held different views on the speed of development and the extent to which to compromise with Wahhabi values and practices. Those who favored a slower pace of industrialisation and closer adherence to the Wahhabi interpretation of the Sharia at home also advocated greater support for the Palestinian cause. Led by King Khalid and Prince Abdullah bin Abdul Aziz Al Saud, they represented the Arab nationalist trend. Those who advocated a faster pace of industrialisation and greater religious-cultural liberalisation favored still closer ties with America, culminating in the signing of a long-term security treaty with Washington. They represented the unqualified pro-American trend within the ruling family. There was an uneasy co-existence between these two trends.

In his policy towards Muslim Arab and non-Arab countries, Khalid stayed firmly with Faisal's line. For instance, he refused to recognize Bangladesh which, led by its founder Shaikh Mujibur Rahman, had adopted a secular, democratic constitution in November 1972. The situation changed radically when the August 1975 military coup, involving the assassination of President Rahman and his family, resulted in General Ziaur Rahman seizing power. When he started stressing Islam in public life, Khalid bestowed the Kingdom's recognition on his regime. With this, Saudi Arabia acquired a firm footprint in Bangladesh, thus extending its influence in South Asia. Later, the number of Bangladeshis working in Saudi Arabia rose in line with the rise in the Kingdom's oil revenues.

With the overthrow of Bhutto by the Islamist General Muhammad Zia ul Haq—a man of middling height with receding hairline and a well-trimmed walrus mustache—in July 1977, ties between Riyadh and Islamabad grew even closer. Zia ul Haq outdid Bhutto in his adulation of the late King Faisal by renaming Lyallpur, Pakistan's third largest city, Faisalabad in September.

In neighboring Afghanistan, in the wake of the Marxist military coup in Kabul in April 1978, divisions had surfaced between radicals and moderates in the ruling leftist People's Democratic Party of Afghanistan (PDPA). To end the internecine fighting, the Kremlin started to intervene, at first by dispatching military advisers and elite forces. When that proved inadequate, it sent combat troops from its 40th Army on Christmas Day in 1979. By so doing, it helped the moderate wing to consolidate its hold on power. The Carter administration considered Moscow's move a violation of the agreement between the two superpowers that ruled out extending their influence through military force.

As a consequence, Pakistan became a frontline state in the Cold War, with Saudi Arabia emerging as an integral part of the anti-Soviet alliance led by the US. The subsequent arming and training of the fundamentalist mujahedin in Afghanistan was carried out by Pakistan's Inter-Services Intelligence (ISI), while the arms were procured by the CIA. Riyadh pledged to contribute as much cash as did Washington. It did so through its General Intelligence Directorate, directed by Prince Turki bin Faisal since early 1979, who worked closely with the CIA.

Fearing their exclusion from the United Nations-sponsored negotiations between Kabul, Moscow, Islamabad and Tehran, the seven existing Afghan Islamic parties—all of them Sunni—agreed to form the Islamic Alliance of the Afghan Mujahedin, popularly known as the Afghan Mujahedin, in May 1983. Led by Abdul Rasul Sayyaf, it started operating from the Pakistani city of Peshawar.[8] A tall, heavily-built academic, with a chest-long beehive beard, Sayyaf was an adherent of Wahhabi Islam. His own group, *Ittihad-e Islami* (Islamic Union), was generously bankrolled by Riyadh, and would later clash with the pro-Iranian militia in Afghanistan during the civil war from 1992 to 1996.

The Saudis Back Zia ul Haq's Islamisation

As mentioned above, Zia ul Haq's dispatch of special forces troops to Mecca helped the Khalid regime overpower the militant rebels, which had bolstered Pakistan's standing in Riyadh.[9]

The anti-Kremlin campaign in Afghanistan provided the Saudi regime with an ideal opportunity to mobilise Muslims in the Arab world and beyond to participate in a jihad, and to further propagate Wahhabi Islam, particularly in poor but populous countries such as Pakistan and Egypt. It did so by funding the building of Saudi-style mosques with Wahhabi preachers, and establishing madrassas, religious schools.

On the eve of the founding of Pakistan in 1947, the existing 181 madrassas were antiquated institutions with ill-educated clerics as teachers. Later the failure of the Pakistani government to provide sufficient educational facilities resulted in more predominantly poor students attending madrassas, the religious management of which was patronised by different sects and sub-sects within Islam.

Among the Sunni Muslims of Hanafi jurisprudence prevalent in Pakistan, there were Deobandi and Barelvi branches. Since Ahmad Barelvi (1786–1831) harnessed the leading tolerant Sufi orders within the framework of reformed interpretation of the Sharia, his school was more popular than orthodox Deobandis. The Deobandi interpretation, originating in the Dar ul Uloom madrassa in the north Indian town of Deoband, stressed the external aspects of the Sharia over its inner meanings as favored by most Sufi saints. They believed in applying strictly the injunction of "enjoining good and forbidding evil (Arabic, *amr bil maruf wa nahiy anil munkar*)" derived from a Quranic verse. Thus the Deobandi doctrine was close to the Wahhabi and Salafi doctrines, and shared their hatred of Sufis and Shias. The Deobandi seminaries were affiliated to the long-established *Jamiat Ulema-e Islam* (JUI, Society of Scholars of Islam), an Islamist political party.

In the late 1970s, of the 893 madrassas, about 40 per cent were Deobandi, and some 30 per cent Barelvi.[10]

In general the curriculum of Sunni madrassas included the life of Prophet Muhammad, the Sayings and Deeds of the Prophet, memorising the Quran, the exegesis of the Quran, the Sharia, jurisprudence, Arabic literature, polemics, logic, grammar and mathematics. The primary function of the non-religious subjects was to enable the student to comprehend fully the religious literature. These schools provided poor students with free textbooks, board and lodging, as well as a modest stipend. With the inflow of Saudi funds into these institutions in the 1980s, the curriculum began to combine the local Sunni ideology with moderated Wahhabism as a result of its cross-pollination with the Salafiya doctrine.[11]

The dissemination of such a puritanical version of Islam was at odds with the lifestyles of senior Saudi royals, such as Fahd. However, as the monarch he continued with Khalid's staunch backing for the Islamisation of state and society that Zia ul Haq carried out during his eleven years of military dictatorship until his death in a military plane crash in 1988. Among other things, the number of madrassas ballooned from 893 to 2,801.[12] Two-thirds of these, being Deobandi, were funded by Saudi cash.

Official aid to Pakistan in the social-cultural sphere was matched by large donations from Saudi princes and Wahhabi institutions. Later Saudi religious charities and affluent citizens started funding such ultra-Sunni militant organizations as the Sipah-e-Sahaba Pakistan (Urdu: "Soldiers of the Companions of the Prophet" or SSP). Overall, the resulting societal amity between the Saudi Kingdom and the Islamic Republic of Pakistan reinforced the diplomatic alliance between their respective governments.

By the time of the Soviet withdrawal from Afghanistan in February 1989, the CIA had poured between $3 and $3.30 billion into fostering and sustaining the Afghan Mujahedin. And, having promised to match the American contribution, the Saudi GID went on to fund directly its favorite, Ittihad-e Islami.[13] On top of the official Saudi aid, there were contributions by Islamic charities, foundations, mosque collections, and handouts by the princes. Many of the religious charities were formed by GID in association with leading Wahhabi clerics. Prominent among those who personally tapped the private sources was Osama bin Laden—a richly bearded, white-turbaned follower of Wahhabi Islam, born into the household of Muhammad Awad bin Laden, the chief executive of the Jeddah-based Saudi Binladen Group, a multinational construction conglomerate close to the ruling dynasty. A quarter century on, the tribal belt along the Afghan-Pakistan border remains a hotbed of jihadist terrorism.

A Blip in Saudi Influence in Egypt

King Khalid continued Faisal's policy of assisting Egypt financially. Between 1973 and 1978, Riyadh's financial aid to Cairo totaled $7 billion, almost half of it earmarked for arms purchase.[14] The state-to-state assistance was underpinned by the Saudis funding several Islamic groups and social projects in the impoverished but strategically important country. Later, unwilling to accept President Anwar Sadat's bilateral peace deal with Israel in September 1978, the leaders of the Arab League resolved to cut diplomatic relations with Egypt when it signed a peace treaty with Israel in March 1979. Riyadh's severance of diplomatic ties with Cairo, however, had minimum impact on the flow of Egyptians into Saudi Arabia to serve as doctors, male nurses, accountants and teachers as well as semi-skilled or unskilled workers. They met the vaulting demand in the Saudi Kingdom for Arabic-speaking expats in the wake of the dramatic rise in oil prices of 1973–1974.

So great was the difference in living standards between Egypt and Saudi Arabia that an Egyptian teacher working in the Kingdom on a five year contract earned as much as he would have during all his working life.[15] Following Sadat's abrupt move to liberalise the market economy, inflation soared, impoverishing the vast majority of ordinary Egyptians who received fixed wages. Many of the Egyptians working in the Saudi Kingdom considered its new-found wealth and power as a divine reward showered on Saudis for leading pious lives according to Wahhabi tenets. This dovetailed with the regime's refrain that Almighty Allah had singled out the Holy Land by awarding it gargantuan underground riches. Riyadh-Cairo diplomatic links remained broken until 1989. By then Saudi Arabia had acquired a firm foothold in Pakistan.

Saudi-Iranian Rivalry in Pakistan and Afghanistan

With the Marxist military coup in Afghanistan in April 1978, the influence of the Iranian Shah, Muhammad Reza Pahlavi, ended abruptly. When the Kremlin intervened militarily in Afghanistan in December 1979, Ayatollah Ruhollah Khomeini condemned the invasion vehemently. His government implemented its own anti-Soviet strategy in the neighboring state while eschewing the US-Saudi campaign against the Kabul regime. It aided the Revolutionary Council of the Islamic Union of Afghanistan, containing moderate and radical elements, which set up its government in the central Hazarajat highlands with arms and cash. The ethnic Hazaras, accounting for 15 to 18 per cent of the population, who mostly lived in this region, were Shia. Meanwhile the Iranian government provided shelter to the stream of Afghan refugees pouring across the border and ultimately ended up hosting 1 million of them, most of whom were Sunni.

In Afghanistan, besides the areas controlled by the Peshawar-based Sunni parties there were territories in the central Hazarajat highlands ruled by Shia organizations. They maintained offices in Iranian cities as well as Quetta in the Pakistan province of Balochistan. The Revolutionary Council of the Islamic Union of Afghanistan, which set up its administration in the Hazarajat region in September 1979, consisted of moderate and radical Shia Islamists. In the spring of 1985, Iran urged Afghan Shia groups to unite.[16] But this would happen in Kabul only after the departure of the Soviet troops in February 1989. The result was the founding of *Hizb-e Wahdat* (Arabic: Party of Unity) under Karim Khalili, an ethnic Hazara, with its own militia, armed and trained by Iran.

After the Soviet withdrawal the Afghan Mujahedin fractured along ethnic lines. The constituent seven Afghan factions, originally fostered by foreign powers, had become autonomous. The traditional rivalry between Pashto-speaking Pushtuns, forming 40–45 per cent of the Afghan nation, and Tajiks, accounting for 25–27 per cent of the population, came to the fore. Among the universally Sunni Pushtuns, Gulbuddin Hikmatyar emerged as the most prominent leader. Though most Tajiks were Sunni, their language, Tajik, was akin to Persian, which was the everyday language in Herat. Situated seventy miles from the Iranian border, Herat was the third largest city in the country, most of whose inhabitants were Tajik.

The inter-sectarian fighting between the pro-Riyadh Islamic Union of Sayyaf and the pro-Tehran Wahdat fighters added another dimension to the ongoing conflict between the partisans of Hikmatyar and Ahmad Shah Masoud. Since Afghan Sunni groups were backed by Pakistan and Saudi Arabia financially and militarily, both Hizb-e Wahdat and the Tajik faction led by Masoud received active backing by Tehran.

Despairing of the interminable ethnic fighting among Afghans, Pakistan helped an emerging Sunni fundamentalist group called the Taliban (Pashto: religious students) in the autumn of 1994 to forge ahead as its proxy. Its government encouraged the students in the madrassas set up in the Afghan refugee camps in Pakistan, holding more then 3 million people, to swell the ranks of the Taliban. The group went on to gain the active support of Saudi Arabia. In the ongoing civil war, once the Taliban captured Kabul in September 1996, they consolidated their control of most of Afghanistan. Their opponents combined to form the Northern Alliance which, dominated by Tajiks and led by Masoud, contained Hizb-e Wahdat. Iran backed the Northern Alliance with arms and funds. Thus the Saudi Kingdom and Iran ended up on opposing camps in Afghanistan.

Proxy War in Pakistan

Within weeks of Pakistan recognizing the Khomeini regime, its foreign minister Agha Shahi arrived in Tehran and met the Ayatollah, who went on to declare that ties with Pakistan were "based on Islam." Such cordial relations withered when in 1980 the Carter administration found General Zia ul Haq eager to see Pakistan replace the third pillar in Washington's Middle East strategy that it had lost with the fall of the Shah, the other pillars being Saudi Arabia and Israel.

Domestically, in late 1979, President Zia ul Haq issued Zakat and Ushr Ordinance to be effective from 20 June 1980. It specified compulsory collection of religiously enjoined taxes to be used as charity by the state. Zakat (Arabic, derivative of *zakaa*, to be pure) amounts to 2.5 per cent of the accumulated assets and savings of a Muslim, and *ushr* (Arabic: one-tenth) is the land tax amounting to 10 per cent of the produce. In Pakistan zakat was to be deducted from all bank accounts annually on the eve of the holy month of Ramadan, starting on 14 July 1980.

Shias, emboldened by the Islamic revolution in Shia Iran, protested. They were estimated to account for 10 to 15 per cent of Pakistan's population, according to the *CIA World Factbook*.[17] But being mostly urbanite and forming a very substantial part of the trading community, they were better organised as a sect than the Sunni majority. They now argued that as believers they were enjoined to pay one-fifth of their trading profits to a grand ayatollah of their choice. Led by Arif Hussein Husseini, Shias mounted a nationwide protest which culminated in tens of thousands of them descending on Islamabad by bus and other vehicles, and besieging the federal government's secretariat on 4 and 5 July. Thus cornered, Zia ul Haq exempted the sect from zakat. That restored the peace. But later this episode would be seen as the starting point of sectarian tensions which would turn bloody in the coming decade.

Emboldened by this success, Husseini and Allama Mufti Jafar Hussein went on to establish the Movement for the Implementation of the Jafaria

Jurisprudence, named after the Shias' sixth Imam Jafar al Sadiq, bearing the Urdu title of *Tehrik-e Nafaz-e Fiqah-e Jafaria* (TNFJ). The Zia ul Haq government, whose penal code was derived from the Hanafi jurisprudence of Sunni Islam, viewed the rise of this organization as part of a conspiracy hatched in Tehran to export its revolution. It tried to create a division in the TNFJ, and succeeded. After the split the majority section renamed itself *Tehrik-e-Jafaria Pakistan* (TJP).

Many orthodox Sunnis were angered by the zakat exemption given to Shias. Inter-sectarian tensions rose and led to a Sunni-Shia riot in Karachi in 1983. This was the backdrop against which Zia ul Haq and the ISI encouraged radical elements in the Islamist JUI to form a militantly Sunni group called Sipah-e-Sahaba under the leadership of Haq Nawaz Jhangvi, a Deobandi cleric from the district of Jhang in central Punjab. There feudal lords were often Shia, and bazaar merchants Sunni. The SSP argued that the Shia landed gentry not only exploited its peasants in socio-economic terms but also led them astray in matters of religion, which needed to be challenged. This won the SSP the additional financial backing of Riyadh's General Intelligence Directorate.

In return, the SSP linked its drive to open more pro-Wahhabi mosques and madrassas funded by Riyadh with violent intimidation of Shias. It ignited serious anti-Shia riots in Lahore in 1986 and its activists assassinated Husseini in 1988. This compelled the TNFJ leadership to form an armed wing called the *Sipah-e Muhammad Pakistan* (Urdu: Soldiers of Muhammad; SMP) to carry out tit-for-tat killings. In February 1990, four SMP gunmen shot dead Jhangvi outside his home in Jhang.[18]

This led to violent inter-sectarian clashes as well as the torching of numerous houses and shops in Jhang. In December, Sadeq Ganji, the Iranian Counsel General in Lahore, was assassinated.[19] That assassination received headlines in the international press, highlighting the fact that Saudi Arabia and Iran were engaged in a proxy war in Pakistan. Two months later Jhangvi's successor Isar Qasmi was killed by Shia terrorists in Jhang.

His successor, Ziaur Rahman Farooqi, branched out into parliamentary politics, thus widening the base of the SSP. It won a few seats in the National Assembly in 1993 on the platform of turning Pakistan into a Sunni state. It allied with the Pakistan People's Party which exercised power from 1993 to 1996. Sporadic attacks on Shias during Friday prayers in Punjab claimed seventy-three lives and injured more than 300 in 1994.[20] And yet Farooqi's overarching policy fell foul of the radical elements within the SSP who favored relentless violent anti-Shah drive.

The radicals, led by Riaz Basra, the party's propaganda chief and a veteran of the anti-Soviet jihad, left in 1996 to form the *Lashkar-e Jhangvi* (Urdu, Army of Jhangvi; LeJ) as loyalists to Haq Nawaz Jhangvi. It resorted to terror tactics to press its demand of declaring Shias as non-Muslim, and establishing an orthodox Sunni Islamic system in Pakistan. It emerged as the most lethal faction, operating in extreme secrecy, with its small cells coming together to stage an operation and then immediately dispersing. Unlike all similar groups, it had no links with ISI. So the government found it extremely difficult to eradicate it.

The rationale behind militant Sunnis' attacks on important Shia individuals or gatherings was to provoke Shias to retaliate. That in turn would make Sunnis at large feel threatened and compel them to discard their complacency—stemming from their majority status—and hit back hard.

The net result of the violent and non-violent anti-Shia agitation by the LeJ and the SSP was to escalate inter-sectarian tensions, and compound the already intense hostility between several ethnic groups in the country's largest city, Karachi. The government found the annual inter-sectarian death toll of 800 in the metropolis unbearable, and resorted to blaming India's Research and Analysis Wing, charged with foreign intelligence gathering, for the internecine violence. It closed down the Indian consulate in Karachi.[21] But the mayhem continued.

Farooqi was killed on 18 January 1997, when a bomb attached to a motorcycle exploded upon his arrival to a Lahore courthouse, where he was being tried for the murder of a rival Shia leader. The bombing killed twenty-five and wounded dozens, including the LeJ's second-in-command, Muhammad Azam Tariq. In response, SSP militants set fire to Iranian cultural centers in Lahore and Multan and rioted in parts of Punjab. Between January and May 1997, they killed seventy-five leading Shias.[22] The fanatical denunciation of Shias continued. After becoming the head of the SSP, Tariq said, "If Islam is to be established in Pakistan, then Shias must be declared infidels."[23] The Deobandi madrassas in southern and central Punjab continued to produce recruits for the SSP.[24]

Meanwhile, in the Arab Middle East, President Saddam Hussein had created a major crisis by invading and occupying Kuwait in August 1990. With Saudi Arabia sharing borders with both Kuwait and Iraq, King Fahd had no option but to intervene on behalf of the occupied emirate of Kuwait. He did so when US President George H. W. Bush had moved swiftly to get the UN Security Council to condemn Iraqi aggression and demand immediate Iraqi withdrawal by fourteen votes to none.

8

SAUDI ARABIA AT THE CENTER OF THE TWENTIETH CENTURY'S LAST MAJOR WAR

Saudi Arabia's aid of over $25 billion to Iraq during the Iran-Iraq War far exceeded the $10 billion provided by Kuwait in the form of the oil it supplied to Iraq's customers. Yet it was Kuwait's Emir Jaber bin Ahmad al Sabah who demanded an immediate repayment of the loan in the summer of 1990. This was because the issue was tied up with a dispute about border delineation that the Emirate had with Iraq.

Saddam Hussein's Blitzkrieg on Kuwait

After much debate about these interlinked problems, Emir Jaber al Sabah nominated Crown Prince Saad bin Abdullah al Sabah to head the Kuwaiti delegation to meet its Iraq counterpart led by Deputy President Izzat Ibrahim in Jeddah. After meeting for an hour and a half in the evening they adjourned for prayers, and then for dinner hosted by Saudi King Fahd. Following the King's departure, Ibrahim and the Crown Prince resumed negotiations. The Kuwaiti royal insisted that they discuss the border demarcation first before anything else. This angered the Iraqi leader. Tempers flared. Saad reportedly said, "Kuwait has very powerful friends. You will be forced to pay back all the money you owe us."[1]

Back in Kuwait City, "We were being told that well over 100,000 Iraqi troops [equipped with 2,000 tanks] had massed in the southern region of Iraq and were within minutes of the [Kuwaiti] border," wrote Lt-Colonel Fred L. Hart Jr., an American advisor to the Kuwaiti Land Forces. "The evening of 1 August, we all watched the local English news broadcast which showed the Kuwaiti Crown Prince Saad al Sabah return from Jeddah with the news that Izzat Ibrahim walked out of the talks when he was unwilling to meet Saddam Hussein's demands [of $2.4 billion for the Iraqi oil allegedly stolen from across the border, and a loan of $10 billion from Kuwait]."[2]

Earlier, Iraq's President Saddam Hussein had refused to repay the loans he had received from Kuwait and Saudi Arabia, arguing that he had waged the war with Iran not just to safeguard his country but also to save the thrones of the Gulf monarchs which were threatened by the rising tide of Islamic republicanism stemming from Tehran. In response, the Kuwaiti emir, backed by the United Arab Emirates, flooded the oil market in the spring of 1990, depressing the price from $18 to $11 a barrel. A drop of $1 a barrel reduced Baghdad's annual revenue by $1 billion—a loss Saddam Hussein found intolerable in the face of the urgent demands of postwar reconstruction and jobs for the demobilised soldiers from a wartime army of one million.

"By 2300 hours 1 August 1990, the Chief of US Liaison Office Kuwait Col. John Mooneyham began receiving telephonic reports from US Westinghouse technicians manning a radar observation balloon position just north of Mutla Ridge," continued Hart:

> Their reports showed a mass armor formation resembling an iron pipe several kilometers long and rolling down hill. The technicians were advised to cut the tether and move out smartly…I went up to the roof of our villa around 0030 hrs on 2 August and could see a few flares on the northern horizon, but heard no distant sounds of artillery…By 0500 hrs the Iraqi formation was on the outskirts of Camp Doha [on a small peninsula on Kuwait Bay]. Word spread quickly of the invasion…. By then we had all been notified telephonically or awakened by low flying fighter bombers and the distinct sound of artillery fire. At 0515 hrs I went outside and immediately recognized the smell of cordite in the air and could hear the sounds of war getting closer. Looking to the southwest from my two-story villa rooftop, I could see Kuwait international airport five to seven kilometers away under bombardment by

Iraqi fighter bombers... Iraqi planners failed to coordinate the one hour time difference between Kuwait City and Baghdad, resulting in an uncoordinated attack by Iraqi Special Forces units [who arrived by ship and helicopters] and Republican Guard ground forces [who advanced overland].[3]

During the second stage of the offensive Iraq's fighter aircraft hit key installations in and around Kuwait City while its commandos and airborne units attacked the Emir's residence, Dasman Palace, radio and TV stations, and the Central Bank. At the Dasman Palace, they were reinforced by Iraqi units in armored personnel carriers which had been brought in by landing craft. More Iraqi troops arrived by helicopter and landed on the roof and in the garden of the palace. Among other things they aimed to capture or kill Emir Jaber al Sabah. But the emir, reportedly tipped off about the invasion before its launch, had left the palace earlier along with his entourage for the military General Headquarters to observe the battle there, and then swiftly fled to Saudi Arabia in a convoy of Mercedes-Benz saloons.[4] The fighting at the palace went on until 1400 hours. Among others it claimed the life of the Emir's younger brother Fahd. "I could see from my rooftop that Iraqi armored forces had occupied the palace grounds," concluded Hart.[5]

Iran, now ruled by Ayatollah Ali Khamanei, chosen by the popularly elected Assembly of Experts after the death of Ayatollah Ruhollah Khomeini in June 1989, was quick to condemn Iraq's occupation of Kuwait and called on Saddam Hussein to withdraw his troops from the emirate.[6] Iran's leaders now felt vindicated for having repulsed Saddam's aggression against their country and sustained a long war. During that military conflict, Saddam had wrapped up his war rhetoric in racist terms, describing Persians as inferior to Arabs, with his generals describing Iranians as insects deserving to be eliminated by chemical weapons. Now he showed no qualms in invading a neighboring Arab state. Among other things this brought home to Gulf Cooperation Council (GCC) members the aggressiveness of Saddam Hussein of which Iran had been a victim a decade earlier.

America as Protector of Saudi Arabia

Iraq's invasion of Kuwait prompted the US to step in as the protector of the Saudi Kingdom which, according to the administration of

President George H. W. Bush, was Saddam's next target. At the National Security Council meeting at the White House on 2 August Bush, who had made his first million dollars as an oilman in Texas, argued that with 20 per cent of the world's oil—11 per cent in Iraq and 9 per cent in Kuwait—"Saddam would be able to manipulate world prices [by acting as a swing producer] and hold the United States and its allies at his mercy. Higher fuel prices would fuel inflation, worsening the already gloomy condition of the US economy."[7]

At Washington's behest, the UN Security Council imposed economic sanctions on Iraq and occupied Kuwait on 6 August, thus removing 4.8 million bpd of oil from the market. The price doubled to $22 a barrel (or $42 in 2017's terms). Kuwait's emir Shaikh Jaber al Sabah set up his royal court in exile in the Saudi resort city of Taif. From there he dispatched his foreign minister Sabah al Ahmad al Sabah to Tehran. Among other things he offered apologies to his hosts for aiding Saddam Hussein's government in the Iran-Iraq War.[8]

On his part, Bush focused on pushing the line that Saddam was on the verge of invading Saudi Arabia despite the fact that he had signed a non-aggression pact with the Kingdom in March 1989, and that he vehemently denied any intention to breach that agreement.[9] Therefore Bush had to come up with irrefutable evidence to convince Fahd. He claimed to have it in the form of the pictures taken by US surveillance planes and satellites which showed Iraqi armored personnel carriers (APCs) and troops amassed in the desert along the Saudi border, with five APCs inside the Saudi territory. But since these vehicles were in an area where the border lacked proper delineation their presence was most probably unintentional.[10]

Armed with the overhead pictorials, which required expertise to interpret, US Defence Secretary Dick Cheney flew to Jeddah. During a meeting with Fahd at the latter's palace on 6 August, he succeeded in scaring the monarch by telling him that Iraq had positioned surface-to-surface missiles in Kuwait aimed at Saudi targets. But inviting American armed forces to Saudi Arabia was a momentous call for Fahd to make. In the past US military personnel had worked inside the Kingdom; but since their numbers were small they were virtually invisible to the general public. This time, however, they had to be stationed in massive numbers on Saudi territory but under their own flag. That would violate an injunction by Prophet Muhammad later recorded in the Hadiths that "Let there be no two religions in Arabia."[11] Fahd needed to consult the members of the Council of Senior Ulema (COSU). Ultimately he agreed to invite US armed forces, albeit subject to three conditions: President Bush should state in writing that American troops would leave Saudi Arabia when the Iraqi threat was over; the US would obtain Saudi approval before launching any offensive military action against Iraq; and the Bush administration should keep the Saudi invitation secret until the first American troops had landed on the Saudi soil. After consulting Bush over the telephone, Cheney agreed.[12]

On 9 August the Saudi government belatedly admitted the earlier arrival of the US soldiers in the Kingdom just as the members of COSU, chaired by Shaikh Abdul Aziz bin Abdullah bin Baz, met in Riyadh. On 13 August COSU issued its approval of Fahd's decision. "The Council … has been aware of the great massing of troops on the Kingdom's borders," stated its communiqué. "This has prompted the rulers of the Kingdom… to ask Arab and non-Arab countries to deter the expected danger." Since "It is the duty of the good Muslim ruler to deter aggression and the incursion of evil," continued the communiqué, COSU lent its support to "all the measures [already] taken by the ruler."[13] COSU did so only after it had been briefed by King Fahd that he had obtained a written agreement from President Bush that the US-led Coalition forces would advance into Iraqi-occupied Kuwait only after obtaining the approval of the Saudi monarch, and that all American soldiers would leave the Kingdom once Kuwait had been liberated.

It came as no surprise that bin Baz and COSU delivered what King Fahd wanted. After all, bin Baz lived in a two story building inside a compound on royal grounds in Shumyasi. Other COSU members lived in spacious homes presented to them by richly-endowed foundations or affluent patrons.[14] In these new circumstances the traditional Wahhabi-Al Saud alliance remained in place.

Among those who criticised the decision of COSU were Salman al Awda and Safar bin Abdul Rahman al Hawali, the foremost non-establishment senior Wahhabi scholars, and the leading figures of the Sahwa movement. Their stance would coincide with that of the Iranian government following a totally unexpected move by Saddam Hussein. On 16 August a high level Iraqi delegation arrived in Tehran with a letter by him addressed to his Iranian counterpart Ali Akbar Hashemi Rafsanjani. According to Baghdad Radio, in that letter the Iraqi leader offered to recognize Iran's disputed pre-war land and fluvial borders, release all Iranian prisoners of war (PoWs), and start withdrawing Iraqi troops from about 1,000 square miles of occupied southwestern Iran from 17 August. A bullish foreign minister of Iran, Ali Akbar Velayati, told Tehran Radio, "This is the biggest victory of the Islamic Republic of Iran throughout its history." An Iranian spokesman said the government would review Iraq's proposal "with optimism," predicting that it it would lead to a "lasting and just peace."[15] Saddam Hussein made this sweeping offer in order to shift the bulk of his 300,000 troops guarding the frontier with Iran to Kuwait.

Iran viewed the build-up of the US-led anti-Iraq coalition with rising anxiety and disapproval. Its government welcomed Iraqi Foreign Minster Tariq Aziz in Tehran on 9 September to underscore Iraq's resolve to normalise relations with Iran. Three days later Khamanei declared that opposition to the US military presence in the Persian Gulf region was a Muslim jihad. "Anyone who fights America's aggression, its greediness and its plans to encroach on the Persian Gulf region has engaged in jihad in the cause of Allah, and anyone who is killed on that path is a martyr."[16] On 28 September massive crowds gathered in Tehran and marched toward the Tehran University prayer grounds shouting anti-American slogans. They had responded to the call made by the state-sponsored Committee to Coordinate Islamic Propaganda, broadcast repeatedly on Tehran Radio.[17]

Since its founding in 1979, the Islamic Republic had opposed the military involvement of foreign powers in the Gulf, arguing that the Muslim states of the region should form an alliance similar to the North Atlantic Treaty Organization (NATO) to safeguard the area militarily. This could be achieved by expanding the existing GCC to admit Iran. Such a scenario did not appeal to Saudi Arabia which would stand to lose its leadership role in the GCC to a Shia-majority republic.

For now, however, despite its best efforts, the Iranian government failed to dissuade President Hafiz Assad of Syria, a long time strategic ally of the Islamic Republic, from joining the US-led Coalition against Iraq. Assad committed 14,500 ground troops to the Arab-Islamic forces led by General Khalid bin Sultan Al Saud. In return, he received $2.2 billion in aid from Saudi Arabia, the Kuwait government in exile, and the UAE.[18]

By the end of 1990 the Pentagon, leading a coalition of twenty-eight nations, including thirteen Arab and Muslim ones, assembled the most lethal fighting machine since the Second World War: 775,000 Western and 220,000 Arab and Muslim troops (most of them stationed on Saudi soil), equipped with 4,000 tanks and 2,900 warplanes and combat helicopters, and deploying 107 warships in the Persian Gulf, the northern Arabian Sea and the Gulf of Oman, the Red Sea and the eastern Mediterranean. It faced 545,000 Iraqi troops in Kuwait and southern Iraq, equipped with 4,200 tanks and 150 combat helicopters, supported by 55 combat-ready warplanes.[19]

The Arab-Islamic part of the Coalition included Pakistan and Bangladesh. Islamabad dispatched 11,000 troops to Saudi Arabia. Bangladesh, meanwhile, ruled by a general of the Islamic Bangladesh Nationalist Party since 1975, worked so closely with Riyadh that its President, Abdul Rahman Biswas, had no problem getting the parliament to sanction the dispatch of 2,300 soldiers to the Saudi kingdom. From then on, there was a steady increase in Riyadh's financial aid to Dhaka.

Significantly, the Arab-Islamic forces, commanded by General Prince Khalid bin Sultan Al Saud, operating in coordination with General Norman Schwarzkopf, leading the Western forces, were posted between the Kuwaiti border and American forces further south.[20]

The War and Its Consequences

During the 43-day war, which began on 16 January 1991 and was code-named Operation Desert Storm, the Coalition mounted 106,000 air sorties, dropping 141,000 tons of explosives, and fired 315 cruise missiles. The Arab Monetary Fund estimated the damage to Iraq's infrastructure at $190 billion. The total estimated Iraqi dead were 57,600 to 62,600. Between 2,000 and 5,000 Kuwaitis, most of them civilian, died. The Coalition lost 376 troops.[21]

While the Iran-Iraq armed conflict ended up as the longest conventional warfare of the twentieth century, the 1991 Gulf War, fought in essence for the control of oil prices, proved to be that century's last major armed conflict. It also had several unintended consequences. It impacted on the November 1992 US presidential poll. After his impressive victory in this war, President Bush's approval rating soared to 91 per cent. His re-election seemed so certain that leading Democrat politicians did not enter the race for the party's nomination. Into this vacuum stepped the little known governor of the obscure southern state of Arkansas, Bill Clinton. In much the same way that Islamic Iran had done in 1980, now Saudi Arabia, a non-Western country, ended up playing a critical role in shaping the political history of its protector, the United States.

The discovery of Iraq's advanced infrastructure for the development and manufacture of chemical, biological and nuclear weapons by International Atomic Energy Agency (IAEA) inspectors would lead to Iran accelerating its four-year-old super-secret program to produce an atom bomb. (Conversely when, in the aftermath of the Anglo-American invasion of Iraq in March 2003, Washington concluded in October that Iraq's nuclear project had ended in 1991, the government in Iran discontinued its own nuclear program in the autumn of 2003, according to US intelligence agencies. This meant that the origin of Tehran's nuclear drive was to find a deterrent to the nuclear danger that Iran faced from Saddam's Iraq—and was unrelated to Israel.)

"The war brought into focus so many things: it raised our consciousness and gave us an opportunity for soulsearching,' said Khalid Meena, editor of the pro-regime *Arab News*. "All sections of society are having this experience."A Saudi source, knowledgeable about the goings-on in the army, said, "There are more and more bearded soldiers... More and more leaflets and clandestine letters criticizing the behavior of the royal princes, the perverse way the [Saudi] embassies are run, the widespread corruption among highranking officials and members of the royal family are distributed in the army's garrisons."[22] Domestically, the growing disaffection of Saudis, caused by the overwhelming presence of US troops on Saudi soil, and the economic downturn, would compel King Fahd to decree a Basic Law of Government (constitution) for the Kingdom a year after the end of the 1991 Gulf War—and sixty years since the founding of Saudi Arabia. This declared the Quran and the Sunna as the constitution of the kingdom to be governed by the male descendants of Abdul Aziz bin Abdul Rahman Al Saud. The monarch is the head of state and of the council of ministers, and is also the commander-in-chief of the military. He appoints the prime minister and other members of the cabinet. There was no provision for a legislature, political parties or trade unions. However, the Basic Law provided for the appointment of a Consultative Shura Council of sixty members and its chairman by the monarch for a four-year term. In August 1993 Fahd did so. It was a toothless, advisory body. When the Speaker of the council was offered the gift of a parrot during a foreign tour, he is said to have replied, "No, thank you; I have sixty of them already."[23]

In the wider region, the Muslim Brotherhood branches in most Arab countries opposed Fahd's military alliance with non-Muslim America. The Saudi government responded by reducing its financial aid to the Brotherhood. This would prove to be the beginning of a process that would end with Saudi Arabia declaring the Brotherhood a terrorist organization in 2014.

During the seven-month long Kuwait crisis and the subsequent war, the Saudi Kingdom was able to fill only two-thirds of the 4 million bpd gap left in oil exports following the UN sanctions on Iraq. This led to a spike in petroleum prices—causing the Third Oil Shock after the ones in 1973–1974 and in 1979–1980—and an economic recession in 1991–1992, one of the main reasons for Bush's defeat by Clinton. In Saudi Arabia itself, the huge expenses incurred by the government in fighting the 1991 Gulf War, the rearming of the Kingdom that followed the conflict and the sharply reduced prices of oil led Fahd's cabinet to raise foreign loans to balance the budget in 1994. With that, the government lost its tool of silencing the opposition by bribing its leaders at a time when between 1982 and 1993, the per capita GDP fell from $13,625 to $7,386.[24]

The Aftermath of the 1991 Gulf War

Shortly after the end of the 1991 Gulf War, Riyadh restored diplomatic ties with Tehran. In April, President Rafsanjani, a moderate cleric elected to high office in July 1989—a month after the death of Ayatollah Ruhollah Khomeini—flew to Saudi Arabia to meet King Fahd. Back-channel talks between the feuding states had started earlier. In September 1990, Velayati met his Saudi counterpart Saud al Faisal at the United Nations in New York. The Saudi foreign minister agreed to raise the quota to 45,000 for Iran's pilgrims and proposed that the Iranians hold their rally but in a fixed place, where the message from their Supreme Leader could be read to the assembled. The Saudis repeated the offer during the GCC meeting in Doha in December 1990, which Iran attended as an observer. In the end the two sides settled for 115,000 Iranian pilgrims instead of 45,000 according to the original formula. It was also understood that the rallied pilgrims would not criticise Muslim governments. Soon after the end of the 1991 Gulf War on 28 February, the two sides resumed diplomatic relations.[25]

One of the pilgrims to the Hajj, which started on 21 June, was Velayati. He met King Fahd twice in Jeddah. Arguing that the GCC ought to be strengthened in order to deter aggression against any of its members in the future, he suggested expanding the GCC to include Iran. Fahd lent him a sympathetic ear.[26] He left the Kingdom express-ing "great optimism" about the future of ties between the two coun-tries. In early August Saudi Arabia and Iran decided to exchange ambas-sadors,[27] but there was no prospect of expanding the GCC. Iran's earlier optimism was based on the fact that the GCC had agreed with Egypt and Syria in early March to create a joint peacekeeping force to maintain post-war security in the Gulf region. That vanished when the GCC reversed its decision. As a result, Egypt withdrew its 20,000 soldiers from the Saudi Kingdom on 5 May 1991. Three days later, Vice President Cheney arrived in the region to confirm a series of bilateral defense ties with each of the Gulf monarchies, including a formalised defense agreement with Saudi Arabia.[28] This nipped in the bud Iran's plan to become part of a regional security arrangement to be devised by the countries around the Gulf except Iraq, and to facilitate the departure of American forces from the region.

By early May 1991 all non-Saudi forces had left Saudi Arabia—except 37,000 US troops, including air force personnel, and American warplanes based at the Prince Sultan Airbase in Al Kharj, 50 miles (80 km) south-east of Riyadh.[29] This met with disapproval by large sections of Saudi society whose means of expressing it were very limited. Among other things this would motivate such hardline Wahhabis as Osama bin Laden to assert that King Fahd had "sided with Jews and Christians" and committed "an unforgivable sin." He denounced the House of Saud as *munafiq* (i.e., deviant Muslims). The growing popular-ity of his attacks on the Saudi royal family helped strengthen Al Qaida, his extremist Islamist organization.

The continued presence of US troops in the Kingdom was justified by the Pentagon on the grounds that they were helping to enforce the southern no-fly zone in Iraq below the 32nd parallel. This rationale convinced nobody in Saudi Arabia. The southern no-fly zone was imposed by President Bush in August 1992 as part of Operation Southern Watch which was mounted to punish Saddam Hussein for his lack of cooperation with the UN inspectors charged with finding and destroying chemical, biological and nuclear weapons and the facilities to manufacture them. So what was the justification for the presence of US troops between 28 February 1991 and the launching of the Operation Southern Watch, many Saudis rightly asked.

In the Kingdom, there were public manifestations of discontent. In a tape-recorded sermon, Safar al Hawali argued that "What is happening in the Gulf is part of a larger Western design to dominate the whole Arab and Muslim world."[30] The best known of the public demonstrations were in Buraidah in the northern Qasim Province. On 17 May 1991, the provincial governor, Prince Abdul Ilah bin Abdul Aziz, banned Shaikh Salman al Awda from delivering his Friday sermons because earlier he had been stridently critical of the autocracy of the House of Saud and the continued presence of American forces. Two days later thousands of his supporters, led by the local ulema and mutawwa, mounted a noisy demonstration in Buraidah. The National Guard broke up the march and made many arrests. To the consternation of the ruling family, Shaikh bin Baz backed Awda, and an influential group of clerics petitioned the monarch to dismiss the governor of Qasim.[31]

On 24 May it was revealed that during his meeting with King Fahd a week earlier, Shaikh bin Baz had passed on to him a petition, titled "Letter of Demands," signed by nearly 400 leading clerics, judges and academics. Their ten-point petition combined the call for an impartially nominated consultative assembly to decide all domestic and foreign affairs, with demands for Islamisation of all social, economic, administrative, and educational systems, reform of the judicial system, punishment of all those who have enriched themselves by illegal means "whoever they are, wherever they are, without any exception of rank," the creation of Islamic cultural centers throughout the Muslim world with the task of challenging the Western, non-Islamic press and propaganda, keeping the *umma* (Islamic community) out of non-Islamic pacts and treaties—as well as reforming the military into an independent armed forces, backed by a sophisticated armament industry and military academies, and the diversification of modem arms procurement sources.[32]

The demands to diversify sources of arms procurement and eschew treaties and alliances with non-Muslim states implied damning criticism of Riyadh's alliance with the leading Western powers. The religious luminaries were thus advising King Fahd to end close ties with the West, particularly the US. They had the support of Crown Prince Abdullah bin Abdul Aziz Al Saud and Prince Salman bin Abdul Aziz Al Saud, the influential governor of Riyadh Province; and they were opposed by Prince Sultan bin Abdul Aziz Al Saud, the defense minister, and his two sons, Prince Khalid and Prince Bandar, all of them favoring closer ties with America. They also advised the monarch to take firm action against the rebellious preachers of Buraidah.

King Fahd prevaricated. But, reminded of his promise in late 1979 to establish a Consultative Council and a Basic Law "within months", he did so in March 1992 with the publication of the 83-article Basic Law. The fully nominated four-year tenure Consultative Council did not come into existence until August 1993.

Nonetheless, the continued presence of US forces in the Saudi Kingdom provided Awda and Hawali with a solid basis for their criticism of the regime. Their views were echoed by academics who sought to uphold human rights. Encouraged by the holding of the first multi-party general election in the recently united Yemen in April 1993, six Saudis, including Awda and Hawali, formed the Committee for the Defence of Legitimate Rights (CDLR). It became the first opposition organization openly to challenge the monarchy, accusing the government and senior ulema of not doing enough to protect the legitimate Islamic rights of Muslims. Calling on citizens to report official acts of injustice to it, the CDLR demanded elections based on universal suffrage. The government arrested its head, Professor Muhammad al Masari, and sacked others from their jobs. After its proscription in the Kingdom, the dissident Masari fled to Britain, and launched an extensive fax campaign to receive information from Saudi Arabia, much of it on the corruption rampant among Saudi royals, and then faxed it back to supporters there.

To curb the rising opposition, the authorities resorted to repression. In September 1994 they arrested 200 non-violent political dissidents, including Awda and Hawali and fifty of their followers in the Sahwa movement. The CDLR, operating in London, revealed inter alia that there were 300 political prisoners in Saudi Arabia by early 1995.[33]

In the Kingdom, the brutally suppressed opposition turned violent. The first sign came on 13 November 1995 when a car bomb attack on the US Office of the Program Manager in charge of the National Guard Modernisation Program killed six people, including five American officers.[34]

By then the seventy-three-year-old Fahd had grown obese and lethargic, sleeping through the day and spending the night with obsequious cronies in his three-billion dollar worth palace in Jeddah where they were intrigued and fascinated by the antics of fish swimming in an elaborate aquarium. He avoided Riyadh since a fortune-teller had once told him that he would die there. Fahd had taken to giving long, rambling descriptions of his arthritic knees in the middle of important meetings. When a stroke incapacitated him on 29 November, he appointed Crown Prince Abdullah bin Abdul Aziz—a tall, bespectacled man with a permanently dyed mustache and a goatee beard—as Regent.

Crown Prince Abdullah was not part of Fahd's inner circle which was limited to his six blood brothers, known as the Sudairi Seven since their mother was the formidable Hussa bint Ahmad al Sudairi. She married King Abdul Aziz in 1920. By 1941 she delivered seven sons which made her the most valued wife of the monarch. Her beauty and charm were enhanced by her strong personality. She tried to instill a sense of group feeling among her sons, and urged them to stick together, which they did. The Sudairi Seven included Sultan (Defense Minister since 1963), Nayef (Interior Minister since 1978), Salman (governor of Riyadh Province since 1963), Abdul Rahman (Deputy Defense Minister) and Ahmad (Deputy Interior Minister). In contrast, Abdullah's power base lay in his command of the National Guard which was administered by a ministry that stood apart from the Ministry of Defence. Though on Fahd's recovery the Sudairi Brothers compelled Abdullah to step down from the regency, the situation changed when Fahd suffered a more severe heart attack in 1997. From then on, there was far less of Fahd's imprint on administration, and Abdullah became the de facto ruler of the Kingdom.

Fahd's Thaw with the Saudi Shias

The rising tensions between Saudi Arabia and Iran in the wake of the bloody Mecca rioting in July 1987 impacted on the Shias in the Kingdom's Eastern Province who came under increased official pressure. Hassan al Saffar and other leaders of the Organisation of Islamic Revolution in the Arabian Peninsula (OIRAP) decided to move from Tehran to Damascus where the Syrian President Hafiz Assad belonged to the Alawi sub-sect within Shia Islam. They continued to smuggle anti-regime pamphlets into the Eastern Province—until September 1990 when, in response to Saddam Hussein's invasion and occupation of Kuwait, they reverted back to the earlier title of the Reform Movement of Saudi Arabia. And, fearing an attack on the Kingdom by Iraq, Saffar called on his followers to rally behind the government to fight Saddam's regime. Many Saudi Shias volunteered to join the army and the civil defence force. The renamed moderate organization called for peaceful reform and democracy, and pledged to submit petitions to the King to improve the status of Shias.

At the initiative of Saffar, more than 150 Saudi-exiled Shias from Iran, Syria, Britain and America gathered in the Damascus suburb of Ghouta in July 1993 to consider a back channel proposal for reconciliation from King Fahd who had noted the moderation in the rhetoric of the Reform Movement. By a large majority they agreed to negotiate provided the monarch agreed to release 400 Shias held as political prisoners and allow 1,200 to 1,500 others to return to the Kingdom. Saffar then flew to Tehran to consult Iranian leaders who, intent on thawing relations with Riyadh, gave him a green signal. This in turn encouraged Fahd to play for time. In his appointments to the fully nominated First Shura Consultative Council he included Jamal al Jishi, a Shia. President Rafsanjani persuaded Fahd to cut Saudi oil output to raise petroleum prices which helped cash-strapped Iran.[35] Fahd met several of Saffar's emissaries and agreed inter alia to an order excising derogatory terms for Shias from textbooks, removing some other forms of overt discrimination, and permitting self-exiled Shias to return home.[36]

Saffar returned to Qatif, and in October he oversaw the disbanding of the Reform Movement. Two years later, in 1995, Grand Mufti Abdul Aziz bin Baz would invite Saffar to his home in Riyadh, a momentous gesture. But at its root, Wahhabi hatred of Shias at the clerical as well as popular level did not subside, and kept appearing in its virulent form over the next few decades.

In 1992, the Iranians' Hajj ritual had passed off peacefully against the background of Rafsanjani's statement that the political aspect of the pilgrimage could not be allowed to impact negatively on "other dimensions of the pilgrimage," implying that these were spiritual.[37] In 1993 the Iranian pilgrims' leader, Muhammad Muhammadi-Reyshahri, appointed by Rafsanjani, called on his followers to pray with Sunni brothers in congregational prayer, thus breaking with the tradition of praying separately. Iran's moderation emboldened the Saudis to enforce their ban on the holding of a rally for the Iranian pilgrims. Even Ali Akbar Nateq-Nouri, the hardline Speaker of Iran's Parliament, failed to protest. "We believe [the Saudi decision] was due to pressure by others from outside, compelling Saudi Arabia to prevent the rally. But this will not give way to a severance in our relations. We should daily improve our ties with regional and neighboring countries, and we should mutually resolve bilateral issues."[38] Tehran's quiet acceptance of the latest restrictions led the Saudi government to halve Iran's Hajj quota of 115,000 pilgrims in 1994.

9

SAUDI-IRANIAN DÉTENTE

King Khalid had a passion for falcons, rearing and training them as hunting birds. But far more widely known was the passion his Second Deputy Prime Minister, Abdullah bin Abdul Aziz, had for horses. Having learned to ride as a boy, he went on to groom, train and even shoe some of his horses in his youth. He then established the Equestrian Club in Riyadh in 1965. Many years later his stables at his sprawling Janadriyah Farm on the outer fringes of the city would contain up to 1,000 horses in air-conditioned stables. The different sections of the complex focused on horse breeding, racing and show jumping. He was known to relax when assessing young thoroughbred yearlings, and had been overheard telling guests that "their whinnying is music to my ears."[1] He maintained a weekend residence and office in the complex, and often hosted visiting dignitaries there. US Presidents George W. Bush and Barack Obama were his guests there respectively in January 2008 and June 2009. When asked if he spent time with his horses by John Brennan, Counterterrorism Adviser to Obama, Abdullah threw up his hands to complain. "I see them on television when they race," he said. "I love horses. Every couple of weeks I get to see them, and then I have a very calm and restful sleep.[2]

Abdullah was close to the tribes, and possessed a Bedouin soul. In the Bedouin tradition, Abdullah was egalitarian. It was the custom of the royal family members to receive petitioners every evening at their palaces. Over time commoners had resorted to extreme forms of deference to the royals, attempting to kiss hands while crying in supplication. The Bedouin in Abdullah loathed the sight of grown men groveling. Armed with a slender bamboo camel stick, Abdullah stood at the front of the line-up of the petitioner. He would thwart any attempt at kissing his hand or prostration by tapping the supplicant's head, hand or another body part. His habit of retreats at his desert camp, Rawdat al Khraim, near Riyadh set him apart from other senior princes who spent summers in their Mediterranean palaces.

Abdullah was a child of a union between Ibn Saud and one of the three women of the House of Rashid who had been widowed by the fighting between Ibn Saud and his rival Muhammad bin Rashid of the Shammar tribe in 1921. To reconcile his defeated foe, Ibn Saud married Fahda bint Asi Al Shuraim of the Shammar tribe. Abdullah was born two years later. Soon after the beautiful, formidable Hussa bint Ahmad al Sudairi started delivering a string of sons who came to monopolise Ibn Saud's love and attention. Abdullah was neglected particularly after the death of his mother when he was only six. In later years Abdullah would attribute his stutter to the fierce scolding he received from his authoritarian father, Abdul Aziz, for something that had caused him annoyance. It was thus that Abdullah came to be known to his critics as the Stuttering Horseman. His more numerous admirers lauded the critical role he had played in the royal battle between King Saud and his challenger Faisal, the Crown Prince and the Premier, in 1964 as described in an earlier chapter.

Saudi National Guard, a Force for All Eventualities

An armed force drawn from the most loyal of the Najd-based tribes, the National Guard was the new name given to the White Guard, formed in 1932, after the dissolution of the Ikhwan established by Ibn Saud. The need to rename, rearm and retrain this force, to be administered by its own ministry, arose in the aftermath of the overthrow of the monarchy in North Yemen in September 1962. Its mission was redefined as repulsing both domestic and foreign threats to the Saudi monarchy. National Guard personnel were billeted outside the main urban centers, and its officers were the most pampered outside the royal family. In contrast, army garrisons were deliberately sited away from cities and near the borders. Thus the National Guard, generously supplied with anti-tank rockets and anti-aircraft missiles, were strategically equipped to block rebellious troops advancing from distant garrisons, and to shoot down warplanes taking off from airbases near the borders.

As the kingdom's most reliable armed force, the National Guard deals with anything that remotely threatens the regime—be it a strike, a demonstration, a tribal revolt or disaffection in the military. Unsurprisingly, therefore, it was at the forefront of quelling the uprising by hard line Wahhabi militants in Mecca and defiant demonstrations by Shias in the Eastern Province in November 1979.

Starting in the early 1980s, Abdullah oversaw a thorough reorganization and retraining of the National Guard by the Pentagon as well as private US defense contractors. This program was accelerated after the 1991 Gulf War. Hence the anti-regime Al Qaida terrorists targeted the US Office of the Program Manager in charge of National Guard modernisation in Riyadh, killing five American officers. At that time the National Guard was 57,000 strong with 20,000 tribal levies in reserve. By comparison, the regular army had 70,000 soldiers.[3]

All along Abdullah pursued his overarching objective of turning the National Guard into a fully-integrated, self-contained entity with an extensive civilian infrastructure of schools, hospitals and housing colonies. "He [Abdullah] saw the Guard primarily as a way to develop and educate Saudis," said Abdul Rahman Abu Haimid, who supervised the Guard's civil works with the rank of deputy commander for twenty-four years. "Our hospitals, our schools, our housing, our training—everything had to be the very best. He would insist on testing the prototypes for the various housing units to make sure that families would be happy in them."[4] Abdullah ordered that every Guard base should feature active adult education units. He also continued to resist any attempt to amalgamate the National Guard with the regular military. The powerful Sudairi Seven did not press the point. They were well aware that the National Guard was the ultimate guarantor of the survival of the House of Saud. They also accepted the equilibrium in the royal family's power balance that a non-Sudairi commander of the Guard brought. On his part, when Abdullah, the heir apparent, found himself being left out of the loop by the Sudairi Brothers when deciding high level policy, he chose not to protest while brooking no interference in running the National Guard.

Islamic Revolutionary Guards, the Iranian Regime's Ultimate Guarantor

Following Ayatollah Ruhollah Khomeini's 6 May 1979 decree to form the Islamic Revolutionary Guard to safeguard the revolution, it came into existence on 16 June. The IRGC helped suppress armed resistance and protest demonstrations by ethnic Arabs (in the oil-rich Khuzistan) and Kurds, demanding regional autonomy. In order to maintain internal security, it curbed the activities of the leftist groups which had earlier participated actively in the anti-royalist movement. It also helped the civilian authorities to purge all un-Islamic elements from the civil service, military and oil industry.

After the resignation of the government of Mahdi Bazargan in the wake of radical students' takeover of the US Embassy in Tehran, on 4 November 1979, IRGC accelerated the drive to purge the regular army of officers whose loyalties to the revolutionary regime were suspect. "The Iranian army… still has a royalist organization that has no connection at all with the current revolutionary Islamic regime," said Abbas Zamani, the IRGC commander. Apparently, there was much scope for a purge in the military. On the first anniversary of the revolution in February 1980, Defense Minister Mustapha Ali Chamran announced that 7,500 military personnel, mostly of high rank, had been dismissed during the past two months. But that was not enough since every officer who had received military training by the Pentagon was suspect. Their number ran into many thousands. Later the Constitution vested the authority to appoint the IRGC's commander with the Supreme Leader, who embodied the revolution.

Soon after the militant students' seizure of the American Embassy, Khomeini issued a decree to establish a paramilitary volunteer militia, *Niruyeh Muqqawwat Baseej* (Persian: "Resistance Force Mobilization"), commonly known as the Baseej. It was formed in April 1980, and was open to males below the age of eighteen and those above forty-five, as well as women. The regime used the country's 9,000 mosques as recruiting centers for Baseej and the IRGC. Most of those who joined had grown up in poor neighborhoods. With the outbreak of war with Iraq in September 1980, the IRGC was drafted into conventional warfare. Its battlefield achievements received more coverage on state-run radio and television than those of the military.

To thwart any incipient rivalry between the IRGC and Baseej, the Majlis incorporated the Baseej into the IRGC in February 1981, thus turning it into an auxiliary of the older, more powerful organization. Initially the Baseej was assigned to assist internal security and law enforcement, provide social services, organise religious ceremonies and act as morality police.

Politically, as 1981 unrolled, tensions between President Abol Hassan Bani-Sadr, who owed his success in the presidential contest to the backing Khomeini had given him, and the Majlis, dominated by the Islamic Republican Party (IRP), rose. Bani-Sadr attempted to cultivate his own base but failed. He then moved close to the leftist Mujahedin-e Khalq (Persian: People's Mujahedin, MeK) led by Masoud Rajavi. When the MeK refused to surrender its arms to the Islamic regime, it came in conflict with Khomeini.

To thwart the Iranian parliamentarians' move to impeach Bani-Sadr, the MeK and other smaller leftist and secular groups brought 200,000 pro-Bani-Sadr supporters to central Tehran on 19 June 1981. The government deployed IRGC troops to break up the demonstration. In the violent skirmishes that followed, thirty people, including fourteen guards, were killed.[5] The next day Bani-Sadr was impeached by 177 votes to one. Khomeini dismissed him. With that open warfare erupted between the government and the MeK. In late July Bani-Sadr and Rajavi flew clandestinely to Paris.

Rajavi devised a political-economic plan to overthrow the regime. It involved debilitating the Majlis through assassinations of IRP leaders, weakening the IRGC through repeated attacks, isolating Tehran by striking at rail and bus traffic, and destroying food reserves by burning storage silos. The Paris headquarters of the MeK claimed that in the two months since 20 June, party activists had killed 500 IRGC personnel and 40 Majlis deputies.[6] The IRGC was to play a critical role in frustrating MeK's strategy while the government resorted to executing MeK prisoners. The IRGC guarded all government and revolutionary buildings, which were illuminated by searchlights at night. On 8

COLD WAR IN THE ISLAMIC WORLD

February 1982 the IRGC raided an MeK hideout in Tehran and killed ten central committee members of the organization, thus decapitating its leadership. This virtually finished off MeK. By then it claimed to have killed 1,200 religious and political leaders of the regime. And the government put the number of MeK members it had executed at 4,000 whereas the MeK came up with a figure twice as high.[7]

The IRGC and Baseej were part of Iran's human wave strategy, involving 200,000 combatants. By staging a series of human waves on central fronts, the Iranians succeeded in encircling the Iraqi forces and destroyed three armored Iraqi divisions, regaining 24,500 sq km of Iranian territory. This tactic involved pressing forward waves of about 1,000 combatants, rocket propelled grenade launchers, at intervals of 200 to 300 meters with the aim of exhausting the ammunition supplies of the Iraqi troops and then overpowering them.[8]

During the next year about a fifth of 2.4 million volunteers did so. Often young Baseej members volunteered to act as vanguards in the human wave tactics that the Iranians mounted against the enemy, performing such dangerous tasks as removing mines. The teenagers had grown up in an environment of revolutionary fervor and were more dedicated to Islam than adult males. This, combined with adolescent daring and a romantic view of war explained their urge to be in the front line. "For them war is like a movie, with bullets whizzing past them but not through them," said one volunteer who had been to the front. "They are so macho that they don't even helmets and get blown up. But [they] feel they are on their way to heaven."[9] Unsurprisingly, the fatality rate among them was very high.

Meanwhile, after the establishment of its own ministry, the IRGC formed an elite division with the specific purpose of protecting Tehran against a possible military coup. The war had provided an opportunity for the IRGC to acquire battle experience and become proficient in handling heavy weapons and aircraft. In the spring of 1982 the IRGC was 170,000 strong and included both ground and air forces. It remained the regime's most reliable and most effective fighting force.[10]

During the tanker warfare phase, beginning in 1984 in the Iran-Iraq military conflict, Tehran integrated IRGC Navy's speedboats with sea mines, land-based anti-ship cruise missiles, and aircraft to attack civilian tanker shipping in the Gulf to undermine its foe, Iraq. The specific task of IRGC Navy was to deploy swarm tactics and speedboats to harass oil tankers off Kuwait and Saudi Arabia. By the time the Iran-Iraq War ended in 1988, the IRGC Navy had a large inventory of small fast attack craft and armed personnel who specialised in hit and run tactics on sea. It also had an ample arsenal of coastal defense and anti-ship cruise missiles and mines.

All told, by the late 1980s, the IRGC had proved its mettle in maintaining internal security and fighting an external foe. In that sense the decade-old IRGC of Iran was superior to Saudi Arabia's US-trained National Guard dating back to the founding of the Kingdom in 1932.

As in the case of Iran's military, the IRGC had a political-ideological department. Its task of infusing the ranks with Islamic ideology, as determined by Khomeini, was performed by the mullahs attached to each IRGC base through weekly sermons. This was a contrast to what prevailed in the Saudi Kingdom. There the stress was on impressing the personnel in the military as well as the National Guard to be loyal to the House of Saud, which based its legitimacy on the approval of the state-appointed Council of Senior Ulema (COSU). These differences stemmed from the varying circumstances in which the two regimes, both claiming Islamic legitimacy, had become major players in the Gulf.

After a hectic dozen years, covering the revolutionary movement, the founding of the Islamic Republic, waging the twentieth century's longest conventional war, and the death of Khomeini, Iranians craved normalcy, reconstruction and peaceful co-existence with neighbors. The newly elected President Ali Akbar Rafsanjani, who had his hand on the nation's pulse, registered the national mood, and acted accordingly, focusing at first on the economy and reconstruction.

Rafsanjani's Pragmatic Moderation

As a result of economic liberalisation introduced by President Ali Akbar Rafsanjani, Iran's annual growth rate in 1990–1991 soared to 10.5 per cent while inflation fell to 8 per cent. Guided by him the Majlis amalgamated police, gendarmerie and revolutionary Komitehs into the Law Enforcement Forces. In February 1992 at his behest, Supreme Leader Ayatollah Ali Khamanei decreed that there should be one head of the military and the IRGC, to be called the Chief of Staff of the Armed Forces General Command. In the region, the Hajj pilgrimage in Mecca in late May 1993 passed off peacefully with the Iranian pilgrims refraining from staging any demonstrations. Two weeks later the incumbent Rafsanjani won the presidential contest albeit with 64 per cent of the vote compared to 94 per cent in the previous poll. After his re-election he turned his attention to improving ties with Saudi Arabia where Abdullah bin Abdul Aziz Al Saud was the Crown Prince.

As the fruit of a union between two rival dynasties—Al Saud (father) and Al Rashid (mother)—Abdullah was by nature a reconciler. He was given to defusing internal tensions by conciliating political and religious dissidents at home. He seemed equally willing to bury the hatchet with the Islamic Republic. He found common ground with Rafsanjani in that both had ruled out friendly relations with Iraq so long as Saddam Hussein remained president.

The stampede during the stoning ceremony in Mina required of Hajj pilgrims on 23 May 1994, causing 270 deaths, had nothing to do with the Iranian contingent, which behaved peacefully. Soon afterwards, Rafsanjani deputed his son, Mahdi Rafsanjani, to confer with Crown Prince Abdullah at his summer retreat in Casablanca, Morocco, along with Iran's ambassador to Germany, Hussein Mousavian. They reviewed several aspects of Saudi-Iranian relations with Abdullah over four days. They briefed Rafsanjani in Tehran. Having judged that the preliminary exchange was satisfactory, Abdullah invited Mousavian and Mahdi Rafsanjani to Jeddah for further talks. To fit Abdullah's work pattern his interlocutors held late night sessions. He was in the habit of dividing his sleep in two parts—between midnight and the dawn prayer, and a long siesta during the afternoon.

The three of them agreed that Iraq was one corner of a strategic triangle, the other corners being Iran and Saudi Arabia, and that a stable Iraq was in the interest of both Riyadh and Tehran. When Abdullah referred to Iran's meddling in the politics of the Eastern Province, Mousavian alluded to the Saudis' interference in the Sunni-majority Iranian province of Sistan-Balochistan. The conferees settled for twice-a-year meetings between their countries' foreign ministers, and an annual exchange of visits by the heads of state. They also agreed to form a joint security commission. As a sign of goodwill, Abdullah gifted a piece of the *kiswa*, the black and gold fabric that covers the Kaaba and is renewed every year. Mousavian briefed Rafsanjani who went along with what he had agreed with Abdullah. But during their brief meeting with the ailing King Fahd, Mousavian and Mahdi Rafsanjani were exposed to an important caveat. Fahd told them that the Kingdom would not pursue building normal relations with Iran if that would undermine Riyadh's strategic interests with "another country"—a thinly disguised reference to the United States. Then the Iranian dignitaries did the Umrah (short Hajj) pilgrimage in Mecca as guests of Abdullah. In Tehran, President Rafsanjani and Mousavian conferred with Supreme Leader Khamanei, who sanctioned the deal that had been cut with the Saudis. He was moved to learn that Abdullah planned to build a summer home for his family near the Caspian Sea. He went on to buy a plot there, but a princely mansion did not materialise. Meanwhile, Abdullah's family visited Iran and Rafsanjani's family made a trip to the Saudi Kingdom.[11]

This was the background against which, at the behest of the Saudi Kingdom, the seventh summit of the Organisation of the Islamic Conference in Casablanca in December 1994 decided to hold the next triennial meeting in Tehran. Seen in the context of the internal dynamics of Saudi policy-making, this development showed that in the ongoing debate in the 1990s about the Kingdom's stance toward Iran, Abdullah prevailed over Defense Minister Prince Sultan bin Abdul Aziz who, along with his son Prince Bandar, then Saudi ambassador to the US, advocated an active anti-Tehran policy. Their advocacy dovetailed with the stance of President Bill Clinton's administration in the region, encapsulated in the Dual Containment doctrine adopted in May 1993. "'Dual Containment' derives from an assessment that current Iraqi and Iranian regimes are both hostile to the American interests in the region," explained Martin Indyk, Special Assistant to the President on Near East and South Asian Affairs. "Accordingly, we do not accept the argument that we should continue the old balance of power game, building up [one] to balance the other."[12]

Determined to play the reconciler in the region, Abdullah had opted for pursuing positive engagement with Iran even at the expense of displeasing Washington. After he became the de facto regent in the wake of the stroke that Fahd suffered on 19 November 1995, Riyadh's relations with Tehran became warmer.

Khobar Towers Bombing, a Blip

On 25 June 1996 terrorists blew up a fuel tanker truck parked near the low-walled compound of the eight-story residential complex, called the Khobar Towers, housing US Air Force personnel and their families near the King Abdul Aziz Air Base near Dhahran. The powerful explosion tore the face off one side of the Towers, killing nineteen airmen and injuring 372.[13] This attack highlighted the continued presence of US forces in the Kingdom which many Saudis came to equate with the presence of the Soviet soldiers in Afghanistan in the 1980s. It cast a shadow over improving Saudi-Iranian relations after Washington blamed Tehran for the attack. However, in the absence of cast-iron evidence provided by the US, Abdullah, the de facto regent of the Kingdom, chose to downplay the incident. The subsequent manhunt failed to find the culprits. But the Saudi government combined transferring US warplanes and personnel to the Prince Sultan Air Base at Al Kharj, situated sixty miles south of Riyadh, in a desert region. It would become the lynch-pin of the Pentagon's Middle East air command. Five years later, American forces' presence at this desert site would be exposed, deeply embarrassing the government.

According to Bruce Riedel, a US deputy assistant secretary of defence, who arrived at the devastated scene within hours, senior Saudi officials in Dhahran pinned the responsibility on Ahmad Ibrahim al Mughassil. A Shia native of Qatif, he was the military commander of the Hizbollah al Hijaz, also known as the Saudi Hizbollah, which was monitored by the Saudi intelligence. He was chosen by the Iranian government first to identify US facilities in the kingdom, and later to mastermind a terrorist assault on a high-profile military facility in coordination with the IRGC and the Lebanese Hizbollah, a Shia militia. He started the surveillance of the Khobar Towers and the nearby King Abdul Aziz Air Base in early 1994, and commuted between Eastern Province, Damascus and Lebanon while maintaining close contact with his Iranian handlers. According to the indictment issued by the US Department of Justice in 2001, cited by Riedel, while based in Damascus, Mughassil visited Dhahran periodically to oversee the surveillance and recruit local Shias for the attack. The ten metric ton bomb was most probably built by an expert of the Lebanese Hizbollah. On the appointed day, Mughassil parked the truck containing the massive bomb near the low protective wall of the Khobar Towers. The explosion he triggered by remote control was so powerful that the front wall of the residential tower collapsed. Mughassi allegedly fled to Iran. In its investigation, the US was denied full cooperation by Riyadh since—in Riedel's estimation—Crown Prince Abdullah reckoned that, armed with solid evidence of Tehran's involvement US President Clinton would order air strikes on Iranian targets which would in turn lead to retaliatory Iranian air strikes on Saudi Arabia. The Kingdom's Interior Minister Prince Nayef bin Abdul Aziz had his own reason not to share all the information on Saudi Hizbollah with the Americans, fearing that that would expose weaknesses in his ministry. However the Clinton Administration made enough progress in its investigation by June 1999 that, using Sultan Qaboos of Oman as the intermediary, it informed Tehran that it had credible information gathered by the FBI that the IRGC and Lebanese Hizbollah were involved in the terrorist attack. The Iranian government denied any involvement adding, curiously, that it was confident that there would be no further attacks. This did not satisfy Washington. Clinton retaliated by instructing the CIA to expose all IRGC and Iranian intelligence officers serving around the world under cover. This seemed to have chastened Tehran.[14]

Iranians Back Reformist Khatami

The victory of Sayyid Muhammad Khatami, a fifty-four-year-old black-turbaned reformist cleric, over his conservative rival Majlis Speaker Ali Akbar Nateq-Nouri—believed to be the favorite of Supreme Leader Khamanei—by an impressive margin of 44 per cent in the May 1997 presidential poll reassured the Saudi government. His surprise victory was welcomed in the West as well. "This clearly was an interesting election in Iran—unexpected to Iranians and unexpected to those who follow Iran," said Madeleine Albright, the Secretary of State since January 1997.[15] She had succeeded Warren Christopher who, as Deputy Secretary of State in the Carter Administration, had developed deep animosity towards Iran over the hostage crisis. Under Albright, Washington adopted a policy of "parallel responses", promising a positive US response to an amicable gesture by Tehran. With that, Saudi policymakers saw a window of opportunity to thaw US-Iran relations.

The positive comment by Clinton and Albright on Khatami's election went down well among the Saudi royals who were also pleased to note that Khatami retained many of Rafsanjani's ministers and advisers to run his team. Khamanei's decision to name Rafsanjani chairman of the Expediency Consultation Council System, charged with conciliating differences between the President and the Majlis, was another positive sign for Riyadh. A month after Khatami was sworn in as President in August, Saudi Arabia allowed Iran Air to resume flights to the Kingdom.

Khatami would combine his policy of détente in the region with a campaign for broader international dialogue. His call to the UN during his September 1998 speech to the General Assembly to declare a year of "Dialogue Among Civilizations" would be accepted with 2001 so named.[16]

A multi-linguist, Khatami was a man of many parts. He was born in the household of Sayyid Ahmad Khatami, a descendant of the Prophet Muhammad, in the central Iranian city of Yazd. After obtaining a degree in Western philosophy at Isfahan University, he acquired a master's in education from Tehran University. Then, as required by law, he was drafted into the Imperial Army where he served as a second lieutenant for two years. He then spent seven years studying Islamic sciences in the holy city of Qom, and qualified as mujtahid, one who applies interpretative reasoning to the Sharia. In 1978 the religious establishment in Qom sent him to Hamburg to head the Islamic Center that ran a Shia mosque. There he learnt German and English. He was a member of the Association of the Militant Clergy. After the revolution he was elected to the First Majlis. Ayatollah Ruhollah Khomeini appointed him chairman of the state-run Kayhan Newspapers. In 1982 he was named Minister of Culture and Islamic Guidance. He was confirmed in that post by two subsequent parliaments. When the conservative-dominated 1992 Majlis objected to his liberal views, he resigned. President Rafsanjani then appointed him an adviser to the Presidential Office while he also served as head of the National Library. Such a curriculum vitae was set to impress both religious and secular leaders in foreign capitals.

On 26 November 1997, Khatami invited King Fahd to the summit of the OIC in Tehran on 9–11 December. But, having suffered a near-fatal heart attack earlier in the month, Fahd declined. Instead, Crown Prince

Abdullah led a large Saudi delegation at the OIC gathering. Khatami embraced him with kisses on both cheeks at Tehran's airport.

Tehran Hosts Islamic Summit

With the full turnout of the leaders of the fifty-five members of the OIC addressed by the UN Secretary-General Kofi Annan, Iran achieved a diplomatic coup. President Khatami set the harmonious tone of the conference. "Islamic and Western civilizations are not necessarily in conflict and contradiction," he declared. Citing Greek and Roman roots of the West, he said, "We should never be oblivious to the careful acquisitions of the Western civil society."[17]

It was in that spirit that Crown Prince Abdullah stated that "We have to eliminate the obstacles which block the way [toward amity] and giving counsel on a reciprocal basis between Muslim countries." He condemned terrorism and extremism in the Muslim world. He praised "the immortal achievements of the Muslims of Iran and their invaluable contributions," and added that, "It is no wonder that Tehran is hosting this important Islamic gathering." He condemned terrorism and extremism in the Muslim world. He stated that "I do not think it would be difficult for the brotherly Iranian people and its leadership and for a big power like the United States to reach a solution to any disagreement between them. ...There is nothing that will make us more happy than to see this sensitive part of the world enjoy stability, security and prosperity...If the United States asks us we will not hesitate to contribute to efforts to bring stability to the region."[18] But the disagreements between Iran and the US were too fundamental to be resolved by a third party tied to Washington.

Abdullah held two rounds of private talks with Khatami. During the second round Khatami departed from protocol by calling on the Saudi leader in his suite for a meeting that lasted forty-five minutes. He reportedly advised his host that Iran must convince Washington that it was no longer a threat to the Gulf monarchies. Since Abdullah also had a meeting with Khamanei, known for his hostility towards America, which he routinely described as "the arrogant power," it was assumed that he offered the same advice to the Supreme Leader as well. If so, as a graceful host, he would have lent Abdullah a sympathetic ear, nothing more.

American diplomats regarded the prestige that Iran gained from hosting the OIC summit as a setback to their policy of isolating Tehran. Much as they disliked the event they could not ignore it altogether. The State Department had nice words to say about the condemnation of terrorism in the Tehran Declaration which, pointedly, distinguished terrorism from "struggle of people against colonialism or alien domination or foreign occupation." Responding to this overture, at his 14 December press conference Khatami referred to "the great American people," and added that he wanted a dialogue in "the not too distant future." The next day Clinton said that he would welcome that "as long as we have an honest discussion of all relevant issues"—meaning Iran's sponsorship of international terrorism, its efforts to acquire nuclear weapons, and its opposition to the Middle East peace process.[19] There was no mention of the subjects that were of interest to Tehran.

On 7 January 1998, Khatami gave an interview to CNN in two parts—an unedited speech, followed by questions by Christiane Amanpour, an American journalist of Iranian origin. Khatami said, "First there must be a crack in this 'wall of distrust' between the two governments," and that "we must definitely consider the factors that led to severance of relations and try to eliminate them." He added, "If negotiations are not based on mutual respect, they will never lead to positive results." Specifically, he proposed an increase in the exchange of cultural, academic and sports delegations. In his answers to Amanpour, he described the hostage-taking of American diplomats as "a tragedy."[20]

The next day, the US state department spokesman, James Rubin, confirmed that top US officials had watched the program. He said, "President Khatami's extensive comments with respect to US civilization and values were interesting. We appreciated the spirit in which those remarks were offered. We also noted the president's comments that the conduct of relations between nations must be based on mutual respect and dignity; we agree. …We noted with interest his regret concerning the hostage taking. We welcome his statement that this period in Iranian history is over and that rule of law should be respected domestically and internationally. On terrorism, Khatami's rejection and condemnation of all forms of terrorism directed at innocents was noteworthy."[21]

These events were enough to convince Abdullah that Iran's leaders had accepted his advice and acted accordingly. This in turn set the foundation for an eventual amity between Riyadh and Tehran.

Saudis' Red Carpet for Rafsanjani

In the ongoing Saudi-Iranian reconciliation process, extending over a few years, Rafsanjani played an active role. In the second half of February 1998, accepting an official invitation, he led a large delegation on a ten-day tour of Saudi Arabia to warm bilateral relations. His party included members of Khamanei's inner circle, important Majlis deputies, and Oil Minister Bijan Namdar Zanganeh and his deputies.

Rafsanjani's historic visit came at a time when oil prices had plunged to their lowest levels in nearly four years. There was reduced demand in the Asian market caused by a dramatic drop in the so-called tiger economies of south-eastern Asian nations. The UN oil-for-food deal allowed Iraq to sell oil abroad in 1996 after a gap of six years. The northern hemisphere had a mild winter. Finally there was oversupply of petroleum because Saudi Arabia, aided by Kuwait and the United Arab Emirates, had raised the OPEC output ceiling by 10 per cent to 27.5 million barrels per day (bpd) at the OPEC's Jakarta meeting in November 1997.

Rafsanjani had meetings with Fahd, Abdullah and Defense Minister Prince Sultan bin Abdul Aziz. He visited the Consultative Shura Council and talked to its luminaries. He held a series of meetings with businessmen in Riyadh, Jeddah and Dammam. He toured the industrial city of Jubail in Eastern Province, and later conferred with Shia leaders.[22] While giving extensive coverage to the ground-breaking tour of the Saudi Kingdom by a high Iranian official, who had been an intimate confidante of Ayatollah Khomeini for many years, the state-run Iran Republic News Agency (IRNA) referred to King Fahd as the Custodian of Two Holy Mosques, which the Saudi monarch had decreed twelve years earlier.

In the religious sphere, Rafsanjani met Grand Mufti Shaikh Abdul Aziz bin Baz. And, during their Umrah in Mecca, he and his aides were given the rare privilege of praying *inside* the Kaaba. Taking their cue from the Royal Court, the obsequious Saudi media attached the honorific of "His Reverence the Shaikh" to Rafsanjani. To some Wahhabi clerics, such deference to a Shia mullah was beyond the pale. Among them was Shaikh Abdul Rahman Hafizi. He devoted almost half of his sermon at the Friday prayers in the Prophet's Mosque in Medina, broadcast live, to attacking Shias, Ayatollah Khomeini and Iran's Islamic revolution, well aware that Rafsanjani was in the congregation. A report by IRNA said that Rafsanjani, familiar with Arabic, walked out in protest. Later when Abdullah apologised for Hafizi's speech to Rafsanjani in private, Rafsanjani reportedly said, "In Iran we have many clergymen like that; if in the Kingdom there is only one, there is no need to worry." Nonetheless, Abdullah got the offending cleric sacked—an action that went unmentioned in the Saudi media but was much applauded by the Iranian media. Overall, the mood to conciliate with the Saudi Kingdom was so strong that even the hard line Ayatollah Ahmad Jannati in his Friday prayer sermon in Tehran said that "We have had differences with Saudi Arabia in the past," but "these cannot remain. [Now] we should work together and join as Muslim brothers... We Muslims must wake from our slumber and join together."[23]

In its report on the Fahd-Rafsanjani talks, IRNA said that "The Saudi king told Ayatollah Rafsanjani that Iran and Saudi Arabia as two important nations of the world and also of the region must collaborate in every issue of their mutual interest including oil, OPEC, and regional matters." It added that King Fahd "promised that his country would have closer cooperation with Iran for maintaining oil prices at reasonable rates in the future." At the same time, IRNA quoted Rafsanjani as saying that "mutual good understanding between petroleum exporting countries would certainly prevent a downturn in oil prices," and that "the Muslim world can rely on its own indigenous resources to solve those problems without the interference of non-Muslim alien powers." The last statement was de rigueur for an Iranian official of any standing since this was the core of Tehran's policy as stated in its constitution. The report of the state-run Saudi Press Agency (SPA) differed from IRNA's. It merely stated that the two leaders had "discussed relations between the Kingdom of Saudi Arabia and the Islamic Republic of Iran and issues in the Islamic and international arenas," and provided no details.[24] Following Zanganeh's meeting with his Saudi counterpart, Ali Naimi, they issued a joint statement expressing willingness to work together towards reversing the oil price downturn. "Mountains of ice were melted during my visit," said Rafsanjani, summarizing his experience. "I felt that Saudi Arabia too has realized that the way to solve our regional problems is through cooperation with Iran."[25]

Multiple Areas of Cooperation

On the eve of the Hajj on 6 April 1998, the Saudi monarch invited Khatami to be his guest for the pilgrimage for which the Kingdom had raised Iran's quota. Because of his earlier commitments, Khatami could not accept the offer, and added that he would come "as soon as possible".

After this annual ritual Iran's Supreme Leader Khamanei declared it a success for the Iranian pilgrims, and added that ties with the Saudi Kingdom were "good," hoping that diplomatic relations with Riyadh would improve by the day within "an acceptable framework." At the same time he asserted that "We do not give up our basic beliefs at any price and cannot [therefore] forgo the 'Disavowal of Infidels' at Hajj ceremonies—we try rather to perform it as much as possible."[26] Here again Khamanei was restating the interpretation about "Disavowal of Infidels" that the Islamic Republic's founder, Khomeini, had offered. The current Supreme Leaders described it as part of "our basic beliefs." The next month, May, the two countries inked a Comprehensive Cooperation Agreement which covered economic, commercial, technical, scientific, cultural, and sports fields and also included cooperation in providing consular services, expansion of communications services, air and sea transport and environmental issues.[27]

As required by law, the State Department issued its annual report on the countries listed as state sponsors of terrorism in May 1998, with Iran being one of them.[28] It described Iran as "the most active sponsor of state terrorism in 1997." It provided money and arms to radical Palestinian Hamas and Islamic Jihad. And its agents carried out the assassinations of at least thirteen leaders of Mujahedin-e Khalq and the Kurdistan Democratic Party of Iran. Operating from the quasi-independent Iraqi Kurdistan protected by the US, these organizations staged pin-prick attacks on Iran.[29] This routine US report had no impact on the evolving Saudi-Iranian cordiality. It is worth noting that since at least the early 1970s Israel carried out targeted assassinations abroad of those it believed had attacked its citizens or interests, later extending its list to those Arabs or Iranian nuclear physicists believed to be engaged in the development of atomic bombs.[30] At the OPEC meeting on 23 March 1999, Saudi Arabia, backed by Iran, succeeded in an agreement to cut overall OPEC output of 23 million bpd by 1.7 million bpd with four non–OPEC countries—Mexico, Norway, Oman and Russia—reducing their production by 400,000 bpd. The petroleum price improved from $13 a barrel to $18, raising Iran's oil income by $2.5 billion to $13 billion, and enabling it to reduce its long and short-term loans by a quarter to $11.6 billion.[31] Meanwhile high level visits by Saudi and Iranian ministers to their respective capitals continued. The Kingdom's Foreign Minister Saud Al Faisal spent two days in April to confer with his Iranian counterpart Kamal Kharrazi.

Far more significant was the five-day visit that Saudi Defence and Aviation Minister Sultan bin Abdul Aziz undertook in early May 1999. After his interaction with Prince Sultan, Iran's Defence Minister Admiral Ali Shamskhani described Prince Sultan's visit as "a turning point in our relations," and proposed a military pact with Riyadh to defend the Gulf region. This has been Tehran's agenda since the 1979 revolution. Sultan moved quickly to cool Shamskhani's ardor. "It is too early to look at defense pacts," he said. "The option of a defense pact is not viable between two states whose relations were severed for years", he argued. "We should start with economic, social and cultural cooperation." To reassure the remaining Gulf monarchies, Sultan asserted that "Any direct cooperation with Iran to guarantee the protection of the Gulf is quite inadmissible." As a minor concession, though, he agreed to exchange military attaches.[32]

Sultan's meeting with Iran's Vice President Hassan Habibi on improving trade and cultural ties was fruitful. Among other things they agreed to increase flights between the two states.[33]

When King Fahd invited President Khatami to the Kingdom, some of Khamanei's close aides advised against acceptance. But they were overruled when Rafsanjani intervened in favor of accepting the invitation. It was the first time that the serving President of the Islamic Republic of Iran was so honored by Saudi Arabia. On 15 May Khatami was welcomed at Jeddah international airport by King Fahd, then confined to a wheelchair, Crown Prince Abdullah, and other senior princes who showered him with embraces and kisses on both cheeks. During his three-day stay Khatami had cordial talks with them as well as other senior members of the government, and rounded off his trip with Umrah in Mecca.

Following his meeting with Khatami, King Fahd declared that "The door is wide open to develop and strengthen relations between the two countries in the interests of the two peoples and the Muslim world" As required by diplomatic protocol, Khatami extended an invitation to Fahd to visit Tehran. However, given the precarious health of the monarch, such a trip was unlikely. After his talks with Iran's Foreign Minister Kharrazi, Prince Saud Al Faisal said that that there was potentially no limit to the extent of ties between the two states. He then added an important caveat just as Defense Minister Sultan had done. "The main ingredient for establishing solid relations is confidence-building. For that we need to settle outstanding problems peacefully and amicably."[34]

In sum, the main purpose of Rafsanjani's extended trip in February 1998 was to build a bridge between Saudi Arabia and Iran. Using his charm and shrewdness he achieved that goal, and much traffic flowed across that bridge in the succeeding months. The unspoken agenda of Khatami was to cap economic, cultural and diplomatic ties with a bilateral security pact. Given a history of hostility and tensions between Tehran and Riyadh, this was a Herculean task. The idea of military cooperation between Saudi Arabia, which had depended on the US for its external security since 1943, and the Islamic Republic of Iran, where hostility towards America was an article of faith, was too far-fetched to be considered seriously. Yet, Iran's politicians and media kept harping on the subject, which in the Casablanca talks had appeared under the heading of "joint security commission." In return, Saudi officials started explaining publicly that any such compact would apply to internal security and mutual non-interference in the other country's internal affairs, and that this was their final word.

And so it happened. But to assuage Iran's disappointment, Saudi Interior Minister Prince Nayef bin Abdul Aziz traveled to Tehran in April 2001 to sign the "security" agreement with his Iranian counterpart, Abdolvahed Mousavi-Lari. It covered countering organised crime, terrorism and drug trafficking. When at their joint press conference it was pointed out that it did not cover extradition of suspected criminals, Nayef found himself having to deny that this omission had anything to do with the 1996 Al Khobar bombing. There were persistent reports that the Saudi government was sceptical about Tehran's denials in that terrorist act. But it was unwilling to let that slow down the advance towards cordial relations with Tehran.[35] A by-product of this stance was that there was an easing of official pressure on Saudi Shias in Eastern Province.

The Tehran-Washington Minuet

During his visit to New York to address the UN General Assembly in September 1998, Khatami explained to a group of US journalists that a dialogue among peoples and cultures was different from political dialogue. Iran had no intention of engaging in a political dialogue with an American administration until it had taken "concrete steps to change its policies towards Iran."

President Clinton stated in April 1999 that, somehow, a way had to be found to get dialogue started. In August, John Lambert of the State Department, speaking in Persian on US-funded Radio Liberty, said that the United States was ready to enter into negotiations with Iran "without any preconditions". Tehran was not satisfied. As a sign of goodwill, it wanted Washington's policy changed on the following areas: the 1996 Iran-Libya Sanctions Act, continued freezing of Iran's assets in America, pressuring Iran's neighbor to adopt anti-Tehran policies, and beaming hostile propaganda at Iranian audiences. Later that month Clinton reportedly addressed a letter to Khatami through Sultan Qaboos of Oman. In it he requested assistance from Iran, based on the report by FBI director Louis Freeh that the three Saudi suspects in the Al Khobar bombing, believed to be linked to the Saudi Hizbollah, had taken refuge in Iran. The FBI was not satisfied with the information given by Riyadh, and wanted to question these suspects. The Iranian government repeated its earlier denial of any involvement in this bombing.[36]

The impact of Clinton and Albright welcoming reformists' success in the Majlis election in early 2000 was countered by the US Senate passing almost unanimously the Iran Non-Proliferation Act which had been adopted unanimously by the House of Representatives in September

1999. It authorized the US President to take punitive action against individuals or organizations known to be providing material aid to Iran's weapons of mass destruction program. On 13 March Clinton renewed his executive order of 1995 barring trade with Iran because "Its support for international terrorism, its efforts to undermine the Middle East peace process, and its acquisition of nuclear weapons," continued to threaten the national security and economy of the United States.[37]

Then, in the now familiar pattern, came a step forward. In her speech to the Princeton-based American-Iranian Council, on 17 March 2000, Albright admitted that America had created a climate of mistrust with Tehran by playing a "significant role" in the 1953 coup against Muhammad Mussadiq and providing longstanding support for Muhammad Reza Shah Pahlavi. She regretted the past "shortsightedness" in US policy, particularly the Iran-Iraq War, when Washington backed Baghdad. She then held out an olive branch. She promised to "increase efforts" towards "a global settlement of Iran's claims of its frozen assets in America"—a departure from the case-by-case basis used by the Iran-US Claims Tribunal in the Hague since 1981. She also announced that the US was lifting its ban on imports of Iranian carpets, caviar, pistachios and dried fruit, thus reversing a decision taken in early 1987 by the Ronald Reagan administration. (However at $85 million these Iranian exports were only 8 per cent of the total.) "I call upon Iran to join us in writing a new chapter in our shared history," she concluded. The Iranian response was mixed. "Iran thinks it [Albright's speech] is positive and welcomes it," said Hamid Reza Asefi, the foreign ministry spokesman. He added that Iran would now allow imports of US food and medicine. But Khamanei was not satisfied since it did not include an apology. Taking a middle position, Foreign Minister Kharrazi later welcomed certain elements of Albright's speech, but added that her initiative was "polluted" by continued American interference in Iran's internal affairs,[38] the latest example being the State Department's condemnation of how the Iranian authorities had dealt with the student protest in July 1999 followed by a Senate resolution to that effect.

In short, there was some relaxation in tension between Tehran and Washington but there was no sign of the easing of the long-running stalemate that Saudi Crown Prince Abdullah wished for.

With George W. Bush, a Republican, succeeding Clinton in the White House in January 2001, the end of the Tehran-Washington minuet seemed imminent. Before his election, Bush was coached on the politics of the Middle East by the neo-conservative Richard Perle, a staunch anti-Iran supporter of Israel. Bush was therefore expected to adopt an uncompromising policy toward Tehran, and show none of the flexibility Clinton had.

In contrast, Abdullah remained a fixture in the Riyadh-Washington-Tehran triangulation, with his pledge to Tehran to help ease its relations in the Arab world in return for continued moderation in its foreign policy. Abdullah encouraged Bahrain, Qatar and the United Arab Emirates (UAE) to warm their relations with Tehran. As a result, Qatar received Khatami as a state guest in May 1999. Kuwait and Oman, the remaining members of the Gulf Cooperation Council, had already forged cordial ties with Iran.

THE GULF RIVALS' EASTWARD MARCH

"Down in the plain, a blur of smoke, trees, and houses announced Mashhad, the holy city of the Shias," wrote Robert Byron in his classic *The Road to Oxiana*, on 21 November 1933. "A gold dome flashed, a blue dome loomed, out of the cold autumnal haze. Century by century since Imam Reza was interred beside Caliph Harun al Rashid, this vision has refreshed the desert-weary sight of pilgrims, merchants, armies, kings, and travelers—to become the last hope of several dozen fretful passengers in a damaged motor-bus."

At the shrine, Byron continued, "Turcomans, Kazakhs, Tajiks and Hazaras throng its approaches, mingling with the dingy crowds of pseudo-European Persians. The police are frightened of these fanatics, so that access to the Shrine is still denied to the infidels despite the official anti-clerical policy [of Reza Shah Pahlavi] which is opening the mosques elsewhere."

Two funerals transformed the capital of Khorasan from Tus to Mashhad—meaning Place of Martyrdom—he explained. "In 809 Caliph Harun al Rashid, on his way to quell a rebellion in Merv [in today's Turkmenistan] was taken ill at Tus, died, and was buried in a holy place twenty miles off, which is now Mashhad. In 816 his son Mamoun [al Rashid], based in Merv, summoned the eighth Imam of Shias, Ali al Rida (aka, Reza) of Medina, to proclaim him heir to the Caliphate [in order to end periodic Shia revolts]. But Imam Reza died at Tus while accompanying Mamoun on a visit to his father's grave. In orthodox doctrine, he died of a surfeit of grapes. But Shias believe Mamoun poisoned him [because he had proved very popular]. He was buried next to Harun al Rashid and his tomb became, after that of Imam Ali in Najaf, the holiest place in the Shia world. So the Shrine grew up, and [so did] the city round it."

On 24 December 1933, "Attended by an unhappy police officer, I spent the morning on various roofs examining the Shrine through field-glasses from the other side of the circular street," continued Byron. "There are three main courts, each with four ivans [also spelt ayvan].[1] Two of the courts point north and south; [and] the tile work on these looks like the chintz, dating from the 17th or 18th century. The third court points west—at right angles to the north and south courts. This is the mosque that Gohar Shad [wife of Shah Rukh (1377–1447), son of Tamerlane] built between 1405 and 1418. Above the sanctuary chamber at the end, which is linked by two enormous minarets, rises the sea-blue dome, bulbous in shape, inscribed on the bulge with bold black Kufic, and festooned from the apex with thin yellow tendrils. The mosaic of the whole court appears to be still intact. ... I must and will penetrate this mosque before I leave Persia. But not now. In the spring."

On 7 May 1934, Byron and his companion Christopher Sykes blackened their faces. "A broken-down Victoria [carriage] drove to the main gate of the [Imam Reza] Shrine where we dismounted, but instead of entering, turned to the right up the circular avenue. 'Are you ready?' said the guide, and dived into a dark tunnel. We followed like rabbits, found ourselves in a little yard, scurried down a lighted bazaar full of booths and purchasers, and came out in the great court of the Mosque of Gohar Shad."

The sight mesmerized Byron. "Amber lights twinkled in the void, glowing unseen from the mighty arch before the sanctuary. Reflecting a soft blaze over the gilded entrance to the tomb opposite, and revealing, as the eye adapted itself, a vast quadrilateral defined by ranks of arches. An upper tier rose out of reach of the lights, and, passing through a zone of invisibility, reappeared as a black parapet against the stars. Turbaned mullahs, white-robed Afghans, vanished like ghosts between the orbits of the lamps, gliding across the black pavement to prostrate themselves beneath the golden doorway. A sound of chanting was heard from the sanctuary, where a single tiny figure could be seen abased in the dimness, at the feet of its lustured mihrab... Every circumstance of sight, sound, and trespass conspired to swamp the intelligence. The message of a work of art overcame this conspiracy, forcing it way out of the shadows, insisting on structure and proportion, on the impress of superlative quality, and on the intellect behind them... An epoch, the Timurids, Gohar Shard herself, and the architect Kayamuddin, ruled the night."[2]

The other mosque that Gohar Shard built was in Herat in present day Afghanistan. She spent sixty of her eighty-four years of life in this city which was the capital of an empire stretching from the Tigris to Sinkiang. "Herat stands in a long cultivated plain stretching east and west, being three miles equidistant from the Hari river in the south, and the last spurs of the Paropamisus mountains to the north," noted Byron. "Herat lies midway between the two halves of the empire of Timur Beg [aka, Tamerlane], Persia and Oxiana, and of the two roads which join them, it commands the easier." Gohad Shard married Shah Rukh in 1388, and delivered Ulugh Beg six years later. The people of Herat remembered her not as the builder of outstanding mosques but as "a personality," and for "the versatility of her life."[3]

Little wonder that in today's Herat, the third largest Afghan city after Kabul and Kandahar, the everyday spoken language is Tajik, akin to Persian. When Muhammad Reza Shah Pahlavi extended his influence to the Republic of Afghanistan after 1973–1974, he faced no competition from the Saudi Kingdom. Later, in the civil war that erupted in Afghanistan after the overthrow of the leftist Muhammad Najibullah government in 1992, the pro-Tehran Wahdat militia allied with the Tajik-dominated Northern Alliance led by Ahmad Shah Masoud against the Pushtun-dominated coalition backed by Pakistan and Saudi Arabia.

Afghanistan, a New Battleground

Crown Prince Abdullah bin Abdul Aziz continued the earlier Saudi official policy of aiding the Taliban. In April 1996 the Taliban's spiritual leader, Mullah Muhammad Omar, was annointed as the Commander of the Faithful by 1,200 Sunni clerics and tribal leaders in the southern city of Kandahar. In mid-June 1996, Prince Turki arrived in Kandahar where Taliban leaders secretly discussed with him obtaining further Inter-Services Intelligence (ISI) logistical support, costing $5 million, which they needed in order to capture Kabul before winter set in. Riyadh provided the Taliban with 400 Toyota pick-up trucks and financial aid. And thousands of new recruits from Afghan refugee camps and madrassas arrived to enlist with the Taliban.[4]

Meanwhile, in their Friday sermons, *ulema* in Saudi Arabia boosted support for the Taliban, and collected donations for them at mosques. This continued after the Taliban had captured Kabul on 27 September, overthrowing the regime of President Burhanuddin Rabbani and his defence minister, Masoud—both of them ethnic Tajiks—who were backed by Tehran. At the Royal Court in Jeddah, Grand Mufti bin Baz lobbied on behalf of the Taliban. In return the latter showed their reverence for the House of Saud and Saudi ulema by adopting the Committee for the Propagation of Virtue and the Prevention of Vice, set up four years earlier, and upgraded it to ministerial level by renaming it the Department of the Promotion of Virtue and the Prevention of Vice.

Mullah Omar imposed his fanatically puritanical version of the Sharia on the region under his control. He required women to wear a *burqa*, and men to don salwar-kameez and a turban, grow beards, and attend the mosque for prayers daily. He banned nail polish, lipstick and make-up for women. He closed all girls' schools and forbade women from working outside the home. His blanket ban on music and television resulted in the destruction of audio- and video-tapes as well as television sets. The reason for prohibiting music, singing and dancing was that they aroused lust and led to fornication, thus undermining marital fidelity and stable family structures, the foundations of a truly Islamic social order. He also prohibited such leisure activities as chess, football, kite flying and pigeon racing. The reason for banning kite flying and pigeon racing was that they were done from flat roofs which enabled boys and men to look into the women's quarters of neighboring houses. To prevent idolatry, he ordered the tearing up of all pictures and portraits. He outdid the Wahhabis by banning photography. He outlawed gambling and charging of interest on loans. He prescribed compulsory prayer, and banned all transport during prayer times.[5]

The Taliban's dramatic triumph was viewed negatively in Iran as well as Russia and Central Asia. As expected, Pakistan and Saudi Arabia were quietly jubilant for having trounced Tehran's plans and placed their protégé in power. Unexpectedly, though, instead of raising alarm at the victory of the most diehard Islamic fundamentalist party, US State Department spokesperson Glyn Davies said there was nothing "objectionable" about the domestic policies pursued by the Taliban.[6] This did not surprise foreign observers. With Warren Christopher heading the State Department, the US was locked into a rigidly anti-Tehran stance. "Between 1994 and 1996 the US supported the Taliban through its allies Pakistan and Saudi Arabia politically, essentially, because Washington viewed the Taliban as anti-Iranian, anti-Shia, and pro-Western," wrote Pakistani journalist Ahmed Rashid in his book *Taliban*. "The US conveniently ignored the Taliban's Islamic fundamentalist agenda, its suppression of women and the consternation they created in Central Asia."[7]

While the ruling clerics in Tehran were quick to condemn particularly the Taliban's ban on women's education, describing it as contrary to the Quranic verse which enjoins all believers, irrespective of their gender, to acquire knowledge, the State Department remained silent on the subject for several weeks during which it announced the dispatch of its envoy to Kabul to confer with the Taliban regime.

For the next three months the Taliban captured province after province, often by bribing local warlords with funds supplied first by the Pakistani ISI and later by the Saudi intelligence agency. But their advance further north was stopped by the heavy air and artillery bombardment by Masoud's Tajik forces. The Taliban lost the momentum that had so far gained them a third of Afghanistan.

Enter Osama bin Laden

Once the Taliban had consolidated its position in Kabul, Mullah Omar instructed Prime Minister

Mullah Muhammad Rabbani to talk to Osama bin Laden, the leader of Al Qaida, who, after arriving in Jalalabad in May 1996 after his expulsion from Sudan, had moved to the Tora Bora cave complex near the Pakistani border. As a staunch Wahhabi, he considered Shias heretics. After several meetings with Taliban envoys, during which bin Laden praised the Taliban's achievements and took an oath of allegiance

167

to Mullah Omar, he received the protection of the regime. The ISI worked covertly to bring about an alliance between Omar and bin Laden, who took up residence at the airport near Kandahar. He and Mullah Omar became close friends. Engaging in night-long conversations, they came to share common views, politically and religiously, with Mullah Omar gradually turning against America and the West, and losing interest in gaining their recognition of his regime. Bin Laden started to lend the services of his seasoned Afghan and Arab fighters and his vehicles to the Taliban during the latter's campaigns to extend their realm, and was generous in his cash contributions to them.

Having brought 70 per cent of the country under his jurisdiction by early 1997, Mullah Omar resolved to expel the anti-Taliban forces from the rest of Afghanistan. In April 1997, Taliban Prime Minister Rabbani traveled to Riyadh and met King Fahd. He said, "Since Saudi Arabia is the center of the Muslim world, we would like to have Saudi assistance." In return King Fahd expressed his approval of measures taken by the Taliban especially over the imposition of the Sharia in Afghanistan. Five months later more aid arrived from Riyadh.[8]

The Taliban met stiff resistance in its attempt to seize the northern city of Mazar-e Sharif, the opposition's main base where President Burhanuddin Rabbani had joined Gen. Abdul Rashid Dostum, an ethnic Uzbek. They overcame it by bribing individual commanders. President Rabbani fled to Tajikistan. This provided the rationale for Pakistan formally to recognize the Taliban regime on 26 May 1997, and establish diplomatic relations. Saudi Arabia and the United Arab Emirates (UAE) soon followed suit. Mullah Omar changed the name of the country from the Islamic State of Afghanistan to the Islamic Emirate of Afghanistan.

The loss of Mazar-e Sharif to the Taliban shocked Islam Karimov, the secular president of Uzbekistan, so much that he overcame his antipathy towards Iran. He allowed Tehran—along with the Russians and the Turks—to use Uzbek territory to transfer weapon supplies to Dostum's forces. Thus fortified, Dostum regained Mazar-e Sharif. He combined his National Islamic Movement with Northern Alliance to form the United National Islamic Front. But the Taliban regarded the loss of Mazar-e Sharif as only a temporary setback.

Around this time, Bin Laden declared that he and Al Qaida aimed to target Americans and Jews worldwide and to "liberate" Islam's holiest sites from the Saudi royal family. That prompted King Fahd to dispatch Prince Turki to Kandahar in June 1998 to confer with Mullah Omar. According to Turki, they agreed to form a joint committee to arrange the details of bin Laden's extradition to the Saudi Kingdom.[9]

In the ongoing Afghan civil war, the Taliban, now openly backed by Pakistan and Saudi Arabia, mounted a series of offensives in the spring and summer of 1998. Their fighters regained Mazar-e Sharif, won control of five more provinces centered round Mazar and routed Dostum's forces, leaving only four of the thirty-two provinces in opposition hands. Dostum fled to Turkey, and the National Islamic Front reverted to being the Tajik-dominated Northern Alliance. In the larger context, the emergence of the Taliban as the predominant force in Afghanistan split the region into two camps, with Pakistan and Saudi Arabia on one side; and Iran, Central Asia, Russia and India on the other.

Iran and the Taliban Eyeball-to-Eyeball

Following the Taliban's seizure of Mazar-e Sharif, ten diplomats and one journalist at the Iranian consulate "disappeared." The Taliban claimed that these individuals had been involved in arms transfers to their enemies and had fled the city when they captured Mazar. Tehran alleged that they had been taken to Kandahar, Mullah Omar's headquarters.

Tempers rose sharply in Iran. "We are opposed to the Taliban's vision of Islam," Rafsanjani told the Friday prayer congregation in Tehran. "We are opposed to their ideology and their war mongering." Tehran announced military exercises near Torbat-e Jam, 40 kilometers (25 miles) from the Afghan frontier. "These exercises are not without links to the new situation in Afghanistan," said Major General Yahya Safavi, commander of the Islamic Revolutionary Guard Corps (IRGC), charged with protecting the country's borders.[10] On 1 September 1998, the IRGC started its annual exercises, involving 70,000 troops, near the Afghan border.

Meanwhile, on 7 August 1998 huge bombs exploded at the US embassies in Nairobi and Dar as Salam, killing 227 people, including twelve Americans. The Bill Clinton administration held bin Laden responsible for these blasts, and called on the Taliban to hand him over.

Mullah Omar refused, arguing that bin Laden was a guest not only of the government but the people of Afghanistan.

On 20 August 1998, having obtained reliable intelligence that bin Laden was at the al Badr camp in the Khost region to address 200–300 Al Qaida members, around 2300 hours local time, Clinton ordered strikes at six camps in the Zhawar Killial Badr complex. According to the Pentagon, this complex, covering sixty buildings and fifty caves, constituted training as well as base and support camps. As part of its Operation Infinite Reach, the Pentagon fired, from the Abraham Lincoln aircraft carrier in the Arabian Sea, 75 Tomahawk cruise missiles through Pakistani airspace at six camps. The strikes killed twenty-six people, all of them Pakistanis or Kashmiris. Bin Laden had left the al Badr camp a few hours before the missiles struck. Of the four training camps the two near Khost were used for training Pakistanis and Kashmiris and were run by *Harkat al Mujahedin*, a Pakistan-Kashmiri organization, and the other two—al Farouq and al Badr—were for Arab and other volunteers. Since this vast complex was originally built by the CIA in the 1980s, the Pentagon knew its exact coordinates.[11]

Explaining his actions in a television address, Clinton said there was evidence that these terrorist groups in Afghanistan played a key role in bombing the US embassies, that they had staged terrorist actions against Americans earlier and were planning further attacks and attempting to acquire chemical and other dangerous weapons. From then on, capturing or killing bin Laden became an obsession with the Clinton administration. In late September, at the behest of the US President, Crown Prince Abdullah dispatched Prince Turki to Kandahar, to show Mullah Omar the evidence collected by the FBI that bin Laden was linked to the bombings of the US Embassies in Kenya and Tanzania.

According to Turki, when he met Mullah Omar the latter denied any commitment about extraditing "such an illustrious holy warrior as Osama bin Laden," and wondered why Saudis "didn't prefer to free the world of the infidels". He was furious. "As he continued to insult Saudi Arabia and the royal family, I ended the meeting."[12] The fact that Mullah Omar insulted the House of Saud, one of the Taliban's principal bene-factors, illustrated the extent to which the Taliban leader had come under the spell of bin Laden. Turki returned to Riyadh empty-handed. Saudi Arabia downgraded its diplomatic links to second secretary, asked the Taliban charge d'affaires to leave, and recalled the head of its mission to Afghanistan based in Islamabad. But, tellingly, it did not terminate its relations with the Taliban regime.

Depressingly for Washington, as a consequence of the high profile that bin Laden acquired, many zealots traveled to Afghanistan to swell the ranks of Al Qaida while some rich individuals in Saudi Arabia and elsewhere in the Gulf sent cash through couriers plying between Dubai and Kabul to his network, and contributed generously to Islamic charities in the Gulf which diverted part of their collections to Al Qaida.

As for the Taliban's leaders, having suffered the US missile strikes, they could no longer withstand pressure from Tehran on the issue of its missing diplomats. They admitted that the Iranians had been killed in the storming of the consulate building by "rogue" troops, and that the latter would be arrested and punished.[13] They allowed an Iranian airplane to fly to Afghanistan to collect the corpses of those killed in Mazar-e Sharif.

Nationwide mourning in Iran was followed by the government announcing military maneuvers involving 200,000 troops near the Afghan border. There was much sound and fury. In the end, though, Iran's leaders refrained from invading Taliban territory, because they felt that a war with the Taliban could get transmuted into a Shia-Sunni conflict in the region with unforeseen consequences, and partly because an attack by a foreign country would rally Afghans behind the Taliban regime. Nonetheless, Iran's saber-rattling won plaudits in all the Central Asian capitals, including Tashkent. They felt reassured that Iran, with its military hardened by its eight-year war with Iraq, was the most effective regional power to confront the Taliban militarily, should it come to that.

Prominent among those who argued successfully against military action was President Muhammad Khatami—a reformist who was by temperament moderate and open-minded. It was during his presidency that Iran cooperated with Armenia, for example. This allowed the United Nations Security Council, backed by Washington, to succeed in defusing the situation. In February 1999 the two sides held talks but there was no slackening of tense relations.

The ongoing struggle between Iran and the Taliban, backed by Pakistan and Saudi Arabia, left intact the process of reconciliation between the Islamic Republic and the Saudi Kingdom, with the hitherto anti-Iran defence and interior ministers visiting Tehran to sign important agreements in 1999.

In Pakistan, the military coup orchestrated by General Parwez Musharraf which overthrew the government of Prime Minister Nawaz Sharif in October 1999 left intact Islamabad's policy toward the Taliban. Indeed, after removing President Rafiq Taroor from office and occupying his seat in June 2000, Musharraf tried hard to win recognition of the Taliban by foreign capitals—but to no avail.

For its part, Iran maintained its active opposition to the Taliban—in whose bigoted, intolerant worldview Shias were virtual heretics. As before, Tehran continued its war by proxy with the Taliban by increasing its arms supplies to the anti-Taliban Northern Alliance. But, the cash, fuel, military equipment, technical advice, and military advisers that the Taliban received from Pakistan far exceeded the military aid that the Northern Alliance was getting from Iran and Russia. As a result, the Taliban prevailed on the battle field. Their dramatic success came in September 2000 when they captured Taloqan, where Masoud had his headquarters. This came as a blow to Iran as well as Russia and Tajikistan. In June 2000, aided by the material and technical support by Pakistan's ISI, the Taliban launched a major offensive involving 25,000 soldiers, including 10,000 non-Afghan troops made up of Al Qaida veterans and Pakistani irregulars, to seize Takhar province from the Northern Alliance. But the alliance, assisted by Iran, Russia and India, managed to hold on.

In Washington, Clinton focused on isolating the Taliban diplomatically. On 19 December 2000 the UN Security Council adopted a resolution, sponsored by Washington and Moscow, which described the Taliban-controlled Afghanistan as "the world-center of terrorism." It demanded the extradition of bin Laden, and the shutting down of military training camps for foreigners within a month. The failure to do so would result in the Security Council banning all Taliban international flights, closing Taliban offices abroad and freezing their assets, and imposing an arms embargo against the Taliban.[14] With that Mullah Omar grew closer to bin Laden. And it became increasingly risky for Pakistan and Saudi Arabia to maintain relations with the Taliban regime.

On 20 January 2001, George W. Bush succeeded Clinton as US president. While the UN shut off arms supplies to the Taliban, the Iranian government rushed weapons to the Northern Alliance, now based in Tajikistan's capital, Dushanbe. At the same time it turned a blind eye as Washington's National Security Agency teams and CIA operatives arrived in Dushanbe to assist Masoud. The first ever visit to Dushanbe by US Central Command's combatant commander, General Tommy Franks, in the spring of 2001 gave Iran an inkling of the hardening stance of Bush's administration against the Taliban.[15]

In Riyadh, on 1 September, Crown Prince Abdullah sacked Prince Turki, who as the chief spymaster for twenty-three years had been close to the US, and replaced him with his own half-brother, sixty-eight-year-old Prince Nawwaf bin Abdul Aziz, a royal adviser on Gulf affairs. Ten days later the Saudi-Taliban-Pakistan alliance came to a shuddering halt. Fifteen of the nineteen hijackers involved in the terrorist attacks in New York and Metropolitan Washington turned out to be Saudi citizens. The hijackers crashed two passenger aircrafts into two of the skyscrapers of the World Trade Center in Lower Manhattan, a symbol of America's economic might, and another one into the Pentagon in Washington, the symbol of the unmatched military power of the US.[16] In 80 minutes, 18 million square feet (1.6 million square meters) of office space was reduced to rubble. The attacks killed 2,977 people and injured almost 6,000. They would lead to permanent strict air travel security procedures worldwide, establishment of the Homeland Security Department in the US and an erosion of civil liberties in the West in the name of countering Islamist terrorism, and activate deep-rooted xenophobia among many citizens of Western nations. On a higher level, they touched off two long-running wars, in Afghanistan and Iraq.

On 12 September US President Bush declared a "war on terror" worldwide, and three days later he named bin Laden as the mastermind behind the 9/11 attacks. The latter denied any involvement. This led to the Pentagon's invasion of Afghanistan in October 2001, a war which was ongoing sixteen years later and had cost America $860 billion,[17] followed by the Anglo-American invasion of Iraq in March 2003 at the cost of $815 billion to US taxpayers until its end in January 2014.

Contrasting Reactions to 9/11 in Tehran and Riyadh

Iran's President Khatami was quick to condemn the attacks and called on the international community to "take measures to eradicate such crimes."Tehran's mayor, Murtaza Alviri, sent a message to his New York counterpart, Rudolph Giuliani: "Tehran's citizens express their deep hatred of this ominous and inhuman move, strongly condemn the culprits, and express their sympathy with New Yorkers." Thanking Khatami, the Bush administration invited him to join the anti-terror campaign—by, say, sharing information on bin Laden and the Taliban with it. This was not on—at least not publicly—however much Tehran detested the Taliban. Supreme Leader Ayatollah Ali Khamanei decided to deliver the sermon about 9/11 at the Friday prayer congregation in Tehran. "Mass killing is a catastrophe wherever happens and whoever the perpetrators," he said. "It is condemned without distinction. But if, God forbid, a similar catastrophe is inflicted on Afghanistan, we will condemn it too." Iran favored action against the Taliban under the auspices of the United Nations. Its defence minister, Admiral Ali Shamskhani, explained that, "If strikes against the terrorist bases took place within the framework of the international community, Iran would support it." That is, Iran would participate in any UN-sponsored action against the perpetrators of this criminal act, well aware that UN Security Council Resolution 1368 had a provision to that effect.[18]

In several Iranian cities, huge crowds turned out on the streets and held candlelit vigils for the victims. Two days later the 60,000 spectators who gathered at Tehran's football stadium for a match observed a minute's silence.[19] During his visit to New York to participate in the United Nations' celebration of the year of "Dialogue Among Civilisations," President Khatami gave an interview to the *New York Times* on 9 November. "The horrific terrorist attacks of September 11, 2001 in the United States were perpetrated by cult of fanatics who had self-mutilated their ears and tongues, and could only communicate with perceived opponents through carnage and devastation," he said.[20]

On the eve of the Pentagon's campaign against the Taliban on October 7, codenamed Operation Enduring Freedom, Bush sent a confidential memorandum to Iran through the Swiss embassy assuring it that his Defence Department would not use Iranian air space. The next day, Iran replied that it would rescue any personnel in distress in its territory, thus implying its de facto membership of the coalition. That day, the Bush administration petitioned a federal judge to throw out a $10 billion lawsuit against Iran by the 1979 American Embassy hostages.[21]

It later transpired that Tehran had allowed 165,000 tons of US food aid for the Afghan people to be unloaded at an Iranian port and sent through Iran into Afghanistan. As Bush prepared to invade Taliban-ruled Afghanistan, he received useful intelligence on the Taliban from Iran through back-channels. Tehran also instructed the Tajik warlord Ismail Khan, based in Mashhad, to coordinate his attack on western Afghanistan with the Pentagon—which he then did. [22]

In stark contrast, most Saudis at the popular and official levels went into denial about 9/11, expressed in the statement, "I didn't ask for it, but God brought it." It became a personal matter for many. "To accept that Saudis were major players in 9/11 was like accepting that your son was a serial killer," said Khaled al Maeena, editor of the *Arab News*. "You had to refuse to believe it."[23] They latched on to the rumor that the Jews in New York were warned by agents of Mossad, the intelligence agency of Israel, who perpetrated the atrocity, to stay away from work on 11 September. And 3,000 Jews in New York did so. That was why there were no Jews among those killed at the World Trade Center. In reality, between 270 and 400 Jews died in the attacks. [24]

"Bin Laden was evil and murderous," said Prince Amr Al Faisal. "As a Muslim I fiercely and totally condemn what he did. But the Saudis are a daring people, and it is not surprising that one of the most daring terrorists in the world should be a Saudi. As many Muslims saw it, the falling of the Twin Towers was a lesson to the pride and complacency of the Americans. It gave them just a little taste of what the Muslims have been going through." An insight into the popular view among Saudis was provided by Muhammad al Harbi, a chemistry teacher in the northern city of Buraidah. "The jihad has started," they [his students] were saying. "They were all very supportive and content with the attacks on New York, and clearly were very happy that it had been done by Saudi hands—or so they assumed."[25]

The conventional wisdom accepted by senior Saudi princes was that the attacks were part of a Zionist conspiracy in order to get the US administration so incensed that it would launch a worldwide campaign against Islamic terrorism. This was what the newly appointed US Ambassador to Saudi Arabia, Robert Jordan, an eminent lawyer from Texas, found on his arrival in Riyadh in October 2001. "Many senior princes believed that it was a Jewish plot," he said. "[Interior Minister]

Nayef actually said it was a Zionist conspiracy in a public statement. Even [Crown Prince] Abdullah was suspicious."This was the case after Abdullah had told Bush over the telephone on 16 September that "We in the Kingdom of Saudi Arab are fully prepared to cooperate with you in every way that may help identify and pursue the perpetrators of this criminal incident."[26]

In his meeting with Abdullah, Ambassador Jordan laid out the dossiers prepared by the Federal Bureau of Investigation (FBI). These contained the details of who was on the planes, and the movement of all the hijackers, most of them being Saudi, including surveillance shots from the various airports' security cameras. They were all well-educated, intelligent men in their mid-twenties. Three were law graduates, two were teachers, two were brothers of a provincial police chief, and one was a son of a rich businessman. Unsurprisingly, none of them was Shia. Their surnames—al Hazmi, al Mihdhar, al Hasnawi, al Ghamdi, al Qadi Bani Hammad, and others—seemed familiar to Abdullah, who was well informed about the Saudi tribes. In each case he contacted the father of the listed Saudi hijacker, who confirmed the patrimony of the missing son. He was convinced.[27]

Abdullah had already resorted to damage limitation. He boosted Saudi Arabia's oil quota specified by OPEC by 500,000 barrels per day (bpd), and shipped an extra 700,000 bpd in Saudi tankers to America. As a result, the petroleum price fell from $28 a barrel to $20 within weeks. Unlike Abdullah, Prince Nayef was not convinced. He seemed to agree with Mullah Omar who argued that bin Laden could not have been responsible since he had no pilots. "In Afghanistan, there is no such possibility for training [of pilots]."[28] This ignored the fact that the hijackers had trained at flying schools in America. Astonishingly, Nayef stuck to his view. "We still ask ourselves who has benefited from the 11 September attacks," he said in mid-2002. "I think they [the Jews] were the protagonists of such attacks."[29]

Pentagon's Operation Enduring Freedom

As the US prepared to attack Taliban-administered Afghanistan, the UAE, Saudi Arabia and Pakistan pressured Mullah Omar to hand over bin Laden. He refused. On 22 September the UAE cut its links with the Taliban. Three days later Saudi Arabia did so too, regretting that "the Taliban had used "its high status gained due to the resistance to the Soviets not to build brotherly relations or set up high Islamic values, but to make the land a center to attract and train a number of mis-guided people to carry out criminal acts against the Sharia, to go on with terrorist operations, thus causing harm to Islam and spoiling the name of Muslims."[30] (Since the Taliban came into existence five years after the Soviet withdrawal from Afghanistan, they played no part in resisting the Soviets.) Pakistan, the foster parent of the Taliban, was the last to sever ties with its regime.

Riyadh's words echoed those used repeatedly by Tehran over the years. Yet the Iranian leaders were unhappy at the way they thought Washington was using the crisis to establish a foothold in Central Asia while seeking assistance from Afghanistan's neighbors, including Iran. "How can America that has tampered with Iran's interests, demand help from Iran to attack the suffering, oppressed and Muslim nation of Afghanistan?" Khamanei asked. "It is wrong to say that those who are not with us are with the terrorists. There are countries like Israel, side by side with America, whose leaders commit terrorist acts against Palestinians. No, we are not with you and we are not terrorists."[31]

Following a briefing to the North Atlantic Treaty Organization (NATO) in Brussels by US counter-terrorism specialist Frank Taylor on 2 October, its General Secretary Lord Robertson said: "All roads lead to Al Qaida and pinpoint Osama bin Laden as being involved." This meant that the basis for activating Article 5 of the NATO Treaty—namely, that an attack on a member must originate abroad—had been satisfied, clearing the way for NATO to provide the US "unlimited use of it base facilities, seaports, logistic support, early warning aircraft, extra security for US troops in Europe, and staging of naval show of force in the Eastern Mediterranean."[32]

With this, the Pentagon was all set to launch its Operation Enduring Freedom the next day, using its upgraded command centre which inte-grated data from satellites, aerial drones, air and ground surveillance and other intelligence sources to give commanders a real-time view of the battlefield, at the Prince Sultan Airbase at Al Kharj in Saudi Arabia to coordinate the bombardment, making use of all its aircraft including those stationed at the Saudi base. The Pentagon had poured hundreds of millions of dollars to transform the original airstrip into a sprawling air base, the largest US air base in the Middle East.[33] More than the technical advantage of using the latest state-of-the-art command post was involved. The United States stood to reap a propaganda coup. To have the foremost Islamic state march shoulder to shoulder with America in its war on terror would reassure the Arab and Muslim world that its campaign was not directed against Islam per se. After securing Riyadh's permission for the use of the facility at Prince Sultan Air Base, the US publicized it. By so doing it deeply embarrassed Interior Minister Prince Nayef, who publicly contradicted Washington. A few days later a story by Al Jazeera contradicted Nayef. Indeed, following his visit to Riyadh on 3 October 2001, US Defense Secretary Donald Rumsfeld announced that some countries were helping the US-led coalition overtly and others covertly. In plain English, the Pentagon was allowed to make use of its new command center at the Prince Sultan Airbase as and when it wished.[34]

Crown Prince Abdullah intervened. He ruled out the use of American planes stationed on Saudi soil against Afghanistan, whose government had not threatened the Kingdom. Even Rumsfeld's intervention in person in Riyadh failed to persuade Abdullah. Referring to the oblique statement made by Rumsfeld at a press conference after his meeting with his Saudi counterpart, Prince Sultan, Michael Gordon of the *New York Times* reported that "The comments suggested that the US might be able to use Saudi bases under which the Pentagon could direct bombing attacks [by planes based elsewhere] but could not conduct bombing missions from the Saudi territory."[35] This led to a hurried, personal approach on 4 October by Rumsfeld to Oman's Sultan Qaboos, then camping in the desert at Sham Camp. The Sultan agreed to the transfer of US warplanes to an Omani air base provided Washington allowed the sale of $1.2 billion worth of advanced weaponry to the Sultanate. Rumsfeld completed his whirlwind tour in Cairo on 6 October.

On 7 October the Pentagon started bombing Afghanistan with cruise missiles and aerial munitions. That day Al Jazeera television aired bin Laden's twenty-minute video-tape.

"[W]hat America is tasting now is only a copy of what…our Islamic umma [nation] has been tasting for eighty years, humiliation and disgrace, their sons killed and their blood spilled," he said. "[W]hen the sword fell upon America after eighty years—hypocrisy [i.e. hypocrite Muslims] raised their head high bemoaning those American killers who toyed with the blood, honor and sanctities of Muslims. The least that can be said about those hypocrites[36] is that they are apostates ... Americans have been telling the world they are fighting terrorism. A million children [killed] in Iraq [because of sanctions], this is not a clear issue.[37] But when a little over 10 [Americans] were killed in Nairobi and Dar as Salam, Afghanistan and Iraq were bombed, and the hypocrites stood behind the head of international infidels, America and its allies... I swear to Allah that those living in America will not live in security and safety until we live in our lands and in Palestine, and all the army of the infidel has departed from the Land of Muhammad. Peace be upon him."[38]

On 10 October, the foreign ministers of the Organisation of the Islamic Conference, meeting in Doha, failed to reach a consensus on the US invasion of Afghanistan. Alluding to the complicity of bin Laden in the terrorist outrage, the presiding Qatari foreign minister, Hamad bin Jassem Al Thani, said, "We [OIC members] have some evidence but we do not have sufficient evidence. We did not see anything concrete."[39] By contrast, in Tehran, Khamanei said, "How can you allow innocent civilians to be killed or injured? Since when has it become a norm to send troops to another country and hit its cities with missiles and aerial bombardment because of so-called terrorism in that country?"[40]

The United States, assisted by Britain, continued its aerial offensive day after day. On the night of 12 and 13 November—four days before the start of Ramadan—the Taliban abandoned Kabul in an orderly manner, heading south to Kandahar. Iran became the first country to reopen its embassy in Kabul. It did so within ten days of the flight of the anti-Shia Taliban leaders to Pakistan.[41] Later, during his visit to Tehran, the Interim President Hamid Karzai of Afghanistan would describe the Afghan-Iranian friendship, founded on common culture and language, as "eternal".[42] (The two countries shared a 935 km (581 miles) long border.) Thus, in their competition for supremacy in Kabul in the regional context, the Iranians prevailed at the expense of the Saudis, thanks largely to the military muscle of America.

Fittingly, it was a female announcer, Jamila Mujahid, who announced on Radio Kabul the arrival of the Northern Alliance in the capital. They did so with 6,000 soldiers who entered the Tajik sector of the city where the cheering and welcoming crowds strew them with flowers. This was a moment savored concurrently by two long-time adversaries, Iran and the the United States. Their new-found cooperation continued behind the scenes. At the UN-sponsored conference on Afghanistan, as four major groups of Afghans vied for power, the Americans and Iranians tried to forge a compromise. Iran's Foreign Minister Kamal Kharrazi and his team worked actively with US officials, who included Zalmay Khalilzad, the Afghan-American director for Afghanistan at the National Security Council, to assemble an interim, post-Taliban government in Kabul. It came on 5 December. The conferees agreed to a thirty-member cabinet chaired by Hamid Karzai, a Pushtun, with five deputy chairs, one for each important ethnic group.[43] Saudi Arabia was not part of this process. Later, following an inclusive sectarian policy, Karzai ensured that one of his two vice-presidents was a Shia, much to the satisfaction of Iran.

Tehran awaited a quid pro quo from Washington namely moderation of its hard line stance towards Iran. Nothing of the sort happened. Indeed, in his State of the Union speech to Congress of 29 January 2002, Bush said, "Our second goal is to prevent regimes that sponsor terror from threatening America or our friends and allies with weapons of mass destruction...North Korea is a regime arming with missiles and weapons of mass destruction, while starving its citizens. Iran aggressively pursues these weapons and exports terror...Iraq continues to flaunt its hostility toward America and to support terror... States like these, and their terrorist allies, constitute an axis of evil, arming to threaten the peace of the world."[44] In short, there was no change in the adversarial positions of Tehran and Washington. This reinforced Khamanei's long-held view that America could not be trusted.

However, Operation Enduring Freedom altered Washington's relations with Riyadh to a certain extent, reflecting the disjunction between the Kingdom's official position of support and anti-American public opinion. This could be inferred by Abdullah's address to senior religious and judicial officials on the eve of Ramadan, when he said, "I ask you not to be swept away by emotion or be incited by anyone. The government will handle foreign affairs judiciously and without hasty decisions."[45]

Strained Relations Between Riyadh and Washington

While the Saudi royals agreed with Washington's political position, they were also nervously aware of the popular anger caused in the kingdom by the Christian superpower's military strikes against the poor Muslim country of Afghanistan. Though the Council of Senior Ulema refrained from taking a position on the subject, the imam of the Grand Mosque of Mecca, Shaikh Salih bin Humaid, said, "This issue [of terrorism] calls for new policies [by America], not new wars." He warned that attack on Afghanistan could stir conflict between civilisations and religions.[46]

At the popular level there was much scepticism about bin Laden's guilt, which was privately shared by the Saudi political elite, who blamed Washington's unabashed backing for Israel's suppression of the year-old Palestinians' Second Intifada (Arabic: literally, tremor; figuratively, uprising) as the main reason driving young Saudis into the arms of Islamist extremists. They overlooked the fact that absence of political freedom in the Kingdom had led many educated Saudis searching for a political cause to join the jihad in Bosnia or Chechnya after the victory of the anti-Soviet jihad in Afghanistan. They were the ones who now called bin Laden "the Conscience of Islam." As a senior (unnamed) Saudi lawyer in Jeddah told a visiting reporter from the *New York Times*, "What bin Laden says and what he does represents what Muslims or Arabs want to say and can't. What he says, we agree with it."[47] This was borne out by a secret opinion survey conducted by the Interior Ministry: it showed 95 per cent of educated Saudis in the 25–41 age group supporting "bin Laden's cause."[48] As for those in the lower age group, Mai Yamani, a Saudi Fellow at the Royal Institute for International Affairs, London, said, "The young have been exposed to satellite television and new ideas about the Palestinian Intifada and sanctions against Iraq. The main issues are censorship and double standards. There is a rising demand to participate. Young men and women are saying, 'We are the nation but we are never consulted.' When Osama Bin Laden and others come up with alternatives, they cheer them."[49]

At the official level, differences arose between Riyadh and Washington on the question of freezing assets of organizations alleged to be funding terrorists. On 12 October Washington named twenty-two groups and individuals whose assets it sought to freeze—throughout the world. They included the Muwafaq Foundation, based in Saudi

Arabia, and the Islamic Cultural Institute in Milan, Italy, described as "the main station house of Al Qaida in Europe".[50] Riyadh refused to shut down the Muwafaq Foundation, an Islamic charity, partly because Islam enjoined charity, and the Kingdom had affluent citizens in abundance, partly because the country lacked a supervisory body for banks, and partly because Washington had failed to prove that funds from any Saudi-based charity had gone to Al Qaida.

The Bush administration then pressured Riyadh by leaking embarrassing information on the royal princes' moral and material corruption to the investigative journalist Seymour Hersh of the *New Yorker*, implying further damaging revelations if Saudi Arabia failed to meet its demands on freezing the assets of the US-named charities and providing full backgrounds of the fifteen hijackers. After disclosing that the US National Security Agency had been monitoring the telephone conversations of the king, crown prince and several senior princes since the mid-1990s, Hersh referred to the intercept where the Interior Minister Nayef instructed a subordinate to withhold from the police the evidence of hiring prostitutes—a severe crime—"presumably by the members of the royal family," insisting that the "client list must not be released under any circumstances."[51]

Though the ploy worked, with Riyadh freezing the assets of the Muwafaq Foundation within days of the Hersh article, the US unwittingly reinforced the anti-royalist argument of the bin Laden camp. Incensed, Riyadh denounced "the vicious campaign against the kingdom in the Western media" on 29 October. The White House spokesman said that Bush had telephoned Crown Prince Abdullah to say "I am very pleased with the Kingdom's contribution to the war effort," and that the media citing differences between America and Saudi Arabia were simply incorrect."[52]

This did not satisfy the Kingdom's government. Throwing the cautionary Saudi discretion to the wind, its foreign minister Prince Saud Al Faisal said, "Bush's failure to commit his personal prestige to forging the final peace settlement [between Israel and Palestinians] makes a sane man go mad." All Bush had to do was to set himself up as an honest broker. "Bush cannot be an honest broker and meet only one side [Israeli Premier Ariel Sharon]," he added.[53] Evidently, he found unconvincing Bush's argument that Yasser Arafat had not done "enough" to lower Palestinian violence and root out terrorists during the ongoing Second Intifada.

Prince Bandar's Unshakeable Ties with the Bush Clan

Intriguingly, the tensions created by the leading role of Saudi citizens in the most violent attack on mainland America left intact the close friendships that Prince Bandar bin Sultan, Saudi Arabia's ambassador to the US since 1983, had forged with President George H. W. Bush and his son, George Walker Bush. Together with Bush Senior, he had lobbied for the approval of massive US arms sales to the Saudi Kingdom where Bandar's father Prince Sultan bin Abdul Aziz had been the Defence Minister since 1963. During Bush Senior's presidency Bandar had several lunches with him every year. Bandar was a frequent guest at the Bushes' family retreat in Kennebunkport, Maine, and went hunting with Bush Senior. Lodged in a large, well-guarded mansion in McLean, Virginia, and leading a luxurious life, he came to be known as "the Arab Gatsby" for the big parties he gave. Over the years Bandar had become an integral part of the Bush family and helped forge financial ties between the Bush clan and the House of Saud.

As it happened, President George W. Bush had invited him to the White House on 13 September 2001 to discuss the Middle East peace process. Despite the traumatic 9/11 attacks, that meeting went ahead. It was reported that Bush discussed his administration handing over to the Saudis those captured Al Qaida operatives who failed to cooperate with the FBI. At first Bandar dismissed the reports of Saudi involvement in 9/11 as overblown. Then he received a phone call from CIA director George Tenet on the evening of 12 September telling him that fifteen of the hijackers were Saudis. For the next forty-eight hours, Bandar went to work on two fronts: reputational damage control through an effective public relations campaign, and ensuring that 140 Saudis who were members or associates of the House of Saud and the Saudi Binladin Group were flown out of the United States immediately, even though the Federal Aviation Authority (FAA) had banned all flights and grounded 4,000 commercial aircraft, and another 200,000 private planes.

After a thorough investigation, Craig Unger of the New York-based *Vanity Fair* published an account of how these Saudis were whisked from America. The first inkling came in October 2001 when the *Tampa Tribune* reported that a chartered plane carrying three Saudis flew from Tampa to Lexington on 12 September despite the FAA's ban on all flights, which was lifted on 14 September, initially for private planes only. According to the *New York Times*, members of the extended bin Laden family were driven or flown under FBI supervision first to a secret assembly point in Texas and later to Washington. From there, they flew abroad when airports reopened on 14 September. Other assembly points for the privileged Saudis included Houston, Cleveland, Los Angeles and Newark. Several flights brought the Saudis to Boston's Logan International Airport and Newark Airport on 18 September. The final batches of Saudis flew out from Boston and Newark, the airports that the 9/11 hijackers had used, on 19 September. Those departing were merely identified by FBI agents, and none were subjected to serious interview or interrogation. The FBI also refused to release the departing Saudis' identities. While the FBI denied that it had anything to do with the Saudi repatriations, Bandar told CNN, "With coordination with the FBI, we got them all out."

Despite his best efforts, Unger failed to find out who issued the initial order to prioritise the repatriation of the well-connected Saudis then in the US, and why.[54] Informed speculation centered on Prince Bandar's very close ties to both the Bushes. His role would figure prominently when Bush Junior prepared to invade Iraq in 2003, a move initially opposed by Crown Prince Abdullah.

For now, Abdullah was intent on closing the gap that had developed between his government and the public regarding the Kingdom's relationship with the United States.

The Ongoing Iranian-Saudi Rivalry in Pakistan

Whereas Riyadh quickly adjusted to the downfall of the Taliban in Afghanistan, this was not the case with Islamabad. There was no change, however, in Saudi Arabia and Iran waging a proxy war in Pakistan through inter-sectarian violence, with rival militant groups conducting tit-for-tat assassinations.

Muhammad Azam Tariq, who succeeded Aurangzeb Farooqi as Sipah-e Sahaba (SSP) leader, was a former MP. In Parliament he introduced a bill which sought to include the names of the four Rightly Guided Caliphs (Abu Bakr, Omar, Uthman and Ali) in Pakistan's existing Blasphemy Law. But he failed.[55] He was charged with the murder of several Shia figures in the 1990s and served a two-year jail sentence. As SSP leader, he tightened the group's links with Al Qaida and the Taliban.

Yielding to Washington's pressure in the aftermath of 9/11, on 12 January 2002, Pakistan's military ruler General Parwez Musharraf banned five extremist organizations, including the SSP and the (Shia) Tehrik-e Jafaria Pakistan. Yet Tariq was allowed to contest the October 2002 parliamentary poll from his prison cell, and won. The government released him and he took his seat in the National Assembly when he agreed to back the pro-Musharraf alliance.[56] He kept his promise until his assassination in 6 October 2003 by rival Shia militants. In short, sectarian violence in Pakistan, originating in the Riyadh-Tehran rivalry, revived.

Riyadh's Alarm at Tehran's Nuclear Program

In August 2002 at a press conference in Washington, the National Resistance Council of Iran (NRCI) revealed that Iran was hiding a massive uranium enrichment facility and other sites from the Vienna-based International Atomic Energy Agency (IAEA). The underground facility turned out to be at Natanz, northeast of Isfahan, where a research reactor had been installed many years ago. This discovery provided the George W. Bush administration with a fresh basis to allege that Iran was planning clandestinely to produce nuclear weapons. While enriching uranium does not violate the 1968 nuclear Non-Proliferation Treaty (Official title: Treaty on Non-Proliferation of Nuclear Weapons, NPT), signed by Iran in 1970, the signatory is required to inform the IAEA. But Tehran had not done so. In Riyadh, the NRCI's revelation strengthened the hand of the pro-American Prince Sultan. However, in the summer of 2002 the Bush administration was too focused on planning an invasion of Iraq to ratchet up pressure on Iran.

Both the US and Saudi Arabia had also noted the claim made by Dariush Foroughi, head of the Center for Research on Energy and Environment in Tehran, that Iran possessed 12,000 tones of uranium deposits.[57] Riyadh's anxiety turned into alarm when Iran went public in early 2003 with its plan to enrich locally mined uranium for "peaceful purposes." As for the IAEA, it said that it had known about Iran's plans before. As a signatory to the nuclear NPT, Iran was entitled to enrich uranium up to 5 per cent purity to be used in a civilian nuclear power plant. This failed to assure the Saudis. Their fears of a nuclear-armed Iran achieving its hegemonic ambitions in the Middle East, which had never been fully dispelled, were revived.

Abdullah Equivocal as Bush Targets Iraq

In his address to the UN General Assembly in September 2002—two months after CIA agents had infiltrated Iraq through Jordan to carry out undercover operations against the regime of President Saddam Hussein—US President George W. Bush devoted it exclusively to demonising the Iraqi leader, alleging that he was clandestinely engaged in producing weapons of mass destruction. The UN Security Council Resolution 1441 of 8 November 2002 stated that Iraq had not complied with its previous resolutions, but did not authorize military action against the regime of Saddam Hussein, which would have required a separate, specific resolution as had happened after Iraq's invasion and occupation of Kuwait in August 1990.

Abdullah was opposed to external aggression against any Arab country. Anticipating his refusal to let the Pentagon use Prince Sultan Air Base, its regional Central Command (aka, CENTCOM) built up a back-up air command facility at the French-built Al Udeid Air Base 25 miles (40 km) west of Doha, the capital of Qatar. On 22 November CENTCOM announced the completion of this base amid media fanfare.[58] This facility in Qatar would provide the Saudis with a handy alibi that the US air operations were being coordinated from there.

Over the next several weeks the White House publicly pressured Saddam Hussein to step down of the extent that the UAE joined the exercise in January. This was a non-starter. A haughty, arrogant dictator, Saddam Hussein was never going to take this humiliating step.

In early January Bush decided to invade Iraq and gained the backing of British Prime Minister Tony Blair. On 13 January Dick Cheney and Defense Secretary Rumsfeld briefed Prince Bandar of the President's decision to attack Iraq before informing Secretary of State Colin Powell, a former Chairman of the Joint Chiefs of Staff.[59] Prince Bandar was briefed several times before the invasion as part of securing Riyadh's assistance, and received regular updates as the Pentagon's needs changed. Actually, preparations for US operations inside the Saudi Kingdom started in 2002 when the US Air Force awarded a contract to a Saudi company to supply jet fuel at four airfields or bases inside the country.[60] During his several trips to Riyadh, Bandar kept the Crown Prince Abdullah and the monarch fully informed. Abdullah had to suppress his premonition that destabilising the current regime in Baghdad would lead to the fracturing of Iraq. Even if he had conveyed his fear directly to the White House, Bush was intent on invading Iraq irrespective of what America's Arab allies or the members of UN Security Council said. Being based in Washington, Bandar was not exposed to the universal unpopularity of the planned US war among Saudi citizens.

Iran's Wily Strategy

Aware of the popular sympathy that Iranians had developed for their suffering fellow Muslims in Iraq on account of the impact of long-running sanctions, from 1997 Tehran started to help Iraq smuggle its petroleum through Iranian territorial waters, albeit for hefty fees. President Khatami ensured Iran's participation in bypassing no-fly zones, which began in late summer 2000. By having Foreign Minister Kharazi lead an Iranian delegation in the first Iran Air flight to Baghdad in October 2000, Khatami highlighted the change in his policy. After meeting Saddam Hussein, Kharrazi said that the Iraqi President had expressed his "willingness and determination to normalize relations with Iran." More significantly, Kharrazi added, "We have decided to activate the 1975 [Algiers] agreement in order to set up balanced and goodneighborly relations."[61] So twenty years after Saddam invaded Iran after tearing up the Algiers Accord during a television address, the two neighbors were—as it were—returning to square one. With President George W. Bush lumping together Iran and Iraq as part of the "Axis of Evil," a repulsive phrase, in his State of the Union speech in January 2002, relations between the two countries warmed further.

During the run-up to the Anglo-American invasion of March 2003, however, the Iranian government followed a schizophrenic policy. It gave a green light to the underground Supreme Council for the Islamic Revolution in Iraq (SCIRI), headquartered in Tehran along with its armed wing, called the Badr Brigade since its foundation in 1983, to participate in Washington's pre-invasion destabilisation plans. At the same time it reiterated publicly that any armed action against Iraq had to be sanctioned by the UN Security Council.

Iran needed to do no more. That was not the case with the Saudi Kingdom, which was fully aware of the well-publicized stance the fugitive Osama bin Laden, operating from a hide-out along the Afghanistan-Pakistan border region, had taken. "This Crusade war is primarily aimed at the people of Islam regardless of the removal or survival of the socialist government [of Iraq] of Saddam" he said in his audiotape, aired on Al Jazeera TV channel on 11 February 2003, the high point in the annual Hajj pilgrimage. "The Muslims as a whole or in Iraq in particular, should carry out jihad against the oppressive offensive. It does not hurt that in the current circumstances, the interests of Muslims coincide with those of the socialists in the war against the Crusaders, taking into account our belief and declaration of the apostasy of socialism."[62]

Saudi Arabia's Duplicitous Policy

Against the background of an impending war, the Arab League held a summit in the Egyptian Red Sea resort of Sharm el Shaikh on 1 March 2003. Syria opposed any war without the authorization of a UN Security Council, a stance it shared with Iran outside the Arab world. Saudi Arabia and Egypt led a faction which urged avoidance of war. The final communiqué, adopted unanimously, expressed "total rejection of any attack on Iraq" and called for the crisis to be resolved through international channels. They urged Arabs to "not participate in any military action aimed at Iraq's or any Arab country's safety and territorial integrity", and said that UN inspectors should be given "ample time" to carry out their work. It noted that serious threats to Iraq (by the US) could lead to grave conflagration with grave consequences in the Arab world.[63]

Washington's invasion plans were by now far too advanced to be deflected by an Arab League resolution. In terms of timing, weather was a critical factor, as temperatures soar after the end of March. Moreover once the parliament in Turkey, a NATO member, refused to let US forces use Turkish soil for operations in Iraq along the northern front on 1 March, the direct and extensive involvement by Saudi Arabia became crucial. But in order to show that the Kingdom's rulers were in tune with popular opinion, Abdullah delivered a televised address in which he read out King Fahd's policy statement: the monarch said that the Kingdom will "in no way whatsoever" participate in a war against Iraq.[64] The reality was totally out of synch with this public posture.

On the eve of the Anglo-American invasion of Iraq, codenamed Operation Iraqi Freedom, set to be launched with a blitzkrieg on 20 March 2003, the *New York Times* reported that at the sprawling Prince Sultan Air Base at Al Kharj, 5,500 US troops were posted within a secure perimeter, with the Pentagon's Central Command controlling access to the compound. The base was a hub for US fighter aircraft, E-3 Awacs early warning and in-flight refuelling planes, and other surveillance and reconnaissance aircraft. Contrary to the statements by the Saudis, American officials confirmed the primary air command operations, directed by the Combined Air Operations Center, would remain in Saudi Arabia, where the decision-makers were based. CENTCOM commander General Tommy Franks visited the computer-crammed bunkers at Prince Sultan Air Base on 19 March. Lt. Col. Joseph LaMarca described the operations center as "a multinational organization [which] includes our hosts, who, he said, work in our headquarters building in the actual Combined Air Operations Center," which was then busily identifying Iraqi bombing targets, and readying itself to assess post-bombing damage. He maintained that the operations center would continue to "plan, direct and monitor the execution of all air operations in the Central Command's area of responsibility," which includes Iraq.[65]

Between 250 and 300 US warplanes took off from Saudi Arabia, the officials said. Air and military operations during the war were permitted at the Tabuk air base and Arar regional airport near the Iraq border. General T. Michael Moseley, a top US Air Force general who was a key architect of the air campaign in Iraq, revealed in April 2004 that "We operated the command center at Saudi Arabia. We operated airplanes out of Saudi Arabia, as well as sensors, and tankers." He thanked the Saudis for "their counsel, their mentoring, their leadership and their support." To maintain the facade that Riyadh was not cooperating with the Pentagon, during the war US officials held media briefings about the air campaign in Qatar to make the point that CENTCOM was using its Al Udeid Air Base for its air war. Riyadh allowed cruise missiles to be fired from Navy ships across Saudi air space into Iraq. A few times missiles went off course and landed inside Saudi Arabia. During the conflict, the Saudis provided tens of millions of dollars in discounted oil, gas and fuel for US forces. The sight of a stream of oil delivery trucks stretching for miles outside the Prince Sultan Air Base provided the evidence. In order to counter a rise in petroleum prices because of the likelihood of the Iraqi troops setting alight their oil wells to deprive the invading forces of their use, Abdullah ordered an increase of 1.5 million bpd during the run-up to war.[66]

The US military presence extended to the air bases at Arar and Tabuk near the Iraqi border. These sites hosted American and British tanker aircraft for in-flight refuelling and helicopters for search and rescue missions. Also it was from there that US Special Forces took off during the ground campaign which was launched on 22 March.[67] It is also noteworthy that, according to WikiLeaks, during his 15 March 2009 meeting with US Ambassador to the Kingdom Ford Fraker, and visiting White House officials, Abdullah said, "We (the US and Saudi Arabia) spilled blood together" in Kuwait and Iraq.[68]

On 1 April 2003, with war in the air and on the ground raging, Saudi Foreign Minister Prince Saudi Al Faisal suggested a pause in the fighting. "Stop the war," he said. "Let's sit down, let's have a breather after what we have seen of the destruction." He implied that Saddam Hussein should step down, adding that "Mr Saddam Hussein has asked his people to sacrifice for their country, and if the only thing that keeps the conflict going is his presence, then he should listen to his own advice." In response, Iraqi Vice President Taha Yassin Ramadan called Prince Sultan "a minion and a lackey" of America.[69]

A week later, Baghdad fell to advancing US troops, and Saddam Hussein went into hiding, and would remain at large until December.[70] For all practical purposes the war ended on 16 April although it was not until 1 May that Bush announced a formal end to the hostilities against Iraq. During those four weeks CENTCOM mounted 37,000 air sorties, launched 23,000 precision-guided missiles, fired 750 cruise missiles, and dropped 1,566 cluster bombs, which were coordinated at Prince Sultan Air Base.[71] Many Iraqi generals defected, and the leaderless soldiers scattered. There was thus no formal surrender of Iraq to the victors.

The Post-Saddam Hussein Era: Iran

Once Saddam Hussein's regime was overthrown, there was quiet satisfaction among the Iranian people and politicians. After all, they had
been the first victims of Saddam's aggression. Now Iran's leaders
demanded that the US-led troops should hand over peacekeeping and
holding of elections to the UN. The US had no such intention. Indeed,
in the first flush of the Pentagon's swift victory in Iraq, reports started
emanating from Washington that Iran was next in line among the "axis
of evil" for regime change.

To forestall such a move, Iran made a dramatic—but little known—
approach to Washington. This came in the form of a letter sent through
the Swiss Embassy which represented US interests in Iran. (According
to the Iranians, the missive was a response to a set of talking points that
had come from US intermediaries.) In it Iran expressed willingness to
discuss all subjects of interest to the US, including the issue of Iran's
nuclear program, stabilising Iraq, ending its support for Palestinian militant groups, and helping to disarm Hizbollah. In return, Tehran wanted
an end to Washington's hostile behavior and an official removal of Iran
from its "axis of evil" list. The letter materialised after an intense internal
debate among policy-makers and was endorsed by the officials at the
highest level. According to Seyed Adeli, then a deputy foreign minister
of Iran, "That letter went to the Americans to say that we are ready to
talk, we are ready to address our issues." Nothing came of it.[72] The Bush
White House decided it did not want to talk to a member of "the axis
of evil" and opted instead for bringing about regime change in Iran.

The preliminary step was to destabilize the regime in Tehran by
co-opting the anti regime Iranians settled in America who operated
many Persian language satellite radio and television channels and internet sites. In a concerted move, they named 10 June as the inaugural
date for overthrowing "mullahcracy" in their native land. Disturbances
erupted in Tehran, and continued for the next ten days with declining
support. The number of demonstrators barely exceeded a few thousand. The egregious incitement from America-based exiles' media and
open encouragement by US officials from Bush downwards played into
the hands of Iran's hardliners, and allowed rightwing vigilantes to sav-
agely attack protesters, who were villified by the regime as traitors
acting on the orders of Iran's foreign enemies. Washington's strategy

backfired. It made protesters in particular and reformists in general appear as stooges of the Great Satan, a recipe for political suicide.[73]

That meant the Bush administration's options to undermine the Iranian regime were limited. Iran, on the other hand, continued to play both sides of the fence in Iraq, now occupied by Anglo-American troops, with Paul Bremer acting as Washington's Pro-consul in Baghdad. Directed by Tehran, the leaders of SCIRI (later renamed Islamic Supreme Council of Iraq, ISCI) participated in the 25-member Interim Iraqi Governing Council (IIGC) under Izzedine Salim, a Shia, appointed by Bremer in July 2003. Its schizophrenic stance was encapsulated in the slogan, "No, no to America; no, no to Saddam." Also, al Daawa (official title: *Hizb al Daawa al Islamiya*, Islamic Call Party), a recent breakaway from SCIRI, whose leaders had taken refuge in Tehran over the years, independently decided to participate in the IIGC. At the same time the Iranian government kept up its calls for foreign troops to leave Iraq.

Much to the dismay of the Saudi government, Bremer introduced ethnic-sectarian proportionality in the composition of the IIGC. It had thirteen Shias, eleven Sunnis and one Christian. Among the Sunnis, five were ethnic Kurds and one was a Turcoman. That is, only five IIGC members were Sunni Arabs, who had ruled Iraq since 1638 when Sunni Ottoman Turks incorporated Iraq into their empire. While only a quarter of the Iraqi population, local Sunnis had seized the reins of power, treating the majority Shias as second-class citizens. Now, the nightmare that Saudi royals dreaded had come to pass.

As head of the newly named Coalition Provisional Authority (CPA), Bremer dismissed all military personnel and civil servants, and abolished the ministries of defence and information as well as the military and security courts.[74] This uprooting of the core of the Sunni-dominated, tightly controlled state machinery that Saddam Hussein had perfected over the past quarter century sent shock waves through Saudi Arabia. The contrary was the case in Iran, but its leaders were careful not to give vent to their feeling of satisfaction at Saddam's ousting which would have amounted to endorsing the invasion of Iraq by the hated Americans.

With the eradication of Iraq's repressive bureaucracy which had functioned efficiently under Saddam, the sole leader of the secular Arab Baath Socialist Party, the long-suppressed Sunni Islamist militants became active. They focused on resisting the occupation forces and attacking Shia targets. Among the various Sunni groups pursuing this agenda, the *Jamaat al Tawihid wal Jihad* (Arabic: Society of Divine Unity and Jihad; JTJ) was the most important. Its leader was Abu Mussab Zarqawi (born Ahmad Fadil al Khalalyle in Zarqa, Jordan), an exiled Jordanian. He was based in Falluja, thirty-six miles west of Baghdad, in the overwhelmingly Sunni province of Anbar bordering Jordan, which became the soft belly of the government in Baghdad. The JTJ claimed responsibility for such dramatic acts as the bombing of the United Nations mission in Baghdad in August 2003, and the assassination of the IIGC's president Salim 10 months later. The JTJ took Westerners as hostages and beheaded some. The US raised the bounty on the capture of Zarqawi, dead or alive, from $10 million to $25 million.

In early 2004 the JTJ became an affiliate of Al Qaida and changed its name to Al Qaida in Mesopotamia, AQIM (Arabic: *Tanzim Qaidat al-Jihad fi Bilad al-Rafidayn*). Later it would become a member of the Mujahedin Shura Council, an umbrella organization of six Sunni Islamist groups. It targeted Shia gatherings, starting with a Shia funeral procession in December 2004 in Najaf when its car bomb attacks killed sixty mourners.[75] This caused anger and anguish not only among Iraqi Shias but also in Iran. Tehran increased its weapons supplies to the SCIRI-affiliated Badr Brigade, which had crossed into the Shia-dominated southern Iraq after the defeat of Saddam Hussein. It signaled the start of Iran's rising influence in post-Saddam Iraq, with SCIRI and al Daawa acting as its proxies.

In March 2004 Bremer issued the Transitional Administrative Law which was signed by IIGC members. It provided for an Interim Government headed by an executive Prime Minster to administer Iraq while focusing on holding elections to a Constituent Assembly not later than January 2005.

This did not satisfy Hojatoleslam Muqtada al Sadr, a militant Iraqi Shia cleric. In early April 2004 he called on his Mahdi Army volunteers to mount an armed uprising against the Anglo-American occupiers. Addressing the Friday prayer congregation in Tehran on 9 April, Ayatollah Ali Akbar Rafsanjani described Saddam Hussein's supporters, resisting foreign occupation, as terrorists. "Contrary to those terrorist groups in Iraq, there are powerful bodies which contribute to the security of the [Iraqi] nation," he said. "Among them is the Mahdi Army, made up of enthusiastic, heroic young people."[76]

It was against this backdrop that on 1 June 2004 the formation of the Interim Government was announced. It consisted of executive Prime Minister Ayad Allawi (also spelt, Iyad Allawi), a secular Shia, heading a cabinet of thirty-three ministers, and Ghazi Yawar, a Sunni tribal chief, as President with two deputies. On 28 June, Bremer handed over a "letter of sovereignty" to Iraq's Supreme Court Chief Midhat Mahmoud at a secret location in the heavily guarded Green Zone of Baghdad. In reality, whatever sovereignty was passed on to the Interim Government was at best moot. The security situation did not improve; in fact it got worse. "The United States has reached a dead end in Iraq like a trapped wolf, and it is trying to frighten people by roaring and clawing," said Khamanei in his address to an assembly of clerics in Tehran in early August. "But people of Iraq will not allow it to swallow their country."[77]

The Post-Saddam Hussein Era: Saudi Arabia

Having lost power, political and economic, Iraqi Sunnis and their leaders went into denial. Some of them responded positively to Saddam Hussein's call, issued from the underground, actively to resist the occupation forces. Those who did not join the resistance opted for non-cooperation with the occupiers. They showed scant interest in the elections to the Interim National Assembly, charged with drafting a new constitution, due on 30 January 2005. In contrast, Grand Ayatollah Ali Sistani, the most revered Shia cleric, issued a fatwa on 1 October 2004 declaring that voting was a religious duty of the believers. As a result 70 per cent of Shias (forming 60 per cent of the population) and Kurds (forming 15 per cent of the population) voted compared to a mere 20 per cent of Sunni Arabs.[78] With the Shia United Iraqi Alliance emerging as the majority party, its leader Ibrahim al Jaafari led the coalition government of his group with the Democratic Patriotic Alliance of Kurdistan, headed by Jalal Talabani with seventy-five seats, which excluded the forty-strong Sunni-dominated Iraqi List of Allawi, who had won the financial backing of the Saudi Kingdom. Thus it was the alliance of Shias and Kurds that drafted the constitution of post-Saddam Iraq.

By largely boycotting the poll to the Interim National Assembly, Sunni Arabs paved the way for their exclusion from the future power structure of Iraq. Some embittered Sunnis joined Al Qaida in Mesopotamia. Its leader Zarqawi argued that since the authority to legislate rested with Allah's word as revealed in the Quran, it was illegitimate for the believers to participate in elections. It backed the decision of the Sunni tribal leaders to boycott the poll for the Interim National Assembly in January 2005. The base of AQIM widened as Zarqawi amalgamated his anti-Shia rhetoric with Iraqi patriotism, arguing that non-Arab Iranians were surreptitiously taking over the reins of power in Baghdad. The militant group focused on high-profile and coordinated suicide attacks on Shia crowds which materialised not only during Ashura but also on the birthdays of the five Shia Imams buried in Iraq. In addition to the gilded tombs of Imams Ali and Hussein respectively in Najaf and Karbala, there were shrines of Imams Musa al Kadhim (aka Kazem) in Baghdad, and Muhammad Naqi al Hadi and Hassan bin Ali al Askari in Samarra.[79] Zarqawi's overarching aim was to create insecurity at large. But because of his addiction to violence for violence sake, violating tribal traditions and showing intolerance of those who differed from the AQIM, many Sunni tribal chiefs withdrew their support. To regain the lost ground, in January 2006, Zarqawi created the Islamic World Council to gather all Sunni resistance groups under one banner. He had made scant progress in this direction when he was killed in June in a joint operation by American and Iraqi forces.[80]

Conscious of the rising anti-American sentiment in Saudi Arabia, bin Laden ordered his Saudi-based lieutenants, Khalid Ali bin Ali Hajj and Abdul Aziz al Muqrin, co-founders of Al Qaida in the Arabian Peninsula (AQAP), to target Westerners residing in the Kingdom. They informed him that their network was not fully in place. But bin Laden nonetheless insisted on unleashing a violent campaign.

On 12 May 2003, bombs exploded at three residential compounds for expatriates in Riyadh—Dorrat Al Jadawel, Al Hamra Oasis Village, and the Vinnel Compound maintained by Vinnel Corporation training Saudi National Guard officers—on the outskirts of the capital. The attackers arrived in black sedans loaded with explosives, in two groups, with one shooting dead the security guards for the other to enter the premises. In one case, when they failed to enter the premises, they detonated the explosives at the gate. In another instance, gunmen shot their way into the residential compound, and exploded their lethal cargo to a devastating effect. A 100 meter high column of fire leapt into the sky and there was black smoke everywhere. According to US Ambassador Robert Jordan, at least twelve homes and sixteen apartment complexes were demolished in this compound. All told, twenty-nine people, including nine Americans and nine attackers, died, and nearly 200 were injured.[81] The grisly event shook the regime. Interior Minister Prince Nayef's son, Muhammad, who had been running the ministry's counter-terrorism department, resolved to crush the violent jihadists. Tellingly, the bombings came two weeks after Washington's announcement that it was pulling out most of its troops from Saudi Arabia—thus inadvertently reminding Saudis that the United States had failed to keep its written promise to withdraw its forces from the Kingdom at the end of the 1991 Gulf War.

The terrorist attacks were masterminded by thirty-four-year-old al Muqrin. A native of Riyadh, he underwent military training at an Al Qaida camp in Afghanistan. There he grew close to bin Laden and left Afghanistan in the same year, 1992, as did the Al Qaida leader—to join the jihad in Bosnia. Later he was a member of the hit team that made a failed attempt to assassinate Egypt's President Hosni Mubarak in June 1995 during his visit to Addis Ababa, Ethiopia, to attend the Organisation of African Unity summit. He was arrested there and extradited to Saudi Arabia. He was given a jail sentence of two years which was reduced to one year after he had memorised the Quran. Al Muqrin traveled to Taliban-ruled Afghanistan, and fled after the overthrow of the Taliban regime in December 2001. Back in Saudi Arabia, he made adroit use of the Internet to disseminate his militant ideas. "I have taken it upon myself and I have sworn to purge the Arabian Peninsula of the polytheists," he told an Arabic website in 2003. "They [the Crusaders and Jews] will not have any security until we evict them from the Land of the Two Holy Places (Saudi Arabia) and until we evict them from the land of Palestine and the land of the Muslims, which they pillage and usurp from the east to the west."[82]

On his part, Crown Prince Abdullah convened the first National Meeting for Intellectual Dialogue, which had its own constitution and secretariat, in June 2003. It was open only to Sunni clerics who belonged to the Hanbali school of jurisprudence (which included Wahhabis). Safar al Hawali of the Sahwa movement declined the invitation, but his colleague Salman Awda attended.[83] In September Abdullah expanded the organization to the National Dialogue Forum, consisting of Sunni and Shia clerics, businessmen, educationalists and media executives to debate ways of reforming society. By so doing he adroitly succeeded in diverting the long-repeated demand for reforming monarchy.

With the departure of the last American troops from the Kingdom in September 2003, Prince Muhammad bin Nayef expected AQAP leaders to cease their violent campaign. They did not. On 8 November, during Ramadan, AQAP terrorists stormed past security guards into the affluent, heavily protected Al Mohaya housing compound west of Riyadh, and detonated explosions. As many as twenty-eight people (of whom only four were Westerners, with the vast majority being expatriate Arabs) were killed, and 122 injured. By contrast the official figures were two dead and 87 injured.[84] Among other things these bombings laid to rest the conspiracy theory about the Israeli intelligence agency Mossad being responsible for both Al Qaida and 9/11. In the Kingdom there was all round condemnation of these assaults, including by Shaikhs Salman al Awda and Safar al Hawali, the recently released co-founders of the Sahwa movement.

In the wake of the death of bin Baz in May 1999, and the subsequent vacuum in the theological power structure, the government considered it expeditious to co-opt the Sahwa movement's leaders to serve as an alternative source of religious legitimacy. Therefore it released the much chastened Awda and Hawali and their followers in the summer. Awda and Hawali promised to tone down their political opposition in exchange for the regime tolerating their softened stance with their opinions limited to the non-political aspects of Islam. Two years later, at the behest of the Saudi regime, Awda was invited to host Islam Today. net (Arabic: *al Islam al-yawm*), a program on Dubai-based MBC (Middle East Broadcasting Center), owned by Waleed al Ibrahim, a brother-in-law of King Fahd. Its mandate was to expound Islam-related religious and social subjects, and provide Islamic educational resources in English, Arabic, French and Chinese.[85] This enabled Awda to bolster his religious authority among Saudis and others.

In response to the high profile terrorist assault on the Kingdom, Prince Muhammad bin Nayef intensified his counterterrorist efforts.

This led to the killing of Khalid Ali bin Ali Hajj on 15 March 2004. With that, AQAP leadership passed to al Muqrin. He focused on petroleum facilities in order to damage the economy. An attack on an oil facility in Yanbu left six Westerners dead and ended with the beheading of helicopter engineer Paul Marshall Johnson. A climax came on 28–31 May 2004 when four AQAP militants targeted three premises in Khobar, an oil hub. They took hostages, gave phone interviews to the Al Jazeera TV channel, and ended up killing twenty-two people, including nineteen foreigners working in the oil industry.[86] Soon after, Awda and Hawali joined six senior ulema to denounce Al Qaida violence and its campaign to overthrow the House of Saud.

Al Muqrin also continued the practice of targeting individual Westerners which, in his view, was a significant element of urban guerrilla warfare to frighten and demoralize the enemy. He penned a manual in Arabic which, translated into English by Norman Cigar as *A Practical Course for Guerrilla War*, would be published posthumously. On 6 June 2004, AQAP militants killed Simon Cumbers, a BBC cameraman, and injured BBC journalist Frank Gardner. Two days later they gunned down Robert Jacobs of Vinnell Arabia Corporation in front of his villa. And on 12 June, another American, Kenneth Scroggs, was slain in front of his home. The Interior Ministry ratcheted up its efforts to kill or capture its number one enemy, al Muqrin. Its success came on the night of 18 June when he died in a shoot out with the security forces at a petrol station in Riyadh along with three other co-founders of AQAP.[87] With that, terrorism declined temporarily.

In the regional context, on 27 July 2004, Saudi Foreign Minister Prince Saud Al Faisal welcomed an Iraqi delegation of ministers and the Central Bank governor, headed by Interim Prime Minister Allawi in Jeddah. After his talks with Allawi, the Saudi Foreign Minister said, "We agreed on the resumption of diplomatic representation" severed in 1991.[88] However, a follow-up failed to materialise. On the other hand the promise of Riyadh's grant of $1 billion toward Iraq's reconstruction resulted in Baghdad receiving $300 million over the next year.[89]

Ongoing Terrorism in the Kingdom

Under the leadership of Salih al Awfi, AQAP operators raided the United States consulate in Jeddah, leading to the deaths of five staff and four attackers in December 2004. Awfi was killed by Saudi security forces in a gun-battle in Medina on 18 August 2005 after being detected in a hideout near the Mosque of the Prophet a few hours before a visit by King Abdullah.[90] More car bombs exploded in Riyadh. In response, the government cracked down hard. By the time of King Fahd's death in August 2005, more than ninety-one civilians and 118 militants were killed and nearly 800 injured. After interrogating thousands, the Interior Ministry arrested at least 800 men as suspected terrorists.[91] The government complimented its iron-fist approach toward terrorists with propaganda against Islamist violence, using advertisements and billboards, sponsoring clerical conferences where ulema offered arguments against terrorism based on Islamic precepts, and airing dramas on state-run TV channels, showing the presence of religious militancy in society.[92]

11

IRAN'S NUCLEAR SAGA;

AND IRAQ AVERTS AN INTER-SECTARIAN WAR

It was a bitterly cold night on 12 January 2010 in Tehran's northern-most district of Shemiran along the slopes of the Elborz Mountain. Yet the balding, mustached fifty-year-old Mansour Ali Mohammadi, a phys-ics professor at Tehran University, and his stocky, moon-faced wife Mansoureh Karami, rose from their bed in a well-furnished house to say their dawn prayer. After refreshing themselves with a final, brief stretch of sleep, as Karami started cooking breakfast for her husband and two grown-up children, Ali Mohammadi leafed through the bound PhD thesis that one of his students had given him a week earlier, one more time. He ate breakfast, and while taking his packed lunch from Karami, bid her goodbye, put on the shoes kept near the door, and, clutching his leather satchel, said a final goodbye to his wife.

He opened the front gate, and then started up his car. As he stepped out of his car to shut the gate, an earth-shaking blast, triggered by remote-control, rang out—releasing a lethal spray of steel pellets. The source was a motorcycle parked nearby. Mohammadi collapsed in a pool of blood. The pellets penetrated the PhD thesis as well as the glasses case inside his satchel. The explosion shattered the windows in a nearby four-story building, distorted window frames, and blew off a garage door.

The government suspected the hand of Israel and/or America. Its intelligence agencies went on high alert. Later a tip-off from "a third country" referred to a cell that Mossad, Israel's foreign intelligence agency, had set up inside Iran. With the killing of another nuclear scientist, Majid Shahriari, and the wounding of Fereydoon Abbasi-Davani, a leading official at Iran's Atomic Energy Organisation, on 29 November, the intelligence agencies went into an overdrive.

The next month the authorities arrested Majid Jamali Fashi, a twenty-three-year-old Iranian kick-boxer, for murdering Mohammadi. In his televised confession aired in January 2011, he said that he had been recruited by Israeli agents when he was in the Azeri capital of Baku to participate in an international martial arts competition. He was flown to Israel. "They told me that the subject of the operation is a person involved in making an atomic bomb and that humankind is in danger and you are the savior." He was flattered. At the Mossad station off the Tel Aviv-Jerusalem highway east of Ben Gurion Airport, he was trained to kill his target. It included working with two new Iranian motorcycles, and a replica of Mohammadi's street and house. Once he had accomplished his assigned task, "I was very proud that I have done something important for the world—and then suddenly realised that what I believed in was a lie."[1]

In retrospect, Mohammadi's widow, Karami, recalled that only she and a few others knew that he was engaged in a secret nuclear program, and that he felt that during his Hajj pilgrimage in 2009 he was being followed and filmed. In December 2009, on the eve of his departure for Jordan to attend a highly specialized scientific conference, he feared that he might be kidnapped and felt physically ill, she revealed.[2]

The meticulously planned murder of Mohammadi sent shock waves through Iran's scientific and nuclear community. Conversely, it reassured policy-makers in Riyadh that Israel, the most fervent regional enemy of Iran, had resorted to targeted killings to sabotage Tehran's nuclear activities. On the other hand, they had not taken this factor into account while devising their own strategy to counter Iran's nuclear threat. Instead, they had decided on shoring up their long-established cordial relations with nuclear Pakistan.

Saudis' Military Ties with Pakistan

At the Organisation of the Islamic Conference (OIC) summit in Lahore in February 1974, behind closed doors, Prime Minister Zulfikar Ali Bhutto reportedly told Saudi King Faisal that since the Israeli and Indian atom bombs were meant to intimidate the Muslim world there was an urgent need for an Islamic nuclear bomb. By then the news had leaked that when the Israelis suffered a series of setbacks on the battlefield in October 1973, in the occupied Sinai Peninsula, Prime Minister Golda Meir ordered that all the twenty-five nuclear bombs produced since 1966 be mounted on specially adapted bombers.[3]

King Faisal reportedly agreed to provide cash in exchange for a pledge that Islamabad's nuclear program would henceforth provide a security umbrella for Saudi Arabia against Israel. With that objective in mind he was also believed to have extended financial aid to Iraq after its Vice-President Saddam Hussein became chairman of the Iraqi Atomic Energy Agency in 1974 and had authorized a clandestine nuclear weapons program.[4]

Following protracted negotiations, the Saudi and Pakistani governments signed a three-year military protocol in December 1982. This was overseen by the Saudi Pakistan Armed Forces Organisation in Riyadh. Pakistani soldiers were stationed in Tabuk near the strategic Gulf of Aqba, and in Khamis Mushayet near the South Yemeni border.[5] This was a welcome development for debt-ridden Pakistan since the affluent Saudis paid for the salaries of its soldiers and the maintenance of its military hardware. From Riyadh's viewpoint, the presence of skilled and disciplined Muslim soldiers from Pakistan was far less provocative to Saudi citizens than an American or other Western presence. The Saudi-Pakistan agreement was renewed in 1985 for three years. In 1986, Pakistan's military presence in the Saudi Kingdom was put at one infantry division (13,000 strong) and two armored and two artillery brigades (totaling, 10,000 soldiers). That meant Pakistan accounting for most of the Saudi 12th Armored Brigade near Tabuk.[6] Toward the end of this period, the Saudi government insisted that the Pakistani forces had to be purely Sunni. President General Zia ul Haq rejected the condition, arguing that there could be no sectarian discrimination in the Pakistani military. Following the withdrawal of these combat troops, Pakistan still had up to 5,000 military instructors, technicians and other personnel in the Kingdom under military assistance programs.[7]

Riyadh-Islamabad-Delhi Triangulation

Meanwhile, on 1 March 1987, the London-based *Observer* headlined its front page scoop, "Pakistan has the A-Bomb". It quoted Abdul Qadeer Khan, later called the godfather of the Pakistani atomic bomb, saying, "What the CIA has been saying about the atom bomb is correct. They told us Pakistan could never produce the bomb and they doubted my capabilities, but they now know we have it."[8] The report was by Kuldip Nayar, an Indian journalist who had been invited to Islamabad. In Nayar's interview in Islamabad on 28 January, Khan said, "We have it [an atom bomb] and we have enriched uranium…Weaponized the thing. Put it all together." Nayar replied, "If you have tested, it would be a tremendous warning for India."[9] The story was published around the globe. Since even implicit acceptance of the report would have resulted in Washington cutting off all aid to Pakistan, its government was vehement in its denial. At the same time, General Zia ul Haq resolutely ruled out testing the device in order not to embarrass US President Ronald Reagan who was keen to bolster Pakistan's anti-Soviet jihad in Afghanistan.

In the Muslim world among the countries that approached Pakistan about buying its nuclear weapons technology was Iran. According to one report, nuclear weapons equipment was transferred to Iran for cash between 1988 and 1990 when General Imtiaz Ali was Pakistan's former Chief of Army Staff.[10] No details became available in the public domain. But a well-informed guess was that Pakistan provided a fully functional set of high speed centrifuges for enriching uranium. Since the material used for these contraptions was being updated steadily any Pakistani equipment acquired by Iran would have become obsolete in less than a decade.

In the Gulf region, Saudi Arabia signed the nuclear Non-Proliferation Treaty (NPT) only in 1988 when pressured by Washington, keen to pre-empt any attempt by the Kingdom to obtain nuclear arms technology from Pakistan. Earlier Riyadh had maintained that it would sign the NPT only after Israel had done so. That never happened, and was most unlikely to happen.

The strong bonds between Riyadh and Islamabad remained in place even after the restoration of democracy in Pakistan after Zia ul Haq's death. In December 1988, it brought to power Benazir Bhutto, a daughter of Zulfikar Ali, who had performed the Umrah in March 1985. She was invited to the Kingdom by King Fahd. She arrived in Jeddah in April 1990 at the head of a 45-strong delegation. She met the monarch. Six months later she was dismissed from office by President Ghulam Ishaq Khan on charges of corruption and maladministration.

It was during the tenure of a caretaker government in Islamabad that the crisis precipitated by Iraq's invasion and occupation of Kuwait in August erupted. Following the UN Security Council resolution calling on member-states to assist the Kuwaiti ruler to expel the Iraqis from his emirate, US President George H. W. Bush started assembling a coalition of Western and Muslim countries to achieve this objective. The caretaker government in Islamabad agreed to send 11,000 troops to Saudi Arabia. And after winning the parliamentary poll in October 1990, Prime Minister Nawaz Sharif—a small, rotund man with a flabby face and a balding head—canvassed the Muslim world to support the Saudi-US alliance. During the subsequent 1991 Gulf War, Pakistan deployed its Air Defence Regiment for the protection of vital Saudi military assets in Tabuk, and in order to deter Iraq's air force.

According to the official documents photocopied by senior Saudi diplomat Mohammad A. Khilewi in June 1994, the aggregate sum provided by Riyadh to Iraq's clandestine nuclear weapons program, which ended in 1990 when Iraq invaded and occupied Kuwait, came to about $5 billion. Most of this amount was funneled from the total of $25,734,469,886 with which the Saudi Kingdom provided Iraq during the 1980–1988 Iran-Iraq War, according to the 11 February 1991 Newsletter of the Embassy of Saudi Arabia, Washington, D.C.[11] Following the US-led defeat of Iraq in February 1991, its secret nuclear weapons program would be detected and destroyed.

However, Saudi funding for Islamabad's clandestine nuclear program was supplemented by the military's Inter-Services Intelligence (ISI) channeling some of the CIA cash it received during the anti-Soviet jihad.[12] Pakistan was in a nuclear race with India which, having tested its "atomic device" successfully in May 1974, had resorted to fabricating an atom bomb in 1980. Seven years later, having learned of

Pakistan's success in nuclear armament, India accelerated its own program in that field.

In Delhi, by December 1995, Indian Premier P.V. Narasimha Rao was ready to order an underground test of its atomic bomb. But US President Bill Clinton, informed by the US satellite images of enhanced activity at the Indian test site of Pokhran in the Rajasthani desert, succeeded in persuading Rao to abandon his plan. A consensus had grown among Indian leaders that the only way their country could gain a permanent seat at the UN Security Council was by becoming either a heavyweight economic power or a state with nuclear arms. The first objective was nowhere on the horizon. Therefore it was the logic of the second option that drove Prime Minister Atal Bihari Vajpayee to order nuclear tests in May 1998 once the strategy to evade satellite imaging by the US had been successfully deployed by the Indians.

Vajpayee's Pakistani counterpart in Islamabad, Nawaz Sharif, faced a dilemma. Testing a nuclear weapon would lead to sanctions by the US with adverse consequences for Pakistan's parlous economy. None the less, popular pressure built up.

The only foreign leader that Sharif consulted on the subject was Crown Prince Abdullah, the de facto leader of Saudi Arabia. As a result of the nuclear test, Pakistan would suffer economic sanctions by the US, he explained. To offset the loss, Abdullah granted Pakistan 150,000 oil barrels per day free of charge,[13] and the rest of its petroleum needs on deferred payment terms to be agreed annually. His gesture clinched Sharif's decision to proceed with the tests in the Chagai Hills of Balochistan, about thirty miles from the Iranian border. After the nuclear explosion the Saudi Kingdom heralded Pakistan for becoming "'the first Muslim country to be a nuclear power."[14] Riyadh's concession to Pakistan helped to relieve to some extent the impact of sanctions on it by the US and the European Union.[15] Pakistan's military assistance to the Saudi kingdom in the form of soldiers, expertise and ballistic missiles increased. High-level, bilateral teams of scientists, government officials and military officers conferred periodically to advise Riyadh on developing its nuclear program.

A month later, following a hastily arranged trip to Islamabad, Crown Prince Abdullah held a meeting with Nawaz Sharif. A joint Pakistani-Saudi communiqué mentioned the two leaders dealing with economic issues. This was true in so far as Abdullah agreed to convert the $2 billion Pakistan owed Riyadh as deferred payments during the past five years into a grant.[16] The visit by Saudi Defence Minister Prince Sultan to Islamabad in May 1999 was focused on a single subject. Accompanied by Pakistani Premier Nawaz Sharif and Chief of Army Staff General Pervez Musharraf—a bespectacled, mustached man of medium build with his graying hair parted in the middle—he was given a tour of the Kahuta uranium enrichment plant by Abdul Qadeer Khan. The Saudi minister also visited the plant equipped to assemble the Ghauri missile, which has a range of 1,500 to 2,000 km. It was the first time that an outsider was allowed into the top-secret sites. When the Bill Clinton administration pressed the Saudis for an explanation, they obfuscated.[17]

In November A.Q. Khan traveled to Saudi Arabia, one of forty such trips he would log up before finding himself under house arrest four years later. Such were his high level contacts in the Kingdom that he claimed to have been offered Saudi citizenship, a rare privilege, by one of Abdullah's half-brothers.[18] Washington's suspicion was justified. In February 2004, Khan would confess in a televised interview that he had sold nuclear secrets to Iran, Libya and North Korea.

The Saudis' Input into Pakistani Politics

On 12 October 1999 Musharraf mounted a coup against Sharif. Two weeks later he flew to Saudi Arabia and briefed King Fahd and Crown Prince Abdullah. Only after that did he fill most of the country's ministerial posts. In December 2000 as a result of an agreement negotiated by the Saudis and the Clinton administration to forestall Sharif's execution on a charge of treason, Sharif along with forty members of his extended family went into exile in Saudi Arabia in a deal brokered by King Abdullah. It required Sharif to shun Pakistani politics for ten years. During his exile, after receiving a loan of $33 million from the Saudi Industrial Development Fund, he established a steel mill in 2005 in Jeddah with a capacity to produce 100,000 tons of steel annually.[19]

General Musharraf's authoritarian style of governance was warmly approved by Riyadh. In 2001, Saudi Arabia and Pakistan set up joint ventures to manufacture small arms and ammunition. By then joint military exercises by the two nations had become routine. On 25 May

2002, President Musharraf invited high Saudi officials to attend the test launching of a Ghauri missile with a range of 940 to 1,250 miles, capable of carrying a nuclear warhead.[20] In return for Islamabad's military and security cooperation, Saudi Arabia promised increased investments in Pakistan whose GDP growth often fell behind the rise in its population. In that context remittances sent home by nearly one million Pakistani workers in the Saudi kingdom were of vital importance to the economy. In June, Musharraf, who continued to serve as the Army chief, summed up Islamabad-Riyadh relations thus: "When Pakistan faces any problem, Saudi Arabia is the first shelter to which Pakistan turns."[21] Two months later, following a sensational exposure about Tehran's nuclear program, regional and international attention turned to Iran.

Iran's Nuclear Issue to the Fore

In August 2002 the revelation by the Paris-based National Resistance of Council of Iran (NRCI) of the existence of a secret uranium enrichment complex in Natanz, and the construction of a heavy water production plant in Arak,[22] prompted anxiety in Riyadh. Iran claimed that it was enriching uranium up to 5 per cent purity to be used in a civilian nuclear power plant. In December Tehran agreed to inspections by the United Nations' International Atomic Energy Agency (IAEA).

In February 2003 Iranian President Muhammad Khatami revealed that his government had unearthed uranium deposits, and announced plans to develop a nuclear fuel cycle—that is undertake a series of industrial processes which involve the production of electricity from uranium in nuclear power reactors.[23] (Earlier, in June 2002, Dariush Foroughi, head of the Center for Research on Energy and Environment, had announced that Iran's uranium reserves amounted to 12,000 tons).[24] This set alarm bells ringing in Riyadh. Its interest in Islamabad's nuclear program grew exponentially.[25]

Following an urgent discussion at the highest levels of the national security apparatus in Riyadh, a Saudi strategy paper evolved. On 18 September 2003 the *Guardian* reported that top Saudi officials were debating three options: the Kingdom acquiring a nuclear capability of its own as a deterrent; maintaining or entering into an alliance with an existing nuclear power that would offer protection; and trying to reach a regional agreement on a nuclear-free Middle East.[26]

This report appeared around the time the US alleged that Iran was not complying with international non-proliferation accords. Nonetheless it agreed to support a proposal by Britain, France and Germany—collectively called the European Union (EU) Troika—to give Tehran until the end of October to resolve with "full transparency" all the remaining questions of the IAEA on the nuclear issue, and allow surprise inspections by the IAEA under its Additional Protocol. Following talks between Iran's Foreign Minister Kamal Kharrazi and his EU Troika counterparts in Tehran, the Iranian government announced on 21 October that it had agreed to suspend the enrichment of uranium, and would sign the IAEA's Additional Protocol. Two main considerations drove Iran to be pliant—one negative, the other positive. Its policy-makers feared that the Bush White House would try again to destabilize their regime. And the payback for a successful agreement with the EU Troika on the nuclear issue was a fully-fledged trade and economic cooperation pact with the EU.[27]

On the Saudi side, Crown Prince Abdullah and his accompanying 200-strong entourage, which included Foreign Minister Saud Al Faisal and several other cabinet ministers, arrived in Islamabad on 18 October to be greeted by Prime Minister Mir Zafrullah Jamali. The Jamali-Abdullah meeting was attended by the foreign ministers of both countries. Among the dignitaries at the subsequent luncheon was President Musharraf. During his press conference, referring to the recent meeting in Delhi between Vajpayee and the visiting Israeli Prime Minister Ariel Sharon, Prince Saud warned that Israeli-Indian defence cooperation would inflame the region and escalate the arms race.[28]

As for formal Riyadh-Islamabad nuclear cooperation, different unconfirmed reports gained currency. One version had Pakistan providing Saudi Arabia with nuclear technology along with a promise to pass on to it a nuclear bomb if it felt threatened by a third party's nuclear program in the future. Another version mentioned the Saudi Kingdom purchasing Pakistani nuclear warheads to be placed atop Saudi missiles if Iran became an armed nuclear power. Both governments denied these unconfirmed reports while IAEA Director-General Muhammad El Baradei said in November 2003 that there was "no evidence" that Iran was pursuing a nuclear weapons program.

During 2004, the IAEA kept a close watch on Iran's nuclear program. In February it reported that Iran had experimented with polonium-210, which could be used to trigger the chain reaction in a nuclear bomb, but failed to explain its experiments. And in June, it criticised Tehran for not offering "full, timely and pro-active" co-operation with inspectors. In September, Iran's Supreme Leader Ayatollah Ali Khamanei issued a fatwa that it was "un-Islamic" to use an atom bomb. Two months later, Iran suspended its uranium enrichment program until there was a "grand bargain" between it and the EU Troika, with the EU guaranteeing nuclear, political, and trade concessions to Iran for Tehran's indefinite suspension of its enrichment program.[29] It even allowed IAEA inspectors into the secretive Parchin plant near Tehran in January 2005. While Iran waited for the EU Troika's offer, its politics were overshadowed by the presidential poll on 17 and 24 June 2005. To the surprise of many, Mahmoud Ahmadinejad, the hard line mayor of Tehran, beat the veteran Ayatollah Ali Akbar Rafsanjani by a margin of 62:35 per cent of the vote. This heralded a further hardening of the Iranian position.

By a strange coincidence, King Fahd died on 1 August 2005, and Ahmadinejad was sworn in as president of the Islamic Republic of Iran the next day. Pakistan's President General Musharraf attended the funeral and offered condolences to King Abdullah, as did Muhammad Arif, the First Assistant of Khatami.[30] The closeness of the Riyadh-Islamabad axis could be judged by the fact that following the death of King Fahd, Pakistan declared a seven-day period of official mourning.

Iran's Nuclear Program and Iraq's Sectarian Violence

As Abdullah had been the de facto ruler since 1995, nothing changed in Riyadh. This was not the case in Tehran where a radical conservative succeeded a moderate reformer. Ahmadinejad's election coincided with the rising power of the security and intelligence agencies. He appointed Ali Larijani, a hardliner, to lead the talks with the EU Troika. In the final analysis, however, the authority in this vital matter rested with the Supreme National Security Council charged with formulating policies on defence and national security. Chaired by the president, it consisted of eighteen civilian officials and military commanders, including two representatives of the Supreme Leader. Its decisions had to be ratified by the Leader before they were implemented.

On 6 August 2005, the EU Troika's "grand bargain" boiled down to Iran giving up its right to enrich uranium permanently in return for improved commerce with Tehran and guaranteed supplies of nuclear fuel from Europe for Iran's civilian nuclear power plants. Crucially, there was no mention of Iran's right to enrich uranium as accorded by the NPT. Three days later Ahmadinejad's government rejected the offer. In January 2006 it broke IAEA seals on its uranium enrichment facility at Natanz. The EU Troika ended its talks with Iran. But Iran's government was buoyed by the fact that an independent investigation discovered no evidence that Iran was working on a secret nuclear weapons program, and concluded that traces of bomb-grade uranium in Iran's nuclear facilities came from contaminated Pakistani equipment. Unsurprisingly, Washington dismissed this report.[31]

In February 2006, to the delight of Saudi royals, the thirty-five-strong Board of Governors of the IAEA decided to refer Iran's case to the United Nations Security Council by twenty-seven votes to three.[32] In return, Iran ended voluntary co-operation with the IAEA beyond basic nuclear Non-Proliferation Treaty requirements, and resumed enrichment of uranium In the regional context this was a win for Saudi Arabia, secure in the knowledge that the world's highest security organization was to deal with Iran's nuclear ambitions. In the regional context, as the international crisis with Tehran on the nuclear issue deepened, the unconfirmed reports of Riyadh's unwritten deal with Islamabad, often planted by Israeli officials, appeared periodically to pressure the US to get tough with Iran on its nuclear project.

On the other hand, events in Iraq were going unambiguously in favor of Iran. The new constitution drafted by the Interim National Assembly, elected in January 2005, was ratified in a referendum by 76 per cent of the voters in October. The election to the 275-member Council of Representatives under the new constitution followed in December. It described Iraq as an Islamic, democratic, federal parliamentary republic. It specified Islam as a main source of legislation and stated that no Iraqi law would violate the basic tenets of Islam. It stipulated a parliamentary system with an executive prime minister to be elected by the Council of Representatives. But it also required that all bills passed by this assembly must be approved unanimously by a three-member Presidential Council, consisting of a Shia, a Sunni and a Kurd before it could become law.[33]

Winning 128 seats, the (Shia) United Iraqi Alliance led by Ibrahim al Jaafari, emerged as the largest group, followed by the Democratic Patriotic Alliance of Kurdistan headed by Masoud Barzani with 53 seats, and the (Sunni) Iraqi Accord Front of Tariq al Hashimi with 44 seats. This time Sunnis voted in large numbers. And yet the 15 per cent popular vote garnered by the Iraqi Accord Front was less than a quarter of the combined total of the Shia and Kurdish parties.[34] Thus an impartially implemented electoral system reflected the true strengths of the three major ethnic-sectarian groups—a development that worried the monarchical autocracy of Saudi Arabia.

There were more electoral setbacks in store for the Desert Kingdom. In the first free and fair election in the Palestinian Territories, populated by Sunnis with a small Christian minority, in January 2006 the radical resistance group Hamas won 74 of the 132 parliamentary places compared to 45 secured by the long-established, moderate ruling Fatah movement, backed by Saudi Arabia, on a voter turn-out of 77 per cent.

The resulting Hamas government was not recognized by the US and the EU because they had listed Hamas as a terrorist organization, and it had refused to recognize Israel. They cut off their financial assistance to the Palestinian government of Hamas. Iran stepped in and increased its contribution to Hamas to $23 million.[35] Bowing to Washington's pressure, Saudi Arabia refused to fund the Hamas administration. If it had defied the US, it would have made itself vulnerable to being listed as a sponsor of state terrorism. It therefore ended up mediating between Hamas and Fatah by chairing a meeting between their representatives in Mecca. This led to the formation of a unity government in March 2007 under Hamas leader Ismail Haniyeh. But it failed to secure the recognition of America and Israel. In any case, it proved transient. To abort a plot by the Fatah intelligence chief, Muhammad Dahlan, working in collusion with the US and Israel, to overthrow the Hamas-dominated government, the militia of Hamas in the Gaza Strip mounted a preemptive attack on Fatah from 10 to 15 June, and seized full control of the territory.[36] Iran maintained its support for Hamas, thus establishing a firm footprint in a Sunni Arab territorial entity, which was a bitter pill for the Saudi government to swallow.

In Iraq the intermittent tit-for-tat attacks by Al Qaida in Mesopotamia (AQIM) on Shias and the Mahdi Army and the Badr Brigade on Sunnis became a depressing feature of daily life. The bombing of the gold-domed mosque containing the shrine of Shia Imams Muhammad Naqi al Hadi and Hassan bin Ali al Askari in Samarra in February 2006 triggered low-intensity warfare between Shias and Sunnis. This sensational attack occurred at the time of political stalemate. Jaafari's leadership of the United Iraqi Alliance was challenged by Adel Abdul Mahdi. He defeated his rival by one vote, thanks to the support he secured from those members of the alliance who were associated with the Mahdi Army, which was committed to a speedy ending of the Anglo-American military presence. Disregarding his administration's claim that Iraq became sovereign in June 2004, President George W. Bush publicly opposed the re-election of Jaafari as the Prime Minister. To end the debilitating stalemate, Grand Ayatollah Ali Sistani persuaded Jaafari to step down. The premiership then went to Nouri al Maliki, the spokesman of the alliance. He was regarded by James Jeffrey, Senior Advisor for Iraq to the Secretary of State, to be someone independent of Iran, and easy to maneuver.[37] Maliki assumed office in May 2006.

Even though the Allawi-led Iraqi National List (INL) had only twenty-six seats, he included it in his cabinet. However, Allawi declined a ministerial post, unwilling to serve under Maliki, and spent most of his time in Amman. Instructed by him, INL ministers resigned in 2007.

Once in power, Maliki acted as independently as he could to present himself as an Iraqi nationalist. The first foreign capital he visited was Tehran where he was warmly welcomed by Ahmadinejad and Khamanei. During his subsequent tour of the Gulf States to explain his recently launched Iraq Reconstruction project, he arrived in Jeddah on 1 July to meet King Abdullah. According to the Saudi monarch, he received from Maliki "a written list of commitments for [sectarian] reconciliation in Iraq," but the Iraqi leader failed to follow through.[38] This was not so. Indeed, on 25 July, along with the re-appointed President Jalal Talabani, Maliki announced the formation of the thirty-member National Reconciliation Commission, charged with holding conferences and meetings, and mounting a media campaign for reconciliation.[39]

On the other hand, it was not feasible for Maliki to live down the fact that as a leader of the banned al Daawa party in Iraq, he had taken refuge in Tehran from 1982 to 1990 before moving to Damascus. He publicly described himself as a Shia first then leader of the al Daawa party, and lastly an Iraqi national. He consolidated Shia power, thus alienating disgruntled Sunnis further. Anbar Province had emerged as the bastion of Sunni insurgency with AQIM being the leading actor, funded by its lucrative illicit oil trading.

Zarqawi's successor Abu Ayub al Masri, a former Egyptian military officer, replaced the Islamic World Council with the Islamic State of Iraq, under the leadership of Abu Omar al Baghdadi, a leading extremist ideologue, by co-opting small militant groups. It aimed to seize power in Iraq and transform it into an orthodox Sunni Islamist state. According to a classified US Marine Corps intelligence report in August 2006, Sunnis, "increasingly abandoned by religious and political leaders who have fled to neighboring countries," were desperate, fearful and impoverished. Unlike the Shias and Kurds, they did not possess oil or other natural resources in the areas where they formed a majority. Between Al Qaida violence, Iran's influence, and an expected US drawdown, "the social and political situation had deteriorated to a point" that American and Iraqi troops "are no longer capable of militarily defeating the insurgency in Anbar," it concluded. Among the solutions it proposed were creating a local paramilitary force to protect Sunnis and offsetting Iranian influence in Baghdad.[40]

The change in the balance of power was starkly reflected on the ground in Baghdad, home to a quarter of Iraq's population of 27 million. Before the AQIM assault on the twin shrines in Samarra's Golden Mosque in February 2006, the Mahdi Army and the Badr Brigade reacted defensively to the attacks by Sunni extremists. That changed radically after the Samarra bombing. They went on the offensive, a process that accelerated after Maliki assumed the premier's office in April.[41] Neighborhoods in the eastern sector—most vulnerable to the Shia militias based in Sadr City—lost much of their minority Sunni populations. Even the mixed, middle-class districts started to lose their Sunni residents. By the end of 2006, more than ten neighborhoods that were mixed Sunni and Shia a year earlier became almost completely Shia.[42] Four out of five sectarian acts of violence occurred within thirty miles of Baghdad which had become divided between sectarian enclaves.

The Maliki government condemned anti-Sunni violence but did little in practice to stop it. The fear among Sunni politicians and policy-makers in Washington was that if the emboldened fringe Shia militants were to resort to violence on a wider scale and do so with impunity then the neighboring Sunni countries—Saudi Arabia in particular—might intervene, and ignite a protracted regional armed conflict.

The United States sounded an alarm bell. Stating that the situation in Iraq "could not be graver," President Bush on 10 January 2007 said that "The war on terror cannot be won if we fail in Iraq. Our enemies throughout the Middle East are trying to defeat us in Iraq. If we step back now, the problems in Iraq will become more lethal, and make our troops fight an uglier battle than we are seeing today." The task of additional troops would be "to help Iraqis clear and secure neighborhoods, to help them protect the local population, and to help ensure that the Iraqi forces left behind are capable of providing the security," he added.[43] In his State of the Nation speech to Congress on 23 January 2007, Bush announced that as part of the military surge—described as "The New Way Forward in Iraq"—he had ordered the dispatch of over 21,500 soldiers into Iraq with most of them to be deployed in the capital and Anbar Province.[44] He did so after gaining the consent of Maliki with whom he held weekly video teleconferences.

A few weeks earlier, as the Commander-in-Chief of Iraq, Maliki had set up the Office of the Commander-in-Chief (OCINC) with twenty-four nominees as a consulting body. Within months, the OCINC resorted to circumventing the established chains of command in the ministries of defense, interior and national security. By so doing, it provided Maliki with direct means to dismiss or appoint commanding officers. US military sources in Iraq referred to several instances in which capable Iraqi commanders were detained or forced out of their positions after suppressing Shia militias. This led to reports in the US media that the OCINC was a smokescreen to hide Maliki's Shia agenda. The White House expressed its "concern," and stressed that it was essential for Iraqi democracy to have security forces that would enforce the law fairly "regardless of what group a citizen belongs to." However,

Iraq's Defense Minister Abdul Qadir al Obeidi, a Sunni, denied that the OCINC was overstepping its advisory role. A senior Iraqi army officer was quoted by CNN as saying that "the presence of the Americans was preventing the actions of the Office [of the Commander-in-Chief] from being devastating, but he worried about what would happen when US forces ultimately leave Iraq." At that point, he added, "there will be no restraint on the activities of the Office."[45] His statement would prove to be prescient.

In Washington, the National Intelligence Estimate on Iraq, released by the White House in early February 2007, referred to "certain elements" of civil war in Iraq. These included "the hardening of ethno-sectarian identities, a sea change in the character of the violence and population displacements". It stated that Iran and to a lesser extent Syria were contributing to a worsening of the situation.[46] The last statement chimed with the view of the Saudi government.

And yet Saudi King Abdullah was faced with the fact that a pro-Tehran government was in office in Baghdad. He also took on board the concern of regional states at the escalating Sunni-Shia violence which the Iraqi and American forces had failed to reverse as well as political standoff in Lebanon. He therefore invited Ahmadinejad to the Saudi capital for talks on 3 March 2007. On returning to Tehran after his summit with Abdullah, Ahmadinejad said that "plots carried out by the enemies in order to divide the world of Islam were discussed," and his interlocutor had joined him in condemning them. Earlier the official Saudi Press Agency reported that "The two leaders asserted that the greatest danger threatening the Muslim nation [*umma*] at the present time is the attempt to spread strife between Sunni and Shia Muslims, and that efforts should be exerted to stop such attempts and close ranks."[47] These ameliorative statements, however, made little difference on the ground.

Additional American troops started arriving steadily in Iraq from February 2007. There was also a shift in the White House's policy on counterterrorism. It instructed the Pentagon to focus on protecting civilians rather than on killing the maximum number of enemies. This was crucial to dampen sectarian violence. Given the growing disaffection of the Sunni tribal chiefs with AQIM, there was a good chance of luring them to join the anti-insurgent drive with money and arms.

But US Ambassador Ryan Crocker and the supreme commander of US forces in Iraq, General David Petraeus, needed the consent of Maliki. He refused. Yielding to intense lobbying by Crocker and Petraeus, he later agreed if the Pentagon became the paymaster and refrained from supplying arms to the Sunni tribes. The winning over of these tribes, which started in the spring of 2007, was called the Sunni Awakening (Arabic: *sahwa*). Encouraged by its progress, Pentagon expanded the program, offering $300 a month to volunteers, who were free to buy arms, easily and cheaply available, and man checkpoints and patrol. Additionally, they were required to tip off American and Iraqi troops. In return they were told that they would ultimately be integrated into the state's regular army and police.

Reflecting the resulting change, the Pentagon started to use the term "Concerned Citizens" instead of the Sunni Awakening. "I now have more Concerned Citizens than coalition troops," said Major General Rick Lynch, commander of US-led forces in central Iraq, in October 2007, and he felt confident that his present force of over 21,000 Concerned Citizens would "exponentially grow." He added, "Right now I've got thirty-four concerned citizen groups under contract, and that is costing me $7.5 million every 60–90 days," most of the groups being Sunni.[48] Actually, in less than a year the recruitment area spread from the Sunni tribes in Anbar Province to become an ad-hoc armed force of 65,000 to 80,000 across Iraq.

The overarching strategy remained the same: US forces were to clear an affected area of insurgents, and then the Concerned Citizens/Sunni Awakening groups would hold it. However, Maliki felt uneasy about the Pentagon's program and threatened to curb such activity and bring it under the control of the Iraqi army amid accusations that one Sunni group had resorted to kidnapping, killing and blackmailing in the capital. He did not follow up.

The compounding of the increased US military force with the funding and arming of the Concerned Citizens/Sunni Awakening groups led to a noticeable drop in violence. US troop fatalities dropped from 126 in May 2007 to 23 in December. During the same period Iraqi civilian deaths fell from more than 1,700 to about 500.[49] In 2008, the Pentagon began planning to reduce its troops, then numbering 140,000, starting with their withdrawal from cities and towns to their rural bases.

Politically, reduced bloodshed imbued the Iraqi government with much needed confidence. Maliki pressed the Bush administration to agree to a staged withdrawal of American forces, arguing in June 2008 that sixteen months would be the right time-frame to complete the process. By October, his government felt self-assured enough to take over the responsibility for paying Awakening Council members, who then numbered close to 94,000. But it intended to integrate only a quarter of them into the Shia-led military and police, despite the urging of Washington to absorb all of them.

Little wonder that during his March 2009 meeting with John Brennan, the counterterrorism adviser to President Barack Obama, Saudi King Abdullah expressed "a complete lack of trust in Iraqi PM (Prime Minister) al Maliki and held out little hope for improved Saudi/ Iraqi relations as long as al Maliki remains in office". He had not followed through the commitments for sectarian reconciliation in Iraq he had made. "I don't trust this man," the King stated, "He's an Iranian agent." The King said he had told both Bush and Cheney "how can I meet with someone I don't trust?" Maliki has "opened the door for Iranian influence in Iraq" since taking power, the King said, and he was "not hopeful at all" for Maliki, "or I would have met with him [after 2006]."[50] Unsurprisingly, at the Arab summit in Doha on 28–29 March, Abdullah had deliberately avoided greeting Maliki.

On his part, Maliki continued to consolidate his power in Iraq by projecting himself as a committed nationalist. His success could be judged by the fact that soon after assuming the US presidency in January 2009, Barack Obama announced that all American troops would leave Iraq by the end of 2011. And when on 30 June 2009 US soldiers withdrew from the urban areas to their rural bases, Maliki's government declared it as the National Sovereignty Day.[51] This proved to be more than a symbolic gesture; it strengthened Maliki's diplomatic clout.

On 24 September 2009 a secret cable to the State Department, sent by Christopher Hill, the US Ambassador to Iraq, headlined, "The Great Game, in Mesopotamia: Iraq and Its Neighbors, Part I," covered the ground comprehensively. Alluding to an account of the Oval Office session that Maliki had with Obama in July 2009, the Iraqi leader suggested to the US President that he should ask the Saudis to refrain from intervening in Iraq's affairs. Their efforts to rally the Sunnis, complained

Maliki, were heightening sectarian tensions and providing Iran with an excuse to intervene in Iraqi politics. "For now," continued Hill, "the Saudis are using their money and media power (Al Arabiya and Al Sharqiya TV satellite channels, and other various media they control or influence) to support Sunni political aspirations, exert influence over Sunni tribal groups, and undercut the Shia-led Islamic Supreme Council of Iraq (ISCI) and Iraqi National Alliance (INA)."

Hill pointed out that "Iraqi officials note that periodic anti-Shia outbursts from Saudi religious figures are often allowed to circulate without sanction or disavowal from the Saudi leadership." This reality, continued Hill, "reinforces the Iraqi view that the Saudi state religion of Wahhabi Sunni Islam condones religious incitement against Shia. The suspicion is that these anti-Shia attitudes color Saudi views of a Shia-led Iraq. The Saudis have traditionally viewed Iraq as a Sunni-dominated bulwark against the spread of Shiaism and Iranian political influence. In the wake of bombings in predominantly Shia areas across the country in June 2009 that killed dozens, PM Maliki pointed publicly to one such statement, made by a Saudi imam in May, and noted, 'We have observed that many governments have been suspiciously silent on the fatwa provoking the killing of Shiites.'"

Summarising the briefings of the Embassy's Iraqi contacts, Hill noted that "These contacts assess that the Saudi goal (and to varying degrees most other Sunni states) is to enhance Sunni influence, dilute Shia dominance, and promote the formation of a weak and more fractured Iraqi government."

Hill went to offer his assessment of Iran. "Iranian influence in Iraq remains pervasive, as Tehran manipulates a range of levers to mold Iraq's political, religious, social, and economic landscape," he observed. "Iranian efforts are driven by a clear determination to see a sectarian, Shia-dominated government that is weak, disenfranchised from its Arab neighbors, detached from the US security apparatus and strategically dependent on Iran."

Hill then distinguished Iran's modus operandi from that of Iraq's Sunni Arab neighbors. "Iranian influence is not aimed, unlike that of some Sunni Arab neighbors, at fomenting terrorism that would destabilize the government," he noted. "It will naturally create nationalistic Iraqi resistance to it (both Shia and more broadly), if other outsiders do not intervene to stoke Sunni-Shia sectarian tension; and has been frozen in place to some extent in the past few months by the [post-presidential] political turmoil inside Iran."[52]

Abdullah's action in Iraq was part of a bigger anti-Iran, anti-Shia policy that came to light when the Saudi foreign ministry was hacked by a group calling itself the Yemeni Cyber Army in 2015. The hackers released a number of sample document sets on file-sharing sites, but these were deleted by the Saudi government's censorship tools. Subsequently they passed on more than half a million Saudi cables and other documents to WikiLeaks, covering 2010 to early 2015. Then WikiLeaks started releasing the material in tranches of tens of thousands of documents at a time, starting with 70,000 documents on 19 June 2015.[53]

Saudis' Anti-Iran, Anti-Shia Obsession Exposed

Two months later (in November 2015), the Saudi Foreign Ministry admitted to a breach of its computer networks. Riyadh found the leaked documents so embarrassing that it made spreading them a criminal offence. A summary provided by Ben Hubbard and Mayy El Sheikh of the *New York Times*, and published two days after Iran's 14 July nuclear deal, encapsulated Riyadh's ongoing anti-Iran and anti-Shia crusade. While Saudi Arabia maintained that some documents were fabricated, most contained correct names and phone numbers. When contacted by the *New York Times*, many individuals and organizations mentioned in the cables verified their contents.

The leaked Saudi cables, covering the period between 2010 and early 2015, revealed in forensic detail how the Kingdom has spent billions of dollars to implement its two-track religious agenda, devised by top officials from the Foreign, Interior and Islamic Affairs Ministries, the intelligence service and the Royal Court, and coordinated by the Supreme Council for Islamic Affairs, an inter-ministerial body. One track focused on disseminating the Saudi brand of Sunni Islam by putting foreign clerics on the Kingdom's payroll, building mosques, schools and study centers, and undermining foreign officials and news media seen as threats to Saudi interests. The other track focused on undermining Shia Islam and Iran.

There was a standard procedure for financing the religious agenda. The Foreign Ministry conveyed funding requests to the Interior Ministry and the intelligence agency to vet potential recipients. The Mecca-based, Saudi-funded World Muslim League helped coordinate strategy, and Saudi diplomats abroad supervised the projects. Alternatively, prompted by the World Muslim League, Saudi diplomats identified sympathetic overseas Muslim leaders and organizations, distributed funds and religious literature, trained clerics and hired them as salaried employees to work in their home countries. The cables named fourteen new clerics to be employed in Guinea and showed that contracts had been signed with twelve others in Tajikistan.

"We are talking about thousands and thousands of activist organizations and preachers who are in the Saudi sphere of influence because they are directly or indirectly funded by them," said Usama Hasan, a senior researcher in Islamic studies at the Quilliam Foundation in London to the *New York Times*. "It has been a huge factor, and the Saudi influence is undeniable."

Following the Foreign Ministry's instructions, Saudi embassies in Asia, Africa and Europe monitored the activities of the Iranian missions in minute detail. An example was the Saudi embassy in Colombo, Sri Lanka, reporting a meeting between the Iranian ambassador and a group of Muslim scholars, which started at 7:30 p.m.

In the ideological field, a clutch of Saudi cables expressed grave concern that Iran was seeking to turn Tajikistan into "a center to export its religious revolution and to spread its ideology in the [Central Asian] region's countries." The Saudi ambassador in Dushanbe suggested that Tajik officials could restrict Iranian support "if other sources of financial support become available, especially from the Kingdom." A cable from Riyadh to the Saudi embassy in Dushanbe stated that the government was keeping a close watch on Iran's moves in Russia. Unsurprisingly, the Saudi embassy in Tehran sent daily reports on local news coverage of the Kingdom. In one cable it suggested that Saudi Arabia should start a Persian-language television station and send pro-government clerics to tour Iran.

The leaked cables revealed that between 2010 and 2013, King Abdullah tried to force Iran's Arabic-language satellite television station, Al Alam, off the air. These attempts included issuing royal decrees aimed at stopping the broadcasts, pressuring the Riyadh-based satellite provider Arabsat to discontinue the channel, and using "technical means" to weaken the channel's signal so it did not reach Bahrain and the Kingdom's Eastern Province, where discrimination against Shias was rampant. The Saudi monarch's efforts failed. After being dropped by two Arab satellite providers, Al Alam management succeeded in finding a European satellite provider. "We are broadcasting normally" said a Beirut-based manager of Al Alam to the *New York Times*. "The only disruption we have [now] is when we broadcast a show about Bahrain."

In 2012 the Saudi Foreign Ministry instructed its ambassadors in Africa to send reports on Iranian activities in their countries. The Saudi ambassador to the largely Christian Uganda filed a detailed report on "Shia expansion." A cable from Mali, a predominantly Muslim country, warned that Iran was appealing to the local Muslims, who knew little of "the truth of the extremist, racist Shia ideology that goes against all other Islamic schools."

At the same time, Riyadh did not overlook countries where Muslims were a tiny minority such as China (1.6 per cent) and the Philippines (5 per cent). The Saudi embassy in Beijing was asked to suggest "practical programs that can be carried out to confront Shia expansion in China." The cables from Manila included suggestions to "restrict the Iranian presence." In flood-stricken Thailand, the Saudi foreign minister requested funds from the Treasury, arguing that "it will have a positive impact on Muslims in Thailand and will restrict the Iranian government in expanding its Shia influence."

Meanwhile, King Abdullah had kept his eye firmly fixed on Iran's progress in the nuclear field, and to counterbalance it had deepened the Kingdom's interest in the politics of Pakistan, which was steadily expanding its arsenal of atomic bombs.

Abdullah Intervenes in Pakistani Politics

On 1 February 2006, Abdullah, leading a delegation of ministers, top civil servants and business magnates, arrived in Islamabad to be greeted by President Musharraf and Prime Minister Shaukat Aziz. After receiving Pakistan's highest award, the *Nishan-e-Pakistan* (Urdu: "Emblem of Pakistan"), he signed an economic co-operation accord with Pakistan, a country for which the Saudi kingdom was the largest oil supplier.

To Musharraf's discomfiture, in May 2006 Sharif and Benazir Bhutto signed the Charter of Democracy, drafted jointly by their aides, during their meeting in London. They announced that their political parties would contest the elections promised by Musharraf in 2007. This alliance between long-time rivals materialised after the conciliatory call that Bhutto, self-exiled in Dubai since April 1999, made on Sharif in Jeddah in February 2005.[54] According to the secret cable sent by the US consulate in Jeddah on 12 September 2007, published by WikiLeaks, the Saudi intelligence chief Prince Muqrin told US Ambassador to Saudi Arabia, Ford M. Fraker, that there was a verbal agreement that after five years, he and Sharif would negotiate reduction in the ten year period for Sharif's abstinence from Pakistani politics.[55] On 23 August 2007 the Pakistan Supreme Court ruled that Sharif was free to return home. In an undisguised intervention in Pakistan's internal affairs, Prince Muqrin held a press conference in Islamabad on 8 September. When reminded of the Supreme Court ruling, he said, "Which comes first, the agreement with us or the Supreme Court?" He added that Saudi Arabia would "welcome" Sharif if he was deported by the Pakistani government. When Sharif arrived at Islamabad airport, he was arrested and put on a plane bound for Jeddah.[56]

But when the Bush administration persuaded Musharraf to let Benazir Bhutto return to Pakistan on 18 October, the Saudi government found itself in a quandary. If Sharif's rival could go home, it was unthinkable for Riyadh to keep Sharif in the Kingdom against his will. On his part, ignoring Washington's advice, Musharraf declared an emergency on 3 November, ostensibly to counter the rising influence of jihadist terrorism. As a consequence the general election due in late November was postponed to early January 2008. This riled the domestic opposition united under the umbrella of the Movement for the Restoration of Democracy.

King Abdullah summoned Musharraf to Riyadh on 20 November. According to WikiLeaks, on that day, Adel al Jubeir, the Saudi Ambassador to Washington, invited the US charge d'affaires Michael Gfoeller to his residence in Riyadh, and informed him that Musharraf would meet the monarch, Foreign Minister Prince Saud Al Faisal, and Prince Muqrin. "The purpose of these meetings is to get a read-out of the situation [in Pakistan] and present our point of view to him," al

Jubeir said. "*We in Saudi Arabia are not observers in Pakistan, we are partici-pants.*" He added that the Saudi government would control Sharif's movements in the Kingdom in future. Giving his assessment of the situation in Pakistan, he remarked that neither Sharif nor Bhutto was a viable replacement for Musharraf. "With all his flaws, he [Musharraf] is the only person that you or we have to work with now." He described Pakistan as "very tribal, much like our own country." Given the fact that Pakistan possessed both nuclear weapons and delivery vehicles, the Kingdom's policy there boiled down to a drastic choice: "We can either support Musharraf and stability, or we can allow [Osama] bin Laden to get the bomb." As a senior advisor to King Abdullah for eight years, al Jubeir represented the monarch's views, according to the US charge d'affaires.[57]

This secret cable sent from the US Embassy in Riyadh cut through the traditional opacity that was characteristic of Saudi policy-makers. It put an official stamp on their strong preference for authoritarian rulers and their disdain for the democratically elected leaders who could not assure stability. Jubeir's remark about Pakistani society being tribal was patently ill-informed. The elements of tribalism could be detected only in the provinces of Balochistan and Khyber Pakhtunkhwa which together formed only one-fifth of the country's population.

The United Nations Sanctions Iran

In April 2006 Ahmadinejad announced that Iran had succeeded in enriching uranium to 3.5 per cent purity. In June, China, Russia, and the United States joined the EU Troika to offer another proposal for comprehensive negotiations with Iran. This was again rejected by Tehran. In its Resolution 1696 passed under Chapter VII of the United Nations, in July 2006, the UN Security Council demanded an end to Iran's uranium enrichment-related and reprocessing activities. Iran refused to comply.

When Iran defied the Security Council's resolution in December 2006 to suspend enrichment-related and reprocessing activities and cooperate with the IAEA, the Council followed up with Resolution 1747 on 24 March 2007. It increased the sanctions placed in December 2006, banned Iran's arms exports and froze the assets and restricted the travel of individuals engaged in Iran's nuclear program. This reassured the Saudi government about the seriousness with which the UN was handling Tehran's nuclear activities.

Its mood changed when, on 3 December 2007, US National Intelligence chief Mike McConnell released an unclassified summary of a new National Intelligence Estimate (NIE) of Iran's nuclear intentions and capabilities, based on the consensus of all sixteen US spy agencies. It concluded with "high confidence that Iran had halted its nuclear weapons program four years earlier, in the autumn of 2003, and had not resumed work on nuclear weapons as of mid-2007." This conclusion was based on Iran's military communications intercepted by the United States.[58]

The report made sense. The driving force for militarisation of Iran's nuclear program was Saddam Hussein's ambitions to produce an atom bomb. By the autumn of 2003, when it became abundantly clear after a thorough search of Iraq by the occupying Anglo-American troops that the Iraqi leader had destroyed all facilities for producing weapons of mass destruction, Iran's government discontinued its tentative moves toward producing an atomic bomb.

By chance, on 3 December 2007 Ahmadinejad was in Doha at the invitation of Qatar's Emir Hamad Al Thani to attend the annual two-day Gulf Cooperation Council summit as a guest. In his address to the summit, Ahmadinejad presented a twelve-point proposal, which included cooperation in the scientific, cultural and economic spheres, leading to a free trade agreement. "We are proposing the conclusion of a security agreement," he said, adding that insecurity would affect all countries bordering the Gulf. "We want peace and security…based on justice and without foreign intervention."[59] The key phrase was "without foreign intervention," which translated into GCC states terminating their ongoing defense cooperation agreements with the US—a non-starter, principally for Saudi Arabia. Later when he was asked to comment on Washington's NIE on Iran, he said that the issue of Iran's nuclear program was "closed", and that his country was prepared for any eventuality. "We do not feel threatened at all, but we are prepared," he added.[60]

His words played well with radicals in Iran, but left Abdullah and his inner circle fuming. All the same, outwardly Abdullah showed no sign of any cooling towards Ahmadinejad. Indeed, he invited the Iranian president to the Hajj pilgrimage, starting on 18 December 2007. Ahmadinejad thus became the first serving president of Iran to receive such an invitation, which he accepted readily.

At the UN Security Council resolutions passed in March 2007 and March 2008 imposed gradual sanctions on Iranian individuals and entities believed to be involved in the country's nuclear and missile programs. In September 2008 the Security Council adopted Resolution 1835 restating the demands made in July 2006, but without imposing additional sanctions. All these resolutions were passed under Chapter 7 of the UN charter and were based on the premise that Tehran's nuclear program was illegitimate and a threat to international peace and stability.

To leave nothing to chance, by then President Bush had authorized a clandestine cyber program to access Natanz's industrial computer controls to obtain a blueprint of how it worked. Once that was achieved, a joint US-Israeli team started building a worm to attack the Natanz plant and make its centrifuges, which enrich uranium, run out of control. The resulting Stuxnet worm would then be introduced into the Natanz facility with contaminated computer drives around June 2009.[61]

In September, when pressured, Tehran admitted that it was constructing a uranium enrichment plant into a mountainside at Fardow near the holy city of Qom, but insisted that it was for peaceful purposes. The next month five permanent UN Security Council members and Germany offered Tehran a proposal to enrich its uranium abroad. Iran showed interest. The subsequent talks to agree the details dragged on for many months, and finally collapsed in May 2010 when Iran refused to stop enrichment per se, its right under the nuclear NPT. Three months earlier Ahmadinejad had announced that Iran had enriched uranium to 20 per cent which was required for the nuclear research reactor built in Tehran in 1967 to produce medical isotopes. In June the Security Council passed Resolution 1929 imposing a complete arms embargo on Iran.[62]

Abdullah's Duplicitous Policy on Iran

On 2 March 2008 Ahmadinejad became the first Iranian president to undertake a state visit to Iraq since the establishment of the Islamic

Republic in 1979. In contrast to the visit by President Bush who was flown by helicopter from Baghdad airport to a heavily protected American compound, Ahmadinejad rode in a motorcade to the compound of Iraqi President Jalal Talabani, an ethnic Kurd, guarded by local forces.

There he declared that he had arrived to open a "new chapter" in Iraqi-Iranian relations. In response, Talabani stated that "economic, oil, political and security issues" were all on the table. At a joint press conference with his guest, Prime Minister Maliki said, "I think that the level of trust [between Iraq and Iran] is very high. And I say frankly that the position Iran has taken recently was very helpful in bringing back security and stability." When an Arab reporter referred to the Bush administration's statements that Iran supplied arms to Shia militias, Ahmadinejad said, "You can tell Mr. Bush that making accusations about others will increase the Americans' problems in the region. They will have to accept the facts in the area. The Iraqi people do not like the Americans." On another occasion Ahmadinejad stated that the American occupation had resulted in terrorists flocking to Iraq. The next day he signed agreements for energy supplies and other investment projects in Iraq to help its reconstruction drive.[63]

The growing cordiality between Baghdad and Tehran greatly worried both Riyadh and Washington. In addition, there lurked the fearful prospect of Iran managing to fabricate an atom bomb, which the Saudi royals dreaded most. Yet there was very little they could do directly to stop Iran's nuclear program. All they could do was to urge Washington to get tough with Tehran on this issue. They tried hard behind the scenes but their clandestine efforts became public knowledge with the release by WikiLeaks of the first cache of 220 US diplomatic cables on 28 November 2010, which were published by the *New York Times* and the *Guardian* among others.

The cable sent by the American Embassy in Riyadh on 20 April 2008 summarised the talks between US Ambassador to Iraq, Ryan Crocker, US General David Petraeus, commander of the multinational forces in Iraq, and King Abdullah along with his ministers of foreign affairs, interior and intelligence on 14–15 April, and the conversation between the US charge d'affaires and Adel al Jubeir, Saudi Ambassador to Washington, on 17 April. The text under the sub-heading "The Need to Resist Iran" referred to Abdullah and his senior ministers agreeing that "the Kingdom needs to cooperate with the US on resisting and rolling back Iranian influence and subversion in Iraq. The King was particularly adamant on this point, and it was echoed by the senior princes as well." The text then summarized al Jubeir's remarks. "Al Jubeir recalled the King's frequent exhortations to the US to attack Iran and so put an end to its nuclear weapons program. 'He told you [Americans] to cut off the head of the snake,' al Jubeir recalled to the charge d'affaires, adding that working with the US to roll back Iranian influence in Iraq is a strategic priority for the King and his government."[64] On its part, America had imposed oil and trade sanctions over Iran's alleged sponsorship of terrorism as far back as 1995.

King Abdullah was unhappy about the turn of events in Pakistan in 2008 on two counts. That year saw the return of democracy in Pakistan after eleven years of military dictatorship, and that led to the election of Asif Ali Zardari, a Shia, to presidency. Unable to hide his hatred of Zardari, Saudi King Abdullah told the visiting US National Security Adviser, James Jones, that Zardari was the "rotten head" that was infecting the whole body.[65]

A Sudden Internal Challenge to Khamanei

Instead of investing cash from record high oil prices, Ahmadinejad, untutored in economics, consumed it by raising pensions and salaries and giving cheap loans. And, by using the everyday language of the people and touring each of the thirty-one provincial capitals, addressing rallies there and collecting petitions from citizens, he widened his popular base. He also rallied the nation on the issue of Iran's right to enrich uranium for peaceful purposes. Over-confident of his public standing, his government allowed three 90-minute TV debates between him and each of his three challengers during the run-up to the presidential poll on 12 June 2009. This gave an unprecedented opportunity for opposition views to be aired before an audience of 50 million. It dramatically enhanced the chances of reformist Mir Hussein Mousavi, a former Prime Minister during the 1980–1988 Iran-Iraq War. He eviscerated Ahmadinejad for mismanaging the economy and reversing the social-cultural liberalisation introduced by Khatami.

At 84 per cent, the voter turn-out was the second highest in the Republic's history. It meant that more of the upper-middle and upper class Iranians—often secular—went out to vote than before. This favored Mousavi. So the official result, announced post-haste, giving 62.5 per cent of the ballots to Ahmadinejad to Mousavi's 33.9 per cent stunned most Iranian and foreign analysts. Tens of thousands took to streets in Tehran and other large cities to protest against the widely suspected poll-rigging, with some angry participants vandalising and burning buses. The authorities closed the Tehran bureau of the Dubai-based Al Arabiya TV channel for a week. In response, pro-Ahmadinejad voters rallied in central Tehran. Mousavi lodged a complaint with the twelve-member Guardian Council election authority, a body of senior clerics and judges. It agreed to carry out a partial recount a day after an estimated three million supporters of Mousavi—who rejected the Guardian Council's decision while demanding a fresh poll—poured into the streets in the largest protest since the 1979 revolution on 15 June. The government banned foreign media reporting from the streets of Tehran, confining them to their hotels and offices. The next day there were pro- and anti-Ahmadinejad demonstrations. The regime closed universities in Tehran, blocked certain websites, and cut mobile signals. It mobilised its police force and the far more numerous Baseej volunteers, the shock troops used to end public protest. They often drove into the demonstrating crowds on motorcycles, and beat the participants with clubs, metal batons and baseball bats. Although an auxiliary force of the IRGC, Baseej volunteers, operating as vigilantes, did not wear uniform, and were fanatically loyal to the Supreme Leader.

On 18 June when more than 100,000 protesters held a candlelight vigil in the capital following Mousavi's call for a day of mourning for those killed in protests,[66] the Ansar Hizbollah, forming the core of the Baseej, issued a call for a demonstration against the "seditious conspiracy" being carried out by "agitating hooligans." It invited "the vigilant people who are always in the arena to make their loud objections heard in response to the babbling of this tribe," on the following day, Friday.[67] In his sermon to the Friday prayer congregation, Supreme Leader Ayatollah Khamanei said the presidential poll was legitimate and that the large voter turnout and resulting success for Ahmadinejad was a "divine assessment," adding that the margin of victory—over 11 million votes—was too large to have been manipulated. He warned that protests would no longer be tolerated.[68]

The opposition rejected Khamanei's assertion. But far fewer people protested while the security forces became more vicious, sometimes using live ammunition to disperse crowds, and killing ten protesters, including Neda Agha-Soltan, a young Iranian student, whose death covered by a YouTube video went viral, and who became a symbol of the opposition[69]—now called the Green Movement, named after the color favored by Mosavi.

On 29 June the Guardian Council, following its random counting of 10 per cent of the ballots, certified the results of the disputed election. That triggered a fresh wave of protests despite the official ban on street marches.

A week after Ahmadinejad was sworn in for a second term as President on 5 August, a spokesman for the judiciary said that 4,000 persons were arrested during the post-election protests, and that all but 300 who were "involved in the riots" were detained only for a few days. While the government admitted the deaths of "about thirty" protesters, the opposition estimated the figure at sixty-seven, according to the testimony from the bereaved families. Most of those arrested were held in the notorious jails of Evin and Kahrizak. There were so many complaints of abuse of the prisoners at the Kahrizak detention center that Khamanei ordered its immediate closure. Iran's Parliament and judiciary also appointed committees to investigate the post-election unrest and the government's response.[70] In short, after blatantly rigging the poll for reasons which remain obscure because of the opacity of what transpires at the office of the Supreme Leader, Khamanei pulled out all the stops to crush the popular protest that arose spontaneously.

Iran's Growing Isolation Boosts Riyadh

In the face of Tehran's refusal to suspend uranium enrichment, UN Security Council started extending sanctions against Iran in the financial sector. Its resolution in March 2008 called on member-states to monitor the activities of Iranian banks and inspect Iranian ships and aircraft for breach of its arms embargo. More specifically, the Saudis were reassured by Washington's continued hostility toward Tehran despite the succession of Bush by Barack Obama, a Democrat, as US President in January

2009. Repeating its conclusion in the earlier years, the State Department said in its annual country reports on terrorism in May that Iran remained the "most active state sponsor of terrorism" in the world. The main culprit, it said, was the Al Quds unit of Iran's Islamic Revolutionary Guard Corps (IRGC) which was aiding Shia militias in Iraq and maintaining close links with Hizbollah in Lebanon.[71]

Earlier, on 12 January 2010 the Iranian media coined the term "a nuclear martyr," when reporting the assassination of Mansour Ali Mohammadi, a physics professor at Tehran University, outside his home in north Tehran. On the eve of the thirty-first anniversary of the Islamic Revolution on 10 February 2010, Ahmadinejad announced that Iran had succeeded in enriching uranium to 20 per cent purity from the previous level of 3.5 to 5 per cent. This, he claimed, was required as fuel for the US-supplied nuclear reactor built in Tehran in 1967 to produce medical isotopes for the treatment of cancer.[72]

Four months later, on 9 June 2010, the UN Security Council Resolution 1929 imposed a fourth round of sanctions on Iran. It included tighter financial curbs and an expanded arms embargo by barring Tehran from purchasing such heavy weapons as attack helicopters and missiles, banned Iran from any activities related to ballistic missiles, and authorized the inspection and seizure of shipments violating these restrictions. It also extended the asset freeze to the IRGC and Islamic Republic of Iran Shipping Lines and recommended member-states to prohibit the opening of Iranian banks and prevent Iranian banks from entering into relationship with their banks if it might contribute to the nuclear program. The resolution was adopted by twelve votes to two—Turkey and Brazil—opposing, with Lebanon abstaining.[73] Russia and China cooperated with the three Western members with veto power on the understanding that they would not act beyond this resolution. This was not to be, with the US and the European Union later imposing further unilateral sanctions on the Islamic Republic. In Tehran Ahmadinejad dismissed the resolution as "a used handkerchief which should be thrown in the dustbin."[74]

Saudi Kingdom's Unresolved Domestic Challenge

Terrorist activity continued after Abdullah succeeded Fahd in August 2005. Indeed, a potentially most damaging attack on the Saudi oil industry occurred in February 2006. Two Al Qaida in Arabian Peninsula (AQAP) operatives, wearing the uniforms of Saudi Aramco guards and driving company pick-up vans, managed to cross two of the three perimeter gates of the Abqaiq oil facility which processed 7 million barrels per day to be loaded into tankers for export. It was only at the last gate that they were challenged. The subsequent gun battle lasted two hours, resulting in the deaths of the terrorists and two security guards, and damage to pipelines. Had the infiltrators succeeded in their mission to blow up part of the vast plant, oil futures would have risen by a hefty $20 a barrel.[75] The subsequent crackdown by the Saudi authorities forced many of the group's several hundred members to seek refuge in Yemen.

Anti-American feeling among ordinary Saudis was on the rise against the background of incipient sectarian warfare between Sunnis and Shias in US-occupied Iraq. In February 2007, 99 Saudi lawyers, professors and activists released a petition, titled "Milestones on the way to constitutional monarchy". It so angered the government that it arrested nine ringleaders for assembling to form a political party. However, to show that he had noted the popular sentiment against America, King Abdullah used his opening speech at the Arab League summit in Riyadh on 27–28 March 2007 to state that "In the beloved Iraq blood is spilled between brothers under an illegitimate foreign occupation and despicable sectarianism that threatens civil war."[76] With this, Abdullah, who had cooperated with President Bush in the latter's invasion of Iraq, surpassed himself in egregious hypocrisy. His statement came two-and-a-half years after UN secretary general Kofi Annan declared that the US-led war on Iraq was illegal on two counts: it was not sanctioned by the UN Security Council, and it was not in accordance with the UN's founding Charter.[77]

On the sixth anniversary of 9/11 (September 2007), the Saudi cleric Salman al Awda addressed an open letter to Osama bin Laden in his weekly program *Al haya kalima* (Life is a Word) on MBC. "How many innocent children, women, and old people have been killed, maimed, and expelled from their homes in the name of Al Qaida?", asked Awda rhetorically. "The image of Islam today is tarnished. People around the world are saying how Islam teaches that those who do not accept it must be killed. They are also saying that the adherents of Salafi teachings kill Muslims who do not share their views."[78] On 1 October 2007, Grand Mufti Abdul Aziz bin Abdullah Al Shaikh issued a fatwa prohibiting Saudis from engaging in jihad abroad, and warned that undertaking such a mission without the ruler's authorization constituted serious offense.[79] The reference to jihad outside the Kingdom related to those Saudi citizens who after traveling to Iraq participated in Islamist terrorism against the American occupiers.

The impact of the state's strategy on AQAP was minimal. Its planned major terrorist act during the Hajj season in December 2007 was foiled only at the last minute, according to official sources. Earlier, on 27 April, the government arrested 172 AQAP members from seven cells who were planning attacks on military bases and oil refineries. By early 2008 more than 4,000 suspected terrorists were interrogated. In April, further large groups of suspects were taken into custody. By the autumn the authorities claimed to have foiled as many as twenty-five plots and killed or captured 260 operatives including all except one of the twenty-six ring leaders.[80]

Along with its police action against jihadists, the Interior Ministry introduced a rehabilitation and re-education program for the detainees, treating them as young men with twisted minds, rather than political radicals. A distinction was made between those who had joined a jihad abroad and the ones involved in domestic attacks, the latter considered as misled Saudi sons. "These young people have been sick," said Prince Muhammad bin Nayef. "We view their problem as a virus in their brain... Among our detainees we have about 20 per cent who refuse to change... But we help those who are willing to be helped. We bring in psychiatrists. We bring in clerics who show them where they have misread the Quran. They have lots of religious lessons. We bring in all the family."[81] The end-purpose of the rehabilitation program was to enable the reformed man to settle down with a wife and raise a family. The Ministry gave him SR 60,000 ($16,000) to cover the current bride price, with the family encouraged to find a suitable wife for him. Between 2004 and the autumn of 2008, almost 100 clerics, backed by thirty psychologists, were drafted in to run the rehabilitation program. Of the 2,000 detainees who went through it, 700 were freed after their renunciation of jihadist beliefs. At the outset, 1,400 detainees had refused to participate in the project.[82]

In August 2009 Bin Nayef was lucky to escape a meticulously planned assassination attempt during Ramadan. Abdullah Hassan al Asiri, a Saudi AQAP activist, returned to Jeddah from Yemen and offered to surrender personally to Bin Nayef as two dozen other AQAP radicals had done before. In addition, he presented himself as someone who could persuade other militants in Yemen to surrender. That led to his meeting with the prince at his private residence in Jeddah on Friday, 28 August. He went through the metal detector, and a patting of his body by the guards. The plastic explosive PETN that he was hiding in his underwear went undetected, and so did his chemical fuse. During the meeting he used the prince's mobile phone to call his comrades in Yemen to tell them that he was standing near Bin Nayef. After finishing the call, he handed the phone to the prince. At that moment, the plastic bomb blew up, tearing al Asir in seventy-three parts but, miraculously, injuring his target only slightly. Bin Nayef, holding the phone, heard "Allahu Akbar" at the other end in celebration of his presumed death.[83]

Bin Nayef had worked in close cooperation with counterterrorism officials in Washington. During his 15 March 2009 meeting with King Abdullah in his private palace in Riyadh, John Brennan described Prince Bin Nayef as "an outstanding counterterrorism partner," according to WikiLeaks.[84] And yet AQAP would remain active in the Saudi Kingdom as evidenced by the arrest of its 249 members and seizure of $600,000 cash in late November 2010.[85]

Abdullah's Unvarnished Take on Iran

As a prologue to the 90-minute 15 March discussion summarised in the secret cable on 22 March 2009 sent by the US Ambassador to Saudi Arabia, Ford Fraker, King Abdullah said, "Thank God for bringing Obama to the presidency," which has created "great hope" in the Muslim world. Under the sub-heading "Iran: Heated Exchange," the document read: "The King noted that Iranian FM Manouchehr Mottaki had been 'sitting in that same seat (as Brennan) a few moments ago.' The King described his conversation with FM Mottaki as 'a heated exchange, frankly discussing Iran's interference in Arab affairs.' When challenged by the King on Iranian meddling in Hamas affairs, Mottaki apparently protested that 'these are Muslims.' 'No, Arabs' countered the King, 'You as Persians have no business meddling in Arab matters.' When Mottaki said the Iranians wanted to improve relations, the King responded by giving Mottaki an ultimatum. 'I will give you one year [to improve ties], 'after that, it will be the end.'"

When Brennan told the monarch that President Obama wanted to hear his thoughts on Iran, "Abdullah asserted that Iran is trying to set up Hizbollah-like organizations in African countries, observing that the Iranians don't think they are doing anything wrong and don't recognize their mistakes. 'I said (to Mottaki) that's your problem,' recounted the King…He described Iran not as 'a neighbor one wants to see,' but as 'a neighbor one wants to avoid.' He said the Iranians 'launch missiles with the hope of putting fear in people and the world.' A solution to the Arab/ Israeli conflict would be a great achievement, the King said, but Iran would find other ways to cause trouble. 'Iran's goal is to cause problems,' he continued. 'There is no doubt something unstable about them.' He described Iran as 'adventurous in the negative sense,' and declared 'May God prevent us from falling victim to their evil.' Mottaki had tendered an invitation [to him] to visit Iran, but Abdullah said he replied 'All I want is for you to spare us your evil.' Summarizing his history with Iran, Abdullah concluded: 'We have had correct relations [with Iran] over the years but the bottom line is that they cannot be trusted'."

Abdullah went on to reveal that in 2006 "Iran's Supreme Leader Khamanei had sent his adviser Ali Akbar Velayati with a letter asking for Abdullah's agreement to establish a formal back channel for communication between the two leaders. Abdullah said he had agreed, and the channel was established with Velayati and Saudi FM (Foreign Minister) Saud Al Faisal as the points of contact. In the years since, the King noted, the channel had never been used."

When Brennan assured Abdullah that the United States would seek his advice in dealing with the multiple issues in the Middle East, he asked if that included Iran. "Brennan responded that it did. Brennan said that we had our eyes wide open to Iranian ambitions, that we were not naive to the dangers Iran posed to Saudi Arabia, and that Iran could not be allowed to succeed in its destabilizing activities." He further observed that the US-Saudi partnership had to remain strong and that together, and with others, "we needed to thwart Iran's nuclear ambitions." Abdullah responded, "That is important."[86]

Obama started his five-day trip to four countries on 3 June with Saudi Arabia, being "the place where Islam began," a gesture that pleased Abdullah. At Riyadh airport, he exchanged a light embrace and a double-kiss with King Abdullah, who presented him with a large gold medallion known as the King Abdul Aziz Collar. After spending the afternoon with his host, he headed to the monarch's Al Janadriyah Farm, where Abdullah gave him a brief tour of his sprawling equestrian estate.[87] Altogether, Abdullah had good reason to believe that he had established a warm rapport with the first African-American president of the United States.

Abdullah took the initial bonhomie with the young US president as a licence to keep pressing his administration to move against Iran militarily. This became quite intolerable to the US Defence Secretary Robert Gates. During his meeting with French foreign minister Bernard Kouchner in Paris in February 2010 to coordinate Washington's efforts to impose UN sanctions on Iran, Gates remarked that the Saudis always wanted to "fight the Iranians to the last American," adding that now it was time for them to "get into the game."[88]

Evidently, Abdullah was not privy to the resolve of Obama who, as a senator for Illinois, had called Bush's invasion of Iraq a "dumb war," not to start the third US-led war in the Middle East by ordering military strikes against Iran. In that he had the backing of Gates, a Republican, who had succeeded Donald Rumsfeld as Defense Secretary under Bush in 2007. Obama focused on non-military means to contain Iran's nuclear ambitions. Under his presidency the joint American-Israeli operation to undermine Iran's nuclear program by using computer technology, launched in mid-2007, remained in place. Its existence became public on 26 September 2010 when Iranian officials admitted that the Stuxnet virus had hit computers at the Russian-built nuclear power plant near Bushehr, which would delay production of electricity for several months. The report in the *Daily Telegraph* added that Iran may be suffering wider sabotage aimed at slowing its nuclear advances, referring to a series of unexplained technical glitches that had reduced the number of working enrichment centrifuges at the Natanz plant.[89]

Two months later, following the killing by unidentified motorcyclists of Majid Shahriari, reportedly running a "major project" for Iran's Atomic Energy Organisation, and the wounding of Fereydoon Abbasi-

Davani, listed as a top official linked to his country's nuclear program by the UN Security Council, Ahmadinejad saw "the hand of the Zionist regime and Western governments" in the attacks. At the same time he acknowledged for the first time that Iran's nuclear program had been disrupted recently by malicious computer software that attacked its centrifuges.[90] The Stuxnet virus had damaged nearly 1,000 centrifuges, about a fifth of the total at Natanz, before it was detected and removed.

While both Israel and America were aligned with the Saudi Kingdom in their policy on Tehran's nuclear program, this was not the case in the diplomatic arena when it came to dealing with post-Saddam Iraq. There, for diverse reasons, both Tehran and Washington shared the common goal of establishing a stable, democratic Iraq, in which, by virtue of their numbers, Shias were bound to the dominant party in the national government. This was too bitter a pill for Saudi Arabia to swallow.

Abdullah Frustrated in Iraq

Irrespective of the overt changes in Riyadh's stance towards Tehran, its clandestine strategy of countering Iran's influence with cash had continued uninterrupted. Riyadh still maintained close contacts with Ayad Allawi. At its behest, in early 2009, he formed *Al Iraqiyya List* (Iraq Nationalist Movement), an alliance that included Sunni Vice-President Tariq al Hashimi and his Sunni followers. During the run-up to the 7 March 2010 general election, King Abdullah rolled out the red carpet for him on 23 February, and was reportedly generous in funding his political party. Tellingly, Allawi visited all the neighboring countries except Iran.[91] The Al Iraqiyya List secured two more seats than the eighty-nine won by Maliki's purely Shia group, the State of Law Coalition, with al Daawa as its leading constituent, in the 325-member legislature. Stalemate ensued. It was in mid-May that, following its partial recount of ballots, the Electoral Commission declared that the poll had been fraud-free.

Despite his best efforts, Allawi failed to win the support of the majority in the chamber—much to the frustration of Saudi royals. The resulting deadlock continued for six months. During this period there was a spurt in the terrorist activities of AQIM despite—or perhaps because of—the killings of al Masri and al Baghdadi by US airstrikes near Tikrit in northern Iraq on 18 April. Four days later a series of bomb explosions in Sadr City, a poor Shia area in Baghdad, claimed sixty lives. Coordinated bomb blasts at twenty-three sites in the capital and seven elsewhere on 10 May resulted in nearly 100 fatalities. But the scheduled withdrawal of US combat troops continued as planned, the last such soldier leaving on 30 August.

Iran's leaders swung into action by getting Muqtada al Sadr—pursuing further theological studies in Qom after his Mahdi Army had been disbanded forcibly by Maliki's security forces in March 2008—to drop his opposition to Maliki continuing as Prime Minister. This came about after Sadr's religious guide, and General Qassim Suleimani, commander of the IRGC's Al Quds (Arabic name of Jerusalem) Force,[92] prevailed upon the radical cleric to serve the higher goal of consolidating Shia power in Iraq by combining with Maliki's State of Law Coalition. Maliki signaled his desire for reconciliation with Sadr by sending his chief of staff and a senior al Daawa leader to Qom.[93]

This was the backdrop against which Maliki arrived in Tehran on 17 October, ostensibly to energise the limping reconstruction of Iraq, to talk to Ahmadinejad. He then met with Khamanei. The state TV quoted Khamanei telling his guest, "Formation of a government as soon as possible and establishment of full security are among the important needs of Iraq because development and reconstruction of Iraq ... can't be achieved without these two." Maliki described Iraqi-Iranian relations as "strategic". He said, "We ask Iran and our neighbors to support our reconstruction and to boost economic and commercial co-operation, which will help improve stability in our region."[94]

On the other side of the spectrum, in his 17 October CNN interview, Maliki's rival Allawi nailed his anti-Iran colors to the mast. He said that Iran was "trying to destabilize the region by destabilizing Iraq, and destabilizing Lebanon and destabilizing the Palestinian issue". He added that "This is where unfortunately Iraq and the rest of the greater Mideast is falling victim to these terrorists who are definitely Iran-financed and supported by various governments in the region."[95] This was just what the Saudi royals wished to hear.

Continuing his trip to Iran, Maliki went to Qom on 18 October to mend fences with Sadr. However, the combined total of the State of the Law Coalition and the seventy-strong (Shia) National Iraqi Alliance, dominated by Sadr's followers, was 159 deputies, still short of a majority. That was why the state-run MENA news agency in Cairo reported on 19 October that during their talks, Egypt's President Hosni Mubarak and Maliki had discussed efforts to form a national unity government in Iraq.[96] Since Mubarak was close to the US, this indicated the Obama White House's preference for a national unity administration in Baghdad.

Back in Iraq, this idea was supported by Masoud Barzani, the directly elected president of the Kurdistan Regional Government since 2007. Barzani ended up brokering a power-sharing deal between Maliki and Allawi which was signed in the Kurdish regional capital of Erbil on 15 November. It contained the proviso that Allawi would be offered the presidency of the proposed National Council for Strategic Policies (NCSP), in principle to act as a check on the Maliki government, whose composition and exact powers were to be decided later.[97] The subsequent horse-trading between various factions of the two major blocs for ministries was so intense that it was only on 21 December that Maliki announced a cabinet of thirty-five ministers. The sectarian-ethnic composition of the cabinet was twenty Shias, ten Sunnis, four Kurds and one Christian.[98] Though far less than half the Shia population among Iraqi Arabs, Sunnis headed half as many ministries as Shias.

In the absence of a consensus as to who should run the much coveted ministries of defence, interior, and national security, Maliki took charge of these on an ad hoc basis. With consensus proving elusive, he became the de facto minister of defence and interior and minister of state for national security. As the commander-in-chief, who headed the Iraqi National Command, he bypassed the chain of command and made all commanders report to him directly. All told, Maliki's prime ministerial office directly controlled the military and paramilitary forces, intelligence agencies, and the national elements of the police.[99] Among other things, Maliki purged the National Intelligence Service of its Iran division, ending his government's ability to monitor and check its large eastern neighbor.

He dashed the hopes of the US administration that all the members of the Sunni Awakening councils would be absorbed into the state's security forces for providing critical assistance in averting a fully-fledged sectarian war. His government continued the policy of confiscating the weapons of former Sunni Awakening council members on the grounds that they lacked authorizing permits. Moreover, according to the Pentagon, most of the 40,000 such fighters who were offered employment by the autumn of 2010 found temporary, menial jobs. Only about 9,000 ended up working for the security forces. This led some of them to drift towards Islamist insurgent groups, which paid well.[100]

The sharply increasing monopolising of power by Maliki alarmed policy-makers as well as Allawi. Since the NSCP did not appear in the constitution, it needed to be amended accordingly, or a separate law could be passed by Parliament. For the first option, a preliminary two-thirds of cabinet ministers had to agree before the amendment could be put to referendum for approval by a simple majority.[101] This allowed Maliki to stall, which he did for several months. When it came to the second option, major differences arose between Maliki's State of Law Coalition and Allawi's Al Iraqiyya. Maliki's faction argued that the NCSP was basically a consultative body; otherwise, it would become a government within the government. Al Iraqiyya disagreed. Secondly, voiding the promise made in Erbil (also spelled Irbil), the State of Law Coalition insisted that the head of the NCSP be elected by its nineteen members.[102] In contrast, Al Iraqiyya advocated election of the NCSP's head by Parliament. As a result, a draft law on the establishment of the NCSP did not progress from its first reading in Parliament on 12 August 2011.[103] In disgust, Allawi threw in the towel on 7 October 2011. "There is no partnership in our country," he declared. "On the contrary, there is power monopolization."[104]

By then the Middle East had been convulsed by the rise of a grass roots, revolutionary demand for democracy, in which protesters used social media as a highly effective tool—and its reversal by Saudi Arabia working in collusion with domestic counterrevolutionary forces.

12

THE ARAB SPRING—REVERSED BY A SAUDI-BACKED COUNTERREVOLUTION

Emboldened by the toppling of the Tunisian and Egyptian dictators, Saudi dissidents used social media to declare 11 March 2011, a Friday, as a "day of rage." Confident of aborting such demonstrations in Riyadh, the government issued visas to foreign journalists. "I took a taxi from our hotel at midnight on Thursday to find police cars with their lights flashing parked at five-meter intervals along all the main streets of Riyadh," reported BBC Newsnight correspondent, the late Sue Lloyd Roberts.

I was pulled over by the police for merely filming on my mobile phone. On Friday, the city woke up to the sight of more police on the streets than people, and the atmosphere was tense. The anti-government "day of rage" rallies calling for democratic reforms—not revolution—in this oil-rich Kingdom of Saudi Arabia were supposed to start after midday prayers, but people stayed away. "It was hardly surprising, given that over the past few days there had been warnings in the newspapers of the punishments demonstrators could expect—lashings and imprisonment. And then there is the surveillance and intimidation." Yet, continued Roberts, "It was reported that police opened fire on protests in the eastern provinces—home to the Shia minority—on Thursday night. We went to the eastern town of Dammam to meet the families of political prisoners—some of whom have been held without trial for up to 16 years. Opposition activists say there are some 30,000 political prisoners in Saudi Arabia; the government puts the figure at one third of that," continued Roberts. We didn't know we were being followed by the security forces, and after we had finished filming we were arrested and our tapes taken from us. The message is clear—people should not protest, and if they do, journalists should not report it. On Friday [11 March], I was due to meet one of the demonstration organizers who said he would accompany me to see the protests. But an hour before the rally was due to begin, I received a text message. "My emails and mobile phone are being monitored. I cannot meet you. I am sorry. This is a sad day for Saudi Arabia."

The government claims people have no need to demonstrate because they have a method of government that works. But one opposition spokesman described his country to me as "a police state masquerading as a theocracy." We journalists were herded into buses on Friday and taken to see the "day of rage" non-event.

Helicopters hovered overhead, there were road blocks and cars being searched, hundreds of police cars and thousands of police—but not a demonstrator in sight. Suddenly, as we were all getting bored of filming each other, a solitary man in his 40s, dressed in casual Western-style t-shirt and jeans approached us. "We want freedom. We want democracy," he shouted. "Why are you saying this, in front of all the police?" I asked him. "I shall go to jail, I know," he replied, shaking with nerves and frustration. "But the whole country is a jail. I had to speak out." Within a few minutes, the man was surrounded by a dozen or more journalists; he was the only one in Riyadh on Friday giving a press conference. There were so many of us [journalists] there that there was nothing the police could do except speak nervously into their mobile phones and then shepherd us all back into our buses. But I refused to go and accompanied the man to his car. I asked for his phone number and shall call him at home—but I don't expect him to answer.[1]

The "day of rage" came in the wake of the success that peaceful demonstrators had won on the wave of earlier triumph achieved after street protests in Tunisia in mid-December 2010. This unexpected development breached the compact that the Saudi government had reached with Sahwa movement leaders.

Neutralising the Force of the Arab Spring Tide

King Abdullah was recuperating from two major operations on his spinal cord in New York in late 2010—initially at a luxury hotel in the city—when the dictatorial Tunisian President Zine al Abidine Ben Ali was forced to flee after weeks of mass protests. Abdullah offered Ben Ali refuge in the Saudi Kingdom instantly, and he fled to Jeddah. A week later Abdullah flew to the Moroccan city of Casablanca to continue his convalescence. By then, buoyed by the success of popular protests in Tunisia, demonstrators in Egypt intensified their peaceful campaign against the autocratic President Hosni Mubarak.

As pro-democracy demonstrations built up in Cairo's vast Tahrir Square, Abdullah telephoned Mubarak on 29 January 2011. "No Arab or Muslim can tolerate any meddling in the security and stability of Arab and Muslim Egypt by those who infiltrated the people in the name of freedom of expression, exploiting it to inject their destructive hatred," he said. "While condemning this [infiltration] the Kingdom of Saudi Arabia as well as its people declares [that] it stands with all its resources with the government of Egypt and its people." In reply, Mubarak assured him that the situation was under control.[2] While hundreds of thousands of Egyptians marched peacefully in Cairo on 4 February to demand an end to President Mubarak's thirty-year rule, Saudi Arabia's Grand Mufti Sheikh Abdul Aziz Al Sheikh said, "This chaos comes from enemies of Islam and those who follow them," adding that demonstrations led to bloodshed and stealing.[3]

When, having lost the confidence of the military high command, Mubarak reluctantly stepped down on 11 February, Abdullah offered him refuge in a Saudi palace, which he politely declined, choosing to retire to the presidential palace in the Egyptian sea resort of Sharm el Sheikh. To his disappointment, Abdullah failed to win unanimous backing for his stance in the Kingdom. Shaikh Salman Awda, for instance, disagreed with the official policy, and publicly supported the Arab Spring movement. As a result, he was taken off the Islam.net television program.

On 9 February nine professors, lawyers and social activists formed the Islamic Umma Party (Arabic: *Hizb al Umma al Islami*). Intent on participating in the ongoing regional, peaceful movement for political reform, the founders listed their goals: direct elections to parliament, an independent judiciary, separation of powers, promotion of human rights, including free speech and right to peaceful protest, and promotion of civil society as well as Islamic values in domestic and foreign policies. They petitioned the Royal Court for a licence. A week later seven of the signatories were arrested.[4]

Around the same time a petition, titled "Towards a State of Rights and Institutions", containing the same manifesto as the Islamic Umma Party's appeared. The major difference was that it was signed by about thirty intellectuals of different political groups, with Islamists being the largest. They included Awda and Waleed Abu al Khair, a leading human rights lawyer.[5]

The Saudi monarch acted as soon as he returned to Riyadh on 22 February. He announced a $37 billion package to aid state employees and the young and the poor. This sum provided a 15 per cent pay rise for all government employees—around two-thirds of the workforce who were Saudi nationals; $10.7 billion for the Saudi Development Fund which provides interest-free loans to Saudis who want to build homes, get married or start small businesses; and extra funds for social security and those studying abroad.[6] The official claim that 60 per cent of Saudi citizens owned a house was believed to be twice the actual figure. In his package Abdullah raised the loans to be given by the Real Estate Development Fund from SR 300,000 to SR 500,000 whereas the average house price in Riyadh was SR 1.23 million.[7]

By this time, many young Saudis had hooked up with Egyptian and other Arab activists through Facebook and Twitter. Thus for the first time the push for political reform came from outside the narrow Saudi intellectual circle. The Free Youth Coalition's page started referring to the movement as the Hunayn revolution, referring to the Battle of Hunayn in which Prophet Muhammad defeated the Hawazin tribe following the Muslim conquest of Mecca.[8] The government was alarmed by the calls made on Facebook for a Day of Rage on Friday 11 March in Riyadh. Away from the capital, the protest by Shias in the Eastern Province, inspired by peaceful pro-reform demonstrations by Shias in neighboring Bahrain, had been gathering momentum since mid-February.

The regime devised a comprehensive strategy to meet the challenge. It marshalled the religious establishment and its own means of propaganda as well as deploying its security and intelligence agencies to abort the proposed demonstration in the capital. "There are legitimate ways for advice and reform that bring benefits and avoid evils, and writing petitions with the aim of intimidating and causing division … is not one of them", declared the Council of Senior Ulema on 6 March. "Reform and advice should not be through demonstrations and other means that foster chaos and division in the community…Demonstrations are forbidden religiously.["9] The state intelligence agency destroyed several Facebook pages and hacked others, adding Shia references to the content of pages supporting the Day of Rage to show that it was Shias who were behind the demonstration. Official sources also claimed that the opposition movement was part of Iran's conspiracy to destabilize the Kingdom. Prince Nayef intimidated the normally vocal non-establishment Islamist elements into silence. And the National Guard was deployed nationally, with additional attention paid to the Eastern Province. These tactics worked. Support for the 11 March protest demonstration after the mid-day prayer melted away.

Abdullah followed up his all-out repressive act with another palliative to his subjects. In a rare television speech he announced a package of the staggering sum of $93 billion. It included two months salary as a bonus to all state employees, the introduction of a minimum wage for government jobs, and an additional 60,000 personnel to the security agencies, and a further 66,000 teachers and health workers.[10] There was an increase in subsidies for fuel, food and utilities, and the introduction of unemployment benefits of SR 2,000 a month, something the government had earlier resisted.[11] It was worth noting that this package included $1.2 billion of patronage for the religious establishment. Equally importantly, the regime made a concerted move to increase the number of Saudi nationals in the private sector—a plan known as Saudisation. As part of his political reforms, Abdullah announced that the much postponed local elections would be held in September, with voting restricted to male adults. In that month he promised to extend the franchise to women at the next poll four years later.[12] In January 2013, he would appoint thirty women to the advisory Consultative Council, known locally as the Shura Council.

Saudis' Critical Role in the Military Coup in Egypt

After routing the plans of Saudi supporters of the Arab Spring, King Abdullah continued his counter-revolutionary drive, refusing to accept the turn of events in post-Mubarak Egypt. In Cairo, once the 21-member Supreme Council of the Armed Forces (SCAF), led by Field Marshal Muhammad Hussein Tantawi, took over from the deposed Mubarak on 11 February 2011, it appointed a committee to recommend changes to the constitution to assure free and fair elections for parliament and president. These amendments were ratified in a referendum in late March. When SCAF dragged its feet on naming the election dates, street pressure built up. SCAF then promised a presidential election in June 2012.

In the run-up to the second round of this poll, voters had the option of choosing Muhammad Morsi, a leader of the Muslim Brotherhood with a track record of opposing the autocracy of Hosni Mubarak and his predecessors, or Ahmed Shafiq, a former Air Force commander and minister of aviation under Mubarak who promoted him to prime minister during the last days of his presidency. Unsurprisingly, therefore, Shafiq had the backing of the commanders of the security and law enforcement forces, who verbally instructed their ranks to vote for him. In the region, King Abdullah covertly supported him. Yet, in the first free elections in the sixty year history of republican Egypt, held on 16–17 June 2012, Morsi defeated Shafiq, winning 51.73 per cent of the ballot against Shafiq's 48.27 per cent.[13] Within hours of his defeat, Shafiq fled to Abu Dhabi along with his family, fearing prosecution for bribe-taking during his tenure as minister of aviation.

From the mid-1950s to 1990, Saudi Arabia was the prime financial and ideological backer of the Brotherhood, which originated in Egypt in 1928. It provided a haven to them when President Gamal Abdul Nasser cracked down on them after surviving an assassination attempt by a Brotherhood cell in 1954. In Saudi Arabia they designed and largely manned the education system in an almost universally illiterate society. Riyadh's backing of the Brotherhood stopped in the Kingdom and elsewhere when its leaders opposed the stationing of American troops on Saudi soil on the eve of the US-led coalition's military campaign to oust occupying Iraqis from Kuwait in January 1991. Since then the Brotherhood has renounced violence, and in Egypt it participated in parliamentary politics, believing that Sharia law can be introduced in an Arab country through the ballot. The blending of democracy and political Islam was what earned the Brotherhood the undying hostility of Saud royals since it undercut the legitimacy of the dynastic rule in which citizens had no input.

In Cairo, to his credit, within two weeks of assuming the presidency, Morsi flew to Jeddah where he had fruitful meetings with King Abdullah and Crown Prince Salman. It seemed the Saudi royal family had decided to respect the democratic choice of Egyptians. But this would prove to be a mirage.

Overall, though, in line with the Brotherhood's election manifesto, Morsi was set to give a new direction to Egypt's foreign policy and be more independent than his predecessor. Instead of making Washington his first foreign capital to visit outside the region, he flew to Beijing, seeking financial aid. On his way back, he attended the Non-Aligned Movement (NAM) summit in Tehran in August 2012 because Egypt was scheduled to take over the NAM's chairmanship for the next three years from Iran. During Mubarak's long rule, Cairo's relations with Tehran had remained frozen while he successfully presented himself as a bulwark against Iranian influence in the Arab world—much to the enthusiastic approval of Saudi royals. In Tehran Morsi and his Iranian counterpart Mahmoud Ahmadinejad agreed to upgrade their bilateral diplomatic relations, which had been re-established after a thirty-year break, immediately after Mubarak's deposition, by rededicating their respective embassy premises.[14] Conversely, the Saudis were frustrated when Morsi gave his Iranian counterpart the red carpet treatment on the latter's arrival in Cairo to attend the OIC summit in February 2013.

"Egypt is a very important country in the region and the Islamic Republic of Iran believes it is one of the heavyweights in the Middle East," said Ali Akbar Salehi, the foreign minister of Iran accompanying the president. "We are ready to further strengthen ties." On his part, Ahmadinejad called on Shaikh Muhammad Sayyid Tantaoui, the rector of Al Azhar University, the seat of the highest Sunni scholarship, which does not admit Shia students.[15] Later when an Al Azhar spokesman chided Ahmadinejad for using divisive sectarian language, one of his aides interjected. "We didn't agree on this," he said, as the Iranian leader nodded and replied: "We agreed on unity, brotherhood."[16]

Given the hostility toward Iran that Abdullah nursed, Morsi's reversal of Mubarak's strong opposition to the Islamic Republic upset him and Crown Prince Salman. As a result, their intelligence chief Prince Muqrin bin Abdul Aziz turned his attention to destabilising the Morsi government, which was also being targeted by counter-revolutionary elements in Egypt. Though self-exiled in the UAE, Shafiq became the symbolic civilian head of these Egyptian forces. He secured the support of UAE President Shaikh Khalifa bin Zayed al Nahyan, who was opposed to the Muslim Brotherhood's program to demand and participate in democratic elections in the Arab world.

It was around that time that Prince Muqrin along with Khalid al Tuwaijri, president of the Royal Court and the Saudi monarch's gatekeeper—charged with executing the Kingdom's policy on Egypt—seemingly started to plan the ouster of Morsi in conjunction with General Abdul Fattah el Sisi, the armed forces' commander-in-chief and Defense Minister of Egypt. Sisi was not reconciled to the presidency of Morsi which broke the chain of military rule since the founding of the republic in 1952. However, he and his fellow generals concluded that it would be politically astute to launch a military coup in the wake of anti-Morsi street protests. To that end, in late April, a grassroots organization called *Tamarod* (Arabic: rebellion) cropped up, urging citizens to sign a petition calling on Morsi to resign. It was soon infiltrated by former Mubarak supporters and intelligence agents, collectively called *mukhabarat* (Arabic, intelligence), working under Interior Minister Muhammad Ibrahim who was allied with Sisi.

Carefully orchestrated street demonstrations were scheduled to reach a climax on 30 June 2013, the first anniversary of the Morsi government. There were widespread rumors that Saudi Arabia and the UAE were bankrolling them. In an exclusive interview with the *Guardian*, Morsi declined to name which countries were meddling in Egypt's affairs, but maintained that it was happening. "Asked whether he was referring to Saudi Arabia and the United Arab Emirates, Morsi replied: 'No, I am talking in general terms. Any revolution has its enemies and there are some people who are trying to obstruct the path of the Egyptian people towards democracy. I am not saying it's acceptable, but we observe it everywhere'."[17] Apparently, for diplomatic and other reasons, Morsi was unwilling to go on record blaming either the Saudi Kingdom or the UAE.

Evidence of the UAE channeling cash to bolster anti-Morsi demonstrations would surface in March 2015 in the form of audio-recording of telephone conversations between Sisi's top aide, General Abbas Kamel, and General Sedky Sobhy, the military chief of staff, regarding a bank account controlled by senior defence officials that had been used by Tamarod.

"Sir, we will need 200 tomorrow from Tamarod's account—you know, the part from the UAE, which they transferred," Kamel told

Sobhy. The conversation on Sobhy's side could not be heard. But he mentioned intelligence services or mukhabarat. "What do you mean by mukhabarat, sir? The mukhabarat guys?" Kamel replied. "Do you remember the account that came for Tamarod?" He then said to Sobhy, "We will need only 200 from it—yes, 200,000 [Egyptian Pounds, $30,000]"[18]

Sisi struck on 3 July. He arrested Morsi and held him incommunicado. To King Abdullah's delight, this marked a total victory of the counter-revolution in Egypt. He as well as Shaikh Sabah al Ahmad al Sabah of Kuwait rushed to congratulate Sisi and put together an aid package worth $12 billion, four times as much as the military and economic grants from the US and the EU combined, to bolster the Sisi regime.[19]

The military junta unleashed brutal repression of Morsi's backers operating under the National Coalition for the Support of Legitimacy, and demanding his restoration to presidency, through peaceful sit-ins in two public squares. Its savagery reached a peak on 14 August when Interior Ministry troops cleared the sit-in in Cairo's Rabaa Square, killing 814 people and injuring nearly 4,000. According to Human Rights Watch, the Rabaa Square massacre was "one of the world's largest killings of demonstrators in a single day in recent history."[20]

"Let the entire world know," proclaimed King Abdullah, "that the people and government of the Kingdom of Saudi Arabia stood and still stand today with our brothers in Egypt against terrorism, extremism and sedition, and against whomever is trying to interfere in Egypt's internal affairs." Abdullah's statement was an oblique rebuke to Qatar which officially and through Al Jazeera satellite television channel had backed the Muslim Brotherhood as well as the Arab Spring demonstrations. On the other hand he had reason to note approvingly the fact that despite repeated promises by Shaikh Hamad bin Khalifa Al Thani to hold elections to a partly-elected parliament, the emirate had not progressed beyond municipal elections. Nor did Shaikh Tamim bin Hamad Al Thani, who succeeded his father in 2013, show any inclination towards democratising his regime.

Riyadh and Tehran Clash in Bahrain

In stark contrast to King Abdullah's fervent opposition to the Arab spring, Iran's Supreme Leader Ayatollah Ali Khamanei hailed it as a reprise of the Islamic Revolution in Iran, calling it the Islamic Awakening. Their divergent interpretations came to a head in the tiny, island kingdom of Bahrain, ruled by the Sunni Al Khalifa family since 1783. Since the inauguration in 1986 of the sixteen mile long Fahd Causeway between Saudi Arabia and Bahrain, which became independent in 1971, the island kingdom had become linked to Saudi Arabia in several ways. In Bahrain the opposition, representing most of the Shias, forming 70 per cent of the citizenry, had for many years protested against discrimination and the immigration of Sunni Arabs and Pakistanis. The Shias held only 13 per cent of high-ranking public posts. At the end of October 2009, a two-mile human chain of over 2,000 Shias lined the capital Manama's eastern waterfront to protest against "political naturalisation," the awarding of nationality to foreign, especially Sunni Arab and South Asian, members of the military and security forces.[21]

Inspired now by the success of peaceful demonstrators in Cairo's Tahrir Square in deposing Mubarak on 11 February 2011 the Bahraini opposition, led by Al Wefaq party, called for a demonstration on 14 February in the central Pearl Roundabout of Manama. It was a huge success, with the protesters refusing to leave the square until Al Wefaq's demands for an elected government and a constitutional monarchy were met. On 17 February, security forces retook control of the Pearl Roundabout by using tear gas canisters and rubber bullets, killing four civilians. As tanks and soldiers took up positions around Manama, all elected parliamentarians of Al Wefaq, the largest group in the parliament's lower house, resigned. Following a large funeral procession for the dead demonstrators, the authorities relented and let protesters camp at Pearl Roundabout. On 22 February, Martyrs Day, the number of protesters, shouting "the people want the downfall of the regime (Arabic: *As Shaab Yoreed Eskaat al Nizam*)!" in a demonstration, sponsored by a coalition of seven opposition groups, marching from the Mall to the Pearl Roundabout reached 150,000 in a country with a population of 1.2 million, of whom only 525,000 were citizens.[22] Responding to the popular pressure, King Hamad bin Isa Al Khalifa released political prisoners. Thus encouraged, on 3 March tens of thousands of demonstrators demanded the resignation of the hard line Prime Minister Khalifa bin Salman Al Khalifa, who had held office since independence in 1971. The next day protesters camped outside the Financial District.

Encouraged by the events in Bahrain, and calls by non-establishment clerics in Saudi Arabia, the Shias in Qatif demonstrated on 24 February to demand the release of Shias detained without charge since the 1996 Al Khobar bombing. Three days later almost 3,000 local Shias put their names down on three petitions separately calling for a constitutional monarchy, an elected parliament with full legislative authority, and a revision of the Basic Law.[23] This was enough to alarm the authorities in Riyadh who, like their counterparts in Manama, blamed the pro-democracy demonstrations on a "foreign country," a thinly disguised reference to Iran.

Two days earlier, in Saudi Arabia's Eastern Province, after Friday prayers hundreds of Shia protesters, waving the flags of Saudi Arabia and Bahrain, marched in Qatif, Safwa, Awamiyah, and other places, demanding the release of the "forgotten prisoners". Many Shia activists stressed that these demonstrations were independent of the Day of Rage announced anonymously on social media elsewhere in the Kingdom. All the same, the protesters were disbanded by the security forces armed with Sten guns.[24] Evidently, the unrest in Bahrain was impacting on the Eastern Province of Saudi Arabia.

On 8 March, three hard-line Shia groups called for the abolition of the monarchy and founding of a democratic republic through peaceful means. Three days later their supporters' march to the Royal Court in Riffa, the second largest city, was blocked by the security forces, while tens of thousands participated in an Al Wefaq procession in Manama. The government repeated its claim that Iran was behind the non-violent uprising but provided no evidence. Unsurprisingly, therefore, the Saudi regime urged King Hamad to use maximum force to crush the demand for a democratic government under a constitutional monarchy, fearing that the contagion of democracy would infect the Eastern Province, threatening the future of the House of Saud. Yielding to its urgings, King Hamad appealed to the GCC for help on 13 March, the day its riot police deployed tear gas and rubber bullets to remove protesters from the Pearl Roundabout and the Financial District.

The next day the GCC contrived to send troops to Bahrain under the aegis of the Peninsula Shield Force, set up to assist the member-states against external aggression. Instantly, Riyadh provided 1,000 soldiers mounted on armored personnel carriers for the mission. These troops entered Bahrain from the Saudi mainland via the causeway, to be followed later by token contingents from the UAE and Kuwait, ostensibly "to secure key installations" in the island kingdom. To ensure that the Bahraini protesters got the message, a Saudi official declared that "This is the initial phase. Bahrain will get whatever assistance it needs. It's open-ended." On the other side, the statement issued by Bahrain's opposition groups said that "We consider the entry of any soldier or military machinery into the Kingdom of Bahrain's air, sea or land territories a blatant occupation."[25] Setting aside partisan interpretations, it was indisputable that this intervention marked the first time that an Arab government requested and received foreign military help during the Arab Spring.

In Iran, President Ahmadinejad equated the Saudis' military move with Saddam Hussein's invasion of Kuwait in August 1990 which would later lead to his downfall. Appearing on state television, he said, "What has happened [in Bahrain] is bad, unjustifiable and irreparable," and added that "The people's demands for change must be respected."[26]

Backed by the armored Saudi troops, King Hamad declared a state of emergency. While thousands marched to the Saudi embassy in Manama protesting the GCC intervention, clashes occurred between gun-toting Bahraini soldiers and demonstrators. On the morning of 16 March, Bahrain's troops and riot police, backed by tanks and helicopters, advanced behind clouds of tear gas, and set alight the protesters' white tents in Pearl Roundabout amidst thickening black smoke. Three protesters were killed and hundreds injured by live ammunition and rubber bullets. The authorities imposed a 4pm to 4am curfew in most of the country and jammed mobile phones as soldiers entered Shia villages outside Manama.[27] The ongoing crackdown included the arrest of more than 1,000 protesters, including seven opposition leaders.

During the month-long uprising King Hamad remained confident that the Obama administration would do nothing more than hand-wringing, combined with words of caution and the need to temporise. Little wonder, then, that when Jeffrey Feltman, the US Assistant Secretary of State for the Near East, arrived in Manama on 14 March with a mandate to mediate between the two sides, he found it hard to meet with government officials, let alone persuade them to negotiate with the opposition.[28] The salient fact was that the regional strategy of the Pentagon rested on its retaining Manama as its naval base. Since 1971, the rulers of Bahrain had extended the use of Manama's docks to the Pentagon under several contracts and titles. In 1995, following the US Navy's re-launching of its Fifth Fleet after fifty-eight years it chose the Naval Support Activity Bahrain in Manama at its base.[29] Given these factors, and Bahrain's physical link to the Saudi Kingdom, it was almost inevitable that the will of the House of Saud would prevail in the Sunni-ruled island, and award Riyadh a clear victory over Tehran.

However a far weightier and longer battle between Saudi Arabia and Iran was in the offing in Syria.

A Protracted Battle for Syria

It was the events in Syria's southern town of Deraa near the Jordanian border that caught the imagination of protesters nationally. On 6 March 2011 the local police arrested fifteen teenage pupils for spraying on their school walls the slogan they had seen on their television screens: "The people want the downfall of the regime (Arabic: *As Shaab Yoreed Eskaat al Nizam*)!" They were tortured in detention. On 15 March their families and others marched to demand their release. Three days later confrontation escalated after Friday prayers outside the Omari Mosque when security forces used water cannons and tear gas, followed by live fire, killing four people, to disperse the crowd.[30] This event would soon inspire anti-regime demonstrators elsewhere to chant the slogan, "With our souls, with our blood, we sacrifice for you, O Deraa."

On 20 March angry crowds in Deraa set alight the offices of the ruling Baath Party, and demanded the release of political prisoners as well as an end to the Emergency Law imposed by Baathist leaders after seizing power in 1963. President Bashar Assad, a member of the minority Alawi sub-sect within Shia Islam, dispatched senior officials to Deraa to reassure the local tribal chiefs that he was committed to bringing to justice those who had opened fire. He sacked the local governor and security chief, and ordered the release of the detained students. The tell-tale signs of torture on the students' bodies incensed their parents and their friends. On 24 March the government ordered a cut in taxes and increased state salaries. The next day, Friday, tens of thousands turned out for the funerals of those killed. To disperse them security forces opened fire and killed fifteen more people. A group of enraged protesters tore down the statue of Hafiz Assad, father of Bashar, who had ruled Syria from 1970 to 2000, and who relied on appointing Alawis, some 13 per cent of the population, as heads of the military, police and intelligence agencies. In his speech on 30 March, Bashar Assad said the questions of reform and economic grievances had been overshadowed by a small number of saboteurs who had sought to spread dissension among Syrians, as part of an external conspiracy, to undermine Syria's stability.[31]

Next month, Assad dismissed the cabinet and lifted the Emergency Law, in place since 1963, under which security forces detained and tortured people with impunity. But days later, the crackdown against protesters was stepped up. In May soldiers, supported by tanks, were deployed in restive cities to combat "armed criminal gangs". By mid-May, the death toll had reached 1,000, including dozens of security personnel.[32] Despite the state's ruthless efforts, and pledges by Assad to launch a "national dialogue" on reform, the civilian uprising continued unabated in almost every part of Syria. Opposition supporters had taken up arms, at first in self-defence and then to oust loyalist forces from their areas. Assad denied ordering the military to kill or be brutal in its crackdown on anti-regime protesters, claiming that his forces used live fire only when they were shot at.

Among the regional leaders who agreed with Assad's interpretation was Saudi King Abdullah. Wedded to the status quo, he stood by Assad's regime. But on 8 August he reversed his stance, and withdrew Saudi Arabia's ambassador from Damascus. "What is happening in Syria is not acceptable for Saudi Arabia," he said. "Syria should issue and enact reforms that are not merely promises but actual reforms."[33] Ten days later US President Barack Obama endorsed Abdullah's call. Interestingly, on 27 August Iran's foreign minister Ali Akbar Salehi was quoted as saying, "The government should answer to the demands of its people, be it Syria, Yemen or other countries. The people of these nations have legitimate demands, and the governments should answer these demands as soon as possible."[34]

But the contexts in the two cases were quite different. Syria had tightened its historic cordial ties with Iran in a series of agreements and pacts between 2004 and March 2007. In the aftermath of the US invasion of Iraq in March 2003, the two countries signed a strategic cooperation agreement. At the end of the visit to Tehran by the Syrian Prime Minister, Naji al Otari, in February 2005, he and Iran's Vice-President, Muhammad Reza Aref, announced that their countries had formed a mutual self-defence pact to defend their national borders and confront domestic threats.[35] In June 2006, they inked a military cooperation pact followed by yet another agreement in March 2007.[36]

Finding the Assad regime facing an existential threat, Tehran offered Damascus technical support to monitor internet communications, as well as advising on methods of crowd control, and supplying it batons and riot police helmets. Behind the scenes, Iran's Al Quds force, the external arm of the Islamic Revolutionary Guard Corps (IRGC), provided technical and material support for Syria's crackdown on demonstrators. But Iran's assistance made little difference.

By the year-end, Assad had abrogated the Baath Party's constitutional monopoly over power and held local elections on a multi-party basis. On the other hand, by then the death toll had exceeded 5,000 in a continuing crackdown, according to the United Nations. In his long, televised speech on 10 January 2012, Assad drew a parallel between the recent bombings in the capital and the Islamist revolt by the Muslim Brotherhood, whose armed struggle against the Alawi-dominated regime reached a peak with an unsuccessful attempt to assassinate President Hafiz Assad in June 1980. Led by Hafiz Assad, the Parliament passed a law which made membership of the Brotherhood a capital offence. Armed with this draconian law the security forces went on a rampage, meting out summary justice. As a consequence, the Islamist rebellion petered out. Now his son, Bashar, denounced the Syrian rebels, invariably Sunni, who formed 70 per cent of the Syrian population as terrorists and traitors. "There can be no let-up for terrorism—it must be hit with an iron fist," he declared. "There's no tolerance of terrorism or of those who use weapons to kill."[37] This marked the next phase of the violent turmoil in Syria, with regional powers intervening actively through proxies.

Intervention by Regional Powers

During the popular street protests in Tunisia and Egypt, Qatar and its highly influential Al Jazeera satellite TV channel had backed the Muslim

Brotherhood or its surrogate. Since most of Syria's local rebel groups were offshoots of the Brotherhood outlawed in 1982, Qatar started supplying them with arms channeled through Turkey, whose Islamist Prime Minister Recep Tayyip Erdogan was friendly with the Brotherhood. The first shipment of arms and equipment carried by Qatari Air Force's massive C-130 transport aircraft from Al Udeid Air Base landed at Esenboga Airport near Ankara on 3 January 2012. The clandestine airlift picked up after the November presidential poll in the United States, whose CIA officers assisted Qatar in procuring weapons. Those posted in Turkey worked with Turkish intelligence counterparts to help decide which rebel groups would receive weapons. Not to be seen lagging behind its tiny neighbor, Qatar, Saudi Arabia resorted to supplying weapons and equipment to anti-Assad groups functioning as the Free Syrian Army (FSA), led by defecting officers from Syria's military, from November 2012 onwards, to be channeled through Jordan and Turkey. By March 2013 over 160 military cargo flights by Jordanian, Saudi and Qatari pilots touched down at airports in Turkey and Jordan. "A conservative estimate of the payload of these flights would be 3,500 tons of military equipment," said Hugh Griffiths, of the Stockholm International Peace Research Institute, adding that it was "a well-planned and coordinated clandestine military logistics operation."[38]

According to a top-secret United States National Security Agency document, accessed by whistleblower Edward Snowden, the rocket attacks on the Presidential Palace, Damascus International Airport, and a government security compound on 18 March 2013, the second anniversary of the civil war, were personally ordered by Prince Salman bin Sultan, son of the long-serving Defence Minister. He had procured 120 tons of explosives and other weaponry for the FSA, instructing it to "light up Damascus" and "flatten" the airport.[39] Elsewhere, bolstered by ample supplies, the rebels intensified their campaign of ambushes, roadside bombs and assaults on isolated outposts and expelling Assad's forces from large parts of rural Syria. Meanwhile anti-Assad leaders and several US officials and lawmakers argued that accelerating clandestine arms shipments to the insurgents was necessitated by the weapons being supplied to the Syrian government by Iran and Russia. But the contexts were poles apart.

By virtue of its 2005 self-defence treaty, the Islamic Republic was required to assist Assad to counter domestic threats. Logistically, it was easy for Iran to dispatch weapons and other military equipment to Syria in defiance of the UN Security Council Resolution 1929. The Iraqi government of Premier Nouri al Maliki allowed Iran's over flights carrying military supplies to the Assad regime. He authorized oil shipments to the cash-strapped Assad regime at half the market price.[40] Later he would permit a free flow of Iraqi Shia volunteers, trained by Iran's Al Quds officers, to Syria, ostensibly to protect the holy shrine of Sayyida Zainab, a granddaughter of the Prophet Muhammad, in a Damascus suburb.[41] In the opposition camp, logistically, it was easy for the Syrian insurgents to buy or receive free of charge arms, ammunition and explosives from Sunni tribesmen and militants in neighboring Iraq across the porous border. In addition, the militantly Sunni Al Qaida in Mesopotamia (AQIM) went on to set up its own Syrian branch, named *Jabhat al Nusra* (Arabic: The Nusra Front).[42]

Russia's ties to Syria have deep roots. Historically, given its military links with the Soviet Union since 1956, Syria stayed out of the American orbit during the Cold War. After the 1991 collapse of the Soviet Union, maintaining cordial relations with Moscow became business as usual for Damascus, with the Kremlin continuing to be the chief arms supplier to Syria. More recently, after losing its naval facility in the Libyan port of Benghazi in March 2011, Moscow was keen to retain its naval facilities in the Syrian post of Tartus, dating back to the Cold War, in order to maintain a naval presence in the Mediterranean.

To fulfill its existing contracts, Russia had shipped to Syria advanced, SA-17 surface-to-air missiles (SAM), and short-range missiles. Rebuffing Western pressure, Moscow said that it would be honouring its previously agreed contract which included sophisticated S-300 SAMs.[43]

Mindful of how the Western powers had misused the United Nations Security Council resolution in March 2011 to establish no-fly zones in Libya to protect civilians and to overthrow the Muammar Gaddafi regime, Russia, backed by China, had vetoed Western-sponsored resolutions on Syria at the Council. Playing on the frustration of the three Western permanent members of the Council, Saudi Arabia, Qatar and other pro-Washington Arab countries kept pressing President Obama to reverse his decision against intervening militarily in Syria.

This created great anxiety in the Syrian government. Official nervousness reached a peak when on 18 July 2012 a suicide car attack directed at the National Security headquarters in Damascus killed the defence minister Daoud Rajha and several heads of the intelligence agencies. On 23 July, Jihad Makdissi, a Syrian Foreign Ministry spokesman, said at a televised news conference that "Any stock of WMD [weapons of mass destruction] or unconventional weapons that the Syrian Army possesses will never, never be used against the Syrian people or civilians during this crisis, under any circumstances. These weapons are made to be used strictly and only in the event of external aggression against the Syrian Arab Republic." By so doing, he offered direct confirmation of what the CIA had said in its 2011 report to Congress. "Syria has had a CW [chemical weapons] program for many years and has a stockpile of CW agents, which can be delivered by aerial bombs, ballistic missiles, and artillery rockets," noted the document. "We assess that Syria remains dependent on foreign sources for key elements of its CW program, including precursor chemicals." Five years before, the CIA had stated that Syria's chemical weapons arsenal included "the nerve agent sarin, which can be delivered by aircraft or ballistic missile." Earlier in July 2012, in his private meeting with Kofi Annan, the UN's special envoy for Syria and former UN secretary general, Assad had told him that any chemical weapons were stored in a safe place and they had not been mixed for use, and that they would not be deployed except in the case of foreign invasion.[44]

Four weeks later, at an impromptu news conference at the White House, President Obama said "We have been very clear to the Assad regime, but also to other players on the ground, that a red line for us is we start seeing a whole bunch of chemical weapons moving around or being utilized. That would change my calculus. That would change my equation. We're monitoring that situation very carefully. We have put together a range of contingency plans."[45]

By early 2013, Iran's Al Quds Force of its IRGC helped transform hundreds of local pro-government Popular Committees in Syria into a well-structured, 60,000-strong National Defense Forces of salaried militiamen as an auxiliary to the regular army. Their strength would rise to 100,000. They manned checkpoints, patrolled, and assisted in counter-insurgency operations. The more promising recruits were trained in urban guerilla warfare not only by the officers of Al Quds Force but also the Lebanese Hizbollah (also spelled Hezbollah, Party of

Allah) at bases in Syria, Lebanon, and Iran. The Hizbollah militia, formed in 1985, had participated in the Lebanese civil war which ended in 1990.

Iran played a critical role in the creation of Hizbollah. It was the Iranian ambassador to Syria who acted as a catalyst to the merger of several Shia groups who had resisted Israel during its invasion of Lebanon in 1982. As Hizbollah escalated guerrilla attacks on Israeli targets in southern Lebanon it received increasing military aid from Tehran, channeled through Syria. By the spring of 1987, the armory of its military wing—called *al Muqawama al Islamiya* (The Islamic Resistance)—included cannons as well as anti-tank and anti-aircraft missiles. In 1991 it had 3,500 militiamen posted in southern Lebanon.[46] It also became the leading Lebanese recipient of financial assistance from Iran, which funded its health, education and other public services. In domestic politics, it secured eight of the 27 seats reserved for Shias in the 1992 Lebanese parliamentary elections. As a result of its alliance with Amal, a moderate Shia group, Hezbollah won all Shia seats, bar one, in the 1996 general election. It intensified its guerrilla activities against Israel occupying southern Lebanon to the point that Israel withdrew from the area in May 2000 as required by a UN Security Council Resolution in 1978. Many years later, it would get entangled in the Syrian civil war for sectarian reasons.

Having ceded most of Aleppo, the largest city and commercial-industrial hub of Syria, to opposition forces in July 2013, the Syrian government resolved to expel rebel Free Syrian Army fighters from parts of Damascus. After achieving that aim, it decided to mete out collective punishment against the residents of Sunni suburbs around the capital, which had become FSA strongholds.

Chemical Weapons and Obama's "Red Line"

The Syrian army focused on Ghouta, a conservative Sunni region about 6 km (3.7 miles) east of the center of Damascus—the scene of ongoing clashes for more than a year, with the military launching repeated missile assaults to dislodge the rebels. In the early hours of 21 August, the Ein Tarma, Zamalka and Muadhamiya neighborhoods of Ghouta were hit by surface-to-surface missiles carrying warheads of sarin nerve agent. Of the 3,600 people who showed neurotoxin symptoms, associated with chemical nerve agents, 502 died, according to the Syrian Observatory for Human Rights, a London-based group with a network of informers in Syria.[47]

Immediately, the opposition claimed that the chemical attack was launched by the military, pointing out two locations from which the missiles had been fired. Its plan was to weaken the rebels before a major conventional attack with tanks, armored personnel carriers and attack planes, it argued. The government denied responsibility, arguing, unconvincingly, that the rebels' mishandling of poison gas had led to the tragedy. Russian officials accused the rebels of staging the attack in order to provoke international military intervention.

In his CNN interview on 23 August, Obama said that when chemical weapons are used, "that starts getting to some core national interests that the United States has." On 28 August he stated that "There need to be international consequences," and two days later he suggested the possibility of taking "limited, narrow" military action. He ordered the Pentagon to develop target lists. Five US destroyers were in the Mediterranean ready to fire cruise missiles at Syrian targets. Obama's statements were warmly welcomed by Saudi Arabia which, since May 2013, had overtaken Qatar as the foremost paymaster for arms and ammunition for the opposition. Adel al Jubeir, the Saudi ambassador to the US, told friends and his superiors in Riyadh that Obama was at last ready to strike Assad's regime. Having "figured out how important this is, he will definitely strike," Jubeir told an interlocutor in Washington.[48]

Not to be caught unawares, by 28 August the Syrian government had transferred its General Staff Command headquarters from central Damascus to bunkers in the foothills of the Anti-Lebanon Mountains north of the capital, and moved various commands to schools and underground bunkers. The barracks and housing compounds for the elite units of the army located in the suburbs of Damascus were evacuated and troops and their families were relocated inside the capital.[49] At the White House, officials were busily building the case that Assad had committed a crime against humanity. But on 29 August, the British Parliament denied Prime Minister David Cameron its endorsement for a possible attack on Syria by 285 to 272 votes. Cameron said he would respect the Parliament's decision.[50]

The unexpected setback for Cameron, who had repeatedly condemned Assad for massacring his own people, prompted a rethink on Obama's part. In his inaugural speech in January 2009, he had committed the United States to multilateralism, which had been discarded by his predecessor George W. Bush, who had acted unilaterally in Iraq. Obama would later tell Jeffrey Goldberg of the *Atlantic* that he found himself recoiling from the idea of a military attack not sanctioned by international law or US Congress. On 31 August, therefore, he announced that he would ask Congress to authorize a strike beforehand.[51] His decision came as a surprise to some of his advisers, and disappointed the Gulf monarchs. Obama's domestic critics said that he was losing his nerve and passing the buck for his own red line.

A few days later Secretary of State John Kerry headed to Europe, and Obama flew to St Petersburg along with his national security adviser, Susan Rice, for the G20 summit, with a common agenda. They would assemble backing from allies for a statement condemning the 21 August chemical attack, blaming Assad for it, and calling for an unspecified response. This was not to be. In St Petersburg, those who opposed military strikes against Syria without a UN Security Council mandate included the five-strong BRICS powers—Brazil, Russia, India, China and South Africa—along with Indonesia, the world's largest Muslim nation, and Argentina.[52] German Chancellor Angela Merkel, the European leader Obama respected most, told him that Germany would not participate in a Syria campaign. Among those who backed the idea of military strikes Saudi Arabia was the most enthusiastic, followed by France. During their one-on-one conversation on 5 September in St Petersburg, President Vladimir Putin asked Obama what if Syria offered to surrender its stockpiles of poison gas to the international community. Obama replied that they should then instruct their top diplomats to explore the offer.

After her return to Washington, Susan Rice briefed Kerry, then in London, who was planning to speak with his Russian counterpart Sergey Lavrov. When a reporter asked Kerry if Syria could avoid military strikes, Kerry replied in the affirmative provided Assad promptly handed over his chemical weapons, and added that "He isn't about to do it, and it can't be done." During their telephone conversation, Lavrov referred to Kerry's comments. Kerry remarked that he was making a debating point. Never the less, Lavrov said that he planned to make a public proposal that Syria should allow international monitors to control the chemical weapons and ultimately give them up. If this was a serious proposal, then the Obama administration would consider it, replied Kerry.[53]

On 10 September, officials at the White House noted with dismay the result of a *Wall Street Journal*/NBC poll that only 33 per cent of Americans favored military action against Syria, clearly indicating that the US public was increasingly wary of foreign entanglements and doubtful that an attack would benefit America.[54] Reflecting popular opinion, US Congress was highly unlikely to give a go-ahead to Obama.

As scheduled before, the President delivered a televised address on the night of 10 September. After providing a background to his decision to consider a limited military attack on the Assad regime, and then asking Congress for authorization, he revealed that Syria had agreed to sign the 1997 Chemical Weapons Convention (CWC), an arms control treaty that outlaws the production, stockpiling, and use of chemical weapons and their precursors. He asserted that "I've spent four-and-a-half years working to end wars, not to start them."[55] He added that he had asked the leaders of Congress to postpone a vote to authorize the use of force while his administration pursued the path of diplomacy offered by Russia.[56]

After two days of negotiations in Geneva, Kerry and Lavrov agreed a deal on 13 September. It specified "immediate and unfettered access" to inspectors of the Organization of the Prevention of Chemical Weapons furnished with a comprehensive list of weapons from Syria. The weapons would be put under international control and removed or destroyed in a process that would begin within a week and be completed by mid-2014. (In the event, the inspectors completed their job in June 2014.) Lavrov explained that any violations by Syria would be notified to the Security Council from the board of the Chemical Weapons Convention before sanctions, short of the use of force, were considered.[57]

Though Kerry stressed that since the US President, as the commander in chief, has the right to defend the United States and its interests regardless of what happens in Congress, and the threat of using force remained open to America, on balance the Geneva agreement favored the Kremlin. It put any American attack firmly on the back burner. It also brought the UN Security Council, earlier skirted by the Obama White House, center-stage as the primary agency to implement and supervise the deal. Moscow also managed to spare the Assad regime the degradation of its military capabilities that would have resulted from the Pentagon's strikes and weakened its capabilities in fighting the insurgents.

The Obama White House had a good reason to take into account the interests of the Kremlin because Russia was one of the six major powers engaged in negotiating with Iran on its nuclear program. In September 2013 Obama's officials were engaged in super-secret talks with their Iranian counterparts in Oman to work out details on how to relieve Tehran from the crippling sanctions in return for reduction in its activities in the nuclear field.

Obama's Economic Pressure on Iran Pays Off

Shortly after his inauguration as President in January 2009, Obama exchanged letters with Iran's Supreme Leader, Ayatollah Ali Khamanei, but nothing came of this even though the President quietly shelved the US project to subvert Iran, the one initiated by President George W. Bush after listing it as one the three members of the "Axis of Evil". In July 2009 Iran arrested three American hikers near the Iraqi border, accusing them of espionage. As the White House tried to secure their release, Sultan Qaboos bin Said of Oman, enjoying friendly relations with Tehran, volunteered to help. One of the Americans, Sarah Shourd, was released in September 2010 on a bail of $500,000 deposited in an Iranian bank in the Omani capital Muscat, and was allowed to return to the US via Oman.[58] The release of the remaining two hikers, Shane Bauer and Joshua Fattal, who had been tried and sentenced to eight years imprisonment, came a year later after the posting of a $930,000 bail by Oman.

In June 2011, Fereydoun Abbasi-Davani, Head of Iran's Atomic Energy Agency, said that "This year, under the supervision of the [International Atomic Energy] Agency, we will transfer 20 per cent enrichment from the Natanz site to the Fordow site and we will increase the production capacity by three times."[59] The existence of the Fordow plant, dug into a mountainside near the holy city of Qom, in order to render it immune from American or Israeli air strikes, was confirmed by Iran only in September 2009. Its latest decision was open to two interpretations: it was bent on moving forward to the 90 per cent enriched uranium needed for an atom bomb, or planning to use this fact on the ground to bolster its bargaining power in any fresh talks with the six global powers.

As the US President and Congress considered a plan to strangle Iran's oil lifeline, the world's third largest petroleum exporter, the Saudi oil minister Ali Naimi, repeatedly stated that the Kingdom "will use [its] spare production capacity to supply the oil market with any additional required volumes" to make up for the loss of Iran's exports.[60] The US National Defense Authorization Act for Fiscal Year 2012, signed into law by Obama on 31 December 2011, also included sanctions against the central bank of Iran, Bank Markazi, the clearing-house for Iran's oil exports. The provision, effective from 1 June, penalised foreign financial institutions that did business with Bank Markazi, forcing Iran's trading partners to choose between buying oil from it or being excluded from any dealings with US companies.[61]

During his visit to Venezuela, on 10 January 2012, Ahmadinejad brushed aside Western alarm over Iran's decision to start 20 per cent uranium enrichment work at its Fordow plant as "exaggerated and politically motivated."[62] On 23 January 2012 European Union (EU) foreign ministers declared that Iran had "failed to restore international confidence in the exclusively peaceful nature of its nuclear program." Therefore, the EU has decided to ban the import, purchase and transport of Iranian crude oil and petroleum products as well as related finance and insurance. The existing contracts would be phased out by 1 July. The prohibition also applied to investment and the export of key equipment and technology for Iran's petrochemical sector.[63]

A far more severe blow to Tehran came in March when Iranian banks were disconnected from SWIFT (Society for Worldwide Interbank Financial Telecommunication). SWIFT, based in La Hulpe, an outer suburb of Brussels, is used worldwide to transmit payments and letters of credit across borders through the banking system.[64] Iran's exclusion from SWIFT severely damaged its ability to conduct foreign trade and money transfers.

Iran's threat to retaliate by blocking the Strait of Hormuz, through which about a third of the global oil exports pass daily, proved hollow.

Indeed, it resumed diplomatic talks with the six world powers in April 2012 in Istanbul. The negotiators adopted a step-by-step process with reciprocal actions in order to create momentum towards a long-term solution. But the two subsequent rounds of talks proved sterile. Western sanctions on Iran's petroleum exports hit the country hard. Tehran's oil revenues fell by more than $40 billion in 2012, with its exports declining by 40 per cent from the 2011 figure.[65] Reflecting this downturn, the free market value of the Iranian rial fell by half from 13,500 rials to one US dollar in 2011 to 26,100 a year later.

The main beneficiary of Tehran's economic woes was Saudi Arabia which increased its oil market share at Iran's expense. More importantly, by now, the negotiating countries with Iran had tacitly adopted its agenda to deprive Tehran of the *capability* of fabricating a nuclear weapon in the future since their intelligence agencies had concluded that Iran's Supreme Leader Khamanei had decided not to build an atom bomb.

The economic downturn in Iran created a division between the government and the general public. While Ahmadinejad maintained a defiant stance by informing the IAEA in January 2013 that he intended to upgrade uranium enrichment centrifuges, thus purifying uranium at a faster rate, the faltering economy coupled with high inflation had turned public opinion dovish on the subject. This forced the Ahmadinejad government's hand, and it returned to the negotiating table. Iran's talks with the five permanent UN Security Council members and Germany (P5+1), chaired by the EU's High Foreign Policy Chief Catherine Ashton, were held in the Kazakh capital of Almaty on 26–27 February 2013.

Of the six major powers, it was the United States which counted most. What was needed then was negotiations between Iran and America which, given their historical animosity, needed to be conducted behind the scenes. That was where mediation by Sultan Qaboos was welcomed by both sides. Personally authorized by President Obama, William Burns, Deputy Secretary of State, and Jake Sullivan, chief foreign policy adviser to Vice-President Joe Biden, led a small team of technical experts on their flight to Muscat in mid-March. There, they met an Iranian team of diplomats, national security aides, and nuclear technical experts. Kerry visited the Omani capital in May ostensibly to push a military contract with the Sultanate.

On 14 June Hassan Rouhani, a moderate cleric who had led the nuclear team from 2003 to 2005 under President Muhammad Khatami, won the presidential poll outright with 50.7 per cent of the vote. He had campaigned on a platform of easing crippling economic sanctions, and an end to Iran's isolation from the West, with which he was familiar since he had obtained his doctorate from Glasgow University. As a result, the pace and intensity of the clandestine American-Iranian talks picked up. After Rouhani assumed the presidency in early August, four top-secret meetings were held during the next three months.

Intriguingly, in a public speech on 17 September, Khamanei approved the use of "heroic flexibility" in diplomacy. In his speech before the UN General Assembly, Rouhani offered "time-bound and results-oriented" talks on the nuclear question.[66] On 28 September Obama spoke by phone to Rouhani who was in New York to address the UN General Assembly where, on the sidelines, Kerry met his Iranian counterpart Muhammad Javad Zarif.[67] Little wonder, then, that two clandestine meetings between Iranian and American officials were held in Oman in October.

At the resumed talks between Iran and the P5+1 in October 2013 in Geneva, the new Iranian delegation was led by foreign minister Zarif. Following two more rounds in as many months Zarif signed a Joint Plan of Action with Catherine Ashton, setting out a road map for the final deal. Iran agreed to curb uranium enrichment above 5 per cent and give IAEA inspectors better access in return for releasing $7 billion of Iran's frozen overseas assets. While the prospects for relaxation of tensions between Iran and the world powers brightened, as a prelude to a final settlement of the nuclear issue, the mood in Riyadh darkened.

Despite the silence maintained by the three concerned parties toward the talks by erstwhile adversaries, unconfirmed reports of these negotiations started circulating in the Gulf region in the summer. The most interested spectators to the long-running contentious issue of Iran's nuclear program were Saudi Arabia and Israel. For different reasons, both of them were resolved to ensure that Iran did not fabricate an atomic bomb. Their best strategy lay in exerting pressure on Washington to deal forcibly with Iran to prevent it from becoming a nuclear state. This, they concluded, would be most effectively achieved if a credible case could be built to show that if Iran acquired its own nuclear weapon then Saudi Arabia would follow suit with the active assistance of its traditional ally, Pakistan.

So, as if on cue, on 6 November 2013, BBC Television's *Newsnight*, hosted by Mark Urban, declared that Saudi Arabia could obtain nuclear bombs "at will" from Pakistan. "Earlier this year, a senior NATO decision-maker told me that he had seen intelligence reporting that nuclear weapons made in Pakistan on behalf of Saudi Arabia are now sitting ready for delivery," stated Urban. "Last month Amos Yadlin, a former head of Israeli military intelligence, told a conference in Sweden that if Iran got the bomb, 'the Saudis will not wait one month. They already paid for the bomb, they will go to Pakistan and bring what they need to bring'." Later in the program Urban said that the information given by the NATO official was believed to have originated in Israel. The timing of this information planted by Israel while talks on Iran's nuclear program were believed to be progressing well seemed suspiciously convenient.[68] The plain truth was that a written nuclear agreement between Riyadh and Islamabad has never been confirmed; nor has it been shown, if it existed, how it would ever be implemented.

After preparatory technical talks were held in Geneva on 7–8 November, Iran and its six interlocutors met at the foreign minister level there later that month. After five days of intensive negotiations, they announced an agreement titled the Joint Plan of Action, commonly known as the Interim Geneva Agreement. It was to become effective on 20 January 2014.

Iran agreed to the following: all uranium enriched beyond 5 per cent will be diluted or converted to uranium oxide; no new uranium at the 3.5 per cent enrichment level will be added to its present stock; 50 per cent of the centrifuges at Natanz and 75 per cent at Fordow will be left inoperable. In addition, Iran will grant the inspectors of the UN watchdog, the IAEA, daily access to the Natanz and Fordow plants. The IAEA will also have access to Iran's uranium mines and centrifuge production facilities. Tehran will address IAEA questions regarding possible military dimensions of its nuclear program and furnish concomitant data as part of an Additional Protocol. In return, Iran will receive relief from sanctions of approximately $7 billion and no further sanctions will be imposed. The accord allowed Iran to purchase spare parts for its aging airline fleet. Also sanctions on the automobile industry and those on associated services will be suspended.[69] The accord set a six-month time frame for a more comprehensive follow-up agreement between Iran and the P5+1.

Between Iran and the US, each side stressed that it got the better of the other. Zarif said the threat of US military strikes was gone. Kerry disagreed. Zarif argued that the agreement explicitly recognized Iran's right to enrich uranium. Kerry again disagreed, though he did so implicitly. As a signatory to the nuclear Non-Proliferation Treaty, Iran was entitled to nuclear power. The long-running dispute boiled down to *how* Iran was to exercise that right.

Politically, the Iranian deal makers had to cover themselves against a counter-attack by hardliners at home. In his nationally televised speech to the students of Shaheed Beheshti University in December, Rouhani said "Nuclear energy is our absolute right, yes but the right to progress, development, improving people's livelihood and welfare is also our definite right." Khamanei had welcomed the deal and said the negotiators "deserved to be appreciated and thanked." In the United States, the latest Reuters-Ipsos opinion poll showed support for the Geneva Accord by a 2 to 1 margin, with only 20 per cent favoring military action against Iran if the deal failed. In early December Zarif finished a four-day whirlwind tour of the capitals of Kuwait, Qatar, Oman and the United Arab Emirates (UAE) to brief them on the accord and allay fears. He wrote in his Facebook post that he was ready for negotiations with Saudi Arabia whenever Riyadh was ready and added that talks would be "beneficial for both countries, the region and the Muslim world." Earlier, the Saudi cabinet had said, "If there is goodwill, this agreement could represent a preliminary step toward a comprehensive solution to the Iranian nuclear program."[70] Unsurprisingly, there was no pick-up of Zarif's offer by the Saudi Kingdom. Tehran and Riyadh remained locked in a bitter struggle in Syria.

In April 2014 the IAEA said that Iran had neutralized half of its 20 per cent enriched uranium stockpile as agreed earlier. Four months later the sixth and final round of nuclear negotiations between Iran and the P5+1 group started in Vienna, but failed to meet the November 2014 deadline for the final deal.

Syrian Civil War, 2014

The ongoing Syrian civil war became more complicated in 2014, with the emergence of the Islamic State in Iraq and Syria (ISIS; also known as Islamic State in Iraq and the Levant, ISIL) as a major player. Having seized the provincial capital of Raqqa—located 230 miles east of Damascus—from other Syrian rebels on 14 January, ISIS declared it its capital city.

ISIS was the latest incarnation of Al Qaida in Mesopotamia, having evolved from Islamic State in Iraq in April 2013 under the leadership of Abu Bakr al Baghdadi, who succeeded Abu Omar al Baghdadi after the latter's death in May 2010. A native of Baghdad, Abu Bakr al Baghdadi (born 1971) obtained a doctorate in Quranic Studies from Saddam University in the capital. He was arrested by US forces in February 2004 as Ibrahim Awad Ibrahim al Badry, his name at birth. He was freed in December as a "low level prisoner". In the Islamic State in Iraq's leadership he served as the head of its Sharia Committee until his elevation to the top post. Taking advantage of the civil war in Syria, he extended the violent activities of his organization to Syria. In April 2013 he announced the formation of ISIS.

Both ISIS ideology and Wahhabi Islam shared their pathological hostility to Shias, who were condemned as apostate for their practice of praying at the tombs of saints, and whose mosques and gatherings were frequent targets of its suicide bombings. Another common ideological point with Wahhabism was the commitment to the principle of *hisba*, which is synonymous with "commanding right and forbidding wrong" (*al-aamr bi-l-maaruf wa-l-nahi aan al-munkar*). It designates the prime duty of Muslims to encourage their fellow believers to abide by the teachings of Islam and punish those who do not. The leaflets distributed by ISIS in Mosul said that in accordance with Sharia law women must stay indoors, and be accompanied by a male member of the family when venturing outside, and that the hands of thieves would be chopped off.[71] Later on, ISIS would replicate the restrictions that were imposed in Ikhwan colonies established by Abdul Aziz bin Abdul Rahman Al Saud in the 1920s. That meant a ban on smoking, singing or dancing, listening to music, and wearing gold or silk—coupled with an obligatory performance of Islamic rituals.

In its intensified armed struggle against the government of Iraqi Prime Minister Nouri al Maliki, ISIS captured Anbar Province's leading cities of Falluja and Ramadi by early 2014. That put Maliki on the defensive. In his public speech in mid-February he claimed that Saudi Arabia and Qatar were offering cash to recruit fighters in Falluja to win more territory for ISIS. Citing unnamed analysts and US officials, the *Washington Post* reported that over the past two years citizens in Saudi Arabia and Kuwait had quietly contributed vast sums of money to and joined the ranks of ISIS and other jihadist groups fighting Assad's regime in Syria.[72]

Maliki went further. In his interview with France 24 television on 8 March, he said, "I accuse them [Saudi Arabia and Qatar] of inciting and encouraging the terrorist movements. I accuse them of supporting them politically and in the media, of supporting them with money and by buying weapons for them." He also blamed Saudi Arabia and Qatar for launching Syria's civil war through Al Qaida-linked groups that now operated on both sides of the Iraqi-Syrian border. "They are attacking Iraq through Syria indirectly. They absolutely started the war in Iraq, they started the war in Syria." According to him, ISIS had been one of the biggest fighting forces in Syria's civil war.[73]

ISIS had achieved this status by overpowering less extreme jihadist groups battling the Syrian military. To a certain extent this worked to the advantage of Assad's regime. In May 2014, the Syrian army regained control of previously rebel areas of Homs. It also made gains in Aleppo and consolidated its control of western Aleppo.

The Syrian government held the presidential poll under the new constitution in the areas under its control on 3 June. Also many thousands of Syrians living abroad, who were entitled to vote, cast their ballots. According to official sources, voter turn-out was 73.4 per cent—with Assad securing 10,319,723 ballots, or 88.7 per cent of the total, and his two rivals 7.5 per cent. The delegation of officials from more than thirty countries, including legislators and dignitaries from Iran, Russia and Venezuela, toured polling stations. Kerry called the election "a great big zero." By contrast, a joint statement issued by the visiting delegations, and read out by Alaeddin Boroujerdi, head of the Iranian parliament's Committee on National Security, said that "These elections have happened in … a transparent, democratic way… These elections in Syria pave the way for a new stage of stability and national agreement in this country after more than three years of war imposed by foreign parties."[74]

The subsequent jubilation in Tehran at Assad's re-election subsided sharply on 9 June when ISIS captured Mosul, the second largest city of Iraq, and seized a huge arsenal of US-made arms and ammunition as well as $429 million in cash from the Central Bank. Armed with advanced weaponry, ISIS forces rapidly marched southward. Their officers made a point of filming their ranks shooting dead Shia prisoners of war, and uploading the images.[75] This was an important tactic of ISIS leaders to demoralise its enemy.

In Riyadh there was schadenfreude among King Abdullah and senior princes, who were glad to see the emergence of powerful Sunni forces to challenge Maliki's Shia-dominated administration, two-and-a-half years after the US pullout from Iraq.

The dramatic victory of ISIS came at a time of political flux in Baghdad in the aftermath of the general election on 30 April. The result announced in mid-May showed the State of the Law Coalition (SLC) winning 92 of the 328 seats. The members of the al Daawa party, the largest constituent of the SLC, opted for Haider al Abadi as the party chief instead of Maliki. In his interview with the *Huffington Post*, Abadi said, "We are waiting for the Americans to give us support. If US air strikes [happen], we don't need Iranian air strikes. If they don't, then we may need Iranian strikes."[76] The Parliament elected Muhammad Fuad Massum, a Kurdish leader, as President, and he took office on 24 July in the midst of a military crisis in Iraq.

When ISIS militia besieged Samarra, sixty-five miles north of Baghdad, alarm bells rang not only in Tehran but also Washington. ISIS "could pose a threat eventually to American interests as well," Obama said in a televised address, but vowed not to be "dragged back into a situation in which, while we're there keeping a lid on things, and after enormous sacrifices by us, as soon as we're not there, people end up acting in ways that are not conducive to the long-term stability and prosperity of the country."[77] He would soon dispatch several hundred US armed forces personnel to Iraq to assess how best the Pentagon could support the Iraqi Security Forces.

By contrast, the Iranian government sent General Qassim Suleimani of its Al Quds Force to Baghdad to assist with the defence of the capital. He met with Shia militia leaders, eager to join the anti-ISIS campaign, and Sunni tribal chiefs in control of Baghdad's western

271

approaches. In the face of the lethal hostility of ISIS, encouraged by Suleimani, various Shia militias in Iraq coalesced under the umbrella of the 140,000-strong Popular Mobilization Forces (Arabic: *Al Hashd Al Shaabi*), overseen by the Interior Ministry. Iran started flying drones over Iraq to assist the government in Baghdad. The state-run Islamic Republic News Agency quoted General Hossein Salami of the Islamic Revolutionary Guard Corps (IRGC) as saying that his forces were "in full combat readiness" to join the fight in Iraq if necessary.[78] By the end of July the IRGC had increased its supply of arms and funds to proxy Shia groups, and Shia fighters operating as the Popular Mobilization Forces had spread south from Samarra to Baghdad and down into the farming communities south of the capital.[79]

In addition, Iran provided aid to the Iraqi defence ministry. A close study of video footage of Russian-made Sukhoi Su-25 "Frogfoot" ground attack jets, posted by the Iraqi authorities in early July, showed that these originally belonged to Iran's IRGC whose insignia and serial numbers had been camouflaged. Seven such warplanes used to be part of the Iraqi Air Force under Saddam Hussein and were flown to Iran for safekeeping during the 1991 Gulf War. They were not returned after the war, and became part of the IRGC's air force.[80]

Heady with a string of dramatic military victories, on 24 June, ISIS announced the establishment of a worldwide Caliphate with al Baghdadi, called Caliph Ibrahim, as its caliph, and ISIS itself was renamed Islamic State. (In the popular media, however, ISIS remained very much in place while in the Arabic speaking world, it was Daesh, the acronym for *al-Dawla al-Islamiya al-Iraq al-Sham*, an Arabic verb, meaning creating disunity.) On the first Friday of Ramadan, which fell on 4 July, ISIS released a 22-minute video of al Baghdadi's sermon from the pulpit of the leading mosque of Mosul. After welcoming the establishment of Islamic State, he said, "Appointing a leader is an obligation on Muslims, and one that has been neglected for decades." He added that "I am your leader, though I am not the best of you, so if you see that I am right, support me, and if you see that I am wrong, advise me."[81]

On 7 August Obama authorized targeted airstrikes against ISIS in Iraq, along with airdrops of aid to refugees. Four days later Iraqi President Massum appointed Abadi as the Prime Minister-designate. Maliki objected, and reneging on his promise not to seek a third term of office, refused to step down. By then soldiers of Iran's Al Quds Force were guarding the golden-domed shrine of two Shia Imams in Samarra, and offering resistance to ISIS forces elsewhere. The power struggle in Baghdad gave Tehran increased leverage to shape Iraqi politics—a fact noted with trepidation in Riyadh. When Iran favored Abadi, Maliki vacated his post on 13 August, and promised to back his erstwhile rival.

Later that month ISIS beheaded two American citizens and posted a video in each case. By the time Obama came up with an overarching anti-ISIS strategy and explained it in a televised address on 10 September—two days after Abadi's "national salvation government" was sworn in—the Pentagon had launched 154 air strikes in Iraq and deployed over 1,100 troops and advisers in non-combat roles. "If left unchecked, these [ISIL] terrorists could pose a growing threat beyond that region—including to the United States," said Obama. "While we have not yet detected specific plotting against our homeland, ISIL leaders have threatened America and our allies." After stating that the United States will conduct a systematic campaign of airstrikes against these terrorists, he said, "I will not hesitate to take action against ISIL in Syria as well as Iraq." He announced that he will send an additional 475 service members to Iraq to help identify ISIL targets in Iraq and Syria by using US drones and helicopters.[82]

As before, Obama was intent on making this campaign a multilateral project. At the NATO summit in Wales on 4–5 September his approach to NATO allies had a good response. And he sought active co-operation in the Gulf region as well, starting with Saudi Arabia. He called King Abdullah before delivering his TV address and sought his kingdom's participation.[83] Thus the US-led anti-ISIS air campaign consisted of 15 participants—eight NATO members, including Turkey, and Egypt and six Gulf monarchies, including Saudi Arabia. Of its 305 combat aircraft, Riyadh placed a dozen under the Pentagon's command.

From now on, Obama treated ISIS as the number one enemy of the United States. According to the CIA, ISIS, controlling a third of Iraq and a quarter of Syria, commanded 20,000 to 31,500 fighters, way up from its previous estimate of 10,000.[84] With that, toppling Assad became a low priority issue for Washington. The contrary was the case in the Saudi Kingdom.

The US-led air strikes on ISIS and smaller jihadist groups prompted the leaders of al Nusra Front, Ahrar al Sham and other Syrian rebel groups to explore the prospect of uniting to face a common danger on 1 November 2014. These talks failed, however. The continued divisions within the broad jihadist camp helped the Syrian government. For instance, it retook the Jhar and Mahr gas fields near Homs from ISIS which had benefited from these fields financially.

In mid-December, General James Terry, commander of the Combined Joint Task Force in Iraq, announced that there had been 1,361 air strikes against ISIS so far.[85] As a result of these bombing raids ISIS had failed to capture more territory either in Syria or Iraq since early September. Around the same time it was reported that Iran had launched airstrikes against ISIS forces along its border with Iraq in an attempt to display its growing military influence in the region in the face of Washington's resurgent role.[86] Both Iranian and American sources emphasized that there had been no coordination between the two sides or sharing of intelligence. Among other things, this reassured the Saudis who feared such an eventuality even if agreed temporarily.

The twenty third day of the following year witnessed the death from lung cancer of Abdullah bin Abdul Aziz Al Saud, the monarch and regent of the Desert Kingdom for twenty years. His successor, Salman bin Abdul Aziz Al Saud, would upend the House of Saud in more ways than one while ratcheting up the rivalry with Iran.

13

MULTI-FRONT COLD WAR BETWEEN RIYADH
AND TEHRAN

The sad-eyed seventy-nine-year-old Salman, wearing a de rigueur dyed black mustache and a goatee beard, stood as tall as Ibn Saud, and resembled his father more that any of his full and half-brothers. As the governor of Riyadh for forty-eight years (1963–2011), Salman acted as a mediator in the vastly expanded Saudi royal family, riven by a complex network of competing factions as they battled for the control of important ministries and governorships. This gave him a unique insight into the power plays within the House of Saud. He went on to deploy it to shake up the traditionally cautious, incremental way the Kingdom had been administered since its inception. On ascending the throne, with his net worth of $17 billion, he became the third richest monarch in the world after Bhumibol Adulyadej, King of Thailand, and Hassanal Bolkiah, Sultan of Brunei. Besides his over-generous royal stipend and profitable financial holdings in the Kingdom's petroleum industry, he inherited a sizable proportion of late King Abdullah's $18 billion fortune.[1]

"Game of Thrones" in the Desert Kingdom

Salman was one of the seven blood brothers born to Hassa al Sudairi.[2] Given the Sudairi Seven's mutual loyalty, and their superiority in terms of their size compared to any other group of blood brothers, they had emerged as the powerhouse of the royal family. Salman's predecessor, King Abdullah, being a child of Fahda al Shraim, was not part of this blood brotherhood. Yet going by strict seniority, he named two of the surviving Sudairis—the shrewd-eyed Sultan and flabby-faced Nayef—as successive Crown Princes, only to see them die in October 2011 and June 2012 respectively, the latter as a result of diabetes and poor blood circulation.[3] After polling each member of the 37-strong Allegiance Council separately in March 2014, Abdullah named the wide-eyed, mustached, moon-faced (non-Sudairi) Prince Muqrin bin Abdul Aziz as the Deputy Crown Prince, with Salman bin Abdul Aziz as the Crown Prince, the status accorded to him in June 2012.

The upending of the dynastic protocol that King Salman accomplished within the first 100 days of his rule proved to be a curtain-raiser to the final act in the real life "Game of Thrones" in Saudi Arabia on 21 June 2017. On that day, at Mecca's royal palace, King Salman elevated his son Muhammad to Crown Prince at the expense of his older cousin, Muhammad bin Nayef, who was also stripped of his position as the Interior Minister. His successor was one of his nephews, thirty-three-year-old Abdul Aziz bin Saud bin Nayef. Since he lacked experience in law enforcement, intelligence or counterterrorism matters, King Salman would soon after reduce the jurisdiction of the Interior Ministry to traffic fines, drug enforcement and passport control, and establish a new organization called the State Security Presidency, to report to him directly.[4] Meanwhile, the new Crown Prince and his ousted cousin made a show of solidarity in front of state television cameras, with Bin Salman kneeling in front of the older royal and vowing: "We will not give up on taking your guidance and advice." In return, Bin Nayef said, "I am content."[5] This was pretence of the highest order.

When Bin Nayef returned to his palace in Jeddah he found that the guards loyal to him had been replaced by the ones owing their loyalty to Bin Salman. He was barred from traveling abroad.[6] Bin Salman's prime aim was to prevent him from flying to Washington, where he had high level contacts, and spilling the beans about how his downfall was engineered by Bin Salman and his father, providing valuable insights into political chicanery within the opaque Saudi inner circle.

Committed to displaying unity in the House of Saud, royals had become past masters in pretending and creating feints to hide their real feelings and motivations, thus masking the ongoing rivalries that existed between different branches of the ruling dynasty, rooted in the many wives that Ibn Saud acquired. After Muhammad bin Salman had been named Deputy Crown Prince by his father on 15 April 2015, he told an interlocutor that he did not expect to become king until he was fifty-five, which was roughly the then age of Crown Prince Muhammad bin Nayef.[7] Reality was starkly different. From the moment Bin Salman became Deputy Crown Prince, he colluded with his father to undermine Bin Nayef.

"The Prince" Among Princes

Standing in front of his vast office desk in a loose ankle length shirt, called a *thobe*, but shorn of the Arab head dress—a square, checked cotton scarf held down by a round black hosepipe-like rope, called an *agal*—his rich black beard and fast receding hairline made Muhammad bin Salman (known in diplomatic circles as MBS) look older than his age. By his own account, both his parents were strict taskmasters. His father made him read a book a week, and his mother, Fahda bint Falah bin Sultan al Hithalayn—nearly twenty years junior to her husband when she married him as his third and last wife in 1984—had her staff arrange extracurricular courses and field trips for him as well as sessions with intellectual mentors. Unlike his four elder half-brothers, who enrolled at Western universities, he obtained his undergraduate degree in law in 2007, at the age of 22, from King Saud University, Riyadh, where the medium of instruction is Arabic, except for medicine and engineering, which are taught in English. However, the Languages Unit provides English language support at all levels. Going by Bin Salman's references to the writings of Sir Winston Churchill in his January 2016 interview with *The Economist*,[8] it seems he availed of this facility. He proudly described himself as someone who belonged to the generation that grew up playing video games and later became an avid user of the products of Apple Inc.

After his graduation, at his father's urging he joined the office of the cabinet's legal adviser. He found bureaucrats too lethargic and hidebound when he tried to get certain company laws and rules changed. When he failed to win a promotion after two years he left to work for his father who was then the governor of Riyadh. As the gatekeeper for his father's office, he upset the old guard who complained to King Abdullah. In October 2011 the eighty-four-year-old Crown Prince Sultan bin Abdul Aziz, who had run the defence ministry for forty-eight years, died of cancer and Alzheimer's disease. Abdullah named Prince Salman as defence minister but ruled out his son Muhammad's presence in the ministry. So the young, restless prince went on to reorganise his father's foundation for building affordable houses. In June 2012, after the death of Crown Prince Nayef, Prince Salman inherited his office. The new Crown Prince appointed his favorite son, Muhammad, his chief of court, thus paving the way for the young prince to get close to the eighty-nine-year-old, ailing King Abdullah. In his dying days, the monarch ordered Muhammad bin Salman to clean up the defence ministry, then riddled with corruption.

Working with two American management consultancies, Bin Salman changed the procedures for weapons procurement, by putting the legal department in the driving seat. Sidelining this department had led to faulty contracts being signed, which fostered widespread corruption. Bin Salman sent back dozens of contracts for revision, and went on to set up a separate office to analyse arms deals. Later, while briefing reporters from *Bloomberg Businessweek*, the director general of the defence minister's office, Fahad al Eissa, said, "Many weapons purchases had been misconceived and inappropriately vetted, with no clear purpose. We are the fourth-largest military spender in the world, yet when it comes to the quality, we are barely in the top twenty."[9]

On assuming the throne in January 2015, Salman handed over the defence ministry to Muhammad. Reportedly afflicted with dementia, which caused him periodic memory losses, Salman was able to concentrate for only a few hours in a day. His son helped by acting as a strict gatekeeper. After a week the king appointed him head of the Council for Economic and Development Affairs (CEDA) which, replacing the earlier Supreme Economic Commission, was mandated to coordinate economic reforms to tackle low petroleum prices. Two months later, King Salman's cabinet decided to transfer the Public Investment Fund from the Finance Ministry to CEDA. It named a new board of directors with Bin Salman as its chairman. Yet more powers were to be placed in the hands of the young prince on 1 May. On that day the monarch dissolved the Supreme Council for Petroleum and Mineral Affairs and established a ten-member Supreme Council of Saudi Aramco, which was split off from the Oil Ministry. Unsurprisingly, the new body was to be chaired by Muhammad bin Salman. The intent, according to senior officials, was to see that the oil behemoth was better monitored, audited and governed as part of radical economic reforms.

In mid-April 2016, in the course of his briefing to *Bloomberg Businessweek*, Bin Salman shed light on the hitherto opaque governance of the Saudi Kingdom. "From the first twelve hours [of Salman's rule], decisions were issued. In the first ten days, the entire government was restructured."[10] A day after acceding the throne, King Salman ordered the merger of his court with that of the Crown Prince Bin Nayef, with a committee led by his son Muhammad to implement his decree.[11] This meant that the Crown Prince had to rely on the goodwill of the Deputy Crown Prince to see the monarch.

Bin Nayef was kept in the dark on matters of vital importance. When, on 26 March 2015, Bin Salman spearheaded an air campaign in neighboring Yemen to oust the Houthi rebels from the capital, Sanaa, after forging a coalition of several Gulf monarchies and Egypt, he kept Bin Nayef out of the loop. Equally, he ignored Prince Mutaib bin Abdullah, minister of the National Guard, who was then out of the country.

When invited by President Barack Obama to a summit of Gulf monarchs at Camp David in May 2015 for a briefing on the talks between Iran and six world powers on Tehran's nuclear program, King Salman deputed Bin Nayef to attend along with Bin Salman. When in his interview with the Saudi-owned Al Arabiya TV channel, Obama said that the younger Prince Muhammad was "wise beyond his years," he boosted Bin Salman's inflated ego at the expense of his much older cousin.[12] Despite his denials, Bin Salman's rivalry with Crown Prince Bin Nayef became a subject of gossip among the Kingdom's chattering classes and the rest of the Arab world. However, this power struggle was one-sided because the young Muhammad had thoroughly eclipsed his namesake cousin, who was senior to him by twenty-six years.

When Salman had a meeting with Obama in the White House on 4 September 2015, he was accompanied not by the Crown Prince but his Deputy Crown Prince son, Muhammad. Savoring the compliment Obama had paid the young prince, Bin Salman violated diplomatic protocol by delivering a soliloquy about the failures of American foreign policy during the Oval Office meeting.[13]

Soon after his return to Riyadh, King Salman sacked Saad al Jabri, a minister of state, who was Bin Nayef's top adviser. According to WikiLeaks, Jabri had acted as the point-man of Bin Nayef since at least 2006, and had been the kingdom's main intelligence contact with the US and other Western nations. Jabri's transgression was that he had questioned Bin Salman's tactics in Yemen which had led Al Qaida in the Arabian Peninsula (AQAP) to grow stronger there, and created fresh pressures from Yemeni refugees and insurgents along the Saudi border.[14] Whereas in theory Bin Nayef was empowered to administer political and security affairs, in reality his writ did not run beyond the interior ministry, which included the feared *Mabahith al Aam* (Arabic: General Investigative Directorate), popularly known as the secret police.

To placate Bin Nayef's bruised ego, the monarch sent him to New York to deliver a speech at the United Nations (UN) General Assembly on 21 September. On his return journey, the Crown Prince paid a state visit in Ankara. If those official assignments reassured Bin Nayef to a certain extent, that feeling disappeared before the year-end. On 15 December Bin Salman announced that thirty-four Muslim nations had joined a Saudi-led military alliance to fight terrorism, and that a joint operations center would be set up in Riyadh to counter extremism in Afghanistan, Egypt, Iraq, Libya, and Syria. Except for Egypt, none of these countries appeared on the list. As for the alliance, twenty-three of the participants were African nations, and all of them had been recipients of Saudi financial aid.[15] Unsurprisingly, Iran was not a member of this alliance; nor was Indonesia, the largest Muslim nation in the world.

In the Saudi Kingdom counterterrorism had been the domain of Prince Bin Nayef since 2003, but Bin Salman's newly created body had no role for him or his resourceful Interior Ministry. Bin Nayef found this rebuff intolerable, but he lacked direct access to the king where he could express his feelings in private. He left the kingdom along with his family for his villa in Algeria, a sprawling compound an hour's drive north of Algiers. Though he was in the habit of taking a short hunting vacation annually in Algeria, this time he stayed away for six weeks, mainly incommunicado, often failing to respond to messages from Saudi officials and close associates in Washington. Even John Brennan, the CIA director, whom he had known for many years, had difficulty reaching him.[16] None of this made an iota of difference to the plan of Salman and his favorite son to undercut Bin Nayef even when, as feared by him, Bin Salman's war against the Shia Houthis had turned into an expensive, embarrassing stalemate.

Riyadh's Military Intervention in Yemen

During the Arab Spring turmoil that led to the stepping down of Yemeni President Ali Abdullah Saleh after thirty-two years in power in February 2012, the Zaidi Shia rebels, loyal to Abdul Malik al Houthi, swelled. These dissenters, based in north-west Yemen, had been at odds with the central government since 2004, leading to several rounds of fighting between them and the army. During the longest period of combat, from August 2009 to February 2010, the Saudi military joined the Yemeni army to curb the rebels. When pro-democracy protests started a year later, the Houthis participated in them. In the nation-wide turmoil that followed, the size of the armed and unarmed Houthis swelled to 120,000. They extended their traditional control of Saada province to the Zaidi-majority provinces of Hajjah and Amran along the Saudi border, much to the alarm of Riyadh.[17]

As part of the agreement that Saleh signed with the mediating Gulf Cooperation Council, Vice President Abd Rabbu Mansour Hadi, a Sunni, followed Saleh after a presidential election in which he was the sole candidate. In line with the GCC-brokered agreement, he set up a National Dialogue Conference (NDC) as a forum to solve the country's political problems in order to create a basis for a new constitution and fresh elections before the end of his two-year transition period. This proved to be a Herculean task for the politically inept Hadi. Yet parliament extended his tenure by a year in January 2014.

This was not acceptable to the Houthis. They advanced toward the capital Sanaa, where the deposed Saleh quietly rejoiced at the threat they posed to Hadi who had failed to gain the loyalty of the army. As a result of cuts to state subsidies in August, fuel prices rose sharply. This led to anti-Hadi demonstrations in the capital. It was in these circumstances that the insurgent Houthis besieged Sanaa on 21 September. They met no resistance from the demoralised and disunited army, or the disaffected politicians. Yet their leaders decided to sign a deal with Hadi, brokered by the United Nations representative, Jamal Benomar, to form a unity government and draft a new constitution. However, the subsequent negotiations dragged on for many weeks.

Frustrated, on 22 January 2015, Houthi leaders compelled Hadi to resign. And a week later they seized the presidential palace and placed Hadi under virtual house arrest. At the UN Security Council, responding to the GCC's lobbying, Jordan along with Britain tabled a resolution on Yemen. Passed unanimously on 15 February, it deplored the Houthis' decision to dissolve Parliament and take over Yemen's administration, and called on the militia to withdraw from government institutions.[18] Houthi leaders ignored the resolution, but allowed Hadi to escape his detention.

Hadi fled to his hometown of Aden, withdrew his resignation, and denounced the Houthi takeover as an unconstitutional coup. The Houthis named a Revolutionary Committee to assume the powers of the presidency along with the long-established General People's Congress, a political party to which Saleh and Hadi belonged. The ruling Committee inaugurated direct air flights between Sanaa and Tehran, offered Iran port facilities, and signed a lucrative oil deal with the National Iranian Oil Company.[19]

This seemed to be enough evidence for Saudi officials and media to start describing Shia Houthis as proxies of Iran. Actually, Houthis' Zaidi sub-sect within Shia Islam is different from Iranians' Twelver sub-sect—so named because of the number of Shia Imams revered by the members of this group. The list begins with Imam Ali and ends with Muhammad al Qassim, who as an infant disappeared in the Iraqi city of Samarra in 837 CE. Zaidis share the first four Imams of the Twelvers, but follow a different line with Zaid, son of Muhammad bin Hanafiya who was a step brother of Imam Hussein, the third Imam.[20] Historically, therefore, there have been no religious or political contacts between the Shias in Yemen and those in Iran.

Now, in early March 2015, the Saudi government was alarmed when Saleh—a Shia of the Zaidi sub-sect with a flair for manipulating competing Sunni tribal leaders through patronage and coercion to retain his presidency for thirty-two years, and still controlling most of the elite Republican Guards—joined the Houthi camp. Together these forces started marching south towards Aden.

On 25 March, Hadi fled Aden by boat, and arrived in Riyadh where the defence ministry had already rallied Egypt and six other Arab countries to mount Operation Decisive Storm against the anti-Hadi forces the next day. Apart from Oman, the other members of the GCC had responded positively to Bin Salman's invitation, as had four Arab recipients of Saudi aid—Egypt, Jordan, Morocco, and Sudan. While staying out of the coalition, Sultan Qaboos of Oman allowed it the use of Omani airspace and closed Oman's border with Yemen. Contrary to Bin Salman's expectation that the shock and awe of the Saudi-led coalition's air offensive would put the Houthi-Saleh alliance to flight from Sanaa, his adversaries showed remarkable staying power. Indeed, they launched artillery and mortar attacks across the border at Saudi urban centers in the Asir region, and made small ground incursions. They also continued their march to capture Aden.

It emerged later that preparations for a massive offensive against the Houthi-Saleh alliance had begun several weeks earlier. In early March Adel bin Ahmad al Jubeir, the Saudi ambassador to the US, called on President Obama, seeking his urgent assistance for a new war in the Middle East. Iran, he claimed, was aiding Houthi rebels in Yemen, who were attempting to set up ballistic missile sites in the range of Saudi cities. The Kingdom along with its Gulf neighbors was about to launch an offensive in support of Yemen's weak government led by Hadi—a campaign most likely to be short. Since Obama did not see Yemen's civil war jeopardizing US national security he let his close advisers debate the issue. Those who opposed cooperation with the Saudis argued that the Riyadh-led campaign would be long, bloody and indecisive. And those who offered the counter-argument said that the White House needed to appease King Salman as it inched towards completing a nuclear agreement with Tehran. Calming the nerves of Salman won the day. Obama instructed the Pentagon to support the upcoming Saudi-led military offensive short of putting boots on the ground. It ended up providing the coalition airborne intelligence, surveillance and reconnaissance, operational planning, maritime interdiction, medical support and aerial refueling.[21]

To its great disappointment, Saudi Arabia failed to co-opt Pakistan in its military plan. On 5 March King Salman went out of his way to greet Pakistani Prime Minister Nawaz Sharif at Riyadh International

Airport along with his full cabinet. During his meeting with Sharif he called for the participation of Pakistani warships, aircraft and ground troops in the military intervention he was planning to make in the ongoing civil war in Yemen to defeat the Houthi rebels. Sharif agreed to put the request before the National Assembly.

After five days of debate, on 10 April parliamentarians unanimously backed the resolution that "Pakistan should maintain neutrality in the Yemeni conflict." Many lawmakers viewed the Saudi move as part of its anti-Shia policy and its ongoing rivalry with Iran in the region. Noting that extremist Sunni jihadists continued to target Shia gatherings in Pakistan, killing hundreds, the legislators in Islamabad stayed out of the Saudi-led coalition in order not to deepen the Sunni-Shia divide in their country, which had the second largest Muslim population in the world. Tellingly, during the debate Iran's Foreign Minister Muhammad Javad Zarif arrived in Islamabad, and met the Prime Minister as well as the Army Chief General Raheel Sharif. Given the military's counter-terrorism campaign against the Pakistani Taliban and tensions with India, Raheel Sharif found his hands tied, making him unable to help Riyadh. While confirming the Parliament's decision, the Prime Minister expressed his preference for a diplomatic solution to the Yemeni conflict.[22] Zarif won, and Bin Salman lost. It was hard for King Salman to accept the rebuff from Islamabad, which meant missing out on deploying its battle-hardened soldiers. He had to console himself with the imposition of a naval blockade of Yemen by Egypt and the United States.

The Saudi government gave the US only a few hours advance warning before the start of its bombing campaign on 26 March. And yet Washington readily lined up with France and Britain at the UN Security Council for a resolution on Yemen. Resolution 2216, passed under Chapter VII on 14 April, by 14 votes to none, with Russia abstaining, called on the Houthis to withdraw from all areas seized during the latest conflict, relinquish arms seized from military and security institutions, cease all actions falling exclusively within the authority of the legitimate Government of Yemen and fully implement previous Council resolutions. It called on all Yemeni parties to resume the UN-brokered political transition.[23] This resolution strengthened the diplomatic hand of Saudi Arabia. In addition, it conferred legitimacy to American and British military personnel working with the Saudi command-and-control center for coalition airstrikes. But it had little immediate impact on the ground fighting.

Unintended Consequences of the Saudis' Yemen Offensive

Having hastily intervened in the long drawn out and convoluted Yemeni civil war, Bin Salman found himself without a clear strategy or exit plan.[24] But, when questioned on the subject by *The Economist* in January 2016, he replied that the decision to go forward with the intervention had been taken by the Council of Ministers and the Council of Security and Political Affairs, and approved by King Salman, and that all he did as Defence Minister was to implement it[25] His statement clashed with the fact that Prince Mutaib bin Abdullah, commander of the 100,000-strong National Guard, was out of the country in late March, and was neither consulted nor informed in advance by Bin Salman.

At the outset Bin Salman ruled out putting Saudi boots on the ground in Yemen. He had failed to learn a cardinal principle of military strategy: to seize control of territory from the enemy, a ground offensive must follow an air campaign. As a result, his military intervention in the Arab world's poorest nation, with its per capita annual GDP of $1,340, turned into a brutal quagmire, draining the Saudi treasury of $6 billion a month.

Bin Salman was so haughtily confident of achieving his declared aim of defeating the Houthi-Saleh alliance within six months, that in late June he went on a pre-planned two-week vacation in The Maldives. Ashton Carter, defence secretary of the United States, which had agreed to support the Saudi-led campaign in Yemen, had trouble reaching him for days during part of his sojourn.[26] Bin Salman rented the exclusive Velaa private island with its six-star luxury hotel. He also took over the nearby island as a base for his extensive staff and support team of bodyguards and advisers. For entertainment, he was reported to have hired such A-list celebrities as Shakira, Rihanna, and Jennifer Lopez. The cost of his profligate holiday was put at $8 million.[27]

In Yemen, after four weeks of relentless air strikes, the Saudi Defence Ministry claimed that the coalition's action had "successfully eliminated the threat" to the Kingdom's security posed by the ballistic missiles and heavy weaponry of the Houthis and their allies led by Saleh. The intervention by Egyptian warships in the crucial Aden region gave the pro-Hadi forces an irreversible edge over the Houthis and their allies. And yet, on 27 April, a Saudi air raid on the village of Shaaf, twenty miles south of Saada in north Yemen, involved dropping a deadly US-supplied CBU-105, a cluster bomb unit that contains 10 high-explosive sub-munitions, designed to be used exclusively on military targets. When dropped, this bomb fragments into 10 high-explosive sub-munitions which scatter over a large area and explode on hitting the ground. A video recording of the remnants of the cluster bomb posted on YouTube was investigated by the New York-based Human Rights Watch, which established its exact location.[28] Later UN Secretary General Ban Ki-moon would warn that the use of cluster bombs could amount to a war crime.

Having bombed almost all military and security targets, the coalition warplanes started hitting civilian airports. This led the Office for the Coordination of Humanitarian Affairs (OCHA) to urge the coalition to stop targeting airports and sea ports in order to facilitate arrival of humanitarian aid into Yemen. The appeal fell on deaf ears.

Politically and diplomatically, it became crucial for the Saudis and their allies to return Hadi to Aden. Here the military of the United Arab Emirates (UAE), ordered by Crown Prince Muhammed bin Zayed al Nahyan, stepped into the breach. Along with the Saudi defence ministry, it planned an amphibious landing of a UAE brigade equipped with tanks, artillery and attack helicopters along the shores of Aden. On 14 July 2015—the day Iran's nuclear deal was signed in Vienna—the Saudis and the Emiratis landed on the beaches of Aden. In less than a week, along with the local pro-Hadi forces equipped earlier with air-dropped arms, they succeeded in expelling most of the anti-Hadi forces from Aden. On 22 July the first aircraft to arrive at the re-opened Aden airport was a Saudi military transporter, carrying aid and weapons.[29] By 26 July the Saudi-led coalition controlled all of Aden.

Coincidentally, that day King Salman led a contingent of 1,000 of his relatives, staff and military officials and their families for a three-week holiday, costing $100 million. His destination was the sandy shore of Vallauris along the Mediterranean in the south of France. While the inner circles of Salman and his favorite son Muhammad occupied the monarch's massive seafront mansion, around 700 guests stayed at lavish hotels in Cannes. The French authorities sealed off the beach to allow

King Salman and the Deputy Crown Prince to holiday in private. Members of the public were barred from coming within 300 meters (985 feet) of the monarch's villa by sea. Scanning the sea, unobstructed, with his high powered binoculars, Bin Salman spotted a 440-foot yacht in the distance. He liked it instantly, and dispatched an aide to buy the vessel, called *Serene*, owned by Yuri Shefler, a Russian vodka tycoon. The deal was done within hours, at a price of 420 million euros ($494 million), according to an investigative report by the *New York Times* in December 2017. Its source was a trove of records from 13.4 million files, leaked on 5 November 2017, originating with Appleby, a law firm in the British Overseas Territory of Bermuda, called the Paradise Papers. These disclosed the hidden secrets of some of the globe's richest individuals and corporations. Specifically, among other things these files showed how groups of lawyers, bankers and accountants in Germany, Bermuda and the Isle of Man worked fast to swiftly transfer ownership of the yacht to Eight Investment Company Limited. It was managed by Bader Al Asaker, head of Bin Salman's personal foundation.[30] The Russian seller packed and left soon after. This was a dramatic example of Bin Salman's impulsive nature, and his huge appetite for an obscenely luxurious lifestyle.

While the architects of the Saudi-led military charge indulged their fancies on the balmy shores of southern France, the focus of the ground fighting in Yemen turned to the southwestern province of Taiz along the Red Sea, with its southern most point overlooking the strategic Strait of Mandab, or *Bab al Mandab* (Arabic: Gate of Tears), and the oil-rich Marib Province east of Sanaa.

Simultaneously, using land routes from the Saudi Kingdom, the coalition built up military supplies in Safer at the farthest end of the dagger shaped Marib province. In August its massive military camp there was primed to use Marib as a staging post to expel the Houthis from Sanaa. But its plans went awry on 4 September. On that day the Houthis, controlling a fifth of the province, struck the coalition's Safer camp with a Soviet-era, short-range ballistic missile, and destroyed the arms depot, killing forty-five Emirati, ten Saudi and five Bahraini soldiers.[31] The incensed UAE government retaliated with a series of punishing attacks on enemy targets. But the coalition decided not to revive its earlier plans.

The pouring of arms and ammunition by the Saudis, Emiratis and Kuwaitis into the Hadi camp contrasted sharply with the clandestine ways Iran replenished the much smaller arsenals of the anti-Hadi forces, since its arms deliveries were outlawed by the UN Security Council Resolution 2216. It resorted to using desert tracks in Oman to send its allies weapons after these had been smuggled across the narrow Strait of Hormuz by small sea vessels, or *dhows*, into Omani territory.

The six-month deadline mentioned by Bin Salman to expel the Houthi-Saleh alliance from Sanaa ended in mid-September 2015 with no sign of success on the horizon. Even the arrival of Hadi in Aden during that month turned out to be a mere stop-over on his way to New York to address the UN General Assembly which recognized him as the Yemeni head of state. He returned not to Aden, but to Riyadh, where Bin Salman, who at first had flaunted his military leadership by meeting the generals in the field with the press in tow, had ceased to do so.

Bin Salman's failure in Yemen emboldened those royals, senior as well as junior, who disapproved of his egregiously luxurious lifestyle. One of them summarised his thoughts in Arabic, and posted them online in the form of open letters. Among the tens of thousands who read these documents was the Cairo-based journalist Hugh Miles, who is fluent in Arabic. He published a summary in the *Guardian* on 28 September. The first letter claimed that "The king is not in a stable condition and in reality the son of the king [Muhammad bin Salman] is ruling the kingdom." It referred to Bin Salman's spendthrift ways and reckless foreign policy, which included staging air raids "against a defenceless people" in Yemen. It called on the thirteen surviving sons of Ibn Saud—specifically Princes Talal, Turki and Ahmed—to unite and remove the leadership in a palace coup, before choosing a new government from within the royal family. The second document revealed that "Four or possibly five of my [the author's] uncles will meet soon to discuss the letters. They are making a plan with a lot of nephews and that will open the door. A lot of the second generation [of the House of Saud] is very anxious." The royal writer claimed to have received widespread support from both within the royal family and society at large. And yet only one other royal went on to publicly endorse his call for a palace coup.[32]

Ultimately, posting online letters of protest proved to be a sterile exercise. Removing a sitting monarch from the throne was a monumental task even when the king and his crown prince were engaged in an all out power struggle as was the case with King Saud and Crown Prince Faisal—as narrated in a previous chapter.[33] Four days earlier, on 24 September, the world's attention turned to the worst ever stampede during the Stoning the Devil ritual of the Hajj pilgrimage in Mina.

Worst Hajj Disaster Fuels Iran's Fury

The stampede claimed 2,411 lives—as reported by the Associated Press, based on media reports and official comments from thirty-six of the over 180 countries that sent citizens to the Hajj—more than three times the official figure of 769.[34] It occurred when two waves of pilgrims traveling in opposite directions collided. The authorities' failure to provide a credible explanation for the accident led to well-informed speculation. "Talking to pilgrims on the ground yesterday, the main reason for this accident was that the King in his palace in Mina was receiving [local and foreign] dignitaries, and for this reason they closed two entrances to where the stoning happens," said Muhammad Jafari, an adviser to the London-based Hajj & Umrah Travel, in his interview with the BBC. "These were the two roads where people were not able to proceed. You have a stream of people going in and if you stop that stream, and the population builds up, eventually there is going to be an accident. It is the fault of the Saudi government because any time a prince comes along, they close the roads, they don't think about the disaster waiting to happen." The colliding waves contained pilgrims inter alia from Iran, Mali, Nigeria, and Egypt.[35]

With 464 deaths, Iran suffered the highest fatalities, followed by Mali (312), Nigeria (274) and Egypt (190). Tehran immediately called for an international Islamic fact-finding committee on the tragedy. King Salman ignored this proposal. Instead, he ordered Bin Nayef to conduct an inquiry and submit a report. In due course he did so. But this document would remain a state secret like many others. When Iran floated the idea of transferring the administration of the holy cities of Mecca and Medina from Saudi Arabia to some form of international Islamic stewardship, Riyadh was swift to dismiss it.[36]

In May 2016 the Saudi government announced that Iranians would be barred from the upcoming Hajj pilgrimage due in September because Iran had failed to sign an agreed Hajj memorandum of understanding (MOU) about logistics and security. Riyadh said that there was an agreement on it issuing electronic visas in the absence of Saudi diplomatic missions in Iran, adding that Tehran had made "unacceptable" demands, including the right to organise demonstrations "that would cause chaos". On the eve of the Hajj pilgrimage, Ayatollah Ali Khamanei issued a most vitriolic condemnation of the House of Saud on his website. "Saudi rulers … are disgraced and misguided people who think their survival on the throne of oppression is dependent on defending the arrogant powers of the world, on alliances with Zionism and the US," he wrote. Accusing them of turning themselves into "small and puny Satans," he stated that they "tremble for fear of jeopardizing the interests of the Great Satan (America)", and added that "Because of Saudi rulers' oppressive behavior towards God's guests, the world of Islam must fundamentally reconsider the management of the two holy places and the issue of Hajj. …The world of Islam, including Muslim governments and peoples, must familiarize themselves with the Saudi rulers and correctly understand their blasphemous, faithless, dependent and materialistic nature."[37] The vehemence of Khamanei's attack strengthened the hands of hard-liners among Saudi policymakers, such as Bin Salman.

Unlike the catastrophe of the last Hajj, the one in 2016 proved to be a tranquil affair. And, as Interior Minister, Bin Nayef took much deserved pride, hoping that his performance would help seal his position as heir to the throne.

Saudi Shias' Protest Echoes in Iran

Unsurprisingly, when pondering air strikes on the Shia Houthis in Yemen, neither of the two rivals at the top in Riyadh, being staunch Wahhabis, gave any thought to the implication of Saudi military intervention in Yemen on Shias in the Kingdom. The Saudi-led blitzkrieg, code-named Operation Decisive Storm, on the Houthis was denounced by Saudi Shias in the Eastern Province. Their earlier protest, ignited by the events in neighboring Bahrain in February–March 2011, subsided. Some months later the government started arresting Shia activists. That inflamed feelings among Shias. And in early October Saudi security forces fired live ammunition to disperse demonstrators in Awamiyah—a settlement of 30,000 Shias led by the richly bearded, white-turbaned Shaikh Nimr Baqr al Nimr, who carried the title of an ayatollah in the Shia religious hierarchy. While condemning the use of firearms on unarmed civilians, he declared that "The weapon of the word is stronger than the power of bullets." He coupled his criticism of the House of Saud with a demand for parliamentary elections. Weekly protest marches occurred after Friday prayers in the Shia villages of the Qatif region. In late November–early December the security forces shot dead four young Shias. Their funerals turned into the biggest demonstrations the Eastern Province had witnessed in three decades. In early January, al Nimr denounced a list of twenty-three alleged activists published by the Ministry of Interior, and warned that the government would be overthrown if it continued its month-long crackdown against protesters. [38]

The authorities put al Nimr under 24/7 surveillance, with a police car trailing any vehicle in which he traveled. On 6 July when al Nimr was on his way from his farm to his brother's house in Qatif, the police tried to arrest him and his co-passengers. In the altercation that followed, al Nimr was shot in the leg and arrested. Activists posted pictures on the Internet of a grey-bearded man they identified as Nimr inside a vehicle. He was covered with what appeared to be a blood-stained white sheet. In the subsequent protest demonstration, two participants were shot dead by the police. On 11 July thousands of Shias turned out for the funerals of the dead men. They carried Bahraini flags and chanted "Qatif and Bahrain are one people", "Down with the House of Saud", and "Down with Muhammad bin Fahd", referring to the governor of the Eastern Province. [39]

Al Nimr was held for eight months before being charged with thirty-three offences, including "disobeying the ruler," "inciting sectarian strife," and, "encouraging, leading, and participating in demonstrations". On 23 December 2013, his lawyer informed the Special Criminal Court that the defendant was unable to respond to the charges because he did not have a pen and paper. Neither his lawyer nor his family was informed prior to the last court session on 22 April 2014. On 15 October 2014, al Nimr was sentenced to death for "seeking 'foreign meddling' in [Saudi Arabia], 'disobeying' its rulers and taking up arms against the security forces". After his appeal to the Appellate Court was rejected in March

2015 leading Shia religious dignitaries from Iraq, Iran and Lebanon condemned the death sentence.

Shia Muslims all over the globe staged peaceful rallies and petitioned the UN Secretary-General to prevent al Nimr's execution. There were street demonstrations in Saudi Arabia, Bahrain, Iran, India and Iraq. None of this mattered. On 25 October 2015, the Supreme Religious Court of Saudi Arabia upheld al Nimr's death sentence. Its ruling also applied to six other Shia activists. Along with Al Qaida terrorists, they were to be beheaded in a public square. Iran's deputy foreign minister, Hossein Amir-Abdollahian, warned in an interview on state television that "the execution of Sheikh Nimr would mean Saudi Arabia facing a heavy cost".[40] It was now left to King Salman to commute al Nimr's execution. That could happen only if a recommendation to that effect was made by the Interior Minister, Prince Muhammad bin Nayef. That was most unlikely since, in his latent but real rivalry with Bin Salman, he could not afford to be seen to be a less fervent Wahhabi than his younger cousin. Regional tensions rose sharply on 2 January 2016 when the Saudi government added al Nimr and three other Shia dissidents to a batch of forty-three Al Qaida militants who had committed violent terrorist acts. The terrorists were beheaded, and the Shia dissidents were also executed. They were all buried in unmarked graves.

An enraged Khamanei tweeted, "This oppressed scholar had neither invited people to armed movement, nor was involved in covert plots. The only act of #SheikhNimr was outspoken criticism," adding that "the unfairly-spilled blood of oppressed martyr #SheikhNimr will affect rapidly and Divine revenge will seize Saudi politicians." While condemning Saudi Arabia's "medieval act of savagery" in executing al Nimr, the Islamic Revolutionary Guard Corps predicted the "downfall" of the Saudi monarchy. Iran's foreign ministry summoned the Saudi charge d'affaires in Tehran in protest. And the Saudi foreign ministry lodged a complaint with the Iranian envoy in Riyadh about Tehran's "blatant interference" in the Kingdom's domestic affairs. Iranian newspapers strongly denounced the execution of al Nimr, with the reformist *Sharq* fearing that this "irresponsible" act could exacerbate sectarian tensions in the region, and advised the Iranian government not to get drawn into Riyadh's "dangerous game". On the other side, *Al Riyadh* declared that no "incitement of harm or sedition" should be tolerated irrespective of the culprit's affiliations. Grand Ayatollah Ali Sistani of Iraq called the execution an "unjust aggression". In Beirut, Hassan Nasrallah, leader of the Hizbollah movement, accused the House of Saud of trying to trigger a civil war between Sunni and Shia Muslims across the world. In Washington, reflecting the views of President Obama, State Department spokesman John Kirby appealed to the Saudi government to respect and protect human rights, and ensure fair and transparent judicial proceedings. He urged it to permit peaceful expression of dissent and, along with other leaders in the region, redouble efforts to reduce regional tensions.[41]

Iran lost whatever high moral ground it gained because of the obduracy of the Saudi Kingdom when an enraged mob in Tehran attacked the Saudi Embassy, ransacked it and set alight a part of it. In response, Riyadh cut its diplomatic ties with Iran. The Hassan Rouhani government resorted to damage limitation. It sacked General Hassan Arabsorkhi, head of police Special Forces in Tehran, and Safar Ali Baratlou, a senior security official, for failing to stop the ransacking of the Saudi Embassy. It immediately arrested forty suspected rioters, with the total rising to 100 later on.[42] By then the long-ailing Saudi foreign minister Prince Saud Al Faisal was dead, and a commoner, Adel al Jubeir, was promoted to succeed him in July 2015. This provided Bin Salman increased leverage on deciding the policy that the Kingdom should follow in Syria's civil war. He opted to raise the stakes against Bashar Assad.

Bin Salman's Syria Move Goads Putin to Bolster Assad

Once Obama had described Islamic State as America's number one enemy in June 2014, his administration's interest in toppling Assad waned. He urged the Gulf States to aid the Iraqi government by sending combat troops to Iraq. They ignored his call. By late 2014 it had dawned on US policy-makers that the only realistic alternative to Assad was a regime dominated by jihadist extremists. Little wonder then that Obama's $500 million program for the training of opposition fighters committed to creating a democratic polity in Syria, conceived in mid-2014, made little progress. The number of volunteers, carefully vetted, was small, with the State Department insisting that they fight ISIS as the primary enemy.

This was disappointing news for the Saudis who complained that the Obama White House, needing the support of Iran against ISIS in Iraq, and hopeful of an accord over its nuclear program, was losing interest in removing Iran's client regime in Damascus. In the region Turkey's leader Recep Tayyip Erdogan agreed with Riyadh's interpretation during his meeting with King Salman in Riyadh on 2 March 2015. They resolved that a strong, coordinated initiative must come from the regional powers to oust Assad. Bin Salman was only too willing to give Riyadh an enhanced profile in Syria's civil war. The result was the creation of the Jaish al Fatah, or the Army of Victory, a command structure for seven jihadist groups in Syria, on 24 March under the leadership of a Saudi cleric Abdullah al Muhaysini. They included Jabhat al Nusra, an affiliate of Al Qaida, and Ahrar al Sham, which shared Al Qaida's Salafi ideology. Together these two groups contributed nearly 90 per cent of the fighters in Jaish al Fatah. This coalition proved very effective.

Riyadh financed the purchase of CIA-procured TOW anti-tank missiles, which largely powered a rebel offensive against Assad in the summer. Jaish al Fatah made inroads into regime-held territory, capturing Idlib and other towns and villages in the province adjoining Turkey. The Nusra Front provided over 3,000 battle-hardened fighters for the offensive which put the insurgents in a position to launch an offensive against Latakia, the bastion of the Assad regime.[43] This unnerved the government in Damascus.

In the face of intensified battering by the opposition, Syria's military and its auxiliary militia, the National Defence Forces, found themselves increasingly short of manpower. Evading call-up had become commonplace, with the number of absentees put at 70,000 by the Syrian Observatory for Human Rights. Deaths, defections and draft-dodging had cut the Syrian military, 300,000 strong in March 2011, by half. Of the estimated 230,000 people killed in the war more than a third were soldiers and their supporting militiamen. This was the backdrop against which Assad conceded in a televised address to a select audience in the capital on 25 July 2015 that his army had been forced to abandon some areas in order to retain others in the war.[44] Apparently, the reinforcements sent by Iran and the Lebanese Hizbollah had proved inadequate to cover the shortfall in manpower.

Assad appealed to Russia for urgent military assistance, as did the Iranian government. The Russian President Vladimir Putin was resolved not to let the Syrian regime collapse, and see the Kremlin lose its last toehold on the Mediterranean coast at Tartus. Russia's military planners decided to fill the gaping hole left by Syria's threadbare air force, shore up its air defences, and boost its depleted arsenal of tanks and armored vehicles. To do this, they turned one of Russia's footholds on a foreign soil, Khmeimim (also spelled Hmeimim) airbase near the port of Latakia, into a forward operating base, in mid-September, and shipped to it warplanes, attack helicopters, tanks, artillery, and armored personnel carriers. The Kremlin also deployed its most advanced S-400 surface-to-air missiles there.[45] Putin ruled out sending combat troops to Syria. Officially Russia's military intervention in the Syrian civil war started on 30 September 2015. And its peak, about 5,000 Russian air force personnel would be involved.

In coordination with the pro-Assad ground forces, Russian warplanes bombed the targets of ISIS and the jihadist constituents of Jaish al Fatah. By the end of 2015, the battlefield scene started to shift in Assad's favor chiefly because the opposition fighters lacked anti-aircraft missiles. Their foreign backers could not supply them these weapons in the face of unremitting opposition from Obama. He argued that once the Syrian rebel factions came to possess these missiles they could fall into the hands of jihadist terrorists who would end up targeting civilian aircraft to a devastating effect.

Over the past few years United Nations' attempt at peace-making in Syria had failed mainly because, at the insistence of Saudi Arabia, Iran was excluded from multilateral talks. After the collapse of two such conferences in Geneva, the third UN-sponsored peace conference was scheduled in Geneva on 29 January 2016. In order to forge a powerful anti-Assad front, Bin Salman, working with Jubeir, convened a conference of all opposition groups, except the Nusra Front, on 10 December. King Salman welcomed the delegates in Riyadh. Two days later the attendees issued a communiqué which called on Assad to step down at the start of a "transitional period." It backed a "democratic mechanism through a pluralistic regime that represents all sectors of the Syrian people which would not discriminate on religious, sectarian or ethnic grounds" The delegates of Ahrar al Sham—a 20,000-strong Islamist militia—walked out when their argument that there could be no final settlement without the post-Assad state basing itself on the

Sharia law was rejected by most of the participating political factions.[46] In any case, the subsequent UN-sponsored peace conference in Geneva failed when the Syrian government delegates rejected the idea of Assad stepping down before the setting up of a transitional authority.

In the final analysis, talks at a negotiating table reflect the balance of force on the battlefield. There, boosted by overt Russian military involvement along with increased backing to the Syrian infantry by Iran and the Lebanese Hizbollah, the Assad government made steady gains. By September 2016, most major Syrian cities were back in government hands, and rebel-held eastern Aleppo was under attack.

On the diplomatic front, following Russia's forceful intervention in Syria, the region's balance of power shifted. Between October 2015 and August 2016, top officials from Saudi Arabia, the UAE, Qatar, Bahrain, and Turkey held talks with Putin. The first to do so, in October, was Bin Salman. He and Putin met at the Russian president's dacha in the Black Sea resort of Sochi. The two agreed that they shared the common goal of preventing "a terrorist caliphate [ISIS] from getting the upper hand." When Jubeir mentioned his concern about the rebel groups the Russians were targeting, Putin expressed readiness to share intelligence, which meant future cooperation between their militaries and security services.[47] Later that day, Sheikh Muhammad Al Nahyan, the deputy supreme commander of the UAE's armed forces, called on Putin. "I can say that Russia plays a very serious role in Middle Eastern affairs," he stated, adding that, "There is no doubt that we have a privileged relationship [with it]." The ruler of Qatar, Emir Tamim bin Hamad Al Thani, went a step further after meeting Putin at the Kremlin in January 2016: "Russia plays a main role when it comes to stability in the world." Along with Jordan, Qatar had been providing the CIA with bases for training and arming anti-Assad insurgents. A month later, the next Gulf chief to call on Putin in Sochi was King Hamad bin Isa al Khalifa of Bahrain, which has hosted the US Navy's Fifth Fleet since 1971. He presented a "victory sword" of Damascene steel to the Russian leader. After their talks, Foreign Minister Sergey Lavrov reported that the two countries had agreed to boost economic and military ties.[48]

On 9 August, Turkish President Erdogan flew to St Petersburg to meet "my dear friend" Putin. Their relations had fallen to a low point when the Turks shot down a Russian warplane over northern Syria in November 2015. But on the following 15 July, Putin was the first foreign leader to call Erdogan to congratulate him on aborting an attempted military coup—something no Western leader did. "We are always categorically opposed to any attempts at anti-constitutional activity," Putin explained after three hours of talks with Erdogan.[49] By so doing, he inadvertently offered an explanation for his earlier unqualified backing for the constitutional Syrian government of Assad. Erdogan and Putin agreed to mend their strained economic relations. In a striking reversal, Erdogan stopped calling on Assad to step down.

In practice, his gesture had no significance for the Syrian president. As it happened, around this time he was planning a bold move in the war.

Assad's Recapture of Eastern Aleppo, a Turning Point

In early September, Assad's government decided to retake rebel-held eastern Aleppo, containing a quarter of a million civilians (compared to 1.5 million in government-controlled western Aleppo), in coordination with Iraq and Iran. Consequently, over 1,000 Iraqi Shia militants traveled from Iraq to the suburbs of Aleppo to join another 4,000 Shia fighters, trained by Iran, already there. Together they formed half of the Assad regime's ground force of 10,000.[50] The Syrian army's offensive started on 22 September and was coordinated with the Russian air force. It gained about a sixth of eastern Aleppo.

Determined to retain their hold over the highly symbolic urban territory of Aleppo, rebel commanders forbade civilians from fleeing at pain of death in order to inhibit the devastating air raids by Russian warplanes. But Assad was hell-bent on retaking eastern Aleppo. In his interview with Daria Aslamova of the Moscow-based tabloid *Komsomolskaya Pravda*[51] on 12 October, he talked of "cleaning" the besieged Aleppo. "It's going to be the springboard, as a big city, to move to other areas, to liberate other areas from the terrorists. This is the importance of Aleppo now," he said. It would provide important political and strategic gains for his regime, he added. He revealed that early on the Saudis told him: "If you move away from Iran and you announce that you disconnect all kinds of relations with Iran, we're going to help you. Very simple and very straight to the point."[52] Among other things this showed Saudi rulers' failure to grasp the length and depth of Damascus-Tehran ties dating back to the 1979 revolution in Iran. They were so used to practising cheque-book diplomacy that they could not comprehend that there were certain loyalties, based on deep-rooted national interests, which could not be bought with cash.

In eastern Aleppo, the insurgent fighters, estimated to number 8,000 to 10,000, were retreating or giving up more readily than had been expected. Saudi Arabia and Qatar could not come to their rescue with arms and ammunition for logistical and diplomatic reasons. Their supply lines were severed by Syrian troops, and Turkey had adopted a neutral stance in the civil war. Little wonder that the government forces broke through the enemy's defensive lines and advanced rapidly to capture all but 5 per cent of eastern Aleppo by 13 December 2016. With UN mediation, a ceasefire was announced to allow the evacuation of civilians and rebels. But it lasted only a day. It was revived on 15 December. During the next week, 34,000 civilians and rebel fighters were bussed out to rebel-held territory in the countryside west of Aleppo and in Idlib province. On 22 December the Syrian army declared that it had retaken full control of Aleppo. "This victory represents a strategic change and a turning point in the war against terrorism on the one hand and crushing blow to the terrorists' project on the other," read its statement. In Moscow, Defence Minister Sergey Shoigu announced that since September 2015 its warplanes had carried out 18,800 sorties, and had "liquidated 725 training camps, 405 weapon factories and workshops, 1,500 pieces of terrorist equipment, and 35,000 fighters."[53]

In his *Komsomolskaya Pravda*, Assad said that "What we've been seeing recently during the last few weeks, and maybe few months, is something like more than Cold War [between Russia and the West]. I don't know what to call it, but it's not something that has existed recently, because I don't think that the West and especially the United States has stopped their Cold War, even after the collapse of the Soviet Union."[54]

Assad's observation was imprecise. The relationship between Russia and the West is best described as competition in some areas and cooperation in others. For instance, Russia had consistently worked with the West on the issue of Iran's nuclear project, agreeing fully that Tehran must not be allowed to build an atomic bomb. And along with five other global powers it had left it to the United States to negotiate the thorny points with Iran while continuing to complete its contract with the Islamic Republic to build a civilian nuclear power plant under the supervision of the International Atomic Energy Agency (IAEA). The end result was the signing of the 109-page Joint Comprehensive Plan of Action (JCPOA) on 14 July 2015. It had taken an inordinately long time to materialise, however.

Joint Comprehensive Plan of Action

In April 2014 the IAEA said that Iran had neutralised half of its 20 per cent enriched uranium stockpile as agreed in the Joint Plan of Action of November 2013. Four months later the sixth and final round of nuclear negotiations between Iran and the P5+1 group started in Vienna, but failed to meet the November 2014 deadline for the final deal. Extended negotiations revealed differences among the five permanent members of the UN Security Council. Russia tilted toward Iran whereas France insisted on a robust deal with detailed checks. China urged all sides to meet one another halfway. And the United States, after threatening to walk away on 30 March 2015 if current negotiations failed to yield a political framework accord, was once again at the center of the talks.

The bottom line for the US and five other powers—Britain, China, France, Germany and Russia—had been to keep Iran at least one year away from being able to produce enough nuclear fuel for a single weapon. A year was universally considered enough warning time to prevent an Iranian race for an atom bomb by re-imposing tight economic pressure or, if need be, to stage a few bombing raids by the Pentagon. The hard-knuckle bargaining that marked high-level negotiations over several days at the Swiss resort of Lausanne centered chiefly around three contentious points: the length of restrictions on Tehran's nuclear program within the general agreement; the pace or modality of lifting UN sanctions on Iran; and the penalty for Iran in case of its non-compliance with the agreed protocol. Iran wanted the life of the agreement to be ten years with restrictions on its nuclear program to apply over that period. The six global powers favored fifteen years. They wished to extend the limitations on Tehran for a further five years on the assumption that, with advanced centrifuges available to Iran, its break-out time to produce an atom bomb would be reduced. Iran's leaders rejected prolonged curbs on their centrifuge development, arguing that would make their country dependent on foreign technology.

On the modality of lifting UN sanctions on Iran, Ayatollah Khamanei outlined his position, on 30 March, with his website message saying that "sanctions must be lifted in one go, not as a result of future Iranian actions." He seemed to take on board the open letter that 47 US Republican Senators addressed to him on 9 March, warning that "The next president [after Barack Obama] could revoke such an executive agreement with the stroke of a pen, and future Congresses could modify the terms of the agreement at any time." Foreign Minister Muhammad Zarif, head of Iran's negotiating team, described the letter as a propaganda ploy, adding that revocation by a future US administration would violate international law. None the less, this would happen when on 13 October 2017, US President Donald Trump refused to certify that Iran was complying with all the terms of the agreement, a precondition for the suspension of sanctions by Washington—something he was required to do every 120 days according to US law.[55] In the spring of 2015, President Obama found it "somewhat ironic" to see some members of US Congress form "an unusual coalition" to make common cause with the hardliners in Iran. Actually, these hardliners had been quiet, noting Khamanei's repeated backing for the Iranian negotiators.

According to the latest *Washington Post*-ABC News poll, 59 per cent backed an agreement in which the United States and its negotiating partners lifted major economic sanctions in exchange for restrictions on Iran's nuclear program, with 31 per cent opposing a deal.[56]

Well aware of the anxiety that Saudi Arabia and other members of the GCC had about lifting sanctions on Iran, Obama hosted a one-day GCC summit at Camp David on 14 May 2015. He gave them a preview of the international agreement that was being finalised in Switzerland. He pledged Washington's continued cooperation in addressing Tehran's "destabilizing activities in the region," and reiterated that Washington would side with GCC partners against an external attack. He also assured Gulf rulers that that his administration was seeking only a "transaction" with Tehran on the nuclear issue and not a "broader rapprochement". He offered active assistance in forging a region-wide anti-missile defence system under central command to abort Iran's missile attacks.[57] Separately, a week later, much to the Saudis' satisfaction, the Republican-majority US House of Representatives passed a resolution barring Obama from waiving or suspending US sanctions on Iran until the end of his term on 20 January 2017.[58]

Meanwhile, the hard-nosed bargaining between Iran and the six world powers that followed in Lausanne went beyond the deadline of 30 June to end two weeks later with an agreement, to become effective on 18 October. Yukiya Amano, the IAEA director general, signed a separate "roadmap" agreement with Tehran, requiring the agency to resolve any outstanding concerns by the end of 2015.

Of its nearly 20,000 centrifuges, used to separate out the most fissile isotope U-235, at its Natanz and Fardow facilities, Iran was allowed to run only 5,060 of the oldest and least efficient machines at Natanz for ten years. Iran's current uranium stockpile was to be reduced by 98 per cent to 300 kg (660lbs) for fifteen years, and it had to keep its level of enrichment at 3.67 per cent suitable as fuel for nuclear power plants. Research and development will be permitted only at Natanz for eight years. The Fardow facility will be converted to a nuclear, physics and technology center. Its 1,044 centrifuges will produce radioisotopes for use in medicine, agriculture, industry and science. As for the Arak heavy water plant in the making, following its dismantling, Iran agreed not to redesign its reactor in a way that it could produce weapons-grade fuel. All spent fuel will be shipped out of the Islamic Republic during the lifetime of the reactor. On the highly contentious issue of IAEA's access to military sites, there was compromise. IAEA inspectors will be able to request visits to such sites with the proviso that access was not guaranteed and could be delayed. In return, all restrictions on Iranian banks will cease; Iran's $100 billion overseas assets, held mainly in banks in China, India, Japan, South Korea and Turkey and frozen since 2012 under sanctions, will be released after the IAEA has closed its Iran file satisfactorily; the oil embargoes, financial restrictions and trade restrictions imposed by the UN (but not the United States) will be waived; the UN arms embargo will end after five years; and most limitations on Tehran's current nuclear activities will cease after 2025.[59] Iran accepted that sanctions would be snapped back if an eight-member panel determined by a majority vote that it was violating the deal.[60]

The final closing of the IAEA's file on its decade-long nuclear probe on Iran would occur on 15 December 2015.

The peaceful end to the twelve-year standoff over Iran's nuclear program, an international landmark, was welcomed instantly in world capitals, except Tel Aviv and Riyadh. Iranian state television announced that Khamanei had voiced his "appreciation and thanked the Iranian nuclear negotiators for their honest and diligent efforts."[61] As news of the final agreement reached Tehran early on 14 July, there were public celebrations in the streets. Prior to that many Iranians spent hours glued to their televisions which aired speeches by Rouhani and Obama. "Suddenly we saw Barack Obama on the Islamic Republic Television station in a live broadcast," said Mahin, a fifty-eight-year-old retired teacher. "Just imagine Iran broadcasting a live speech by the president of the Great Satan." Sadegh Zibakalam, a leading political scientist, compared the JCPOA to three earlier turning points in the Islamic Republic's history: the occupation of the US embassy in Tehran in 1979, the start of the Iraq war in 1980, and the 1997 election of reformist President Muhammad Khatami, which galvanised the public demand for greater social and political freedoms.[62]

In New York, the UN Security Council endorsed the JCPOA on 22 July 2015. And ninety days later came the official Adoption Date of 18 October. Globally, the leading winners were Rouhani, Obama and Putin; and the foremost losers were Salman, Benjamin Netanyahu, and the self-proclaimed Caliph, Abu Bakr al-Baghdadi. Rouhani claimed that his country's right to develop peaceful nuclear energy had secured international recognition, and its isolation from the West had ended. "This deal demonstrates that American diplomacy can bring about real and meaningful change," said Obama. "Let us never negotiate out of fear. But let us never fear to negotiate." The JCPOA vindicated what many considered to be the premature awarding of a Nobel peace prize to him in 2009. Assad hailed the deal as a "major turning point" in the history of Iran, the region and the world, calling it a "great victory". Tehran's enhanced regional position in the wake of this agreement was set to strengthen its demand for recognition as a key player in the Middle East, including negotiations about the future of Syria. Putin declared that the world had "breathed a huge sigh of relief" when the deal was finalised.[63]

In sharp contrast, Riyadh's initial silence about the JCPOA indicated deep anxiety about a rapprochement between Washington and Tehran. According to Prime Minister Netanyahu, lifting sanctions gave "Iran a jackpot, a cash bonanza of hundreds of billions of dollars, which will enable it to continue to pursue its aggression and terror in the region and in the world". In the capital of ISIS, al Baghdadi feared enhanced pressure on his forces following fresh options for cooperation between America and Iran.[64]

Five days before the JCPOA's adoption date, Iran's parliament passed the bill approving it. The vote, taken after sharp exchanges between the opposing sides, was 161 in favor and 59 against, with 13 abstentions.[65] Following the IAEA's certification that Iran had done what was required under the deal on 15 December 2015, the EU was set to adopt a regulation for the lifting of sanctions and President Obama to issue waivers for sanctions. This would happen on 22 January 2016.

In keeping with his word to the Saudi monarch during their September 2015 meeting, President Obama approved the sale of PAC-3 (Patriot Advanced Capability) surface-to-air missiles to Saudi Arabia. Such a step was required by a law passed by Congress in 2008 to ensure that Israel continued to maintain a "qualitative military edge" over its traditional adversaries in the Middle East. All weapons sales to the Middle East were, therefore, weighed on how they will affect Israel's military superiority.[66] The Obama administration had concluded that since Gulf monarchies considered Iran as much of a threat to their survival as Israel, allowing them to purchase advanced US weaponry aided Israel's security. In October the Saudi government signed an agreement with the Obama administration for the purchase of 320 Patriot PAC-3 missiles produced by Lockheed Martin Corporation.[67] And the following month the US authorized the $1.29 billion sale of precision munitions for the Saudi Kingdom specifically meant to replenish stocks used in Yemen.[68] The Obama administration was keen to minimise civilian casualties in the Saudi-led military campaign in Yemen.

The Saudis' Quick-fix Strategy in Yemen Gets Bogged Down

The Saudi-led coalition's indiscriminate bombing of civilian targets had damaged 39 hospitals, including one run by Medecins Sans Frontieres

(MSF), in Saada province on 27 October 2015. "This attack is another illustration of a complete disregard for civilians in Yemen where bombings have become a daily routine," said Hassan Boucenine, head of the group's mission in Yemen.[69]

This was the background against which President Hadi was flown to Aden in mid-November and lodged in the presidential palace. It was in the intensifying clashes between the two sides in the adjoining Taiz Province, on 14 December, that the Houthis hit a Saudi military camp, as mentioned above.[70] A report by United Press International (UPI) said that the dead included fifteen to forty employees of Blackwater, a US private security firm renamed Academi since 2011.[71] By then the UAE had hired 400 Eritrean and 450 predominantly Colombian mercenaries to serve as a protection force for its combat troops in Aden after training them to handle grenade launchers and armored vehicles.[72] This was one of the several unintended consequences of Saudi Arabia's military intervention in Yemen.

The deadly missile attack occurred a day before the start of a week-long ceasefire between the warring sides, during which they reportedly exchanged hundreds of prisoners, on the eve of peace talks.[73] These were held in the Swiss village of Macolin near Berne under the chairmanship of the UN's special envoy to Yemen, Ismail Ould Cheikh Ahmed. Soon after the opening session a spokesman for the forces loyal to Saleh said that the port of Hodeidah was bombarded by the coalition's naval vessels during the agreed week-long ceasefire. On 18 December the Houthi-Saleh delegates declared that they would resume talks only after the UN had condemned the Hadi government's breach of the truce. That did not happen. That led Ahmed to "suspend" the talks indefinitely.[74]

In January 2016 the UN-appointed panel of experts reported that the Saudi-led coalition had targeted civilians with air strikes in a "widespread and systematic" manner. It documented 119 coalition sorties that violated international law, many of which involved multiple strikes on such civilian objects as schools, health facilities, wedding parties and camps for the displaced. In addition, it found that civilians fleeing coalition air raids had been chased and shot at by helicopters. It concluded that civilians were also being deliberately starved as a war tactic, and called for an investigation into human rights abuses by the coalition.[75]

On 27 February, a coalition air strike hit a busy market in Khulqut Nihm, twenty miles north of Sanaa, killing thirty people. Video footage depicting the aftermath of the attack showed incinerated bodies, including children, along with dead sheep and rubble. An eye witness said that there was no apparent military target in or near the market.[76]

The Saudis were nowhere near achieving their goals of expelling the Houthi-Saleh forces from Sanaa, handing over the capital to Hadi, and containing the Houthis in the north. On the contrary, the rebels were so firmly rooted in the capital that they invited in Western correspondents to see for themselves. "At a police station in Sanaa, Yemeni security officials put a US-made cluster bomb unit on display," reported Orla Guerin of the BBC. "They claim it was dropped in the western suburbs in January 2016 scattering deadly bomblets over a civilian area. They produced several [bomblets] from a pink plastic shopping bag. The coalition has denied using the weapons, which have been banned by more than 100 countries."[77]

Around this time two correspondents of the *New York Times* provided an explanation as to why the coalition's air strikes continued to hit civilian sites. Fearful of enemy ground fire, the inexperienced Saudi pilots flew at high altitudes to avoid being hit. But this reduced the accuracy of their bombing and increased damage to civilian property and life. "We offer them coaching [in flying low but safely], but ultimately it's their operation," said General Carl E. Mundy, the deputy commander of Marines in the Middle East.[78]

Tension remained high along the Yemeni-Saudi border. When subjected to punishing air raids by the coalition's jets, Houthi-Saleh partisans responded with indiscriminate shelling of the Saudi territory adjacent to Yemen, making the area insecure for civilians. This drove the tribal leaders on both sides of the border to alleviate the increasingly unbearable situation. Using their prestige in their respective communities they managed to act as mediators between the Houthis and the Saudi government. They arranged the exchange of seven Houthi prisoners for a captured Saudi officer on 8 March after a week of secret preparatory talks. The reports of Houthi delegates arriving in Saudi Arabia to discuss larger prisoner exchanges were not acknowledged officially in Riyadh. Nonetheless these enabled Bin Salman and Jubeir to reassure US Secretary of State, John Kerry, during their meeting with him at King Khalid Military City, that their government supported the efforts of the UN Special Envoy to bring all parties to the negotiating table in pursuit of a peaceful political transition in Yemen.[79]

As before, the warring camps agreed to a week long ceasefire starting on 10 April before the start of the UN-brokered talks, this time in Kuwait, which remained part of the Saudi-led coalition. Earlier, the World Health Organization (WHO) reported that during the year-long conflict over 6,200 people had been killed and 30,000 wounded, and that more than 21 million Yemenis—82 per cent of the population—were in need of humanitarian aid.[80]

The UN-sponsored negotiations dragged on for more than three months. The only tangible outcome was the two aides agreeing to hand over half of the prisoners they held. As a consequence, in mid-June, Houthi and pro-Hadi forces exchanged nearly 200 prisoners in Taiz.[81] Most of the inconclusive discussion between the warring parties, focusing on the type of government to run Yemen during a transition period, proved sterile. The main stumbling-block was the status of Hadi who insisted on retaining his presidency until fresh elections were held under a new constitution.

Feeling frustrated at the stalled talks, on 28 July the Houthi-Saleh camp announced the formation of an alternative government under the title of the High Political Council. It had ten members divided equally between the Houthis and the General People's Congress (GPC) to manage the country's affairs in all political, military, economic and administrative areas on the basis of the existing constitution. So far the Houthis had been supervising regions they controlled through a Revolutionary Committee with the GPC's participation. The UN Special Envoy declared that the move violated Security Council Resolution 2216, which called on the Houthis "to refrain from further unilateral actions that could undermine the political transition in Yemen."[82] This was the third failed attempt by the UN to end Yemen's civil war.

Overall, the Houthi-Saleh alliance administered most of Yemen's northern half while Hadi's forces shared control of the rest with Southern separatists and various tribes—with AQAP jihadists operating in the south-east with impunity because of the intensified violence between the two principal antagonists. For all practical purposes the territorial situation reverted to what it had been before the unification of North and South Yemen in 1990.

Riyadh's Mounting Toll of Civilian Casualties in Yemen

A report by the Yemen Data Project, a group of academics and human rights activists, analysed 8,600 Saudi-led air attacks between March 2015 and the end of August 2016. Of these, 3,577 were listed as having hit military sites and 3,158 such non-military sites as schools, hospitals, markets, mosques, culture centers, camps for displaced persons, poultry farms, bridges, power plants, airports, seaports, and factories producing potato chips, yogurt, tea, paper tissues, ceramics, cement, and Coca-Cola. And 1,882 incidents were listed as "unknown" when a hit site could not be classified as military or civilian. The survey listed 942 attacks on residential areas, 114 on markets, 34 on mosques, 147 on school buildings, 26 on universities and 378 on transport. The records updated to the end of September showed 356 air strikes targeting farms, 174 hitting markets, and 61 targeting food storage sites.[83]

Responding to the most comprehensive survey by an independent body, Jubeir said that the Houthis had "turned schools and hospitals and mosques into command and control centers. They have turned them into weapons depots in a way that they are no longer civilian targets." His statement could not explain why a school building in Dhubab in Taiz Province was hit nine times and a market in Sirwah in Marib Province twenty-four times, as reported by the Yemen Data Project.[84]

On 8 October the coalition's air strike at a funeral hall hosting the wake of Ali al Rawishan, father of the Houthi-appointed Interior Minister Gawal al Rawishan in Sanaa, set a record. It killed more than 140 people, and injured 525 others. The casualties included senior military and security officials of the Houthi-Saleh alliance. "The place has been turned into a lake of blood," said Murad Tawfiq, one of the rescuers collecting in sacks hundreds of body parts strewn in and around the building. The carnage drew strong condemnation not only from the UN but also the European Union and the US. While acknowledging the Saudi-led coalition's responsibility for the deadly air assault, its spokesman attributed it to "faulty intelligence".[85]

The funeral hall atrocity tipped Washington's stance from strong support for the coalition's campaign and restoration of Hadi's presidency toward a more nuanced approach. "US security cooperation with Saudi Arabia is not a blank check," said NSC spokesman Ned Price. "In light of this and other recent incidents, we have initiated an immediate review of our already significantly reduced support to the Saudi-led Coalition and are prepared to adjust our support so as to better align with US principles, values and interests, including achieving an immediate and durable end to Yemen's tragic conflict." His reference to "already significantly reduced" US support for Riyadh probably referred to the withdrawal in June of many American personnel assigned to a joint US-Saudi planning cell established to coordinate the provision of military and intelligence support for the campaign. Clarifying the current position, White House press secretary Josh Earnest said on 12 October that "this [US] assistance that we provide is primarily logistical support. We do share some intelligence with them, but the United States does not do targeting for them."[86] It was important for the White House to stress that it had nothing to do with a string of targets that clearly violated International law.

A week before the UN Security Council's discussion of Yemen on 31 October, the UN Envoy to Yemen, Ismail Ould Cheikh Ahmed, presented a road map to peace. It consisted of turning the presidency into a ceremonial post, forming a national unity government, a phased removal of the Houthi-Saleh forces from the cities captured by them in 2014 and 2015 under UN supervision, and gradually moving toward presidential and parliamentary elections. To Washington's annoyance, Hadi rejected the plan since it required his virtual abdication. On its part, the Houthi-Saleh alliance sought Hadi's immediate resignation and the formation of a unity government with a significant role for it. Riyadh demanded that the Houthi-Saleh alliance must hand over their heavy weapons to a third party, and sought a guarantee that a unity government would prohibit the deployment of weapons that could threaten Saudi territory or international waterways.[87]

In late November, an eye witness account of the Saudi-led coalition's devastation of Yemen's civilian infrastructure in the Houthi-Saleh-controlled territory was provided by Ben Hubbard of the *New York Times*. Brig. Gen. Sharaf Luqman, a spokesman for Houthi-allied military units, talked to Hubbard in his car because the Defence Ministry headquarters had been bombed. "We have lost everything, our infrastructure, and we have nothing left to lose," he said. "Now it is a long war of attrition." Many ministry buildings were badly damaged by the coalition, and those still standing were virtually empty, their employees staying home. They did so out of fear of being bombed and also because they had not received their salaries since September. To tackle the problem the Houthis had resorted to appointing their activists as supervisors over the civil servants and policemen who reported for work. The territory administered by the Houthi-Saleh alliance contained members of many Sunni tribes. It seemed that Riyadh's military intervention had helped unify diverse Yemeni elements against a common foe. "What brought the [multi-sectarian] army together with Ansar Allah [God's Helpers]?" asked Tariq Muhammad, a policeman in the town of Hajjah, using the official name for the Houthis. "The aggression against the country: that is what caused us to come together as one hand." Given this, Houthi-Saleh loyalists were very much in control of the area they had seized. "During our 10-day trip to Sanaa and nearby provinces, it was clear that the Houthis were in charge," reported Hubbard. "Their authorities issued our visas, determined what sites we could visit and assigned us a minder to make sure we stuck to the program. Houthi checkpoints dotted the roads, sometimes less than a mile apart... While this slowed traffic, Houthi security measures have put a stop to the suicide bombings and assassinations that used to be frequent in the capital, perhaps their greatest achievement in governing."[88]

The overarching strategy of the Houthi-Saleh alliance was in essence defensive, to survive against all odds with the much-coveted Sanaa as its capital. It faced an acute banking crisis when, on 18 September, Hadi ordered the Central Bank governor to move the bank from Sanaa to Aden after accusing the Houthi-Saleh alliance of adding thousands of militiamen to the Ministry of Defence's payroll, consuming $100 million a month in foreign reserves. All through the turmoil dating back to early 2011, the Central Bank, capable of stabilizing the economy and receiving foreign currencies, had functioned normally. It paid salaries regularly to 1.2 million civil servants and soldiers, thereby sustaining a quarter of the population. After the relocation of the bank, the Hadi government promised to cover the salaries of only those public workers who were employed before September 2014 when Houthis captured Sanaa. In practice this did not happen. On the other side, to meet the financial crisis, the Houthi-Saleh government set up its own central bank, ordered the authorities in their controlled territory to send their revenues from taxes and fees to it, cut the salaries of its employees by half, and appealed to citizens to donate funds to the bank while creating a system whereby people could donate Yemeni rials by text messages from their mobile phones.[89]

Meanwhile, the mounting civilian deaths in Yemen started to weigh heavily on the Obama administration. In mid-December 2016 it blocked the sale of some 16,000 guided munitions kits, used to upgrade dumb bombs to smart bombs that can more accurately hit targets, by Raytheon Corporation. In addition, the White House decided to curtail some intelligence sharing with Riyadh which could potentially lead to even more civilian casualties.[90] Riyadh drew comfort from the fact that the navies of several Western nations interdicted weapons caches bound for the Houthi-Saleh alliance. American officials said in October 2015 that US Navy ships had interdicted five Iranian arms shipments bound for Yemen. In late February an Australian ship interdicted a dhow bound for the Somali port of Caluula used as a transit point for shipments to Yemen. Its cargo included 2,000 AK-47 assault rifles, and various machine guns. Another interdiction by a French ship on 20 March revealed a cargo of more than 2,000 assault rifles. And eight days later USS *Sirocco* interdicted a dhow carrying 1,500 assault rifles and 200 rocket launchers. The weapons pipeline outline by the London-based Conflict Armament Research, funded by the EU, showed flows from Iran to a few small transshipment ports in the semi-autonomous Puntland region of the Somalia coast. From these ports, contraband is picked up by small vessels bound for other ports in Somalia or Yemen.[91]

The US Navy's press release of 5 April 2016 noted that for the third time in recent weeks, American and other international naval forces operating in the Arabian Sea had seized illicit shipments of weapons originating in Iran for delivery to the Houthi-Saleh forces in Yemen via Somalia. The arms caches included AK-47 assault rifles, sniper rifles, general purpose machine guns, rocket-propelled grenade launchers, mortar tubes, and anti-tank missiles.[92] Iran's denials do not carry much weight. Noticing that the Houthi-Saleh alliance was being squeezed on different fronts, it was politically incumbent on Tehran to show that it stood by the anti-Saudi forces in their hour of acute need. To its satisfaction, Saudi Arabia faced intensifying international criticism for the ongoing military intervention in Yemen led by it. Along with continuing reports of civilian casualties and displacement were the persistent shortages of food, medicine, and water suffered by ordinary Yemenis, the unexpectedly high resilience of the Houthi-Saleh alliance, and the advances made by AQAP and the local branch of ISIS.

14

TRUMP FUELS GULF RIVALS' COLD WAR

2017 opened a chapter when the attention of those living in America as well as elsewhere turned to the successor of President Barack Hussein Obama: Donald John Trump.[1] For the first time in American history, its chief executive in Washington was a businessman, a real estate tycoon, who had never before served as an elected official, and was a novice in public affairs, particularly in the field of international relations. In office he turned out to be thoroughly undisciplined with no patience or interest in learning, refusing to read briefing papers, and firing off tweets on Twitter, jumping wildly from subject to subject, fight to fight, depending on what he had seen on news broadcasts on cable TV.[2]

A Demagogic Populist Wins the White House

On 7 December 2015, Donald Trump called for "a total and complete shutdown of Muslims entering the United States until our country's representatives can figure out what is going on." He had previously proposed surveillance against mosques and said that he was open to the idea of establishing a database for all Muslims living in America. His campaign manager Corey Lewandowski told CNN that the ban would apply not just to Muslim foreigners looking to immigrate to the US, but also to Muslims looking to visit the US as tourists. "Everyone."

Trump's sweeping proposal came in the aftermath of a deadly mass shooting in San Bernardino, California, by suspected Islamic State sympathisers and the day after President Obama asked the nation not to "turn against one another" out of fear.[3]

Addressing an election rally in Bluffton, South Carolina, on 16 February 2016, Trump said, "It wasn't the Iraqis that knocked down the World Trade Center. It wasn't the Iraqis. You will find out who really knocked down the World Trade Center,' cuz they have papers in there that are very secret. You may find it's the Saudis, okay? But you will find out." The next morning on Fox and Friends program he said, "Who blew up the World Trade Center? It wasn't the Iraqis; it was Saudi— take a look at Saudi Arabia, open the documents." He was referencing the 28 pages that were redacted from the official 2002 Joint Inquiry into the 9/11 attacks. Those pages were widely believed to implicate Saudi elites in financing the attacks.[4]

After the US Senate passed, by voice vote, the Justice Against Sponsors of Terrorism Act (JASTA), allowing families of 9/11 victims to sue the Saudi government, on 16 September 2016 following a voice vote by the House of Representatives a week earlier, Obama vetoed it on 23 September. He argued that JASTA could put the United States, its taxpayers, its service members, and its diplomats at "significant risk" if a similar law was adopted by other countries. Trump condemned Obama's veto, calling it "shameful... [it] will go down as one of the low points of his presidency," adding that as president he would sign the legislation.[5] But such a need did not arise. On 28 September the Senate overrode the veto by 97 votes to one, and the House by 348 to 77 votes. JASTA came into force two days later. As a result, 1,500 injured survivors and 850 family members of 9/11 victims would file a class action lawsuit against the Kingdom of Saudi Arabia on 20 March 2017, alleging that the Saudi government had prior knowledge that some of its officials and employees were Al Qaida operatives or sympathisers.

Trump nursed a grievance against the Desert Kingdom on another issue. As early as June 2015, he tweeted: "Saudi Arabia should be paying the United States many billions of dollars for our defense of them. Without us, gone!"[6] Nine months later he got a chance to deal with the subject at length during his interviews with Maggie Haberman and David E. Sanger, which were published in the *New York Times* on

26 March 2016. He argued that without US protection, Saudi Arabia would cease to exist, and that being "a monetary machine," it should reimburse Washington for the amount the Pentagon spent to protect the kingdom.[7]

Saudi policy-makers had no intention of getting entangled in the internal affairs of America. Nonetheless, during his visit to Washington in July, Saudi Foreign Minister Adel al Jubeir rejected Trump's comments, telling CNN that the Saudi kingdom "carries its own weight" as an ally.[8] Bare facts spoke for themselves. A country of 30 million, Saudi Arabia had the third highest defense budget in the world, after America and China in 2015.[9]

But Trump persisted. Three months *after* assuming the presidency in January 2017, he complained that Saudi Arabia was not treating the United States fairly, and that Washington was losing a "tremendous amount of money" defending the kingdom.[10]

New York Times reporters sought Trump's views on Iran's nuclear agreement with six world powers. He said that deal was "not [for] long enough," and asserted that he would never have given $150 billion back to Tehran.[11]

A fact-checker at the *New York Times* or any other US media organization would have pointed out three salient facts to Trump: America was one of the six global powers negotiating with Iran; all six of them had to agree on each of the many points under discussion. The amount in the negotiations was $100 billion, not $150 billion; and, more importantly, since Iran's $100 billion overseas assets were held mainly in banks in China, India, Japan, South Korea and Turkey and frozen since 2012 under sanctions, the unfreezing of this amount had nothing to with Washington.

The Jaw-dropping U-turns of Trump

On 27 January the White House published President Trump's executive order titled "Protection of The Nation From Foreign Terrorist Entry Into The United States." It put in place a ninety-day ban on entry to the US from citizens of Iran, Iraq, Syria, Yemen, Sudan, Libya and Somalia. The absence from the banned list of the Saudi Kingdom at which Trump had earlier pointed an accusing finger regarding 9/11 attacks surprised many.

When, on ABC News, David Muir asked why Afghanistan, Pakistan and Saudi Arabia did not feature on the banned list, Trump replied: "We're going to have extreme vetting in all cases. And I mean extreme."[12] The implication was that Saudi Arabia was in the grey zone. The Executive Order blocked the travel plans of some 60,000 Muslim US visa holders and was immediately challenged in the American courts.

On 14 February a federal judge suspended the original order in Virginia because it was probably motivated by "religious prejudice" and not "rational national security concerns", thus violating the First Amendment of the Constitution which guarantees freedom of worship. In support of the verdict, the judge cited Candidate Trump's 7 December 2015 call for a blanket prohibition on the entry of all Muslims into the US, as well as comments by Trump's advisers before and after the election, as evidence. "The 'Muslim Ban' was a center-piece of the president's campaign for months, and the press release calling for it was still available on his website as of the day this Memorandum opinion is being entered," stated the ruling.[13] Conse-quently, Trump issued a new Executive Order—a more detailed, nar-rowly focused order, applying to six Muslim majority countries, after the exclusion of Iraq. It was still open to judicial challenge.

Tellingly, while controversy about Trump's Muslim travel ban raged in America, the Saudi government chose not to lobby for an emer-gency Organisation of Islamic Cooperation (OIC) summit. In its agenda the parochial interests of the Saudi Kingdom mattered far more than the rights of the broader Muslim population worldwide.

Saudi Arabia had noted with great approval Trump's decision to reverse the foreign policy achievements of Obama who had fallen from favor with Riyadh particularly after Washington's nuclear deal with Iran and the Obama administration's scrutiny of Riyadh's repeated targeting of civilian sites in Yemen. This was considered sufficient common ground for the scheduling of a meet-and-greet meeting between the Saudi Deputy, Crown Prince Muhammad bin Salman, and Trump in Washington. The original arrangement was upgraded to a working lunch between the two at the recommendation of Jared Kushner, the son-in-law of and senior adviser to Trump. Kushner, an Orthodox Jew and a real-estate tycoon, had been assigned the task of conciliating Israelis and Palestinians. He envisaged Saudi Arabia aiding the process even though the Kingdom did not recognize Israel. Nevertheless the working lunch between Trump and Bin Salman and their close aides at the White House went well, with Trump reportedly promising to lift the suspension of some 16,000 guided munitions kits imposed by the previous administration to boost Washington's support to Riyadh in its military campaign in Yemen. It set the scene for Saudi Arabia to become Trump's first foreign destination as president. It was hard to reconcile this decision with the ruling of a judge in Virginia nearly a month earlier that Trump's 27 January travel ban was based on religious prejudice against Muslims.

As Trump's travel plans firmed up, King Salman and his favorite son prepared to welcome the American president in spectacular fashion. They went all out to massage the ego of the narcissist Trump with excessive flattery, to underscore their anti-extremist credentials in the eyes of the new administration in Washington and to build an anti-Iran front among Muslim nations.

As a preview of the lavish welcome that awaited the President and his entourage in Riyadh, the management of the Ritz Carlton Hotel projected a five-story-high image of Trump onto its façade, pairing it with a similarly huge and flattering photo of King Salman.[14] On arrival in Riyadh on 20 May, the American guests found the capital's streets lined for miles with alternating US and Saudi flags. In addition, the city was splashed with billboards carrying pictures of Trump and Salman over the slogan "Together we prevail." But against whom? That was left to the imagination of the spectator.

After Trump's one-on-one talk with Salman, the two leaders signed documents which included an arms deal which the White House described as worth $350 billion over the next decade. A day earlier Pentagon officials had told The Associated Press that "the immediate sale" was worth $110 billion and included "Abrams tanks, combat ships, missile defense systems, radar, and communications and cyber security technology."[15] But even the lower figure of $110 billion turned out to be a highly exaggerated. Many of the items listed as part of the package had already been offered to Riyadh during the Obama administration, including a Patriot Missile Defense System, multi-mission Surface Combatants, attack helicopters, and artillery systems. Thus what was publicized as a new deal was in reality mostly a mix of offers already made by the US and promises yet to be fulfilled.[16] The end-purpose of mentioning high figures for US weaponry was to emphasise the Trump administration's uncritical support for Riyadh, its hostility to Tehran, and its focus on "jobs, jobs, jobs," as Trump kept trumpeting. Before tucking into his dinner, an awkward looking Trump brandished a sword in an all-male sword dance, a speciality of the Desert Kingdom.

The high point of Trump's visit was the speech he delivered to the Arab Islamic summit. The Saudi government invited the heads of 57 member-states of the Organisation of Islamic Cooperation except Iran, Syria and the Palestinian Authority. Of the fifty-four countries attending the summit in Riyadh on 21 May, Azerbaijan, Bahrain and Iraq were Shia-majority states.[17]

"We must be united in pursuing the one [overarching] goal ... to conquer extremism and vanquish the forces of terrorism,"Trump told his audience. "The true toll of ISIS, Al Qaida, Hizbollah, Hamas, and so many others, must be counted not only in the number of dead. It must also be counted in generations of vanished dreams... A better future is only possible if your nations drive out the terrorists and extremists." He then turned to the specific target he had in mind. "From Lebanon to Iraq to Yemen, Iran funds, arms, and trains terrorists, militias, and other extremist groups that spread destruction and chaos across the region. For decades, Iran has fueled the fires of sectarian conflict and terror. ...Among Iran's most tragic and destabilizing interventions have been in Syria." He concluded his denunciation of the Islamic Republic thus: "The Iranian regime's longest-suffering victims are its own people. Iran has a rich history and culture, but the people of Iran have endured hardship and despair under their leaders' reckless pursuit of conflict and terror."[18]

It so happened that the suffering and despairing citizens of Iran had exercised their right to choose their leader for the next four years on 19 May. Indeed, this was the twelfth time these oppressed Iranians had been given the chance to elect their executive president since the 1979 Islamic revolution. Now, they re-elected Hassan Rouhani as president by a margin of 57 to 39 per cent, defeating his conservative rival Ebrahim Raisi. Four rounds of televised debates by the contestants had preceded the polling.[19]

After the speeches came the inauguration of the Global Center for Combating Extremist Ideology. This was done, symbolically, with

Salman, Trump, and Egyptian President Abdel Fattah el Sisi touching a futuristically glowing orb. After that Trump had a series of much-publicized bilateral meetings with Arab leaders, starting with Sisi. Speaking through a translator, Sisi said to Trump, "You are a unique personality that is capable of doing the impossible." Smiling broadly, Trump replied, "I agree!"[20] Arab leaders had registered the fact that Trump had an unquenchable appetite for self-glorification. They found it easy to flatter him since they were themselves often surrounded by sycophants.

Haughty Bin Salman Throws Down a Gauntlet to Iran

King Salman and the Deputy Crown Prince were buoyed by the fact that Trump had appointed retired US Marine general James Mattis as his Secretary of Defense. Mattis was vehemently anti-Iran, describing the Islamic Republic as "the single most enduring threat to stability and peace in the Middle East." In August, 2010 President Obama asked Mattis, the freshly appointed commander of the US Central Command, CENTCOM, his priorities. He replied "Iran, Iran, and Iran." His hatred stemmed from the fact that US Marines, posted in Iraq after 2003, had suffered many casualties caused by an Iran-made singularly lethal device, known as an explosively formed penetrator (EFP), which fired a molten copper bullet capable of piercing armor, used by local Shia forces. Little wonder that as defense secretary Mattis opted for more vigorous support for the Saudi-led intervention in Yemen, including additional planning assistance and more intelligence sharing.

Trump's animus toward Iran sharpened once he had imbibed the view of his first National Security Adviser, Michael Flynn, another former general. He conflated Tehran-backed Shia radicalism with Sunni jihadism, ignoring theological conflict between Sunnis and Shias, because it fitted his bigoted anti-Iran stance. In his speech to the Arab Islamic summit Trump would lump Iran and Sunni jihadis together as part of the same evil of terrorism.[21]

These factors emboldened Bin Salman to take an aggressively anti-Iran stance publicly. This came on 1 May 2017 in his hour long interview on the Dubai-based, Saudi-owned Al Arabiya television channel, which was aired simultaneously on several Saudi-owned satellite networks. Given his repeated claims that the Houthis in Yemen were puppets of Iran, he was asked if he saw a possibility for direct talks with Tehran. In his reply, he referred to a Twelver Shia belief of waiting for the arrival of the 12th Hidden Imam, who disappeared around 873 CE, as al Mahdi, or the Messiah, to bring justice to the world: "How can I come to an understanding with someone, or a regime, that has an anchoring belief built on an extremist ideology?" he asked rhetorically. He went on to assert that "We are a primary target for the Iranian regime," and accused it of seeking to take over Islamic holy sites in Saudi Arabia. "We won't wait for the battle to be in Saudi Arabia. Instead, we'll work so that the battle is for them in Iran."[22]

Within weeks this would translate into the Saudi government brutally crushing the simmering Shia protest in Awamiyah, the birth place of Ayatollah Nimr al Nimr, who was executed in January 2016. In the same interview, putting a brave face on the grinding, expensive stalemate in the Yemen conflict, Bin Salman claimed that Saudi forces could uproot the rebels "in a few days," but that doing so would kill thousands of Saudi troops and many civilians. So, he said, the coalition is waiting for the rebels to tire out. "Time is in our favor," he concluded.[23]

Trump's vehement attack on Iran at the Islamic Arab Summit triggered a chain of events which would over the next several months lead to results that countered the trumpeted aims of Bin Salman and the US president.

On 23 May Qatari Emir Tamim bin Hamad Al Thani attended a military graduation ceremony in Doha. Later that day the state-run Qatar News Agency (QNA), reportedly carried remarks by the ruler on several sensitive regional issues and Qatar's relationship with Trump. Emir Tamim was quoted as saying "there is no wisdom in harboring hostility towards Iran," and that his relationship with the Trump administration was "tense" despite a cordial meeting he had with the US president in Riyadh two days earlier. Before the talk, Trump said "One of the things that we will discuss is the purchase of lots of beautiful military equipment because nobody makes it like the US," adding that "And for us, that means jobs and it also means, frankly, great security back here, which we want.[24] This was a reference to the sale of up to seventy-two Boeing F-15 fighter jets to Qatar for $21.1 billion, approved by the Obama administration in November.[25] Now the same Emir Tamim was quoted as saying that he did not believe Trump would last long in office.

He described Qatar's ties with Israel as "good", and hoped to help broker a peace deal in the Israeli-Palestinian conflict. The QNA story attributed to Emir Tamim positive statements about Hizbollah and Hamas as well as the Muslim Brotherhood. These remarks were picked up by several other news outlets and broadcasters in the Arab world, triggering hostile reactions in Saudi Arabia and the UAE. Their governments blocked the main website of Qatar's Al Jazeera, which they had long considered as being critical of them.[26]

The contradiction between Qatar hosting Hizbollah and Hamas as well as the Muslim Brotherhood and simultaneously maintaining cordial relations with Israel was so egregious that the supposed QNA story should have been seen straightaway as fake. The Qatari authorities said so by claiming that the QNA website had been hacked. There was no question of Emir Tamim making all these alleged statements because he did not deliver a speech at the graduation ceremony. This was immaterial to the Saudi and Emirati media. They used the fake story to slam Qatar. The Jeddah-based *Okaz* daily screamed: "Qatar splits the rank, sides with the enemies of the nation." And Riyadh's *Arab News* reported that the comments sparked "outrage" among other Gulf States.[27]

Taking advantage of the media war, Bin Salman and UAE Crown Prince Muhammad bin Zayed Al Nahyan co-opted Bahrain and Egypt to move against Qatar. On 5 June, they severed diplomatic ties with Qatar, closed all borders, sea lanes and air space to Qatar; prohibited their citizens from traveling to Qatar, and banned all Qatari residents from traveling to their countries. Saudis in particular claimed to be focused on Qatar's alleged role in financing terrorist groups in the region. The move stunned officials and residents of the tiny emirate.

By contrast, the impulsive Trump, uninformed on the subject, instantly accepted the Saudi move at face value. He even went on to take credit for it. "During my recent trip to the Middle East I stated that there can no longer be funding of Radical Ideology. Leaders pointed to Qatar—look!" ran his tweet.[28] Trump's hasty conclusion, based on flawed memory and bordering on incompetence, was exposed the same day by none other than the Pentagon. On 6 June its spokesman renewed praise of Qatar for hosting a vital US air base and for its "enduring commitment to regional security."[29]

In fact, military cooperation between Doha and Washington started in early 1992 in the wake of the 1991 Gulf War. In 1996, Qatar built the Al Udeid Air Base 25 miles southwest of Doha, at a cost of over $1 billion. Through a secret agreement, the Qatari Emir, Hamad Al Thani, let the Pentagon use this base in its air campaign against Al Qaida and the Taliban after the 9/11 attacks. This became known only in March 2002, when US Vice President Dick Cheney stopped there during a trip to the region with a group of reporters. In 2003 the Qatari-American military relationship was dramatically upgraded when the Bush administration started preparing for its invasion of Iraq. Saudi Arabia's de facto ruler at the time, Crown Prince Abdullah bin Abdul Aziz, refused to let the Pentagon use the state-of-the-art operations facility at Al Kharj Air Base it had prepared for air strikes against Iraq. The Qatari emir came to Washington's rescue. He allowed the Pentagon to transfer all its equipment from Al Kharj to Al Udeid Air Base.[30] It would become the forward headquarters of CENTCOM, the Pentagon's key facility in the region. In June 2017, Al Udeid held no less than 10,000 US troops, 100 warplanes and some 100 British Royal Air Force personnel. They carried out air strikes on ISIS targets in Afghanistan, Syria and Iraq.[31]

Resistant to admitting a mistake or a defeat, Trump continued blindly to follow the Saudi lead. On 10 June he accused Qatar of being a "funder of terror at a very high level," and demanded a cutoff of that cash flow in order for Qatar to rejoin the circle of responsible nations. In Doha, Dana Shell Smith, the US ambassador to Qatar, retweeted a statement from the US Treasury Department praising Qatar for cracking down on extremist financing. Now Qatar expressed its readiness to sign on to fresh proposals being drafted by the Treasury Department to strengthen controls against the financing of militant groups.[32]

The contradictory stances of the Trump administration remained on track. On 15 June US Defense Secretary Mattis signed a $12bn deal to supply Qatar up to 36 Boeing F-15 combat aircraft with his Qatari counterpart Khalid al Attiyah. "This is of course proof that US institutions are with us but we have never doubted that," said a Qatari official in Doha. "Our militaries are like brothers."[33]

On 21 June, King Salman precipitated a diplomatic earthquake in the Gulf by elbowing out Muhammad bin Nayef as crown prince and replacing him with his favorite son, Muhammad. Determined to stay calm and reasonable, the thirty-seven-year-old Qatari Emir Tamim sent a cable of congratulations to the Saudi monarch "on the occasion of the selection of his royal highness Prince Muhammad bin Salman Al Saud as Crown Prince," expressing hope for "brotherly relations between the two brotherly countries"—a message reported by state-run Qatar News Agency and posted on social media.[34] Emir Tamim had ascended the throne in June 2013 after the voluntary abdication of his father, Hamad, a unique event in the history of the Arabian Peninsula. But Bin Salman, the architect of the anti-Qatar drive, was on a pre-determined trajectory. Implementing a previously agreed plan, on 22 June the anti-Qatari axis issued a list of thirteen sweeping demands to be accepted by Qatar within ten days in return for abandoning the diplomatic and trade embargo.

Bin Salman Reveals His Anti-Iran Mindset

Tellingly, the list was topped by the demand, "Curb diplomatic ties with Iran and close its diplomatic missions." The attempt to drive a wedge between Qatar and Iran was doomed to fail on purely economic grounds. Qatar shares the North Dome–South Pars gas field with Iran. At 3,750 sq miles, it is the largest field of its kind in the world, with its South Pars section, measuring about a third of the total, lying in Iran's territorial waters. The aggregate recoverable gas reserves of this field are the equivalent of 230 billion barrels of oil, second only to Saudi Arabia's reserves of conventional oil. Income from gas and oil provide Qatar with more than three-fifths of its GDP and seven-eighths of its export income. With a population of just 2.4 million, of whom only 300,000 are citizens,[35] Qatar's per capita GDP, at $74,667, was the highest on the planet. As such, Doha could not afford to become an adversary of Iran.

The third demand read, "Shut down Al Jazeera and its affiliate stations." Al Jazeera television has long unnerved Saudi Arabia and the other autocratic Arab monarchies. Broadcasting in Arabic and English, the channel is available in 100 countries, giving Qatar a profile and reach far beyond the Arab world. Al Jazeera was the brain-child of Qatari Emir Hamad bin Khalifa Al Thani who seized power in a bloodless coup in June 1995 while his father, Emir Khalifa bin Hamad, was in Switzerland. In a concerted move, Emir Hamad abolished the ministry of information, eased media censorship and allocated $140 million over the next five years for an independent 24-hour satellite TV news channel. Al Jazeera (Arabic: The Peninsula), started broadcasting in Arabic in November 1996, with its English channel going on air ten years later. From the start, its reporting staff consisted almost wholly of BBC-trained journalists who had lost their jobs seven months earlier when the Rome-based Orbit television, owned by a Saudi prince, cancelled its contract to produce news in Arabic for the BBC. Al Jazeera smashed the Middle Eastern mould of television news tied to local information and intelligence agencies. Two weekly discussion programs *The Opposite Direction* and *The Other Opinion* debated controversial subjects including religion and politics, Arab relations with Israel, and the role of monarchs in the Arab world. During the Arab Spring uprisings in 2011, Al Jazeera was the prime source of reliable news. The soaring popularity of Al Jazeera led several Arab governments to allow more leeway to state-controlled or -guided media in their countries. Nonetheless, Al Jazeera remained a thorn in the side of authoritarian regimes, particularly in Egypt and Saudi Arabia.

The list of Saudi-led demands challenged the sovereignty not just of Qatar, but also of Turkey. High on the list of demands was "Immediately terminate the Turkish military presence in Qatar and end any joint military cooperation with Turkey inside Qatar." The Turkish Defense Minister Fikri Isik described the ultimatum as unacceptable interference in Ankara's relations with Doha. Turkey was targeted by the anti-Qatar Axis because, ruled by Recep Tayyip Erdogan, leader of the Islamist Justice and Development Party since 2003, it had emerged as a strong supporter of the transnational Muslim Brotherhood. Its candidate, Muhammad Morsi, won the first free and fair presidential election in Egyptian history in June 2012. His overthrow by the generals a year later was applauded by Riyadh which announced a $12 billion rescue package for the military regime. By contrast Tehran condemned the military coup against the popularly elected president.

In March 2014 Saudi Arabia declared the Brotherhood a terrorist organization. Its hostility against it stems from the fact that the latter's leaders demonstrated in Egypt that Sharia rule could be established in a Muslim country by the ballot box, and reiterated that ultimate power lies with the people, not a dynasty. It is worth noting that the Brotherhood was not on Washington's list of terrorist organizations.[36]

While Turkey lined up with Qatar, most Muslim countries remained neutral. Indonesia, the most populous Muslim nation, called for dialogue between Riyadh and Doha to defuse the crisis. So did Pakistan despite the fact that Prime Minister Nawaz Sharif had maintained close relations with the Saudi royals for many years. Even within the six-member Gulf Cooperation Council, Kuwait and Oman stayed above the fray. Kuwait did so because 30 per cent of its 1.23 million citizens are Shia. It also has had an elected parliament since 1962 in which opinions are freely expressed. Oman could not afford to alienate Iran, given that its territorial waters overlap those of Iran in the strategic Straits of Hormuz.

Apart from America, no other Western nation backed the anti-Qatari move by Riyadh and its three Arab allies. Doha's twelve-year-old sovereign wealth fund, operating as the Qatar Investment Authority (QIA), had assets worth $335 billion. A third of these were invested in the emirate, with the bulk scattered across the globe.[37] It owns the Santa Monica-based Miramax, a film producing and distributing company. It was the fourth largest investor in US office space, mainly in New York and Los Angeles, and it owns almost 10 per cent of the Empire State Building's owner, Empire State Realty Trust Inc. QIA also owns London's tallest building, the Shard, the famed Harrods stores, and a quarter of the properties in the upscale Mayfair neighborhood. Its wholly-owned Paris Saint-Germain Football Club had won four French soccer league titles. It was the largest shareholder of Germany's Volkswagen AG. And in the biggest office transaction in Singapore, valued at $2.5 billion, it acquired the highly prestigious Asia Square Tower.

Overall, the four members of the anti-Qatar Axis rushed into their drastic action against Doha without assessing objectively its geopolitical and economic strengths as well as its military ties with Washington; and soft power as exercised by Al Jazeera. To help it overcome the consequences of the Saudi-led boycott, within a week three Iranian ships, carrying 350 tonnes of fruit and vegetables, were set to sail from the port of Dayyer for Doha.[38] This was in addition to five Iranian cargo planes, loaded with 450 tonnes of perishable food, that had landed in Doha.

ISIS Targets Shias—in Iran and Saudi Arabia

A few weeks after his address to the Islamic Arab summit, President Trump's thesis of conflating Iran-backed Shia radicalism with Sunni jihadism to form the same evil of terrorism fell apart.

On 7 June six ISIS gunmen and suicide bombers, dressed as veiled women, attacked the Parliament complex, and mausoleum of Ayatollah Ruhollah Khomeini, the founder of the Islamic Republic of Iran, in Tehran, killing at least seventeen people and injuring more than fifty. Three months earlier, ISIS operatives in eastern Iraq had posted a video in Persian on their social media networks which contained the threat that "We will invade Iran and return it to Sunni control." This video heaped abuse at Iran's Supreme Leader Khamanei and condemned his regime for protecting its nearly 9,000 Jews, who are entitled to one member in Parliament. "Iran shouted slogans against America and Israel in order to deceive the Sunnis, while the Jews of Iran live in security under the protection of the Iranian state," stated the commentator.[39]

Less than two weeks later, Iran fired six Zolfaghar ballistic missiles from its western provinces at an ISIS command center and a suicide car-bomb making facility in Syria's eastern city of Deir el Zour, 370 miles away, over Iraqi airspace. It coordinated the attack with Iraq, Syria and Russia.[40]

Within months of declaring its caliphate in Mosul, Iraq, in June 2014, ISIS operatives had tried to cross into Iran after recruiting followers from among Iran's Sunni Kurdish minority. And long before the Obama administration geared up to help the government in Baghdad fight ISIS,[41] Iran had trained, funded and armed Iraqi Shias to combat the rabidly anti-Shia ISIS. Tellingly the Persian language ISIS video showed the execution of captured Iraqi Shia militiamen.

It is worth noting that when it came to selecting targets in the Saudi kingdom, the ISIS branch in that country chose Shia mosques. The first ISIS suicide bomb attack occurred on 22 May 2015 in al Qadeeh village in Eastern Province during Friday prayers. The blast left at least twenty-one people dead and more than eighty injured. The online ISIS statement said "the soldiers of the Caliphate" were responsible and forecast "dark days ahead" for the Shias.[42]

Following the rapid advance of Bin Salman in the ruling family's hierarchy, Shias in the Kingdom were subjected to incendiary speeches by Wahhabi preachers. For instance, on 31 March 2015, in an online audio recording, captioned, "Imam of the Grand Mosque in Mecca calls for all-out war against Shias," Shaikh Abdul Rahman al Sudais said, "Our war with Iran...is truly sectarian... If it was not sectarian, we will make it sectarian… Our disagreement with Rafidha [another term for Shias] will not be removed, nor our suicide to fight them… as long as they are on the face of the earth."[43]

Awamiya, the birth place of Ayatollah Nimr al Nimr, who was executed in January 2016, had emerged as an enduring flashpoint between the government and the minority Saudi Shias, with a most of the fifty-one Shias killed between March 2011 and May 2017 being residents of Awamiya.[44] The town's four hundred year old quarter, bounded by a sturdy wall built for protection from raiders, or Musawara (Arabic: walled fortress), became a bastion of militant Shias, ready to resist the state by force of arms if necessary, its abandoned houses and narrow winding streets proving an ideal environment. The policy-makers in Riyadh concluded that Musawara needed to be razed to deprive Shia terrorists of their safe haven. But to mask their real motive they declared that many of the 480 buildings in Musawara were unsafe and that the old neighborhood needed to be redeveloped. Locals were sceptical. With their town ringed by checkpoints since the pro-democracy demonstration in 2011, their alienation from the state had grown apace.

On 10 May security forces moved to evict the residents of Musawara from their homes, claiming that the neighborhood had become a haven for those committing terrorist acts and selling weapons and illegal drugs. Violence broke out when Shia activists, some of them armed, offered resistance. Security forces patrolled the town's streets in armored vehicles to protect themselves against fire by militants who accused them of frequently firing randomly towards homes and cars during their confrontation with gunmen in the area. Local activists pointed out several houses and shops which had been set alight or damaged by security forces. Townspeople were incensed when the government meted out collective punishment by frequent power and water cuts.

The ongoing security operation in Awamiya, shielded from local and foreign media, came under the jurisdiction of Prince Abdul Aziz bin Saud on 21 June when King Salman dismissed Prince Muhammad bin Nayef as Interior Minister. His thirty-one-year-old replacement was loyal to the freshly promoted Crown Prince Bin Salman. With that, the drive to depopulate the Musawara neighborhood and raze its buildings intensified. The civilian fatalities caused by mortar shelling, which flattened entire blocks, and sniper fire rose steadily. In late July elite troops reinforced the security personnel deployed earlier. With that the fight between the government and armed Shia militants reached a peak. The state won. Thousands of people living outside the walled Musawara quarter fled.

On 2 August journalists, escorted by Special Forces in armored vehicles, were chaperoned to Awamiya. They witnessed the Musawara neighborhood transformed into a war zone. They found rusted-out cars lying half-flattened next to wrecked homes pocked with hundreds of bullet holes. Though the casualty figures were not published, an Interior Ministry representative said that eight members of a police rapid reaction team and four Special Forces troops had died during the latest campaign. According to Shia activists, five fighters and twenty-three civilians were killed in the fighting, and more than 20,000 had fled or been evacuated to safer towns and villages. Reporters noticed the posters of Ayatollah al Nimr all over Awamiya. Photocopied portraits of "martyrs" were tacked on to lamp posts and buildings. "The land which is mixed with the blood of martyrs gets sufficiently watered by God's light to defeat the mighty," read graffiti along one rubble-strewn street.[45] "Eighty houses were demolished, and we still have about 400 more to go," acting mayor Essam Abdullatif al Mulla told the BBC correspondent Sally Nabil two weeks later.[46]

However Bin Salman's swift success in eradicating the last vestige of Shia resistance in the Kingdom contrasted sharply with the continuing stalemate in Yemen in which he had invested a great deal of money, military muscle and his prestige.

A Rift in the Saudi-led Coalition in Yemen

Like all long-running armed conflicts the one in Yemen started yielding unintended consequences. Differences surfaced between the Saudi Crown Prince and his principal ally, the UAE's Crown Prince Bin Zayed Al Nahyan, on the status of President Hadi.

When Riyadh-based Hadi flew to Aden, the temporary capital of his exiled government, in early February 2017, his plane was refused permission to land by the commander of the International Airport. He was an appointee of the UAE government whose troops and mercenaries were the dominant force in southern Yemen. In addition, the UAE had gained the backing of the tribes in the south who wanted to undo the 1990 unification of North Yemen and South Yemen. Unwilling to accept the UAE's veto, Hadi loyalists fought UAE forces at the airport—a confrontation which ended with the mediation of Saudi Arabia. At the behest of Bin Salman, Hadi flew to Abu Dhabi in late February to meet Prince Bin Zayed to settle who controlled Aden's airport. Their brief meeting ended in acrimony, with Hadi telling his interlocutor that the Emiratis were behaving "like an occupation power in Yemen rather than a force of liberation". After his return to Riyadh, he dismissed two officials close to the UAE: the governor of Aden, and the commander of the forces of the UAE-run Security Belt.[47] Bin Salman tried in vain to reconcile the feuding parties in southern Yemen. The splits in the Saudi camp raised the morale of the Houthi-Saleh alliance in Sanaa.

Hadi decided to assert his authority by returning to Aden in August, but was turned away from Riyadh International Airport. Indeed, to keep the UAE on board with Riyadh in Yemen, Bin Salman barred Hadi along with his sons, ministers and military officers from returning to their homeland. The official reason was the continuing hostility between Hadi loyalists and UAE forces. The imposition of an official ban became known on 6 November when the Associated Press published a well-sourced report on the subject.[48]

The two-and-a-half year long Saudi-led coalition's military intervention in Yemen had created an unprecedented humanitarian crisis. Of the 28 million Yemenis, 17 million needed food assistance, with 7 million at risk of famine. Three million had lost their homes.[49] More than two-thirds of the population lacked access to clean water and sanitation. Because of the breakdown of the health service, compounded by a strike of sanitation workers who had not been paid for months, Yemen suffered the worst outbreak of cholera recorded by the WHO since 1949. Whereas it took Haiti seven years—from 2010 to 2017—to record 815,000 cholera cases, Yemen exceeded that figure in six months. "There's no doubt this is a man-made crisis," said Tamer Kirolos, the Yemen director for Save the Children NGO, in October 2017. "Cholera only rears its head when there's a complete and total breakdown in sanitation."[50]

On 11 October, the Saudis allowed a Russian medical team to land at Sanaa airport to operate on the seventy-five-year-old Ali Abdullah

Saleh whose serious injuries sustained in a failed assassination attempt six years earlier had not fully healed. "Saudi-led coalition intervenes to save seriously ill Saleh's life!" crowed the Saudi press which noted that it was the second time Riyadh had done so.[51] But why? Bin Salman and his father were hoping to fracture the Houthi-Saleh alliance against the background of the well-armed, disciplined Houthis systematically taking over Saleh's bases and fighters. Saleh chafed at the loss but could do little to reverse the trend.

The Fateful Early November 2017

On 1 November a Saudi air raid on a market in Saada killed 25 people.[52] In response, on 3 November, the Houthi-Saleh alliance fired a modified Scud surface-to-surface missile at Riyadh which was intercepted in flight by a US-supplied Patriot missile. The following day, Saad Hariri, the Sunni Prime Minister of Lebanon, summoned to Riyadh by Bin Salman, surprised the regional capitals by announcing his resignation via video from the Saudi capital in protest against Iran's undue influence in Lebanese politics, adding that he feared assassination.[53] That same day King Salman stunned domestic audiences by establishing a supreme committee overnight to investigate public corruption, chaired by Bin Salman. It was charged with launching "investigations, issuing arrest warrants, travel bans, disclosing and freezing bank accounts and tracking funds." According to a statement issued by the public prosecutor, Saud al Mojeb, a month later, 320 people had been subpoenaed and the bank accounts of 376 people had been frozen. Of these 159 business leaders, including eleven members of the royal family, were detained at the five-star Ritz Carlton Hotel in Riyadh where they were forbidden from contacting their lawyers.[54] Among those who saw their bank accounts frozen was Bin Nayef, the former crown prince, believed to have a net worth of some $6 billion, and some of his immediate relatives.[55]

On 6 November in his CNN interview, Saudi Foreign Minister Jubeir claimed that the missile aimed at Riyadh had been smuggled into Yemen in parts, assembled in Yemen by operatives from Hizbollah and the Islamic Revolutionary Guard Corps (IRGC) of Iran, and fired from Yemeni soil by Hizbollah technicians. He described the firing of this missile as an "act of war" by Iran. "Iran cannot lob missiles at Saudi cities and towns and expect us not to take steps."[56] Tehran dismissed the accusation. The Saudi-led coalition responded to the 3 November Scud missile attack by pounding Sanaa with repeated air strikes, thus adding to more than 8,670 Yemenis killed, and nearly 50,000 injured, in the war.[57] On 6 November it re-imposed its blockade of ports and airports in the territory controlled by the Houthi-Saleh alliance, thus worsening the already severe humanitarian crisis.

On 9 November the United Nations Security Council called for the blockade to be lifted, warning that otherwise Yemen would face "the largest famine the world has seen for decades". Riyadh was unmoved. A week later the heads of the World Food Program, UNICEF and the WHO, noted that supplies including medicines, vaccines and food were waiting to enter Yemen. "Without them, untold thousands of innocent victims, among them many children, will die," they warned. Also without imported fuel, Yemen's water and sanitation networks would collapse at a time when it was battling cholera. Behind-the-scenes Western powers lobbied Saudi Arabia, with Britain calling specifically for the reopening of Hodeidah, the entry point for 80 per cent of aid reaching the country. Riyadh responded by claiming that Hodeidah was a conduit for weapons shipments to Houthi rebels. It demanded guarantees that UN inspectors would stop arms shipments as a precondition for reopening Hodeidah. After a review of inspection procedures by the UN and Saudis, Riyadh announced on 22 November that it would lift the blockade on humanitarian supplies, but not on commercial ships.[58]

The latest crisis worsened the suffering of the hapless Yemeni public. Their rancour against the Houthis increased particularly when the cash-strapped government failed to pay the already reduced salaries of state employees. Tensions between Houthis and Saleh partisans that had been building up over months escalated to fighting in Sanaa on 29 November. The city's streets turned into a battlefield and residents stayed indoors to avoid injury or death. The Saudi-led coalition intensified its airstrikes over Yemen, with dozens of airstrikes aimed at Houthi positions inside Sanaa and in other northern provinces.

On 2 December in his interview with Yemen al Yom (Yemen Today) television channel, affiliated with his camp, Saleh denounced Houthis as a "coup militia". He then held out a conditional olive branch. "I call upon the brothers in neighboring states and the alliance to stop their aggression, lift the siege, open the airports and allow food aid and the saving of the wounded and we will turn a new page by virtue of our neighborliness," he said. "We will deal with them in a positive way and what happened to Yemen is enough."[59] In Riyadh, Hadi applauded Saleh's dramatic switch-over. But the euphoria in the Saudi-led coalition proved flecting.

Saleh's interview turned out to be his last public speech. Later that day when Houthi soldiers seized his house in the capital, they found him missing. Once their commander learned that Saleh's destination was his home village of Bait al Ahmar, he set a desert ambush for Saleh's motorcade. Saleh along with his companions was killed on 4 December. His corpse was dumped in the back of a pick-up truck, and a video recording the scene was uploaded online. In a televised speech, Abdul Malik al Houthi, the Houthi leader, said Saleh had been killed because he was a traitor. "Today is the day of the fall of the conspiracy of betrayal and treason," he said, "It is a dark day for the forces of the [Saudi-led] coalition."[60] The five-day long clashes left at least 230 people dead with thousands more injured. Houthis celebrated Saleh's death in public. That event also killed the Saudi strategy of breaking the rebel alliance between Saleh and the Houthis. By happenstance, Bin Salman's plan to push back against Tehran's influence in Lebanon, exerted through its proxy Hizbollah over the past three decades, also came to nought around the same time.

The Rise and Rise of Hizbollah

Hizbollah's rising popularity among Shias, the largest Muslim community in Lebanon, was attested by the general election in May–June 2005. As part of the Amal-Hizbollah alliance, called The Resistance and Development Bloc, it secured fourteen of the twenty-seven Shia seats. This vote was called in the febrile aftermath of the assassination of Rafiq Hariri, a construction tycoon and former (Sunni) prime minister, in Beirut. It caused a political earthquake. Accusing fingers were pointed at Hizbollah, allied with Syria, as the mastermind behind the attack. Among other things the US put Hizbollah back on its list of terrorist groups after having removed it after Hizbollah's condemnation of the 9/11 attacks.

A series of anti-Syrian demonstrations culminated in a massive one in Beirut on 14 March 2006. The resulting 14 March Alliance demanded the withdrawal of 14,000 Syrian troops and intelligence agents who had been there since 1976. Western powers backed the demand as did Saudi Arabia. On 27 April Syrian President Bashar Assad withdrew his soldiers and agents.

Earlier, a demonstration and a rally by various pro-Syria groups in Beirut on 8 March had led to the formation of the 8 March Alliance. It thanked Syria for ending the civil war of 1975–1990, and for backing Lebanese resistance to Israel's occupation of southern Lebanon. Hizbollah was part of this alliance which was backed by Iran. This bloc also included the Free Patriotic Movement, a Christian party founded by Michel Aoun, a former army general, which in 2005 won 31 of the 58 Christian seats in parliament. In February 2006 Aoun signed a memorandum of understanding with the Hizbollah leader, Hassan Nasrallah, on relations between the two parties centered round a defence strategy to protect Lebanon from the Israeli threat.[61] The 8 March Alliance won 56 seats in the impending general election which was supervised by the United Nations. But the rival 14 March Alliance, generously funded by Riyadh, secured 72 seats, and went on to form the government.

As an integral part of the anti-Israel axis led by Iran, Hizbollah fortified a three mile-wide strip along the Israeli-Lebanese border with numerous bunkers, booby-traps, land mines, and closed circuit TV cameras to watch the enemy forces. During its war with Israel in July–August 2006, it was from these bunkers that Hizbollah fired their anti-tank missiles at Israel's armor. Its spirited fight with Israel raised its prestige in the Lebanese public despite the wide scale damage wrought on Lebanon's civilian infrastructure and properties. Emir Hamad of Qatar stepped forward to help financially all those who had lost their homes and businesses, irrespective of their sectarian affiliation. Iran rushed to replenish the diminished armory of Hizbollah which emerged as a strong advocate of Palestinian rights—which Saudi King Abdullah had failed to advance in his dealing with US President George W. Bush.

Emir Hamad put to use the goodwill he had earned in 2006 when a political impasse in central Beirut over the election of the successor to Emile Lahoud, which started in October 2007, turned violent on 6

May. The nationwide clashes between the two sides claimed 200 lives. To avert Lebanon descending into fully fledged civil war, Emir Hamad invited the rivals to Doha. The concord reached on 21 May favored Hizbollah. It was allowed to continue bearing arms as a means of protecting Lebanon from Israel's military designs and to maintain its own telecommunications system.[62]

From then on, during the periodic crises in the region, Hizbollah's position became unassailable. It was dogged by the Special Tribunal on Lebanon (STL), set up by the United Nations Security Council, to investigate the killing of Hariri and bring the guilty to justice. The 14 March Alliance, led by billionaire Saad Hariri, who held dual Lebanese-Saudi nationality, scored 71 seats in the June 2009 general election compared to 57 seats by the 8 March Alliance, now led by Hizbollah; but the majority party won only 44.5 per cent of the popular vote, and the minority party 55.5 per cent.[63] As a son of Rafiq, who had made his fortune as a construction magnate in Saudi Arabia, Saad was intimately involved with the business in the Desert Kingdom, and was close to the House of Saud. Now, aware of the lower popular vote for the 14 March Alliance, he opted for a national unity cabinet resulting from the Doha Agreement. In November he led a new cabinet of twenty-five ministers, with ten from the 8 March Alliance, and five named by President Michel Suleiman, considered neutral between the two competing blocs. When Hariri refused to convene a cabinet meeting to discuss possible indictments to be issued by the STL, 8 March Alliance ministers resigned, and his government fell in January 2011.[64] The subsequent government of Najib Mikati was dependent on the goodwill of Hizbollah. This was a bitter pill for the Saudi government to swallow. The defeated Saad Hariri spent three years in self-exile, dividing his time between Saudi Arabia and France. He returned to Beirut from Riyadh in August 2014.

By then Lebanon had become entangled in Syria's civil war. After initially denying that their militia was actively working with the Assad regime, Hizbollah leaders had to come clean in June 2013. Their fighters played a major role in the Syrian government's recapture of the border town of Qusair used as a transit point for weapons to the rebels from Sunni-dominated north-eastern Lebanon.[65] At that time, Hizbollah had 7,000 soldiers and 20,000 reservists. In addition to penetrating the army and security services, it had placed allies in most government ministries and state-owned enterprises. Its estimated annual income ranged between $800 million and $1 billion, with 70 to 90 per cent coming from Tehran, and the rest from private Shia donors, and business networks in Lebanon. It paid salaries to 60,000 to 80,000 people working for its charities, schools, clinics and other institutions besides its military and security apparatus.[66]

With the ascendancy of Prince Muhammad bin Salman, Riyadh abandoned its traditional policy of competing with Tehran behind the scenes, freely using its cash weapon, and opted for an openly aggressive stance. It called on the Lebanese government to condemn Iran and Hizbollah which, it claimed, were exercising undue influence in Lebanon's foreign policy and national security. It was an overly unrealistic demand, which was ignored. Saudi Arabia then cancelled its pledged aid of $4 billion to Beirut, with $3 billion earmarked for the Lebanese Army to end "the stranglehold of Hizbollah on the state". On 2 March 2016, Riyadh capped its pressure on Beirut by declaring Hizbollah a terrorist organization. By then, 8,000 Hizbollah soldiers had served in Syria on short deployments.[67] Saudi Arabia's decision put Saad Hariri in a bind. As a politician in touch with realities on the ground, he knew that Hizbollah could not be ignored, and advocated dialogue with it.[68]

At the same time his efforts to prop up Suleiman Tony Franjieh as a rival to Aoun were faltering. This was a contrast to the strengthening of ties between Aoun and Nasrallah who had been meeting regularly to review events in Lebanon and Syria. To please Nasrallah, Aoun had taken to tailoring his statements to suit Iran's regional interests. On the other side, when Saudi Arabia's ambassador in Beirut completed his term that summer, Riyadh did not name his successor.

But as momentum built up for Aoun's presidency, the Saudis dispatched a senior envoy to Beirut to discuss a compromise: it offered tacit approval of Aoun as president if he agreed to ask Hariri to form the next government. Once Nasrallah agreed to the Saudi offer, MPs met on 31 October and elected Aoun president by casting 83 votes in his favor in the second ballot. The news was greeted by pro-Aoun demonstrations in the Hizbollah stronghold of Beirut's southern suburbs as well as the streets of Damascus, where Assad, who had met Aoun three times in Damascus, had strongly backed his bid for presidency.[69] This was a watershed moment in Hizbollah's history because it legitimised it as a nationalist party with support across sects—a departure from the traditional description of it as a sectarian organization. In the regional context this was a clear win for Tehran over Riyadh. As promised, Hariri formed a national unity government in which two of the five Shia ministers were from Hizbollah, the rest from Amal.

To help Hariri consolidate his position, King Salman dispatched Prince Khaled Al Faisal, the governor of Mecca, to Beirut. By meeting Aoun, Hariri and other government officials, the Saudi envoy showed the Kingdom's support for the Lebanese state. In early January 2017 Aoun paid a state visit to Riyadh to ease Lebanese-Saudi tensions further and King Salman agreed to send a new ambassador to Beirut.[70]

In his TV interview in Cairo during his visit to the city in February 2017, Aoun blamed Israel for the need to support Hizbollah in "a complementary role to the Lebanese army…As long as the Lebanese army is not strong enough to battle Israel … we feel the need for its existence."[71] In 2016, the strength of Hizbollah's active duty troops, at 20,000, was, on paper, less than a third of the Lebanese army's 65,000. But Hizbollah had 25,000 reservists. These armed personnel were highly motivated and equipped with more up-to-date weapons than regular soldiers. Hizbollah's armory included not only thousands of anti-tank missiles, but also more than 120,000 rockets and surface-to-surface missiles as well as dozens of drones.[72]

Hizbollah's growing involvement in the Syrian civil war, especially when the Assad regime started to gain an upper hand over the opposition, backed strongly by Saudi Arabia, was viewed as a challenge by Prince Bin Salman. In keeping with his impetuous nature, he summoned Hariri, and on 4 November 2017 pressed him to resign. He did not bother to brief France or the United States on his move, a failing which would inter alia lead to his diplomatic defeat. He failed to note that these Western powers were keen not to destabilize Lebanon partly because as a country with a population of a mere 4.3 million, it had taken in more than one million Syrian refugees.

In his televised address from Riyadh on Al Arabiya, Hariri slammed Iran and Hizbollah for meddling in Arab affairs, declaring that "Iran's arms in the region will be cut off." He accused Tehran of spreading chaos, strife and destruction throughout the region. He went on to express fear for his life and claimed that the atmosphere in Lebanon was similar to that which existed before his father, Rafiq Hariri, was assassinated in 2005.[73] Tehran vehemently denied the charge. The next day the Lebanese Army issued a statement saying that intelligence in its possession along with its ongoing investigations had not revealed "the presence of any plan for assassinations in the country."[74] When Hariri failed to return to Lebanon, many claimed that he was being held in Riyadh against his will, and that he had aired his televised speech under duress. Lebanese President Aoun called on Hariri to submit his resignation in person. Meanwhile, when the Saudi minister Thamer al Sabhan arrived in Washington a few days after Hariri's sudden resignation, US State Department officials criticised him for implementing a rash act likely to destabilize Lebanon.[75] However, the fault lay with the ultimate decision-maker in Riyadh, Prince Bin Salman.

His strong arm tactics backfired. Leaders of different factions and even some members of the Hariri clan objected to the Saudis swapping Lebanese politicians at will. "We are not herds of sheep, nor a plot of land whose ownership can be moved from one person to another," said Nouhad Machnouk, the interior minister and an ally of Hariri. "In Lebanon, things happen though elections, not pledges of allegiances," referring to the standard practice in the Saudi Kingdom. The Lebanese leaders' stance won the backing of Western and Arab governments led by France and Egypt, which led to the end of Hariri's two-week long virtual house arrest in Riyadh.

After brief stops in Cairo and Paris, he returned to Beirut in time for the celebration of Lebanon's Day of Independence (from France) on 22 November. After his meeting with Aoun, Hariri announced that he was putting his resignation on hold to allow for dialogue with other political leaders. He added that the dialogue would focus on the principle that Lebanon should keep out of conflicts in the region. After a cabinet meeting on 5 December, Hariri stated that the government had recommitted to dissociate "from any dispute and conflicts or wars, and not to interfere in the internal affairs of the Arab states, in order to preserve the relationship between Lebanon and its Arab brethren." He withdrew his resignation. Actually, a policy of "disassociation" from regional conflicts was first adopted in 2013 to insulate Lebanon from the war in Syria. But this official stance was ignored by Hizbollah as well as Hariri's party, the Future Movement, which backed the rebels in Syria.[76] Now, with Syria completely liberated from ISIS forces, Assad needed negligible assistance from Hizbollah, if at all. Thus, the month-long episode ended with Prince Bin Salman chalking up an undisputed failure in his series of rash foreign policy adventures.

The deadlock in the Yemen war continued, and Saudi-Qatari relations remained frozen. In Syria, the Saudi Kingdom had retreated to the point of having no input of note. To its continued frustration, Iran remained an important player in Syria.

Saudis' Lie Balanced by Iranians' Unconvincing Denial

Saudi Arabia's claim to have downed a Scud missile fired by the Houthis at Riyadh International Airport on 4 November turned out to be a lie. Addicted to his habit of latching on to a success story, Trump had tweeted, "Our system knocked the missile out of the air. That's how good we are. Nobody makes what we make, and now we're selling it all over the world." But a forensic analysis of photos and videos of the strike available on social media by a research team at the East Asia Nonproliferation program of the Middlebury Institute of International Studies led by Jeffrey Lewis—and shared with the *New York Times*—contradicted Trump's chutzpah. The missile, seen in the video released by the Houthis, was a Burqan-2, a variant of the Scud missile used throughout the Middle East, with a range of 600 miles, and a payload of a 1,400-pound warhead. To survive the stresses of its long flight, the missile was designed to separate into two pieces when nearing its target. The tube, which propels it for most of its trajectory, falls away, and the smaller warhead, harder to hit, continues toward the target. The research team concluded that the missile's warhead flew unimpeded over US-supplied Patriot defense batteries and almost hit the airport. Indeed, it exploded so close to the domestic terminal of the King Khalid International that customers jumped out of their seats. A study of the debris, scattered in downtown Riyadh, twelve miles from the airport, showed that the missile defense batteries either missed the incoming missile or hit its harmless rear section. The evidence of a successful interception provided by the Saudis was most likely the missile ejecting its tube as intended.[77]

Equally, Tehran's denials about supplying Scud missiles to the Houthis turned out to be false. A confidential report by the UN sanctions monitors' panel submitted on 24 November concluded that their study of the remnants of the four Scud missiles fired by the Houthis between 19 May and 4 November at Saudi Arabia had been designed and manufactured by Iran. However, they failed to produce evidence as to the identity of the broker or supplier of the missiles. "Design characteristics and dimensions of the components inspected by the panel are consistent with those reported for the Iranian designed and manufactured Qiam-1 missile," the Panel noted. It said that it had gathered evidence that the missiles were transferred to Yemen in pieces and assembled there by missile engineers working with the Houthi-Saleh allies. It added that the missiles most likely were smuggled into Yemen along "the land routes from Oman or Ghaidah and Nishtun in Mahrah governorate of southern Yemen after ship-to-shore transshipment to small dhows, a route that has already seen limited seizures of anti-tank guided weapons."[78]

While submitting the panel's report to the Security Council, UN secretary general Antonio Guterres, said that there was evidence that Iran was supplying ballistic missiles to Houthi rebels in defiance of UN Resolution 2231 of 20 July 2015 which called on Iran not to undertake any activity related to ballistic missiles designed to be capable of delivering nuclear weapons, and that the UN was investigating. He referred to President Trump's decision on 13 October not to certify Iran's nuclear agreement under US law, which created "considerable uncertainty" about its future, but added: "I am reassured that the United States has expressed its commitment to stay in [the deal]." Among others, British officials were deeply concerned that if Washington decided to push to impose wider sanctions on Tehran for breaches of UN resolutions relating to Yemen it could potentially endanger the 2015 nuclear deal, goading Iran to walk away from the agreement.[79]

Hizbollah-Saudi Arabia-Israel

With IRGC experts working with the Houthis to assemble the Scud parts supplied by Iran, and operate the missile, there was no need to involve Hizbollah in the venture. Therefore Jubeir's inclusion of

Hizbollah seemed to be a ploy to encourage Israel, maintaining a close watch on Hizbollah to its north, to make an aggressive move against the militant group. This added credibility to persistent rumors that Israel and the Saudi Kingdom had forged clandestine contacts. On 19 November, in his interview with Army Radio, Yuval Steinitz, a member of the Israeli Prime Minister's security cabinet, revealed that Israel has had covert contacts with Riyadh. "When we fought to get a better nuclear deal with Iran, with only partial success, there was some help from moderate Arab countries vis-à-vis the United States and the Western powers to assist us in this matter," Steinitz said. "And even today, when we press the world powers not to agree to the establishment of an Iranian military base in Syria on our northern border, the Sunni Arab world is helping us."[80] A few days earlier, Israel's military chief, Lt. Gen. Gadi Eisenkot, in an interview with the Saudi-owned *Elaph* online newspaper, claimed that Iran was the "biggest threat to the region" and was seeking "to take control of the Middle East." He added that Israel was ready to share "intelligence information" with Saudi Arabia since their countries had a common interest in standing up to Iran.[81] Avigdor Lieberman, the defense minister of Israel, went further. On his Facebook page on 18 November he called for a coalition of "moderate states" in the Middle East against Iran along the lines of the US-led anti-ISIS coalition.[82]

On the diplomatic side, in mid-November the Beirut-based *Al Akhbar* (The News) published a leaked letter from Jubeir to Bin Salman in which he set out the conditions that would have to be satisfied for normal diplomatic relations between Riyadh and Tel Aviv. These included inter alia "military equivalence" between the two states. Since Israel is the only country with nuclear weapons in the Middle East, the Kingdom must acquire this deterrent or seek to remove Israel's. The Kingdom would also propose that Jerusalem (al Quds) be placed under international control administered by the United Nations.[83] None of these conditions was likely to be met. Nearer home in Qatar, too, there was no prospect of Bin Salman scoring a success.

Qatar Tightens Links with Turkey and Iran

Following mediation by President Trump, Qatar's Emir Tamim and Bin Salman had a telephone conversation on 8 September, according to the state media of both countries. "During the call, the Emir of Qatar expressed his desire to sit at the dialogue table and discuss the demands of the four countries to ensure the interests of all," the state-run Saudi Press Agency (SPA) reported. But the next day SPA quoted a spokesman of the Saudi foreign ministry saying, "What was published on the Qatar News Agency is a continuation of the distortion of the Qatari authority of the facts. The Kingdom of Saudi Arabia announces the suspension of any dialogue or communication with the authority in Qatar until a clear statement is issued clarifying its position in public."[84]

Addressing the UN General Assembly in New York on 19 September, Emir Tamim said, "The countries who imposed the blockade on the State of Qatar interfere in the internal affairs of many countries, and accuse all those who oppose them domestically and abroad with terrorism. By doing that they are inflicting damage on the war on terror. We have refused to yield to dictations by pressure and siege." Later he held a meeting with Trump in which he was careful to emphasise the strong Qatar-US relationship. At their joint press conference, Emir Tamim said, "As you said, Mr President, we have a problem with our neighbors", adding that with Trump's intervention, "hopefully we can find a solution for this problem." The chances for reconciliation were slim. An official from one of the members of the anti-Qatari axis said it was "unfortunate that Emir Tamim continues to talk about a blockade when even he in the same speech acknowledged that his shipping lanes are open."[85]

While Saudi-Qatari relations remained frozen, the ties between Qatar, Iran and Turkey blossomed. Iran's strategic importance was highlighted on 27 November when Turkey, Iran and Qatar signed a trade-transport agreement, with Iran named as transit country for trade between Qatar and Turkey.[86] The move helped neutralise Riyadh's efforts to isolate Qatar economically.

As the rotating chair of the GCC, Kuwait invited Qatar to the annual two-day GCC summit on 5 December. Emir Tamim attended, being the only ruler to do so besides the host Emir Sabah al Ahmad Al Sabah. Other members sent their foreign ministers. The closed door meeting ended after a brief session on 5 December. It unanimously condemned the Houthis for killing Ali Abdullah Saleh, and called on Yemenis to "get rid of the Houthi militias who are following and being backed by Iran."

It condemned "all terrorist actions carried out by Iran and its continued interference in the internal affairs of Arab countries."[87]

In contrast to his string of failures in foreign policy, Bin Salman forged ahead with consolidating his power at home. He garnered rising popularity among the young, given the demographic profile of two-thirds of Saudi citizens being below thirty, by liberalising some socio-cultural aspects of daily life. His steps included re-opening cinemas closed since the early 1980s, allowing musical concerts, lifting the ban on women driving not only cars but also trucks, and ending the arrest powers of the much-dreaded religious police. These measures went hand in hand with his scaling back of the already limited civil and political rights of citizens.

Bin Salman Curbs Religious and Secular Dissidents

During summer of 2017 at a super-secret, high level conclave of the most senior royal princes, Bin Salman noted continued resistance to his elevation as heir to the throne. He and King Salman resolved to suppress it. An indication of this came by the way the government treated a comment by Shaikh Salman al Awda. He welcomed a report that suggested the row between Qatar and Saudi Arabia may be resolved. "May God harmonize their hearts for the good of their people," he tweeted to his 14 million followers. It generated nearly 2,000 responses, 15,000 likes, and 13,000 retweets. Within hours of this post he was detained.[88] Among others detained was Awad al Qarni, another popular cleric who was banned from writing on Twitter in March 2017 on the grounds that he was posting content on social media which was likely to jeopardise public order. Along with Awda, he had expressed support for reconciliation with Qatar.[89] They were singled out among leading Islamic scholars for their continued sympathy for the Muslim Brotherhood. During the subsequent crackdown thirty people, viewed as critics of Bin Salman, were arrested.

They included writers, a poet, intellectuals and two women, according to lists being circulated on social media by Saudi activists. The arrests were seemingly confirmed in a vague statement published by the state-run news agency on 12 September. The statement said arrests were made after the State Security Presidency monitored the activities of a group of people acting "for the benefit of foreign parties against the security of the kingdom and its interests." The official Council of Senior Ulema (COSU) rushed to back the government. On its Twitter account, it said that Saudi Arabia was founded on the words and deeds of Prophet Muhammad "so there is no place for political parties or ideologies".[90] This was the backdrop against which Crown Prince Bin Salman and his father struck in early November at the business elite likely to challenge the supremacy of Bin Salman after his father's death.

Midnight Arrests in Riyadh

A benign interpretation of Bin Salman's intentions was that he needed to be more autocratic with more centralising of power to see through the social and economic changes he wished to implement in Saudi society. "Life is too short and a lot of things can happen," he told Thomas Friedman of the *New York Times* in late November. "And I am really keen to see it [change] with my own eyes—and that is why I am in a hurry."[91] Sceptical insiders had a different take on this. Since nobody could be absolutely sure what would follow after the death of King Salman, both he and his favorite son wanted Bin Salman to ascend to the throne during the monarch's lifetime. That meant Salman abdicating in favor of his heir. Hence the unseemly haste.

In his long interview with Friedman, Bin Salman said that one of the first acts of his father—supposedly untainted by charges of corruption—was to order his team secretly to gather all the information about corruption at the top. At the end of a two-year-long investigation the team produced a list of about 200 names. Once the evidence was checked, Attorney General Saud al Mojeb moved on 4 November within hours of the establishment of the Anti-Corruption Committee. "We show them [the detainees] all the files that we have and as soon as they see those about 95 per cent agree to a settlement," which means signing over cash or shares of their business to the Saudi state treasury. "About 1 per cent," he added, "are able to prove they are clean and their case is dropped right there. About 4 per cent say they are not corrupt and with their lawyers want to go to court. Under Saudi law, the public prosecutor is independent. We cannot interfere with his job: the king can dismiss him, but he is driving the process ... We have experts making sure no businesses are bankrupted in the process"—to avoid causing unemployment. "How much money are they recovering?" asked Friedman. According to the public prosecutor, it could eventually "be around $100 billion in settlements," said Bin Salman.[92]

High level corruption existed in different forms but centered round government contracts for supplies or for infrastructure projects. In most instances, leading businessmen, including royals, took large cuts of contracts in public and private sectors, or invoiced far more than the actual cost of a project and siphoned off the difference. In other cases, the government signed contracts for public works with private firms, and paid them even when a project was unfinished.[93]

Bin Salman's admirers argued that his action was meant to reassure potential foreign investors that the days were over of obtaining lucrative Saudi contracts by bribing influential princes or businessmen to act as middlemen, and henceforth all dealings with the Saudi public sector would be above board. But his critics pointed out that his preemptive strike had created uncertainty among the rich elite, causing capital flight. No matter, COSU rushed to endorse the monarch and Bin Salman on the arrests. It said that "The Sharia instructs us to fight corruption and our national interest requires it."[94]

Senior ulema seemed to have woken up from a long slumber. Corruption had a long history in the Kingdom. It surged after the full nationalisation of Aramco which enabled the House of Saud and its hangers-on to exploit the renamed Saudi Aramco for their personal benefit. The most lucrative way was to secure kick-backs on oil sales. For instance, the Saudi government ordered one of the former constituents of Aramco to sell oil at $32 a barrel to Petromonde, a Japanese company which then sold it to a Japanese refinery at $34.63, with $2.63 a barrel going to Petromonde as commission. On investigation Petromonde turned out to be a London-based company with the same phone and telex numbers as Al Bilad, owned by Prince Muhammad bin Fahd, son of the then Crown Prince.[95]

But this turned out to be chicken-feed when the classified cables of the US Embassy in Riyadh were put into the public domain by WikiLeaks. In the 30 November 1996 cable the authors referred to "a handful of the senior most princes," controlling several billion in annual expenditures in "off-budget" programs with no ministry of finance oversight or controls." This information was based on what self-made (non-Sudairi) Prince Al Waleed bin Talal revealed to the US Ambassador, explaining that "through these off-budget programs, five or six princes control the revenues from one million barrels per day (bpd) of the Kingdom's 8 million bpd of crude oil production."[96] Seemingly, those who acquired this rich treasure were among Fahd's full (Sudairi) brothers and this underhand practice started in the early days of the nationalised Saudi Aramco. (In his interview with the *Wall Street Journal* in November 2013, Al-Waleed bin Talal denied the persistent rumors that his Kingdom Holding Company was an investment front for other Saudi royals keen to guard their anonymity.[97]

The classified November 1996 cable from the US Embassy in Riyadh opened with the sentence: "Saudi princes and princesses, of whom there are thousands, are known for the stories of their fabulous wealth—and tendency to squander it." The document explains that the most common mechanism for distributing Saudi Arabia's wealth to royals is the budgeted system of monthly stipends that members of the Al Saud family receive. Managed by the Ministry of Finance's "Office of Decisions and Rules," which acts like a kind of welfare office for Saudi royalty, the royal stipends in the mid-1990s ran from about $800 a month for "the lowliest member of the most remote branch of the [royal] family" to $200,000–$270,000 a month for one of the surviving sons of Abdul Aziz Ibn Saud.[98] "Bonus payments are available for marriage and palace building," continued the cable, which estimated that the system cost the government, with an annual budget of $40 billion at the time, about $2 billion a year.[99]

"In the end," noted the authors of the cable, "royals still seem more adept at squandering than accumulating wealth. Despite the handouts, there are more commoner billionaires than royal billionaires in the kingdom. The wealthiest royals and their personal fortunes by our estimates are Al Waleed bin Talal bin Abdul Aziz, $13 billion; King Fahd, $10 billion; Defense Minister Prince Sultan bin Abdul Aziz, $10 billion; Khalid bin Sultan bin Abdul Aziz, $2 billion."[100]

All told, the profligacy, incompetence and avarice of the royals from the highest to the lowest had caused wastage of tens of billions of dollars of oil income over the past two decades. On the other hand, between 1981 and 2001, per capita income in the Kingdom slumped by three-quarters, from $28,000 to $6,800.[101]

As one of the very few persons familiar with the innermost work-ings of the monarchical system, the word of Bin Salman on the arrest of scores of the top businessmen and princes carried much weight. But the key question he was not asked was: why early November 2017? It was worth noting that while setting up the Anti-Corruption Com-mittee, King Salman reshuffled the cabinet, replacing the Sandhurst-trained Prince Mutaib bin Abdullah as Minister of the National Guard, made up exclusively of tribes loyal to the House of Saud, with a Bin Salman loyalist—Prince Khalid bin Abdul Aziz bin Muhammad Al Saud. By so doing the father and son duo tightened their grip on all institutions of security and intelligence: defence, National Guard, and interior ministries as well as the State Security Presidency.

Bin Salman came to believe that with the backing of the Trump administration—"the right person at the right time," in his words—the Saudi Kingdom and its Arab allies were gradually building a coalition to challenge Iran. He wrapped up his anti-Iran obsession with a bizarre interpretation of recent European history. Iran's "supreme leader is the new Hitler of the Middle East," he told Friedman. "But we learned from Europe that appeasement doesn't work. We don't want the new Hitler in Iran to repeat what happened in Europe in the Middle East." What matters most to Bin Salman, according to Friedman, was what the Saudi government did domestically to bolster its strength and economy.[102]

The economy was to be restructured according to the Vision 2030 document that Bin Salman had published to great fanfare. It envisaged the country being weaned away from its almost total reliance on oil, creating millions of jobs for young Saudi citizens, and building up the domestic defense industry from a very low base. All this would take, at the minimum, ten years.

Meanwhile, repeating his past behaviour in foreign affairs, Bin Salman inadvertently acted in a similar fashion domestically. While in public he led a much-trumpeted crackdown on corruption and self-enrichment by the elite, he was found to have made a surreptitious record-breaking art purchase, according to an investigation by the *New York Times* on 7 December. Acting through a close friend and a distant cousin, Prince Bader bin Abdullah bin Muhammad bin Farhan Al Saud, Bin Salman paid $450.3 million for Leonardo da Vinci's portrait of Jesus Christ, "Salvator Mundi." This amount was more than twice the previous record of $179.4 million for a painting by Pablo Picasso at a public auction. Christie's did not disclose the name of the buyer.[103]

The same day, the Abu Dhabi branch of the Louvre, which opened in November, announced that it would display Leonardo's "Salvator Mundi" without mentioning whether the painting was a gift or a loan, or obtained on a rental basis.[104] The man behind the Abu Dhabi Louvre project was Crown Prince Muhammad bin Zayed, a close ally of Bin Salman.

The embarrassing disclosure had a religious dimension in a ruling dynasty affiliated to the ultraconservative Wahhabi school of Islam, and was likely to damage Bin Salman's standing even among establishment clerics. "Salvator Mundi" is a reverential rendering of Jesus Christ who is regarded as one of the prophets, not the savior of the world. Furthermore depiction of a prophet, including Muhammad, is strictly forbidden in Islam.

While the full implications of Bin Salman purchasing a painting of a prophet had to be felt across different sections of Saudi citizens, Trump had acted in a manner similar to Bin Salman.

So far Trump's trust-building process in the Middle East seemed to be on track. With his first foreign visit to Saudi Arabia, he built up good ties with the Sunni states; he maintained close relationships with Israel; and he was making progress even with the sceptics in the Palestinian Authority. And then, on 6 December, with his precipitate announcement of recognising Jerusalem as the capital of Israel, he demolished it all.

Trump's Jerusalem Bombshell Diminishes Riyadh's Islamic Standing

By so doing Trump legitimised the annexation and colonisation of East Jerusalem since the 1967 Arab-Israeli War—in violation of international law. In 1947, when the UN voted to partition Palestine into Jewish and Arab states, Jerusalem was defined as a separate entity under international supervision. In the Arab-Israeli War of 1948–1949 it was divided into western and eastern sectors under Israeli and Jordanian control respectively. In the June 1967 Arab-Israeli War, Israel captured the eastern side, expanded the city's boundaries and annexed it in 1980—an act that was rejected by the UN Security Council. All along Washington maintained strict neutrality on the subject. Following the Israeli-Palestinian Liberation Organization in September 1993, which accepted the two-state solution to resolve the Israeli-Palestinian conflict, the final status of Jerusalem was to be decided by the two parties. In October 1995 US Congress passed the Jerusalem Embassy Relocation Act. It allowed the President to issue a waiver every six months to keep the embassy in Tel Aviv in the interests of national security. President Barack Obama signed the last such waiver on 1 December 2016. Trump followed his example only once.

Trump's decision was criticised by UN Secretary General António Guterres as well as the EU. As the rotating president of the Organisation of Islamic Cooperation, Turkey called an emergency OIC summit in Istanbul. More than fifty heads of state or government attended. Among them were the Qatari Emir Tamim Al Thani and the Lebanese President Michel Aoun, a Christian. But neither the Custodian of the Two Holy Mosques, Saudi King Salman, nor his assertive Crown Prince, attended. Instead Saudi Arabia was represented by its Minister of Islamic Affairs, Endowments, Call and Guidance, Shaikh Saleh bin Abdul Aziz Al a Shaikh. "Jerusalem is and will forever be the capital of the Palestinian state," said Mahmoud Abbas, president of the Palestinian Authority. "We do not accept any role of the United States in the political process from now on, because it is completely biased towards Israel." In his speech, Iran's President Hassan Rouhani said that the only reason Trump had dared to recognize Jerusalem as the capital of Israel was because some in the region were seeking to establish ties to Israel—a thinly disguised reference to Saudi Arabia. The final communiqué declared East Jerusalem as "the capital of the state of Palestine" and invited "all countries to recognize the state of Palestine and East Jerusalem as its occupied capital". It described Trump's move "as an announcement of the US administration's withdrawal from its role as sponsor of peace" in the Middle East, and declared it as legally "null and void" and "a deliberate undermining of all peace efforts" that would give impetus to "extremism and terrorism".[105]

On 18 December, at the UN Security Council the resolution demanding that the Trump administration rescind its decisions to recognize Jerusalem as Israel's capital and to move the American Embassy there, backed by fourteen of the fifteen members, was vetoed by Washington. As a Security Council member, Egypt called for an emergency session of the UN General Assembly on 21 December. Donald

Trump threatened to cut financial aid to those who backed the resolution sponsored by Turkey and Yemen. The Council described Trump's step "null and void" and reaffirmed ten Security Council resolutions on Jerusalem, dating back to 1967, including requirements that the city's final status must be decided in direct negotiations between Israel and the Palestinians. It demanded that "all states comply with Security Council resolutions regarding the holy city of Jerusalem, and not to recognize any actions or measures contrary to those resolutions". Of the 193 members, 128 voted in favor of the resolution, and nine against, with 35 abstaining. The list of those who backed the resolution included such major Muslim recipients of US aid as Egypt and Afghanistan.[106]

With that died the prospect of Bin Salman realising his grand plan of Saudi Arabia and its Arab allies steadily building a powerful coalition to confront Iran.

15

CONCLUSIONS

To fully comprehend the changing relations between Saudi Arabia and
Iran, it is important to note their histories. Iran's recorded chronicles
go far back in ancient times. Fast forward to 1501 when, after capturing Tabriz in Azerbaijan, Shah Ismail I Safavi extended his domain from
Baghdad to Herat, Afghanistan, and adopted Twelver Shia Islam as the
state religion. Thus contemporary Iranian identity dates back to 1501.
By contrast, the First Saudi State, called the Emirate of Diriya, was
established in 1744. And the final Kingdom of Saudi Arabia appeared
on the Iranian/Persian radar only in 1924 when Abdul Aziz bin
Abdullah Al Saud (aka, Ibn Saud) captured Mecca and Medina after the
dissolution of the Ottoman Empire.

A Historical Perspective

Long before the defeat of the Ottoman Empire in the First World War,
Britain had become the dominant Western power in the Arabian
Peninsula and Iran. It acquired this role in order to safeguard the sea
lanes to its Indian colony. Britain was the first Western nation to recog-
nize Ibn Saud as part of the Treaty of Jeddah signed in May 1927,
whereby the Saudi monarch accepted Britain as the "protector" of the
Arab principalities in the Gulf and Oman. By then, the Anglo-Persian
Oil Company, owned by the British government, was well established

in Iran with Reza Shah Pahlavi as the monarch since 1925. Iran maintained normal diplomatic ties with America.

In 1928, the United States rejected Ibn Saud's request for recognition as an independent monarch. It reversed its decision in 1931, and signed a basic treaty of friendship and navigation with Saudi Arabia in November 1933. That was six months after Ibn Saud awarded an oil concession to the Standard Oil Company of California (Socal). Seven years lapsed before Washington named its nonresident consul to Saudi Arabia. With the outbreak of the Second World War in 1939, and the resulting steep drop in Muslim pilgrims to Mecca as well as oil production, the Saudi king's financial position became dire. Caltex, the American oil combine, helped by paying him advances against future royalties which were running at an annual rate of $2 million before the war. It also appealed to President Franklin Roosevelt to help solve his financial crisis.

A possibility arose with the passing of the US Lend-Lease Act in March 1941. It authorized the president to sell, exchange, lend, lease, or otherwise hand over military equipment to friendly nations under attack by the Axis Powers. Saudi Arabia did not fall in this category. Ibn Saud's chance came when US Congress approved a $425 million loan to Britain in July. Roosevelt instructed the administrator of the Federal Loan Agency to "tell the British [that] I hope that they can take care of the king of Saudi Arabia." Consequently Britain's payments to Saudi Arabia rose forty-fold in three years: from $403,000 in 1940 to $16.6 million in 1943.[1] Far more importantly, on 18 February 1943, Roosevelt signed a document saying, "I hereby find the defense of Saudi Arabia is vital to the defense of the United States."[2]

Since then this statement has been endorsed by all succeeding presidents, Democrat or Republican. In January 2009, during his private meeting with his successor, Barack Obama, at the White House, US President George W. Bush advised Obama to accord Saudi Arabia special attention. Obama did so during his first term in office. But in his second term, he came to question this State Department orthodoxy—as revealed by Jeffrey Goldberg in his 19,500-word long article, "The Obama Doctrine," based on several interviews with Obama, published in *The Atlantic* in April 2016.

"Obama's frustration with the Saudis informs his analysis of Middle Eastern power politics," noted Goldberg. "At one point I observed to him that he is less likely than previous presidents to axiomatically side with Saudi Arabia in its dispute with its arch-rival, Iran. He didn't disagree.

"Iran, since 1979, has been an enemy of the United States, and has engaged in state-sponsored terrorism, is a genuine threat to Israel and many of our allies, and engages in all kinds of destructive behavior," the president said. "And my view has never been that we should throw our traditional allies"—the Saudis—"overboard in favor of Iran." But Obama went on to say that the Saudis need to "share" the Middle East with their Iranian foes. "The competition between the Saudis and the Iranians—which has helped to feed proxy wars and chaos in Syria and Iraq and Yemen—requires us to say to our friends as well as to the Iranians that they need to find an effective way to share the neighborhood and institute some sort of cold peace," he said. "An approach that said to our friends "You are right, Iran is the source of all problems, and we will support you in dealing with Iran" would essentially mean that as these sectarian conflicts continue to rage and our Gulf partners, our traditional friends, do not have the ability to put out the flames on their own or decisively win on their own, and would mean that we have to start coming in and using our military power to settle scores. And that would be in the interest neither of the United States nor of the Middle East."[3]

To be sure, the problem was not one-sided. In the Saudi Kingdom, serious challenges to the regime have risen on ideological grounds either from hard line Wahhabis operating outside the state-sponsored religious establishment, or as a result of the impact of a regional, non-violent, democratic movement such as the Arab Spring of 2011. By resorting to an armed rebellion as in 1979, or terrorism, starting in 2005, Wahhabi religious zealots have highlighted the vulnerability of the royal dynasty. Even otherwise, on the ideological front, the key challenge to the House of Saud is to justify the monarch's title of the Custodian of the Two Holy Mosques, which implies his spiritual leadership of all Islam, and his self-acquired role to protect and propagate the sole true religion, which is regarded as all-encompassing. The House of Saud is extremely sensitive to any challenge on that front. It comes down heavily when a non-establishment Wahhabi religious leader crosses the red line and questions, even obliquely, the Islamic legitimacy of the royal family.

The red lines are sharply drawn and ferociously enforced. Criticism of the House of Saud or the ruling dynasty of other Gulf Arab states is not tolerated. And neither are the Internet sites that organise political opposition or question the ruling family's conception of Islam, which is endorsed at critical times by the state-appointed Council of Senior Ulema, all of them being Wahhabi.

At the same time the demands of administering a modern state are too complex and multifarious to be tailored to meet the strict codes of a faith founded in the seventh century. The exacting task of navigating this perilous course is a challenge that is inherent in the very existence of the House of Saud and its reliance on America—a predominantly Christian country with a secular constitution—as the ultimate guarantor of its external security, and thus its survival. The ruling dynasty is finding it increasingly onerous to reconcile its alliance with the United States and the maintenance of an Islamic image at home. Unsurprisingly, when the military alliance with Washington becomes overtly clear as in the continued presence of American troops on Saudi soil, the protest by non-establishment clerics becomes vehement.

Saudis' Protector, Iran's "Great Satan"

Riyadh's intimate links with Washington put it at odds with the Islamic Republic, which adopted "Neither East nor West" as the guiding principle of its foreign policy. After the collapse of the Soviet Union in 1991, Iran treated the subsequent Russian Federation as a neighbor, which was no longer atheist, and therefore worth cultivating. By contrast, Tehran's adversarial stance toward America, somewhat moderated after the death of Ayatollah Ruhollah Khomeini, who routinely called America "Great Satan," remained in place.

It was an article of faith among Iran's leaders that a non-Muslim state—no matter how powerful—should have no role in the defense of any of the littoral Muslim states in the Gulf region. This boiled down to a zero sum equation between Tehran and Washington. What was a plus for the US was a minus for Iran; and vice-versa. The Islamic Republic has stuck to this doctrine in principle throughout its existence. It has paid a price for its obduracy in terms of economic sanctions. But these measures, along with a long war with Iraq, compelled Iran to become self-reliant. As a result, there was a spurt in its civilian and military industries. Also the contribution of oil and gas to its GDP declined to a mere 15 per cent, about a third of the current figure for Saudi Arabia.

Riyadh's intimate links with the US exposes it to the ideological challenge by the Islamic Republic of Iran. It tries to counter this by highlighting Iran as a state of Shias, a minority among the world's 1.6 billion Muslims. It is worth noting that Article 12 of the Iranian constitution, which describes Islam and the Twelver Jaafari school as the country's official religion, accords "full respect" to Hanafi, Shafii, Maliki, and Hanbali schools of Sunni Islam as well as Zaidi (Shia), with their followers being free to act in accordance with their own jurisprudence in performing their religious rites.

As followers of the Wahhabi school within the puritanical Hanbali jurisprudence in Sunni Islam, Saudi royals are particularly hostile toward Shias at home and abroad. In contrast to their Saudi counterparts, Iranian leaders stress what unites Shias and Sunnis rather than what divides them. In their rivalry with the Saudi Kingdom, they refrain from making any reference to their sectarian affiliation. Every year Iran observes Islamic Unity week which bridges the gap between the two birthdays of Prophet Muhammad, one accepted by Sunni ulema and the other by their Shia counterparts.

Tehran's record speaks for itself. With cash and weapons, it has aided Hamas, which is purely Sunni since there are no Shias in the Gaza Strip or the West Bank. It has maintained cordial relations with the transnational Muslim Brotherhood, an Islamic movement that originated in 1928 in an almost universally Sunni Egypt. Ideologically, the Islamic Republic shares republicanism with the Brotherhood. The Saudi government, once the prime financial and ideological backer of the Brotherhood, fell out with its leadership in 1991 when the latter opposed the stationing of US troops on Saudi soil on the eve of the 1991 Gulf War.

Iran's chance to intervene in Palestinian politics, which riles Saudi policy-makers, came because of the failure of the Saudis' argument that only by remaining in the American camp can they influence US policy on the Middle East. That became clear during the Palestinians' Second Intifada (2000–2005) when King Abdullah's lobbying of the Bush White House proved fruitless.

The Saudi government chafed at the prestigious diplomatic gain Tehran made by providing money and arms to Hamas which it could not do since Hamas had been listed as a terrorist organization by the US.

Cold War Between Riyadh and Tehran

Diplomatic competition between Saudi Arabia and Iran got going in 1975, and escalated to a Cold War after the founding of the Islamic Republic of Iran four years later. It was King Faisal, who, riding the wave of petro-dollars resulting from the quadrupling of oil prices in 1973–1974, started a concerted drive to have a footprint in Muslim countries outside the Arab Middle East. He succeeded in Pakistan.

In a similar campaign, Muhammad Reza Shah Pahlavi gained influence in adjoining Afghanistan using money as the prime means to achieve it. After his overthrow, the Islamic Republic pursued the aim of gaining influence in the Muslim states of the Middle East and South Asia by using a variety of means except cash handouts. The list included rhetorical propaganda through state-controlled broadcasting media, appeals to Islamic solidarity with a view to eliminating Western influence, advancing republicanism in the Arab Gulf monarchies (Ayatollah Ruhollah Khomeini ruled that monarchy is un-Islamic), and advancing radicalism among the Palestinians in their ongoing conflict with Israel. Being listed by the US as a country that sponsors state terrorism since 1985 made it free to support financially and militarily Hamas.

Altogether, the long-running cold war between Riyadh and Tehran has, inadvertently, replicated the pattern of the US-Soviet Cold War. The two superpowers cooperated to sign the Strategic Arms Limitation Treaty I in May 1972 while continuing their competition to win over the recently liberated countries in Asia and Africa. In the Islamic world, this has meant Saudi Arabia and Iran competing for influence in the Middle East and beyond.

In 2017, Iran had the upper hand in the Arab Middle East despite the fact that after the detente between the two Islamic heavyweights from May 1993 to December 2001, Saudi Arabia had intensified its efforts to counter Iranian influence in the region. Tehran made gains for various reasons. Besides its deployment of an armory of tactics, it had the advantages of geopolitics and demography. It has land borders with six countries in South Asia, the Caucasus, and the Middle East, and a fluvial border with Russia in the Caspian Sea. Although Shias are only 15 per cent of the Muslim population worldwide, in the region covering the eight littoral states of the Persian Gulf, Yemen, Levant (Syria and Lebanon), Jordan, and Palestine, Shias total about 116 million. Their overall numbers are slightly larger than Sunnis' in an aggregate population of 226 million, including 6 million Christians. They constitute a clear majority in Iran, Iraq and Bahrain. Iran made gains by default in the aftermath of Washington's disastrous invasion of Iraq in 2003, and as a result of the Saudi Arabia-led diplomatic and commercial blockade on Qatar in 2017.

All in all, in the multi-front Cold War, Iran gained the upper hand in Iraq, Syria, Lebanon and Qatar. In the long-running civil war in Yemen between Iran-backed Houthi rebels, occupying the capital of Sanaa, and the government of Riyadh-based President Abd Rabbu al Hadi, the situation remains murky. There is, however, a general agreement that a clear-cut military victory for one side is most unlikely. It is hard to see how, in the interim political agreement to lead to UN-supervised elections, the Houthis can be excluded, since they have proved to have far more staying power than all the other parties in the civil war as well as outside powers had anticipated.

Backed by the virulently anti-Iran US President Donald Trump, Saudi Arabia's brash Crown Prince Muhammad bin Salman has tried to counter Tehran's supremacy, with little success so far. His military intervention in Yemen has turned into an expensive quagmire. His hasty move to punish Qatar for maintaining normal relations with Iran by getting the UAE, Bahrain and Egypt to cut off commercial and diplomatic links with Doha has proved counterproductive. His move has thrown Qatar into the welcoming arms of Iran and strengthened military cooperation with Turkey, a leading Sunni nation. Qatar's plans to host the 2022 FIFA World Cup in Doha remain on track, with several large Turkish construction companies playing an important role in the building of stadiums.

The Saudi Crown Prince failed in his attempt to destabilize Lebanon which is ruled by a national unity government with pro-Iran Hizbollah ministers. Bin Salman has not yet grasped a cardinal rule of diplomacy. Before trying to bend a foreign government to your will, you must calculate its strengths and weaknesses dispassionately.

All along a basic flaw in Saudi diplomacy has been its almost total reliance on cash handouts. But financial incentives are effective only up to a certain point. A good example is Pakistan. While maintaining close links with Riyadh, Pakistan's President General Zia ul Haq refused to exclude Shia soldiers from the contingents he agreed to send to the Saudi Kingdom in the 1980s. He stated point blank that he could not make a distinction between Sunni and Shia soldiers in his country's military.

When Bin Salman tried to build up a powerful coalition to intervene in Yemen in March 2015, he and King Salman approached Pakistan. But, realising that the Saudi government's move was driven by its pathological hatred of Shias, the lawmakers in Islamabad rejected the Saudi call. They were well aware of the influence of the minority Shias in the national institutions as well as repeated attacks on soft Shia targets by the local, militantly Sunni jihadist groups.

Nearer home, Kuwait refused to join Bin Salman's drive against Qatar for maintaining normal ties with Tehran in June 2017, because its ruler was conscious of the fact that 30 per cent of Kuwaiti citizens were Shia.[4] But the overall perspective that Saudi royals hold of Shias is highly skewed. They see a threatening Shia crescent arising in the midst of a Sunni region.

The Spectre of The Shia Crescent

During his March 2009 meeting with John Brennan, Counterterrorism Adviser to President Obama, King Abdullah pointed out that "some say the US invasion handed Iraq to Iran on a silver platter; this after we fought Saddam Hussein."[5] Handing over something is a deliberate act. What happened in the aftermath of US President George W. Bush's disastrous invasion of Iraq in March 2003 was rather an unintended consequence of the war.

It is worth recalling that in his January 2002 State of the Union speech, Bush had included Iran along with Iraq as part of his Axis of Evil. Bush invaded Iraq on the ground that Saddam was building weapons of mass destruction. By so doing—knowingly or inadvertently—he advanced the agenda of Israel, intent on ensuring that neither Iraq nor Iran ever possessed a nuclear weapon. After Iraq, it was to have been Iran's turn for violent regime change. But the problems in the wake of the bloody overthrow of Saddam Hussein proved so over-whelming that the Bush administration had to limit itself to tightening up economic sanctions on Iran.

Politically, Bush and his team failed to realise that once they had introduced free and fair elections in post-Saddam Iraq, the majority Shias—who had been suppressed since 1638, when the Sunni Ottoman Turks incorporated Iraq into their empire—would gain power through the ballot. In short, Iran found a friendly Shia-dominated government in post-Saddam Baghdad, because of a serious, strategic blunder made by the US president, who was less than honest with the American public on this subject. It is worth remembering here that Ayatollah Ruhollah Khomeini's attempt in the late 1970s to rally Shias in Iraq to overthrow Saddam Hussein's regime had failed.

There was still another instance of an unintended consequence of military action benefiting Tehran. This time it was Israel's invasion of south Lebanon in April 1978. It was in the aftermath of this incursion that Iran's ambassador to Syria, Ali Akbar Mohtashemi, acted as a catalyst for several Shia groups to found Hizbollah four years later. Its leaders issued their organization's charter in 1985. As for Tehran's long-lasting strategic alliance with Damascus, it is underscored not only by the shared sectarian affiliation of Shia Islam but also an anti-imperialist ideology. In the late 1970s, Syrian President Hafiz Assad was the first Arab leader to recognize the Islamic Republic of Iran. Born in a poor Alawi peasant household, Assad had grown up as a socialist, and developed close relations with the Soviet Union while remaining wary of the United States. In 1979 he rightly regarded the post-Shah regime in Tehran as anti-imperialist. The ties between Tehran and Damascus tightened during the eight-year-long Iran-Iraq War. Syria provided vital intelligence on Iraq to Iran, and the Islamic Republic sold oil at discount rates to Syria. As explained in an earlier chapter,[6] the formal pacts between the two countries cover not only assistance in the case of foreign aggression but also serious domestic threats to the respective regimes' survival. In the case of Yemen, it was the military intervention by the Saudi-led coalition that drew the Houthis—who are Zaidi Shias, not Twelvers—and Iran together. The series of setbacks chalked up by Riyadh in foreign policy have contrasted with the smooth run enjoyed so far by Bin Salman in reforming the socio-cultural lives of Saudi citizens.

Bin Salman Shines at Home

At the time of the unveiling of his Vision 2030 blueprint in April 2016, Bin Salman backed the Kingdom's ban on women driving. He claimed that "the Saudi community" was "not convinced about women driving". He argued that "Women driving is not a religious issue as much as it is an issue that relates to the community itself that either accepts it or refuses it." He offered no evidence—such as an opinion survey of all Saudis, male and female—to support his statement.[7] But around the same time, depriving the feared religious police, the mutawwa, of their power to arrest had proved very popular, particularly among the young. In September 2017, at Bin Salman's behest, King Salman issued a decree to lift the ban, effective nine months later.[8]

There was, however, no overt sign of any change of opinion on this issue by the country's highest religious and legal authority Grand Mufti Shaikh Abdul Aziz bin Abdullah Al Shaikh. "Allowing women to drive could open the floodgates that would not be controllable," he said. "Allowing them to drive could also mean women could leave their houses alone and go to places without the knowledge of their families, and this could of course imply several evils."[9] The blind, bearded, seventy-five-year-old Grand Mufti seemed too coy to say openly that a woman driving off on her own would be free to have extra-marital sex. Actually, his predecessor, Grand Mufti Abdul Aziz bin Abdullah bin Baz, had said in his "Ruling on Females driving cars," that "Allowing women to drive contributes to the downfall of society" by encouraging mixing of the sexes and "adultery, which is the main reason for the prohibition of these practices." His fatwa was recorded on the official fatwas website, www.alifta.com.[10] The stress is basically on discouraging adultery which, in the opinion of these ulema, occurs when unrelated men and women mix socially.

Anticipating opposition from diehard Wahhabi ulema, Bin Salman carried out "a pre-emptive strike," in the words of an unnamed cleric recorded during his phone interview with the *New York Times* in early November. "All those who thought about saying no to the government got arrested."[11] It was unclear what the grounds for these arrests were. But then again arbitrariness was an integral part of an absolute monarchy. "It's not like they held a referendum and said, 'Do you want to go this way or that way?'" added the same unnamed cleric.[12]

CONCLUSIONS

In his interview with Thomas Friedman of the *New York Times*, the Crown Prince referred to the time of Prophet Muhammad when music was performed and the genders mixed freely. "The first commercial judge in Medina was a woman."[13] Being on such solid ground, he could have chosen to debate the issue with a non-establishment, hard line cleric on television to make his case in public.

Unlike in Iran, where Shia grand ayatollahs have an independent economic financial source of income, resulting from receiving one-fifth of the trading profits from their followers, clerics in a Sunni state, such as Saudi Arabia, depend on the state for their livelihood. Given this tradition, it was no surprise that the official Council of Senior Ulema in Saudi Arabia had become a handmaiden of the monarchy. It had been virtually divested of having any input in the defence and national security policies of the realm, or even expressing doubts on the official stance. Now it was being deprived of its right to have a say in socio-cultural matters. It had no choice but to acquiesce. In the past it had repeatedly declared that opposing the ruler amounted to *fitna*, sedition, which was illegitimate in Islam.

All told, the recent socio-cultural changes in the Saudi Kingdom could not be interpreted as the Saudi version of the Arab Spring. Millions of ordinary Arabs mounted non-violent demonstrations for political and civil rights in early 2011, an unprecedented phenomenon. In the case of Bin Salman, however, liberalisation of the social order went hand in hand with the curtailing of civil and human rights as illustrated by his wholesale detention of Wahhabi clerics likely to disagree with him. Earlier, he had used an iron hand to crush the last remnant of any resistance by Saudi Shias in the Eastern Province. He had shown himself to be fiercely intolerant of criticism, direct or oblique.

Also, his all-consuming hatred of Iran blinded him to certain egregious events in the Kingdom. In his interview with the *Guardian* in late October 2017, Bin Salman blamed the 1979 Islamic Revolution in Iran for the ultra-conservative mould of the Saudi state and society.[14] This showed his lack of grasp of the recent history of his own country. The key reason for the adoption of hard line conservatism was the seizure of the Grand Mosque in Mecca on Islamic New Year of 1400—20 November 1979. It was the most serious domestic ideological challenge to the Saudi monarchy in its history. As explained above,[15] having crushed the armed rebellion, the Saudi government considered it politic to examine the criticisms leveled at it by Juheiman al Utaiba, most of which were subtly endorsed by Grand Mufti Abdul Aziz bin Abdullah bin Baz. It also noted the widely held public view that Allah had intervened on the first day of Islamic Year 1400 to end the un-Islamic proliferation of photographs of human beings in the Kingdom.[16]

In his eagerness to paint himself in Churchillian colors, Bin Salman called Ayatollah Ali Khamanei the "New Hitler", vowing not to appease expansionist Iran, but to confront it.[17] It was ironic to find a crown prince invested with unfettered, hereditary power calling the supreme leader of the Islamic Republic, chosen for an eight-year term by the popularly elected Assembly of Experts.

Before upping the ante in the current Cold War with Iran further, Bin Salman would be well advised to refashion the social and economic profile of the Kingdom as envisaged in his Vision 2030 unveiled in April 2016. It includes plans to sell shares in Saudi Aramco to create the world's largest sovereign wealth fund. A year-and-a-half later, Bin Salman, as chairman of the Public Investment Fund (PIF), announced plans to build a $500 billion mega city, Neom—measuring 26,500 sq km, on Saudi Arabia's Red Sea coast, adjoining Jordan and Egypt—by 2025. Focusing on energy and water, biotechnology, food, advanced manufacturing and entertainment, it will be a city of robots and renewables.[18] The Kingdom's PIF was trying to entice foreign corporations to invest in its mega projects. However, implementing these overambitious plans *and* raising the temperature in the Cold War with Iran are mutually exclusive objectives. Even the slightest hint of any further deterioration in Riyadh-Tehran relations will scare foreign investors who are currently ambivalent about making large investments in the Desert Kingdom.

As for Bin Salman the person, the thirty-two-year-old Crown Prince about to ascend the throne is set to rule for five decades, barring assassination or a fatal accident. As such, the current level of hostility between the two Islamic heavyweights—the Saudi Kingdom and the Islamic Republic of Iran—is unlikely to be moderated in the near future.

16

EPILOGUE

The testimonies given to *New York Times* correspondents by more than a dozen of those detained in Riyadh as part of the anti-corruption drive in early November 2017 as well as their family members provide a reliable and coherent narrative of a most extraordinary event in Saudi history.

A Hyped Anti-Graft Strike: An Unvarnished Account

Most of those arrested ended up as nominal "guests" of the swanky Riyadh Ritz Carlton Hotel at the end of a meticulously executed secret plan. Some were invited to a dinner hosted by King Salman; and others were summoned for a meeting with Crown Prince Muhammad bin Salman. The less fortunate were handcuffed in their homes and led like criminals to vehicles waiting outside.

Each detainee had an armed guard posted outside the open door of his room. He had access to TV but not to the Internet or his phones. More disturbingly, he was barred from calling his lawyers while he was held incommunicado for several days. Later he was permitted to reassure his family through short, monitored phone calls. His room was stripped of curtain cords and glass shower doors to prevent any attempt to commit suicide. Since many of those detained were overweight or had health problems, a doctor was drafted in. And, soon after, a tailor arrived to take their measurements for new clothes.

The alleged wrongdoings by the detainees included paying and accepting kickbacks, inflating government contracts, extortion and bribery. Armed with files, Royal Court officials pointed out the assets they had allegedly stolen from the government. Handicapped by the absence of his lawyers, the accused was unable to defend himself properly or negotiate freely. "It is just like playing Monopoly with a bunch of guys," explained Jamal Khashoggi, a self-exiled Saudi journalist. "But you are in charge of everything, you can change the rules,and everyone has to stay at the table and play with you."[1]

The case of Prince Alwaleed bin Talal, with a net worth of $17.4 billion, including shares in Apple, Twitter, and Newscorp, whose arrest shocked international business circles, provided eye-opening details. At a pre-dawn hour on 4 November, when he was asleep at a desert camp, he was summoned by the Royal Court to see the monarch. On his return to his mansion in Riyadh, his guards were dismissed and his phones were taken from him. He was driven to the Ritz Carlton Hotel. A Saudi official told Reuters that the allegations against Bin Talal included money laundering, bribery and extorting officials.[2]

As the day unrolled, similar calls to see King Salman or the Crown Prince lured in scores of Saudi personalities. They included some of the Kingdom's wealthiest and most powerful men—such as Prince Mutaib bin Abdullah; Khalid al-Tuwaijri, a former head of the Royal Court; Bakr Bin Laden, chairman of the construction behemoth Saudi Binladin Group; and Fawaz Alhokair, who owned the country's franchises of Zara, the Gap, and dozens of other stores. Their relatives panicked while the managers of their far-flung businesses drew up contingency plans to keep operations running, unsure of how long their bosses would be away.

When the BBC reported that Bin Talal had been kept in a prison-like cell outside the hotel and mistreated, Bin Salman's office arranged for the Reuters bureau in Riyadh to videotape an interview with him. Its reporter Katie Paul did so on 27 January in the prince's "office" in his luxury suite. Looking thinner and sporting a scruffy salt-and-pepper beard, he pointed out his dining room and held up a Diet Pepsi before taking a sip. "I'm very comfortable because I'm in my country," he said, rather self-consciously. "I'm in my city, so I feel at home. It's no problem at all. Everything's fine." He claimed that his detention had been a "misunderstanding" that would be cleared up soon. "Rest assured this is a clean operation that we have and we're just in discussion with the government on various matters that I cannot divulge right now. But rest assured, we are at the end of the whole story." So it was. A few hours later he was set free. He returned to his mansion in Riyadh only to find it placed under armed guard. By and large he remained silent on what really happened to him at Ritz Carlton. "It is something he wants to forget," one associate said. Nonetheless, it was widely believed that to gain his freedom he handed over a fair share of his vast fortune to the state.[3]

During their detention, many were subjected to coercion. And a lesser number were deprived of sleep, roughed up and interrogated with their heads covered while their interrogators pressured them to sign over large assets. The aggregate sum thus collected from 326 detainees, according to the Public Prosecutor, Shaikh Saud al Mojeb, would amount to $106.6 billion, and include real estate, company shares, cash and other assets. At least seventeen detainees were hospitalized as a consequence of physical abuse. One of them, Major-General Ali al Qahtani, a sixty-year-old National Guard officer, died. Those who saw his corpse said that his neck was twisted in a way that indicated it had been broken, and that his body was badly bruised and distended, showing signs inter alia of burn marks resulting from electric shocks. His value to the interrogators lay in the fact that he was a top aide to Prince Turki bin Abdullah, a former governor of Riyadh, and that he could provide damaging information about a son of a former monarch, Abdullah bin Abdul Aziz. Members of the Qahtani and Abdullah families were afraid to discuss Qahtani's death publicly for fear of further retribution.[4]

Their fear was justified. The released detainees were forced to wear ankle bracelets so that their movements could be traced. Their mansions were guarded by soldiers over whom they had no control. The ban on their travel extended to their wives and children. They were also denied access to their bank accounts. An unnamed former detainee sank into depression as his business collapsed. "He signed away everything, even the house he is in," a family member of his told the New York Times.[5]

Bin Salman's Multiple Motives

The most wide-ranging repressive move against the high and mighty was presented by Saudi officials as a concerted drive to root out graft. This was only partly true. King Salman and the Crown Prince had multiple motives to do what they did in a baneful strike planned and executed with military precision.

One of the primary reasons was to settle once and for all a family feud, to eliminate a rival power center, and squash any chance of the descendants of former King Abdullah ascending the throne. King Salman had moved swiftly to dismiss Prince Mishaal bin Abdullah and Prince Turki bin Abdullah, the respective governors of Mecca and Riyadh. That had left Prince Mutaib bin Abdullah as the commander of the National Guard. Unsurprisingly, he found himself locked up inside the Ritz Carlton. His ordeal lasted a little over three weeks. After his release, a Saudi official said that Prince Mutaib had reached "an acceptable settlement agreement". The undisclosed amount he had paid was believed to be equivalent of more than $1 billion. The accusations against him included embezzlement, hiring non-existent employees, and awarding contracts to his own firms, including a $10 billion deal for walkie-talkies and bulletproof military gear for the National Guard.[6]

Another primary aim was to reshuffle radically the main actors in the economy in order to secure the lead role for Bin Salman. That explained the arrest of Bakr bin Laden, chairman of a mega construction corporation, Saudi Binladin Group, with 100,000 employees and an annual turnover of $30 billion, along with several family members. After detaining five of the Bin Laden brothers, who led the company, the government seized effective control of its board by forcing them to transfer a substantial part of their holdings to the state in a settlement with the Public Prosecutor. They were released on 14 January, and instructed to report to a government-appointed committee.[7]

And still; another motive behind Bin Salman's action was to monopolize the broadcasting media, dominated by Middle East Broadcasting Center (MBC), owned largely by its chairman Waleed al Ibrahim, and based in Dubai. It was the largest free-to-air Arab TV network with several channels, and had 50 percent market share in Saudi Arabia and an audience of 140 million in the Arab world. While

MBC was not very profitable, its extensive network enabled it to sway Arab public opinion.

In 2015 Prince Bin Salman sought to buy MBC. Ibrahim demanded $3 to $3.5 billion whereas the Crown Prince put the cap at $2.5 billion. When negotiations bogged down, Bin Salman hired the accounting firm PwC UK and the law firm Clifford Chance to draft a sales document. In October 2017 a team of PwC UK accountants arrived at MBC's head office to vet the company's books. This seemed to be a sign of progress. So when a confidante of Bin Salman invited Ibrahim to Riyadh at the end of that month, the MBC chairman assumed that a final deal was in the offing. He arrived in the Saudi capital in his private jet only to find that his meeting with the Crown Prince had been cancelled. When he tried to return to Dubai the officials at the airport informed him that his aircraft was grounded and that commercial flights to Dubai were unavailable. On 5 November, however, Ibrahim's meeting with Bin Salman was reconfirmed. But instead of closing the deal, Ibrahim found himself locked up inside the world's most luxurious prison. This was also the fate of most of the other MBC shareholders and board members.

At his TV network, Ibrahim was an effective buffer against interference by Saudi government because of his filial links to the ruling family. His sister, Jawhara, was married to King Fahd. As a result, when he set up MBC in 1991, in London, he received state loans from the Kingdom. After he moved the MBC base from London to Dubai in 2002, it took off. Later his nephew Prince Abdul Aziz bin Fahd became a shareholder in MBC. But in the anti-corruption sweep up this did not help Ibrahim because Prince Abdul Aziz too was detained.

Though Ibrahim was released on 26 January he did not fly back to Dubai. In Riyadh MBC representatives conferred with Clifford Chance's lawyers to finalize an agreement to reduce Ibrahim's share in the company to only 40 percent—as a prelude to removing him as a director.[8] Thus MBC was set to follow the fate of the Saudi Binladin Group which was taken over by the state.

With the meteoric rise of Bin Salman, which caused disaffection among many senior princes, the intelligence agencies were put on high alert. Stark evidence of their efficacy came on 4 January when security services arrested eleven princes after their refusal to leave the historic

Qasr Al Hokm palace in old Riyadh. They were held at Al Hair maximum security prison pending their trial. They had gathered at this palace allegedly to object to a decree which ordered the government to stop paying the electricity and water bills of princes. A few days later, in his voice message on Whatsapp, Prince Abdullah bin Saud questioned the authenticity of the charges against the detained princes, arguing that all of them had "great financial capabilities, far from concerns and financial problems, and were raised by their fathers to be obedient" to the monarch. He explained that when the princes had arrived at the old palace they were barred from entering by the guards in a provocative manner, and that some of them were "overcome by the excitement of youth," leading to fistfights. Prince Abdullah ended his message with praise of the leadership of King Salman and the Crown Prince, and criticized "the attempts of some to create division and schism within the royal family." When his voice message went viral, he was removed as head of the Maritime Sports Federation, a decision made by the General Sport Authority Chairman Turki Al Shaikh.[9]

The final details of the anti-graft drive were announced by Mojeb on 29 January. Of the 381 people detained at Ritz Carlton, fifty-five were witnesses. Of the rest, all but fifty-six were released after being cleared completely or surrendering significant assets to the government. Those with unsettled cases chose to defend themselves in court along with their lawyers. They were transferred to prison cells.[10] Forming 17 percent of the detainees, they were four times as numerous as the 4 percent of the total mentioned by Bin Salman in his interview with Thomas Friedman of the *New York Times* two months earlier.[11]

Bin Salman's admirers attributed the ant-corruption campaign to his attempt to appease ordinary Saudis citizens who were bearing the brunt of austerity measures, and paying a 100 percent tax on tobacco products and energy drinks, and a 50 percent tax on soft drinks since mid-2017. They had resorted to complaining privately and on social media that there was no corresponding curtailment of the privileges enjoyed by royals. There was little doubt that the government's move against the rich and mighty was warmly received by the common man although, in the absence of public opinion surveys, the approval rate could not be quantified.

On the other hand, the government's ad hoc strategy in the crackdown damaged confidence in the governance system that the private sector had. It was unlikely to be restored in the near future. While it was refreshing to see the state at last holding the elites to the rule of law, it was counterproductive to use coercive, potentially illegal, methods to apply the hurriedly enacted law.

All in all, in his relentless drive to monopolize power—political, security forces, intelligence, economic, and media—Bin Salman was transforming the royal family's authoritarian regime into a totalitarian one.

Yet the Western states were at best muted in their disapproval of Bin Salman's governance style. They were keen to maintain cordial relations with the heir apparent poised to ascend the throne. Among Western leaders, US President Donald Trump was an enthusiastic backer of the Crown Prince.

Given Bin Salman's visceral hatred of Iran, it was not surprising that Trump lent his support to the protests that erupted suddenly in the Islamic Republic on 28 December 2017.

Unrest in Iran, Rooted in Distorted Economy

In a series of tweets, Trump called on the Iranian government to "respect people's rights", allow them free expression, cease restricting the Internet and social media, warning it that "the world is watching" and that it was "time for a change". On 3 January, he capped these statements with a pledge of support for the Iranians attempting to "take back" their government. "You will see great support from the United States at the appropriate time!" he said sweepingly.[12]

Trump's aggressive intervention in the Iranian protest contrasted with the measured response of the major European states. In separate statements they called on the Tehran government to permit peaceful protests and refrain from carrying out mass arrests. They resisted Trump's pressure to sign a joint statement with the United States to condemn Iran.[13] Trump's pathological hatred of Iran and Iranians was so widely known in the Islamic Republic that his rapid-fire pro-protest tweets provided ammunition to the regime to claim that the protesting demonstrators were acting as agents of foreign government.

The reality was that economic grievances of the working and lower middle classes, rooted in high inflation and lack of jobs, had been building up for some years. Over the past six months the authorities had allowed Iran's currency, the rial, to depreciate; and that fueled inflation of such basic necessities as eggs by 40 percent. The trigger for the street protest was the publication of the draft budget for the financial year starting on 21 March 2018. It was widely debated on Telegram, the country's most used social media outlet. Among other things the budget proposed ending the monthly cash subsidy of $12 each for 30 million people and raising fuel prices by 50 percent. In sharp contrast was the proposed allocation of $15 million to the grandson of Ayatollah Ruhollah Khomeini, the founder of the Republic, to publish his grandfather's works.[14]

The protest started on 28 December in Mashhad, a city of two million which was a bastion of hardliners. Several hundreds gathered to denounce recent price hikes, the poor state of the economy, the widening inequality, and corruption. Within days, aided by the social media, protest demonstrations took place in many provincial towns as well as Tehran. These turned increasingly political, with demonstrators shouting such anti government slogans as "Free political prisoners," and "Care for us and leave Palestine."

At first, Iranian President Hassan Rouhani was unfazed. On 31 December he said that "the people are completely free to make criticism and even protest," and coupled it with a warning against creating chaos in the process.[15] But the protest movement had acquired a momentum of its own, spreading to eighty cites and towns. It gave the ideological opponents of the regime a chance to advance their agenda. In the words of Eshaq Jahangiri, the First Vice-President, "The ones who trigger political moves in the streets may not be the ones who will put an end to it, since others may ride the wave they have started, and they must know that their action will backfire on them."[16]

The government put restrictions on Instagram, one of the social media tools deployed to mobilize protesters, and Telegram used by an estimated 40 million Iranians. But when the protest movement did not subside, it implemented a two-track strategy it had turned to previously: deploy the troops of the Islamic Republican Guard Corps (IRGC) as well as the ranks of the Baseej militia, and organize pro-regime demonstrations. It dispatched IRGC units to provinces most affected by unrest. By 7 January, the residents in various urban centers contacted by Reuters said that street protest had subsided.[17] What set this bout of protest apart from the one in mid-2009 in the wake of a rigged presidential poll—called the Green Movement—was that it was spontaneous and scattered, and lacked central leadership.

To hammer home the regime's overall popularity, the state-run television showed pro-government rallies in Ahvaz, the capital of the south-western province of Khuzestan, Ilam in the west, and in the central Iranian cities of Arak and Shahr-e Kord, with hundreds of people in Shahr-e Kord clutching umbrellas in heavy snowfall, shouting "Death to America", "Death to Israel", and "Death to seditionists."They had taken their cue from the Supreme Leader Ayatollah Ali Khamanei's claim that "All those who are at odds with the Islamic Republic have utilized various means, including money, weapons, politics and intelligence apparatuses, to create problems for the Islamic system, the Islamic Republic and the Islamic Revolution."[18]

On 7 January IRGC Commander Muhammad Ali Jafari announced "the end of the sedition".The violent clashes between protesting demonstrators and security forces claimed twenty-two lives—mainly protesters, and the rest security guards. Most of the 1,000 people arrested were released while the leaders of the unrest were locked up by the judiciary.The authorities lifted restrictions on Instagram. But security officials and lawmakers decided that access to Telegram would remain restricted until the messaging service agreed to ban "hostile, anti-Iranian channels promoting unrest." Many Iranians accessed Telegram by using virtual private networks and other tools to bypass government filtering of the Internet.[19]

In the cold light of the restored normalcy, the government realized that it had failed to address the rickety performance of the financial institutions which had impoverished many investors. Khamanei would go on to acknowledge responsibility for the growing number of victims of these entities, and state that "These appeals must be dealt with and heard out. I myself am responsible; and all of us must follow this approach."[20]

However, the root cause of the malaise was the distortion of the economy caused by the long war with Iraq and decades of sanctions of varying severity. Religious foundations headed by senior most clerics, the IRGC, the military and the police had emerged as big players in the economy of the country of 80 million whose GDP ranked twenty-seventh in the world.

After the 1979 Islamic Revolution, the regime nationalized banks along with several other industries. It also established a clutch of quasi-official holding companies under the Supreme Leader, topmost clerics, or high-ranking military commanders. Over the next few decades many of these economic entities evolved into sprawling conglomerates with a substantial presence in the private sector. This happened because of the favorable access to capital, tax exemptions, and political connections they enjoyed. The largest of these controlled by the Supreme Leader was estimated to constitute 15 to 20 percent of the economy, with the IRGC accounting for about a third of the total.[21] (According to the Washington-based Foundation for Defense of Democracies, the IRGC controlled 20 to 40 percent of the economy through significant stake in 229 companies.) The state's favorable treatment made these holding companies vulnerable to mismanagement and inefficiency as well as insider dealings and other forms of corruption.

Following the Iran-Iraq War in the 1980s, the government permitted the IRGC to enter the private sector. It set up a construction company called Khatam Al Anbia (Arabic: Seal of the Prophet). It built roads and ports, and became involved in defense industry. During the second administration of US President Barack Obama, as a result of the US-led sanctions on the Islamic Republic because of its controversial nuclear program, Iran found itself cut off from international credit. With foreign firms leaving and foreign banks unwilling to finance trade or investment in Iran, the government turned to the IRGC to keep the economy afloat. The IRGC took over the oil projects from such foreign companies as Royal Dutch Shell, managed to sell petroleum to some willing countries and, deploying complex means, channelled sorely-needed hard currencies into Iran The IRGC also acquired the task of running the telecommunication networks. As a result Khatam Al Anbia's workforce shot up to 135,000 people.[22]

During the presidency of the reformist Muhammad Khatami, the government opened up the banking sector, and let religious foundations establish loosely regulated savings and loans entities to serve the poor. Its next move was to allow the creation of private banks and the partial sale of state bank shares.

The vastly expanded financial sector sharpened competition, and encouraged some to gamble with depositors' funds or run Ponzi schemes. Such activities went unchecked because the holding companies were led by religious foundations, the IRGC or other semiofficial investment funds of the state. Many of them funneled their funds into the ballooning property market, gave loans to influential friends, or extracted high interest rates from desperate borrowers. When the inevitable bursting of the real estate balloon followed, hundreds of thousands of depositors lost money. The regulators directed many of the failing companies into mergers with larger banks to try to absorb their losses. That in turn lumbered the banking sector with bad loans and overvalued assets. In December 2017 the International Monetary Fund (IMF) warned that Iran's banks and lenders needed urgent restructuring and recapitalization. It called for write-downs of overvalued assets and a stop on loans to insiders. The enormity of the problem was such that the cash needed to prop up banks would lead to a substantial hike in public debt, it stated.[23]

With the implementation of Iran's nuclear deal with six world powers in January 2016, and the ending of EU sanctions, there was a spurt in Iran-EU trade. This reduced the need for the government to rely on the IRGC for economic reasons, and strengthened the hands of Rouhani. In July 2017, it was announced that the government had decided to reduce Khatam al Anbiya's annual budget and that in future it would have to compete with private contractors. Three months later it failed to win two major oil and shipping projects because its bids were higher than those from the competing French and South Korean companies.[24]

To reduce the power and privilege that the IRGC had acquired over decades, Rouhani sought and gained the support of Khamanei who was concerned about the prevailing corruption. He upbraided officials for letting corruption grow at all levels of the political system, and instructed the executive authority to approach foreign countries for investments and new enterprises. This was the background to the IRGC's intelligence agency's arrest of several former IRGC officers on suspicion of corruption during the summer of 2017.[25]

Three weeks after the first street protest in Mashhad, Defense Minister General Amir Hatami told the state-run English daily newspaper *Iran* that Ayatollah Khamanei had ordered the regular military and the IRGC to withdraw from businesses not directly affiliated to their duties. This raised the possibility that these institutions privatizing some of their vast holdings. Hatami added that starting this process would depend on "market conditions.[26] This seemed to be a trial balloon partly to placate Rouhani who had been advocating this approach before the unrest without much success.

Iran's Proxy Wars

Iran remained fully engaged in the wars in Syria and Yemen though its proxies. Advisers from the IRGC's Al Quds force were posted at Syria's military bases, with their commanders arriving at the front lines to lead battles. In general Al Quds officers worked as trainers or overseers of various militias, whose ranks in early 2018 numbered 20,000, including 6,000 from Hizbollah. Tehran continued to supply advanced, high-precision missiles to Hizbollah over land to target Israel's sensitive infrastructure. Israel hit the Iranian convoys almost every month. In order to avoid such strikes, Iran resorted to using some ostensibly humanitarian aid shipments to supply arms to Hizbollah. Overall, the Islamic Republic and its allies followed a dual track strategy: to consolidate a land corridor from Iran to the Mediterranean through Iraq, Syria and Lebanon; and to construct underground works in Syria and southern Lebanon to produce high precision missiles. Referring to the threat posed by such weapons and the opening of a new Israeli front along southern Syria, Yaakov Amidror, a former national security adviser of Israel, said "Each one is problematic; together, they are devastating."[27]

Iran also introduced such new technologies in Syria as drones for surveillance and even to attack the enemy. When an Iranian drone flew into Israeli airspace in early February 2018, the resulting flare-up ended quickly, with the drone destroyed and an Israeli jet downed after bombing sites in Syria on 10 February.[28]

Iranian leaders made no secret of their plan to reinforce the axis of resistance against Israel and America. By forging links with local forces that shared their goals and received their funds and expertise, they enhanced their influence in the Arab world while lessoning the threat to their own forces and territory. Unsurprisingly, this caused much anxiety in America, Israel and Saudi Arabia, who failed to devise an overarching strategy to counter it.

Yet there was an altogether different rationale driving Tehran's policy. This was articulated by Iraqi Prime Minister Haider al Abadi in his interview with the *Independent* in October 2017. "The Iranians are under the impression that others want to topple them and this is understandable," he said. "To protect themselves they have to fight outside their borders."[29] The Iranians pursued their strategy through proxies and an adroit manipulation of local forces.

The need to exercise their manipulative skills arose in the aftermath of the parliamentary poll in Iraq in May 2018. The strength of the State of the Law coalition, led by Nouri al Maliki, the

bête noire of Saudi royals, plummeted from 92 in the previous election to 25. The freshly created Fatah (Arabic: Victory) Alliance led by pro-Tehran Hadi al Amiri garnered 47, second only to the Muqtada al Sadr-led Sairoon (Arabic: On the Move) Alliance of the Sadrist Movement and the Communist Party at 54, up from 34 won previously by the Sadrist Movement on its own. The third in size at 42 was Al Nasr (Arabic: Victory) Alliance led by Prime Minister Abadi. The two Kurdish parties between them garnered 43 seats. The emergence of the alliance headed by Sadr as the largest group was a surprise to all, and a setback for Iran. As a fiery cleric, Sadr had violently resisted US occupation of Iraq after the 2003 war. More recently, by objecting to Iran's interference in his country's internal affairs, he underscored his Iraqi nationalism. He had also been the foremost critic of the prevalent, rampant corruption. In February 2018, as he contemplated forging an alliance with the Communist Party on a platform of a graft-free governance system and non-interference in Iraq's domestic affairs by outsiders, a warning was issued by Ali Akbar Velayati, the leading foreign policy adviser to Khamanei. "We will not allow liberals and Communists to govern in Iraq," he declared in a speech in Iraq.[30] A son of a Grand Ayatollah, Muqtada was hardly a liberal. This blatant interference by Iran, verging on arrogance, proved counterproductive. And yet though the leader of the Sairoon Alliance in Parliament was to be invited by the President to form the government, his chances of cobbling together a coalition supported by the required majority of 165 MPs were slim. The President's second choice was bound to be Amiri. Since the Kurdish parties had been friendly with Iran for several decades, he had a better chance of co-opting them in his proposed coalition, particularly if he agreed to let Abadi—acceptable to the Washington-Riyadh axis—remain the prime minister.

In war-torn Yemen it was bullet, nor ballot, that shaped the hapless country's fate. Following the assassination of Ali Abdullah Saleh on 4 December 2017, Houthi leaders consolidated their grip over the territory they had held in alliance with Saleh. It included the port of Hodeidah which was the main entry point for the imports of food, medicine and fuel. Yemenis were dependent on all of their fuel and medicine and 90 percent of their food on foreign supplies. Therefore blockading of the Hodeidah port by the Saudi-led coalition from 6 November onwards was viewed by many observers as tantamount to using starvation as a tactic of war. This led to an international outcry. Riyadh relented in the third week of December. On 27 December the Saudis claimed that five vessels carrying fuel had entered Hodeidah and that coalition forces had given ten permits to transfer humanitarian aid to Yemen through land crossings. However, much of the goodwill thus earned by Riyadh was lost when it emerged that on that very day two air raids by the anti-Houth coalition had killed 68 civilians. The first struck a crowded market in Taiz province, killing 54 civilians, including eight children, and the second in the province of Hodeidah, taking a toll of 14 lives.[31]

Soon thereafter, the Aden-based government of President Abd Rabbu Mansour Hadi (in self-exile in Riyadh) faced pressing financial and political challenges. Its Central Bank struggled to pay public sector salaries because of dwindling foreign exchange reserves. Prime Minister Ahmed Obeid bin Daghr appealed for help. King Salman ordered the Saudi Arabian Monetary Authority to deposit $2 billion in the Yemeni Central Bank. This allowed Daghr to present the first budget since 2014 on 21 January stating that it included salaries for the military and civilians in twelve out of twenty-one provinces.[32]

But five of the twelve provinces were under the control of the competing Southern Transitional Council (STC) led by Maj.-Gen. Aidrus Zubaidi. He had been sacked as the governor of Aden by Hadi in April 2017 for being loyal to the secessionist Southern Movement which wanted to undo the 1990 unification of North and South Yemen. On 26 December, the Southern National Assembly of 303 members, meeting in Aden, called on the Daghr cabinet to step down. When it refused to do so, the STC declared on 21 January that it would overthrow the Hadi-Daghr government within a week. In the subsequent fighting from 28 to 30 January, the STC captured all of Aden, and kept Daghr captive in the presidential palace. While the Houthis rejoiced at the turn of the events, alarm bells rang in Riyadh. The Saudi-led coalition mediated a quick settlement between the rivals on terms that were not disclosed. The STC turned over Aden to the Hadi government during the next week.[33] On 16 February the STC allowed Daghr to fly to Riyadh to join Hadi in exile. By then Yemen had fractured into three mini-states and several enclaves of the terrorist Al Qaida in Arabian Peninsula—not to mention hardline Saleh loyalists in his elite Republican Guards who would form the core of the National Resistance Council led by the former president's nephew, Brigadier-General Tariq Saleh.

Among foreign officials who monitored the situation closely, the UN envoy Ismail Ould Cheikh Ahmed was the most important. In his briefing to the UN Security Council on 27 February, he put the blame for the failure of the latest round of peace on the Houthis' unwillingness to make concessions on the proposed security arrangements. A day earlier Russia vetoed a British-sponsored resolution at the Council that condemned Iran for violating the arms embargo on Yemen, and demanded additional measures against Tehran. Immediately afterward, the Council unanimously adopted the Russian-drafted resolution on a rollover of the Yemen sanctions regime for one year. The sanctions included an asset freeze against designated individuals and entities and a travel ban.[34]

With the Yemen civil war showing no sign of de-escalation, and the chances of political settlement looking bleak, the patience of US lawmakers was wearing thin. In a rare move Senators attempted to invoke the 1973 War Powers Act. It called on Trump to withdraw any US troops in Yemen, or affecting Yemen, within thirty days. The Senate majority leader, Republican Mitch McConnell, argued that invoking of the War Powers Act was misconceived because Washington's support to the Saudi-led coalition did not involve introduction of US forces. The Pentagon did nothing more than provide targeted intelligence to the coalition's bombing campaign and assist with refueling its bombers in air. On the other side, Senator Bernie Sanders, a leading contender for Democratic nomination for President in 2016, said, "The Constitution is clear; the US Congress decides whether we go to war. There is no question in my mind that by aiding Saudi Arabia the way we are doing that we are assisting in war." By a vote of 55 to 44, the measure was referred back to the Senate Foreign Relations Committee for further debate.[35] By coincidence the debate took place on the 15th anniversary of the invasion of Iraq during the Presidency of George W. Bush.

What Senators did not know was that following the Houthis' firing of a modified Scud missile with a range of 600-plus miles at Riyadh International Airport on 4 November 2017, Crown Prince Bin Salman renewed his previous request that the White House dispatch troops to assist his forces combat the Houthi threat. In early December it became public knowledge that the Saudis' claim that their air defense personnel had shot down the incoming missile in mid-air with the US-supplied Patriot missile was false. A forensic analysis of the photos and videos of the strike posted to social media by a team of missile experts at the Middlebury Institute of International Studies showed that the missile's warhead flew unimpeded over Saudi defense batteries and that it exploded so near the airport's domestic terminal that the waiting travelers jumped out of their seats.[36]

Responding to Bin Salman's latest appeal, the Trump White House dispatched a team of US Army's commandos, Green Berets, to help locate and destroy caches of ballistic missiles and launch sites of Houthis. The Green Berets deployed US surveillance planes along the Saudi-Yemeni border to gather electronic signals to track the Houthi weapons and their launch sites.

This was a marked escalation of the Pentagon's assistance against the Houthis, who had conducted no operations outside Yemen, and who had not been classified as belonging to a terrorist organization by the State Department. In his testimony to the Senate Foreign Relations Committee on 17 April, Robert S. Karem, assistant secretary of defense for international security affairs, revealed that the US had about fifty military personnel in Saudi Arabia.[37]

To avenge the repeated killings of civilians by the Riyadh-led coalition, Houthis had intensified their ballistic missile attacks. In the first four months of 2018, they launched over thirty missiles—almost as many as in all of 2017—mainly against Saudi airports, military installations and oil infrastructure. Houthis had taken to assembling parts of missiles smuggled through ports along the western coast. The Saudis and the Americans needed to locate the sites where missiles were stored. This required large intelligence data which they lacked. Hitting the launch sites was even more difficult since mobile missile launchers were easily hidden inside culverts or beneath highway overpasses, and could be moved quickly from one location to another. To counter the threat effectively required a well-orchestrated system involving satellites, ground troops, and strike aircraft. That was not in the offing.[38]

Having failed to expel the Houthis from Sanaa, the military planners in the Saudi-led coalition focussed on retaking Houthi-held Hodeidah whose port was the main entry for the smuggled parts for ballistic missiles. Starting in early April, in a concerted move, the UAE-funded National Resistance Council forces along with the tribal fighters loyal to President Hadi launched an offensive along the western coast. Their steady progress brought them within ten miles of Hodeidah by the end of May. They planned to breach the road linking Hodeidah with Sanaa, and then besiege the port city. The Houthis' loss of Hodeidah could be the tipping point in the civil war, according to many defense experts. At the same time, Martin Griffiths, the UN special envoy for Yemen, finalizing his peace proposal after meeting with the leaders of all Yemeni factions, warned that a battle over Hodeidah would "take peace off the table".

The improved position of the Saudi-led coalition was noted by Tehran. Having resisted attempts by major EU states to engage Iran in talks about its involvement in Syria and Yemen, it made a concession. In his interview on the state-run TV channel, Iran's Deputy Foreign Minister, Seyed Abbas Araqchi, revealed in late May that "On humanitarian grounds and because of dire situations faced by the people of Yemen, we have entered talks with four European countries—France, the UK, Germany and Italy."[39]

However, there was no chance of Iran ceasing its arms supplies to Houthis through long-established circuitous logistical methods.

Bin Salman's Expensive Charm Offensive in the West

By contrast, open, legitimate sales of weapons by the United States to Saudi Arabia were highlighted by Trump at the Oval Office on 20 March with the Crown Prince Bin Salman sitting by his side.

Trump displayed a poster listing military aircraft, worth $12.5 billion, that his administration had agreed to sell to the Saudi Kingdom. "Saudi Arabia is a very wealthy nation," he said. "And they're going to give the United States some of that wealth hopefully, in the form of jobs, in the form of the purchase of the finest military equipment anywhere in the world." During their working lunch along with senior US officials, Bin Salman was advised to settle his dispute with Qatar, and minimize civilian casualties and human suffering in the Saudi-led coalition's war in Yemen.[40] His responses to this counsel were not reported by the White House spokesperson.

Earlier, during Bin Salman's visit to London in early March, the sale of British arms to Riyadh was the focal point of the protestors. The United Kingdom had sold £4.6 billion ($6.5 billion) worth of aircraft, helicopters, drones, grenades, bombs and missiles to the Saudi Kingdom since March 2015, according to the Campaign Against the Arms Trade.[41] Anticipating adverse publicity, the Saudi embassy in London mounted an expensive pro-Bin Salman campaign with a number of propaganda trucks driving around London displaying his image and promoting the hashtag #WelcomeSaudiCrownPrince, while digital billboards on the M4 highway from Heathrow airport carried the message—"He is bringing change to Saudi Arabia".[42] The British government treated him as the de facto ruler of his country, and arranged a lunch with Queen Elizabeth II. In his talks with the British Prime Minister Theresa May, he was keen to secure Britain's cyber expertise to help him tackle the cyber threat from Iran.[43]

Bin Salman's first foray into a Western country lasted three days while the details of his two-week long tour of America were being finalized by the Saudi Embassy in Washington. Working in conjunction with six public relations and lobbying firms, retained on an annual retainer of nearly $7 million,[44] it drew up an impressive list of American personalities the Crown Prince was scheduled to see in five cities as well as meetings with the editorial boards of the *New York Times*, *Wall Street Journal*, *Washington Post* and *Los Angeles Times*. After leaving Washington he discarded his traditional Saudi dress for a business suit with an open-neck shirt to stop looking exotic to Americans.

Saudi print and broadcasting media gave fulsome coverage to his tour of the US. Official reports wee issued by the Saudi embassy in

Washington and the state-run Saudi Press Agency (SPA). The embassy had the international audience in mind, and the SPA domestic. Their different approaches were captured by the way they reported the Crown Prince's meeting with religious leaders in New York, which included two rabbis. The embassy's English version mentioned this. But the SPA version in the Arabic version censored the names and affiliations of the participants, or that the meeting included rabbis. The SPA version was carried verbatim by the state-run Al Arabiya TV channel and several Saudi newspapers.[45] It was the Israeli newspaper *Haaretz* which, citing a leaked copy of Bin Salman's itinerary, reported that the Crown Prince was scheduled to meet on 30 March Jewish leaders from the pro-Israeli American Israel Public Affairs Committee, Conference of Presidents of American Jewish Organizations, Jewish Federations of North America, and America Jewish Committee.[46] The state-run Press TV of Iran highlighted this event.

During his meeting with editors and reporters of the *New York Times* on 27 March, Bin Salman said, "We know the target of Iran. If they have a nuclear weapon, it's a shield for them to let them do whatever they want in the Middle East, to make sure that no one attacks them or they will use their nuclear weapons."[47]

In his interview with the Crown Prince, published on 2 April, Jeffrey Goldberg of the *Atlantic* asked if he believed "the Jewish people have a right to a nation-state in at least part of their ancestral homeland" Bin Salman replied," I believe that each people anywhere has a right to live in their peaceful nation. I believe the Palestinians and the Israelis have the right to have their own land. But we have to have a peace agreement to assure the stability for everyone and to have normal relations." Referring to the interests that could bring Saudi Arabia and Israel closer, he noted that that cooperation against Iran was only one of them. Since Israel was a big economy compared to its size, and one that was growing, "there are a lot of interests we share with Israel and if there is peace, there would be a lot of interest between Israel and the Gulf Cooperation Council countries and countries like Egypt and Jordan." He repeated his sweeping broadside against Ayatollah Khamanei. "I believe the Iranian supreme leader makes Hitler look good. Hitler didn't do what the supreme leader is trying to do. Hitler tried to conquer Europe. The supreme leader is trying to conquer the world."[48]

To set the official record straight, according to the Saudi Press Agency, King Salman called Trump to restate "the Kingdom's steadfast position towards the Palestinian issue and the legitimate rights of the Palestinian people to an independent state with Jerusalem as its capital." Crucially, the monarch refrained from making any mention of Israel.[49]

To stress his commitment to Palestinians and to Jerusalem as a holy city to Muslims, Salman would describe the Arab League summit held on 15 April in Dhahran[50] as the "Al Quds" [Jerusalem] summit. Arab leaders criticized the White House's decision to recognize Jerusalem as Israel's capital and transfer the US embassy there from Tel Aviv. Significantly, on the eve of the summit, *Al Riyadh* newspaper, close to the Royal Court, published an editorial which argued that "the Arabs must realize that Iran is more dangerous to them than Israel," and that "The Arabs have no other option than reconciliation with Israel, signing a comprehensive peace agreement and freeing themselves up to tackle the Iranian project in the region."[51] It was most unlikely that the Dhahran resolution would spur any Arab government to action, least of all the one in Riyadh. Fixated on its anti-Iran campaign, it was resolved not to vex President Trump during the run-up to the deadline of 12 May when he had to decide whether to recertify that Iran was complying with its nuclear deal. Israel's intense lobbying of the White House to withhold recertifying had the backing of Saudi Arabia.

Regarding the Crown Prince's tour of America, which ended on 9 April, the official reason was, primarily, to attract US corporate investment in the Kingdom's infrastructure projects and, secondarily, to remake the image of Saudi Arabia among Americans. To this end, tens of millions of dollars from the Saudi treasury were spent. In New York all rooms at the luxury Plaza Hotel were taken to accommodate the Crown Prince Prince's entourage, consisting of a large contingent of security personnel, at an enormous cost. Later the Saudis took over the Four Seasons Hotel in Beverly Hills, Los Angeles, while Bin Salman stayed at a private mansion. The tariff at this five-star hotel, with 285 guest rooms and luxury suites, started at of $615 a night. The Saudi visitors also rented the entire Four Seasons Hotel in Palo Alto near the campuses of Google and Facebook.[52]

Throwing petro-dollars at American hotels was easy but altering the popular view of Saudi Arabia in the United States was a hard sell. This became clear on 29 March. On that day Judge George Daniels of the US District Court for the Southern District of New York ruled that there was a reasonable basis to allow legal action seeking billions of dollars in damages from the Kingdom by the families of nearly 3,000 killed and about 25,000 people injured in the 9/11 attacks. They and the affected businesses and insurers had filed twenty-five lawsuits against the Saudis in 2017.

Saudi Arabia argued that the plaintiffs could not show the Kingdom or any Saudi-affiliated charities were behind the attacks, and claimed sovereign immunity. In the opinion of Daniels, however, the Justice Against Sponsors of Terrorism Act (JASTA), enforced in September 2016, had narrowed the scope of the legal doctrine of foreign sovereign immunity.[53] With the case set to drag on for a few years, there was a slim chance of the ominous cloud over Saudi-American relations at the popular level disappearing.

Saudi royals, however, could take comfort in the fact that the negative image of Iran among Americans had become embedded. The arrival of Trump at the Oval Office had strengthened that view with the president casting the Islamic Republic in bad light at every opportunity.

In addition to effectively tearing up the Iran nuclear deal on 8 May, Trump announced the re-imposition of American sanctions in place before the landmark 2015 Iran denuclearization agreement,—officially called the Joint Comprehensive Plan of Action (JCPOA). These covered the Islamic Republic's energy, banking and other sectors, with a provision for penalizing foreign businesses worldwide trading with or investing in Iran. He did so in an eleven-minute TV address explaining his decision. It ignored several salient facts. Among these was the set of ten quarterly reports by the inspectors of the International Atomic Energy Agency (IAEA) that Iran was in compliance with the JCPOA. Another was the French foreign ministry's reaffirmation that "All activity linked to the development of a nuclear weapon is permanently forbidden by the [JCPOA] deal."[54] Altogether Trump's address contained ten such false or misleading statements as Iran is on the "cusp of acquiring the world's most dangerous weapons."[55]

Before his rash move on Iran, Trump had angered the 28-member European Union (EU) by refusing to grant it exemption from the tariffs he imposed on steel and aluminum imports in March. An American president is authorized to take such action to protect national security. EU officials argued that their bloc was an ally of the United States, with all EU members, except one (Sweden), being members of the 29-strong NATO led by Washington—but to no avail.

"We are witnessing today a new phenomenon: the capricious assertiveness of the American administration," said Donald Tusk, President of the European Council, on the eve of the EU summit in Sofia, Bulgaria, on 16 May. "Looking at the latest decisions of President Trump, some could even think, 'With friends like that, who needs enemies?'" After the summit Tusk announced that EU members agreed unanimously to stay in the agreement as long as Iran remains fully committed: "Additionally, the [European] Commission was given a green light to be ready to act whenever European interests are affected." Jean-Claude Juncker, president of the EU's executive arm, the European Commission, said that to protect EU companies doing business with Iran, he would turn to a plan last used to shield European businesses active in Cuba facing sanctions: "the 'blocking statute' process, which aims to neutralize the extraterritorial effects of US sanctions in the EU." He did so on 18 May. The 1996 statute prohibits EU companies and courts from complying with foreign sanctions laws and stipulates that foreign court verdicts based on these laws are null and void in the EU. Juncker added that the European Investment Bank will also provide a funding stream for businesses working in Iran.[56]

As it happened, on 16 May the National Iranian South Oil Company signed an agreement with London-based Pergas International Consortium to develop the Keranj field in the oil rich Khuzestan province over the next decade.[57]

The EU's split with Trump on the JCPOA was welcome news in Tehran. Unsurprisingly, therefore, in the wake of Trump's 8 May decision, Beijing was the first foreign capital visited by Iran's foreign minister Mohammad Javad Zarif along with top oil officials. After meeting with his counterpart, Wang Yi, both sides stated they would remain in the JCPOA.[58]

Given the military cooperation between Tehran and Moscow in Syria, there was no question of Russia opting out of the JCPOA. Indeed, actively assisted by Iran and Russia, Syrian President Assad recaptured the Eastern Ghouta region in rural Damascus, home to

400,000 people, on 14 April after a two-month long campaign, involving a suspected chemical attack on the enclave's main town of Douma.[59] In response to the Assad government's chemical attack on Douma on 7 April the US, France and Britain fired missiles at the alleged chemical weapons sites a week later.)

The news of the EU-US split on the JCPOA went down badly in Saudi Arabia, which had been buoyed by Trump's exit from the Iran deal. Earlier, it had noted warmly the appointment of John Bolton as Trump's National Security Adviser. Bolton's super-hawk stance against Tehran was aptly captured in the headline of his op-ed for the *New York Times* on 26 March 2015, "To Stop Iran's Bomb, Bomb Iran."[60] He went on describe the JCPOA as a "diplomatic Waterloo." The backing for his vehemently anti-Iran stance would come from Mike Pompeo who became the Secretary of State on 26 April.

The appointments of Bolton and Pompeo to high office in Washington won a hearty approval by Israel. During the week following Trump's tearing up of the JCPOA, Israel engaged in a feverish diplomatic activity centered round the unveiling of the US embassy in Jerusalem on 14 May 2018, the 70th anniversary of the founding of the State of Israel. The landmark event was attended by 800 guests, who included Trump's daughter, Ivanka, and her husband Jared Kushner. Most EU ambassadors stayed away. US officials mingled with their Israeli counterparts complimenting one another on their mutual devotion to peace and stability.

In stark contrast, fifty miles to the south of Jerusalem, Israeli soldiers killed sixty-two unarmed Palestinian protestors, and injured 2,400, along the double-fenced border with Gaza following the unofficial but widely discussed "mowing the lawn" policy of unrestrained force to crush those who backed Hamas. The massacre on 14 May—commemorating al Nakba (Arabic: Catastrophe), when 750,000 Palestinian were forced from their homes during the formation of Israel—brought the total of Palestinian deaths to 117 since the Great Return March launched on 30 March in pursuit of their right of return to their original homes.[61]

"Israeli regime massacres countless Palestinians in cold blood as they protest in world's largest open air prison," tweeted Iran's Foreign Minister Muhammad Javad Zarif. "Meanwhile, Trump celebrates move of US illegal embassy and his Arab collaborators move to divert attention. A day of great shame."[62]

There was little doubt that the unnamed "Arab collaborators" included Saudi Arabia. But irrespective of the earlier state of Riyadh-Washington relations during Trump's presidency, Saudi Arabia moved fast to uphold the Palestinian cause. It strongly condemned the massacre of unarmed Palestinians by Israeli forces. In addition, King Salman urged the Arab League secretary-general, Ahmed Abul Gheit, to convene an emergency meeting of Arab foreign ministers in Cairo. The session was chaired by Saudi Foreign Minister Adel al Jubeir, who said, "Our meeting today comes at a time of utmost importance as the US has moved its embassy to Jerusalem,"The Arab League demanded an international investigation into the "crimes" against the Palestinians committed crimes committed by Israel.[63]

International outrage was expressed at the special session of the 47-member UN human rights council in Geneva on 18 May. Its director-general, Zeid Ra'ad al Hussein, pointed out that many of the Palestinians injured and killed in the protests "were completely unarmed [and] were shot in the back, in the chest, in the head and limbs with live ammunition." By twenty-nine votes in favor and to two (America and Israel) opposed, the Council condemned "the disproportionate and indiscriminate use of force by the Israeli occupying forces against Palestinian civilians," and set up a commission of inquiry to produce a final report by March 2019.[64]

The first foreign capital that Mike Pompeo visited as Secretary of State was Riyadh.There he urged his counterpart, al Jubeir, the Crown Prince and the monarch to end their spat with Qatar. He did so at a time when Saudi Arabia was considering delineating its border with Qatar with a moat.[65] Pompeo's exhortation was a far cry from Trump describing Qatar as a financier of terrorists as alleged by Saudi Arabia and its allies in June. Since then Qatar had inked agreements with the US on sharing information on terrorists and terrorist financing. At the same time its ruler Tamim Al Thani expended millions of dollars to beef up his roster of lobbyists in Washington, and invite influential American power brokers to Doha. As a result he secured a meeting with the US President on 9 April when his host expressed strong support for his emirate.[66] Trump conveniently overlooked the fact that Qatar had developed strong ties with Iran in the aftermath of the Saudi-led embargo against it. That move was a prelude to regime change in Doha, according to the claim made by Emir Tamim in his interview with US broadcaster CBS in late October.[67]

The Trump administration came to view the unresolved Qatari crisis as a hurdle to devising a sharply anti-Iran policy by a unified Gulf Cooperation Council to be adopted at a GCC summit in Washington in April. Bin Salman along with his close ally, the UAE's Crown Prince Muhammad bin Zayed Al Nahyan let it be known that they would decline such an invitation because a pre-requisite for that meeting would have been an end to their Qatar embargo, which was tantamount to accepting defeat at the hands of Doha. For Bin Salman, facing failures in his foreign ventures in Yemen and Lebanon was one thing; but to accept the same fate in the case of a tiny neighbor would have been too much of humiliation.

However, a speech by Pompeo at the conservative Heritage Foundation in Washington on 21 May lifted the mood in Riyadh. He announced that the US would pile on additional punitive measures on Iran. And he listed twelve demands that the Islamic Republic must meet. It should give a full account of its alleged past work on nuclear weapons development; cease enriching uranium altogether, stop launches of nuclear-capable ballistic missiles; terminate its support for Hamas, Hizbollah and the Palestinian Islamic Jihad; pull out all forces under Iranian command from Syria; and stop supporting Houthis in Yemen.[68] In short, Iran should surrender the salient elements of sovereignty in order to satisfy the Trump administration. Seemingly, Pompeo failed to see that his demands were similar to the thirteen demands the Saudi-led alliance made of Qatar almost a year ago. It was ironic that having upbraided Saudi Arabia's top policy-makers for creating an unprecedented crisis in the GCC he was, inadvertently, following into their footsteps by making totally unrealistic demands of Tehran.

In the Kingdom's domestic scene, however, things were going well for Bin Salman in his drive to reform the polity's economic and social make-up. On 18 April, Saudi Arabia inaugurated its first cinema since 1980 with a private screening of *Black Panther*, set in a fictional African nation of Wakanda, in a converted concert hall in the capital. The movie was centered round a young royal who transforms a nation.[69] The parallel with Bin Salman was too apparent to be missed.

The select audience watched a version which had been subjected to strict Saudi censorship. It covered not just drugs and gambling but also any sort of intimacy and love between genders which were deemed to violate Islamic morals. Though censorship of movies was the norm in the Islamic Republic since its founding, its strictness was not as extreme as in the Saudi Kingdom.

Overall, though, there was much greater buzz in the Saudi air on a subject that affected half the population: women's right to drive. As 24 June, the date for ending the ban on women driving, approached, the dark side of Bin Salman's reformist campaign emerged. In a repeat of what had happened on 26 September 2017—they day the decision about women driving was announced—the authorities ordered female activists not to speak out in its favor. The two interpretations of this move were that the Crown Prince wanted to monopolize the credit for this liberalizing step, and that the government was wary of giving conservative ulema an opportunity to express their opposition in public. To leave nothing to chance, the authorities arrested eleven activists about a month before 24 June. All but two detainees were women and they had been in the vanguard for women's rights. However, four of them were released. The remaining seven had led a petition that the female guardianship system, which treated adult women as legal minors, be abolished.[70]

This ran counter to the fatwa issued by Saudi Grand Mufti Shaikh Abdul Aziz al Shaikh in September 2016. He ruled that removing the guardianship system would be a crime against Islam's teachings, and that recent tweets and hashtags calling for its abolition were "an evil call that goes against the Sharia and the instructions of the Prophet."[71]

The continued detentions of women's rights activists were accompanied by a smear campaign against them in the state-guided newspapers, accusing the campaigners of treason and implying that they had been funded by Qatar. The *Okaz* ran a double-page spread featuring some of the detainees. Also a hashtag, #AgentsofEmbassies, and a graphic featuring the activists' faces, was disseminated via social media.[72]

It was worth noting that in Shia Iran guardianship had a very limited application. A mother is the guardian of her son until he is two years old and of her daughter until she is seven. Father is the guardian of a son after the age of two and an unmarried daughter above the age of seven. In the case of a marriage of a minor, the father or grandfather is the guardian.[73]

Thanks to the diligence of the sympathizers of women's rights activists, and their extensive use of Twitter, the fate of the detainees became public knowledge. Both the New York-based Human Rights Watch and the London-based Amnesty International followed their cases closely. By contrast, even these stalwart organizations had lost interest in the fate of the thirty Saudis clerics, writers and intellectuals who were thrown behind bars in the summer of 2017 for daring to express their opposition to the policies of the Royal Court. They had become non-persons, the early victims of a totalitarian regime in the making.

NOTES

PROLOGUE

1. It was on the night of 26–27 Ramadan that the first divine revelation was made to Prophet Muhammad.
2. Staff writer, Al Arabiya English, 21 June 2017, http://english.alarabiya.net/en/News/gulf/2017/06/21/Saudi-Arabia-extends-Eid-Al-Fitr-religious-holiday-by-a-week-.html
3. Ben Hubbard, *New York Times*, 21 June 2017, "Saudi King Rewrites Succession, Replacing Heir With Son, 31," https://www.nytimes.com/2017/06/21/world/middleeast/saudi-arabia-crown-prince-mohammed-bin-salman.html
4. Martin Chulov and Julian Borger, *Guardian*, 21 June 2017, "Saudi king ousts nephew to name son as first in line to throne," https://www.theguardian.com/world/2017/jun/21/saudi-king-upends-tradition-by-naming-son-as-first-in-line-to-throne
5. AFP, 22 June 2017, "Qatar's Emir congratulates Saudi crown prince Muhammad bin Salman," http://www.financialexpress.com/world-news/qatars-emir-congratulates-saudi-crown-prince-Muhammad-bin-salman/730098/
6. Martin Chulov and Julian Borger, Guardian, 21 June 2017, ""Saudi king ousts nephew to name son as first in line to throne," https://www.theguardian.com/world/2017/jun/21/saudi-king-upends-tradition-by-naming-son-as-first-in-line-to-throne
7. Ben Hubbard, *New York Times*, 2 May 2017, "Dialogue With Iran Is Impossible, Saudi Arabia's Defense Minister Says," https://www.nytimes.com/2017/05/02/world/middleeast/saudi-arabia-iran-defense-minister.html
8. Al Jazeera, 21 June 2017, "Muhammad bin Salman named Saudi Arabia's crown prince," http://www.aljazeera.com/news/2017/06/saudi-arabia-appoints-king-salman-son-crown-prince-170621033707437.html
9. The term Sudairi clan refers to seven sons born to King Abdul Aziz bin Abdul Rahman Al Saud and his wife Hussa bint Ahmad al Sudairi, and their descendants.

1. INTRODUCTION

1. Since a lunar Islamic year is 11 days short of a solar year, an Islamic century equals 97 solar years.
2. Reporters Without Borders, 2017 RSF ranking, https://rsf.org/en/ranking
3. The other Shia-majority countries are Azerbaijan, Bahrain and Iraq.

4. SIPRI, 5 April 2016, "World military spending resumes upward course," http://www.converge.org.nz/pma/milexrel2016.pdf and http://www.sipri.org/

5. Democracy Index 2015, http://www.yabiladi.com/img/content/EIU-Democracy-Index-2015.pdf. The Index is composed of electoral process and pluralism, functioning of government, political participation, political culture and civil liberties.

6. Karen Elliot House, *On Saudi Arabia: Its People, Past, Religion, Fault Lines—and Future*, Alfred A. Knopf, 2012, p. 9.

7. Reporters Without Borders, 2017 RSF ranking, https://rsf.org/en/ranking

8. Karen Elliot House, *On Saudi Arabia*, p. 100.

9. The *kiswa* is renewed every year.

10. The term Wahhabi was originally coined by the Ottoman Turks, the adherents of the Hanafi school of Sunni Islam.

11. Following the death of Muhammad bin Ibrahim Al Shaikh, the office of the Grand Mufti, to be named by the monarch, remained unfulfilled until 1993. But his two sons ran the justice ministry until 2009. Abdul Aziz bin Abdullah bin Baz served as the Grand Mufti from 1993 until his death six years later.

12. Sami Moubayed, *Under the Black Flag: At the Frontier of the New Jihad*, I.B. Tauris, London and New York, 2015, p. 29.

13. The word "*imam*" means, literally, model—one whose example or leadership should be followed.

14. The Islamic era starts at the sunset of 15 July 622 CE, the start of the *hijra*, migration, of Prophet Muhammad from Mecca to Medina; and an Islamic year is denoted by AH.

15. For the narrative about the Ashura, see Dilip Hiro, *A Comprehensive Dictionary of the Middle East*, Interlink Publishing Group, Northampton, MA, 2013, pp, 67–68.

16. Dilip Hiro, *A Comprehensive Dictionary of the Middle East*, p. 676.

17. Samra Hussain, 5 July 2014, "A Sunni Muslim prays at a Shia mosque," http://www.nairaland.com/1800031/experience-sunni-muslim-woman-praying

18. Differences in Prayer between Sunni and Shia, http://people.opposingviews.com/shia-mosque-vs-sunni-mosque-9660.html

19. US State Dept Report on Human Rights in Saudi Arabia, http://www.state.gov/documents/organization/171744.pdf

20. Robert Lacey, *Inside the Kingdom: Kings, Clerics, Modernists, Terrorists, and the Struggle for Saudi Arabia*, Arrow Books, London, 2010/Penguin Books, New York, 2010, p. 40).

21. Max Rodenbeck, "Unloved in Arabia," *New York Review of Books*, September 30 2004. http://www.network54.com/Forum/242875/message/1096582797/Unloved+in+Arabia

22. Will Worley, Independent, 14 April 2016, "Saudi Arabia strips religious police of powers of arrest and says they must be 'kind and gentle'," http://www.independent.co.uk/news/world/middle-east/saudi-arabia-strips-religious-police-of-powers-of-arrest-and-says-they-must-be-kind-and-gentle-a6983816.html)

23. Dilip Hiro, *Holy Wars: The Rise of Islamic Fundamentalism*, Routledge, Abingdon and New York, 2013, pp.110–111.

24. Awadh Al Badi, "Saudi-Iranian Relations: A Troubled Trajectory." http://futureislam.com/blog/saudi-iranian-relations-a-troubled-trajectory-2/

25. Dilip Hiro, *Holy Wars: The Rise of Islamic Fundamentalism*, Routledge, Abingdon and New York, 2013, p.115.

26. Dilip Hiro, *A Comprehensive Dictionary of the Middle East*, Interlink Publishing Group, Northampton, MA, 2013, pp. 681–682.

27. Education in Saudi Arabia, US Library of Congress, 1993, http://countrystudies.us/saudi-arabia/31.htm

28. Ibid.

29. Dilip Hiro, *Inside the Middle East*, Routledge and Kegan Paul, London, 1982/McGraw Hill, New York, 1983, pp. 14–15.

30. U.S. Library of Congress, 1993, Population, Saudis and Non-Saudis, http://countrystudies.us/saudi-arabia/19.htm

31. Ali M. Ansari, *Modern Iran Since 1921: The Pahlavis and After*, Routledge, Abingdon and New York, 2007, p. 62.

32. Dilip Hiro, *Iran Under the Ayatollahs*, Routledge, Abingdon and New York, 2011, p. 53

33. Ibid., p. 61.

34. Ibid., pp. 60–61.

35. Misagh Parsa, *Social Origins of the Iranian Revolution*, Rutgers University Press, New Brunswick, NJ, 1989, p. 64.

36. World Bank Overview of Iran, 1 April 2017, http://www.worldbank.org/en/country/iran/overview

37. Forbes.com, December 2016, Saudi Arabia Profile, https://www.forbes.com/places/saudi-arabia/

2. BLACK GOLD AND AMERICA SHAPE IRAN AND SAUDI ARABIA

1. Dilip Hiro, *Blood of the Earth: The Battle for the Earth's Vanishing Oil Resources*, Nation Books, New York, 2007/ Politico's Publishing, London, 2008, pp. 19–20.

2. Dilip Hiro, *A Comprehensive Dictionary of the Middle East*, Interlink Publishing Group, Northampton, MA, 2013, pp. 516–517.

3. John Leyne, BBC News, 18 August 2008, "Oil discovery transformed Iran," http://news.bbc.co.uk/1/hi/world/middle_east/7569352.stm)

4. David Holden and Richard Johns, *The House of Saud*, Sidgwick & Jackson, London, 1981, p.118.

5. *Aramco World*, February 1963, http://archive.aramcoworld.com/issue/196302/the.search.began.in.1933.htm

6. Mary Norton, *Aramco World*, May–June 1988, "Well Done, Well Seven," http://archive.aramcoworld.com/issue/198803/well.done.well.seven.htm

7. Hiro, *Blood of the Earth*, p. 86.

8. David Holden and Richard Johns, *The House of Saud*, Sidgwick & Jackson, 1981, pp.128–129.

9. Cited in Daniel Yergin, *The Prize: The Epic Quest for Oil, Money and Power*, Simon & Schuster, New York and London, 1991, p. 401.

10. William Eddy, *F.D.R. Meets Ibn Saud*, American Friends of the Middle East, New York, 1954, p. 34; Holden and Johns, *The House of Saud*, p. 138; Robert Lacey, *The Kingdom*, Hutchinson, London, 1981, p. 272. When the memorandum of the five-hour conversation was later put on record, it showed that Roosevelt promised that he would do "nothing which might prove hostile to Arabs," and that he would not alter America's basic policy in Palestine without "full and proper consultation with both Jews and Arabs." But Roosevelt died on 12 April 1945.

11. Yergin, *The Prize*, p. 404.

12. Dilip Hiro, *Inside the Middle East*, Routledge and Kegan Paul, London, 1982/McGraw Hill, New York, 1983, pp. 79–80.

13. Rasoul Sorkhabi, GeoExPo, Issue 4, Volume 7, 2010, "The King of Giant Oil Fields," http://www.geoexpro.com/articles/2010/04/the-king-of-giant-fields

14. Cited in L. P. Elwell-Sutton, *Persian Oil*: A Study in Power Politics, Lawrence & Wishart, London, 1955/ Greenwood Press, 1976, Santa Barbara, CA, 1976, p. 119.

15. Yergin, T*he Prize*, pp. 451–452.

16. Manuchehr Farmanfarmaian and Roxane Farmanfarmaian, *Blood and Oil: Inside the Shah's Iran*, Modern Library, New York, 1999, pp. 184–185.

17. Dilip Hiro, *The Iranian Labyrinth: Journeys through Theocratic Iran and Its Furies*, Nation Books, New York, 2005/*Iran Today*, Politico's Publishing, London 2006, p. 195.

18. Dilip Hiro, *Iran Under the Ayatollahs*, Routledge and Kegan Paul, London and Boston, 1985, p. 40.

19. This US-Iran arrangement, secured by an American President's executive order, did not require the Senate's consent, and was within the parameters of the Eisenhower Doctrine announced in January 1957. For this doctrine, see Hiro, *A Comprehensive Dictionary of the Middle East*, p. 167.

20. Hiro, *The Iranian Labyrinth*, p. 195

21. Hiro, *Blood of the Earth*, p. 91.

22. Dilip Hiro, *The Essential Middle East: A Comprehensive Guide*, Carroll & Graf Publishers, New York, 2003, p. 269, p. 560.

23. Hansard 1803–2005, 12 March 1928, "King Ibn Saud: HC Deb 12 March 1928, Vol 214 cc1495-", http://hansard.millbanksystems.com/commons/1928/mar/12/king-ibn-saud

24. Leon Hesser, *Nurture the Heart, Feed the World: The Inspiring Life Journey of Two Vagabonds*, BookPros, Austin, TX, p. 104.

25. Sanderson Beck, *Mideast & Africa 1700–1950: Ethics of Civilization, Volume 16*, World Peace Communications, Santa Barbara, CA, 2010, http://www.san.beck.org/16-4-Arabia,Iraq.html

26. Holden and Johns, *The House of Saud*, p. 202.

27. Robert Morse, "The Rich, Royal Way of King Saud," *Life* Magazine, 9 November 1962, p. 21, antiques.gift/life-magazine-november-9-1962-cover-u-thant-with-british-ambassador_5875518.html

28. Farrukh Abbas 31 March 2015, "To liberate all Jerusalem, the Arab peoples must first liberate Riyadh," Gamal Abdul Nasser, https://twitter.com/farrukh_abbas12/status/5 82882928209723392?lang=en

29. Mark Weston, *Prophets and Princes: Saudi Arabia from Muhammad to the Present*, John Wiley, Hoboken, NJ; and Chichester, UK, 2008, pp. 179–180.

3. FAISAL'S ENDURING IMPRINT; THE SHAH'S VAULTING AMBITION

1. NBC News, 21 May 2017, "Trump Receives Royal Welcome in Saudi Arabia," http://www.nbcnews.com/slideshow/president-trump-s-royal-saudi-welcome-n762616

2. Hiro, *Iran Under the Ayatollahs*, p.20.

3. King Faisal's statement is recorded in the official Saudi journal *Umm Al Qura*, Issue 2193, 20 October 1967, http://www.muqatel.com/openshare/Wthaek/Khotob/Khotub13/AKhotub119_6-1.htm_cvt.htm#القرى%20أم

4. Kerry-Brown BCCI Report, BCCI, the CIA and Foreign Intelligence. https://fas.org/irp/congress/1992_rpt/bcci/11intel.htm

5. Weston, *Prophets and Princes*, p. 180.

6. Like his father Ibn Saud, Prince Saud sired many offspring. Of the 121 children he sired, 52 sons and 55 daughters survived him.
7. Hiro, *Inside the Middle East*, p. 82.
8. Hiro, *A Comprehensive Dictionary of the Middle East*, p. 46.
9. Kerry-Brown BCCI Report, BCCI, the CIA and Foreign Intelligence. https://fas.org/irp/congress/1992_rpt/bcci/11intel.htm
10. Al Arabiya News, 12 August 2010, "Saudi king limits clerics allowed to issue fatwas." https://www.alarabiya.net/articles/2010/08/12/116450.html
11. Because the war started after sunset on 5 October 1973, it was 6 October according to the Islamic and Jewish calendars. For Jews 6 October was Yom Kippur, the Day of Atonement. Thus the war became known in Israel as the Yom Kippur War.
12. Hiro, *A Comprehensive Dictionary of the Middle East*, p. 508.
13. Holden and Johns, *The House of Saud*, p. 380.
14. Juan De Onis, "Faisal Killer Is Put To Death," *New York Times*, 19 June 1975. http://www.nytimes.com/1975/06/19/archives/faisals-killer-is-put-to-death-prince-is-beheaded-before-a-crowd-of.html
15. Ibid.
16. Laudan Nooshin (ed.), *Music and the Play of Power in the Middle East, North Africa and Central Asia*, Ashgate Publishing, Singapore, p. 94.
17. Joseph Finklestone, Joseph Finklestone Obe, *Anwar Sadat: Visionary Who Dared*, Routledge, Abingdon and New York, 1996, p. 158.
18. Hiro, *Blood of the Earth*, p. 115.
19. Clifford Krauss, "Oil Prices Explained: Signs of a Modest Revival," *New York Times*, June 2. 2016, http://www.nytimes.com/interactive/2016/business/energy-environment/oil-prices.html
20. Steven Emerson, *The American House of Saud*, Franklin Watts, New York and London, 1985, p. 136.
21. Hiro, *Iran Under the Ayatollahs*, pp. 302–303.
22. Ibid., p. 303.
23. Ibid., p. 304.
24. Anthony Lewis, *New York Times*, 2 March 1971, "British Reaffirm a Firm Persian Gulf Plan." http://www.nytimes.com/1971/03/02/archives/british-reaffirm-persian-gulf-plan-assert-they-will-terminate.html?mcubz=0
25. Hiro, *Iran Under the Ayatollahs*, p. 307.
26. Ras al Khaima joined the federation only in February 1972.
27. Hiro, *Iran Under the Ayatollahs*, p. 333.
28. Ibid., p. 304.
29. Ibid., p. 333.
30. Andrew Scott Cooper, The *Fall of Heaven: The Pahlavis and the Final Days of Imperial Iran*, Henry Holt, New York, 2016, p. 263.
31. Hiro, *A Comprehensive Dictionary of the Middle East*, p. 499.
32. Iran's oil income shot up from $450 million in 1963 to $4.4 billion in 1974. See Hiro, *Iran Under the Ayatollahs*, p. 54.
33. Scott Cooper, The *Fall of Heaven*, pp. 263–264.
34. Marvin Zonis, *Majestic Failure The Fall of the Shah*, University of Chicago Press, 1991, p. 66.
35. Hiro, *A Comprehensive Dictionary of the Middle East*, pp. 271–272.
36. Dilip Hiro, *Holy Wars: The Rise of Islamic Fundamentalism*, Routledge, New York, 1989, p. 249.

4. AN ISLAMIC REVOLUTION IN IRAN; INITIAL MISREADING BY THE SAUDIS

1. Shia clerics, who did not claim lineage from Prophet Muhammad, wear white turbans.
2. PBUH stands for "Peace Be Upon Him".
3. Ruh Allah Khumayni, *Islam and Revolution* (tr. Hamid Algar), Mizan Press, Berkeley, CA, 1981, p. 170.
4. Hiro, *The Iranian Labyrinth*, p. 120.
5. Khumayni, *Islam and Revolution*, p. 170.
6. Hiro, *Iran Under the Ayatollahs*, p.73.
7. Ministry of Islamic Guidance, *The Dawn of Islamic Revolution: Volume I*, Tehran, nd, pp. 254–255.
8. Ali-Reza Nobari (ed.), *Iran Erupts*, The Iran-America Documentation Center, Stanford, CA, 1979, p. 196.
9. Hiro, *Iran Under the Ayatollahs*, pp. 78–79.
10. Ibid., p. 81.
11. Ibid., p. 83.
12. Ibid., pp. 84–85.
13. Ibid., pp. 86–87.
14. Khumayni, *Islam and Revolution*, pp. 246–247.
15. In March 1980, President Anwar Sadat invited the Shah to Cairo. He died there of cancer on 27 July, leaving behind his widow, Farah Diba, and their only son, Reza Cyrus.
16. Hiro, *Iran Under the Ayatollahs*, p. 93.
17. Asked when exactly he expected the revolution to succeed, Ayatollah Murtaza Pasandida, the elder brother of Khomeini, replied. "I did not expect the revolution to succeed at all." Interview in Qom, December 1979.
18. Hiro, *Iran Under the Ayatollahs*, p. 95.
19. Hiro, *Inside the Middle East*, p. 337.
20. Awadh Al Badi, "Saudi-Iranian Relations: A Troubled Trajectory." http://futureislam. com/blog/saudi-iranian-relations-a-troubled-trajectory-2/
21. Hiro, *Iran Under the Ayatollahs*, p. 154.
22. Ibid., p. 110.
23. Al Badi, "Saudi-Iranian Relations." http://futureislam.com/blog/saudi-iranian-relations-a-troubled-trajectory-2/
24. Hiro, *Iran Under the Ayatollahs*, p. 119.
25. Hiro, *A Comprehensive Dictionary of the Middle East*, p. 704.
26. The literal meaning of *Rahbar-e Inqilab* is Leader of the Revolution. But in order to distinguish him from the common noun "leader," the English language media use the term Supreme Leader.
27. Hiro, *Iran Under the Ayatollahs*, pp. 120–122.
28. Al Badi, "Saudi-Iranian Relations." http://futureislam.com/blog/saudi-iranian-relations-a-troubled-trajectory-2/
29. Hiro, *Iran Under the Ayatollahs*, p. 318.
30. Ibid., p. 318.

5. IRAN'S SECOND REVOLUTION; A MILLENNIAL CHALLENGE TO THE HOUSE OF SAUD

1. The entire cache was later published in 54 volumes in English and Persian.

2. Lacey, *Inside the Kingdom*, pp. 16–17.
3. Hiro, *Holy Wars: The Rise of Islamic Fundamentalism*, pp. 129–130.
4. Holden and Johns, *The House of Saud*, p. 522.
5. Ziauddin Sardar, *Mecca: The Sacred City*, Bloomsbury, London, 2015, pp. 330–331.
6. Yaroslav Trofimov, *The Siege of Mecca: Mecca: The Forgotten Uprising in Islam's Holiest Shrine and the Birth of al-Qaeda*, Doubleday, New York, 2007/Allen Lane, London, 2007, p. 173; and pp. 188–197, and 209–213.
7. Irfan Husain. *Fatal Faultlines: Pakistan, Islam and the West*, Arc Manor Publishers, Rockville, MD, 2011, p. 129.
8. Sardar, *Mecca*, pp. 331–332.
9. Philip Taubman, *New York Times*, 21 November 1979, "Mecca Mosque Seized by Gunmen Believed to Be Militants From Iran." http://www.nytimes.com/1979/11/21/archives/mecca-mosque-seized-by-gunmen-believed-to-be-militants-from-iran.html?mcubz=0
10. Yaroslav Trofimov, Macrohistory and World Timeline, "The Siege of Mecca: The Forgotten Uprising in Islam's Holiest Shrine and the Birth of al Qaeda." http://www.fsmitha.com/review/trofimov2.html
11. BBC News, 21 November 1979, "Mob destroys US embassy in Pakistan." http://news.bbc.co.uk/onthisday/hi/dates/stories/november/21/newsid_4187000/4187184.stm
12. John Kifner, *New York Times*, 25 Nov 1979. "Khomeini Accuses US and Israel Of Attempt to Take Over Mosques." http://www.nytimes.com/1979/11/25/archives/khomeini-accuses-us-and-israel-of-attempt-to-take-over-mosques.html?mcubz=0
13. Lacey, *Inside the Kingdom*, p. 44.
14. Ibid., pp. 40–41.
15. Falah Abdullah al Mdaires, *Islamic Extremism in Kuwait: From the Muslim Brotherhood to Al-Qaeda and other Islamic Political Groups*, Routledge, Abingdon, 2010, p. 200.
16. Hiro, *Iran Under the Ayatollahs*, p. 319, citing *Guardian*, 30 April 1980.
17. *Washington Post*, 25 April 1980; *Daily Telegraph*, 26 April and 2 May 1980; and *Guardian*, 2 May 1980.
18. Hiro, *Iran Under the Ayatollahs*, p. 335.
19. Karen Elliot House, *On Saudi Arabia: Its People, Past, Religion, Fault Lines—and Future*, Knopf, New York, 2012/Vintage, London, 2013, p. 48.
20. Ibid., p. 47.
21. Lacey, *Inside the Kingdom*, p. 85.
22. Ibid., p. 49.
23. Paul Aarts and Carolien Roelants, *Saudi Arabia: A Kingdom in Peril*, Hurst, London, 2015, p. 34.
24. Aarts and Roelants, *Saudi Arabia*, p. 11.
25. Abduallah Al Shihri and Aya Batrawy, *Independent*, 11 December 2016, "Saudi Arabia to allow cinemas to open in kingdom for first time in 35 years." http://www.independent.co.uk/news/world/middle-east/saudi-arabia-cinemas-opening-35-year-ban-movies-films-theatres-freedoms-conservatism-islam-a8103216.html
26. Lydia Smith, *Independent*, 9 December 2017, "Saudi Arabia hosts first-ever concert by female performer." http://www.independent.co.uk/news/world/middle-east/saudi-arabia-first-female-performer-concert-hiba-tawaji-womens-rights-middle-east-a8099646.html
27. Sardar, *Mecca*, p. 48.
28. See Chapter 13, p. 277.
29. Aarts and Roelants, *Saudi Arabia*, p. 41.

30. Hiro, *Iran Under the Ayatollahs*, p. 199, citing *Sunday Times*, 26 Sept. 1981.
31. Dilip Hiro, *The Longest War: The Iran-Iraq Military Conflict*, HarperCollins, London, 1989/ Routledge, New York, 1991, pp. 26–27.
32. BBC Foreign Broadcast Information Service, 18 April 1980; *Washington Post*, 18 April 1980.
33. Hiro, *The Longest War*, p. 36.
34. Hiro, *Iran Under the Ayatollahs*, p. 337, citing *Daily Telegraph*, 4 Feb. 1981.
35. Hiro, *The Longest War*, pp. 38–39.
36. Hiro, *A Comprehensive Dictionary of the Middle East*, p. 487.
37. Ibid., pp. 494–495.

6. THE IRAN-IRAQ WAR STEELS KHOMEINI'S REGIME

1. *Toronto Star*, 28 September 1986.
2. See also "martyrdom" in Hiro, *A Comprehensive Dictionary of the Middle East*, p. 406.
3. Hiro, *The Iranian Labyrinth*, pp. 251–252.
4. The *Guardian*, July 22, 1983; *New York Times*, 29 March, 1984.
5. Hiro, *Blood of the Earth*, p. 129.
6. UPI, 24 September 1981, "Saudi Arabian security forces Thursday attacked Iranian pilgrims in…." http://www.upi.com/Archives/1981/09/24/Saudi-Arabian-security-forces-Thursday-attacked-Iranian-pilgrims-in/4372370152000/
7. Hiro, *Iran Under the Ayatollahs*, p. 337, citing *The Times* (London), 21 December 1981.
8. Hiro, *Iran Under the Ayatollahs*, p. 338, citing the *Daily Telegraph*, 19 January 1983.
9. John Roberts, *Los Angeles Times*, 17 January 1988, "With Oil Income Slashed, Saudis Also Drill a Deficit." http://articles.latimes.com/1988-01-17/opinion/op-36465_1_saudi-arabia
10. Sandra Mackay, *The Saudis: Inside the Desert Kingdom*, Houghton Mifflin, Boston, MA/ Harrap, London, 1987, p. 378.
11. Hiro, *Iran Under the Ayatollahs*, p. 248, citing Islamic Republic News Agency, 2 November 1983.
12. Hiro, *Iran Under the Ayatollahs*, p. 339.
13. Hiro, *The Iranian Labyrinth: Journeys through Theocratic Iran and Its Furies*, pp. 221–222.
14. Hiro, *Inside the Middle East*, p. 85.
15. Hiro, *The Longest War: The Iran-Iraq Military Conflict*, p. 132.
16. Ibid., pp. 135–136.
17. Hiro, *A Comprehensive Dictionary of the Middle East*, p. 202.
18. *Toronto Star*, 28 September, 1986.
19. Hiro, *Blood of the Earth*, pp. 124–125.
20. Hiro, *The Longest War*, p. 183.
21. BBC News, 10 March 2005, "Iran 'given Pakistan centrifuges'." http://news.bbc.co.uk/1/hi/world/south_asia/4336559.stm
22. Itamar Rabinovich (ed.), *Middle East Contemporary Survey, 1987*, Moshe Dayan Center, Tel Aviv University, p. 173, https://books.google.co.uk/books/about/Middle_East_Contemporary_Survey_1987.html?id=CKNrjrfWJ90
23. John Kifner, *New York Times*, 2 August 2, 1987, "400 Die as Iranian Marchers Battle Saudi Police in Mecca; Embassies Smashed in Tehran." https://www.nytimes.com/1987/08/02/world/400-die-iranian-marchers-battle-saudi-police-mecca-embassies-smashed-teheran.html
24. Sandbox: Martin Kramer on the Middle East, http://martinkramer.org/sandbox/

reader/archives/khomeinis-messengers-in-mecca/, citing Radio Tehran, 3 August 1987, quoted in BBC Summary of World Broadcasts, 5 August 1987.

25. Martin Kramer, Sandbox: "Khomeini's messengers in Mecca." http://martinkramer. org/sandbox/reader/archives/khomeinis-messengers-in-mecca/
26. Hiro, *A Comprehensive Dictionary of the Middle East*, p. 225.
27. Ibid., p. 203.
28. Ibid., p. 204.
29. Ibid.
30. *Tehran Times*, 21 April 1983.
31. Hiro, *Iran Under the Ayatollahs*, p. 237.

7. THE SAUDI-IRANIAN RACE TO INFLUENCE THE MUSLIM WORLD

1. *Time*, 1 October 1985, "Asia: Silent Guns, Wary Combatants," http://content.time. com/time/magazine/article/0,9171,834413,00.html
2. From the past pages of *The Dawn*: 1966 Fifty years ago, Tribute to Saudi King Faisal, www.dawn.com/news/1253124
3. Karl R. DeRouen, *Defense and Security: A Compendium of National Armed Forces and Security Policies*, ABC-CLIO, Santa Barbara, CA, 2005, p. 572.
4. Sabha E. Nagib, "Impact of Indo-Pakistani Wars on the Middle East," *World Affairs*, Vol.135, No.2, Fall 1972, p.131.
5. S. M. Burke, *Pakistan's Foreign Policy: An Historical Analysis*, Oxford University Press, London and New York, 1973, p.214.
6. Roham Alvandi, *Nixon, Kissinger, and the Shah: The United States and Iran in the Cold War*, Oxford University Press, New York, 2014, pp. 61–62.
7. Michael T. Kaufman, *New York Times*, 6 February 1981, "22 Countries Avail Themselves Of Pakistani Soldiers".
8. Dilip Hiro, *Apocalyptic Realm: Jihadists in South Asia*, Yale University Press, London and New Haven, Conn., 2012, p. 62.
9. Irfan Husain. *Fatal Faultlines: Pakistan, Islam and the West*, Arc Manor Publishers, Rockville, MD, 2011, p. 129.
10. Tariq Rahman, "Madrassas: Religion, Poverty and the Potential for Violence in Pakistan", http://ipripak.org/journal/winter2005/madrassas.shtml
11. See Chapter 5, p. 83.
12. Hasan Mansoor, *Dawn*, 31 July 2015, "Report on the state of madressahs in Pakistan launched,"https://www.dawn.com/news/1197466
13. Neamatollah Nojumi, *The Rise of the Taliban in Afghanistan: Mass Mobilization, Civil War, and The Future of the Region*, Palgrave-Macmillan, Basingstoke, UK, and New York, 2002, p. 188. Between 1980 and 1992, the aggregate sum of $10 billion would be funneled to the Afghan Mujahedin, Ahmed Rashid, *Taliban: The Story of the Afghan Warlords*, Pan Books, London, 2011/*Taliban: Militant Islam, Oil and Fundamentalism in Central Asia*, Yale University Press, New Haven, Conn., 2011, p. 18.
14. Gad G. Gilbar, *The Middle East Oil Decade and Beyond*, Routledge, Abingdon, UK, and New York, 1997, p. 67.
15. Laudan Nooshin (ed.), *Music and the Play of Power in the Middle East, North Africa and Central Asia*, Routledge, Abingdon, UK, and New York, 2009, p. 95.
16. Dilip Hiro, *Holy Wars: The Rise of Islamic Fundamentalism*, Routledge, New York, 1989/ Paladin Books, London, 1989; Re-issued, 2013; p. 260.
17. CIA: The World Factbook, Pakistan, 2010 estimate, Muslim (official) 96.4 per cent

(Sunni 85–90 per cent, Shia 10–15 per cent), other (Christian and Hindu) 3.6 per cent, https://www.cia.gov/library/publications/the-world-factbook/fields/2122.html

18. Stanford University, Mapping Militant Organizations: Sipah-e-Sahaba Pakistan, http://web.stanford.edu/group/mappingmilitants/cgi-bin/groups/view/147

19. Abbas Rashid. 01 December 1996, "The Politics and Dynamics of Violent Sectarianism," https://www.tni.org/en/article/the-politics-and-dynamics-of-violent-sectarianism

20. Abbas Rashid. 01 December 1996, "The Politics and Dynamics of Violent Sectarianism," https://www.tni.org/en/article/the-politics-and-dynamics-of-violent-sectarianism

21. Dilip Hiro, *Apocalyptic Realm: Jihadists in South Asia*, Yale University Press, London and New Haven, Conn., 2012, p. 201.

22. S.V.R. Nasr, "The Rise of Sunni Militancy in Pakistan: The Changing Role of Islamism and the Ulema in Society and Politics," Modern Asian Studies, Vol. 34, No. 1 (2000), p. 178.

23. Hassan Abbas, *Pakistan's Drift into Extremism: Allah, the Army, and America's War on Terror*, M.E. Sharpe, New York, 2005, p. 205.

24. Zahid Hussain, *Frontline Pakistan: The Struggle with Militant Islam*, Columbia University Press, New York, 2007, p. 94.

8. SAUDI ARABIA AT THE CENTER OF THE TWENTIETH CENTURY'S LAST MAJOR WAR

1. Pierre Salinger, with Eric Laurent, *Secret Dossier: The Hidden Agenda behind the Gul War*, Penguin Books, Harmondsworth, UK/Viking Penguin, New York, 1991, pp. 70–75.

2. LTC Fred L. Hart Jr., "The Iraqi Invasion of Kuwait: An Eyewitness Account." http://www.desertstormartillery.com/eyewitness01.html

3. Ibid.

4. Michael S. Casey, *The History of Kuwait*, Greenwood, Westport, Conn., 2007, p. 89.

5. Hart Jr., "The Iraqi Invasion of Kuwait".

6. Gayle Young, United Press International, 28 September 1990, "Iranians protest US military presence." http://www.upi.com/Archives/1990/09/28/Iranians-protest-US-military-presence/5706654494400/)

7. Bob Woodward, *The Commanders*, Simon & Schuster, New York and London, 1991, p. 226.

8. Jamal S. Suwaidi (ed.), *Iran and the Gulf: A Search for Stability*, I.B, Tauris, London and New York, 1996, p. 146.

9. Dilip Hiro, *Desert Shield to Desert Storm: The Second Gulf War*, HarperCollins, London, 1992/ Routledge, New York, 1992, p. 114.

10. Lacey, *Inside the Kingdom*, p. 132.

11. This statement was cited inter alia by Shaikh Saleh al Fawzan, a Wahhabi professor of the Sharia at the Imam Muhammad bin Said Islamic University in Riyadh. See Stephen Schwartz, 21 September 2004, "Is Saudi Arabia Holy Soil?" http://www.islamicpluralism.org/1150/is-saudi-arabia-holy-soil

12. Hiro, *Desert Shield to Desert Storm*, p. 116. Walter Pincus, Washington Post Service, 3 August 1998, In *A World Transformed*, co-authored by George H. W. Bush and Brent Scowcroft, Bush wrote that in order to keep secret the Cheney-Fahd agreement he did not inform Congress until the troops were actually in Saudi Arabia. "I was less worried about Congressional notification than keeping our word with the Saudis and getting our forces in place as safely as possible."

13. Lacey, *Inside the Kingdom*, p. 133.
14. Ibid., p. 130.
15. Steve Coll, *Washington Post*, 16 August 1990, "Saddam Offers to Conclude Full Peace with Iran." https://www.washingtonpost.com/archive/politics/1990/08/16/saddam-offers-to-conclude-full-peace-with-iran/6b87c9d2-e36f-454e-a103–09c112c6f546/?utm_term=.2f5edba03550
16. Nick Williams, *Los Angeles Times*, 13 September 1990, "Iranian Ayatollah Urges Holy War Against US Buildup." http://articles.latimes.com/1990–09–13/news/mn-371_1_holy-war
17. Gayle Young, United Press International, 28 September 1990. http://www.upi.com/Archives/1990/09/28/Iranians-protest-US-military-presence/5706654494400/
18. Hiro, *Desert Shield to Desert Storm*, p. 326.
19. Hiro, *A Comprehensive Dictionary of the Middle East*, p. 206.
20. Hiro, *Blood of the Earth*, p. 179.
21. Hiro, *A Comprehensive Dictionary of the Middle East*, p. 207.
22. Cited in *Middle East International* (London), 7 June 1991, p. 11.
23. Judith Miller, *God Has Ninety-Nine Names: Reporting from a Militant Middle East*, Simon & Schuster, New York, 1996, p. 121.
24. Saudi Arabia, per capita GDP (current US $ in 2014). https://www.indexmundi.com/facts/saudi-arabia/gdp-per-capita
25. Martin Kramer, Sandbox: "Khomeini's messengers in Mecca." http://martinkramer.org/sandbox/reader/archives/khomeinis-messengers-in-mecca/
26. Peter W. Wilson and Douglas F. Graham, *Saudi Arabia: The Coming Storm*, M.E. Sharpe, New York, 1994, p. 118.
27. Hiro, *Desert Shield to Desert Storm*, p. 424.
28. Dilip Hiro, *Neighbors, Not Friends: Iran and Iraq after the Gulf Wars*, Routledge, London and New York, 2001, p.196, citing the *Economist*, 5 December 1992, pp. 39–40.
29. Hiro, *Blood of the Earth: The Battle for the World's Vanishing Oil Resources*, Nation Books, New York, 2007/ Methuen, London, 2008, p.130.
30. Cited in Samuel P. Huntington, *The Clash of Civilizations and the Remaking of World Order*, Simon & Schuster, New York, 1996, p. 249.
31. Hiro, *Desert Shield to Desert Storm*, Paladin, London, 1992/Routledge, New York, 1992, p. 423.
32. *New York Times*, 27 May 1991 and 6 July 1991.
33. Hiro, *A Comprehensive Dictionary of the Middle East*, p. 136.
34. Ibid., p. 466.
35. Toby Matthiesen, *The Other Saudis: Shiism, Dissent and Sectarianism*, Cambridge University Press, Cambridge and New York, 2014, pp. 156 and 159.
36. Vali Nasr, *The Shia Revival: How Conflicts within Islam Will Shape the Future*, W. W. Norton, New York, 2007, p. 238.
37. Martin Kramer, Sandbox: "Khomeini's messengers in Mecca." http://martinkramer.org/sandbox/reader/archives/khomeinis-messengers-in-mecca/
38. Ibid.

9. SAUDI-IRANIAN DÉTENTE

1. Welcome to the Stables of HM King Abdullah & Sons, Saudi Arabia. http://www.janadriafarm.com/
2. Public Library of US Diplomacy, Secret: Counterterrorism Adviser Brennan's Meeting

with Saudi King Abdullah, Ref: Riyadh 427; 22 March 2009. https://wikileaks.org/plusd/cables/09RIYADH447_a.html_

3. Hiro, *Dictionary of the Middle East*, p. 199.
4. Cited in Lacey, *Inside the Kingdom*, p. 184.
5. Hiro, *Iran Under the Ayatollahs*, p.192.
6. Ibid., p. 193.
7. Hiro, *A Comprehensive Dictionary of the Middle East*, p. 437.
8. Hiro, *Iran Under the Ayatollahs*, p. 209.
9. Ibid., p. 251, citing *Toronto Star*, 12 March 1984.
10. Hiro, *Iran Under the Ayatollahs*, p. 251.
11. Banafsheh Keynoush, *Saudi Arabia and Iran: Friends or Foes?*, Palgrave Macmillan, New York, 2007, pp. 137–138.
12. Cited in Hiro, *Neighbors, Not Friends*, p. 69.
13. Associated Press, 26 August 2015, "Saudi arrested in 1996 Khobar Towers truck bombing that killed 19 US servicemen." http://www.usnews.com/news/politics/articles/2015/08/26/suspect-in-1996-khobar-towers-bombing-arrested
14. Bruce Riedel, Al Monitor, 26 August 2015,"Why did it take Saudi Arabia 20 years to catch Khobar Towers bomber?" http://www.al-monitor.com/pulse/originals/2015/08/saudi-arabia-terrorist-capture-mughassil.html
15. Cited in Hiro, *Neighbors, Not Friends*, p. 227.
16. Elaine Sciolino, *New York Times*, 10 November 2011, "Iran Chief Rejects Bin Laden Message."http://www.nytimes.com/2001/11/10/world/iran-chief-rejects-bin-laden-message.html
17. Cited in Hiro, *Neighbors, Not Friends*, p. 230.
18. Anthony H. Cordesman and Arleigh A. Burke, CSIS, June 2001, "Saudi Arabia and Iran." https://csis-prod.s3.amazonaws.com/s3fs-public/legacy_files/files/media/csis/pubs/saudi_iran.pdf
19. Hiro, *Neighbors, Not Friends*, p. 231, citing *Middle East International*, 19 December 1997, p. 10.
20. Ibid., pp. 9–10.
21. Ibid., pp. 231–232.
22. Fahad M. Alsultan and Pedram Saeid, *The Development of Saudi-Iranian Relations Since the 1990s: Between Conflict and Accommodation*, Routledge, 2016, p. 115.
23. Ibid., pp. 115–116.
24. Anthony H. Cordesman and Arleigh A. Burke, CSIS, June 2001, "Saudi Arabia and Iran," https://csis-prod.s3.amazonaws.com/s3fs-public/legacy_files/files/media/csis/pubs/saudi_iran.pdf
25. Alsultan and Saeid, *The Development of Saudi-Iranian Relations Since the 1990s*, p. 117.
26. BBC News, 21 April, 1998, "Iranian leader hails improving ties with Saudi Arabia." http://news.bbc.co.uk/1/hi/world/middle_east/81197.stm
27. Anthony H. Cordesman and Arleigh A. Burke, CSIS, June 2001, "Saudi Arabia and Iran." https://csis-prod.s3.amazonaws.com/s3fs-public/legacy_files/files/media/csis/pubs/saudi_iran.pdf
28. Other counties on the list were Cuba (since 1982), Libya (since 1979), North Korea (since 1988), Sudan (since 1988), and Syria (since 1979).
29. Hiro, *Neighbors, Not Friends*, p. 233, citing *Washington Post*, 1 May 1998.
30. For details, see the entry on "Mossad," in Dilip Hiro *A Comprehensive Dictionary of the Middle East*, pp. 427–429.
31. Hiro, *Neighbors, Not Friends*, p. 254.

32. Alsultan and Saeid, *The Development of Saudi-Iranian Relations Since the 1990s*, p. 119.
33. Anthony H. Cordesman and Arleigh A. Burke, CSIS, June 2001, "Saudi Arabia and Iran." https://csis-prod.s3.amazonaws.com/s3fs-public/legacy_files/files/media/csis/pubs/saudi_iran.pdf
34. BBC News, 17 May 1999, "Iran and Saudi Arabia strengthen ties." http://news.bbc.co.uk/1/hi/world/middle_east/345834.stm
35. Anthony H. Cordesman and Arleigh A. Burke, CSIS, June 2001, "Saudi Arabia and Iran", https://csis-prod.s3.amazonaws.com/s3fs-public/legacy_files/files/media/csis/pubs/saudi_iran.pdf, citing *Washington Post*, 17 April 2001.
36. Hiro, *Neighbors, Not Friends*, p. 251, citing *Washington Post*, 29 September 1999.
37. Ibid., pp. 256–257.
38. Ibid., p. 257.

10. THE GULF RIVALS' EASTWARD MARCH

1. An *ivan* is a huge open-fronted hall with pointed vaults and high facades often used in mosque architecture in Persia.
2. Robert Byron, *The Road to Oxiana*, Macmillan, London, 1937, p. 83, p. 122, p. 123, and p. 206.
3. Ibid., pp. 88 and 215.
4. Ahmed Rashid, *Taliban: Islam, Oil and the New Great Game in Central Asia*, I. B. Tauris, London and New York, 2000, p. 72.
5. Dilip Hiro, *Apocalyptic Realm: Jihadists in South Asia*, Yale University Press, London and New Haven, CT, 2012, p. 79.
6. Dilip Hiro, *War Without End: The Rise of Islamist Terrorism and the Global Response*, Routledge, London and New York, p. 251, citing *Middle East International*, 25 October 1996, p. 16.
7. Rashid, *Taliban*, p. 176.
8. Ibid., p. 202.
9. *Spiegel*, 8 March, 2004, SPIEGEL Interview: "And then Mullah Omar screamed at me." http://www.spiegel.de/international/spiegel/spiegel-interview-and-then-mullah-omar-screamed-at-me-a-289592.html
10. Inter-Press Service, 31 August 1998.
11. Hiro, *War Without End*, p. 275, citing *Financial Times*, 22–23 August 1998; *International Herald Tribune*, 27 August 1998.
12. *Spiegel*, 8 March, 2004, "SPIEGEL Interview: "And then Mullah Omar screamed at me." http://www.spiegel.de/international/spiegel/spiegel-interview-and-then-mullah-omar-screamed-at-me-a-289592.html
13. It transpired later that the rogue soldiers were to be punished not for killing the Iranians but for destroying evidence of Iran's interference in Afghanistan's internal affairs.
14. Hiro, *War Without End*, pp. 291–292, citing *Middle East International*, 26 January 2001, p. 17.
15. Dilip Hiro, *Inside Central Asia: A Political and Cultural History of Uzbekistan, Turkmenistan, Kazakhstan, Kyrgyzstan, Tajikistan, Turkey and Iran*, Overlook/Duckworth, New York and London, 2011, p. 385.
16. The hijackers of the fourth plane, heading for the Capitol in Washington D.C., were overpowered by the airline's crew and passengers, leading to the crash of the aircraft in a field in Pennsylvania.

17. For my book on this war, codenamed Operation Enduring Freedom, I chose the title, *War Without End*.

18. Hiro, *War Without End*, p. 311, citing *International Herald Tribune*, 14 and 17 September 2001; and *Washington Post*, 25 September 2001.

19. Gordon Corera, BBC News, 25 September 2006, "Iran's gulf of misunderstanding with US." http://news.bbc.co.uk/1/hi/world/middle_east/5377914.stm

20. Elaine Sciolino, *New York Times*, 10 November 2011, "Iran Chief Rejects Bin Laden Message." http://www.nytimes.com/2001/11/10/world/iran-chief-rejects-bin-laden-message.html

21. Hiro, *Inside Central Asia*, p. 386.

22. Ibid.

23. Robert Lacey, *Inside the Kingdom: Kings, Clerics, Modernists, Terrorists, and the Struggle for Saudi Arabia*. Arrow Books, London, 2010/Penguin Books, New York, 2010, p. 228.

24. Going by the 1,700 victims whose religion was listed, Jews accounted for about 10 per cent of the 2,700 New Yorkers killed on the ground. The figure of 400 was obtained by examining the last names of those who perished. See also, Gary Rosenblatt, *The Jewish Week*, "The Mitzvah To Remember (09/05/2002)." https://web.archive.org/web/20021010020906/http://www.thejewishweek.com/bottom/specialcontent.php3?artid=362

25. Cited in Lacey, *Inside the Kingdom*, p. 229.

26. Hiro, *War Without End*, p. 328, citing *New York Times*, 17 September 2001.

27. Lacey, *Inside the Kingdom*, pp. 228 and 232.

28. Hiro, *War Without End*, p. 313, citing *Observer*, 16 September 2001.

29. Lacey, Inside the Kingdom, 2010, p. 231.

30. Hiro, *War Without End*, p. 332, citing *Washington Post*, 26 September 2001.

31. Ibid., p. 333, citing *New York Times*, 27 September 2001.

32. Dilip Hiro, *War Without End*, 2002, p. 334, citing *International Herald Tribune*, 3 and 5 October 2001.

33. Craig S. Smith, *New York Times*, 20 March 2003, "Threats And Responses: A Command Post."http://www.nytimes.com/2003/03/20/world/threats-responses-command-post-reluctant-saudi-arabia-prepares-its-quiet-role-us.html?mcubz=1

34. Hiro, *Blood of the Earth*, pp. 140–141.

35. Hiro, *War Without End*, p. 334.

36. A hypocrite (*munafiq*) is the one who claims to be Muslim but is not because of his/her failure to follow Islamic injunctions. According to the Quran (4: 144) ("Surely hypocrites will be in he lowest reaches of the fire [of Hell]; you will not find for them any helper."

37. Estimates given by the World Health Organization in March 1996 were "500,000 dead during 1990–1994," and by UNICEF in July 2000, "500,000 dead during 1991–1998," *Guardian*, 10 October 2001.

38. Hiro, *War Without End*, p. 338, citing Reuters, 7 October 2001, and *Daily Telegraph*, 8 October 2001.

39. Only the foreign ministers of Egypt, Pakistan and Saudi Arabia said they were satisfied that Osama bin Laden was responsible. *Financial Times*, 11 October 2001.

40. Hiro, *War Without End*, pp. 344–345, citing *Guardian*, 9 October 2001.

41. Ibid., p. 364.

42. BBC News, 25 February, 2002, "Afghan leader thanks Iran." http://news.bbc.co.uk/1/hi/world/middle_east/1838368.stm

43. Hiro, *War Without End*, pp. 365–366.

44. BBC News, 30 January, 2002, "Full text: State of the Union address." http://news.
   bbc.co.uk/1/hi/world/americas/1790537.stm

45. Hiro, *War Without End*, p. 359, citing Associated Press, 16 November 2001, Reuters,
   16 November 2001.

46. Hiro, *War Without End*, p. 342, citing *Washington Post*, 8 October. 2001. On 7 October
   a bomb in Al Khobar killed one American and injured several more.

47. Ibid., p. 342, citing *New York Times*, 6 October 2001.

48. Ibid., p. 342. This figure was leaked to the *New York Times* by a US intelligence source,
   and was published on 28 January 2002.

49. Ibid., p. 342, citing *Sunday Times*, 21 October 2001.

50. The Milan-based organization's office turned out to be a run-down two-story warehouse off a grey, polluted road in Milan. *Financial Times*, 13–14 October 2001.

51. *New Yorker*, 22 October, pp. 13–25.

52. Hiro, *War Without End*, pp. 343–344, citing *New York Times*, 9 November 2001.

53. Ibid.

54. Craig Unger, *Vanity Fair*, October 2003, "The War at Home: Saving the Saudis: https://
   www.vanityfair.com/news/2003/10/saving-the-saudis-200310; and Craig Unger, *House
   of Bush, House of Saud: The Secret Relationship Between The World's Two Most Powerful Dynasties*,
   Scribner, New York and London, 2004, pp, 10–11.

55. Stanford University, Mapping Militant Organizations, Sipah-e-Sahaba Pakistan. http://
   web.stanford.edu/group/mappingmilitants/cgi-bin/groups/view/147

56. Ibid.

57. *Hamshahri* (Tehran), 23 June 2002, "Iran's Uranium Reserves, 44 Billion Barrels of
   Crude Oil." http://www.parstimes.com/business/uranium_reserves.html

58. Dilip Hiro, *Secrets and Lies: Operation "Iraqi Freedom" and After*, Nation Books, New York,
   2004/Politico's Publishing, London, 2005, p. 100.

59. Bob Woodward, *Plan of Attack: The Definitive Account of the Decision to Invade Iraq*, Simon
   & Schuster, New York and London, 2004, pp. 270–271.

60. Associated Press, 25 April 2004, "New Details on Saudi Help in Iraq War." http://
   www.foxnews.com/story/2004/04/25/new-details-on-saudi-help-in-iraq-war.html

61. Dilip Hiro, *The Iranian Labyrinth: Journeys through Theocratic Iran and Its Furies*, Nation
   Books, New York, 2005/ *Iran Today*, Politico's Publishing, London, 2006, p, 238, citing *International Herald Tribune*, 16 October 2000.

62. Cited in Hiro, *Secrets and Lies*, p. 312.

63. BBC News, 1 March 2003, "Public spat mars Arab summit." http://news.bbc.co.uk/1/
   hi/world/middle_east/2811403.stm

64. Radio Free Europe, Newsline: 19 March 2003, "Is Saudi Arabia Encouraging Hussein
   Exile?" https://www.rferl.org/a/1142s78.html

65. Craig S. Smith, *New York Times*, 20 March 2003, "Threats And Responses: A Command
   Post."

66. Associated Press, 25 April 2004, "New Details on Saudi Help in Iraq War." http://
   www.foxnews.com/story/2004/04/25/new-details-on-saudi-help-in-iraq-war.html

67. Lacey, *Inside the Kingdom*, 2010, p. 291.

68. Public Library of US Diplomacy, Secret: Counterterrorism Adviser Brennan's Meeting
   With Saudi King Abdullah, Ref: Riyadh 427; 22 March 2009. https://wikileaks.org/
   plusd/cables/09RIYADH447_a.html

69. Congressional Research Service: Alfred B. Prados, Saudi Arabia: Current Issues and
   U.S. Relations, 3 April 2003. http://www.iwar.org.uk/news-archive/crs/19494.pdf

70. The United States offered a $25 million award for information leading to his arrest.

Betrayed by an accomplice, he was arrested in December 2003 by American troops in a farm fifteen miles from his home town of Tikrit where he was hiding in an underground cellar. Following his trial under the Interim Iraqi government in the US-occupied Iraq, relating to the killing of 148 Shia residents of Dujail, the site of a failed assassination attempt on him in 1982, Saddam Hussein was sentenced to capital punishment in November 2006. He was hanged the following month.

71. Hiro, *A Comprehensive Dictionary of the Middle East*, p. 216.
72. Gordon Corera, BBC News, 25 September 2006, "Iran's Gulf of Misunderstanding with US." http://news.bbc.co.uk/1/hi/world/middle_east/5377914.stm
73. Hiro, *The Iranian Labyrinth*, p. 329.
74. Hiro, *Secrets and Lies*, p. 312.
75. Hiro, *A Comprehensive Dictionary of the Middle East*, pp. 733–734.
76. Hiro, *The Iranian Labyrinth*, p. 240, citing Reuters, 9 April 2004.
77. Ibid., p. 240, citing *Sunday Times*, 8 August 2004.
78. Hiro, *Secrets and Lies*, p. 548.
79. Hiro, *A Comprehensive Dictionary of the Middle East*, p. 734.
80. Ibid., pp. 563–564.
81. BBC News, 13 May, 2003, "Saudi bombing deaths rise." http://news.bbc.co.uk/1/hi/world/middle_east/3022473.stm
82. Rob L. Wagner, *The Saudi Gazette*, 20 June, 2004, "Bitter High School Dropout Who Became a Flamboyant Killer." https://sites.google.com/site/roblwagnerarchives/bitter-high-school-dropout/
83. Lacey, *Inside the Kingdom*, p. 271.
84. CNN, 9 November 2003, "Saudi official blames Riyadh attacks on al Qaida." http://edition.cnn.com/2003/US/11/08/saudi.explosion/
85. Muslim 500: Shaikh Salma Al Ouda, http://themuslim500.com/profile/sheikh-salman-al-ouda
86. Abdul Hameed Bakier, "Lessons from Al Qaida's Attack on the Khobar Compound," Terrorism Monitor Volume: 4 Issue: 16, 11 August 2006. http://www.jamestown.org/programs/tm/single/?tx_ttnews%5Btt_news%5D=871&tx_ttnews%5BbackPid%5D=181&no_cache=1
87. Wagner, *The Saudi Gazette*, 20 June, 2004, "Bitter High School Dropout Who Became a Flamboyant Killer."
88. *Dawn*/AFP, 28 July 2004, "Saudi Arabia, Iraq agree to resume ties." https://www.dawn.com/news/365909/saudi-arabia-iraq-agree-to-resume-ties
89. United States Institute Of Peace Special Report: Joseph Macmillan, "Saudi Arabia and Iraq Oil, Religion, and an Enduring rivalry." https://www.usip.org/sites/default/files/McMillan_Saudi%20Arabia%20and%20Iraq_SR%20157.pdf
90. BBC News, 19 August 2005, "Profile: Saudi al-Qaeda." http://news.bbc.co.uk/1/hi/world/middle_east/4166612.stm
91. Jon B. Alterman and William McCants, "Saudi Arabia: Islamists Rising and Falling." https://csis-prod.s3.amazonaws.com/s3fs-public/legacy_files/files/publication/141215_Chapter6_Alterman_McCants_ReligiousRadicalism.pdf, p. 157
92. Sherifa Zuhur, *Saudi Arabia*, ABC-CLIO, Santa Barbara, CA, 2012, p. 69.

11. IRAN'S NUCLEAR SAGA; AND IRAQ AVERTS AN INTER-SECTARIAN WAR

1. Scott Peterson, *Christian Science Monitor*, 17 July 2014. "Covert war against Iran's nuclear scientists: a widow remembers," www.thetruthseeker.co.uk/?p=100935

2. Ibid.

3. Hiro, *A Comprehensive Dictionary of the Middle East*, pp. 410–411.

4. Khidhir Hamza, "Inside Saddam's secret nuclear program." Bulletin of the Atomic Scientists September 1998, p. 29, https://books.google.co.uk/books/about/Bulletin_of_the_Atomic_Scientists.html?id=rwsAAAAAMBAJ

5. Dr Hamid Hussain, "Arab-Pakistani Security Cooperation." http://brownpundits.blogspot.co.uk/2015/04/arab-pakistani-security-cooperation.html

6. Shashank Joshi, *The Permanent Crisis: Iran's Nuclear Trajectory*, Routledge, Abingdon and New York, 2015, p. 109.

7. Barbara Crossette, *New York Times*, 14 August 1990, "Pakistanis Agree to Join Defense of Saudi Arabia." http://www.nytimes.com/1990/08/14/world/confrontation-in-the-gulf-pakistanis-agree-to-join-defense-of-saudi-arabia.html

8. Cited in Adrian Levy and Catherine Scott-Clark, *Deception: Pakistan, the United States and the Global Nuclear Weapons Conspiracy*, Atlantic Books, London, 2007, p. 151. The *Observer* paid Kuldip Nayar a miserly £350 ($500) for his sensational exclusive story.

9. Levy and Scott-Clark, *Deception*, p. 151.

10. Sharon Squassoni, Arms Control Today, "Closing Pandora's Box: Pakistan's Role in Nuclear Proliferation." https://www.armscontrol.org/act/2004_04/Squassoni

11. Mohammed Al Khilewi: "Saudi Arabia Is Trying to Kill Me," *Middle East Quarterly*, September 1998, pp. 66–77. http://www.meforum.org/409/mohammed-al-khilewi-saudi-arabia-is-trying-to.ki

12. The CIA funnelled money to the Afghan Mujahedin via the ISI in cash in order not to leave a paper trail.

13. Joshi, *The Permanent Crisis*, p. 110.

14. Jane Perlez, *New York Times*, 10 July 1999, "Saudi's Visit to Arms Site in Pakistan Worries US." http://www.nytimes.com/1999/07/10/world/saudi-s-visit-to-arms-site-in-pakistan-worries-us.html

15. Farhan Bokhari, Stephen Fidler, and Roula Khalaf, *Financial Times*, 5 August 2004, "Saudi oil money joins forces with nuclear Pakistan". http://www.ft.com/cms/s/0/33019f30-e67c-11d8-9bd8-00000e2511c8.html#axzz2pYUMP2Wc

16. Alexander's Gas & Oil Connections, 7 November 2003, "Pakistan and Saudi Arabia extend crude oil deal." http://www.gasandoil.com/news/2003/11/nts34828

17. Jane Perlez, *New York Times*, 10 July 1999, "Saudi's Visit to Arms Site in Pakistan Worries US." http://www.nytimes.com/1999/07/10/world/saudi-s-visit-to-arms-site-in-pakistan-worries-us.html

18. Simon Henderson, "The Nuclear Handshake," Washington Institute for Near East, November 8, 2013. http://www.washingtoninstitute.org/policy-analysis/view/the-nuclear-handshake

19. *Gulf News*, 2 July 2001, "The Steel mill will get a loan of SR122 million from Riyadh", http://gulfnews.com/news/uae/general/sharifs-likely-to-set-up-steel-mill-in-saudi-arabia-1.420631; and http://www.mesteel.com/cgi-bin/w3-msql/company.htm?id=hillmetalsest

20. *The Hindu*, 26 May 2002, "Pak. test-fires Ghauri missile." http://www.thehindu.com/2002/05/26/stories/2002052603660100.htm

21. Devin T. Hagerty, *South Asia in World Politics*, Rowman & Littlefield, Lenham, MD, 2005, p. 63.

22. *Iran's Strategic Weapons Programmes: A Net Assessment*, The International Institute for Strategic Studies, London, 2005, p. 16.

23. A nuclear cycle consists of mining uranium ore (in which only seven out of 1,000 ura-

nium atoms are the lighter fissile isotopes U235, the rest being the heavier U238), pro-
cessing it into uranium oxide (yellow cake), transforming it into uranium tetraflouride
(UF$) gas, and then uranium hexaflouride (UF6), followed by enriching UF6 to vary-
ing degrees of U235 purity: 3.5 to 4 per cent for use in nuclear power reactors, 10 to
20 per cent for research reactors, and 90 percent–plus for nuclear weapons.

24. *Hamshahri* (Tehran), 23 June 2002, "Iran's Uranium Reserves, 44 Billion Barrels of
    Crude Oil." http://www.parstimes.com/business/uranium_reserves.html
25. BBC News, 27 November 2003, "Timeline: Iran Nuclear Crisis." http://news.bbc.
    co.uk/1/hi/world/middle_east/3210412.stm
26. Ewen MacAskill and Ian Traynor, *Guardian*, 18 September 2003, "Saudis consider
    nuclear bomb." https://www.theguardian.com/world/2003/sep/18/nuclear.saudiara-
    bia
27. BBC News, 27 November 2003, "Timeline: Iran Nuclear Crisis." http://news.bbc.
    co.uk/1/hi/world/middle_east/3210412.stm
28. Global Security: "Saudi Arabia Special Weapons." https://www.globalsecurity.org/wmd/
    world/saudi/index.html
29. Hiro, *A Comprehensive Dictionary of the Middle East*, p. 416.
30. Khaled Almaeena, Arab News, 3 August 2005, "King Fahd Laid to Rest." http://www.
    arabnews.com/node/270970
31. BBC News, 24 September 2005, "Timeline: Iran Nuclear Crisis." http://news.bbc.
    co.uk/1/hi/world/middle_east/4134614.stm
32. Hiro, *A Comprehensive Dictionary of the Middle East*, p. 116.
33. Ibid., p. 275.
34. Iraqi parliamentary election, December 2005. https://ipfs.io/ipfs/QmXoypizjW3
    WknFiJnKLwHCnL72vedxjQkDDP1mXWo6uco/wiki/Iraqi_parliamentary_
    election%2C_December_2005.html
35. Hiro, *A Comprehensive Dictionary of the Middle East*, p. 416.
36. Ibid., p. 228.
37. Ibid., pp. 401–402.
38. Public Library of US Diplomacy, Secret: Counterterrorism Adviser Brennan's Meeting
    With Saudi King Abdullah, Ref: Riyadh 427; 22 March 2009. https://wikileaks.org/
    plusd/cables/09RIYADH447_a.html
39. ABC News/AFP, 22 July 2006, "Iraq announces national reconciliation commission."
    http://www.abc.net.au/news/2006-07-22/iraq-announces-national-reconciliation-
    commission/1808110?pfmredir=sm
40. Dafna Linzer and Thomas E. Ricks, *Washington Post*, 28 November 2006, "Anbar Picture
    Grows Clearer." http://www.washingtonpost.com/wp-dyn/content/article/2006/
    11/27/AR2006112701287.html
41. At the local government level, of the fifty-one members elected in the January 2005
    election, only one member was Sunni.
42. Sabrina Tavernise, *New York Times*, 23 December 2006. "District by District, Shias Make
    Baghdad Their Own." http://www.nytimes.com/2006/12/23/world/middleeast/
    23Shias.html?mcubz=1
43. The White House, Office of the Press Secretary, 10 January 2007, "Fact Sheet: The
    New Way Forward in Iraq." https://2001-2009.state.gov/p/nea/rls/78567.htm
44. President Bush Delivers State of the Union Address, January 23, 2007. https://web.
    archive.org/web/20130507084817/http://georgewbush-whitehouse.archives.gov/
    news/releases/2007/01/20070123-2.html

45. Arwa Damon, CNN, 1 May 2007, "Shadowy Iraq office accused of sectarian agenda." http://edition.cnn.com/2007/WORLD/meast/05/01/iraq.office/
46. BBC News, 2 February 2007, "Elements of 'civil war' in Iraq." http://news.bbc.co.uk/1/hi/world/middle_east/6324767.stm
47. BBC News, 4 March 2007, "Mid-East vow to curb sectarianism." http://news.bbc.co.uk/1/hi/world/middle_east/6415605.stm
48. AFP, 16 October 2007, "US buys 'concerned citizens' in Iraq, but at what price?" https://web.archive.org/web/20080907015324/http://afp.google.com/article/ALeqM5iMzKGlyT_ahqRjtyXrAUrKIQLncA
49. Stephen Biddle, Jeffrey A. Friedman and Jacob Shapiro, 12 July 2012, "Testing the Surge: Why Did Violence Decline in Iraq in 2007?" http://www.mitpressjournals.org/doi/10.1162/ISEC_a_00087
50. Public Library of US Diplomacy, Secret: Counterterrorism Adviser Brennan's Meeting With Saudi King Abdullah, Ref: RIYADH 427; 22 March 2009. https://wikileaks.org/plusd/cables/09RIYADH447_a.html
51. Hiro, *A Comprehensive Dictionary of the Middle East*, p. 402.
52. US embassy cable—09BAGHDAD2562 (original version), "The Great Game, in Mesopotamia: Iraq and its Neighbors, Part I," Created: 24 September 2009. http://cables.mrkva.eu/cable.php?id=226620
53. WikiLeaks publishes the Saudi Cables, 19th June 2015. https://wikileaks.org/saudi-cables/press
54. Ramananda Sengupta, *The Rediff Special*, 18 May 2006, "What are Benazir and Nawaz Sharif up to?"http://www.rediff.com/news/2006/may/18ram.htm
55. *Dawn*, 20 May 2011, "Nawaz Sharif feared arrest after deportation in '07." http://www.dawn.com/news/630373/nawaz-sharif-feared-arrest-after-deportation-in-07
56. Human Rights Watch, New York, 10 September 2007, "Pakistan: Musharraf Illegally Forces Sharif Back Into Exile."https://www.hrw.org/legacy/english/docs/2007/09/10/pakist16832.htm
57. *Guardian*, 1 December 2010, "US embassy cables: Saudi influence in Pakistan," 20 November 2007. https://www.theguardian.com/world/us-embassy-cables-documents/130876
58. Stockholm International Peace Research Institute, *SIPRI Yearbook, 2008: Armaments, Disarmament and International Security 2008*, Oxford University Press, Oxford, 2008, p. 348.
59. Abu Zainab, *Arab News*, 10 Dec 2007, "GCC aims for Greater Integration." http://susris.com/articles/2007/ioi/071210-gcc-summit.html
60. Ibid.
61. Hiro, *A Comprehensive Dictionary of the Middle East*, p. 417.
62. Ibid.
63. Richard A. Oppel Jr. and Ahmad Fadam, *New York Times*, 3 March 2008, "Ahmadinejad, in Iraq, Chides Bush on Iran Criticism." http://www.nytimes.com/2008/03/03/world/middleeast/03iraq.html
64. *Guardian*, 28 November 2010. "US embassy cables: Saudi king urges US strike on Iran." https://www.theguardian.com/world/us-embassy-cables-documents/150519
65. Declan Walsh, *Guardian*, 1 December 2010, "WikiLeaks cables: Saudi Arabia wants military rule in Pakistan." https://www.theguardian.com/world/2010/dec/01/saudis-distrust-pakistan-embassy-cables
66. CNN.com: "2009 Iran presidential elections." http://edition.cnn.com/2009/WORLD/meast/06/16/iran.elections.timeline/index.html

67. Neil MacFarquhar, *New York Times*, 18 June 2009, "Shadowy Iranian Vigilantes Vow Bolder Action." http://www.nytimes.com/2009/06/19/world/middleeast/19Baseej.html?_r=1&ref=global-home

68. CNN.com: 2009 Iran presidential elections. http://edition.cnn.com/2009/WORLD/meast/06/16/iran.elections.timeline/index.html

69. *Financial Times*, 11 June 2010, "Timeline: Iran's post election protests." https://www.ft.com/content/533d966e-755a-11df-a7e2-00144feabdc0

70. BBC News, 11 August 2009, "Iran admits 4,000 June detention." http://news.bbc.co.uk/1/hi/world/middle_east/8195586.stm

71. BBC News, 1 May 2009, "Iran 'leading terrorist sponsor'." http://news.bbc.co.uk/1/hi/world/americas/8028064.stm

72. Arms Control Association: History of Official Proposals on the Iranian Nuclear Issue. https://www.armscontrol.org/factsheets/Iran_Nuclear_Proposals

73. BBC News, 10 June 2010, "Ahmadinejad: New UN Iran sanctions 'fit for dustbin'." http://www.bbc.co.uk/news/10280356

74. Ibid.

75. Hiro, *Blood of the Earth*, p. 350, citing AP, 25 February 2006.

76. Delinda C. Hanley, *Washington Report on Middle East Affairs*, May–June 2007 "Saudi Arabian King Abdullah Challenges Arab League to Solve Mideast Conflicts." http://www.wrmea.org/2007-may-june/saudi-arabian-king-abdullah-challenges-arab-league-to-solve-mideast-conflicts.html

77. Ewen MacAskill and Julian Borger, *Guardian*, 16 September 2004. "Iraq war was illegal and breached UN charter, says Annan." https://www.theguardian.com/world/2004/sep/16/iraq.iraq

78. Muslim Matters, 18 September 2007, "Shaykh Salman al-Oudah letter to Osama bin Laden. http://muslimmatters.org/2007/09/18/shaykh-salman-al-oudahs-ramadan-letter-to-osama-bin-laden-on-nbc/

79. Bruce Riedel and Bilal Y. Saab, *The Washington Quarterly*, Spring 2008, pp. 33–46, "Al Qaida's Third Front: Saudi Arabia." https://muse.jhu.edu/article/232365

80. Sherifa Zuhur, *Saudi Arabia*, ABC-CLIO, Santa Barbara, CA, 2012, p. 70; and Bruce Riedel and Bilal Y. Saab, *The Washington Quarterly*, Spring 2008, pp. 33–46, "Al Qaida's Third Front: Saudi Arabia." https://muse.jhu.edu/article/232365

81. Lacey, *Inside the Kingdom*, p. 257.

82. Bruce Riedel and Bilal Y. Saab, *The Washington Quarterly*, Spring 2008, pp. 33–46, "Al Qaida's Third Front: Saudi Arabia." https://muse.jhu.edu/article/232365

83. From Peter Bergen, CNN, 30 September 2009, "Saudi investigation: Would-be assassin hid bomb in underwear;" http://edition.cnn.com/2009/WORLD/meast/09/30/saudi.arabia.attack/index.html?iref=24hours; and Karen Elliot House, *On Saudi Arabia*, p. 193.

84. Public Library of US Diplomacy, Secret: Counterterrorism Adviser Brennan's Meeting With Saudi King Abdullah, Ref: Riyadh 427; 22 March 2009. https://wikileaks.org/plusd/cables/09RIYADH447_a.html

85. Sherifa Zuhur, *Saudi Arabia*, ABC-CLIO, Santa Barbara, CA, 2012, p. 70.

86. Public Library of US Diplomacy, Secret: Counterterrorism Adviser Brennan's Meeting With Saudi King Abdullah, Ref: Riyadh 427; 22 March 2009. https://wikileaks.org/plusd/cables/09RIYADH447_a.html

87. Jeff Zeleny and Helene Cooper, *New York Times*, 3 June 2009, "Rival Messages as Obama Lands in the Mideast." http://www.nytimes.com/2009/06/04/world/middleeast/04prexy.html?mcubz=1

88. WikiLeaks 15, "Gates: Saudis always want," 8 February, 2010. http://friday-lunch-club.blogspot.co.uk/2010/12/wikileaks-15-gates-saudis-always-want.html

89. *Daily Telegraph*, 29 Sept 2010, "Computer virus forces Iran to delay production of nuclear energy." http://www.telegraph.co.uk/news/worldnews/middleeast/iran/8033452/Computer-virus-forces-Iran-to-delay-production-of-nuclear-energy.html

90. William Yong and Robert F. Worth, *New York Times*, 29 Nov 2010, "Bombings Hit Atomic Experts in Iran Streets." http://www.nytimes.com/2010/11/30/world/middleeast/30tehran.html?mcubz=1

91. Hiro, *A Comprehensive Dictionary of the Middle East*, p. 24.

92. As the founder of the Islamic Republic of Iran, Ayatollah Ruhollah Khomeini called the last Friday in Ramadan as the Jerusalem Liberation Day. This continues. It was the long term objective of an elite force within the Islamic Revolutionary Guard Corps to free Jerusalem from Zionist occupation. Meanwhile, it was the task of its Al Quds unit to help liberate the regional Muslim states from secular or pro-Western regimes.

93. Martin Chulov. *Guardian*, 17 October 2010, "Iran brokers behind-the-scenes deal for pro-Tehran government in Iraq." https://www.theguardian.com/world/2010/oct/17/iraq-government-iran-tehran-deal

94. Al Jazeera, 19 October 2010, "Iraqi PM courts Iran during visit," http://www.aljazeera.com/news/middleeast/2010/10/2010101854658131883.html

95. Ibid.

96. VOA, 20 October 2010, "Iraqi PM Meets With Turkey's Leaders." https://www.voanews.com/a/iraqi-pm-meets-with-turkeys-leaders-105457303/172395.html

97. Ben Van Heuvelen, *Atlantic*, 16 June 2011, "Iraqi Prime Minister Accused of Plot to Frame Opposition Leader as Terrorist." https://www.theatlantic.com/international/archive/2011/06/iraqi-prime-minister-accused-of-plot-to-frame-opposition-leader-as-terrorist/240543/

98. House of Commons Library, Ben Smith, 19 January 2011, "Iraq at the creation of its new government." http://researchbriefings.files.parliament.uk/documents/SN05834/SN05834.pdf

99. Anthony H. Cordesman and Sam Khazal, *Iraq in Crisis*, Rowman & Littlefield, Lanham, MD, 2014, p. 221.

100. Timothy Williams and Duraid Adnan, *New York Times*, 16 October 2010, "Sunnis in Iraq Allied With US Rejoin Rebels." http://www.nytimes.com/2010/10/17/world/middleeast/17awakening.html

101. Amendment to the Constitution of Iraq. https://en.wikipedia.org/wiki/Amendment_to_the_Constitution_of_Iraq

102. The members of the proposed National Council for Strategic Policies were the President and two Vice-presidents, the Prime Minister and his two deputies, the Speaker of Parliament and his two deputies, the President of the Kurdish Autonomous Region, the President of the Supreme Judicial Council, and two members from each of the four major parliamentary blocs.

103. RFE/RL, 12 August 2011, "Iraqi Parliament Debates New 'Strategic Policy Council.'" https://www.rferl.org/a/iraq_strategic_policy_council/24294945.html

104. AK News, "Allawi renounces Iraq national strategic policy council," 7 October 2011. http://aknews.com/en/aknews/4/265701/

12. THE ARAB SPRING—REVERSED BY A SAUDI-BACKED COUNTERREVOLUTION

1. Sue Lloyd Roberts, BBC Newsnight, 11 March 2011, "Saudi Arabia show of force

stifles 'day of rage' protests." http://news.bbc.co.uk/1/hi/programmes/newsnight/942 2550.stm

2. David Batty and Alex Olorenshaw, *Guardian*, 29 Jan 2011, "Egypt protests—as they happened." http://www.theguardian.com/world/2011/jan/29/egypt-protests-government-live-blog

3. Reuters, 5 February, 2011, "Saudi top cleric blasts Arab, Egypt protests: report." http://www.reuters.com/article/2011/02/05/us-egypt-saudi-idUSTRE71410L2011 0205

4. Human Rights Watch, "Saudi Arabia: Free Political Activists: Secret Police Crackdown on Founders of First Political Party," https://www.hrw.org/news/2011/02/19/saudi-arabia-free-political-activists

5. Human Rights Watch: "Saudi Arabia: Drop Charges Against Human Rights Lawyer." https://www.hrw.org/news/2011/09/11/saudi-arabia-drop-charges-against-human-rights-lawyer

6. BBC News, 23 February 2011, "Saudi king offers benefits as he returns from treatment." http://www.bbc.co.uk/news/world-middle-east-12550326

7. Elliot House, *On Saudi Arabia*, p. 176.

8. Stéphane Lacroix, "Saudi Islamists and the Arab Spring." http://eprints.lse.ac.uk/56725/1/Lacroix_Saudi-Islamists-and-theArab-Spring_2014.pdf

9. Ibid.

10. Elliot House, *On Saudi Arabia*, p. 160.

11. Ibrahim Elbadawi and Hoda Selim, *Understanding and Avoiding the Oil Curse in Resource-rich Arab Economies*, Cambridge University Press, Cambridge, and New York, July 2016, p. 179.

12. Martin Chulov, *Guardian*, 25 September 2011, "Saudi women to be given right to vote and stand for election in four years." https://www.theguardian.com/world/2011/sep/25/saudi-women-right-to-vote

13. Muhammad Morsi garnered 13.23 million votes and Shafiq 12.347 million.

14. Madhyamam.com/IANS, 5 February 2014, "Iran President Ahmadinejad begins historic Egypt visit." http://www.madhyamam.com/en/node/8826

15. Al Azhar Mosque and University were established in 977 in Cairo when it was the capital of the Fatimid Caliphate (969–1171) whose rulers claimed descent from Fatima, the daughter of Prophet Muhammad married to Imam Ali, the founder of Shia Islam. Al Azhar University's refusal to accept Shias as students was therefore incomprehensible.

16. Kareem Fahim and Mayye el Shaikh, *New York Times*, 5 February 2013, "Ahmadinejad Visits Egypt, Signaling Realignment." http://www.nytimes.com/2013/02/06/world/middleeast/irans-president-visits-egypt-in-sign-of-thaw.html?_r=0

17. David Hearst and Patrick Kingsley, *Guardian*, 30 June 2013, "Egypt's Mohamed Morsi remains defiant as fears of civil war grow." http://www.guardian.co.uk/world/2013/jun/30/egypt-mohamed-morsi-defiant-civil-war

18. David D. Kirkpatrick, *New York Times*, 1 March 2015, "Recordings Suggest Emirates and Egyptian Military Pushed Ousting of Morsi." http://www.nytimes.com/2015/03/02/world/middleeast/recordings-suggest-emirates-and-egyptian-military-pushed-ousting-of-morsi.html

19. David Hearst, *Guardian*, 20 August 2013, "Why Saudi Arabia is taking a risk by backing the Egyptian coup." https://www.theguardian.com/commentisfree/2013/aug/20/saudi-arabia-coup-egypt

20. Human Rights Watch, 12 August 2014, "Egypt: Rab'a Killings Likely Crimes against

Humanity." https://www.hrw.org/news/2014/08/12/egypt-raba-killings-likely-crimes-against-humanity

21. Digby Lidstone, *Financial Times*, 9 November 2009, "Shia population: Fed up with immigration and discrimination." https://www.ft.com/content/2a4a99be-ccbd-11de-8e30-00144feabdc0

22. Sarah A. Topol, AOL News, 22 February 2011, "Thousands Join Bahrain Protests; King to Free Some Political Prisoners." https://web.archive.org/web/20110425023326/http://www.aolnews.com/2011/02/22/thousands-join-bahrain-protests-king-to-free-some-political-pri/

23. Timeline of Unrest in Eastern Province from Jan 2006—Dec. 2011. https://wikileaks.org/gifiles/attach/14/14872_Timeline%20of%20Un.doc

24. Ibid.

25. Ethan Browner and Michael Slackman, *New York Times*, 14 March 2011, "Saudi Troops Enter Bahrain to Help Put Down Unrest." http://www.nytimes.com/2011/03/15/world/middleeast/15bahrain.html

26. Patrick Cockburn, *The Independent*, 17 March 2011, "Bahrain protesters driven out of Pearl Square by tanks and tear gas." http://www.independent.co.uk/news/world/middle-east/bahrain-protesters-driven-out-of-pearl-square-by-tanks-and-tear-gas-2244165.html

27. Ibid.

28. Marina Ottaway, Carnegie Endowment, 4 April 2011, "Between the United States and Saudi Arabia." http://carnegieendowment.org/2011/04/04/bahrain-between-united-states-and-saudi-arabia-pub-43416

29. Hiro, *A Comprehensive Dictionary of the Middle East*, p. 403.

30. Hugh Macleod and a reporter in Syria, *Global Post*, 25 April 2011, "Syria: How it all began." https://www.pri.org/stories/2011-04-23/syria-how-it-all-began

31. Ibid.

32. BBC News, 21 October 2015, "Syrian President Bashar al-Assad: Facing down rebellion." http://www.bbc.co.uk/news/10338256

33. Al Jazeera, 8 August 2011, "Saudi Arabia calls for Syrian reforms." http://www.aljazeera.com/news/middleeast/2011/08/201187213922184761.html

34. Nada Bakria, *New York Times*, 27 August 2011, "Iran Calls on Syria to Recognize Citizens' Demands." http://www.nytimes.com/2011/08/28/world/middleeast/28syria.html

35. Ewen MacAskill and Duncan Campbell, *Guardian*, 17 February 2005, "Iran and Syria confront US with defense pact." http://www.theguardian.com/world/2005/feb/17/usa.syria

36. Mona Yacoubian, US Institute of Peace, 1 May, 2007, "Syria's alliance with Iran." http://www.usip.org/publications/syria-s-alliance-iran

37. Anthony Shadid, *New York Times*, 10 January 2012, "Syrian Leader Vows 'Iron Fist' to Crush 'Conspiracy.'" http://www.nytimes.com/2012/01/11/world/middleeast/syrian-leader-vows-to-crush-conspiracy.html

38. C. J. Chivers and Eric Schmitt, *New York Times*, 25 March 2013, "Arms Airlift to Syria Rebels Expands, With Aid From CIA." http://www.nytimes.com/2013/03/25/world/middleeast/arms-airlift-to-syrian-rebels-expands-with-cia-aid.html

39. Murtaza Hussain, *Intercept*, 24 October 2017, "NSA Document says Saudi Prince directly ordered coordinated attack by Syrian Rebels on Damascus." https://theintercept.com/2017/10/24/syria-rebels-nsa-saudi-prince-assad/

40. European Council on Foreign Relations, 24 June 2013, "Syria: the view from Iraq." http://www.ecfr.eu/article/commentary_syria_the_view_from_iraq136

41. Dilip Hiro, YaleGlobal Online, 13 December 2016, "Fall of Eastern Aleppo Marks Turning Point for Syrian Civil War."http://yaleglobal.yale.edu/content/fall-eastern-aleppo-marks-turning-point-syrian-civil-war

42. BBC News, 14 June 2013, "Who is supplying weapons to the warring sides in Syria?" http://www.bbc.co.uk/news/world-middle-east-22906965

43. Ibid.

44. Neil MacFarquhar and Eric Schmitt, New York Times, 23 July 2012, "Syria Threatens Chemical Attack on Foreign Force," http://www.nytimes.com/2012/07/24/world/middleeast/chemical-weapons-wont-be-used-in-rebellion-syria-says.html?pagewanted=all

45. James Ball, Washington Post, 20 August 2012, "Obama issues Syria a 'red line' warning on chemical weapons." https://www.washingtonpost.com/world/national-security/obama-issues-syria-red-line-warning-on-chemical-weapons/2012/08/20/ba5d26ec-eaf7-11e1-b811-09036bcb182b_story.html

46. Hiro, A Comprehensive Dictionary of the Middle East, p. 243.

47. BBC News, 24 September 2013, "Syria chemical attack: What we know." http://www.bbc.co.uk/news/world-middle-east-23927399

48. Jeffrey Goldberg, Atlantic, April 2016, "The Obama Doctrine." http://www.theatlantic.com/magazine/archive/2016/04/the-obama-doctrine/471525/

49. Khaled Yacoub Oweis, Reuters, 28 August 2013, "Syria evacuates most army buildings in Damascus: residents."http://www.reuters.com/article/us-syria-crisis-army-preparations/syria-evacuates-most-army-buildings-in-damascus-residents-idUSBRE97R0R320130828

50. BBC News, 20 August 2013, "Syria crisis: Cameron loses Commons vote on Syria action." http://www.bbc.co.uk/news/uk-politics-23892783

51. Michael Crowley, Politico.com, 11 October 2016, "Obama's 'red line' haunts Clinton, Trump." http://www.politico.com/story/2016/09/obama-clinton-syria-red-line-228585

52. Dilip Hiro, TomDispatch.com, 29 September 2013,"The Mystery of Washington's Waning Global Power. http://www.tomdispatch.com/blog/175753/tomgram%3A_dilip_hiro,_the_mystery_of_washington%27s_waning_global_power/

53. Peter Baker and Michael R. Gordon, New York Times, 10 September 2013, "An Unlikely Evolution, From Casual Proposal to Possible Resolution." http://www.nytimes.com/2013/09/11/world/middleeast/Syria-An-Unlikely-Evolution.html

54. Neil King Jr., Wall Street Journal, 10 September 2013, "Poll Finds Support Fading for Syria Attack." http://online.wsj.com/article/SB1000142412788732359500457906528426144861 4.html

55. Syria did so on 13 September 2013. That reduced the number of non-signatories to the Chemical Weapons Convention in the Middle East to two: Israel and Egypt.

56. BBC News, 10 September 2013, "Transcript: Obama's address to the nation on Syria."https://www.cbsnews.com/news/transcript-obamas-address-to-the-nation-on-syria/

57. Conal Urqhart, Guardian, 14 Sept 2013, "Syria crisis: US and Russia agree chemical weapons deal." https://www.theguardian.com/world/2013/sep/14/syris-crisis-us-russia-chemical-weapons-deal

58. Jeremy Jones and Nicholas Ridout, Oman, Culture and Diplomacy, Edinburgh University Press, Edinburgh, 2013, pp. 178–179.

59. Robin Pomeroy and Mitra Amiri, Reuters, 8 June 2011, "'Defiant Iran plans big rise in nuclear enrichment." http://www.reuters.com/article/us-iran-nuclear-enrichment/defiant-iran-plans-big-rise-in-nuclear-enrichment-idUSTRE7572R620110608

60. Thijs Van de Graaf, Middle East Policy Council Journal, Fall 2013, Volume XX, Number 3,

"The 'Oil Weapon' Reversed? Sanctions Against Iran and U.S.-EU Structural Power." http://www.mepc.org/oil-weapon-reversed-sanctions-against-iran-and-us-eu-structural-power?print

61. Carol E. Lee and Keith Johnson, *Wall Street Journal*, 4 January 2012, "US Targets Iran's Central Bank." http://www.wsj.com/articles/SB1000142405297020470204720204577132923798499772

62. Michael Theodoulou, *The National*, 11 January 2012, "Ahmadinejad makes light of fears over Iran's uranium enrichment." https://www.thenational.ae/world/mena/ahmadinejad-makes-light-of-fears-over-iran-s-uraninium-enrichment-1.579421

63. BBC News, 23 January 2012, "Iran: EU oil sanctions 'unfair' and 'doomed to fail'." http://www.bbc.co.uk/news/world-europe-16693484

64. Reuters Staff, 12 Feb 2016, "Iranian banks reconnected to SWIFT network after four-year hiatus." https://www.reuters.com/article/us-iran-banks-swift/iranian-banks-reconnected-to-swift-network-after-four-year-hiatus-idUSKCN0VQ1FD

65. Van de Graaf, "The 'Oil Weapon' Reversed?".

66. BBC News, 20 December 2016, Iran Profile—Timeline. http://www.bbc.co.uk/news/world-middle-east-14542438

67. BBC News, 28 September 2013, "Iran nuclear: Obama and Rouhani speak by phone." http://www.bbc.co.uk/news/world-middle-east-24304088

68. Mark Urban, "Saudi nuclear weapons 'on order' from Pakistan," BBC Newsnight, 6 November 2013, http://www.bbc.co.uk/news/world-middle-east-24823846"; and Julian Borger, "Does Pakistan have nuclear weapons ready to ship to Saudi Arabia?", *Guardian*, 7 November 2013. https://www.theguardian.com/world/julian-borger-global-security-blog/2013/nov/07/pakistan-saudi-nuclear-proliferation?CMP=twt_gu

69. BBC News, 24 November 2013, "Iran agrees to curb nuclear activity at Geneva talks." http://www.bbc.co.uk/news/world-middle-east-25074729

70. Dilip Hiro, YaleGlobal Online, January 21, 2014, "Will the Iran Nuclear Deal Thrive or Wither?" http://yaleglobal.yale.edu/content/will-iran-nuclear-deal-thrive-or-wither

71. Martin Chulov, *Guardian*, 13 June 2014, "Iranian general visits Baghdad to assist with defense of Iraq capital." https://www.theguardian.com/world/2014/jun/13/iran-general-assists-with-preparing-baghdad-defence-from-insurgents-isis

72. Abigail Hauslohner, *Washington Post*, 13 June 2014, "Jihadist expansion in Iraq puts Persian Gulf States in a tight spot."https://www.washingtonpost.com/world/jihadist-expansion-in-iraq-puts-persian-gulf-states-in-a-tight-spot/2014/06/13/e52e90ac-f317–11e3-bf76-447a5df6411f_story.html?utm_term=.c12f2fc2cab6

73. Reuters Staff, 9 March 2017, "Iraqi PM Maliki says Saudi, Qatar openly funding violence in Anbar." https://www.reuters.com/article/us-iraq-saudi-qatar/iraqi-pm-maliki-says-saudi-qatar-openly-funding-violence-in-anbar-idUSBREA2806S20140309

74. Staff writer, *Al Arabiya News*, 4 June 2014, "Assad wins landslide 88.7% election victory." http://english.alarabiya.net/en/News/middle-east/2014/06/04/Assad-readies-for-Syria-vote-count-victory-.html

75. Babak Dehghanpisheh, Reuters Insight, 3 August 2014, "Iran's elite Guards fighting in Iraq to push back Islamic State." http://uk.reuters.com/article/uk-iraq-security-iran-insight/insight-irans-elite-guards-fighting-in-iraq-to-push-back-islamic-state-idUKKBN0G30GG20140803

76. Mehdi Hassan, *Huffington Post*, 30 June 2014, "Haider Al-Abadi: Bomb Isis, Or We'll Ask Iran To Do It, Top Iraqi Politician Warns United States." http://www.huffingtonpost.co.uk/2014/06/30/iraq-haider-al-abadi-isis-iran-airstrikes-unites-states_n_5543252.html

77. Spencer Ackerman and Paul Lewis, *Guardian*, 13 June 2014, "Obama 'urgently' considering air assault on targets in Syria and Iraq" https://www.theguardian.com/world/2014/jun/13/obama-urgent-air-assault-isis-syria-iraq

78. Hauslohner, "Jihadist expansion in Iraq puts Persian Gulf States in a tight spot."

79. Dehghanpisheh, "Iran's elite Guards fighting in Iraq to push back Islamic State."

80. Jonathan Marcus, 2 July 2014, "'Iranian attack jets deployed' to help Iraq fight Isis." http://www.bbc.co.uk/news/world-middle-east-28125687

81. BBC News, 5 July 2014, "Isis chief Abu Bakr al-Baghdadi appears in first video." http://www.bbc.co.uk/news/world-middle-east-28177848

82. Dan Roberts and Spencer Ackerman, *Guardian*, 11 September 2014, "Barack Obama authorizes air strikes against Isis militants in Syria." https://www.theguardian.com/world/2014/sep/10/obama-speech-authorise-air-strikes-against-isis-syria

83. *Arab News*, 11 Sept 2014, "King Abdullah receives call from President Obama." http://www.arabnews.com/saudi-arabia/news/628521

84. Richard Spencer and Peter Foster, *Daily Telegraph*, 11 Sept 2014, "10 Arab states join the US in battle against ISIL." http://www.telegraph.co.uk/news/worldnews/middleeast/saudiarabia/11090799/10-Arab-states-commit-to-share-US-led-fight-against-ISIL.html

85. Chloe Sommers, CNN, 19 Dec 2014, "Pentagon has a new name for ISIS." http://edition.cnn.com/2014/12/18/politics/pentagon-now-calls-isis-daesh/?cid=ob_articlesidebarall&iref=obinsite

86. Dion Nissenbaum, Benoît Faucon and Matt Bradley, *Wall Street Journal*, 3 December 2014, "Iran Attacked Islamic State Forces in Iraq, US Not Coordinating With Tehran on Airstrikes." https://www.wsj.com/articles/pentagon-officials-believe-iran-attacked-islamic-state-forces-in-iraq-1417623790

13. MULTI-FRONT COLD WAR BETWEEN RIYADH AND TEHRAN

1. Bill Treadway, "Ranking The Net Worth Of Saudi Royalty From Lowest To Highest." http://www.rantnow.com/2015/11/29/ranking-the-net-worth-of-saudi-royalty-from-lowest-to-highest-2/

2. Hassa al Sudairi gave birth to thirteen children.

3. King Abdullah had followed the protocol of consulting the Allegiance Council he had set up in 2007, composed of Ibn Saud's 18 surviving sons and other 19 chosen by the groups of surviving sons of the dead fathers to represent the deceased male parent. On ascending the throne the new king was required to submit his nomination for the Crown Prince to the Council which could reject him and offer an alternative. Lacey, *Inside the Kingdom*, p. 270.

4. *The Hindu*/AP, 15 September 2017, "Saudi Arabia cracks down on critics of crown prince." http://www.thehindu.com/news/international/saudi-arabia-cracks-down-on-critics-of-crown-prince/article19689934.ece

5. *Daily Telegraph*, 21 June 2017, "Saudi king upends royal succession and names son Mohammed bin Salman as first heir to throne." http://www.telegraph.co.uk/news/2017/06/21/saudi-king-upends-royal-succession-names-son-mohammed-bin-salman/

6. Ben Hubbard, Eric Schmitt and Mark Mazzetti, *New York Times*, 29 June 2017, "Deposed Saudi Prince Is Said to Be Confined to Palace." https://www.nytimes.com/2017/06/28/world/middleeast/deposed-saudi-prince-mohammed-bin-nayef.html

7. Cited in David Ignatius, *Washington Post*, 13 October 2105. "A Storm Brews in Saudi

Arabia." https://www.washingtonpost.com/opinions/a-storm-brews-in-saudi-arabia/2015/10/13/886328c0-71e1-11e5-9cbb-790369643cf9_story.html

8. *The Economist*, 6 January 2016, "Transcript: Interview with Muhammad bin Salman." http://www.economist.com/saudi_interview

9. Staff Writers, *Bloomberg Businessweek*, 25 April 2016, "The \$2 Trillion Project to Get Saudi Arabia's Economy Off Oil." http://www.bloomberg.com/news/features/2016-04-21/the-2-trillion-project-to-get-saudi-arabia-s-economy-off-oil

10. Staff Writers, *Bloomberg Businessweek*, 25 April 2016, "The \$2 Trillion Project to Get Saudi Arabia's Economy Off Oil." http://www.bloomberg.com/news/features/2016-04-21/the-2-trillion-project-to-get-saudi-arabia-s-economy-off-oil

11. Staff writer, *Al Arabiya News*, 1 May 2015, "Saudi king orders merging of royal courts," http://english.alarabiya.net/en/News/middle-east/2015/05/01/Saudi-king-orders-to-merge-royal-courts.html

12. David Kirkpatrick, *New York Times*, 6 June 2015, "Surprising Saudi Rises as a Prince among Princes."http://www.nytimes.com/2015/06/07/world/middleeast/surprising-saudi-rises-as-a-prince-among-princes.html?_r=0

13. Mark Mazzetti and Ben Hubbard, *New York Times*, 15 October 2016, "Rise of Saudi Prince Shatters Decades of Royal Tradition." https://www.nytimes.com/2016/10/16/world/rise-of-saudi-prince-shatters-decades-of-royal-tradition.html

14. David Ignatius, *Washington Post*, 13 October 2105, "A Storm Brews in Saudi Arabia." https://www.washingtonpost.com/opinions/a-storm-brews-in-saudi-arabia/2015/10/13/886328c0–71e1–11e5–9cbb-790369643cf9_story.html

15. BBC News, 15 Dec 2015, "Saudis announce Islamic anti-terrorism coalition."http://www.bbc.co.uk/news/world-middle-east-35099318

16. Mark Mazzetti and Ben Hubbard, *New York Times*, 15 October 2016, "Rise of Saudi Prince Shatters Decades of Royal Tradition."*https://www.nytimes.com/2016/10/16/world/rise-of-saudi-prince-shatters-decades-of-royal-tradition.html

17. Hiro, *A Comprehensive Dictionary of the Middle East*, pp. 249–250.

18. Michelle Nicholas, Reuters, 15 February 2015 "UN council demands Houthis withdraw, end Yemen violence." http://www.reuters.com/article/us-yemen-crisis-un/u-n-council-demands-houthis-withdraw-end-yemen-violence-idUSKBN0LJ14E20150215

19. Bruce Riedel, Brookings, 29 April 2015, "Yemen's war shakes up the Saudi palace." https://www.brookings.edu/blog/markaz/2015/04/29/yemens-war-shakes-up-the-saudi-palace/

20. Hiro, *A Comprehensive Dictionary of the Middle East*, p. 732.

21. Mark Mazzetti and Eric Schmitt, *New York Times*, 13 March 2016, "Quiet Support for Saudis Entangles US in Yemen." https://www.nytimes.com/2016/03/14/world/middleeast/yemen-saudi-us.html

22. Bruce Riedel, *Al Monitor*, 13 April 2015, "Why Pakistan said no to King Salman." http://www.al-monitor.com/pulse/originals/2015/04/yemen-conflict-parliament-resolution.html

23. Security Council 7426TH Meeting, 14 April 2015. "Security Council Demands End to Yemen." https://www.un.org/press/en/2015/sc11859.doc.htm

24. Besides Saudi Arabia, the coalition contained four other Gulf Cooperation Council members: Jordan, Egypt, Sudan and Morocco.

25. *The Economist*, 6 January 2016, "Transcript: Interview with Muhammad bin Salman." http://www.economist.com/saudi_interview

26. Mark Mazzetti and Ben Hubbard, *New York Times*, 15 October 2016, "Rise of Saudi

Prince Shatters Decades of Royal Tradition." https://www.nytimes.com/2016/10/16/world/rise-of-saudi-prince-shatters-decades-of-royal-tradition.html

27. Breaking Island News, 9 July 2015, "Maldives: Saudi Prince celebrates in Style with $8 million Private Party." http://www.privateislandnews.com/maldives-saudi-prince-celebrates-in-style-with-8-million-private-island-party/

28. Human Rights Watch, May 3, 2015, "Yemen: Saudi-Led Air Strikes Used Cluster Munitions." https://www.hrw.org/news/2015/05/03/yemen-saudi-led-air strikes-used-cluster-munitions

29. *The Economist*, 25 July 2015, "The kingdom fears a resurgent Iran as sanctions come off." http://www.economist.com/news/middle-east-and-africa/21659759-kingdom-fears-resurgent-iran-sanctions-come-proxies-and-paranoia

30. Nicholas Kurlish and Michael Forsythe, *New York Times*, 16 December 2017, "World's Most Expensive Home? Another Bauble for a Saudi Prince." https://www.nytimes.com/2017/12/16/world/middleeast/saudi-prince-chateau.html

31. Hakim Almasmari, *The National*, 8 September 2015, "Why Marib province is crucial to coalition victory in Yemen." http://www.thenational.ae/world/middle-east/why-marib-province-is-crucial-to-coalition-victory-in-yemen

32. Hugh Miles, "Saudi royal calls for regime change in Riyadh," *Guardian*, 28 September 2015. http://www.theguardian.com/world/2015/sep/28/saudi-royal-calls-regime-change-letters-leadership-king-salman

33. See pp. 35–38.

34. *US News*, 10 December 2015, "AP Count: Over 2,400 killed in Saudi Hajj stampede crush." http://www.usnews.com/news/world/articles/2015/12/10/ap-count-over-2-400-killed-in-saudi-Hajj-stampede-crush

35. Gianluca Mezzofiore, "Mecca hajj stampede: Road closures for Saudi Arabia King Salman blamed for Eid-al-Adha catastrophe," *IB Times*, September 25, 2015. http://www.ibtimes.co.uk/mecca-hajj-stampede-road-closures-saudi-arabia-king-salman-blamed-eid-al-adha-catastrophe-1521183

36. The Economist Intelligence Unit, 2 October 2015, "Saudi-Iranian hajj dispute is war by other means." http://country.eiu.com/article.aspx?articleid=953556479&Country=Iran&topic=Politics_1

37. *Dawn*/AFP, 5 September 2016, "Khamenei calls for ending Saudi Arabia's control over Hajj." https://www.dawn.com/news/1282226

38. Toby Matthiesen, *Guardian*, 23 January 2012. "Saudi Arabia: the Middle East's most under-reported conflict." https://www.theguardian.com/commentisfree/2012/jan/23/saudi-arabia-shia-protesters

39. Al Jazeera English, 12 July 2012, "Saudi Shia protesters mourned by 'thousands'." http://www.aljazeera.com/news/middleeast/2012/07/201271252423623334.html

40. *Guardian*/Reuters, 25 October 2015, "Saudi Arabia Supreme Court upholds death sentence on Shia cleric." https://www.theguardian.com/world/2015/oct/25/saudi-arabia-supreme-court-upholds-death-sentence-on-shia-cleric

41. BBC News, 3 January 2016, "Iran: Saudis face 'divine revenge' for executing al-Nimr." http://www.bbc.co.uk/news/world-middle-east-35216694

42. CBS News/AP, 24 January 2016, "Iran arrests 100 people over attack on Saudi embassy."https://www.cbsnews.com/news/iran-arrests-100-people-over-attack-on-saudi-embassy/

43. Kim Sengupta, *Independent*, 12 May 2015, "Turkey and Saudi Arabia alarm the West by backing Islamist extremists the Americans had bombed in Syria." http://www.inde-

pendent.co.uk/news/world/middle-east/syria-crisis-turkey-and-saudi-arabia-shock-western-countries-by-supporting-anti-assad-jihadists-10242747.html

44. BBC News, 26 July 2015, "Syria: President Assad admits army strained by war." http://www.bbc.co.uk/news/world-middle-east-33669069

45. Dilip Hiro, Tomgram, "Unipolar No More." http://www.tomdispatch.com/post/176196/tomgram%3A_dilip_hiro%2C_unipolar_no_more/v

46. Alastair Dawber, *Independent*, 10 December 2015, "Meeting of Syrian rebel groups in Saudi Arabia ends in chaos as Islamist militia Ahrar al-Sham walk out." http://www.independent.co.uk/news/world/middle-east/meeting-of-syrian-rebel-groups-in-saudi-arabia-ends-in-chaos-as-islamist-militia-ahrar-al-sham-walk-a6768566.html

47. RT.com, 11 October 2015, "Putin and Saudi defence minister meet in Russia, agree on common goals in Syria."https://www.rt.com/news/318324-putin-saudi-goals-syria/

48. Dilip Hiro, Tomgram, 11 October 2016, "Unipolar No More." http://www.tomdispatch.com/post/176196/tomgram%3A_dilip_hiro%2C_unipolar_no_more/

49. Shaun Walker and Jennifer Rankin, *Guardian*, 9 August 2016, "Erdogan and Putin discuss closer ties in first meeting since jet downing." https://www.theguardian.com/world/2016/aug/09/erdogan-meets-putin-leaders-seek-mend-ties-jet-downing-russia-turkey

50. Fox News/*Wall Street Journal*, 6 October 2016, "Iraqi militia fighters pour into Syria to support Assad." http://www.foxnews.com/world/2016/10/06/iraqi-militia-fighters-pour-into-syria-to-support-assad.html

51. Komsomol is the abbreviation of the kommunisticheskiy soyuz molodyozhi, Communist Youth Organization; Pravda means Truth.

52. Daria Aslamova, *Komsomolskaya Pravda*, 12 October 2016, "President Bashar Al-Assad's interview given to Russia's *Komsomolskaya Pravda*. https://www.kp.ru/daily/26594/3609878/

53. BBC News, 22 December 2016, "The Syrian army says it has retaken full control of Aleppo, following the evacuation of the last group of rebels." http://www.bbc.co.uk/news/world-middle-east-38408548

54. Daria Aslamova, *Komsomolskaya Pravda*, 12 October 2016, "President Bashar Al-Assad's interview given to Russia's *Komsomolskaya Pravda*. https://www.kp.ru/daily/26594/3609878/

55. Mark Landler and David E. Sanger, *New York Times*, 13 October 2017, "Trump Disavows Nuclear Deal, but Doesn't Scrap It." https://www.nytimes.com/2017/10/13/us/politics/trump-iran-nuclear-deal.html

56. Scott Clement and Peyton M. Craighil, *Washington Post*, 30 March 2015, "Poll: Clear majority supports nuclear deal with Iran." https://www.washingtonpost.com/world/national-security/poll-2-to-1-support-for-nuclear-deal-with-iran/2015/03/30/9a5a5ac8-d720-11e4-ba28-f2a685dc7f89_story.html?utm_term=.ed39bac6ee94

57. Reuters, 15 May 2015, "Obama vows to 'stand by' Gulf allies amid concern over Iran threat." http://www.arabianbusiness.com/obama-vows—stand-by-gulf-allies-amid-concern-over-iran-threat-592848.html?tab=Articlm. Nothing came of the region-wide anti-missile defence system because of the simmering differences between GCC states regarding territorial disputes along their borders which inhibited them from compromising their exclusive control over defence.

58. Siobhan Hughes, *The Wall Street Journal*, 11 September 2015, "U.S. House Votes Against Approving Iran Nuclear Deal." http://www.wsj.com/articles/u-s-house-votes-against-approving-iran-nuclear-deal-1441993085

59. BBC News 14 July 2015, "Iran nuclear talks: Historic' agreement struck" http://www.

bbc.co.uk/news/world-middle-east-33518524; and Michael R. Gordon and David E. Sanger, *New York Times*, 14 July 2015, "Deal Reached on Iran Nuclear Program; Limits on Fuel Would Lessen With Time." http://www.nytimes.com/2015/07/15/world/middleeast/iran-nuclear-deal-is-reached-after-long-negotiations.html?_r=0

60. BBC News, 14 July 2015, "Iran nuclear crisis: Six key points." http://www.bbc.co.uk/news/world-middle-east-32114862

61. Claire Phipps, Matthew Weaver and Raya Jalabi, *Guardian*, 14 July 2015, "Agreement to end 12-year standoff over Iran's nuclear program." https://www.theguardian.com/world/live/2015/jul/14/iran-nuclear-talks-deal-historic-vienna-live-updates

62. Tehran Bureau correspondent, *Guardian*, 16 July 2015, "Warning from Iran's hardliners mars celebrations of nuclear deal." https://www.theguardian.com/world/iran-blog/2015/jul/16/iran-judiciary-warning-nuclear-deal-celebrations

63. Ian Black, *Guardian*, 14 July 2015, "Iran nuclear deal: the winners and losers," https://www.theguardian.com/world/2015/jul/14/iran-nuclear-deal-the-winners-and-losers

64. Ibid.

65. Saeed Kamali Dehghan, *Guardian*, 13 October 2015, "Iranian parliament passes bill approving nuclear deal." https://www.theguardian.com/world/2015/oct/13/iranian-parliament-passes-bill-approving-nuclear-deal

66. Mark Mazzetti and Helene Cooper, *New York Times*, 18 April 2015, "Sale of U.S. Arms Fuels the Wars of Arab States." https://www.nytimes.com/2015/04/19/world/middleeast/sale-of-us-arms-fuels-the-wars-of-arab-states.html

67. Andrea Shalal, Reuters, 14 October 2015, "Saudi Arabia signs deal for 320 PAC-3 missiles—Lockheed." https://www.reuters.com/article/usa-saudi-lockheed/saudi-arabia-signs-deal-for-320-pac-3-missiles-lockheed-idUSL1N12E20K20151014

68. Warren Strobel and Jonathan Landay, Reuters, 10 October 2016, "Exclusive: As Saudis bombed Yemen, US worried about legal blowback." https://www.reuters.com/article/us-usa-saudi-yemen/exclusive-as-saudis-bombed-yemen-u-s-worried-about-legal-blowback-idUSKCN12A0BQ

69. Associated Press, 28 October 2015, "Doctors Without Borders says Saudi-led airstrikes bomb Yemen hospital." http://www.foxnews.com/world/2015/10/28/doctors-without-borders-says-saudi-led-airstrikes-bomb-yemen-hospital.html

70. BBC News, 14 December 2015, "Yemen conflict: Gulf commanders 'killed in missile strike." http://www.bbc.co.uk/news/world-middle-east-35091675

71. Fred Lambert, UPI, 15 December 2015, "Saudi, Emirati military commanders, dozens others killed in Houthi rocket strike in Yemen." http://www.upi.com/Top_News/World-News/2015/12/15/Saudi-Emirati-military-commanders-dozens-others-killed-in-Houthi-rocket-strike-in-Yemen/2061450200128/

72. Emily Estelle, Critical Threats, 3 December 2015, "2015 Yemen Crisis Situation Report: December 2." http://www.criticalthreats.org/yemen/yemen-crisis-situation-reports-december-2-2015

73. BBC News, 16 December 2015, "Yemen conflict: Warring parties 'exchange prisoners." http://www.bbc.co.uk/news/world-middle-east-35110869

74. *Guardian*, 18 December 2015, "Yemen's UN-sponsored peace talks suspended after ceasefire violation." https://www.theguardian.com/world/2015/dec/18/yemens-un-peace-talks-suspended-ceasefire-violation

75. BBC News, 27 January 2016, "Yemen conflict: Saudi-led coalition targeting civilians, UN says." http://www.bbc.co.uk/news/world-middle-east-35423282

76. Shuaib Almosaw and Kareem Fahim, *New York Times*, 27 February 2016. http://www.

nytimes.com/2016/02/28/world/middleeast/yemeni-civilians-killed-by-Air strike-on-market-witnesses-say.html

77. Orla Guerin BBC News, 26 March 2016, "A year of war that has set Yemen back decades." http://www.bbc.co.uk/news/world-middle-east-35901321
78. Mark Mazzetti and Eric Schmitt, *New York Times*, 13 March 2016. "Quiet Support for Saudis Entangles U.S. in Yemen." http://www.nytimes.com/2016/03/14/world/middleeast/yemen-saudi-us.html?ref=topics
79. Al Arabiya News/AFP, 11 March 2016, "Kerry holds talks on Syria, Yemen in Saudi Arabia." http://english.alarabiya.net/en/News/middle-east/2016/03/11/Kerry-heads-to-Saudi-France-for-Syria-and-regional-talks.html
80. Nick Gladstone, *New York Times*, 28 March 2016, "Saudis Announce Prisoner Swap With Houthis in Yemen Conflict." http://www.nytimes.com/2016/03/29/world/middleeast/saudis-announce-prisoner-swap-with-houthis-in-yemen-conflict.html
81. Reuters, 19 June 2016, "Yemen, warring sides swap 194 prisoners in Taiz." https://www.reuters.com/article/US-yemen-security-taiz-idUSKCN0Z409I
82. Reuters, 28 July, 2016, "Houthi-led bloc says to set up body to run Yemen with peace talks stalled." http://www.reuters.com/article/us-yemen-security-presidency-idUSKCN1081SC
83. Iona Craig, *Guardian*, 12 December 2017, "Bombed into famine: how Saudi air campaign targets Yemen's food supplies."
84. Ewen MacAskill and Paul Torpey, *Guardian*, 16 September 2016, "One in three Saudi air raids on Yemen hit civilian sites, data shows." https://www.theguardian.com/world/2016/sep/16/third-of-saudi-air-strikes-on-yemen-have-hit-civilian-sites-data-shows
85. BBC News, 9 October 2016, "Yemenis protest after funeral hall attack" http://www.bbc.co.uk/news/world-middle-east-37603795; and Nadia Khomami, *Guardian*, 8 October 2016, "Airstrikes on Yemen funeral kill at least 140 people, UN official says." https://www.theguardian.com/world/2016/oct/08/saudi-led-coalition-airstrike-hit-yemen-funeral-officials-say
86. Jeremy M. Sharp, *Eurasia Review*, 12 December 2016, "Yemen: Civil War And Regional Intervention—Analysis." http://www.eurasiareview.com/12122016-yemen-civil-war-and-regional-intervention-analysis/
87. Jeremy M. Sharp, *Eurasia Review*, 12 December 2016, "Yemen: Civil War And Regional Intervention—Analysis." http://www.eurasiareview.com/12122016-yemen-civil-war-and-regional-intervention-analysis/
88. Ben Hubbard, *New York Times*, 26 Nov 2016, "Plight of Houthi Rebels Is Clear in Visit to Yemen's Capital," http://www.nytimes.com/2016/11/26/world/middleeast/houthi-rebels-yemen.html
89. Nasser al Sakkaf, *Middle East Eye*, 19 October 2016. "Yemen's Dim Economy: Two Central Banks, No Pay," http://www.middleeasteye.net/news/yemen-s-dim-economy-two-central-banks-no-pay-735673393; and Jeremy M. Sharp, *Eurasia Review*, 12 December 2016, "Yemen: Civil War And Regional Intervention—Analysis." http://www.eurasiareview.com/12122016-yemen-civil-war-and-regional-intervention-analysis/
90. Helene Cooper, *New York Times*, 13 December 2016, "U.S. Blocks Arms Sale to Saudi Arabia Amid Concerns Over Yemen War." https://www.nytimes.com/2016/12/13/us/politics/saudi-arabia-arms-sale-yemen-war.html
91. *Wargeyska Saxafi*, 9 December 2016, "The Iran-Houthi arms pipeline." https://wargeyskasaxafi.wordpress.com/2016/12/09/report-iranian-arms-sent-to-yemen-via-somalia/

92. US Institute of Peace, 5 April 2016, "US Navy Seizes Iranian Arms Shipment." http:// iranprimer.usip.org/blog/2016/may/23/us-navy-seizes-iranian-arms-shipment

14. TRUMP FUELS GULF RIVALS' COLD WAR

1. In a similar situation in the US presidential poll in November 2000, Democrat candidate Al Gore scored 544,000 votes more than Republican George W. Bush.
2. Peter Baker, *New York Times*, 5 January 2018, "For Trump, Book Raises Familiar Questions of Loyalty and Candor." https://www.nytimes.com/2018/01/05/us/politics/trump-fire-fury-book-loyalty.html
3. Jeremy Diamond, CNN, 8 December 2015, "Donald Trump: Ban all Muslim travel to US." http://edition.cnn.com/2015/12/07/politics/donald-trump-muslim-ban-immigration/
4. Eric Levitz, *New York Magazine*, 17 February 2016, "Donald Trump Suggested Saudi Arabia Was Behind 9/11 Multiple Times Wednesday." http://nymag.com/daily/intelligencer/2016/02/donald-trump-suggests-the-saudis-did-911.html
5. Laura Smith-Spark, CNN, 10 November 2016, "What Trump has said about the world." http://edition.cnn.com/2016/11/09/politics/donald-trump-world-view/
6. Ibid.
7. Maggie Haberman and David E. Sanger, *New York Times*, 26 March 2016; "Transcript: Donald Trump Expounds on His Foreign Policy Views." http://www.nytimes.com/2016/03/27/us/politics/donald-trump-transcript.html
8. Stephen J. Adler, Jeff Mason and Steve Holland, Reuters, 17 April 2017, "Exclusive: Trump Complains Saudis Not Paying Fair Share for U.S. Defense", 27 April, 2017.
9. SIPRI, 5 April 2016, "World military spending resumes upward course."
10. Stephen J. Adler, Jeff Mason and Steve Holland, Reuters, 17 April 2017, "Exclusive: Trump Complains Saudis Not Paying Fair Share for U.S. Defense", 27 April, 2017.
11. Maggie Haberman and David E. Sanger, *New York Times*, 26 March 2016; "Transcript: Donald Trump Expounds on His Foreign Policy Views." http://www.nytimes.com/2016/03/27/us/politics/donald-trump-transcript.html
12. Anwar Iqbal, *Dawn*, 27 January 2017, "Pakistan, Afghanistan visa applicants to face extreme vetting: Trump." https://www.dawn.com/news/1311028
13. Anthony Zurcher, BBC News, 6 March 2017, "Will Trump's new travel ban be halted again in court?." http://www.bbc.co.uk/news/world-us-canada-39149052
14. Anna Giaritelli, *Washington Examiner*, 19 May 2017, "Ritz-Carlton in Riyadh projects five-story portrait of Trump on side of hotel." http://www.washingtonexaminer.com/ritz-carlton-in-riyadh-projects-five-story-portrait-of-trump-on-side-of-hotel/article/2623669
15. Bornie Kristian, *The Week*, Trump Travels Abroad, 20 May 2017. "Trump signs largest arms deal in American history with Saudi Arabia. http://theweek.com/speedreads/700428/trump-signs-largest-arms-deal-american-history-saudi-arabia
16. Defense One, May 2017, "There's Less than Meets the Eye in Trump's Saudi Arms Deal." http://www.defenseone.com/ideas/2017/05/theres-less-meets-eye-trumps-saudi-arms-deal/138055/
17. Fuad Masum, the president of Shia-majority Iraq, was an ethnic Kurd belonging to the Sunni sect.
18. The White House, Office of the Press Secretary, 21 May 2017,. "President Trump's Speech to the Arab Islamic American Summit." https://www.whitehouse.gov/the-press-office/2017/05/21/president-trumps-speech-arab-islamic-american-summit

19. Dilip Hiro, YaleGlobal Online, 25 May 2017, "Saudi Arabia Plays Trump on Iran to Tilt Middle East Balance." http://yaleglobal.yale.edu/content/saudi-arabia-plays-trump-iran-tilt-middle-east-balance

20. David Martosko, Mail Online, 21 May 2017, "Trump shows off buddy act with Mideast leaders as he praises the Egyptian president's shoes—while promising 'beautiful military equipment' to Qatar." http://www.dailymail.co.uk/news/article-4527130/Trump-praises-al-Sisi-s-shoes-promises-arms-Qatar.html

21. Christopher de Bellaigue, New York Times, 11 June 2017, "Will Iran Descend Into Chaos?" https://www.nytimes.com/2017/06/11/opinion/will-iran-descend-into-chaos.html

22. There was no known response from the Iranian authorities to Prince Bin Salman's claim. They would have been justified in pointing out that what Supreme Leader Ayatollah Ali Khamanei had said after the barring of Iranians from the Hajj pilgrimage in September 2016 was nothing more than "the world of Islam must fundamentally reconsider the management of the two holy places and the issue of Hajj."

23. Ben Hubbard, New York Times, 2 May 2017, "Dialogue With Iran Is Impossible, Saudi Arabia's Defense Minister Says." https://www.nytimes.com/2017/05/02/world/middleeast/saudi-arabia-iran-defense-minister.html

24. Gregory Korte, USA Today, 21 May 2017, "In speech to Muslim leaders, Trump condemns 'Islamic extremism'." https://www.usatoday.com/story/news/politics/2017/05/21/trump-muslim-world-speech-saudi-arabia-terrorism/101976694/

25. Dilip Hiro, TomDispatch.com, 6 July 2017, "Two Impulsive Leaders Fan the Global Flames." http://www.tomdispatch.com/blog/176303/tomgram%3A_dilip_hiro%2C_two_impulsive_leaders_fan_the_global_flames/

26. Bethan McKerrran, Independent, 24 May 2017, "Qatar's state news agency blames hackers for fake news story praising Israel and criticizing allies."http://www.independent.co.uk/news/world/middle-east/qatar-news-agency-fake-news-israel-praise-criticise-allies-middle-east-sheikh-donald-trump-a7753026.html

27. Maha El Dahan and William Maclean, Reuters, 24 May, 2017, "Gulf rift reopens as Qatar decries hacked comments by emir." https://www.reuters.com/article/us-qatar-cyber/gulf-rift-reopens-as-qatar-decries-hacked-comments-by-emir-idUSKBN18K02Z_

28. Reuters Staff, 6 June 2017, "Trump says Mideast leaders pointed to Qatar as financing radicalism."https://www.reuters.com/article/us-gulf-qatar-trump/trump-says-mideast-leaders-pointed-to-qatar-as-financing-radicalism-idUSKBN18X1I6

29. Phil Stewart, Reuters, 6 June 2017, "US military praises Qatar, despite Trump tweet."https://www.reuters.com/article/us-gulf-qatar-usa-pentagon/u-s-military-praises-qatar-despite-trump-tweet-idUSKBN18X2G2

30. Dilip Hiro, TomDispatch.com, 6 July 2017, "Two Impulsive Leaders Fan the Global Flames." http://www.tomdispatch.com/blog/176303/tomgram%3A_dilip_hiro%2C_two_impulsive_leaders_fan_the_global_flames/

31. Christina Lamb, Sunday Times, 11 June 2017, "Under siege in the gilded cage of Qatar." https://www.thetimes.co.uk/article/what-is-life-like-during-qatar-blockade-6jljvhthq

32. Dilip Hiro, TomDispatch.com, 6 July 2017, "Two Impulsive Leaders Fan the Global Flames." http://www.tomdispatch.com/blog/176303/tomgram%3A_dilip_hiro%2C_two_impulsive_leaders_fan_the_global_flames/

33. Peter Beaumont, Guardian, 15 June 2017, "US signs deal to supply F-15 jets to Qatar after Trump terror claims." https://www.theguardian.com/world/2017/jun/15/us-signs-deal-to-supply-f-15-jets-to-qatar-after-trump-terror-claims

34. Untutored in diplomatic protocol, US President Donald Trump congratulated Prince Muhammad bin Salman on his elevation, bypassing King Salman, the prime-mover.

35. Wikipedia, the free encyclopedia, https://en.wikipedia.org/wiki/Economy_of_Qatar

36. Tom Gjelten, All Things Considered, NPR, 24 March 2017, "Push To Name Muslim Brotherhood a Terrorist Group Worries US Offshoots." http://www.npr.org/2017/03/24/520299701/push-to-name-muslim-brotherhood-a-terrorist-group-worries-u-s-offshoots

37. Muhammad Sergie, Bloomberg.com, 11 January 2017, "The Tiny Gulf Country With a $335 Billion Global Empire." https://www.bloomberg.com/news/articles/2017-01-11/qatar-sovereign-wealth-fund-s-335-global-empire

38. Foreign Staff, *Daily Telegraph*, 11 June 2017, "Iran sends five planes of vegetables to help Qatar after five Arab nations cut ties over 'extremism' links." http://www.telegraph.co.uk/news/2017/06/11/iran-sends-five-planes-vegetables-qatar/

39. Christopher de Bellaigue, *New York Times*, 11 June 2017, "Will Iran Descend Into Chaos?" https://www.nytimes.com/2017/06/11/opinion/will-iran-descend-into-chaos.html

40. *Independent*, 19 June 2017, "Iran calls missile attack on Syria militants a wider warning." http://independent.ie/world-news/iran-calls-attack-on-syria-militants-a-wider-warning-35840917.html

41. Dilip Hiro, YaleGlobal Online, 25 May 2017, "Saudi Arabia Plays Trump on Iran to Tilt Middle East Balance." http://yaleglobal.yale.edu/content/saudi-arabia-plays-trump-iran-tilt-middle-east-balance

42. BBC News, 22 May 2015, "Saudi Arabia attack: Islamic State claims Shia mosque bombing." http://www.bbc.co.uk/news/world-middle-east-32843510

43. Riyadh Muhammad, *Fiscal Times*, 2 April 2015, "Muslim Cleric Calls All Out War." http://www.thefiscaltimes.com/2015/04/02/Muslim-Cleric-Calls-All-Out-War

44. *The New Arab*, 27 June 2017, "Violence erupts following Saudi demolition of the historic Shia homes."https://www.alaraby.co.uk/english/News/2017/6/27/Violence-erupts-following-Saudi-demolition-of-historic-Shia-homes

45. Noah Browning and Katie Paul, Reuters, 2 August 2017, "Saudi security forces flatten old quarter of Shia town."https://www.reuters.com/article/us-saudi-security-awamiya/saudi-security-forces-flatten-old-quarter-of-shiite-town-idUSKBN1AP21S?il=0

46. Sally Nabil, BBC News, 16 August 2017, "Awamiya: Inside Saudi Shia town devastated by demolitions and fighting."http://www.bbc.co.uk/news/world-middle-east-40937581

47. *Middle East Eye*, 12 May 2017, "Yemen President says UAE acting like occupiers." http://www.middleeasteye.net/news/exclusive-yemeni-president-says-emiratis-acting-occupiers-1965874493

48. Maggie Michael and Ahmed Al-Haj, Associated Press, 6 November 2017, "Saudi barred Yemeni president from going home, officials say." https://www.apnews.com/4e4a659cc61d479d96e9591c80ef13d3

49. David D. Kirkpatrick, *New York Times*, 6 November 2017, "Saudi Arabia Charges Iran With 'Act of War,' Raising Threat of Military Clash." https://www.nytimes.com/2017/11/06/world/middleeast/yemen-saudi-iran-missile.html

50. Kate Lyons, *Guardian*, 12 October 2017, "Yemen's cholera outbreak now the worst in history as millionth case looms." https://www.theguardian.com/global-development/2017/oct/12/yemen-cholera-outbreak-worst-in-history-1-million-cases-by-end-of-year

51. Bruce Riedel, *Al Monitor*, 18 Oct 2017, "Why did Saudi Arabia save Yemen's ex-president again?"https://www.al-monitor.com/pulse/originals/2017/10/saudi-arabia-yemen-save-ali-abdullah-saleh-russia.html

52. Shuaib Almosawa and Nour Youssef, *New York Times*, 1 November 2017, "Airstrike Kills at Least 25 at Market in Yemen." https://www.nytimes.com/2017/11/01/world/middleeast/yemen-saudi-airstrike.html

53. David D. Kirkpatrick, *New York Times*, 6 November 2017, "Saudi Arabia Charges Iran With 'Act of War,' Raising Threat of Military Clash." https://www.nytimes.com/2017/11/06/world/middleeast/yemen-saudi-iran-missile.html

54. Martin Chulov, *Guardian*, 5 December 2017, "Saudi purge sees 159 business leaders held in Riyadh hotel." https://www.theguardian.com/world/2017/dec/05/saudi-purge-sees-159-business-leaders-held-in-riyadh-hotel

55. Al Jazeera and News Agencies, 9 November 2017, "Saudi 'freezes bank accounts' of Muhammad bin Nayef." http://www.aljazeera.com/news/2017/11/saudi-freezes-bank-accounts-Muhammad-bin-nayef-171108210630650.html

56. David D. Kirkpatrick, *New York Times*, 6 November 2017, "Saudi Arabia Charges Iran With 'Act of War,' Raising Threat of Military Clash." https://www.nytimes.com/2017/11/06/world/middleeast/yemen-saudi-iran-missile.html

57. BBC News, 30 November 2017, "Yemen war: Fighting breaks out among allied rebels." http://www.bbc.co.uk/news/world-middle-east-42179313

58. Patrick Wintour, *Guardian*, 24 Nov 2017, "Saudi Arabia still barring aid to Yemen despite pledge to lift siege." https://www.theguardian.com/world/2017/nov/24/saudi-arabia-continues-to-block-humanitarian-aid-to-yemen

59. Reuters, 2 December 2017, "Yemen's Saleh says ready for 'new page' with Saudi-led coalition." https://www.reuters.com/article/us-yemen-security/yemens-saleh-says-ready-for-new-page-with-saudi-led-coalition-idUSKBN1DW08P

60. Shuaib Almosawa and Ben Hubbard, *New York Times*, 4 December 2017, "Yemen's Ex-President Killed as Mayhem Convulses Capital." https://www.nytimes.com/2017/12/04/world/middleeast/saleh-yemen-houthis.html

61. William Harris, *Lebanon: A History, 600–2011*, Oxford University Press, Oxford, 2012, p. 274.

62. Hiro, *A Comprehensive Dictionary of the Middle East*, p. 244.

63. Ibid., pp. 160, 178.

64. In January 2011, the prosecutor of the Special Lebanon Tribunal submitted a sealed indictment for the pre-trial judge Daniel Fransen to confirm. Once this was done, the STL submitted four confidential arrest warrants to the Lebanese government on 30 June. These warrants were believed to name four senior members of Hizbollah. Its leader Hassan Nasrallah questioned the legitimacy of the STL. The warrants could not be served since the named persons went missing. See Hiro, *A Comprehensive Dictionary of the Middle East*, p. 233.

65. BBC News, 14 June 2013, "Who is supplying weapons to the warring sides in Syria?" http://www.bbc.co.uk/news/world-middle-east-22906965

66. Samia Nakhoul, Reuters, 26 September 2013, "Special Report: Hizbollah gambles all in Syria." https://www.reuters.com/article/us-syria-hezbollah-special-report/special-report-hezbollah-gambles-all-in-syria-idUSBRE98P0AI20130926

67. Sam Dagher, *Wall Street Journal*, "Iran 'Foreign Legion' Leads Battle in Syria's North." https://www.wsj.com/articles/iran-foreign-legion-leads-battle-in-syrias-north-1455672481

68. Anne Bernard, *New York Times*, 2 March 2016, "Saudi Arabia Cuts Billions in Aid to Lebanon, Opening Door for Iran." https://www.nytimes.com/2016/03/03/world/middleeast/saudi-arabia-cuts-billions-in-aid-to-lebanon-opening-door-for-iran.html

69. Martin Chulov, *Guardian*, 31 October 2016, "Iran ally Michel Aoun elected as president of Lebanon." https://www.theguardian.com/world/2016/oct/31/michel-aoun-elected-president-lebanon-iran-tehran-saudi-arabia

70. *The National*/AFP, 10 January 2017, "Lebanese president Aoun travels to Riyadh." https://www.thenational.ae/world/lebanese-president-aoun-travels-to-riyadh-1.11457

71. *Times of Israel*, 13 February 2017, "Lebanon needs Hezbollah to counter Israel Threat." https://www.timesofisrael.com/lebanon-needs-Hizbollah-to-counter-israel-aoun/

72. Yaakov Lappin, *Jerusalem Post*, 16 June 2016, "Analysis: Ten Years After War Hezbollah Powerful But More Stretched Than Ever." http://www.jpost.com/Arab-Israeli-Conflict/Analysis-Hezbollah-powerful-but-more-stretched-than-ever-457035

73. Zeina Karam, *Independent*, 4 November 2017, "Lebanon Prime Minister Saad Hariri announces surprise resignation over 'assassination plot'". http://www.independent.co.uk/news/world/middle-east/lebanon-prime-minister-saad-hariri-resignation-resigns-quits-future-movement-surprise-latest-a8037266.html

74. Press TV, 5 November 2017, "Lebanese army says it has not uncovered any assassination plans." http://www.presstv.com/Detail/2017/11/05/541104/Lebanese-army-says-it-has-not-uncovered-any-assassination-plans

75. Ben Hubbard and Hwaida Saad, *New York Times*, 25 Nov 2017, "Lebanon's Vanishing Prime Minister Is Back at Work: Now What?". https://www.nytimes.com/2017/11/25/world/middleeast/lebanon-saad-hariri-iran-saudi-arabia.html

76. Anne Bernard, *New York Times*, 5 December 2017, "It's Official: Lebanese Prime Minister Not Resigning After All." https://www.nytimes.com/2017/12/05/world/middleeast/lebanon-hariri-saudi.html

77. Max Fisher, Eric Schmitt, Audrey Carlsen and Malachy Brown, *New York Times*, 4 December 2017. "Did American Missile Defense Fail in Saudi Arabia?" https://www.nytimes.com/interactive/2017/12/04/world/middleeast/saudi-missile-defense.html

78. Michele Nichols, Reuters, 30 November 2017, "Exclusive: Yemen rebel missiles fired at Saudi Arabia appear Iranian—U.N." https://www.reuters.com/article/us-yemen-security-un-exclusive/exclusive-yemen-rebel-missiles-fired-at-saudi-arabia-appear-ira-nian-u-n-idUSKBN1DU36N

79. Julian Borger and Patrick Wintour, *Guardian*, 14 December 2017, "US gives evidence Iran supplied missiles that Yemen rebels fired at Saudi Arabia." https://www.theguard-ian.com/world/2017/dec/14/us-gives-evidence-iran-supplied-missiles-that-yemen-reb-els-fired-at-saudi-arabia

80. Press TV, 19 November 2017, "Israel minister discloses covert ties with Saudi Arabia for first time." http://www.presstv.com/Detail/2017/11/19/542784/Israel-Saudi-Arabia-Iran-Energy-Minister-Yuval-Steinitz-Army-Radio-covert-contacts

81. Jeffrey Heller, Stephen Kalin, Reuters, 19 November 2017, "Israeli minister reveals covert contacts with Saudi Arabia." https://af.reuters.com/article/worldNews/idAFK-BN1DJ0R3

82. Press TV, 19 November 2017, "Israel minister discloses covert ties with Saudi Arabia for first time." http://www.presstv.com/Detail/2017/11/19/542784/Israel-Saudi-Arabia-Iran-Energy-Minister-Yuval-Steinitz-Army-Radio-covert-contacts

83. *The New Arab*, 14 Nov 2017, "Saudi Arabia plans 'official ties with Israel', leaked document reveals." https://www.alaraby.co.uk/english/News/2017/11/14/Saudi-Arabia-plans-official-ties-with-Israel-leaked-document

84. *Guardian*/Reuters, 9 September 2017, "Saudi Arabia suspends dialogue, saying Qatar 'distorting facts'." https://www.theguardian.com/world/2017/sep/09/saudi-arabia-suspends-dialogue-saying-qatar-distorting-facts

85. Yara Bayoumy and Jeff Mason, Reuters, 19 September 2017, "Qatar emir again urges dialogue, Trump says dispute to be resolved quickly." https://www.reuters.com/

article/us-un-assembly-qatar/qatar-emir-again-urges-dialogue-trump-says-dispute-to-be-resolved-quickly-idUSKCN1BU2IB

86. Dilip Hiro, YaleGlobal Online, 7 December 2017, "Expanding Russia-Iran-Turkey Alliance puts the US on Back Foot." https://yaleglobal.yale.edu/content/expanding-russia-iran-turkey-alliance-puts-us-back-foot

87. *Times of Israel*/Agencies, 6 December 2017, "Two-day Gulf summit ends in minutes as Qatar is snubbed." https://www.timesofisrael.com/two-day-gulf-summit-ends-in-minutes-as-qatar-snubbed/

88. *The Hindu*/AP, 15 September 2017, "Saudi Arabia cracks down on critics of crown prince." http://www.thehindu.com/news/international/saudi-arabia-cracks-down-on-critics-of-crown-prince/article19689934.ece

89. Ibid.

90. Ibid.

91. Thomas L. Friedman, *New York Times*, 23 November 2017, "Saudi Arabia's Arab Spring, at Last."https://www.nytimes.com/2017/11/23/opinion/saudi-prince-mbs-arab-spring.html

92. Ibid.

93. Martin Chulov, the *Guardian*, 5 December 2017, "Saudi purge sees 159 business leaders held in Riyadh hotel." https://www.theguardian.com/world/2017/dec/05/saudi-purge-sees-159-business-leaders-held-in-riyadh-hotel

94. Ben Hubbard, *New York Times*, 5 November 2017, "Saudi Prince, Asserting Power, Brings Clerics to Heel." https://www.nytimes.com/2017/11/05/world/middleeast/saudi-arabia-wahhabism-salafism-mohammed-bin-salman.html

95. *Wall Street Journal*, May 1, 1981.

96. Saudi Royal Wealth: Where do they get all that money, 1996, November 30, 96RIYADH4784_a. https://wikileaks.org/plusd/cables/96RIYADH4784_a.html

97. Matthew Kaminski, *Wall Street Journal*, 22 November 2013, "Prince Al-Waleed bin Talal: An Ally Frets About American Retreat." http://www.wsj.com/articles/SB10001424052702304337404579211742820387758

98. Christopher Helman, "Report Details How Saudi Royals Cream Off Oil Revenue," Forbes, 1 March 2011. http://www.forbes.com/sites/christopherhelman/2011/03/01/report-details-how-saudi-royals-cream-off-oil-revenue/

99. Simon Robinson, "Special Report: U.S. cables detail Saudi royal welfare program," Reuters, 28 February 2011. http://uk.reuters.com/article/us-wiki-saudi-money-idUSTRE71R2SA20110228. Since these stipends started at birth, they also provided an incentive for royals to procreate. Given the annual growth of 3 per cent, the number of princes and princesses doubled every 20–26 years. Anthony H. Cordesman, *Saudi Arabia Enters the 21st Century (Vol. 1): The Political, Foreign Policy, Economic, and Energy Dimensions*, Praeger, Westport, Conn, 2003, p. 143.

100. Saudi Royal Wealth: Where do they get all that money, 1996, November 30, 96RIYADH4784_a. https://wikileaks.org/plusd/cables/96RIYADH4784_a.html

101. Hiro, *Blood of the Earth*, p. 140.

102. Thomas L. Friedman, *New York Times*, 23 November 2017, "Saudi Arabia's Arab Spring, at Last." https://www.nytimes.com/2017/11/23/opinion/saudi-prince-mbs-arab-spring.html

103. David D, Kirkpatrick, Mark Mazzetti, and Eric Schmitt, *New York Times*, 7 December 2017, "Saudi Crown Prince Was Behind Record Bid for a Leonardo." https://www.nytimes.com/2017/12/07/world/middleeast/saudi-crown-prince-salvator-mundi.html. Earlier, Prince Bader had acted as an agent for Bin Salman in the commission

of an elaborate resort complex for the latter's five blood brothers. In addition, the Crown Prince had put Prince Bader in charge of a Saudi media firm controlled by the Salman branch of the House of Saud.

104. Stanley Carvalho, Reuters, 7 December 2017, "Louvre Abu Dhabi to display Leonardo's 'Salvator Mundi'. https://www.reuters.com/article/us-emirates-louvre/louvre-abu-dhabi-to-display-leonardos-salvator-mundi-idUSKBN1E11IO

105. Peter Beaumont, *Guardian*, 13 December 2027, "Palestinians no longer accept US as mediator, Abbas tells summit." https://www.theguardian.com/world/2017/dec/13/recep-tayyip-erdogan-unite-muslim-world-trump-east-jerusalem

106. Peter Beaumont, *Guardian*, 21 December 2017, "UN votes resoundingly to reject Trump's recognition of Jerusalem as capital." https://www.theguardian.com/world/2017/dec/21/united-nations-un-vote-donald-trump-jerusalem-israel

15. CONCLUSIONS

1. Hiro, *Inside the Middle East*, p. 338.
2. Hiro, *Blood of the Earth*, p. 86.
3. Jeffrey Goldberg, "The Obama Doctrine," *The Atlantic*, April 2016. http://www.the-atlantic.com/magazine/archive/2016/04/the-obama-doctrine/471525/
4. Hiro, *A Comprehensive Dictionary of the Middle East*, p. 373.
5. *Guardian*, 28 November 2010, "US embassy cables: Saudi king's advice for Barack Obama." US Riyadh Embassy cable dated 22 March 2009, SECRET RIYADH 000447. https://www.theguardian.com/world/us-embassy-cables-documents/198178
6. See p. 298.
7. Jess Staufenberg, "Saudi Arabia is 'not ready' for women drivers, says deputy crown prince," *The Independent*, 28 April 2016. http://www.independent.co.uk/news/world/middle-east/saudi-arabia-is-not-ready-for-women-drivers-says-deputy-crown-prince-mohammed-bin-salman-a7004611.html
8. Martin Chulov, *Guardian*, 26 September 2017, "Saudi Arabia to allow women to obtain driving licenses." https://www.theguardian.com/world/2017/sep/26/saudi-arabias-king-issues-order-allowing-women-to-drive
9. *Gulf News*, 10 April 2016, Saudi Grand Mufti says women should not drive". http://gulfnews.com/news/gulf/saudi-arabia/saudi-grand-mufti-says-women-should-not-drive-1.1708022
10. See "Ruling on Female driving cars," at www.alifta.com, Part 3, p. 351.
11. Ben Hubbard, *New York Times*, 5 November 2017, "Saudi Prince, Asserting Power, Brings Clerics to Heel." https://www.nytimes.com/2017/11/05/world/middleeast/saudi-arabia-wahhabism-salafism-mohammed-bin-salman.html
12. Ibid.
13. Thomas L. Friedman, *New York Times*, 23 Nov 2017, "Saudi Arabia's Arab Spring, at Last." https://www.nytimes.com/2017/11/23/opinion/saudi-prince-mbs-arab-spring.html
14. Martin Chulov, *Guardian*, 24 October 2017, "I will return Saudi Arabia to moderate Islam, says crown prince." https://www.theguardian.com/world/2017/oct/24/i-will-return-saudi-arabia-moderate-islam-crown-prince
15. See pp. 83–85.
16. Elliot House, *On Saudi Arabia*, p. 47.
17. Thomas L. Friedman, *New York Times*, 23 Nov 2017, "Saudi Arabia's Arab Spring, at

Last." The crown prince has big plans for his society. https://www.nytimes.com/2017/11/23/opinion/saudi-prince-mbs-arab-spring.html

18. Alicia Buller, *Arab News*, 24 October 2017, "Saudi Arabia announces $500 billion city of robots and renewables," http://www.arabnews.com/node/1182501/saudi-arabia

16. EPILOGUE

1. Ben Hubbard, *New York Times*, 27 January 2018, "Billionaire Saudi Prince, Alwaleed bin Talal, Is Freed From Detention." https://www.nytimes.com/2018/01/27/world/middleeast/saudi-arabia-alwaleed-bin-talal.html

2. Rania El Gamal and Stephen Kalin, Reuters, 14 January 2018, "Saudi Prince Alwaleed in settlement talks with government—sources." https://uk.reuters.com/article/uk-saudi-arrest-alwaleed/saudi-prince-alwaleed-in-settlement-talks-with-government-sources-idUKKBN1F308I

3. Ben Hubbard, *New York Times*, 27 January 2018. "Billionaire Saudi Prince, Alwaleed bin Talal, Is Freed From Detention," https://www.nytimes.com/2018/01/27/world/middleeast/saudi-arabia-alwaleed-bin-talal.html

4. Ben Hubbard, David D. Kirkpatrick, Kate Kelly and Mark Mazzetti, *New York Times*, 11 March 2018, "Saudis Said to Use Coercion and Abuse to Seize Billions." https://www.nytimes.com/2018/03/11/world/middleeast/saudi-arabia-corruption-Muhammad-bin-salman.html)

5. Ibid.

6. *Guardian*/Reuters, 29 Nov 2017, "Saudi prince Mutaib bin Abdullah pays $1bn in corruption https://www.theguardian.com/world/2017/nov/29/saudi-prince-miteb-bin-abdullah-pays-1bn-in-corruption-settlement

7. Rania El Gamal and Stephen Kalin, Reuters, 14 January 2018, "Saudi Prince Alwaleed in settlement talks with government—sources." https://uk.reuters.com/article/uk-saudi-arrest-alwaleed/saudi-prince-alwaleed-in-settlement-talks-with-government-sources-idUKKBN1F308I

8. Simeon Kerr, *Financial Times*, 26 January 2018, "Top Saudi broadcaster caught up in Riyadh's corruption shakedown." https://www.ft.com/content/a50075d2–0069–11e8–9650–9c0ad2d7c5b5

9. Vivian Nereim and Glen Carey, Bloomberg, 8 January 2018, "Saudi-Prince Detainees Include Sons of Dairy Billionaire, Sources Say." https://www.bloomberg.com/news/articles/2018–01–08/saudi-princes-detained-are-said-to-include-sons-of-almarai-head

10. Martin Chulov, *Guardian*, 30 January 2018, "Saudi Arabia claims anti-corruption purge recouped $100bn." https://www.theguardian.com/world/2018/January/30/anti-corruption-purge-nets-more-than-100bn-saudi-arabia-claims

11. Thomas L. Friedman, *New York Times*, 23 November 2017, "Saudi Arabia's Arab Spring, at Last." https://www.nytimes.com/2017/11/23/opinion/saudi-prince-mbs-arab-spring.html

12. Saeed Kamali Dehghan and Patrick Wintour, *Guardian*, 3 January 2018, "Thousands of Iranians join counter-protests after week of unrest." https://www.theguardian.com/world/2018/January/03/iranians-counter-protests-week-unrest

13. Ibid.

14. Thomas Erdbrink, David D. Kirkpatrick, and Nilo Tabrizyian, *New York Times*, 20 January 2018, "How Corruption and Cronyism in Banking Fueled Iran's Protests." https://www.nytimes.com/2018/01/20/world/middleeast/iran-protests-corruption-banks.html

15. Azadeh Moaveni, *Guardian*, 1 January 2018, "Iran knows how to silence protests. If only it knew how to listen." https://www.theguardian.com/commentisfree/2018/January/01/iran-silence-protests-learn-listen-young-people

16. Thomas Erdbrink, *New York Times*, 29 December 2017, "Scattered Protests Erupt in Iran Over Economic Woes." https://www.nytimes.com/2017/12/29/world/middleeast/scattered-protests-erupt-in-iran-over-economic-woes.html

17. Michael Georgy, Reuters, 7 January 2018, "Iran Guards say quell unrest fomented by foreign enemies." https://www.reuters.com/article/us-iran-rallies-guards/iran-guards-say-quell-unrest-fomented-by-foreign-enemies-idUSKBN1EW085

18. Sanam Vakil, *Guardian*, 4 January 2018, "How Donald Trump's tweets help Iran's supreme leader." https://www.theguardian.com/commentisfree/2018/January/04/donald-trump-tweets-iran-protesters-sanctions

19. Michael Georgy, Reuters, 7 January 2018, "Iran Guards say quell unrest fomented by foreign enemies." https://www.reuters.com/article/us-iran-rallies-guards/iran-guards-say-quell-unrest-fomented-by-foreign-enemies-idUSKBN1EW085

20. Thomas Erdbrink, David D. Kirkpatrick, and Nilo Tabrizyian, *New York Times*, 20 January 2018, "How Corruption and Cronyism in Banking Fueled Iran's Protests." https://www.nytimes.com/2018/01/20/world/middleeast/iran-protests-corruption-banks.html

21. Ibid,

22. Thomas Erdbrink, *New York Times*, 21 October 2017, "Iran Saps Strength of IRGC With Arrests and Cutbacks." https://www.nytimes.com/2017/10/21/world/middleeast/iran-revolutionary-guards.html

23. Thomas Erdbrink, David D. Kirkpatrick, and Nilo Tabrizyian, *New York Times*, 20 January 2018, "How Corruption and Cronyism in Banking Fueled Iran's Protests." https://www.nytimes.com/2018/01/20/world/middleeast/iran-protests-corruption-banks.html

24. Thomas Erdbrink, *New York Times*, 21 October 2017, "Iran Saps Strength of IRGC With Arrests and Cutbacks." https://www.nytimes.com/2017/10/21/world/middleeast/iran-revolutionary-guards.html

25. Ibid.

26. *Daily Mail*/Associated Press. 21 January 2018, "Iran's Guard may loosen grip on economy." http://www.dailymail.co.uk/wires/ap/article-5294025/Iran-try-loosen-Revolutionary-Guards-grip-economy.html)

27. Ben Hubbard, Iabel Kershner and Anne Bernard, *New York Times*, 19 February 2018, "Iran, Deeply Embedded in Syria, Expands 'Axis of Resistance.'" https://www.nytimes.com/2018/02/19/world/middleeast/iran-syria-israel.html)

28. Ibid.

29. Patrick Cockburn, *Independent*, 16 January 2018, "Trump's escalating threats to Iran risk destabilizing the Middle East."http://www.independent.co.uk/news/world/middle-east/donald-trump-us-iran-nuclear-deal-middle-east-relations-diplomacy-hassan-rouhani-weapons-syria-a8162241.html

30. Michael Gregory, Reuters, 14 May 2018, "Fiery cleric Sadr taps anger over Iran to lead Iraq poll." https://www.reuters.com/article/us-iraq-election-sadr/fiery-cleric-sadr-taps-anger-over-iran-to-lead-iraq-poll-idUSKCN1IF2G8

31. Patrick Wintour, *Guardian*, 28 December 2017, "Saudi-led airstrikes kill 68 civilians in one day of Yemen's 'absurd' war." https://www.theguardian.com/world/2017/dec/28/saudi-led-airstrikes-yemen-war-united-nations

32. Reuters Staff, 21 January 2018, "Yemen sets first budget since 2014." https://

uk.reuters.com/article/us-yemen-security-budget/yemen-sets-first-budget-since-2014-idUKKBN1FA0IT

33. Katharine Zimmerman, "Critical Threats, Yemen Crisis Situation Report," 18 May 2018. https://www.criticalthreats.org/briefs/yemen-situation-report/2018-yemen-crisis-situation-report-may-18

34. Xinhua, 27 February 2018, "UN Security Council adopts Russian-drafted resolution on renewal of Yemen sanctions." http://www.xinhuanet.com/english/2018-02/27/c_137002111.htm

35. Nicholas Fandos, *New York Times*, 20 March 2018, "Senators Reject Limits on U.S. Support for Saudi-led Fight in Yemen." https://www.nytimes.com/2018/03/20/us/politics/senate-yemen-military-support.html)

36. Max Fisher, Eric Schmitt, Audrey Carlsen and Malachy Brown, *New York Times*, 4 December 2017, "Did American Missile Defense Fail in Saudi Arabia?" https://www.nytimes.com/interactive/2017/12/04/world/middleeast/saudi-missile-defense.html

37. Helene Cooper, Thomas Gibbons-Neff and Eric Schmitt, *New York Times*, 3 May 2018,"Army Special Forces Secretly Help Saudis Combat Threat From Yemen Rebels." https://www.nytimes.com/2018/05/03/us/politics/green-berets-saudi-yemen-border-houthi.html

38. Ibid.

39. Patrick Wintour and Saeed Kamali Dehghan, *Guardian*, 31 May 2018, "Battle for rebel-held Yemen port may trigger humanitarian disaster." https://www.theguardian.com/world/2018/may/31/battle-for-rebel-held-yemen-port-may-trigger-humanitarian-disaster

40. Mark Landler, *New York Times*, 20 March 2018, "Saudi Prince's White House Visit Reinforces Trump's Commitment to Heir Apparent." https://www.nytimes.com/2018/03/20/us/politics/saudi-crown-prince-arrives-at-white-house-to-meet-with-trump.html

41. James Landale, BBC News, 7 March 2018, "Why Saudi Crown Prince Muhammad bin Salman's UK visit matters." http://www.bbc.co.uk/news/world-middle-east-43235643

42. Joe Watts, *Independent*, 7 March 2018, "Muhammad Bin Salman: 'Bizarre' PR drive launched by Saudi Crown Prince's backers in face of UK protests over Yemen war." https://www.independent.co.uk/news/uk/politics/Muhammad-bin-salman-uk-visit-protests-pr-publicity-adverts-yemen-saudi-arabia-crown-prince-a8243486.html

43. James Landale, BBC News, 7 March 2018, "Why Saudi Crown Prince Muhammad bin Salman's UK visit matters." http://www.bbc.co.uk/news/world-middle-east-43235643)

44. Eli Clifton, Lobelog, 7 January 2016, "Washington's Multi-Million-Dollar Saudi PR Machine."https://lobelog.com/washingtons-multi-million-dollar-saudi-pr-machine/

45. Glen Carey and Sarah Algethami, Bloomberg, 2 April 2018, "Saudi Prince's US Tour Plays Big at Home."https://www.bloomberg.com/news/articles/2018–04–03/saudi-prince-s-u-s-tour-plays-big-at-home

46. *Haaretz*, 28 March 2018, "Saudi Crown Prince's Full U.S. Itinerary Leaked Online and He Apparently Saved the Best for Last." https://www.haaretz.com/middle-east-news/saudi-crown-prince-s-full-u-s-itinerary-leaked-online-1.5957103

47. Ben Hubbard, *New York Times*, 27 March 2018, "Saudi Crown Prince, on US Visit, Urges Tough Line on Iran." https://www.nytimes.com/2018/03/27/world/middleeast/Muhammad-bin-salman-saudi-prince-interview.html

48. Amir Tibon, *Haaretz*, 3 April 2018, "Saudi Crown Prince: We Share Common Interests

With Israel, but There Must Be Peace With Palestinians." https://www.haaretz.com/middle-east-news/saudi-prince-israelis-have-the-right-to-have-their-own-land-1.5974278

49. Ben Hubbard, *New York Times*, 3 April 2018, "Supported by Saudi Prince Says Israelis Have Right to 'Their Own Land." https://www.nytimes.com/2018/04/03/world/middleeast/saudi-arabia-Muhammad-bin-salman-israel.html

50. The venue was changed from Riyadh to Dhahran in the Eastern Province to avoid the embarrassment of a missile fired by the Houthis striking the Saudi capital during the summit.

51. Agence France-Presse, 17 April 2018, "Arab ire at US on Jerusalem move looks unlikely to spark action." http://www.arabianbusiness.com/politics-economics/394294-arab-ire-at-us-jerusalem-move-looks-unlikely-to-spark-action

52. Tim Arango, *New York Times*, 6 April 2018, "Supported by Oprah, Rupert Murdoch, Harvard: Saudi Prince's US Tour." https://www.nytimes.com/2018/04/06/world/middleeast/saudi-prince-Muhammad-bin-salman-us.html

53. *European News*, 29 March 2018, "US court allows 9/11 victims' lawsuits claiming Saudi Arabia helped plan terror attack." https://www.independent.co.uk/news/world/americas/saudi-arabia-9-11-victims-lawsuit-us-court-allowed-twin-towers-terror-attack-september-a8279236.html

54. Patrick Wintour and Saeed Kamali Dehghan, *Guardian*, 1 May 2018, "Europeans cast doubt on Israel's claims about Iran nuclear breaches." https://www.theguardian.com/world/2018/may/01/europeans-cast-doubt-on-israel-claims-about-iran-nuclear-breaches

55. *Guardian*, 9 May 2018, "The Guardian view on Iran's nuclear deal: Trump creates a narrative for war."https://www.theguardian.com/commentisfree/2018/may/09/the-guardian-view-on-irans-nuclear-deal-trump-creates-a-narrative-for-war

56. Patrick Wintour and Daniel Boffey, *Guardian*, 17 May 2018. "EU sets course for US clash with law blocking Iran sanctions." https://www.theguardian.com/world/2018/may/17/maersk-tankers-pull-out-of-iran-in-blow-to-nuclear-deal.

57. Reuters Staff, 16 May 2018, "Iran signs oil contract with Pergas to develop Keranj field." https://uk.reuters.com/article/us-oil-iran-contract/iran-signs-oil-contract-with-pergas-to-develop-keranj-field-idUKKCN1IH2NZ

58. Chen Aizhu, Reuters, 16 May 2018, "Exclusive: Iran asks Chinese oil buyers to maintain imports after US sanctions—sources."https://www.reuters.com/article/us-iran-nuclear-china-oil-exclusive/exclusive-iran-asks-chinese-oil-buyers-to-maintain-imports-after-u-s-sanctions-sources-idUSKCN1IH0VL

59. First Post/ Agence France-Presse, 15 April 2018, "Syrian Army declares complete retake of rebel-held Eastern Ghouta; clean-up operation underway." https://www.firstpost.com/world/syrian-army-declares-complete-retake-of-rebel-held-eastern-ghouta-clean-up-operation-underway-4432305.html

60. John R. Bolton, *New York Times*, 26 March 2015, "To Stop Iran's Bomb, Bomb Iran." https://www.nytimes.com/2015/03/26/opinion/to-stop-irans-bomb-bomb-iran.html

61. Al Jazeera News, 19 May 2018, "Gaza protests: All the latest updates."https://www.aljazeera.com/news/2018/04/gaza-protest-latest-updates-180406092506561.html

62. Michael Lipin, VOA, 15 May 2018, "Iranian Dissidents Criticize Tehran's Response to Israeli-Palestinian Turmoil."https://www.voanews.com/a/iranians-respond-to-gaza-violence/4394307.html

63. The New Arab, 17 May, "Arab League calls for international probe against Israeli crimes in Gaza massacre." https://www.alaraby.co.uk/english/news/2018/5/17/arab-league-calls-for-international-probe-against-israeli-crimes

64. Peter Beaumont, *Guardian*, 19 May 2028, "UN Human Rights Chief Rebukes Israel as

Egypt Opens Gaza Crossing." http://www.arabamerica.com/un-human-rights-chief-rebukes-israel-as-egypt-opens-gaza-crossing/

65. Gardiner Harris, *New York Times*, 28 April 2018, "Supported by Pompeo's Message to Saudis? Enough Is Enough: Stop Qatar Blockade." https://www.nytimes.com/2018/04/28/world/middleeast/mike-pompeo-saudi-arabia-qatar-blockade.html

66. Gardiner Harris and Mark Landler, *New York Times*, 9 April 2018, "Qatar Charm Offensive Appears to Have Paid Off, US Officials Say." https://www.nytimes.com/2018/04/09/us/politics/qatar-trump-embargo-charm-offensive.html).

67. Bel Trew, *The Times*, 31 Oct 2017, "Saudis want to topple me, says Sheikh Tamim bin Hamad al-Thani." https://www.thetimes.co.uk/article/saudis-want-to-topple-me-says-sheikh-tamim-bin-hamad-al-thani-9h9z07b2x

68. Julian Borger and Heather Stewart, *Guardian*, 21 May 2018, "Iran told: comply with US demands or face 'strongest sanctions in history'." https://www.theguardian.com/us-news/2018/may/21/iran-nuclear-deal-mike-pompeo-us-sanctions

69. Agence France-Presse, 20 April 2018, "Saudi Arabia's first cinema in over 35 years opens with Black Panther." https://www.theguardian.com/world/2018/apr/20/saudi-arabias-first-cinema-in-over-35-years-opens-with-black-panther.

70. Patrick Wintour, *Guardian*, 25 May 2018, "Saudi Arabia arrests key activist in human rights crackdown." https://www.theguardian.com/world/2018/may/25/saudi-arabia-arrests-human-rights-campaigner-mohammed-al-bajadi-women-right-drive

71. Jasmine Bager, Middle East Eye, 28 September 2016, "The camel in the room': Saudi women driving debate on end to guardianship rule."http://www.middleeasteye.net/in-depth/features/camel-room-saudi-women-driving-debate-end-guardianship-rule-317043821

72. Patrick Wintour, Guardian, 25 May 2018, "Saudi Arabia arrests key activist in human rights crackdown." https://www.theguardian.com/world/2018/may/25/saudi-arabia-arrests-human-rights-campaigner-mohammed-al-bajadi-women-right-drive

73. Law Learner, 2 Nov 2012, "Guardianship under Muslim law." inhttp://sanamurtaza.blogspot.com/2012/11/guardianship-under-muslim-law.html

SELECT BIBLIOGRAPHY

Aarts, Paul, and Carolien Roelants, *Saudi Arabia: A Kingdom in Peril*, Hurst, London, 2015.

Abbas, Hassan, *Pakistan's Drift into Extremism: Allah, the Army, and America's War on Terror*, M.E. Sharpe, New York, 2005.

Fahad M. Alsultan and Pedram Saeid, *The Development of Saudi-Iranian Relations Since the 1990s: Between Conflict and Accommodation*, Routledge, Abingdon, and New York, 2016.

Arberry, Arthur J., *The Koran Interpreted*, Oxford University Press, Oxford and New York, 1964.

Robert Byron, *The Road to Oxiana*, Macmillan, London, 1937.

Cordesman, Anthony H., *Saudi Arabia Enters the 21st Century (Vol. 1): The Political, Foreign Policy, Economic, and Energy Dimensions*, Praeger Publishers, Westport, Conn., 2003.

————, *Saudi Arabia Enters the 21st Century (Vol. 2): The Military and International Security Dimensions*, Praeger Publishers, Westport, Conn., 2003.

Hiro, Dilip, *Inside the Middle East*, Routledge and Kegan Paul, London, 1982/McGraw Hill, New York, 1983 (re-issued, 2013).

————, *Iran Under the Ayatollahs*, 1985 (re-issued, 2011).

————, *Holy Wars: The Rise of Islamic Fundamentalism*, Routledge, New York, 1989/ Paladin Books, London, 1989 (re-issued, 2013).

————, *The Longest War: The Iran-Iraq Military Conflict*, HarperCollins, London, 1989/ Routledge, New York, 1991.

————, *Desert Shield to Desert Storm: The Second Gulf War*, HarperCollins, London, 1992/ Routledge, New York, 1992.

————, *War Without End: The Rise of Islamist Terrorism and Global Response*, Routledge, London and New York, 2002.

————, *The Iranian Labyrinth: Journeys through Theocratic Iran and Its Furies*, Nation Books, New York, 2005/ *Iran Today*, Politico's Publishing, London, 2006.

————, *Blood of the Earth: The Battle for the Earth's Vanishing Oil Resources*, Nation Books, New York, 2007/ Politico's Publishing, London, 2008.

————, *A Comprehensive Dictionary of the Middle East*, Interlink Publishing Group, Northampton, MA, 2013.

Holden, David, and Richard Johns, *The House of Saud*, Sidgwick & Jackson, London, 1981.

Karen Elliot House, *On Saudi Arabia: Its People, Past, Religion, Fault Lines—and Future*, Alfred A. Knopf, New York, 2012/ Vintage, London, 2013.

Husain, Irfan, *Fatal Faultlines: Pakistan, Islam and the West*, Arc Manor Publishers, Rockville, MD, 2011.

SELECT BIBLIOGRAPHY

Hussain, Zahid, *Frontline Pakistan: The Struggle with Militant Islam*, Columbia University Press, New York, 2007.

Joshi, Shashank, *The Permanent Crisis: Iran's Nuclear Trajectory*, Routledge, Abingdon and New York, 2015.

Khumayni, Ruh Allah, *Islam and Revolution* (tr. Hamid Algar), Mizan Press, Berkeley, CA, 1981.

Lacey, Robert, *The Kingdom: Arabia and the House of Sa'ud*, Hutchinson, London, 1981/ Harcourt, Brace Jovanovich, New York, 1982.

———, *Inside the Kingdom: Kings, Clerics, Modernists, Terrorists, and the Struggle for Saudi Arabia*. Arrow Books, London, 2010/ Penguin Books, New York, 2010.

Lacroix, Stephan, *The Politics of Religious Dissent in Contemporary Saudi Arabia*, Harvard University Press, Cambridge and London, 2011.

Levy, Adrian, and Catherine Scott-Clark, *Deception: Pakistan, the United States and the Global Nuclear Weapons Conspiracy*, Atlantic Books, London, 2007.

Matthiesen, Toby, *The Other Saudis: Shiism, Dissent and Sectarianism*, Cambridge University Press, Cambridge and New York, 2014.

Al-Rasheed, Madawi, *A History of Saudi Arabia*, Cambridge University Press, Cambridge, 2002.

Ahmed Rashid, *Taliban: The Story of the Afghan Warlords*, Pan Books, London, 2011/ *Taliban: Militant Islam, Oil and Fundamentalism in Central Asia*, Yale University Press, New Haven, Conn., 2011.

Sardar, Ziauddin, *Mecca: The Sacred City*, Bloomsbury, London, 2015.

Suwaidi, Jamal S. (ed.), *Iran and the Gulf: A Search for Stability*, I.B. Tauris, London and New York, 1996.

Trofimov, Yaroslav, *The Siege of Mecca: The Forgotten Uprising*, Doubleday, New York, 2007/ Allen Lane, London, 2007.

Weston, Mark, *Prophets and Princes: Saudi Arabia from Muhammad to the Present*, John Wiley, Hoboken, NJ; and Chichester, 2008.

Wilson, Peter W., and Douglas F. Graham, *Saudi Arabia: The Coming Storm*, M.E. Sharpe, Armonk, NY, 1994.

Yergin, Daniel, *The Prize: The Epic Quest for Oil, Money and Power*, Simon & Schuster, New York and London, 1991.

Zuhur, Sherifa, *Saudi Arabia*, ABC-CLIO, Santa Barbara, CA, 2012.

INDEX

9/11 terrorist attacks, xii, xiv,
173–174, 176–177, 314, 315

Abadan, 97–98
al Abadi, Haider, 271, 272–273
Abbas, Mahmoud, 348
Abbasi-Davani, Fereydoon, 202,
237, 263
ABC News, 300
Abdu, Muhammad, 64
Abdul Aziz bin Abdul Rahman Al
Saud (Saudi king), xxi, 1, 12,
13–14, 16, 23–28, 30, 33, 137,
141, 269, 275, 288, 351–352
Abdul Aziz bin Muhammad bin Said
(Diriya ruler), 8
Abdul Aziz bin Saud bin Nayef Al
Saud (Saudi prince), 276, 327
Abdul Ilah bin Abdul Aziz Al Saud
(Saudi prince), 135
Abdul Muhsin bin Abdul Aziz Al
Saud (Saudi prince), 36
Abdul Rahman bin Abdul Aziz Al
Saud (Saudi prince), 137
Abdullah bin Abdul Aziz Al Saud
(Saudi king), xi, xiii, xv, xxi, 66,
114, 136, 137, 141–142, 170,
173, 196–197, 232, 274, 275,
278, 334, 351, 355

and 9/11 terrorist attacks,
176–177
and Arab Spring, 242–243, 244,
245, 249
and Egypt, 243–247, 249
and Iraq, 188–189, 213, 218,
222, 223, 237, 245
and National Guard, 137
and Barack Obama, 234, 273
and Pakistan, 206–207, 209,
222–223, 24, 228
and Shias, 220–221
and Syria, 254–255, 271
and United States, 75–76, 178,
180, 187, 190, 232, 34,
235–236
Abdullah bin Saud bin Abdul Aziz
Al Saud (Saudi prince), 13
Abu Bakr, 89
Abu Dhabi, 246, 329, 347
Abu Humaid, Abdul Rahim, 143
Abu Musa island, 51
Academi (security company), 304
Addis Ababa, 196
Adeli, Seyed, 191
Aden, 282, 283, 286, 288, 304,
309, 329
Adham, Kamal, 42, 44
Adulyadij. Bhumibol, 275

437

INDEX

INDEX

INDEX

INDEX

INDEX

INDEX

INDEX

INDEX

INDEX